TREASURES OF WISDOM

STUDIES IN BEN SIRA AND THE BOOK OF WISDOM

BIBLIOTHECA EPHEMERIDUM THEOLOGICARUM LOVANIENSIUM

CXLIII

TREASURES OF WISDOM
STUDIES IN BEN SIRA AND THE BOOK OF WISDOM

FESTSCHRIFT M. GILBERT

EDITED BY

N. CALDUCH-BENAGES AND J. VERMEYLEN

LEUVEN
UNIVERSITY PRESS

UITGEVERIJ PEETERS
LEUVEN

1999

ISBN 90 6186 956 0 (Leuven University Press)
D/1998/1869/19
ISBN 90-429-0754-1 (Peeters Leuven)
D/1999/0602/43
ISBN 2-87723-450-9 (Peeters France)

Leuven University Press / Presses Universitaires de Louvain
Universitaire Pers Leuven
Blijde-Inkomststraat 5, B-3000 Leuven-Louvain (Belgium)

© 1999, Peeters, Bondgenotenlaan 153, B-3000 Leuven (Belgium)

PREFACE

On 12 March 1999 Professor Maurice Gilbert S.J. becomes sixty-five years of age. Undoubtedly this is a fine occasion for giving homage to our beloved colleague, friend and teacher with the publication of the present Festschrift and its presentation at the 48th *Colloquium Biblicum Lovaniense* of 1999.

In his zeal for discovering the treasures of Biblical wisdom Maurice Gilbert has dedicated a great part of his scientific work to the study of Israel's sapiential literature, concentrating especially on the Book of Ben Sira (Ecclesiasticus) and the Book of Wisdom. Among his numerous publications on wisdom literature are notably *La critique des dieux dans le livre de la Sagesse (Sg 13–15)* (AnBib, 53) in 1973, the edition of *La Sagesse de l'Ancien Testament* (BETL, 51) in 1979 and its update of 1990, *La Sapienza di Salomone*, 1-2 (Bibbia e Preghiera, 22-23) in 1995 and his two masterly articles: *Sagesse de Salomon (ou Livre de la Sagesse)* and *Siracide* in the *Supplément au Dictionnaire de la Bible*. It comes as no surprise, therefore, that the editors have sought to honour Maurice Gilbert with a volume containing a wide variety of articles on his two favourite books.

Following the list of publications by Maurice Gilbert, the Festschrift offers 32 contributions of philological, thematic, exegetical and intertextual nature, divided in three sections. The first part concerns the Book of Ben Sira, the second the Book of Wisdom, and the third deals with some points of contact between Ben Sira and Qohelet, as well as between Ben Sira and the Qumran literature.

The editors wish to express their sincere and profound gratitude to all contributors for the scientific quality of their work, as well as for their readiness to accept indications and suggestions during the elaboration of this volume. It goes without saying that this gratitude extends also to the editor of the series *Bibliotheca Ephemeridum Theologicarum Lovaniensium* and to the publishers *Leuven University Press* and *Uitgeverij Peeters*, who have made this publication possible.

This Festschrift is a birthday present that testifies to the esteem which Maurice Gilbert enjoys among biblical scholars all over the world. In name of all who have participated directly or indirectly in the preparation of this volume the editors thank our dear colleague, friend, and teacher for all that he has done and continues doing in spreading the love of the Word of God through his untiring search of Wisdom.

Nuria CALDUCH-BENAGES and Jacques VERMEYLEN

CONTENTS

THE BOOK OF BEN SIRA

The Book of Wisdom

BEN SIRA – QOHELET – QUMRAN

INDEXES

FRONTISPIECE: Photograph M. Gilbert (D. Van Acker)

BIBLIOGRAPHY OF M. GILBERT
1970-1998

1970   *La structure de la prière de Salomon (Sg 9)*, in *Bib* 51 (1970) 301-331
        [pp. 326-331 reprinted in *La Sapienza di Salomone*, t. 1, 1995,
        pp. 113-120].

1971   *Volonté de Dieu et don de la Sagesse (Sg 9,17s.)*, in *NRT* 93 (1971)
        145-166 [reprinted in *La Sapienza di Salomone*, t. 1, 1995, pp. 121-
        152].
        Chronique d'Ancien Testament, in *Vie Consacrée* 43 (1971) 50-58.

1972   *La prière de Daniel (Dn 9,4-19)*, in *RTL* 3 (1972) 284-310.
        Chronique d'Ancien Testament, in *Vie Consacrée* 44 (1972) 53-63.
        Report: *Journées Bibliques de Louvain [23-25 août 1972]*, in *RTL* 3
        (1972) 496-500.

1973   *La critique des dieux dans le livre de la Sagesse (Sg 13–15)* (AnBib,
        53), Roma, PIB, 1973.
        Chronique d'Ancien Testament, in *Vie Consacrée* 45 (1973) 41-56.

1974   *Comparaison entre les confessions des péchés de Néhemie 9 et Daniel
        3 Théodotion*, in *Bulletin of the International Organization for Sep-
        tuagint and Cognate Studies* 7 (1974) 23-25.
        La prière d'Azarias (Dan 3,26-45 Théodotion), in *NRT* 96 (1974) 561-
        582.
        Soyez féconds et multipliez (Gn 1,28), in *NRT* 96 (1974) 729-742.
        L'éloge de la sagesse (Siracide 24), in *RTL* 5 (1974) 326-348.
        La nuit pascale (Sg 18,6-9), in *Assemblées du Seigneur*, n.s. 50 (1974)
        52-57 [reprinted in *La Sapienza di Salomone*, t. 1, 1995, pp. 231-
        239].
        La notte pasquale [Sap 18,3.6-9], in *La parola per l'assemblea festiva*
        47 (Brescia 1974) 71-79.
        Le juste traqué (Sg 2,12.17-20), in *Assemblées du Seigneur*, n.s. 56
        (1974) 30-35.
        La sagesse avant tout (Sg 7,7-11), in *Assemblées du Seigneur*, n.s. 59
        (1974) 30-35 [reprinted in *La Sapienza di Salomone*, t. 1, 1995,
        pp. 99-107]. Cf. 1976.
        Chronique d'Ancien Testament, in *Vie Consacrée* 46 (1974) 49-58.
        Vrais et faux prophètes selon l'Écriture, in *La Foi et le Temps* 4 (1974)
        285-307 [reprinted in *Il a parlé par les prophètes*, 1998, pp. 169-
        189].
        Report: *Rencontre entre moralistes et exégètes [8 février 1974]*, in *RTL*
        5 (1974) 127-128.

1975   *Chronique de l'Ancien Testament* (in collaboration with J.L. SKA), in
        Vie Consacrée 47 (1975) 46-58.
        Chronique du Nouveau Testament, in *Vie Consacrée* 47 (1975) 296-310.

1976   *Le Père R. de Vaux et l'histoire ancienne d'Israël*, in *Strumento inter-
        nazionale per un lavoro teologico*, in *Communio* 7 (1976) 90-93.

Roland de Vaux und das Alte Israel, in *Internationale Katholische Zeitschrift Communio* 5 (1976) 444-447.

Prima di tutto la Sapienza, in *La parola per l'assemblea festiva* 56 (Brescia, 1976) 51-59. Cf. 1974.

Ben Sira et la femme, in *RTL* 7 (1976) 426-442.

La conjecture μετριότητι en Sg 12,22a, in *Bib* 57 (1976) 550-553 [reprinted in *La Sapienza di Salomone*, t. 1, 1995, pp. 183-189].

La connaissance de Dieu selon le Livre de la Sagesse, in J. COPPENS (ed.), *La notion biblique de Dieu. Le Dieu de la Bible et le Dieu des philosophes* (BETL, 41), Gembloux, Duculot, and Leuven, University Press, 1976, pp. 191-210 [reprinted in *La Sapienza di Salomone*, t. 2, 1995, pp. 23-50].

La filantropia di Dio (Sap 11,15–12,27). Dispense ad uso degli studenti, Roma, PIB, 1976.

L'Ancien Testament et la morale chrétienne, in M. GILBERT – J. L'HOUR – J. SCHARBERT, *Morale et Ancien Testament* (Lex Spiritus Vitae, 1), Louvain-la-Neuve, Centre Cerfaux-Lefort, 1976, pp. 3-27.

Comment lire les écrits sapientiaux de l'Ancien Testament, *Ibid.*, pp. 131-175.

Chronique d'Écriture Sainte (in collaboration with J.L. SKA), in *Vie Consacrée* 48 (1976) 304-316.

1977 *Chronique d'Écriture Sainte* (in collaboration with J.L. SKA), in *Vie Consacrée* 49 (1977) 301-312.

1978 *Une seule chair (Gen 2,24)*, in *NRT* 100 (1978) 66-89 [reprinted in *Il a parlé par les prophètes*, 1998, pp. 83-98].

Only One Flesh, in *Theology Digest* 26 (1978) 206-209.

Paul VI: In memoriam, in *Bib* 59 (1978) 453-462 [reprinted in *Istituto Paolo VI. Notiziario num. 10* (Brescia, 1985) 100-106].

Jean-Paul I: In memoriam, in *Bib* 59 (1978) 462.

Il convito che fa vivere, in *Rivista di Liturgia* 65 (1978) 643-655.

La disponibilité des prophètes, in *Disponibles. Essais sur une orientation. Au cœur de notre identité*, Roma, Centrum Ignatianum Spiritualitatis, 1978, pp. 45-55.

Le sacré dans l'Ancien Testament, in J. RIES (ed.), *L'expression du sacré dans les grandes religions*, t.1: *Proche-Orient ancien et traditions bibliques* (Homo religiosus, 1), Louvain-la-Neuve, Centre d'Histoire des Religions, 1978, pp. 205-289.

Chronique d'Écriture Sainte (in collaboration with J.L. SKA), in *Vie Consacrée* 50 (1978) 303-319.

1979 *Jérémie écrit aux exilés. Lecture de Jérémie 29*, in *Christus* 26, fasc. 101 (1979) 108-116 [reprinted in *Il a parlé par les prophètes*, 1998, pp. 205-214].

La disponibilité des prophètes, in *Supplément à Vie chrétienne 222: Des hommes disponibles* (Paris 1979) 41-49 [reprinted in *Il a parlé par les prophètes*, 1998, pp. 159-168]. Cf. 1978.

Edition: La Sagesse de l'Ancien Testament (BETL, 51), Gembloux, Duculot, and Leuven, University Press, 1979. Cf. ²1990.

Vingt-cinq années de travaux (avant-propos), *Ibid.*, pp. 7-13.

Le discours de la Sagesse en Proverbes, 8. Structure et cohérence, *Ibid.*, pp. 202-218.

1980   *La prière des sages d'Israël*, in H. LIMET – J. RIES (eds.), *L'expérience
       de la prière dans les grandes religions*. Actes du Colloque de
       Louvain-la-Neuve et Liège 22-23 Nov. 1978 (Homo religiosus, 5),
       Louvain-la-Neuve, Centre d'Histoire des Religions, 1980, pp. 227-
       243 [reprinted in *Il a parlé par les prophètes*, 1998, pp. 333-352].
       Maestri di sagezza e sapienza di Dio, in A. AMATO – G. ZEVINI (eds.),
       Annunciare Cristo ai giovani (Biblioteca di Scienze Religiose, 35),
       Roma, Libreria Ateneo Salesiano, 1980, pp. 91-107 [reprinted in *Il a
       parlé par les prophètes*, 1998, pp. 307-331].
       La Sequela della Sapienza: Lettura di Sir 6,23-31, in *PSV 2: Seguimi!*
       (Bologna, 1980) 53-70.
       *Appendice: La recensione del volume del corso biblico AA 1977/78:
       Stato e comunità religiosa nella tradizione biblica*, in G. DE GEN-
       NARO (ed.), *Amore-Giustizia* (Studio Biblico Teologico Aquilano, 2),
       Napoli, Dehoniane, 1980, pp. 591-600.
       La Sagesse personifiée dans les textes de l'Ancien Testament, in M.
       GILBERT – J.-N. ALETTI, *La Sagesse et Jésus-Christ* (CahÉv, 32),
       Paris, Cerf, 1980, pp. 5-43. Cf. 1981, 1985.
       [*L'éloge de la Sagesse, Sg 7–9* (pp. 33-36), reprinted in *La Sapienza di
       Salomone*, t. 1, 1995, pp. 63-68].
       In memoriam Patris Peter Nober, S.J., in *Bib* 61 (1980) 596-597.
       Psalm 110(109),5-7 (in collaboration with S. PISANO), in *Bib* 61 (1980)
       343-353 [343-356].
1981   *Prolusione al corso sull'antropologia biblica*, in G. DE GENNARO (ed.),
       L'antropologia biblica (Studio Biblico Teologico Aquilano, 3),
       Napoli, Dehoniane, 1981, pp. 25-38 [reprinted in *Il a parlé par les
       prophètes*, pp. 69-80].
       L'antropologia del Libro della Sapienza, Ibid., pp. 245-257.
       Spirito, Sapienza e Legge secondo Ben Sira e il libro della Sapienza, in
       PSV 4: Lo Spirito del Signore (Bologna, 1981) 65-73.
       Les raisons de la modération divine (Sagesse 11,21–12,2), in A.
       CAQUOT – M. DELCOR (eds.), *Mélanges bibliques et orientaux en
       l'honneur de M. Henri Cazelles* (AOAT, 212), Kevelaer, Butzon &
       Bercker, and Neukirchen-Vluyn, Neukirchener Verlag, 1981,
       pp. 149-162 [reprinted in *La Sapienza di Salomone*, t. 1, 1995,
       pp. 165-181].
       La place de la Loi dans la prière de Néhémie 9, in M. CARREZ –
       J. DORÉ – P. GRELOT (eds.), *De la Tôrah au Messie: Études d'exé-
       gèse et d'herméneutique biblique offertes à Henri Cazelles pour ses
       25 années d'enseignement à l'Institut Catholique de Paris (octobre
       1979)*, Paris, Desclée, 1981, pp. 307-316.
       La description de la vieillesse en Qohelet XII,1-7 est-elle allégorique?,
       in J. A. EMERTON (ed.), *Congress Volume Vienna 1980* (SVT, 32),
       Leiden, Brill, 1981, pp. 96-109.
       Jérémie en conflit avec les Sages, in P.-M. BOGAERT (ed.), *Le livre de
       Jérémie. Le prophète et son milieu. Les oracles et leur transmission*
       (BETL, 54), Leuven, University Press and Peeters, 1981, pp. 105-
       118. Cf. 1998.
       *«La Parola di Dio alle origini della Chiesa». L'opera esegetica di
       Mons. Carlo M. Martini*, in *Civiltà Cattolica* 132 (1981) 462-469.

Il linguaggio liturgico cristiano e l'Antico Testamento, in A. PISTOIA –
G. VENTURI et al. (eds.), *Il linguaggio liturgico. Prospettive metodo-
logiche e indicazioni pastorali* (Oggi e Domani. Serie II/7), Bologna,
Dehoniane, 1981, pp. 181-204.

La personificazione della Sapienza negli scritti dell'Antico Testamento,
in M. GILBERT – J.-N. ALETTI, *La Sapienza e Gesù Cristo* (Bibbia
Oggi. Strumenti per vivere la Parola, 21), Torino, Gribaudi, 1981,
pp. 3-38. Cf. 1980.

La Sabiduría personificada en los textos del Antiguo Testamento, in
M. GILBERT – J.-N. ALETTI, *La Sabiduría y Jesucristo* (Cuadernos
bíblicos, 32), Estella (Navarra), Verbo Divino, 1981, pp. 5-43.
Cf. 1980.

Review: *Un commentaire sur Second Isaïe: nature de la réalité
suprême et sens d'une conception de base par P.-É. Bonnard*, in
*Ultimate Reality and Meaning. Interdisciplinary Studies in the Philo-
sophy of Understanding* 4 (1981) 164-165.

1982   *Il cosmo secondo il libro della Sapienza*, in G. DE GENNARO (ed.), *Il
cosmo nella Bibbia* (Studio Biblico Teologico Aquilano, 4), Napoli,
Dehoniane, 1982, pp. 189-199.

Il giudaismo nell'economia della salvezza, in *Civiltà Cattolica* 133
(1982) 454-467.

Le Judaïsme dans le contexte de l'économie du salut, in *La Documentation catholique* 64, t. 79 (1982) 830-836 [reprinted in *Il a parlé par
les prophètes*,1998, pp. 99-118].

L'exégèse spirituelle de Montfort, in *NRT* 104 (1982) 678-691 [reprin-
ted in *La Sapienza di Salomone*, t. 2, 1995, pp. 143-162].

Impegno e fedeltà nella Bibbia, in M. AUGÉ (ed.), *Impegno e fedeltà: i
religiosi si interrogano*, Roma, Rogate, 1982, pp. 7-22 [reprinted in
Il a parlé par les prophètes, 1998, pp. 371-386].

L'enciclica «Dives in misericordia» di Giovanni Paolo II e la Bibbia,
in AA.VV., *Prima lettura della «Dives in misericordia»*. Atti del
Convegno Internazionale Collevalenza, 26-29 novembre 1981, Collevalenza (Perugia), L'amore misericordioso, 1982, pp. 109-121
[reprinted in *La Sapienza di Salomone*, t. 2, 1995, pp. 163-179].

Liturgia penitenziale ed esperienza di Dio nei salmi postesilici, in A.N.
TERRIN (ed.), *Liturgia, soglia della esperienza di Dio?* (Caro salutis
cardo. Contributi, 1), Padova – Abbazia S. Giustina, Messaggero,
1982, pp. 63-76.

La spiritualité de Marie Rivier, in *Osservatore Romano*. Édition hebdo-
madaire en langue française 33/4 (1982) 2.

Honore ton père et ta mère, in *Alliance*, fasc. 24 (nov.-dec. 1982) 20-25.

La sagesse d'Israël. Ben Sirak. Le Livre de la Sagesse (in collaboration)
(Écouter la Bible, 14), Paris, DDB,1982.

Presentation: C. M. MARTINI – A. VANHOYE, *Bibbia e Vocazione*, Brescia, Morcelliana, 1982, pp. 7-8.

1983   *L'adresse à Dieu dans l'anamnèse hymnique de l'Exode (Sg 10–19)*, in
V. COLLADO – E. ZURRO (eds.), *El misterio de la Palabra. Homenaje
de sus alumnos al Profesor D. Luis Alonso Schökel*, Valencia –
Madrid, Cristiandad, 1983, pp. 207-225 [reprinted in *La Sapienza di
Salomone*, t. 1, 1995, pp. 191-217].

La preghiera nel Libro della Sapienza, in G. DE GENNARO (ed.), *La preghiera nella Bibbia. Storia, struttura e pratica dell'esperienza religiosa* (Studio Biblico Teologico Aquilano, 5), Napoli, Dehoniane, 1983, pp. 157-172 [reprinted in *La Sapienza di Salomone*, t. 2, 1995, pp. 93-109].

Bibliographie générale sur Sag., in C. LARCHER, *Le livre de la Sagesse ou la Sagesse de Salomon*, t. I (EB n.s., 1), Paris, Gabalda, 1983, pp. 11-48.

Le Cardinal Augustin Bea, 1881-1968. La Bible, rencontre des chrétiens et des juifs, in *NRT* 105 (1983) 369-383.

La Sapienza si offre come nutrimento (Sir 24,19-22), in *PSV 7: La Cena del Signore* (Bologna, 1983) 51-60.

1984   *La figure de Salomon en Sg 7–9*, in R. KUNTZMANN – J. SCHLOSSER (eds.), *Études sur le Judaïsme hellénistique. Congrès de Strasbourg 1983* (LD, 119), Paris, Cerf, 1984, pp. 225-249 [reprinted in *La Sapienza di Salomone*, t. 1, 1995, pp. 69-97].

Wisdom Literature, in M.E. STONE (ed.), *Jewish Writings of the Second Temple Period*: *Apocrypha, Pseudepigrapha, Qumran Sectarian Writings, Philo, Josephus* (CRINT, 2/1), Assen – Philadelphia, Van Gorcum, 1984, pp. 283-324.

L'amore di Dio per la sua creatura, in *PSV 10: Dio è Amore* (Bologna, 1984) 65-74 [reprinted in *La Sapienza di Salomone*, t. 2, 1995, pp. 83-92].

La loi du talion (Ex 21,13...), in *Christus* 31, fasc. 121 (1984) 73-82 [reprinted in *Il a parlé par les prophètes*, 1998, pp. 145-155].

Le Livre de la Sagesse et l'inculturation, in AA.VV., *L'inculturation et la sagesse des nations* (Inculturation. Études sur l'actualité de la rencontre entre la foi et les cultures, 4), Roma, PUG, 1984, pp. 1-11 (in collaboration with P. SYE IN SYEK and T. NKÉRAMIHIGO) [reprinted in *La Sapienza di Salomone*, t. 2, 1995, pp. 9-22].

Discorso del R.P. Maurice Gilbert, SJ, Rettore: 75 Anniversario della fondazione del Pontificio Istituto Biblico, in *Bib* 65 (1984) 434-437.

In Memoriam Ernst Vogt, SJ (30.1.1903-28.2.1984), in *Bib* 65 (1984) 438-439.

In Memoriam Viliam Pavlovsky, SJ (17.12.1911-13.3.1984), in *Bib* 65 (1984) 440-441.

Review: L. ALONSO SCHÖKEL – J.L. SICRE DIAZ, *Job. Comentario teológico y literario*, Madrid, Cristiandad, 1983, in *Book List, The Society for Old Testament Study* (1984) 48-49.

1985   *Lecture mariale et ecclésiale de Siracide 24,10(15)*, in *Marianum* 47 (1985) 536-542.

«On est puni par où l'on pèche» (Sg 11,16), in A. CAQUOT – S. LÉGASSE – M. TARDIEU (eds.), *Mélanges bibliques et orientaux en l'honneur de M. Mathias Delcor* (AOAT, 215), Kevelaer, Butzon & Bercker, and Neukirchen-Vluyn, Neukirchener Verlag, 1985, pp. 183-191 [reprinted in *La Sapienza di Salomone*, t. 1, 1995, pp. 153-164].

Il giusto perseguitato di Sap 2,12-20: figura messianica, in G. DE GENNARO (ed.), *L'Antico Testamento interpretato dal Nuovo: il Messia* (Studio Biblico Teologico Aquilano, 6), Napoli, Dehoniane, 1985, pp. 193-218 [reprinted in *La Sapienza di Salomone*, t. 1, 1995, pp. 39-61].

L'esprit et la sagesse, in AA.VV., *L'Esprit Saint dans la Bible* (CahÉv, 52), Paris, Cerf, 1985, pp. 19-21 [reprinted in *La Sapienza di Salomone*, t. 1, 1995, pp. 109-112].

Introduction au livre de Ben Sira ou Siracide ou Ecclésiastique [ad usum scholarum], Roma, PIB, 1985.

Paul VI: In memoriam, in *Istituto Paolo VI. Notiziario num. 10* (Brescia 1985) 100-106. Cf. 1978.

A sabedoria personificada nos textos do Antigo Testamento, in M. GILBERT – J.-N. ALETTI, *A Sabedoria e Jesus Cristo* (Cadernos bíblicos, 32), São Paulo, Paulinos, 1985, pp. 9-56. Cf. 1980.

1986   *L'universalité des normes morales selon l'Écriture*, in S. PINCKAERS – C.J. PINTO DE OLIVEIRA (eds.), *Universalité et permanence des lois morales* (Études d'éthique chrétienne, 16), Fribourg, Éditions Universitaires, and Paris, Cerf, 1986, pp. 7-19 [reprinted in *Il a parlé par les prophètes*, 1998, pp. 119-133].

Art. *Sagesse de Salomon (ou Livre de la Sagesse)*, in *DBS* 11 (1986) col. 58-119.

Art. *L'Esprit Saint dans le livre de la Sagesse*, *Ibid.*, col. 153-156.

Saint Jérôme, traducteur de la Bible, in *Commission des Pèlerinages Chrétiens. Annales 1986,* Jerusalem, Notre Dame Center, Christianae, 1986, pp. 81-105 [reprinted in *Il a parlé par les prophètes*, 1998, pp. 9-28].

Har Karkom et le Mont Sinai, in E. ANATI (ed.), *Bollettino del Centro Camuno di Studi Preistorici* 23, Capo di Ponte (Brescia), Edizioni del Centro, 1986, pp. 9-10.

Art. *Gift*, in G. WIGODER (ed.), *Illustrated Dictionary and Concordance of the Bible*, New York – London, MacMillan, 1986, p. 395.

Art. *Wisdom. Ibid.*, pp. 1032-1033.

Ricordo di Pierre Benoit: Dall'esegesi alla teologia, in *Osservatore Romano* (5 maggio 1987) 3.

1987   *La Bible et l'homosexualité*, in *NRT* 109 (1987) 78-95.

La relecture de Gen 1–3 dans le livre de la Sagesse, in F. BLANQUART – L. DEROUSSEAUX (eds.), *La création dans l'Orient ancien* (LD, 127), Paris, Cerf, 1987, pp. 323-344 (+note) [reprinted in *La Sapienza di Salomone*, t. 2, 1995, pp. 111-140].

Jérôme et l'œuvre de Ben Sira, in *Le Muséon* 100 (1987) 109-120.

L'Ecclésiastique: Quel texte? Quelle autorité?, in *RB* 94 (1987) 233-250.

Reflections on Catholic Exegesis and Jewish-Christian Dialogue at the Pontifical Biblical Institute, in C. THOMA – M. WYSCHOGROD (eds.), *Understanding Scripture. Explorations of Jewish and Christian Traditions of Interpretation* (Studies in Judaism and Christianity), Mahwah, NJ, Paulist Press, 1987, pp. 63-77.

Art. *Sagesse, Livre*, in CENTRE INFORMATIQUE ET BIBLE, ABBAYE DE MAREDSOUS (dir.), *Dictionnaire encyclopédique de la Bible*, Turnhout, Brepols, 1987, pp. 1155-1157. Cf. 1995.

Prospettive e istanze nell'esegesi dopo il Vaticano II, in R. LATOURELLE (ed.), *Vaticano II, Bilancio e prospettive. Venticinque anni dopo: 1962/1987,* Assisi, Citadella Editrice, 1987, pp. 289-307. Cf. 1988(2), 1989.

Condanna di un'opera umana, l'idolo (Sap 14,11-21; Is 44,9-20), in
G. DE GENNARO (ed.), *Lavoro e riposo nella Bibbia* (Studio Biblico
Teologico Aquilano, 7), Napoli, Dehoniane, 1987, pp. 97-108
[reprinted in *La Sapienza di Salomone*, t. 1, 1995, pp. 219-229].

1988   *Grégoire de Nazianze et le Siracide*, in *Mémorial Dom Jean Gribomont
(1920-1986)* (Studia Ephemerides «Augustianianum», 27), Roma,
Institutum Patristicum Augustinianum, 1988, pp. 307-314.

Art. *Sapienza*, in P. ROSSANO – G. RAVASI – A. GIRLANDA (eds.), *Nuovo
Dizionario di Teologia Biblica*, Cinisello Balsamo (Milano), Paoline,
1988, pp. 1427-1442.

I Salmi, in A. FANULI (ed.), *La Spiritualità dell'Antico Testamento* (Storia della Spiritualità, 1), Roma, Borla, 1988, pp. 539-580 [reprinted
in *Il a parlé par les prophètes*, 1998, pp. 249-287].

Ouverture et requêtes en exégèse après Vatican II, in R. LATOURELLE
(ed.), *Vatican II: bilan et prospectives vingt cinq ans après (1962-
1987)* (Recherches, n.s. 5), Montréal, Bellarmin, and Paris, Cerf,
1988, pp. 329-349. Cf. 1987.

New Horizons and Present Needs. Exegesis since Vatican II, in
R. LATOURELLE (ed.), *Vatican II. Assessment and Prospectives*, t. I,
New York, Paulist Press, 1988, pp. 321-343. Cf. 1987, 1988.

1989   *Il IV comandamento, «onora tuo padre e tua madre» (Ex 20,12)*, in
V. LIBERTI (ed.), *La famiglia nella Bibbia* (Studio Biblico Teologico
Aquilano, 9), Roma, Dehoniane, 1989, pp. 89-99 [reprinted in *Il a
parlé par les prophètes*, 1998, pp. 135-143].

La procréation; ce qu'en sait le Livre de la Sagesse, in *NRT* 111 (1989)
824-841 [reprinted in *La Sapienza di Salomone*, t. 2, 1995. pp. 59-
82].

Expectativas e instancias en exégesis después del Vaticano II, in
R. LATOURELLE (ed.), *Vaticano II: balance y perspectivas. Veinti-
cinco años después (1962-1987)* (Verdad e Imagen, 109), Sala-
manca, Sígueme, 1989, pp. 221-234. Cf. 1987, 1988(2).

Marie-Joseph Lagrange, in *Azione sociale* [Roma, Settimanale delle
Acli] (7-12 maggio 1989) 8-9.

Lettre au Directeur, in *Bulletin Associated Christian Press* [Jerusalem,
Christian Information Center] (Sept. 1989) 2.

Review: P.W. SKEHAN – A.A. DI LELLA, *The Wisdom of Ben Sira* (AB,
39), New York, Doubleday, 1987, in *Bib* 70 (1989) 272-274.

1990   Art. *Sagesse de Salomon*, in *Dictionnaire de Spiritualité ascétique et
mystique, doctrine et histoire* 14 (1990), 57-72.

Art. *Sagesse (des hommes et de Dieu) I. Ancien Testament*, *Ibid.*, 72-81.

Art. *Sabiduría*, in P. ROSSANO – G. RAVASI – A. GIRLANDA (eds.),
Nuevo Diccionario de Teología Bíblica, Madrid, Paulinas, 1990, pp.
1711-1728.

L'enseignement des sages, in É. CHARPENTIER – A. PAUL (eds.), *Les
Psaumes et les autres Écrits* (PBSB.AT, 5), Paris, Desclée, 1990,
pp. 295-351.

Art. *Esegesi integrale*, in R. LATOURELLE – R. FISICHELLA (eds.), *Dizionario di Teologia Fondamentale*, Assisi, Citadella Editrice, 1990,
pp. 395-403. Cf. 1992.

Quinze lettres du Père Lagrange au Père Lyonnet 1933-1938, in *Bib* 71 (1990) 280-298.

Le pèlerinage d'Iñigo à Jérusalem en 1523, in *NRT* 112 (1990) 660-685. Cf. 1991, 1992.

Edition: *La Sagesse de l'Ancien Testament* (BETL, 51), Leuven, University Press and Peeters, ²1990. Cf. 1979.

Le discours de la Sagesse en Proverbes 8. Structure et cohérence, Ibid., pp. 202-218; Note additionnelle, pp. 414-415.

Une décennie sur les livres sapientiaux: 1979-1989, Ibid., pp. 399-406.

Edition and presentation: M.-J. LAGRANGE, *L'Écriture en Église. Choix de portraits et d'exégèse spirituelle (1890-1937)* (LD, 142), Paris, Cerf, 1990, pp. 7-10.

1991   *Les louanges du Seigneur: commentaire pastoral et spirituel des psaumes du dimanche et des fêtes,* Paris, Desclée, 1991. Cf. 1991, 1992(2).

Ogni vivente dia lode al Signore: commento dei salmi delle domeniche e delle feste, vol. I: *Avvento – Natale – II-IX domenica «per annum»,* tr. by Domenico Ronchitelli (Bibbia e preghiera, 9), Roma, ADP, 1991. Cf. 1992.

The Book of Ben Sira: Implications for Jewish and Christian Traditions, in S. TALMON (ed.), *Jewish Civilization in the Hellenistic-Roman Period* (JSPS, 10), Sheffield, JSOT Press, 1991, pp. 81-91.

Le discours menaçant de sagesse en Proverbes 1,20-33, in D. GARRONE – F. ISRAEL (eds.), *Storia e Tradizioni di Israele. Scritti in onore di J. Alberto Soggin,* Brescia, Paideia, 1991, pp. 99-119.

L'insegnamento dei saggi, in É. CHARPENTIER – A. PAUL (eds.), *I Salmi e gli altri Scritti* (Piccola Enciclopedia Biblica. Antico Testamento, 5), Roma, Borla, 1991, pp. 324-355.

Retiro de seis días con los discípulos de Emaús: Lucas 24,13-35, in *Emaús en Manresa. Biblia y ejercicios,* Roma, Centrum Ignatianum Spiritualitatis, 1991, pp. 20-38. Cf. 1991, 1992.

Con i discepoli di Emmaus (Lc 24,13-35). Punti di meditazione per sei giorni di esercizi, in *Pregare con Ignazio. Bibbia ed Esercizi Spirituali* (Bibbia e preghiera, 8), Roma, ADP, 1991. pp. 19-35.

Confessioni dei peccati nell'Antico Testamento, in *Il Messaggio del Cuore di Gesù* 14 (1991) 695-700 [reprinted in *Il a parlé par les prophètes*, 1998, pp. 289-305].

La peregrinación de Iñigo a Jerusalén en 1523, in *Manresa* 63 (1991) 33-54. Cf. 1990.

Edition and presentation: Marie-Joseph LAGRANGE, *Exégète à Jérusalem. Nouveaux Mélanges d'Histoire Religieuse (1890-1939)* (CRB, 29), Paris, Gabalda, 1991, pp. 7-10.

Review: B. MONTAGNES (ed.), *Exégèse et obéissance. Correspondance Cormier-Lagrange (1904-1916)* (EB, n.s. 11), Paris, Gabalda, 1989, in *Bib* 72 (1991) 142-144.

1992   *Ogni vivente dia lode al Signore: commento dei salmi delle domeniche e delle feste,* vol. II: *Quaresima – Tempo pasquale – Solennità del Signore,* tr. by Domenico Ronchitelli (Bibbia e preghiera, 11), Roma, ADP, 1992. Cf. 1991.

Ogni vivente dia lode al Signore: commento dei salmi delle domeniche e delle feste, vol. III: *X-XXXIII domenica «per annum» – Cristo Re e altre Feste*, tr. by Domenico Ronchitelli (Bibbia e preghiera, 13), Roma, ADP, 1992. Cf. 1991, 1992.

Vint-cinq lettres de M.-J. Lagrange à Robert Devresse (1928-1936), in *RB* 99 (1992) 471-498.

Art. *Exégèse intégrale*, in R. LATOURELLE – R. FISICHELLA (eds.), *Dictionnaire de Théologie Fondamentale*, Paris, Cerf, and Montréal, Bellarmin, 1992, pp. 445-453 [reprinted in *Il a parlé par les prophètes*, 1998, pp. 55-68]. Cf. 1990.

Il pellegrinaggio di Inigo a Gerusalemme nel 1523, in M. LAVRA (ed.), *Ignazio di Loyola e gli Esercizi Spirituali. Atti del convegno nazionale nell'anno ignaziano: 16-18 novembre 1990. Relazioni e documenti di lavoro* (Appunti di Spiritualità, 33. Esercizi Spirituali, XII), Roma, 1992, pp. 68-91. Cf. 1990.

A Six-Day Retreat with the Disciples of Emmaus: Luke 24,13-35, in *Emmaus in Manresa. The Bible and the Exercises*, Gujarat (India), Gujarat Sahitya Prakash, 1992, pp. 10-24. Cf. 1991.

1993　*Pace terrena e pace ultraterrena nel Libro della Sapienza*, in V. LIBERTI (ed.), *La pace secondo la Bibbia* (Studio Biblico Teologico Aquilano, 12), L'Aquila, ISSRA, 1993, pp. 89-96 [reprinted in *La Sapienza di Salomone*, t. 2, 1995, pp. 51-57].

La sequela di Dio e della sapienza nell'Antico Testamento, in S.A. PANIMOLLE (dir.), *Dizionario di Spiritualità Biblico-Patristica. I grandi temi della S. Scrittura per la «Lectio Divina» 4: Apostolo-Discepolo-Missione*, Roma, Borla, 1993, pp. 29-44 [reprinted in *Il a parlé par les prophètes*, 1998, pp. 355-370].

Le grand âge, vu par la Bible, in *La vie spirituelle* 147 (1993) 477-493.

1994　*Cinquant'anni di magistero romano sull'ermeneutica biblica Leone XIII (1893) – Pio XII (1943)*, in M. GILBERT – P. LAGHI – A. VANHOYE, *Chiesa e Sacra Scrittura: Un secolo di magistero ecclesiale e studi biblici* (Subsidia Biblica, 17), Roma, PIB, 1994, pp. 11-33 [reprinted in *Il a parlé par les prophètes*, 1998, pp. 29-53].

Studi sul libro della Sapienza [Aggiornamento bibliografico ed edizione a cura di GIUSEPPE DE CARLO, ofmcap], Bologna, 1994.

Filologia ed esegesi biblica, in *La filologia testuale e le scienze umane* (Atti dei convegni Lincei, 111), Roma, Accademia Nazionale dei Lincei, 1994, pp. 81-89.

1995　*La Sapienza di Salomone*, t.1 (Bibbia e Preghiera, 22), Roma, ADP, 1995. Cf. 1970, 1971, 1974(2), 1976, 1980, 1981, 1983, 1984, 1985(3), 1987.

La Sapienza di Salomone, t. 2 (Bibbia e Preghiera, 23), Roma, ADP, 1995. Cf. 1976, 1982(2), 1983, 1984(2), 1987, 1989, 1993.

L'action de grâce de Ben Sira (51,1-12), in R. KUNTZMANN (ed.), *Ce Dieu qui vient. Mélanges offerts à Bernard Renaud* (LD, 159), Paris, Cerf, 1995, pp, 231-242.

La vecchiaia vista dalla Bibbia, in M. LORENZANI (ed.), *Gli anziani nella Bibbia* (Studio Biblico Teologico Aquilano, 14), L'Aquila, ISSRA, 1995, pp. 1-22.

Qu'en est-il de la sagesse?, in J. TRUBLET (dir.), *La sagesse biblique. De l'Ancien au Nouveau Testament.* Actes du XVᵉ Congrès de l'AC-FEB, Paris 1993 (LD, 160), Paris, Cerf, 1995, pp. 19-60.

La Sapienza biblica: Note semiotiche, in *Atti del Congresso Internazionale: «Semiotica del testo biblico»*: L'Aquila – Forte Spagnolo, 24-30 Giugno 1991, L'Aquila, Edizioni del Gallo Cedrone, 1995, pp. 742-744.

La spécificité de l'université catholique à l'aube du XXIᵉ siècle, in *La Revue Politique* (Bruxelles, janvier-février 1995) 7-21.

Art. *Jesus Sirach*, in E. DASSMANN *et al.* (eds.), *Reallexikon für Antike und Christentum*, t. XVII, Stuttgart, Anton Hiersemann, 1995, col. 878-906.

Art. *Sapienza, Libro*, in R. PENNA (ed.), *Dizionario Enciclopedico della Bibbia*, Roma, Borla and Città Nuova, 1995, pp. 1166-1167. Cf. 1987.

The Divine Promises to the Patriarchs in the Deuterocanonical Books, in A. NICCACCI (ed.), *Divine Promises to the Fathers in the Three Monotheistic Religions* (SBFAnalecta, 40), Jerusalem, Franciscan Printing Press, 1995, pp. 170-174.

Che dice il Nuovo Testamento sull'omosessualità?, in *Lettera sulla cura pastorale delle persone omosessuali. Testo e commenti* (Documenti e studi, 11), Roma, Libreria Editrice Vaticana, 1995, pp. 61-64.

1996   *I saggi della Bibbia*, in G. RAVASI (ed.), *La Bibbia per la famiglia,* V: *Giobbe – Salmi*, Milano, San Paolo, 1996, pp. 28-29.

L'abuso della creazione, in G. RAVASI (ed.), *La Bibbia per la famiglia,* VI: *Proverbi – Qohelet – Cantico dei Cantici – Sapienza – Siracide,* Milano, San Paolo, 1996, pp. 192-193.

Art. *Sexualité*, in *DBS* 12 (1996) 1016-1043.

Art. *Siracide, Ibid.*, 1389-1437.

Les prédictions des prophètes d'Israël, in *Louvain* 70 (1996) 18-20.

1997   *Wisdom of the Poor: Ben Sira 10,19–11,6*, in P. C. BEENTJES (ed.), *The Book of Ben Sira in Modern Research.* Proceedings of the First International Ben Sira Conference, 28-31 July 1996 Soesterberg, Netherlands (BZAW, 255), Berlin – New York, de Gruyter, 1997, pp. 153-169.

La Loi, chemin de la Sagesse, in C. FOCANT (ed.), *La Loi dans l'un et l'autre Testament* (LD, 168), Paris, Cerf, 1997, pp. 93-109.

The Hebrew Texts of Ben Sira a Hundred Years after their Discovery, in *Proceedings of the Irish Biblical Association* 20 (1997) 9-25.

The Last Pages of the Wisdom of Solomon, Ibid., pp. 52-67.

La luce nei testi di Qumran, in J. RIES – Ch.-M. TERNES (eds.), *Simbolismo ed esperienza della luce nelle grandi religioni* (Homo religiosus, II.1), Milano, Jaca Book, 1997, pp. 165-174.

La lumière dans les textes de Qumrân, in J. RIES – Ch.-M. TERNES (eds.), *Symbolisme et expérience de la lumière dans les grandes religions*, Paris, Cerf, 1997 [sub prelo].

1998   Art. *Canon des Écritures*, in J.-Y. LACOSTE (dir.), *Dictionnaire critique de théologie*, Paris, PUF, 1998, pp. 196-200.

Art. *Idolâtrie, Ibid.*, pp. 550-551.

Art. *Résurrection des morts, Ibid.*, pp. 989-990.

Art. *Shéol, Ibid.*, p. 1095.

Jérémie en conflit avec les Sages, in P.-M. BOGAERT (ed.), *Le livre de Jérémie. Le prophète et son milieu. Les oracles et leur transmission* (BETL, 54), Leuven, University Press and Peeters, ²1998, pp. 105-118; Note additionnelle, pp. 427-428. Cf. 1981.

Qohélet et Ben Sira, in A. SCHOORS (ed.), *Qohelet in the Context of Wisdom* (BETL, 136), Leuven, University Press and Peeters, 1998, pp. 161-179.

Introduction, Revision of Translation and Notes of the Wisdom of Solomon and the Wisdom of Ben Sira, in *La Bible de Jérusalem traduite en français sous la direction de l'École biblique de Jérusalem. Nouvelle édition revue et augmentée*, Paris, Cerf, 1998, pp. 1133-1135, 1137-1166, 1167-1169, 1171-1257.

Il a parlé par les prophètes. Thèmes et figures bibliques (Le Livre et le Rouleau, 2), Bruxelles, Éditions Lessius, and Namur, Presses universitaires, 1998. Cf. 1974, 1978, 1979(2), 1980(2), 1981, 1982(2), 1984, 1986(2), 1988, 1989, 1991, 1992, 1993, 1994.

Prêt, aumône et caution, in R. EGGER-WENZEL – I. KRAMMER (eds.), *Der Einzelne und seine Gemeinschaft bei Ben Sira.* Festschrift Friedrich V. Reiterer (BZAW, 270), Berlin – New York, de Gruyter, 1998, pp. 179-189.

Solomon-ei Zihe, 2 (Zihe Munhag Chongseu, 2; Ziheseu,1), tr. by Johan Yeong Sik PAHK, St Pauls, Seoul (Korea), 1998.

On Sesang Manmul-un Zunim-eul Chanmihaeura, 1-3, tr. by Ii, Son Iong, Seoul (Korea), Catholic Publishing House, 1998.

Voir ou craindre le Seigneur? Sir 1,10d, in L. CAGNI (ed.), *Bibbia e Semitistica.* Studi in memoria di Francesco Vattioni, Napoli, Istituto Universitario Orientale. Dipartimento di Studi Asiatici, 1998, pp. 247-252.

Wisdom of Solomon and Scripture, in M. SAEBØ – M. FISHBANE – J.L. SKA (eds.), *Hebrew Bible/Old Testament. The History of its Interpretation*, I/2, Göttingen, Vandenhoeck & Ruprecht, 1998 [sub prelo]

CURRICULUM MAURICE GILBERT

Né le 12 mars 1934 à Gilly (Belgique), d'Auguste Gilbert et de Suzanne Derolaye.
Entré dans la Compagnie de Jésus le 14 septembre 1952.
Ordonné prêtre à Bruxelles, le 6 août 1965.

Candidature en Philosophie et Lettre, Philologie classique, aux Facultés Universitaires Notre-Dame de la Paix, à Namur, 1954-1956.
Licence en Philosophie et Lettres, Philologie classique, à l'Université Catholique de Louvain, 1956-1958.
Licence en Philosophie, aux Facultés Saint-Albert de Louvain, à Eegenhoven-Heverlee, 1958-1960.
Licence en Théologie, aux Facultés Saint-Albert de Louvain, à Eegenhoven-Heverlee, 1962-1966.
Doctorat en Sciences Bibliques, à l'Institut Biblique Pontifical, à Rome, 1967-1973; titre de la thèse publiée intégralement: *La critique des dieux dans le Livre de la Sagesse (Sg 13–15)*, dans la collection «Analecta Biblica», n° 53, Rome, Institut Biblique, 1973, xix-323 p.; mention obtenue: La plus grande distinction.

Chargé de cours à la Faculté de Théologie de l'Université Catholique de Louvain, d'octobre 1971 à juillet 1978.
Professeur d'exégèse d'Ancien Testament à la Faculté Biblique de l'Institut Biblique Pontifical, à Rome, d'octobre 1975 à juin 1993. Professeur ordinaire à partir du 26 décembre 1983.
Directeur de la revue «Biblica», de l'Institut Biblique Pontifical, de septembre 1975 à juillet 1978.
Recteur de l'Institut Biblique Pontifical, à Rome et à Jérusalem, du 26 juillet 1978 au 26 juin 1984.
Directeur de l'Institut Biblique Pontifical, à Jérusalem, du 15 août 1984 au 2 juin 1992.
Professeur invité à l'École Biblique et Archéologique Française, à Jérusalem, d'octobre 1984 à juin 1993.
Professeur invité à la Weston School of Theology, à Cambridge, MA, U.S.A., de septembre à décembre 1987.
Recteur des Facultés Universitaires Notre-Dame de la Paix, à Namur, à partir du 1er août 1993.

La plus grande partie de ma formation s'est déroulée en Belgique, à Namur d'abord, puis à Louvain. L'orientation de ces premières études a été double: la philologie classique, grecque et latine, puis la philosophie et la théologie. Après quoi, l'orientation de mes études spécialisées a été l'exégèse de la Bible, à l'Institut Biblique, à Rome; mes études antérieures de philologie et de théologie trouvèrent là leur épanouissement: l'étude de l'hébreu et du grec bibliques, l'herméneutique des textes de la Bible et la théologie qu'ils véhiculent. Durant ces études spécialisées, en vue d'un enseignement universitaire, je me suis attaché, en particulier pour le doctorat (1970-1973), à l'étude du livre biblique, écrit en grec, de la «Sagesse de Salomon».

Après quelques années d'enseignement de la Bible à l'Université Catholique de Louvain, à temps plein de 1971 à 1975, je fus appelé à l'Institut Biblique de Rome pour y tenir la chaire des livres de sagesse de l'Ancien Testament. Je m'y suis attaché principalement à l'étude du livre de la «Sagesse de Salomon», par des cours, des publications scientifiques et la direction de thèses doctorales de quelques étudiants. Ces dernières années, je suis passé à un autre livre, la «Sagesse de Ben Sira» ou Siracide, connu surtout en hébreu et en grec. Cette dernière recherche, prometteuse, puisqu'elle a déjà donné quelques fruits, est à présent interrompue.

A côté de ces travaux scientifiques de recherche, j'ai toujours voulu consacrer une part de mon temps à des publications destinées au grand public. C'est ainsi que j'ai publié en 1991 un commentaire, accessible à tous, de Psaumes, sous le titre «Les Louanges du Seigneur» (Desclée), dont la presse belge a rendu compte avec intérêt.

Par ailleurs, de 1978 à 1992, je fus appelé à des tâches de gouvernement universitaire à l'Institut Biblique, à Rome d'abord comme recteur, puis à Jérusalem comme directeur de la succursale de cet Institut. Mon séjour à Jérusalem, de 1984 à 1992, m'a conduit à avoir des contacts académiques suivis avec l'Université Hébraïque et avec l'École Biblique des Dominicains, qui m'invitèrent chaque année à donner un cours.

Si je le pouvais, je préparerais à mes temps libres un livre de synthèse sur la sagesse biblique dans son rapport avec la figure du Christ.

M.G.

LETTER OF CARDINAL CARLO M. MARTINI

Milano, 26 giugno 1998

Carissimo Padre Maurice Gilbert, S.J.

Sono molto lieto che si stia preparando un libro in tuo onore e, nel rammarica di non potervi contribuire direttamente per mancanza di tempo e di competenza, voglio esprimere almeno con questa lettera la mia partecipazione ai tuoi festeggiamenti.

È da molti anni che ci conosciamo. Fin dal primo incontro ho ammirato in te quel dono di «saggezza» — cioè di naturale e composto equilibrio, di calma, di maturità di giudizio, di cortesia innata e acquisita (penso all'influsso determinante dei tuoi ottimi genitori, che ho avuto la gioia di conoscere) — che è espresso in tanti modi soprattutto in quei libri «sapienziali» biblici ai quali tu hai poi dedicato tanta parte della tua attività.

Pensado al tuo lavoro scientifico mi vengono alla mente le parole del Sirade: «Conserva i detti degli uomini famosi, / penetra le sottigliezza delle parabole, / indaga il senso recondito dei proverbi, / e s'occupa degli enigmi delle parabole» (Sir 39,2-3). Tu hai dato un contributo decisivo alla nostra conoscenza dei testi della sapienza e della poesia di Israele. Ma la tua preoccupazione è stata non soltanto di approfondire scientificamente le pagine bibliche, ma anche di aprirle alla conoscenza e all'uso dei fedeli. Ho potuto quindi anche come Vescovo approfittare delle tue ricerche e te ne sono vivamente grato.

Ma il Siracide, nel luogo sopra citato, continua: «Svolge il suo compito fra i grandi, / è presente alle riunioni dei capi, / viaggia fra genti straniere, / investigando il bene e il male in mezzo agli uomini» (Sir 39,4). Anche a te è toccato il servizio dell'autorità e della responsabilità. Penso in particolare al tuo Rettorato al Pontificio Istituto Biblico, dove mi sei succeduto mentre io lasciavo il Biblico per andare all'Università Gregoriana e di lì ben presto a Milano come Arcivescovo. Posso dunque ben comprendere quali siano stati i tuoi impegni e le tue preoccupazioni e in particolare quella tensione interiore e quasi lacerazione che si crea in chi si sente diviso tra il servizio dell'autorità, che prende quasi tutto il tempo e le energie, e il servizio alla scienza biblica e alla docenza, che vorrebbe anch'esso tutto il tempo e le energie. Il Siracide parla anche di viaggi e di servizi in altri paesi. Io penso in particolare al tuo servizio a Gerusalemme, una città che è a noi due molto cara e alla quale penso spesso.

Ma a me piace soprattutto quella descrizione dello scriba saggio che segue nel Siracide e che si riferisce alla sua preghiera nascosta: «Di buon mattino rivolge il cuore / al Signore che lo ha creato, / prega davanti all'Altissimo, / apre la bocca alla preghiera» (Sir 39,5). Chi legge i tuoi scritti percepisce che al fondo della tua ricerca c'è la ricerca del Signore, della sua Sapienza e della sua volontà. Questo è ciò che più importa di tutta una vita dedicata alla Scrittura e ai fratelli, quella grazia che ci unisce anche nella lontananza e nella diversità dei cammini.

In questa via ti auguro di camminare ancora a lungo.

Tuo, nel Signore

+ Carlo Maria Card. Martini

IL CARDINALE CARLO MARIA MARTINI
ARCIVESCOVO DI MILANO

THE BOOK OF BEN SIRA

SOME UNCOMMON WORDS
IN THE HEBREW TEXT OF BEN SIRA*

If on one hand the discovery of the Hebrew Mss of Sir in 1896 (= H) has pushed scholars to compare them with the old Greek (= G) and Syriac (= S) versions of the book, on the other hand, as an indispensable preliminary condition for that comparison, it has also required the direct study of the Hebrew language as shown in the Mss[1]. From the beginning this language has been recognised as representative of a transitional phase from the Biblical to the Mishnaic Hebrew[2] and, in any case, closer to the Biblical Hebrew of the more recent writings, characterised by a growing presence of aramaisms[3]. The historical approach to the language in a particular period, including orthography, morphology and especially the syntax[4], recognises above all in the lexicon the field in which it is possible to point out the major innovations and transformations of the language[5]. Conscious of the importance of the lexical novelty for the characterization of the Ben Sira language, the first students of the Mss used to give a list of new words found in them. These novelties regarded mostly shadings of meaning or formations coming from roots already known in the Old Testament[6].

* For the English translation of the paper I acknowledge the competent and generous help of Dr. Susan Whitehouse Zappalà. In this paper the Dictionaries are cited according to the conventional abbreviations.

1. D. STRAUSS, *Sprachliche Studien zu den hebräischen Sirachfragmenten*, in *Schweizerische Theologische Zeitschrift* 17 (1900) 65-80; C.H. TOY, *Remarks on the Hebrew Text of Ben-Sira*, in *JAOS* 23 (1902) 38-43; G.R. DRIVER, *Hebrew Notes on the "Wisdom of Jesus Ben Sirach"*, in *JBL* 53 (1934) 273-290.

2. Cf. recently, A. HURVITZ, *The Linguistic Status of Ben Sira as a Link between Biblical and Mishnaic Hebrew: Lexicographical Aspects*, in T. MURAOKA – J.F. ELWOLDE (eds.), *The Hebrew of the Dead Sea Scrolls and Ben Sira. Proceedings of a Symposium Held at Leiden University 11-14 December1995* (STDJ, 26), Leiden, 1997, pp. 72-91.

3. S. WAGNER, *Die lexikalischen und grammatikalischen Aramaismen im alttestamentlichen Hebräisch* (BZAW, 96), Berlin, 1966, lists as aramaisms in the OT 333 words (pp. 17-121), belonging to pre- and postexilic writings. Among them 50 are occurring in Sir, if we include אתה, נכסים, נתע, עשתון, צרך, קנין, not referred by Wagner to Sir.

4. Cf. S.E. FASSBERG, *On the Syntax of Dependent Clauses in Ben Sira*, and W.Th. VAN PEURSEN, *Periphrastic Tenses in Ben Sira*, in MURAOKA–ELWOLDE, *The Hebrew of the Dead Sea Scrolls and Ben Sira* (n. 2), respectively pp. 56-71 and 158-173.

5. P. JOÜON – T. MURAOKA, *A Grammar of Biblical Hebrew* (Subsidia biblica, 14/I-II), Roma, 1991, p. 9: "The variations in vocabulary and phraseology between one period and another, and one writer and another are the most significant".

6. Besides the exemplary treatment by HURVITZ, *The Linguistic Status* (n. 2), cf. also N.M. BRONZNICK, *An Unrecognized Denotation of the Verb HSR in Ben-Sira and Rab-*

In this way some lists have been prepared, as an appendix to their major publications, by S.R. Driver (1897)[7], Margoliouth (1899)[8], Strack (1903)[9], Lévi (1904)[10], Peters (1905)[11], Smend (1906)[12] and thereafter in an article of comparative philology by G. R. Driver (1934)[13]; Segal also gives us a list of his own, not in an appendix but in the introduction to his commentary[14]. I believe that it would be interesting to check the words in these lists comparing the explanation provided by the authors and the treatment given by the great Hebrew Dictionaries, published in the meantime: *BDB*, Zorell[15], *HALE* (and *HAL*), *DCH* and Alonso Schökel[16], and also Dalman[17] and Jastrow[18] for the post-biblical literature. For the moment I intend to consider only five words starting with *alef*; which let us review, even in a limited manner, a significant trajectory of the biblical studies of this century.

THE VERB אבד (11,12)

The verb אבד, recurring in Sir 8,2.12; 11,12; 14,9; 20,22; 30,40; 41,2.6; 46,18; 49,7, appears in the Lévi and Peters[19] lists for its occurrence in 11,12, where the entire verse says: יש/רשש ואבד מהלך חסר כל

---

binic Hebrew, in R. AHARONI (ed.), *Biblical and Other Studies in Memory of S.D. Goitein* = *HAR* 9 (1985) 91-105.

7. S.R. DRIVER, *Glossary of Words*, in A.E. COWLEY – A. NEUBAUER, *The Original Hebrew of a Portion of Ecclesiasticus (XXXIX.15 to XLIX.11)*, Oxford, 1897, pp. XXXI-XXXVI.

8. G. MARGOLIOUTH, *The Original Hebrew of Ecclesiaticus XXXI.12-31, and XXXVI.22-XXXVII.26*, in *JQR* 12 (1899) 1-33.

9. H.L. STRACK, *Die Sprüche Jesus', des Sohnes Sirachs. Der jüngst gefundene hebräische Text mit Anmerkungen und Wörterbuch*, Leipzig, 1903.

10. I. LÉVI, *The Hebrew Text of the Book of Ecclesiasticus*, Leiden, 1904.

11. N. PETERS, *Liber Jesu filii Sirach sive Ecclesiasticus hebraice*, Freiburg i.B., 1905.

12. R. SMEND, *Die Weisheit des Jesus Sirach erklärt*, Berlin, 1906; ID., *Die Weisheit des Jesus Sirach, hebräisch und deutsch. Mit einem hebräischen Glossar*, Berlin, 1906.

13. G.R. DRIVER, *Hebrew Notes* (n. 1).

14. M.S. SEGAL, ספר בן־סרא השלם, Jerusalem, [3]1972, p. 22.

15. F. ZORELL, *Lexicon hebraicum et aramaicum Veteris Testamenti*, Roma, 1957.

16. L. ALONSO SCHÖKEL, *Diccionario biblico hebreo-español*, Madrid, 1994. Among these Dictionaries only Zorell, Alonso Schökel e *DCH* intend to include the Hebrew text of Ben Sira.

17. G.H. DALMAN, *Aramäisch-neuhebräisches Handwörterbuch zu Targum, Talmud und Midrasch*, Frankfurt a.M., 1897 (reprinted Hildesheim, 1967).

18. M. JASTROW, *A Dictionary of the Targumim, the Talmud Babli and Yerushalmi, and Midrashic Literature*, t. I-II, New York, 1893 (reprinted 1967).

19. LÉVI, *The Hebrew Text* (n. 10), p. 77: poor | *arm* 11,12; PETERS, *Liber Jesu filii Sirach* (n. 11), p. 153: *miser* 11,12; but in the translation says: *marcidus*. The verb אבד occurs in the OT 184 times, and 7 times in the Aramaic portions (A. EVEN-SHOSHAN, *A New Concordance of the Bible*, Jerusalem, 1982, *s.v.*).

וַיּוֹתֵר א[וֹ]נֹש. But in this verse, even before אבד we find a real difficulty in רָשָׁש, for which two diverse interpretations are given fundamentally:

1) רָשָׁש, considered by *BBST* as the only recurrence of the verb רשש in Sir (part. Q), seems that it should be identified with the verb רשש (*BDB*: *Polel*, "beat down, shutter"; *HALE*: "smash, batter to pieces, shatter", *HAL*: *zerschlagen*), that occurs in the OT only in Jer 7,17 and Mal 1,4. Treating this verb under the same entry, Alonso Schökel gets it closer to these passages, although, even translating it with *arrasar* in Jer 5,15 and Mal 1,4, he proposes *empobrecerse, arruinarse* for Sir 11,12, making you think of the better known רוש "be in want, poor" (*BDB*), as has been done in the second interpretation, rather than of רשש. Also the adjective רשיש recurring in 4,19 (*hapax*) is connected with this רשש, and according to the root and the context this must signify "(morally) destroyed, listless, lazy". This interpretative line is followed in 11,12 by Smend[20], Peters[21], Skehan and Di Lella[22].

2) Others consider רשש as a "parallel form"[23] of the verb רוש "to be poor". In this way Lévi, who after having explained in 4,29 that the use of the verb רוש, from which רשיש would be derived, as lazy (*peureux*), is unusual[24], in 11,12 translates directly with "poor" (*pauvre*). Also Segal explains רשש as an intransitive verb or as an adjective "very poor" (רש גדול)[25].

Going back now to אבד we notice that Lévi interprets this as a synonym of the previous רשש that, as we have said, he connects with the root רוש. However, Peters, who follows his interpretation of אבד, but not the one of רשש, moves further apart from him for the collocation of מהלך, interpreted by both as part. Pi. of הלך: with it Peters, together with the others, concludes the hemistich a, while Lévi starts the hemistich b, as we can see from their respective translations: "Tel est pauvre et misérable, Va dénué de tout et riche (seulement) en souffrance" (Lévi)[26]; "Da ist ein Schwächling und *wandernder* Unglücklicher / der

---

20. SMEND, *Die Weisheit des Jesus Sirach* (n. 12), p. 79 : *schlaff* 11,12; the same in the translation, p. 19.
21. N. PETERS, *Das Buch Jesus Sirach oder Ecclesiasticus*, Münster i.W., 1913, p. 96: *Schwächling*.
22. P.W. SKEHAN – A.A. DI LELLA, *The Wisdom of Ben Sira* (AB, 39), New York, 1987. Cf. SKEHAN, p. 235: "broken-down"; in the commentary DI LELLA notes: lit. "beaten down" (p. 239).
23. G.R. DRIVER, *Hebrew Notes* (n. 1), p. 275,
24. I. LÉVI, *L'ecclésiastique ou la sagesse de Jésus fils de Sira. Texte original hébreu édité, traduit et commenté*, t. II, Paris, 1901, p. 22; he explains this unusual meaning by the hypothesis of a retroversion from the Syriac.
25. SEGAL, ספר בן-סרא השלם (n. 14), p. 70.
26. LÉVI, *L'ecclésiastique*, t. II (n. 24), p. 75.

Mangel an 'Kraft' und Überfluß an Schwäche hat" (Peters)[27]. But, for
מהלך, nowadays *BBST* justly proposes reading it as מַהֲלָךְ[28], a substantive already attested in Ezek 42,4; Jonah 3,3; Zech 3,7. But if מַהֲלָךְ is
united to the verb אבד, this can keep its ordinary meaning, without the
need to hypothesize the special meaning registered by Lévi and Peters
for Sir 11,12. The syntagma אֹבֵד מַהֲלָךְ[29] thus means "who is lost on the
way". This is the translation given by *DCH*, even if it wrongly follows
Lévi for the previous רשש; in fact, it translates רשש ואבד מהלך in this
way thus: "poor (!) and about to die, *lit.* about to perish in respect of his
(life-) journey", after having given as the meaning of אבד "die, be destroyed, disappear, be lost"; *HALE*: "become lost, go astray, perish, be
carried off".

THE PLURAL אונים (42,2a)

The two divergent readings of the Mss B and M at the beginning of
the hemistich appear contradictory; it therefore seems convenient to
treat them first separately, and to try to achieve their composition only at
the end. In Ms B we read: לאיש אונים וחסר עצמה. אונים can be plural of
אָוֶן or of אוֹן, that express two opposite concepts, respectively "sorrow"
and "wealth"[30]. As to the context which talks of the suffering man that
finds in death a liberation, we should prefer the plural of אָוֶן and thus
translate: "for the man of sorrows (= that suffers) and that lacks vigour". This is the interpretation of Peters[31], who, differently from Lévi
and Smend, keeps the text, referring to Gen 35,18 and Hos 9,4, two passages that *BDB* puts under אָוֶן, translating them respectively "son of my
trouble or sorrow" (בֶּן־אוֹנִי) and "bread of trouble, sorrow", or "mourning" (לֶחֶם אוֹנִים). Peters is followed by Segal who also goes back to Gen
35,18 and Hos 9,4 and furthermore explains in the same way אדם: אונים
בכל יגון וצער[32]. Zorell also recognises אָוֶן in Gen 35,18 and Ho 9,4, but
does not mention Sir 41,2 neither here nor under אוֹן. Alonso Schökel
instead unifies the two words in one single stem, pointing out that with
the different vocalization the positive (אוֹן: *fortuna*) and negative (אָוֶן:

---

27. PETERS, *Das Buch Jesus Sirach* (n. 21), p. 96.
28. Thus also SMEND, p. 105, and SEGAL, ספר בן־סרא השלם (n. 14), p. 69.
29. This vocalisation given in the Ms indicates the construct state (cf. *BDB*, s.v.)
30. According to the calculation of EVEN-SHOSHAN, the first occurs 77 times, the second 13 times; but he distinguishes an אוֹן II for Gen 35,18; Deut 26,14; Hos 9,4.
31. PETERS, *Das Buch Jesus Sirach* (n. 21), p. 344: "für den *unglücklichen* und
kraftlosen Menschen".
32. SEGAL, ספר בן־סרא השלם (n. 14), p. 276.

desgracia) aspect is specified; this last includes Gen 35,18 and Hos 9,4, but without mentioning Sir 41,2 neither in the one nor the other.

While recognising that אונים should be interpreted according to Hos 9,4, Smend reads in the Ms אננים ("moanings") instead of אונים (exchange between ו and נ) imagining in this way a word not attested elsewhere[33], deriving from the verb אנן *Hitpolal*, which recurs only in Num 11,1 and Lam 3,39, and also in Sir 10,25. But Lévi[34] prefers to derive אונים from און "wealth", underlining the parallelism with עצמה; but to be coherent with the context he corrects לאיש into לאין, making reference to Isa 40,29b: וּלְאֵין אוֹנִים עָצְמָה יַרְבֶּה "and to those who have not wealth (God) increases the vigour". Finally, the different reading of Masada לאין אוינים, correcting the obvious orthographic error אוינים to אונים, confirms Lévi's suggestion[35]. In any case, considering the ambivalence of אונים that can indicate both a negative and a positive concept, if it is put before the negation (לאין) we also get a meaning that is in accordance with the context, provided that the plural of און is read and not that of אָוֶן. Even if G initially seems to concord with B (לאיש = ἀνθρώπῳ) it substantially coincides with M (לאין אונים = ἐπιδεομένῳ, "[to the man] who has needs").

But if, after all, even in B we want to find the fundamental reading of M, where surely, given the presence of the initial negation, we get the plural of און, then, substituting און with אָוֶן we get this *adversative* meaning: "to a man of (who has) wealth, and that (yet) lacks vigour". Differentiating the two positive concepts of wealth and health in this way, since the wealth positivity is cancelled by the lack of health, we get a meaning coherent with the context. *DCH* introduces this passage under און translating B: "man of strength(s)", but adds also the other (negative) possibility, returning however not to אָוֶן but to אֲנֶה "distress" (root אנה "mourn") that recognizes in Gen 35,18 and Hos 9,4, for which *HALE*, instead, proposes the substantive אוֹנִי[36], making it derive from the same root. In any case, even if from the textual-critical point of view the two divergent readings of B and of M must be reconciled, it does not seem correct to harmonize them both under the same stem און as done in *BBST*[37].

33. SMEND, *Die Weisheit des Jesus Sirach* (n. 12), p. 72: "dem Manne, der *seufzt* (= אננים) und kraftlos ist"; p. 61: אננים Traurigkeit 41,2.

34. I. LÉVI, *L'ecclésiastique ou la sagesse de Jésus fils de Sira. Texte original hébreu édité, traduit et commenté*, t. I, Paris, 1898, p. 33: "À qui est *dénué de force* et privé de vigueur".

35. Y. YADIN, *The Ben Sira Scroll from Masada*, Jerusalem, 1965, properly remarks: "The Scroll reading confirms Lévi's suggestion... which was rejected by all other commentators" (p. 18 hebr. = p. 17 engl.).

36. Thus EVEN-SHOSHAN's און II corresponds to אֲנֶה by *DCH*, and to אוֹנִי by *HALE*.

37. *BBST*, p. 77.

The Hitpael of אחר

The particularity in the use of the verb אָחַר in Sir consists in the fact that it is used for the first time in the form of the *Hitpael* in 7,34; 11,11; 32,11, while twice more it is used in the *Piel* form, following the more common use of the Old Testament. To better understand the meaning of this *Hitpael* it is worth examining first the use of the verb אָחַר in the Old Testament (17 times: 1 time *Qal*, 15 times *Piel*, 1 time *Hifil*). In order to initially determine the meaning of the verb, we have to refer to that of the more common adverb/preposition אַחֲרֵי/אַחַר "behind, after"[38] that is stated in a spatial or temporal sense. The first thing that strikes us in the use of אָחַר in the Old Testament is the fact that it is used only in the temporal sense of "to be late" (intr.) and to "detain" (trans.) to various degrees, depending on the context. The use of this verb in its intensive form *Piel* can be explained by the fact that this "to be late" implies a tension in the person being late – the subjet of the verb – and also in the person waiting for him.

Examining the treatment of this voice in the various Dictionaries a certain diversity in the organisation of the various paragraphs is noticeable, also for the only form *Piel*. *BDB* divides the 15 occurrences in two distinct fundamental fields: 1) intensive sense, as indicated by the *Piel*, and 2) causative sense. Also Zorell distinguishes two fundamental areas: transitive sense (3 occur.) and intransitive sense (12 occur.). But, since the distinction criterion changes there is no correspondence between the two areas of the two dictionaries. *HALE*, instead, renounces a basic classification of a formal type and distinguishes simply four meanings between which all the 15 occurrences of the verb are distributed. The first two consider the cases in which the verb has as direct object 1) a person (Gen 24,56: "detain") or 2) a thing (Exod 22,28: "hold back, give hesitantly"), a condition that makes them coincide, except for Deut 7,10, with Zorell's transitive sense. The other two meanings regard the cases in which there is not a direct object governed directly by the verb: 3) "linger (late)" (Prov 23,30; Ps 127,2); 4) "delay, hesitate" (Deut 7,10; Judg 5,28; Isa 5,11; 46,13; Hab 2,3; Ps 40,18; 70,6; Dan 9,19; including the cases with ל + infinitive: Gen 34,19; Deut 23,22; Qoh 5,3). *DCH* goes back to Zorell' classification, distinguishing for the *Piel* the intransitive use (Judg 5,28; Isa 5,11; 46,13; Hab 2,3; Deut 7,10; Prov 23,30; Ps 40,18; Dan 9,19) from the transitive one (Gen 24,56; Ex

---

38. According to EVEN-SHOSHAN אחר occurs in the Old Testament 96 times and אחרי 619 times.

22,28). Then it adds in the par. 3 all the cases in which אָחַר governs an infinitive verb with (Gen 34,19; Deut 23,20; Qoh 5,3) or without לְ (Ps 127,2). A circumstance not pointed out in the dictionaries is that אָחַר in the *Piel* is always preceded by the negative particle לֹא/אַל except when it refers to an action negative in itself, as in Ps 127,2; Isa 5,11; Judg 5,28 (here the interrogative particle מַדּוּעַ precedes). This means that "to be late" is perceived as a negative fact, that it becomes positive when it is preceded by a negation. In addition to the *Piel*'s cases already examined there are two other occurrences, one in *Qal* (Gen 32,5) and one in *Hifil* (2 Sam 20,5). In Gen 32,5 Jacob, coming back from Haran, sends a message to Esau: עִם־לָבָן גַּרְתִּי וָאֵחַר עַד־עָתָּה, "with Laban I have been staying and was delayed till now".

Here אָחַר corresponds to the use of עָמַד in Gen 45,9; Jos 10,19; 1 Sam 20,38 (cf. *BDB* 3.a: "tarry, delay"). Jacob simply states something that already happened, even if the intention is to appease his brother Esau, reminding him of the past vicissitudes; therefore the narrator makes him talk in the *Qal* of אָחַר, also in parallel with the *Qal* of גּוּר (גַּרְתִּי). Instead, in 2 Sam 20,5 we have the *Hifil* (remarked causality) because it is an intentional waste of time which was meant to hinder the adversary plan (very appropriately, *BDB*: "shewed, exhibited delay").

Besides the last two cases taken into consideration, we also have the more ordinary use of אָחַר – as already mentioned – in the *Piel*; and also in Sir this verb is used twice in the *Piel* followed by לְ and infinitive: אל תאחר לשוב אליו, "Do not postpone to go back to him" (5,7); ולא יאחר להשליכה, "And (the fool) shall not delay to throw it (= wisdom) away" (32,17).

Once again אָחַר, is preceded by the negative particle (ולא, אל), and is followed by the infinitive as in Gen 34,19; Deut 23,22; Qoh 5,3; Ps 127,3. In the two cases of Sir 5,7 and 32,17 the sense is "temporal" and indicates the lengthening of an action's duration, as in all the 17 occurrences of אָחַר in the Old Testament. Instead, in all other cases of Sir in which the *Hitpael* is used the "spatial" sense prevails: אל תתאחר מבוכים, "Do not draw aside from those who weep" (7,34); יש עמל ויגע ורץ וכדי כן הוא מתאחר, "One labours, grows weary and runs, and remains more behind (= away from the target)" (11,11).

Coherent with the general rule, this *Hitpael* adds the reflexive value to the usual sense of *Piel*[39], underlining the inconvenience and the misfortune of an action that closes the subject in itself. Also, in the other case in which the *Hitpael* of אָחַר has a "temporal" sense, as it always hap-

---

39. JOÜON – MURAOKA, *A Grammar of Biblical Hebrew* (n. 5), p. 159; W. GESENIUS – E. KAUTZSCH, *Gesenius' Hebrew Grammar* (tr. A.E. Cowley), Oxford, ²1910 , p. 149.

pens in its 17 occurrences in the Old Testament that we have examined above, i.e. אל תתאחר in 32,11, the reflexive aspect is evidenced. The fundamental meaning is similar to what we have in אל תאחר, referring to God in Ps 40,18; 70,6; Dan 9,19; the difference is that here – talking about God – we do not have the reflexive and blameworthy sense which we find instead in Sir 32,11, where it is supposed that "to be late" is an unpleasant action[40].

THE SUBSTANTIVE אכפה IN 46,5b (HAPAX)

From a grammatical point of view אכפה is considered either verb (inf. Qal: Smend, Zorell, Alonso Schökel, HALE) or substantive, vocalised, in turn, as אֶכְפָה (Peters, Lévi, Strack, S. R. Driver) and as אַכְפָה (Dalman, Jastrow, Segal, BBST) respectively. The lacuna present in the Ms therefore is differently reconstructed according to G, being totally absent in S: [מסביו (Smend: איביו; Peters, Segal) אויבים‎/ (Lévi) כאכפה לו צרים

According to Segal אַכְפָה is a feminine form of the אֶכֶף noun which is found in Job 33,7. Nevertheless, he argues that, in this way, the noun results badly connected with the subject of the sentence. In addition, he notes that G's verbal construction (ἐν τῷ θλῖψαι αὐτὸν ἐχθροὺς κυκλόθεν) could correspond either to a suffixed infinitive form כָּאכְפָה or to the perfect form כָּאָכְפוּ[41]. According to Lévi's suggestion, כָּאכְפָה is an infinitive form, even though he points out that the paragogical ה, in this case, is not explainable[42]; therefore, in his "glossary" the אכפה noun only is given[43]. If the noun form is preferred, a nominal clause should be supposed, as it has been rightly translated by DCH under the stem אֲכְפָּה: "when enemies around were pressure to him". Peters translates the noun in a slightly different way: "als in der Not war, Feinde waren ringsum"[44]. Moreover he relies on S. R. Driver[45] for the reading אֲכֵפָה.

With respect to dictionaries, BDB records the אָכַף verb "press, urge", which is found in Prov 16,26 only, and its derivative [אֶכֶף] "pressure",

40. R. ALCALAY, The Complete Hebrew-English Dictionary, Ramat Gan – Jerusalem, 1981, s.v., translates התאחר "to come late", an expression that implicitly possesses a negative connotation.
41. SEGAL, ספר בן־קרא השלם (n. 14), p. 318.
42. LÉVI, L'ecclésiastique, t. I (n. 34), p. 111.
43. LÉVI, The Hebrew Text (n. 10), p.77.
44. PETERS, Das Buch Jesus Sirach (n. 21), p. 393
45. S.R. DRIVER, Glossary of Words (n. 7), p. XXXI.

which is used in Job 33,7 only. Zorell, Alonso Schökel and *HALE* all recognize in Sir 46,5 the verbal form. Moreover, *BDB* and Zorell report both the use of this root as well in Aramaic/Syriac as in Arabic sources, whilst *HALE* only mentions the Accadic parallel; in addition, this labels as Middle Hebrew what *BDB* qualifies as Mishnaic. The most comprehensive documentation is offered, instead, by Wagner[46]. Alcalay records the verb אָכַף "to force, press, compel, burden, weigh on, enforce", also used in *Piel* (to saddle), *Nifal* (to be enforced), *Hifil* (to enforce), as well as all the following derivatives: אַכְפָּתִיוּת, אִכְפָּנוּת, אַכְפַּת, אַכְפָּתִי, אִכְפָּוֹן, אַכְפָּה אָכֵף. In conclusion, it is possible to affirm that this noun has been incorrectly interpreted as a verb, on the basis of G, which, as known, often translates freely.

THE CORRADICALS אָנַס AND אֹנֶס

The root אנס occurs twice in Sir; as a verb in 31,21 and as a noun in 20,4. In the Old Testament it is attested only once as a part. *Qal* in Esther 1,8. *HALE* considers it an Aramaic loan word (*HAL*: *aramäisches Lehnwort*), and refers to Wagner who, in turn, outlines a detailed profile of the root[47]. In *BDB* the verb ("compel, constrain") is treated as *hapax l.* with regard to Esther 1,8, whilst *HALE* cites Sir, both 20,4 and 31,21, under the verbal stem occurring in Esther 1,8. Because of their use in Middle Hebrew, both Dalman and Jastrow record both the verb (*1. Zwingen, gewaltsam tun; 2. Notzüchtigen*: "to bend, force; to do violence; to outrage") as well as the noun (*1. Zwang; 2. Todesfall* : "compulsion, force; unavoidable interference, accident"). With regard to the verb it is worthy of note that it is used in Sir 31,21 within the banqueting context, in tune with Esther 1,8: וְהַשְׁתִיָּה כְדָת אֵין אֹנֵס, "And drinking was according to the law, no one was compelled" (= *RSV*; but lit.: "compelling"). Sir 31,21a says: וגם אם נאסתה במטעמים, "and if you are forced with (= to eat) dainties". The difference consists in the fact that during the meal in Esther 1,8 the "pressure" was avoided as, by contrast, was appreciated according to Sir 31,21a! The use of the noun, absent in the Old Testament, occurs in 20,4: כן עושה באונס משפט כן נאמן לָן עם בתולה, "He who imposes (his) right(s) through violence, is like a eunuch passing the night with a virgin".

---

46. WAGNER, *Die lexikalischen und grammatikalischen Aramaismen* (n. 3), p. 24, who however postulates in Sir 46,5 a verb.

47. WAGNER, *Aramaismen* (n. 3), p. 27.

From a logical point of view the sequence of the two hemistichs must be reversed, and we have to amend the reading כן נאמן in כנאמן (Segal[48], whereas Peters[49] conjectures חמד נאמן; Smend holds the two possibilities[50]); also the first נ must be deleted (dittography). In addition to the noun אוֹנֶס, which, even if it is new, is rather evident in its meaning because of its root, the term נאמן has drawn much attention. Its meaning, evident as part. *Nifal* אמן ("faithful, trustworthy"), is translated by G and S specifically as "eunuch": G εὐνοῦχος, S מהימן. According to Lévi, the present hemistich must have been re-translated from the Syriac into Hebrew, and the translator, misunderstanding the double meaning of מהימן as *eunuque* and as *véridique, fidèle*, would have erroneously chosen the latter giving exactly נאמן and not סריס, which in Hebrew is the specific term to indicate the eunuch. But, as Smend observes, it is not necessary to recur to the Syriac, since in Hebrew too it is possible that the derivative of the same root has undergone the same semantic evolution by acquiring the present special meaning, since the eunuch was also a trustworthy man in the prince's court. However, Lévi's hypothesis has been accepted by Segal, whilst Peters prefers to follow Smend. Finally, with respect to the noun אֹנֶס from which we started, it is only possible to conclude by noting that its use in 31,21 is analogous to that of its corradical verb in 20,4, since in both cases it is a question of "violence" connected with a pleasure: first the table pleasure and then the sexual pleasure.

CONCLUSIONS

Five words selected from the lists of somewhat new words encountered in the Hebrew text of Ben Sira have been analysed. As a matter of fact, all them were not completely new with respect to the Old Testament.

1. In the syntagma אבד מהלך the verb אבד maintains its fundamental meaning "lose, be lost", against the positions of Lévi and Peters.

2. With regard to אונים, it is not possible to attribute to it the same meaning if it is preceded by לאיש (Ms B) or by לאין (Ms M). But, besides the two opposite derivations, either from און or from אֶן, the knowledge of a possible אוֹנִי or אֹנֶה has meanwhile been acquired, having both the negative sense attributed first to אֶן.

48. SEGAL, ספר בן־סרא השלם (n. 14), p. 120.

49. N. PETERS, *Der jüngst wiederaufgefundene hebr. Text des Buches Ecclesiasticus*, Freiburg i.Br., 1898, p. 393.

50. SMEND, *Die Weisheit des Jesus Sirach* (n. 12), p. 21.

3. With respect to the first appearance of אָחַר in *Hitpael*, this use even though not attested before, falls within the general rule regarding the reflexive meaning of *Piel*.

4. The lacuna of the H text in 46,5b reconstructed according to G, does not justify the hypothesis that we have to suppose that the verbal form which we find in this translation, is also in H. Therefore, it is resonable to intend אכפה as a noun, even though not present yet according to this form in the Old Testament.

5. The new noun אֹנֶס is used with the same nuance of meaning intended by the verbal root in both 31,21 and Esther 1,8.

In full agreement with van Peursen's statement that "in any discussion of the language of Ben Sira, one of the main problems is the relationship of the Hebrew of Ben Sira to Biblical Hebrew, Mishnaic Hebrew and Aramaic"[51], I have limited this paper to show only some aspects of this characterization. In conclusion, it seems fitting to stress that the balanced position between tradition and innovation generally observed in Ben Sira's thought, is also confirmed with respect to the language he used, in a transitional phase from the Biblical to the Mishnaic Hebrew,

Studio Teologico S. Paolo   Antonino MINISSALE
Catania

---

51. VAN PEURSEN, *Periphrastic Tenses* (n. 5), p. 158.

AROMAS, FRAGANCIAS Y PERFUMES
EN EL SIRÁCIDA

Personalmente siempre me he sentido atraída por las imágenes que la Sabiduría utiliza para autodescribirse en el espléndido poema conocido como «El Elogio de la Sabiduría» (Sir 24).[1] Me refiero sobre todo a aquellas imágenes "vegetales, ornamentales, perennes, aromáticas y nutritivas"[2] que colorean los vv. 12-17. Árboles, plantas, flores, frutos y perfumes describen el crecimiento y la expansión de la Sabiduría en Israel, a la vez que evocan el idílico paraíso terrenal del libro del Génesis[3]. En el v. 15 la Sabiduría desprende un olor agradable y perfumado que se expande por su heredad e inunda la tienda santa con un sinfín de fragancias. Y es precisamente sobre los aromas, fragancias y perfumes que yo quisiera tratar en este breve artículo.

Podría limitar mi estudio a Sir 24,15 (el perfume de la Sabiduría) e intentar explicar, por ejemplo, el uso que el autor hace de Ex 30,23 y 30,34[4]. He preferido, sin embargo, ampliar el campo de visión y tomar en consideración todo el libro de Ben Sira.

El trabajo que me propongo es de carácter preferentemente filológico. Por lo tanto, su objetivo es el estudio del vocabulario relativo al perfume, teniendo en cuenta las versiones griega, siríaca, sirohexaplar y latina, además del texto hebreo, cuando lo hay[5].

1. Cf. J. MARBÖCK, *Weisheit im Wandel. Untersuchungen zur Weisheitstheologie bei Ben Sira* (BBB, 37), Bonn, Hanstein, 1971, pp. 34-96; O. RICKENBACHER, *Weisheitsperikopen bei Ben Sira* (OBO, 1), Freiburg-Schweiz – Göttingen, Universitätsverlag – Vandenhoeck & Ruprecht, 1973, pp. 111-172; M. GILBERT, *L'éloge de la Sagesse (Siracide 24)*, en *RTL* 5 (1974) 326-348; G.T. SHEPPARD, *Wisdom as a Hermeneutical Construct* (BZAW, 151), Berlin / New York, de Gruyter, 1980, pp. 19-71.

2. V. MORLA ASENSIO, *Eclesiástico. Texto y comentario* (El Mensaje del Antiguo Testamento, 20), Estella-Navarra, La Casa de la Biblia, 1992, p. 126.

3. Cf. A. FOURNIER-BIDOZ, *L'arbre et la demeure: Siracide XXIV 10-17*, en *VT* 34 (1984) 1-10, y M. HIMMELFARB, *The Temple and the Garden of Eden in Ezekiel, the Book of the Watchers, and the Wisdom of Ben Sira*, en J. SCOTT – P. SIMPSON-HOUSLEY (eds.), *Sacred Places and Profane Places. Essays in the Geographics of Judaism, Christianity and Islam* (Contributions to the Study of Religion, 30), New York, Greenwood Press, 1991, pp. 63-78.

4. Cf. SHEPPARD, *Wisdom*, pp. 57-60; P.C. BEENTJES, *Jesus Sirach en Tenach. Een onderzoek naar en een classificatie van parallellen, met bijzondere aandacht voor hun functie in Sirach 45:9-26*, Nieuwegein, Selbstverlag, 1981, pp. 89-90 e ID., *Discovering a New Path of Intertextuality: Inverted Quotations and their Dynamics*, en L. J. DE REGT – J. DE WAARD – J.P. FOKKELMAN (eds.), *Literary Structure and Rhetorical Strategies in the Hebrew Bible*, Assen, Van Gorcum, 1996, p. 40.

5. Para el griego, cf. J. ZIEGLER, *Sapientia Iesu Filii Sirach* (Septuaginta. Vetus

El vocabulario del perfume

En el Sirácida hay 14 términos pertenecientes al mundo de los perfumes. Salvo una excepción (μυρεψός en 38,8), todos los términos están relacionados, directa o indirectamente, con el culto[6]. Cabe señalar que nueve de los citados términos se concentran en 24,15, donde la Sabiduría dice de sí misma:

15a ὡς κιννάμωμον καὶ ἀσπάλαθος ἀρωμάτων[7]
15b καὶ ὡς σμύρνα ἐκλεκτὴ διέδωκα εὐωδίαν,
15c ὡς χαλβάνη καὶ ὄνυξ καὶ στακτὴ
15d καὶ ὡς λιβάνου ἀτμὶς ἐν σκηνῇ.

15a como cinamomo y aspálato aromáticos
15b y como mirra selecta he derramado (dado) perfume,
15c como gálbano y ónice y estacte,
15d y como vapor de incienso en la tienda.

15a
15b
15c
15d

15a como cinamomo y olor (incienso) aromáticos,
15b y como mirra buena he desprendido (perfumado) mi aroma,
15c y como incienso y gálbano y ónice y bálsamo
15d y como buen aceite he derramado (dado) mi aroma.

Testamentum Graecum, 12/2), Göttingen, Vandenhoeck & Ruprecht, ²1980 y A. RAHLFS, *Septuaginta. Id est Vetus Testamentum graece iuxta LXX interpretes*, t. II, Stuttgart, Württembergische Bibelanstalt, ⁷1962, pp. 377-471; para el siríaco, cf. A.M. CERIANI (ed.), *Translatio Syra Pescitto Veteris Testamenti ex codice Ambrosiano sec. fere IV photolithographice edita*, t. II, Mediolani, Pogliani, 1883, pp. 458-485 y B. WALTON (ed.), *Biblia Sacra Polyglotta*, t. VI, London, Thomas Roycroft, 1657, pp. 46-47 (para las variantes); para la sirohexaplar, cf. A.M. CERIANI (ed.), *Codex Syro-Hexaplaris Ambrosianus photolithographice editus*, Mediolani, Pogliani, 1874. pp. 80-96; para el latín, cf. ABADÍA SAN JERÓNIMO (ed.), *Sapientia Salomonis, Liber Hiesu Filii Sirach* (Biblia Sacra iuxta latinam vulgatam versionem, 12), Roma, Typis Polyglottis Vaticanis, 1964, pp. 105-137 y para el hebreo, cf. P.C. BEENTJES (ed.), *The Book of Ben Sira in Hebrew. A Text Edition of all Extant Hebrew Manuscripts & A Synopsis of all Parallel Hebrew Ben Sira Texts* (SVT, 68), Leiden, Brill, 1997. En cuanto a las siglas del aparato crítico en griego, seguimos la edición de Ziegler.

6. Además de E. COTHENET, *Parfums*, en DBS, t. VI, Paris, Letouzey & Ané, 1960, col. 1291-1331, esp. col. 1312-1327: «L'usage des parfums dans le culte», señalamos tres estudios importantes sobre el tema: el clásico M. LÖHR, *Das Räucheropfer im Alten Testament. Eine archäologische Untersuchung* (SKG.G, 4/4), Halle-Saale, 1927; K. NIELSEN, *Incense in Ancient Israel* (SVT, 38), Leiden, Brill, 1986 y más recientemente, W. ZWICKEL, *Räucherkult und Räuchergeräte. Exegetische und archäologische Studien zum Räucheropfer im Alten Testament* (OBO, 97), Freiburg-Schweiz, Universitätsverlag, – Göttingen, Vandenhoeck & Ruprecht, 1990.

7. Excepto O-V 248, los demás códices y manuscritos añaden δέδωκεν ὀσμήν (cf. RAHLFS, *Septuaginta*, t. II, p. 418). Así también L: *aromatizans odorem dedi*.

20a   *sicut cinnamomum et aspaltum aromatizans odorem dedi*
20b   *quasi myrra electa dedi suavitatem odoris.*
21a   *et quasi storax et galbanus et ungula et gutta*
21b   *et quasi libanus non incisus vaporavi habitationem meam*
21c   *et quasi balsamum non mixtum odor meus.*

20a   como cinamomo y aspálato aromáticos perfumé,
20b   como mirra escogida desprendí un olor suave,
21a   y como estoraque, gálbano, ónice y estacte,
21b   y como incienso íntegro (no dividido) perfumé mi habitación
21c   y como bálsamo no mezclado (era) mi olor.

Veamos la lista completa de los términos:

ἄρωμα	perfume (24,15a)
ἀσπάλαθος	aspálato (24,15a)
εὐωδία	buen olor (24,15b; 32[35],8b; 38,11a; 45,16c; 50,15d)
εὐωδιάζειν	dar buen olor, perfumar (39,14a)
θυμίαμα	incienso (45,16c; 49,1a)
κιννάμωμον	cinamomo (24,15a)
λίβανος	incienso (24,15d; 39,14a; 50,9a)
μυρεψός	perfumista (38,8a; 49,1a)
ὄνυξ	ónice (24,15c)
ὀσμή	fragancia (39,14a; 50,15d)
πυρεῖον	incensario (50,9a)
σμύρνα	mirra (24,15b)
στακτή	estacte (24,15c)
χαλβάνη	gálbano (24,15c)

ANÁLISIS DE LOS TÉRMINOS

ἄρωμα

24,15a   ἀρωμάτων   ܪ̈ܝܚܢܐ   *(20) aromatizans*

En la LXX ἄρωμα (17x), generalmente en plural, siempre traduce (a excepción de Cant 1,3) el hebreo בֹּשֶׂם (bálsamo). Dicho sustantivo no suele tener un significado especializado, sino que normalmente se refiere a los perfumes en general: puede designar una planta o hierba aromática, el aroma que de ella se desprende, o simplemente un olor muy suave y agradable. El hebreo בֹּשֶׂם (término que no aparece en Sir) corresponde al siríaco ܒܣܡܐ (buen olor, perfume, incienso)[8].

En Sir 24,15 ἀρωμάτων se refiere al aroma del cinamomo y del aspálato, los dos perfumes que encabezan la lista de imágenes aplicadas a la Sabiduría en este versículo.

8. Cf. COTHENET, *Parfums*, col. 1303 y NIELSEN, *Incense*, p. 67: "It looks as if biblical *bsm* first of all is a general term for odoriferous spice".

ἀσπάλαθος[9]

24,15a   ἀσπάλαθος[10]   ܐܠܒ݂ܟ   (20) aspaltum[11]

ἀσπάλαθος es un *hapax legomenon* en la LXX: solamente se encuentra en Sir 24,15 junto a otros perfumes que se utilizaban para preparar el aceite de la unción (Ex 30,22-33) o el incienso sagrado (Ex 30,34-38)[12]. El aspálato, llamado también "espino de camello" o "cetro rojo" (ἐρυσίσκηπτρον), es un arbusto espinoso de flores rojas, típico del Mediterráneo y del suroeste de Asia, del que se extrae un producto aromático muy apreciado en Oriente[13]. Gracias a las descripciones de Plinio (*Hist. Nat.*-12,52,10 passim) y Dioscórides (*De Mat. Med.* 1,19)[14], sabemos que los antiguos lo utilizaban como ungüento, perfume y también como medicina. El aspálato era además uno de los 16 ingredientes del célebre perfume egipcio conocido con el nombre de *kyphi* (κῦφι)[15].

La versión siríaca utiliza la expresión ܪ݈ܣܡܒܕ ܐܠܒ݂ܟ (aspálato perfumado). La palabra ܐܠܒ݂ܟ, que normalmente significa: vapor, olor, perfume o incienso, aquí parece aludir concretamente al aspálato. Según Löw, ܪ݈ܣܡܒܕ ܐܠܒ݂ܟ podría ser el equivalente de la קִדָּה לְבָנָה (casia blanca) que encontramos en algunos textos rabínicos como, por ejemplo, *Kilayim* 1,8; *'Erubin*, 34b[16].

---

9. Cf. COTHENET, *Parfums*, col. 1302-1303.

10. Los min. 248-672 46 336 534' leen παλαθος (pan hecho a base de frutas), cf. 1Re 25,18. El códice V y el min. 705: απαλαθος y el min. 543: σπαλαθος. Smend piensa que (ἀσ)πάλαθος podría ser un error por (ὡς) κάλαμος (caña), cf. R. SMEND, *Die Weisheit des Jesus Sirach*, Berlin, Reimer, 1906, p. 219. Si se acepta esta última hipótesis, el texto se acercaría mucho a Ex 30,23 LXX (κάλαμος εὐώδης).

11. En algunos códices y ediciones se lee la variante *balsamum* (= ἄρωμα), palabra de significado genérico, en lugar de *aspaltum*.

12. Sobre esta perícopa, cf. el reciente estudio de P. HEGER, *The Development of Incense Cult in Israel* (BZAW, 245), Berlin/New York, de Gruyter, 1997, esp. pp. 127-144.

13. Naomi F. MILLER ha lanzado una nueva hipótesis sobre este arbusto: el aspálato (Alhagi) del que hablan los autores antiguos, incluido Ben Sira, sería en realidad la planta de la alcaparra (Capparis spinosa). Además de la evidencia arqueobotánica, la autora aduce argumentos de tipo lingüístico: el acádico *supalu* (antiguo sumerio *ᵘmunzer*) podría ser el correspondiente del griego ἀσπάλαθος. Cf. *The 'Aspalathus' Caper*, en *BASOR* 297 (1996) 55-60.

14. TEOFRASTO cita el aspálato en una lista de plantas odoríferas utilizadas para elaborar perfumes (*Hist. Nat.* 9,7,3). Ver También, *De Odor.* 33.

15. Cf. F. VIGOUROUX, *Aspalathe*, en *DB*, t. I, Paris, Letouzey & Ané, 1895, col. 1112.

16. Cf. I. LÖW, *Die Flora der Juden*, t. II (Veröffentlichungen der Alexander Kohut Memorial Foundation, 2), Wien-Leipzig, Löwit, 1924, pp. 424-426.

εὐωδία[17]

24,15b	διέδωκα εὐωδίαν[18]	ܐܪܝܚܐ ܕܒܣܡܐ ܝ ܪ	(20) dedi suavitatem odoris
32(35),8b	εὐωδία[19]	——	(8) odor suavitatis
38,11a	εὐωδίαν[20]	——	(11) suavitatem
45,16c	εὐωδίαν	ܒܣܡܐ	(20) bonum odorem
50,15d	ὀσμὴν εὐωδίας	ܠܪܝܚܐ ܕܒܣܡܐ	(17) odorem divinum

En la LXX la palabra εὐωδία por lo general aparece junto a ὀσμή formando la expresión ὀσμὴ εὐωδίας (olor agradable) que traduce el hebreo רֵיחַ (הַ)נִּיחֹחַ (olor apacible, suave). Dicha expresión pertenece al lenguaje técnico del ritual israelita y puede referirse a los holocaustos (Ex 29,18.25), a las oblaciones (Lev 2,2) o a los sacrificios pacíficos (Lev 3,5).

En el Sirácida ὀσμὴ εὐωδίας y su correspondiente רֵיחַ נִיחֹחַ se encuentran solamente en 50,15G (cuando el sumo sacerdote Simón hace la ofrenda del vino) y en 45,16MsB (la elección del sumo sacerdote Aarón) respectivamente.

En 45,16 el latín bonum odorem se acerca al hebreo ריח ניחח (en griego, solamente εὐωδίαν), mientras que el siríaco reduce todo el estico a un solo vocablo (ܒܣܡܐ).

En cuanto a 50,15, el siríaco (ܠܪܝܚܐ ܕܒܣܡܐ, olor agradable) coincide con el griego (ὀσμὴν εὐωδίας), mientras el latín califica el olor de las ofrendas con el adjetivo "divino" (odorem divinum), quizás para sintonizar con el destinatario de las mismas: Excelso Principi. Por lo que al texto hebreo se refiere, en el MsB falta el v. 15 posiblemente por homoioteleuton (cf. 14b y 16d, ambos esticos terminan con la misma palabra: עליון). Pero a pesar de esta laguna en el texto, todo hace suponer la misma expresión que en 45,16MsB: ריח ניחח.

En la LXX εὐωδία (cf. lo dicho antes sobre ὀσμὴ εὐωδίας) presenta connotaciones cultuales muy significativas (cf. Gen 8,21; Num 15; 28; 29). Así también en el Sirácida. A excepción de 24,15, donde el elemento cultual se sitúa en un plano marcadamente simbólico (la función litúrgica de la Sabiduría expresada a través del perfume), el buen olor o olor agradable aparece siempre en un contexto cultual

17. Cf. A. STUMPFF, εὐωδία, en TWNT, t. II, Stuttgart, Kohlhammer, 1935, pp. 808-809.

18. Los min. 315' (315-672) leen ευοσμιαν.

19. V 130* 543 leen ευοδια (cf. 10,5) y b 315' 358 ευδοκια (cf. 20,9).

20. El min. 443 lee ευωχιαν (cf. 3Mac 6,35). Por lo que se refiere al texto hebreo de 38,11a, la única palabra que no se consigue ver por defecto del MsB es la primera del estico, o sea la que correspondería al griego εὐωδίαν.

relacionado directamente con las ofrendas (32[35],8), las libaciones (38,11; 50,15) y los sacrificios (45,16). Mientras en estos textos εὐωδία hace alusión a todo lo que se ofrece en el altar sin distinción alguna, en 24,15b se refiere concretamente a las sustancias aromáticas citadas en el mismo versículo (cinamomo, aspálato, mirra…).

Podemos añadir algunos textos donde εὐωδία aparece como una variante de εὐοδία (buen camino, éxito, suerte)[21]:

10,5a: "En las manos del Señor está el éxito (εὐοδία) del hombre"
         (493-*l* c-679-795 alii: εὐωδία)

20,9a: "Hay quien encuentra el éxito (εὐοδία) en la desgracia"
         (A 253 *L*-248 c alii: εὐωδία)

38,13:   "A veces el éxito (εὐοδία) está en sus manos (de los médicos)"
         (S C 253 *a* c-795 46 307 315' 429 542 543 547: εὐωδία)

43,26a: "Por él (el Señor) tiene éxito (εὐοδία)[22] el mensajero"
         (B 253 46^S 307 315' 443 543 631' 679 705 753 Aeth: εὐωδία)

Si exceptuamos el primer texto citado[23], en los demás casos se impone la lectura de εὐοδία (o del verbo εὐοδόω), ya sea porque el texto hebreo lo confirma (38,13MsB: מצלחה, éxito y 43,26aMsB: צלח, tener éxito), ya sea por el sentido de la frase (20,9a: falta el hebreo).

εὐωδιάζειν

39,14a εὐωδιάσατε ὀσμήν (13c) ܘܝ ܪ (18) *odorem suavitatis habete*

En la LXX εὐωδιάζειν ocurre solamente dos veces: en Sir 39,14 (falta el hebreo) y en Zac 9,17, donde traduce el verbo נוב Polel (hacer crecer, desarrollar).

In Sir 39,14 el verbo εὐωδιάζειν, derivado de εὐωδία, tiene como complemento el sustantivo ὀσμή. Así la expresión εὐωδιάζειν ὀσμήν

---

21. H.J. THACKERAY, *A Grammar of the Old Testament in Greek according to the Septuagint*, t. I: *Introduction, Orthography and Accidence*, Cambridge, Cambridge University Press, 1909, p. 91, § 30: "In Sirach the writing of ω for o is more frequent [que en los demás libros de la LXX] and goes back apparently to the autograph or to an early copy". Ver también, S. DANIEL, *Recherches sur le vocabulaire du culte dans la Septante* (Études et commentaires, 61), Paris, Klincksieck, 1966, p. 197, n. 64: "C'est parce que l'idée de 'succès' (εὐοδία) et l'idée d''agrément' (εὐωδία) sont en définitive très proches l'une de l'autre que la confusion entre les deux termes a pu si aisément être commise par les copistes".

22. Ziegler, Rahlfs y también nosotros, siguiendo el hebreo (también *L a* 542), leemos el verbo εὐοδοῖ (tiene éxito), mientras la mayoría de los códices prefieren εὐοδία. Cf. ZIEGLER, *Iesu Filii Sirach*, p. 330.

23. En 10,5a no tendría que leerse ni εὐοδία, ni mucho menos εὐωδία. El texto hebreo (MsA: ממשלה, poder) y el siríaco (ܫܘܠܛܢܐ, poder) nos inducen a pensar que el término griego adecuado tendría que ser ἐξουσία (poder), sustantivo que en el v. 4 también traduce el hebreo ממשלה.

significa perfumar, dar buen olor, y puede considerarse como un sinónimo de δίδωμι εὐωδίαν (24,15; 38,11) o δίδωμι ὀσμήν, variante de la anterior, que la mayoría de códices y también la versión latina (*odorem dedi*) añaden al final de 24,15a[24] (ver p. 16, n. 7).

Señalemos que en el códice 248 falta el estico completo y que la versión siríaca modifica el texto, dándole un realce mucho mayor (13c) ܢ ܩܘܬ ܚܠ ... ... (como buenos perfumes perfumará vuestra fragancia), (14a) ... ... (como la fragancia del Líbano con sus cedros). ¿Cómo explicar esta curiosa modificación del texto? Es posible que el traductor haya querido jugar con el efecto sonoro de dos términos hebreos muy similares: לְבוֹנָה (incienso) y לְבָנוֹן (Monte Líbano). En siríaco el homónimo ܠܒܢܬܐ puede tener ambos significados: incienso y Monte Líbano[25].

θυμίαμα[26]

45,16c   θυμίαμα   ܘܩܘܛܪܐ   (20) incensum
49,1a εἰς σύνθεσιν θυμιάματος[27] ܐܝܟ ܦܝܪܡܐ ܕܩܘܛܪܐ in compositionem
                                                          odoris

En la LXX θυμίαμα generalmente traduce קְטֹרֶת, derivado de la raíz קָטַר I (hacer subir el perfume de las ofrendas). El sustantivo presenta un amplio abanico de significados: incienso, ofrenda de incienso, humo u olor de las ofrendas, sacrificio en general[28].

En Sir 45,16 el nieto de Ben Sira se aparta del texto hebreo y traduce el verbo ולהקטיר (Hifil de קָטַר, encender)[29] con el sustantivo θυμίαμα. Por su parte, el traductor siríaco — como ya hemos visto antes — reduce todo el estico a un solo término: ܘܩܘܛܪܐ.

---

24. Cf. ZIEGLER, *Iesu Filii Sirach*, p. 238.

25. Cf. J. LIESEN, *Full of Praise. An Exegetical Study of Sir 39,12-35*, Tesis PIB, Rome 1998, pp. 149-150 [manuscrito del autor].

26 Cf. NIELSEN, *Incense*, pp. 50-52 y HEGER, *The Development*, pp. 24-27: «The Association between קָטַר and Incense».

27. *L*-248 leen εἰς σύνεσιν (cf. Is 3,20). A. SCHLATTER, a la luz del hebreo, propone leer ὡς σύνθεσις. Cf. *Das neugefundene hebräische Stück des Sirach. Der Glossator des griechischen Sirach und seine Stellung in der Geschichte der jüdischen Theologie* (BFCT, 1/5-6), Gütersloh, Bertelsmann, 1897, p. 96.

28. Cf. M. HARAN, *The Uses of Incense in Ancient Israelite Ritual*, en *VT* 10 (1969) 113-137, donde el autor distingue entre el incienso como suplemento del sacrificio, el incienso ordinario y el altar del incienso. Heger estudia ampliamente esta clasificación en el segundo capítulo de su obra: «Biblical Incense Rituals (Part I): Haran's Classification» (cf. *The Development*, pp. 48-96). Ver también, M. HARAN, *Temples and Temple-Service in Ancient Israel. An Inquiry into Biblical Cult Phenomena and the Historical Setting of the Priestly School*, Winona Lake, IN, Eisenbrauns, 1978 [reimpr. 1995], pp. 230-245.

29. D. EDELMANN, *The Meaning of qitter*, en *VT* 35 (1985) 395-404.

Más interesante es el segundo texto (49,1), donde θυμίαμα forma parte de la expresión εἰς σύνθεσιν θυμιάματος (en composición de incienso) que traduce el hebreo (MsB) סמים קקטרת (como incienso perfumado, lit.: de perfumes)[30], frecuente en el documento sacerdotal (cf. Ex 30,7; 31,11; 40,27)[31]. La expresión εἰς σύνθεσιν θυμιάματος, referida aquí al rey Josías, nos hace recordar la receta del perfume sagrado en Ex 30,34-38, pero sobre todo nos remite a Ex 35,28 y 38,25 LXX, donde encontramos la misma expresión con alguna ligera variante: τὴν σύνθεσιν τοῦ θυμιάματος.

La versión latina (*in compositionem odoris*) y la sirohexaplar (ܪܟܘܒܐ ܕܒܣܡܐ, en composición de perfumes) coincide, mientras la Peshitta lee ܐܝܟ ܦܝܪܡܐ ܕܒܣܡܐ (como incensario de perfumes), siendo ܦܝܪܡܐ el correspondiente del griego πύρωμα (incensario)[32], palabra que la LXX desconoce (cf. Job 41,12 Aquila).

κιννάμωμον[33]

24,15a	κιννάμωνον	ܩܘܢܡܐ[34]	*cinnamomum*

κιννάμωμον traduce el hebreo קִנָּמוֹן. De fragancia exquisita, el cinamomo es una canela aromática que se extrae de la corteza y de las semillas de una especie de árbol o arbusto originario de Ceilán y Malasia. Importado en Palestina, se utilizaba como condimento en cocina, como perfume (Prov 7,17; Cant 4,14) y como ingrediente del aceite para la unción santa, es decir, para la consagración de los sacerdotes y de todos los objetos del culto junto con sus accesorios (cf. Ex 30,22-33). Al igual que el aspálato, el cinamomo es uno de los ingredientes en la composición del *kyphi*, el perfume sagrado de los egipcios.

En Sir 24,15a la misma Sabiduría se compara con el aroma del cinamomo (y del aspálato).

---

30. Nótese que las preposiciones y la relación de genitivo no concuerdan. Para este último particular, cf. A. MINISSALE, *La versione greca del Siracide. Confronto con il testo ebraico alla luce dell'attività midrascica e del metodo targumico* (AnBib, 133), Roma, PIB, 1995, p. 243.

31. סַמִּים ocurre sólo en plural y nunca designa una sustancia en particular sino los perfumes en general.

32. En Sir 50,9 ܦܝܪܡܐ traduce el hebreo מִנְחָה (ofrenda), posible error por מַחְתָּה (incensario).

33. Cf. COTHENET, *Parfums*, col. 1309 y NIELSEN, *Incense*, p. 64.

34. La Políglota de Walton presenta la siguiente variante: ܩܘܢܡܘܢ.

λίβανος[35]

24,15d	λιβάνου ἀτμίς	ܗܣܪ̈ܟ ܠܒ̈ܟ	(21) libanus non incisus
39,14a	λίβανος	ܝ̈ܡܟ ܪ.ܠܕ̈ܟ	libanus
50,9a	λίβανος	ܠܕ̈ܟܐܘ̈ܟ	——

λίβανος es la traducción del hebreo לְבֹנָה (incienso), atestiguado en todas las lenguas semíticas. El término deriva del verbo לָבֵן I (ser blanco) y, por lo tanto, indica el color blanco de la sustancia. De hecho, del árbol del incienso (λιβανωτός) se extrae una resina blanca con la que se produce el incienso[36]. Poco frecuente en la fabricación de cosméticos, perfumes (Cant 3,6) y medicinas[37], el incienso se utilizaba sobre todo en los ritos religiosos de la mayoría de culturas antiguas.

Las tres ocurrencias de λίβανος en el Sirácida revelan un uso metafórico del término. En 24,15 Ben Sira lo aplica a la Sabiduría, en 39,14 a sus dicípulos[38] y en 50,9 al sumo sacerdote Simón. Es de notar que en la versión griega de este último texto (ὡς πῦρ καὶ λίβανος ἐπὶ πυρείου), la mención del incienso unido al fuego y al incensario, evoca una auténtica escena cultual. El texto del MsB (50,8d), en cambio, omite la mención del incensario (וכאש לבונה על המנחה, como fuego de incienso sobre la ofrenda).

Del punto de vista filológico, el texto más interesante es 24,15d. Notemos que el latín traduce ὡς λιβάνου ἀτμίς (como vapor de incienso) con quasi libanus non incisus (es decir, íntegro, sin división), que en realidad corresponde a ὡς λίβανος (cf. la variante de los min. 248 y 155: λίβανος ἀτμός = ἀτμίς)[39]. Recordemos que en Ex 30,34, el

35. Cf. W. MICHAELIS, λίβανος, λιβανωτός, en TWNT, t. IV, Stuttgart, Kohlhammer, 1942, pp. 268-269 y NIELSEN, Incense, pp. 60-61.

36. W.W. MÜLLER, Zur Herkunft von λίβανος und λιβανωτός, en Glotta 52 (1974) 53-59. En el griego tardío los dos términos (λίβανος, λιβανωτός) se confunden, cf. H. G. LIDDELL – R. SCOTT, A Greek-English Lexicon, Oxford, Clarendon ⁹1968, p.1047.

37. En el mundo grecorromano, sin embargo, el incienso era muy apreciado por sus propiedades curativas. Cf. G.W. VAN BEEK, Frankincense and Myrrh en D.N. FREEDMAN – E.F. CAMPBELL (eds.), The Biblical Archeologist Reader, t. II, Garden City, NY, Doubleday, 1964, pp. 99-126, esp. pp. 114-115.

38. En su comentario N. PETERS, a la luz de Sir 50,8 y Os 14,7, piensa que λίβανος se refiere al Monte Líbano. Cf. Das Buch Jesus Sirach oder Ecclesiasticus (EHAT, 25), Münster, Aschendorff, 1913, p. 327.

39. Veamos la explicación de H. HERKENNE en De veteris latinae Ecclesiastici capitibus I-XLIII, Leipzig, Hinrichs, 1899, p. 192, n. *): "λίβανος ἄτομος (= "tus non incisum", sed indivisum atque integrum) primas tenet secundum Dioscoridem (de materia medica I, 82): πρωτεύει ὁ ἄρρην (sc. λίβανος) καλούμενος σταγονίας, στρογγύλλος φυσικῶς· ἐστὶ δὲ ὁ τοιοῦτος ἄτομος λευκός τε, καὶ θλασθεὶς ἔνδοθεν λιπαρὸς ἐπιθυμιαθείς τε ταχέως ἐκκαιόμενος. Dicitur λίβανος ἄτομος, qui secari non solet, sed talis relinquitur, qualis ex arbore manavit, unde et σταγονίας nominatur. Dicitur

último de los ingredientes citados en la fórmula de composición del incienso litúrgico es el λίβανος διαφανῆς (זַכָּה לְבֹנָה, incienso puro)[40], que se colocaba en la tienda del testimonio (ἐν τῇ σκηνῇ μαρτυρίου). La versión siríaca es más imprecisa, ya que en lugar de la expresión "vapor de incienso" lee "aceite bueno" (ܡܫܚܐ ܛܒܐ), quizás para mantener el paralelismo con 24,15b, donde aparece "mirra buena" (ܡܘܪܐ ܛܒܐ) en una construcción idéntica (ver texto completo en p. 16). El sustantivo ܡܫܚܐ corresponde al hebreo שֶׁמֶן (cf. 45,15b y 50,10b en el MsB).

En nuestro texto la función litúrgica del incienso, y por consiguiente de la Sabiduría, se acentúa por medio de la expresión ἐν σκηνῇ (en la tienda) al final del estico. Mientras la versión siríaca omite la mención de la tienda, la latina prefiere hablar de "mi habitación" (habitationem meam).

Por último, tengamos en cuenta que en griego λίβανος (incienso) también tiene un homónimo Λίβανος (el Monte Líbano): Sir 24,13a; 50,8c y 50,12d. La posible confusión entre los dos términos desaparece gracias al contexto de los textos citados: en 24,13a y 50,12d se mencionan los cedros en forma explícita y en 50,8c se alude a ellos por medio del término βλαστός, retoño, germen, brote (cf. 50,12d: ὡς βλάστημα κέδρων)[41].

μυρεψός

| 38,8a | μυρεψός | | ܡܒܣܡܢܐ | (7) unguentarius |
| 49,1a | ἔργῳ μυρεψοῦ | ܘܡܒܣܡ ܟܪ ܕܡܒܣܡܢܐ | ܘܥܒܝܕܐ | opus pigmentarii |

μυρεψός (en hebreo, רֹקֵחַ) designa la persona que se dedica a preparar perfumes. Según la práctica mesopotámica, el perfumista hace las mezclas de las especias aromáticas, las tritura hasta convertirlas en polvo y las disuelve en agua o aceite[42]. La Biblia habla poco del arte del perfumista, pero por lo que se refiere al perfume sagrado contamos con una información muy detallada. Los textos más significativos están en el

---

autem ἄτομον hoc tus i.e. a ferro intactum ad differentiam Indici, quod cum rotundum sua natura non sit ut illud: κατὰ τὴν ἐπιτήδευσιν στρογγύλον γίνεται nam τέμνοντες αὐτὸ εἰς τετράγωνα σχήματα καὶ βάλλοντες εἰς κεράμεια κυλίουσιν, ἕως ἂν ἀπολάβοι τό στρογγύλον σχῆμα ".

40. En su retroversión, M. S. SEGAL propone: וְכִלְבוֹנַת עָשָׁן (como incienso que arde, humeante), quizás para crear una bonita aliteración con בַּמִּשְׁכָּן. Cf. Sefer Ben Sira Hashalem, Jerusalem, Bialik Institute, ²1958, p. 145.

41. Cf. LIESEN, Full of Praise, p. 150.

42. Cf. al respecto E. EBELING, Parfümrezepte und kultische Texte aus Assur (Sonderdruck aus Orientalia, 17-19), Rom, PIB, 1950, esp. pp. 15-16.

c. 30 del libro del Éxodo, donde el autor nos transmite la receta del aceite de la unción (vv. 22-33) y la del incienso sagrado (vv. 34-38).

En Sir 38,8 el término μυρεψός (MsB רֹקֵחַ Bmg קרח)[43] no presenta ninguna connotación cultual, ya que se refiere al farmacéutico que prepara los ungüentos para los enfermos (G: μεῖγμα, H: מרקחת, S: ܟ̈ܣܡܐ, L: *pigmentum suavitatis*).

En 49,1 el sabio compara el "recuerdo" del rey Josías con el incienso aromático (lit.: composición de perfumes), es decir, con la obra preparada por el perfumista (ἐσκευασμένον ἔργῳ μυρεψοῦ; L: *factam opus pigmentarii*). El texto hebreo del MsB, en cambio, establece la comparación entre el "nombre" de Josías y el incienso aromático, precisando además que el perfumista ha puesto sal en su obra (הממלח מעשׂה רוקח). En Ex 30,35 la sal (TM מֶלַח - LXX μεμιγμένον, mezclado) es el quinto ingrediente en la composición del incienso sagrado[44]. Por su parte, el siríaco traduce libremente y con poco acierto: ܐܝܟ ܦܝܪܡܐ ܕܒܣ̈ܡܐ ܐܬܕܟܝ. ܫܡܗ ܕܝܘܫܝܐ ܒܟ̈ܠ ܒܣ̈ܡܐ ܡܠܝ (el nombre de Josías es como un incensario de perfumes con una mezcla de muchos perfumes).

ὄνυξ[45]

| 24,15c | ὄνυξ | ܛܦܪܐ | (21) ungula |

ὄνυξ (literalmente, uña) traduce el hebreo שְׁחֵלֶת (uña de mar, ámbar) y designa el opérculo de algunos moluscos que los antiguos utilizaban como medicina. De olor muy fuerte y penetrante cuando se quema[46], la uña de mar es el único producto animal destinado a la fabricación del incienso sagrado (cf. Ex 30,34). De hecho, el opérculo se llama ónice (*onyx*), porque tiene la forma de una uña (en latín: *ungula-unguis*, en siríaco: ܛܦܪܐ, en arameo targúmico: טוּפְרָא, en hebreo: צִפֹּרֶן)[47]. Así, en el Talmud de Babilonia (*Kerithoth*, 6a) el segundo ingrediente del perfume sagrado también recibe el nombre de uña (צִפֹּרֶן).

En Sir 24,15c el ónice, así como los demás perfumes mencionados en el versículo, se aplica metafóricamente a la Sabiduría.

---

43. Según la numeración de BEENTJES, 38,8a en G corresponde a 38,7b en el MsB. Cf. *The Book of Ben Sira in Hebrew*, p. 65.

44. Cf. V. HUROWITZ, *Salted Incense*, en Bib 68 (1987) 178-194.

45. Cf. COTHENET, *Parfums*, col. 1309-1310 y NIELSEN, *Incense*, pp. 65-66.

46. Según DIOSCÓRIDES, su olor es parecido al olor del *castoreum*, sustancia segregada por el castor, utilizada en medicina como antiespasmódico (*De Mat. Med.* 2,10). Ver también, PLINIO, *Hist. Nat.* 32,10.

47. HEGER, *The Development*, p. 135, n. 89: "It is also interesting to observe in Latin the philological affinity between 'fingernail' and 'anointing', similar to the Hebrew צפרן, the ingredient of spices. The nail is called 'unguis', and 'unguentum' is ointment".

ὀσμή[48]

39,14a εὐωδιάσατε ὀσμήν[49]　(13c) ‎ܒܣܡ ܪܝܚܗܘܢ‎　　(18) odorem suavitatis
　　　　　　　　　　　　　　　　　　　　　　　　　　　　　　habete
50,15d ὀσμὴν εὐωδίας　　　　　‎ܠܪܝܚ ܒܣܝܡܐ‎　　　(17) odorem divinum

Habiendo ya hablado del término ὀσμή en relación a εὐωδία y a εὐωδιάζειν, ahora añadiremos solamente un particular sobre la interpretación de 39,14a. Retomando las imágenes olfativas aplicadas en 24,15 a la Sabiduría, el sabio exhorta a sus discípulos a "derramar buen olor" en honor del Señor, el mismo buen olor que desprende el incienso del santuario.

Según G. Dwelling, detrás de esta invitación se deja entrever una espiritualización del concepto de sacrificio que se hace mucho más patente en el *Testamento de Leví* 3,6, donde el autor sin rebajar la importancia de los demás sacrificios, otorga la primacía a la ofrenda del incienso. Ésta sería el equivalente en la tierra de la ofrenda razonable y no cruenta de los ángeles en el cielo. Para aplacar la ira de Dios, éstos le ofrecen una «fragancia racional de suave olor» (ὀσμὴν εὐωδίας λογικήν)[50].

En nuestra opinión, la intención del sabio en Sir 39,14a no es tanto presentar una visión espiritualizada del sacrificio, cuanto desarrollar una metáfora, iniciada ya en el versículo anterior con el verbo βλαστήσατε (floreced). Utilizando la metáfora del árbol, los discípulos (como la sabiduría en 24,15) son llamados a florecer, perfumar y dar fruto. En otras palabras, son llamados a crecer en el servicio de la Sabiduría (= del Señor).

πυρεῖον[51]

50,9a　　　　　　ἐπὶ πυρείου[52]　　　　‎ܥܠ ܦܝܪܐ‎　　　　in igni

En la LXX πυρεῖον siempre traduce el hebreo מַחְתָּה (brasero, incensario) del verbo חָתָה (sacar las ascuas de un fuego o transportarlas de un lugar a otro). El sustantivo corresponde al siríaco ‎ܦܝܪܐ‎ y al latín *thuribulum* o también *ignium receptacula* (Ex 27,2; 38,3; Num

48. Cf. G. DWELLING, ὀσμή, en *TWNT*, t. v, Stuttgart, Kohlhammer, 1954, pp. 492-494.
49. Al final de 39,14c leemos: διάδοτε φωνήν (S: ‎ܐܪܝܡܘ ܩܠܟܘܢ‎). En cambio, los códices y manuscritos griegos, y también la Sirohexaplar leen ὀσμήν, debido al influjo de 39,14a.
50. Cf. DWELLING, ὀσμή, p. 494.
51. Cf. E. LEVESQUE, *Encensoir*, en *DB*, t. II, Paris, Letouzey & Ané, 1910, col. 1775-1779, y NIELSEN, *Incense*, pp. 44-45.
52. Variantes: 755: επι πυρος (= L *igni*), 315': επι πυργου.

4,14). El objeto así denominado era una especie de pala de metal, en forma oval o de cuchara, que servía para manejar, trasladar o reunir las brasas del altar del holocausto. El mismo instrumento se convertía en un auténtico incensario, cuando el sumo sacerdote, después de haber retirado el fuego del altar, echaba pequeños granitos de incienso u otros perfumes en la pala (Lev 10,1; 16,12; Num 16,6.17)[53].

In Sir 50,9a, πυρεῖον debe entenderse en este último sentido. Según la descripción del nieto de Ben Sira, el sumo sacerdote Simón aparecía en el altar "como el fuego y el incienso ἐπὶ πυρείου (en el incensario)". Veamos el texto hebreo del MsB: וכאש לבונה על המנחה (como fuego de incienso sobre la ofrenda). Es de notar que aquí no se habla de incensario (מַחְתָּה), sino de la ofrenda del grano (מִנְחָה), dos palabras muy similares de fácil confusión. Podemos suponer que el nieto leyó "incensario" en lugar de "ofrenda" y así lo tradujo[54]. A pesar de la relación existente entre el incienso y la ofrenda del grano (cf. Jer 6,20; 17,26; 33,18; 41,5), la versión griega hace más sentido que el texto hebreo[55]. En cuanto al texto siríaco, su autor consigue expresar la imagen mucho mejor: ܘܐܝܟ ܪܝܚܐ ܕܠܒܘܢܬܐ ܥܠ ܦܝܪܡܐ (y como el aroma del incienso en el incensario), mientras el latín no especifica el objeto donde se quemaba el incienso: *quasi ignis effulgens et tus ardens in igni*. Podemos, pues, resumir la situación textual en la siguiente manera: H (sobre la ofrenda), G y S (en el incensario), L (en el fuego).

σμύρνα[56]

24,15b	σμύρνα ἐκλεκτή	ܣܡܘܪܢܐ ܓܒܝܬܐ	(20) myrra electa

El término σμύρνα (o su equivalente μύρρα)[58] traducen el hebreo מוֹר, de la raíz מרר (ser amargo). Con σμύρνα se quiere indicar la resina de mirra, de sabor amargo y fuerte olor balsámico, que se extrae de

---

53. Este uso se hace más evidente en el término θυμιατήριον (de θυμίαμα, incienso) que corresponde al hebreo מֻקְטֶרֶת (de קָטַר, exhalar perfumes) y al latín *thymiateria*. Cf. al respecto, K. WIGAND, *Thymiateria*, en *Bönner Jahrbücher* 122 (1912) 1-97. El sustantivo θυμιατήριον no se encuentra en el Sirácida. Cf. también, HARAN, *Temples and Temple-Service in Ancient Israel*, pp. 238-241.

54. Cf. nota 31. Según J. H. A. HART, el griego posiblemente ha relacionado πυρείου con πυρὸς σκευός (H: כלי). Cf. *Ecclesiasticus: The Greek Text of Codex 248*, Cambridge, Cambridge University Press, 1919, p. 223.

55. Cf. por oposición, HEGER, *The Development*, p. 186.

56. Cf. COTHENET, *Parfums*, col. 1305-1306 y NIELSEN, *Incense*, p. 61.

57. Algunos min. (253 155 311-548 336 443* 578 672 744) leen μυρνα y el cód. S*: ζμυρναν.

58. Para la doble terminología σμύρνα – μύρρα, cf. W. MICHAELIS, σμύρνα, σμυρνίζω, en *TWNT*, t. VII, Stuttgart, Kohlhammer, 1964, esp. pp. 457-458 y del mismo autor, μύρον, μυρίζω, en *TWNT*, t. IV, Stuttgart, Kohlhammer, 1942, p. 807, n. 2.

diversos arbustos originarios del sur de Arabia y del oeste de Somalia. La mirra se utilizaba como cosmético para embellecer el rostro y el cuerpo (Est 2,12), para perfumar las vestiduras reales (Sal 45,8), el lecho (Prov 7,17) o el cuerpo (Cant 1,13; 5,5), para embalsamar los cadáveres (Jn 19,39-40), y también para paliar el dolor: por ejemplo, mezclada con vino, la mirra actuaba como un analgésico (Mc 15,23)[59].

Ninguno de estos usos encaja en Sir 24,15b, donde la mirra, como los perfumes anteriores, destaca por su función litúrgica (según Ex 30,23 LXX, la σμύρνα ἐκλεκτή es el primer componente del aceite de la unción). Al ser comparada con la mirra selecta, la Sabiduría participa también de esa misma función.

στακτή[60]

| 24,15c | στακτή | ܪܣܡܩܝܣܩܣ | *(21) gutta* |

El término στακτή (del verbo στάζω, gotear) designa la mirra reducida al estado líquido, es decir, el aceite de mirra[61]. En la LXX στακτή traduce cinco términos hebreos distintos: אֲהָלוֹת (áloe), לֹט (láudano), מֹר (mirra), נָטָף (resina balsámica) y נֹפֶךְ (piedra preciosa), lo que hace difícil poder precisar la correspondencia entre los vocablos.

En el Sirácida στακτή (uno de los ingredientes del incienso litúrgico, cf. Ex 30,34), ocurre solamente en 24,15c, un estico en el que las versiones no se ponen de acuerdo:

> G v. 15c: ὡς χαλβάνη καὶ ὄνυξ καὶ στακτή
>   como gálbano y ónice y estacte
>
> S v. 15c: ܘܐܝܟ ܠܒܘܢܬܐ ܘܚܠܒܢܝܬܐ ܘܛܦܪܐ ܘܒܣܡܐ
>   y como incienso y gálbano y ónice y bálsamo
>
> L v. 21a: *et quasi storax et galbanus et ungula et gutta*
>   y como estoraque y gálbano y ónice y estacte

Hagamos algunas constataciones:

— G solamente tiene tres términos, mientras S y L tienen cuatro.
— Gálbano y ónice están presentes en las tres versiones, estacte en G y L, incienso y bálsamo sólo en S, y estoraque sólo en L.

---

59. Cf. VAN BEEK, *Frankincense and Myrrh*, pp. 115-117 y NIELSEN, *Ancient Aromas Good and Bad*, en *Bible Review* 7 (1991) 26-33.
60. Cf. COTHENET, *Parfums*, col. 1306 y NIELSEN, *Incense*, p. 65.
61. Cf. R. O. STEUER, *Myrrhe und Stakte*, Wien, Verlag der Arbeitsgemeinschaft der Ägyptologen und Afrikanisten in Wien, 1933; ID, *Stacte in Egyptian Antiquity*, en *JAOS* 63 (1943) 279-284, donde responde a las apreciaciones de A. LUCAS en *Notes on Myrrh and Stacte*, en *JEA* 23 (1937) 27-33.

— S añade ܠܒܘܢܬܐ (incienso) al inicio del estico y ܩܢܡܘܢ (bálsamo) al final del mismo.

— L comienza la lista con *storax* (estoraque), que en realidad correspondería al griego στύραξ, término que no aparece en la LXX (cf. por contraste, Gen 37,25; 43,11 Aquila y Gen 43,11 Símmaco).

— στακτή corresponde al latín *gutta* y al siríaco ܩܢܡܘܢ (bálsamo).

En cuanto a στακτή, aunque en Ex 30,34 la LXX traduce el hebreo נָטָף con dicho término, los especialistas creen que נָטָף está conectado con צֳרִי, es decir, con estoraque y no con estacte[62]. En la LXX, en cambio, צֳרִי siempre traduce ῥητίνη (resina), cf. por ejemplo, Gen 37,25; 43,11.

χαλβάνη[63]

24,15c	χαλβάνη	ܘܣܠܒܢܝܬܐ	(21) galbanus

El término griego χαλβάνη y el siríaco ܣܠܒܢܝܬܐ (arameo: חֶלְבְּנִיתָא) corresponden al hebreo חֶלְבְּנָה (derivado de חָלָב, leche). De igual manera, el latín *galbanus* depende del griego. El gálbano es la resina lechosa, que se obtiene de la planta conocida en botánica como «Ferula galbaniflua». Según Zohary, es poco probable que este tipo de Ferula (él la describe como "a fetid gum") se utilizara en la preparación de sustancias aromáticas debido a su olor tremendamente desagradable[64].

En Sir 24,15c la mención del gálbano (otro de los ingredientes del incienso sagrado, cf. Ex 30,34) acentúa — como hemos visto con los demás perfumes — la función litúrgica de la Sabiduría.

Este artículo en honor del Prof. Maurice Gilbert, el maestro que me inició en el camino de la sabiduría hace ya algunos años, es solamente una parte de un estudio mucho más amplio sobre el vocabulario cultual en el libro de Ben Sira (los lugares de culto, los ministros del culto y su

---

62. M. ZOHARY, *Plants of the Bible. A complete handbook of all the plants with 200 fullcolor plates taken in the natural habitat*, Cambridge, Cambridge University Press, 1982, p. 192: "The present writer accepts the suggestion of Lagarde (1886) that the Greek name storax derives from the Hebrew Sori". La misma opinión comparte NIELSEN: "It is hard to say wich storax tzorî represents. But it is hardly to be doubted that tzorî is storax. It is very likely that Greek στύραξ is a Semitic loan word in Greek from tzorî" (*Incense*, p. 62).

63 Cf. COTHENET, *Parfums*, col. 1304 y NIELSEN, *Incense*, p. 66.

64 Cf. ZOHARY, *Plants of the Bible*, p. 201: "Despite the Greek, Aramaic and Syriac name *halbane*, cognate with the hebrew *helbenah*, its identification is not yet established".

servicio litúrgico, las ofrendas y sacrificios, los ornamentos sagrados, las actitudes y disposiciones ante el culto…), que espero poder llevar a término en un futuro no muy lejano.

Via Leone Magno 25-27   Nuria CALDUCH-BENAGES, MN
I-00167 Roma

PROVERBIAL SAYINGS/"BETTER"-SAYINGS
IN SIRACH

It is generally recognized that Sirach knew and utilized the Book of Proverbs[1]. That is not the concern of this paper. Rather, a different question is being asked: can we open a window on his *modus operandi* by investigating his utilization of proverbial sayings? Toward that end, this paper will investigate the well-known "better"-saying. The larger question of Ben Sira's style is suggested by the recent discussions concerning proverbial sayings in the Book of Proverbs. And it prompts similar inquiries into the manner of composition of Sirach.

First, the Book of Proverbs. Recent scholarship has attempted to interpret this book on the analogy of the current fashion of investigating the Book of Psalms[2]. That is to say, the *tehillim* are to be interpreted as a book, and not atomized into individual psalms. The research on this aspect of psalm interpretation has been steady, and is far from over. The essential claim is that there is a book context (partial or full) within which a given psalm can and should be interpreted. Similarly with the Book of Proverbs[3]. This work has its own character; it is a collection of collections, to which Proverbs 1–9 was probably prefaced as an introduction. The differences between chaps. 1–9 and 10–29 are particularly noticeable: articulated poems, as opposed to staccato, disparate sayings. Were these collections, especially within 10-31, simply assembled in a haphazard manner, or are there signs of purposeful collocation, or context, even interpretive context, within which they are to be understood? The signs may be catch words uniting usually two or more verses, or themes that extend over several verses or units. A significant stretch, chapters 25–27, has been analyzed by R.C. Van Leeuwen[4]. R.N. Whybray, while differing from Van Leeuwen, also took pains to investigate

1. Cf. H. DUESBERG et I. FRANSEN, *Les scribes inspirés*. Éditions de Maredsous, 1966, pp. 699-711. Although the authors recognize the role of the Torah and Prophets in Sirach, they entitle the chapter, "Le Ben-Sirah Commentateur des Proverbes".

2. See, for example, J.C. McCANN (ed.), *The Shape and Shaping of the Psalter* (JSOTSS, 159). Sheffield, JSOT Press, 1993.

3. See the discussion of this approach in R.N. WHYBRAY, *The Book of Proverbs: A Survey of Modern Study* (History of Biblical Interpretation Series, 1), Leiden, Brill, 1995, pp. 54-61.

4. R.C. VAN LEEUWEN, *Context and Meaning in Proverbs 25-27* (SBLDS, 96), Atlanta, Scholars, 1988.

the collections from this point of view[5]. The same is true of the German commentaries of O. Plöger and A. Meinhold[6].

These and ongoing studies certainly prove that the various collections in the Book of Proverbs were not made in haphazard fashion. At times the rationale for the grouping of some sayings escapes the modern reader, and it is always possible that many random saying were introduced without further consideration. However, in cases where the arrangement of the sayings is intentional, what measure of influence do one or more proverbs exert on each other? Is the meaning of a proverb changed or modified by its association with another saying? I think that the historical literal meaning is *not* changed. That meaning, as far as we can ascertain it, remains the same even in a new context. Deliberate proximity to another proverb does not give it a new meaning. Another proverb may be in conflict with it, or it may bring up a new consideration that must be confronted. But this does not change the meaning of the original proverb. Why? Because every proverbial saying is only a partial view, a small slice into reality. Proverbs can be in conflict with each other, but they must retain their independent meanings in order that there be conflict. One can point to many examples within the Book of Proverbs where this occurs[7]. There is a distinction between the "original" meaning and the application(s), the way(s) a proverb comes to be used. The interpretive context within a collection can provide perhaps another opportunity for the *application* of the basic meaning, but it does not really change it or provide a new meaning. This aspect of levels of meaning is also pertinent to the consideration of the function of proverbial sayings in Sirach. It is very difficult to distinguish the sayings that may be original to him from those he borrowed and simply transmitted. He does provides broad contexts for the sayings. How have these affected the sayings?

Second, the composition of the Book of Sirach. What assumptions are at work in questioning his mode of composition? The most striking difference from Proverbs is that Sirach is not a collection of collections; it

5. Cf. *The Composition of the Book of Proverbs* (JSOTSS, 168), Sheffield, Academic Press, 1994.

6. O. PLÖGER, *Sprüche Salomos (Proverbia)* (BKAT, 17), Neukirchen-Vluyn, Neukirchener, 1984; A. MEINHOLD, *Die Sprüche*, 2 Vols (ZBAT, 16), Zürich, Theologischer Verlag, 1991. See especially the careful studies of J. KRISPENZ, *Spruchkomposition im Buch Proverbia* (EurHS, XXIII/349), Frankfurt a.M., P. Lang, 1989, and R. SCORALICK, *Einzelspruch und Sammlung: Komposition im Buch der Sprichwörter Kapitel 10–15* (BZAW, 232), Berlin, de Gruyter, 1995.

7. Perhaps the most famous example is 26,4-5, about answering/not answering a fool according to his folly.

is an articulation by a single author of several more or less unified poems dealing with a multitude of topics. This statement covers a host of bewildering data. F. V. Reiterer[8] has provided some indication of the wide differences of opinion. For H.-W. Jüngling "biographical notes are the framework of composition". A. Schrader has raised a fundamental question in this respect — are these separate proverbs parts of a larger whole or are they originally independent? Reiterer has observed: "According to Schrader, fundamental theological tensions originate here within the texts, since Sira deals with a collection of originally independent elements that do not originate from Jesus Sirach himself...; in contrast to other statements in the study, this thesis is consistently maintained from start to finish. However in the study, one does not discover what really is genuinely from Sirach; by contrast, see K. W. Burton...: 'The whole of Sirach's text is a well planned symphony, every note, every movement is part of the whole. There are subtleties and allusions throughout which must be seen as notes which give fullness and harmony to his message'". These statements illustrate the wide range of opinion, as well as the difficulty of isolating distinct elements in Ben Sira.

A few observations are in order. First, in a sense Ben Sira's grandson warned us of this difficulty when he indicated in the preface to his translation the wide range of his grandfather's interests in the entire Tanach. This is verified by the "style anthologique," or anthological composition, which is a hallmark of Sirach's work. There is a remarkable coverage of the writings of his biblical predecessors: Wisdom, Torah (and thus the often silent reference to specific legislation) and salvation history (chaps. 44–49)! Second, there is the plethora of literary forms[9]. Merely to raise this question is to enter a prickly area. Much more remains to be done in order to understand the development of thought

8. See the historical summary of recent research by F.V. REITERER in *The Book of Ben Sira in Modern Research* (BZAW, 255), New York/Berlin, de Gruyter, 1997, pp. 23-60; the quotations are taken from pp. 39-40, esp. note 80. He also records on p. 38 that according to A. LEFÈVRE, the work "is 'a collection of proverbs without internal order and about the most diverse circumstances'".

9. A thorough examination of this is a desideratum; it is worth noting that there have been no serious studies of Sirach's literary style since the work of W. BAUMGARTNER, *Die literarischen Gattungen in der Weisheit des Jesus Sirach*, in ZAW 34 (1914) 161-198. In contrast, the literary forms in the book of Wisdom have been subjected to detailed study; e.g., cf. the study by the scholar honored by this Festschrift, M. GILBERT, art. "Sagesse", in *DBS*, t. XI, Paris, Gabalda, 1986, col. 77-87. See also the study of Pseudo-Phocylides in J.J. COLLINS, *Jewish Wisdom in the Hellenistic Age* (OTL). Louisville, KY, Westminster/John Knox, 1997, where the effort to identify literary structure has been labelled "at least partially successful," p. 160.

within the various forms. It is easy enough to point out hymns or numerical proverbs or other commonly accepted forms. But within the long
poems that are unified by a given theme, there can be a number of formulaic statements, such as "do not say," or imperatives, all of which are
as it were diminutive forms contributing to a larger unit. How do they
function within the longer poem? Are they simple additions dictated by
emphasis or by a need for variety? One cannot sell Ben Sira short in the
matter of lengthy compositions. His "praise of the fathers" (chaps. 44–
49), are proof of his creative use of traditional information about Israel's
heroes. Third, a dominant feature in Sirach is the fairly lengthy poems.
An elegant type, that is not easily catalogued except as "alphabetizing,"
is the so-called 22-23 line poem recognized by P. Skehan and Di Lella in
their commentary[10]. Did this or any other type of alphabetizing poem
emerge full blown from the head of Ben Sira? Or was it built up at one
stage or another on the basis of current individual sayings? How were
these accumulated? Are they the creation of the author, or did he draw
them from past tradition or from a current "anthology"? Did he control
a fund of proverbial sayings that he could use *ad libitum.* much as a
modern author might do? Did he compose any original proverbs, whatever be his contribution to their "originality"? By this I mean he could
have taken proverbial sayings and modified them, tilting them in the direction that he desired. This is, of course, a delicate operation: by what
criteria can one establish that a saying has been modified by Ben Sira?
These questions cannot all be answered, but at least they suggest an area
of thought and composition that call for examination. An obvious disadvantage is the state of the text of Sirach: the original Hebrew is incom-
plete, and exists in two general forms (one expanded), while the Greek
translation also exists in two forms, one expanded. That is the situation
that everyone faces in studying this book[11].

Any definition of a proverb is notoriously difficult, and this would be
true also of a proverbial saying[12]. The latter is not necessarily a "proverb", in a commonly accepted meaning of that elusive term, namely a
pithy, aphoristic saying that has gained currency among the public, and
usually characterized by such literary conceits as assonance, etc. While
retaining its character as a proverb, the proverbial saying is broader, less

10. P.W. SKEHAN and A.A. DI LELLA, *The Wisdom of Ben Sira* (AB, 39), New York,
Doubleday, 1987, p. 74 and passim.

11. Cf. *ibid.*, pp, 51-62.

12. A well known description is attributed to Lord John Russell: "one man's wit and
all men's wisdom." An insightful analysis of the biblical proverb is given by J.G.
WILLIAMS, *The Power of Form: A Study of Biblical Proverbs,* in J.D. CROSSAN (ed.),
Gnomic Wisdom (Semeia 17), Chico, CA, Scholars Press, 1980, pp. 35-38.

concentrated, more humble. It is impossible to avoid some subjectivity in this judgment. A typical proverb would be Prov 14,13, "Even in laughter a heart can be sad, and the end of joy, grief". But the proverbial saying is less taut, less disciplined, as it were. It can be a direct imperative or prohibition (frequent in Sirach). As the saying appears in Proverbs, it is usually a bicolon in parallelism, containing a reflection based on experience (Prov 18,17) or even faith (Prov 15,29). Outside the Book of Proverbs one can find various examples of proverbial sayings. Psalm 37, itself an acrostic, provides several instances; 37,16 reads: "Better is the little of the righteous than the abundance of many wicked". This and several other verses of the psalm (e.g., the command to depart from evil in vv. 28-29) one could expect to find in Sirach as well.

THE "BETTER"-SAYING

The "better"-saying is a common form of the proverbial sayings scattered in wisdom literature[13]. It is not usually found in clusters, and hence perhaps it stands out more prominently than other sayings. There is a variant formula occurring in the list in Sir 40,18-26, and the list, as we shall see, is by way of exception. We wish to use this type of saying as as a test-case for Sirach's use of proverbs. The references to the Book of Sirach follow the enumeration of the Greek text of J. Ziegler.

10,27   "Better the laborer who has plenty of goods than the boaster who lacks food" (Greek, instead of Hebrew "gift"in v. 27b). This "better"-saying is similar to Prov 12,9 (better the ordinary person who works for his living [revocalizing the text]). One might surmise that such evaluations derive from a common stock of sayings in favor of the diligent worker as opposed to the lazy person. However, the verse is associated with v. 26 by the catch word, "boast," *mtkbd*. The term fits it into the context since the root, *kbd* (honor, glory), occurs very frequently in vv. 19-31. Hence, even if the saying may originally have belonged in a different context, it is used advantageously here.

16,3cd   "For better is one than a thousand, and to die childless than have ungodly children" (Greek). This saying fits well with the topic of wicked offspring (16,1-2). It is broadened by the following v. 4, which

---

13. The use of the "better"-saying has been studied by J. WEHRLE (for Proverbs) and G. OGDEN (for Qoheleth). The most recent work is by J. WEHRLE, *Sprichwort und Weisheit: Studien zur Syntax und Semantik der TOB... MIN-Sprüche im Buch der Sprichwörter* (ATSAT, 38). St. Ottilien, EOS Verlag, 1993, with a bibliography that covers other studies, such as G. OGDEN (p. 242).

spells out the serious results for the future: "From one intelligent person a city is populated; but wicked descendants make it desolate." In a sense, v. 4 expands v. 3, while joined to it by a catch word ("one" in both the Hebrew and Greek). The appearance of the first person ("my eye" in v. 5) suggests that Sirach is introducing a new topic. He gathers together in vv. 5-10, more from the Old Testament than from visual experience, examples of groups that exemplify the ungodly children of v. 3. This development enables him to move into the theme of divine mercy and divine punishment (vv. 11-14). The "better"-saying is an integral part of the statement concerning offspring in vv 1-4; see Wis 4,1-6 for another treatment.

19,24 "Better is one inferior in intelligence, but (God) fearing, than one who abounds in understanding, but contravenes the law." The saying is certainly not out of context, which unites wisdom with fear of the Lord and fulfillment of the Law (v. 20). The verses develop the failures of *panourgia*, or shrewdness, when it has no moral restraint. Usually understanding is used in a positive sense that includes practical action. Instead, 19,24 seems to be an evaluation of *sunesis/phronēsis* on a purely theoretical level. No matter the desirability of intelligence, it must be accompanied by fear of the Lord, or it is a failure. This evaluation is continued in v. 25 where human cleverness (*panourgia*) leads to duplicity. The point is that the faithful are not to be duped by those more clever than themselves. They have superior wisdom. They are not to be deceived by wily characters (vv. 25-28). Oddly enough, after this description of exterior signs that are really dissembling, Ben Sira gives exterior signs for recognizing the "sensible" (*noēmōn*, v. 29) person (vv. 29-30). But are not these just as ambiguous? See also 13,25-26. All things considered, body language is not as certain as the sages thought; cf. Prov 6:13. The saying in 19,24 is a good choice, and quite fitting in the context.

20,31 See 41,15 where the Hebrew text is provided, and also Ziegler's edition: "Better one hiding folly than one hiding wisdom." The saying that accompanies this verse (20,30; cf. 41,14) is even sharper, for it dismisses hidden wisdom and concealed treasure as worthless (they are worthless because neither of them is utilized in a constructive way). Verse 31 recalls the pungent proverb: "Better an open rebuke than a hidden love" (Prov 27,5). Sir 20,30-31 has little, if any, connection with the context; vv. 24-26 deal with lying (v. 25a is not a "better"-saying); vv. 27-29 point out the profit of wisdom, and v. 29 warns against an old failing, the acceptance of bribes. The addition of vv. 30-

31 looks like a "filler," because it has no context. But they are such perceptive sayings (and somehow came to be repeated in chapter 41), they could have impressed Sirach as observations worthy of emphasis and therefore, repetition. The situation in 41,14-15 is also puzzling; those verses are even more out of context. They appear just before a formal introduction about proper shame (41,14a, 16-22; 41:1-8; cf. Skehan-Di Lella on the alignment of 41,14-15).

Chapter 20 seems to offer more varieties of composition in Sirach than usual. There is the conspicuous stylistic usage of *estin* (Hebrew *yēš,* "there are"; although the Hebrew text is lacking) in 20:5-6, describing the silent person, but especially in 20,9-12, where it occurs seven times. The phrase seems to lend itself to composing a list, as one may also conclude from the usage in 6:8-10 where types of friends are described. Verses 5-6 form part of a self-contained unit (vv. 5-8) dealing with silence. Verses 9-12 form also part of a self-contained unit (vv. 9-17) which describes minor paradoxes: some reversals are gains; some gains are losses; some gifts are not worth having, and so forth. Things are not what they appear to be. A new topic appears in vv. 18-20: speech. Even a proverb, if uttered by a fool, is ineffective because it is untimely (v. 20; cf. Prov 26,7,9, and the general sapiential emphasis on the right time; Prov 15,23b). This fits in well with Sirach's abundant use of the term, *kairos;* see especially Sir 4,20 and 20:6-7. Verses 21-23 are each characterized by the *estin* formula, but the contents are not easily united; v. 21 deals with poverty and vv. 22-23 with shame. Verses 24-26 are concerned with lying. *Pseudos* occurs in each verse, and perhaps "shame" in v. 26 is a catch word with vv. 22-23. The heading found in the Greek before v. 27 is almost a warning not to expect any unity; it is entitled "Proverbial Sayings." There is a catch word, "to please the great" for vv. 27-28, but they are rather different; v. 27 has some relationship to v. 13a, and the two halves of v. 28 have little, if any, relationship to each other. Verse 29 describes the ugly effects of bribery. Verses 30-31 have been treated above; they have only a tenuous connection, if any, with v. 29. This unit, vv. 27-31, lacks the smoothness and inner connection that characterizes so many of Ben Sira's compositions. And when one examines chapter 20 as a whole, it is looks very choppy, as though an artificial arrangement of formulaic repetitions and catch words forms the basis of any unity. This does not deny Ben Sira's talent, but it seems to illustrate *one* pattern of composition.

23,27cd This saying affirms that nothing is better than the fear of the Lord, which is identified with keeping the commandments. It has no

connection with the previous section which deals with sexual conduct
(vv. 16-27; cf. v. 6). It does have the appearance of a sweeping, summary statement. Since it occurs immediately before chapter 24, which is
of primary importance in the book, it may justly be called an "elegant
conclusion", which sums up chapters 1-23 (so Skehan-Di Lella, p. 326).

29,22 "Better the life of the poor person under a modest roof than
rich food among strangers." This fits in with the recommendation to be
satisfied with one's lot in vv. 21-28. The spirit of the saying points out
that the situation of the poor can have a certain advantage. The comparison in line *b* is somewhat unexpected. One would have expected there a
comparison with foods tainted by injustice. Such is a common comparison in Proverbs (cf. Prov 15,16, with the opposition between love and
hatred; 16,19, with the opposition between meek and proud). Here, instead, privacy is extolled over association with (rich) strangers. The reason for the comparison is to instill independence and dignity, because
v. 24 points out that as a guest, presumably at a banquet given by a superior, one is at a disadvantage.

30,14-17 A series of preferences is found here, but only vv. 14 and
17 are "better"-sayings. All four verses extol the advantages of health
over sickness, despite the title before v 16, "On Foods" found in some
Greek mss. Verse 14 voices a straightforward preference for poverty
with health, over riches with sickness. Verse 17 goes beyond v 14. Now
death is better than a miserable life, and the parallelism shows that in the
saying Sheol is viewed as a surcease ("eternal sleep") from physical suffering. This is reminiscent of Job and the use of the motif of Sheol in his
complaint; Job 3,11-23; 14:13. The verses that follow are garbled in
part (cf. the discussion in Skehan and Di Lella), but they seem to be a
continuation of the health theme; those who are ill cannot enjoy their
food.

42,14 The Greek text seems to say that the wickedness of a man is
better than a woman who does good. Commentators have tried to soften
this in various ways, e.g., that hyperbole or paradox is at work here. The
translation in the New American Bible (NAB, formerly the CCD, 1955)
put it differently: "Better a man's harshness (*ponēria*) than a woman's
indulgence (*agathopoios gunē*)". This is also the view of L. Alonso
Schökel in his 1968 fascicle, *Proverbios y Ecclesiastico,* ediciones
cristiandad, Madrid: "Mejor es la dureza del marido que la indulgencia
de la mujer". He admits that this is doubtful, but he notes that the other
version does not agree with the general teaching of Sirach, despite state-

ments like 25,24. The evidence from Masada for v. 14 is not unambiguous. See the discussion in Skehan and Di Lella, p. 480. Whatever be the original reading, the topic of womanly behavior is in harmony with the context of vv. 9-14.

40,18-26   This is a group of ten preferences that abandon the usual formula, "better than" (*ṭôb min*) in favor of "(better) than both" (*mišnēhem; huper amphotera; huper* is used fairly frequently in comparisons in Sirach). The usual formula (*ṭôb min, kreisson*) occurs outside the series in 40,28 (better die than beg; emended reading). The new formula is a strong one, for it compares two things, which are evaluated in a positive manner, with one. The value of the one is all the more enhanced, for it is greater than the two. Indeed, the sayings have the appearance of riddles: what is better than flocks and orchards? what is better than wine and music? Many different answers could be given by way of a guess.

The variation in the formula is welcome. The fact that these sayings occur in a bunch invites wonderment. Where did they come from? It is not impossible for them to be an original composition of Sirach, but it seems unlikely that they were simply invented by him. Rather, they probably represent a traditional grouping of preferences. The perseverance of the formula in each of the ten couplets suggests that they were a specific, fixed, group. Sirach could have simply adopted them because of the tenth couplet about the fear of the Lord, a central theme of his book. This is suggested by what seems to be a deliberate expansion: the addition of two couplets (v. 26cd and v. 27) that also feature the same subject, fear of the Lord, "a paradise of blessing." There is nothing in the chapter that calls for the placement of these ten verses; they would fit in almost anywhere else in the book.

CONCLUSION

The discussion of the above sayings yields no broad insights into Ben Sira's method of composition. This modest attempt illustrates the difficulty of trying to get behind the abundance of sayings transmitted. The restriction to "better-sayings" was necessary in an article of small compass such as this. But the meager concrete results do not disqualify the principle of a closer analysis of Ben Sira's method of composition. His style exhibits a great variety of material, both for form and subject. If enough studies of forms, style, context, etc. are made, there is bound to be progress in this area. A work of the magnitude of Ben Sira, fifty-one chapters no less, is unparalleled in wisdom literature. Job is almost as long, but it has been judged, for fair reasons or foul, to have several additions. However, it has a relatively clear structure. It is not easy to establish a structure for Ben Sira's wisdom. The Book of Proverbs is clearly a collection of collections, with signs of such a fact indicated by titles embedded in the text. There is little agreement about divisions within Ecclesiasticus. The authenticity of chapter 51 of Sirach has been challenged (cf. the colophon in 50,27-29), but the only certain addition seems to be the litany contained in 51,12 (vv. I-XVI) which is found only in the Hebrew ms. B.

Although we have limited ourselves to the "better"-saying, it is appropriate to close with a suggestion that individual verses within a poem deserve to be analyzed for their provenience. For example, one might question the poem in Sir 17,24-32 concerning the Lord's mercy and the appeal to return to him. This standard doctrine draws on the Sheol motif: one must glorify the Lord while one is still alive, and thereby ensure the forgiveness that God is only too ready to impart. How great is this mercy (v. 29)? It seems to be rooted in immortality, *divine* immortality. "For not everything can be found among men, because the son of man is not immortal" (v. 30). And another unusual verse follows immediately: "What is brighter than the sun? Yet it can be eclipsed; and flesh and blood plan evil." The logical progression of thought in these verses is very obscure. I suggest that it derives from Sirach's use of two sayings, not necessarily related to each other. The first deals with human mortality, considered here as a source of human failure to forgive. The second really concerns a solar eclipse; it becomes here a figure of human mortality. With such limitations, only evil is to be expected of flesh and blood. The final verse underscores the difference between the divine world in the heaven (where the sun was eclipsed) and the earthy/ashy reality of humans. Could it be that the density of Sirach's thought derives from a use of three proverbial sayings which he controlled, but which were not linked originally? These are the kinds of questions that arise at many points in a book which is not as obvious as it seems at first sight to be.

It is an honor to offer this article to Maurice Gilbert, S.J. whose mastery of the wisdom literature is manifest in his studies, and those of his students, in the Book of Sirach.

Whitefriars Hall   Roland E. MURPHY, O. Carm.
1600 Webster St. N.E.
Washington, DC, 20017

B. SANHEDRIN 100b
AND RABBINIC KNOWLEDGE OF BEN SIRA

I am grateful to the editors of this volume for the chance to write in celebration of Professor Maurice Gilbert, whose work on the book of Ben Sira has been so influential. Several years ago Prof. Gilbert wrote a programmatic article on Ben Sira in a collection of essays entitled *Jewish Civilization in the Hellenistic-Roman Period*[1]. In this essay, Gilbert posed two questions about the rabbinic citations of the book of Ben Sira. He wrote,

> 1. The rabbinic quotations from that book generally are not literal. Segal reasons that the rabbis quoted from memory[2]. According to M.R. Lehmann, literalness was not required; the quotations were adapted to suit the later context because the book of Ben Sira was not a biblical book[3]. Which theory should we follow?
> 2. Were the quotations taken from a complete edition of Ben Sira without any additions? Or did the rabbis quote a florilegium[4]?

In an effort to begin to answer Gilbert's queries I will look in this essay at one important rabbinic text, B. Sanhedrin 100b, which contains both an extended discussion of the acceptability of reading Ben Sira and a number of "quotations" from the book.

The section on Ben Sira in Sanhedrin 100b begins as a commentary on M. Sanhedrin 10:1 where Akiba notes that those who read the "outside books" (ספרים החיצונים) have no share in the world to come. The first section of the talmudic commentary reports that R. Joseph understood Akiba's statement to forbid reading the book of Ben Sira. Abaye asks R. Joseph why this should be so since Ben Sira contains many things that the rabbis also say, and he adduces a number of passages as examples. The second section again begins with R. Joseph who says in reply to Abaye's objections, "We may expound to them the good things it contains". Another series of quotations follows. Altogether B. Sanhedrin 100b contains, depending on how one counts, ten different

1. Maurice GILBERT, *The Book of Ben Sira: Implications for Jewish and Christian Traditions*, in Shemaryahu TALMON (ed.), *Jewish Civilization in the Hellenistic-Roman Period*, Philadelphia, Trinity Press International, 1991, pp. 81-91.
2. M.H. SEGAL, *The Evolution of the Hebrew Text of Ben Sira*, in *JQR* 25 (1934-1935) 91-149, esp. 135-136.
3. M.R. LEHMANN, *11QPs^a and Ben Sira*, in *RQ* 11 (1983) 239-251, esp. 242-246.
4. GILBERT, *The Book of Ben Sira* (n. 1), p. 85.

passages that purportedly come from Ben Sira. Each deserves some brief description.

1. "Do not strip the skin [of a fish] even from its ear, lest you spoil it, but roast it [all, the fish with the skin] in the fire and eat it with two loaves"[5]. This Aramaic admonishment appears in none of the extant manuscripts of Ben Sira.

2. The second of Abaye's examples comes originally from Sir 42,9-10, a passage about daughters. In both the Masada scroll and Ms B from the Cairo genizah, this passage contains eight cola. The rabbinic quotation, given in Hebrew, contains seven, only six of which parallel the Ben Sira manuscripts. The one colon not found in the manuscripts concerns keeping one's daughter from witchcraft in her old age. In general the outlines of the thought are the same, but the wording and order of the lines differ widely between the rabbinic citation and the manuscripts[6].

3. "Do not let anxiety enter your heart, for it has slain many a person". This third of Abaye's examples is an admonition in Aramaic that has no direct parallel in Ben Sira, although Segal argues that it "is a combination of several lines in our book"[7]. Indeed some of the material from this quotation does occur in somewhat similar contexts in Ben Sira – 30,21 "Do not give yourself over to grief"; 30,23c "For grief has killed [many]"; perhaps 14,1b, "Whose heart has not brought grief upon him" (as Segal corrects the Hebrew)[8]. The similar content of Prov 12,25 cited immediately after this passage may also have influenced the form of the quotation.

4. Abaye's fourth example, which is cited in Hebrew, "Keep the multitude from your house, and do not let everyone enter your house", derives from Sir 11,29. The first half of the citation seems to be a summarizing form of the second half which parallels 11,29a (Ms A) very closely[9].

5. The last of Abaye's citations is, like the first, given in Aramaic and is nowhere to be found in any Ben Sira text. "A thin-bearded man is very astute; a thick-bearded one is a fool. The one who blows in his glass is not thirsty. He who says, 'With what shall I eat my bread'? Take his bread from him. The one who parts his beard no one can overcome".

---

5. The translation here is adapted from I. EPSTEIN, *The Babylonian Talmud*, London, Soncino, 1935.

6. The Masada scroll and Ms B from the Cairo genizah have some textual variants between them. Although some terms are in common between the rabbinic passage and the manuscripts, the manuscripts are much closer to each other than to the rabbinic text.

7. SEGAL, *Evolution* (n. 2), p. 143.

8. *Ibid.*, p. 112.

9. For the Hebrew text of Ben Sira I have used Pancratius C. BEENTJES, *The Book of Ben Sira in Hebrew* (SVT, 68), Leiden, Brill, 1997.

6. In reality the first part of the list of examples of the "good things" from Ben Sira that R. Joseph puts forward is actually comprised of five passages in Hebrew on wives and women.

(a) The first is an almost exact quote of Sir 26,3. Only one word in the Talmud differs from Cairo genizah Ms C (Talmud = בחיק, Ms C = ובחלק). The Talmud also agrees with MS C and the Syriac translation in having the singular "he who fears" rather than the plural of the Greek.

(b) The next section on the evil wife appears to summarize the thought of Sir 25,23-26. One specific part of the citation, the talmudic injunction to divorce such a wife, is not found in the GKI recension of Ben Sira (no Hebrew is extant for these verses), but is found in GKII and the Syriac.

(c) The following sentence reproduces Sir 26,1 almost exactly except that the Talmud has יפה instead of טובה (Ms C) as a description of the good wife.

(d) Next the Talmud cites Sir 9,8a; 9,3b; 9,9a.b; 9,8c. Although the verse order does not agree with Cairo Ms A, the wording of the passages is often very close. Sanhedrin 100b reproduces almost exactly the text of 9,8a, and 9,3b differs substantially only in the verb (Talmud = תלכד, Ms A = תפול). The citation of 9,9a.b is somewhat complicated. The Talmud's אל תט אצל בעלה למסוך עמו יין ושכר is close in form to 9,9a.b in Ms A, עם בעלה אל תטעם ו[...]ב עמו שכור. The Greek translation for this verse, however, is actually an injunction warning against drinking with a married *woman* rather than with her husband (μετὰ ὑπάνδρου γυναικὸς μὴ κάθου τὸ σύνολον). Either the Greek has mistranslated the Hebrew or the Hebrew of Ms A (and the Talmud) is corrupt. Perhaps the talmudic form of the verse has influenced the text of Ms A here[10]. The subsequent sentence in the Talmud is a fairly close representation of Ms A for 9,8c. Sanhedrin 100b reads כי בתואר אשה יפיה רבים הושחתו compared with שחתו רבים[.] בעד אשה. The final talmudic clause "and numerous are those killed by her" looks like a summary of the preceding clause which has no close parallel in Ben Sira.

(e) Although a continuation of the section about women, the next several clauses come from Sir 11,29-34, a section that is textually corrupt in Ms A. The first clause, "and many are the blows sustained by peddlers", is a form of Sir 11,29b in Ms A, which itself probably does not reflect the original Ben Sira[11]. The following sentence takes part of

10. SEGAL, *Evolution* (n. 2), p. 137 suggests that such is the case for Ms A at 11,29c.d.
11. *Ibid.*, p. 137 and G.H. BOX and W.O.E. OESTERLEY, *Sirach*, in R.H. CHARLES (ed.), *Apocrypha and Pseudepigrapha of the Old Testament* (t. I), Oxford, Clarendon, 1913, 357.

11,32a about sparks kindling embers and applies it to "those who seduce
to adultery" rather than to those who enter one's house, the original context in Ben Sira. This sentence seems to end the section treating women.

7. There follows in both the Talmud and Ms A a quotation of Jer
5,27, the talmudic citation probably influencing the development of the
manuscript tradition of Ben Sira[12]. Then comes a citation of 11,29a
about people entering one's house which is identical to the one offered
by Abaye earlier in Sanhedrin 100b.

8. The next section cites Sir 6,6 in a form close to Ms A. The Talmud
reads רבים יהיו דורשי שלומך גלה סודך לאחד מאלף; Ms A has a different
word order for colon a and uses the more generic אנשי instead of דורשי.
In colon b Ms A reads בעל סודך, not גלה סודך as in the Talmud, and it
does not use the preposition before אחד.

9. The Talmud continues with Micah 7,5 and then Prov 27,1b attached to a clause of unknown origin, "Do not worry about tomorrow's
trouble". These quotations are apparently also intended to be part of the
"good things" in Ben Sira.

10. The end of Sanhedrin 100b begins with a short quotation of Prov
15,15, "All the days of the poor are evil", which is followed (in Hebrew) by "Ben Sira said, So are the nights. The lowest roof is his roof,
and on the height of the mountains is his vineyard. The rain of roofs is
on his roof and the earth of his vineyard is on other vineyards". None of
this has any parallel in any manuscript of Ben Sira.

The citations of Ben Sira contained in Sanhedrin 100b are basically of
three different kinds: (1) some represent closely what we find in the
manuscripts of the book, (2) some clearly originate among Ben Sira's
proverbs, but they are characterized by extensive textual variation, corruptions, displacements of order and context, and (3) some do not appear
at all in any Ben Sira manuscript; indeed several biblical passages appear as part of the book's contents. How can this situation be explained?
Both Segal's and Lehmann's solutions, as outlined above by Gilbert, begin with the book's non-canonical status as the basis for explanation.

Segal argues that the only explanation of the rabbinic Ben Sira texts
that makes sense is that "the Rabbis quoted our book from memory"[13].
According to him, since the text of Ben Sira was not canonical scripture
the rabbis took certain freedoms with it that they would not with an authorized text. In the process of homiletical use of the book, the rabbis
combined passages with similar ideas from different places in Ben Sira

12. SEGAL, *Evolution* (n. 2), p. 137.
13. *Ibid.*, p. 135.

or even with verses from the Bible, and they transmitted these combinations orally. Such combinations got included in anthologies of Ben Sira together with other proverbs, many of which were incorrectly ascribed to Ben Sira, and with "miscellaneous popular and even vulgar saws in Aramaic"[14].

Lehmann argues that different "categories of text transmission" help to explain the situation in places like Sanhedrin 100b. He distinguishes "1) authorized (= Biblical) texts, transmitted in scribal reference texts, 2) authorized texts transmitted in non-scribal reference texts (e.g. in legal, liturgical, homiletic, literary texts), 3) unauthorized (= apocryphal) texts, transmitted in non-scribal texts"[15]. For the second of his categories, Lehmann maintains that in such contexts even biblical quotations suffer from changes in vocabulary, grammatical form, conjuntions, etc. The Talmud was not thought of as a "scribal reference text", and thus it belongs to this second category. It utilized biblical texts as adjuncts to legal arguments or in expositional contexts, and the citation of these "authorized texts" did not require the same strictures as did manuscript copies of the Bible. "Undoubtedly", Lehmann says, "the verses were often committed to writing from memory; certainly none of the usual safeguards for faithful transmission of an authorized text were used"[16]. And, of course, if the biblical texts could be subject to such changes, then one ought to expect far more radical changes in the text of books that were, like Ben Sira, unauthorized.

Both Segal and Lehmann, then, develop their understandings of the rabbinic quotations of Ben Sira from slightly different appeals to a nexus of three notions: its unauthorized status, citations from memory, and less-than-careful textual transmission. I do not think, however, that these three notions alone explain the rabbinic quotations of Ben Sira. In additon to these, the texts raise other issues that need to be considered before we can answer the questions raised by Gilbert.

Whether the rabbis did or did not regard Ben Sira as canonical, it is clear that they cite approvingly from the book in a number of contexts[17]. In Sanhedrin 100b, it is clearly the *book* of Ben Sira that is the subject of

---

14. *Ibid.*, p. 135-36.
15. LEHMANN, *11QPs^a and Ben Sira* (n. 3), p. 241.
16. *Ibid.*, p. 242.
17. The literature on the development of the Jewish canon is quite large. For two views, see Sid Z. LEIMANN, *The Canonization of Hebrew Scripture: The Talmudic and Midrashic Evidence* (Transactions of the Connecticut Academy of Sciences, 47), Hamden, CT, Hamden Books, 1976 (see pp. 92-102) and R.T. BECKWITH, *The Old Testament Canon of the New Testament Church and Its Background in Early Judaism*, Grand Rapids, MI, Eerdmans, 1985.

discussion[18]. In other places, however, the rabbis cite proverbs from the book as if Ben Sira were himself a rabbinic sage. In Genesis Rabbah 8, the introductory formula has R. Eleazar quoting Sir 3,21-22 in the name of Ben Sira, ר' אליעזר אמר בשם בן סירא. Other texts offer quotations from the book in the name of rabbinic authorities without any attribution to Ben Sira at all. In Shabbath 11a, for instance, a passage originating in Sir 25,13 is attributed to Rab. Any explanation of rabbinic knowledge of Ben Sira must also take into account the variety of introductory formulae.

When we look at the quotations in Sanhedrin 100b, it seems clear that the dispute between R. Joseph and Abaye centers on ספר בן סירא. But what form of the book was it? The most satisfactory answer is the suggestion of Segal that an anthology of the book is in view. But given the textual forms of the various citations found there, Segal's claim that the rabbis cited from memory is perhaps not nuanced enough. In a number of cases the talmudic form of a passage is very close to the Hebrew manuscripts of Ben Sira. The citations of 6,6, 9,3b, 9,8a.c, 11,29a, 26,1.3 all essentially reflect the text of Ben Sira found either in Ms A or in Ms C. Indeed, the form of 26,3 even agrees with Ms C and the Syriac against the Greek in having a singular rather than a plural subject. In 11,29b, the form of the talmudic passage is related to a text of Ben Sira that is itself already corrupt. Even the passage that summarizes Sir 25,26 witnesses a form of the verse found in the expanded form of the book, in this case Syriac and GII (ms 248)[19]. All of these cases imply some relationship of *texts* to one another and thus a direct connection on the part of the rabbis with the text of Ben Sira. Yet even in some of the instances noted directly above, as well as others, like the citations of Sirach 42 on daughters or 11,32a on sparks and embers, the order of verses or the summarizing nature of the passage indicates manipulation of the text beyond straightforward citation. And how should one account for the non-Ben Sira proverbs?

---

18. Sometimes the book is cited in the same way as scripture. See, as one example, B. Hagigah 13a (citing Sir 3,21-22). B. Baba Kamma 92b has a proverb originally from Sirach cited as כתובים. It is also cited with other scriptural passages. See, for example, Shabbath 153a (with Qoh 9,8); Niddah 16b (with Prov 19,16); Baba Kamma 92b (with Gen 28,9 and Judg 11,3).

19. There is no Hebrew extant for this verse. On the expanded form of Ben Sira, see Patrick W. SKEHAN and Alexander A. DI LELLA, *The Wisdom of Ben Sira* (AB, 39), New York, Doubleday, 1987, pp. 55-62 and C. KEARNS, *Ecclesiasticus or the Wisdom of Jesus the Son of Sirach* in R.C. FULLER (ed.), *A New Catholic Commentary on Holy Scripture*, London, Nelson, 1969, pp. 547-550. The expanded text can be found in the second Greek recension (GII), the expanded Hebrew (HTII) found in the Cairo genizah manuscripts, the Old Latin and the Syriac.

It seems certain that after the Jewish canon was more or less deline-
ated the text of Ben Sira was not handled in the same manner as biblical
texts, but Lehmann's solution of carelessness or lack of precision in
transmission due to the book's non-canonical status does not explain the
situation well enough for earlier centuries. Indeed, the original Hebrew
of Joshua ben Sira suffered from the start, especially at the hands of his
grandson whose translation evidences at times mistranslation and mis-
reading of the Hebrew[20]. Thus, even before any discussions about the
authorized nature of certain books took place among the rabbis, the text
of Ben Sira had its problems, and the book came into the hands of the
rabbis in a far from pristine state. Additionally, it seems to me that
Lehmann's three categories do not really apply to the situation in peri-
ods earlier than the first couple of centuries CE when it is much more
difficult to talk about a canon, especially a tripartite canon of scripture in
Judaism[21]. But while neither Segal's nor Lehmann's explanations entirely resolve all the difficulties of the rabbinic quotations of Ben Sira,
both contribute important elements for a potential solution to the problem.

How then can we adequately account for the passages from Ben Sira
given in Sanhedrin 100b and elsewhere in rabbinic literature? One of
Gilbert's conclusions given in the article cited in the opening of this paper provides the place to begin. There he makes the following remarks
about the various additions to Ben Sira found in the Hebrew, Greek and
other versions:

> These facts suggest that the expanded text of Ben Sira grew little by little.
> We must not imagine only one official second edition, revised and ex-
> panded, but rather a long process of expansion. Not being acknowledged as
> a biblical book in Judaism, the text of the book of Ben Sira could freely
> incorporate doublets and additions, which were not necessarily transmitted
> in all manuscripts and all versions. The expanded text of Ben Sira, there-
> fore, is multiform[22].

---

20. KEARNS, *Ecclesiasticus* (n. 19), pp. 546-47; SEGAL, *Evolution* (n. 2), pp. 93-104.
On the translation technique of the grandson see Benjamin G. WRIGHT, *No Small Dif-
ference: Sirach's Relationship to Its Hebrew Parent Text* (SBLSCS, 26) Atlanta, GA,
Scholars, 1989.

21. On the problems of the development of a tripartite canon, see John BARTON,
Oracles of God: Perceptions of Ancient Prophecy in Israel after the Exile, New York-
Oxford, 1986.

22. GILBERT, *The Book of Ben Sira* (n. 1), p. 88. I have argued in my paper "The Use
of the Wisdom of Ben Sira in Rabbinic Literature," (presented in the Israelite and Christian Wisdom Section at the Annual Meetings of the Society of Biblical Literature, New
Orleans, 1990) that the rabbinic quotations provide evidence for a gradual process of expansion of the text of Ben Sira.

The process of textual variation began in Ben Sira very early. As the text was transmitted into the first and second centuries CE, a number of the errors and variants that we see in the quotations from Sanhedrin, such as changes in word order or vocabulary that better suited developing Hebrew language and style, changes like יפה for טובה in describing a wife, could easily have entered the manuscript tradition. Some of these variants, many of which are present in the Hebrew manuscripts of the book from the Cairo genizah, would be more or less deliberate, others undoubtedly would be the result of the kind of laxity in textual transmission proposed by Lehmann. Both Lehmann's and Segal's articles eloquently document this process. Alongside of these kinds of variations, more extensive differences developed. At times alternative versions of significant parts of or even entire cola developed and entered into the manuscript tradition. One need only scan the places where the Hebrew manuscripts of Ben Sira overlap to find numerous examples of this type of variation[23].

Ben Sira's book certainly seems to have reached such a level of popularity that Jews indeed expounded his proverbs for the good advice they gave and for their benefit for living a life according to the Law. Because of its importance and popularity, the text of Ben Sira's book attracted additional material in the course of its transmission history as the existence of the expanded text shows. The specification in the version of Sir 25,26 in Sanhedrin 100b to "give her [the evil wife] a bill of divorce" (יגרשנה), which is lacking in GI, may show that the rabbis knew the expanded version.

Some of the proverbs of Ben Sira were undoubtedly more popular than others, and people probably used certain types of material more than others. Proverbs on particular topics, like shame, women, or friends, ideally suit popular advice and homiletical contexts. Those who used such proverbs certainly molded them to specific uses or adapted them to differing circumstances, separated out of their original context, and they would cite many of these proverbs from memory. In addition, anthologies of such popular material were created. In these anthologies, material was rearranged, and I imagine it most likely that in them one would find citations like those in Sanhedrin 100b. If the text of the book of Ben Sira itself was handled carelessly because of its non-canonical status, one can only imagine the liberties taken with the book in the creation of anthologies such as Segal describes.

---

23. See, for example, Mss B and B^{mg}, E at 32,18; Mss B and Masada at 41,6; Mss B and A at 15,14. Some of these verses belong to the expanded text of Ben Sira.

We find good examples in two places of how Ben Sira was anthologized, both of which involve advice about women. First is the appearance in Sanhedrin 100b of Sir 42,9-10, 25,23-26 and 26,1.3 on daughters and wives. In these cases the texts range from a close representation of the Hebrew manuscripts (26,1.3) to considerable variation from them (42,9-10) to summation (25,23-26). In the talmudic passages, the order of the verses also differs from the manuscripts. The second example is Ms C from the Cairo genizah. This manuscript is an anthology of Ben Sira that excerpts a number of topics. The section on wives is comprised of 25,8.13.17-24; 26,1-3.13.15.17; 36,27-29. Here the manuscript follows the chapter and verse order of Ben Sira and excerpts the material on wives. In other places, however, that manuscript has passages inserted out of order, most likely for use as general topic headings[24].

Concurrent with the textual development, Joshua Ben Sira himself must have gained a reputation as a great wise person. Such notoriety probably had at least two interrelated results. The first was that he became considered like a rabbinic sage, one who was an expert in the law and who possessed great wisdom. He was subsequently cited as such in rabbinic literature. The second result was that proverbs accumulated around and circulated in his name. Some of these probably never found their way into any complete manuscript of his book, but may well have ended up in the kind of popular anthologies described above and that seem to constitute the ספר בן סירא that was at the center of the dispute between R. Joseph and Abaye in Sanhedrin 100b. These kinds of sayings may have originated in Hebrew or Aramaic. It is interesting in this regard that two of the three major sections of Sanhedrin 100b that are not found in any manuscript of Ben Sira are in Aramaic.

In a similar vein, rabbinic sages probably knew and used some of Ben Sira's more popular adages without any specific attribution, and audiences may have understood the sages to have authored some of them. Such sayings would then be reported as those of rabbinic sages rather than of Ben Sira. Two modern analogies illustrate this process: (1) most Americans know the proverb "A penny saved is a penny earned", but many may have learned it divorced from attribution to its source, Benjamin Franklin in *Poor Richard's Almanac*; (2) because Amos 5,24 is attributed to Martin Luther King, Jr. on his memorial in Atlanta, Georgia, some might think that this biblical verse was actually composed by him[25].

24. On the rationale for the arrangement of the material in Ms C, see Pancratius C. BEENTJES, *Hermeneutics in the Book of Ben Sira. Some Observations on the Hebrew MS. C*, in *EstBíbl* 46 (1988) 45-59.

25. This explanation is a little different from that of Segal (*Evolution* [n. 2], p. 135) who maintains that the rabbis knew the origin of anonymous citations of Ben Sira. He

The ongoing development of the book of Ben Sira was thus a very complicated process. Even if a significant portion of the material that was added to Ben Sira had content that was "inserted to give expression to certain religious ideas not (sufficiently) represented in the original"[26] and thus represents a more systematic recension of the book, it seems clear that numerous changes and additions as well as entire proverbs do not display that content and provide evidence of an ongoing and gradual process that continued to shape the book of Ben Sira well into the first several centuries CE. Indeed, Segal even suggests that the talmudic citation of Sir 11,29c.d influenced Ms A found in the Cairo genizah[27]. In brief compass I have tried to show that several complex but interrelated impulses and processes account for the citations of Ben Sira that we see in Sanhedrin 100b and other rabbinic texts. I do not think that they can be reduced either to memory or to carelessness with the text alone. Memory, all manner of textual manipulation and even invention, played roles in how the book of Ben Sira came to the rabbinic sages. I offer this attempt at some answers to the questions posed above to honor Prof. Gilbert's scholarly career and what will undoubtedly be an influential legacy.

Dept. of Religion Studies   Benjamin G. WRIGHT III
Lehigh University
Bethlehem, PA 18015 USA

says that they were simply "favorite sayings of the particular sages". He makes the assertion on the basis of two verses from Proverbs that are ascribed to Samuel the Little in Abot 4,19. If the book of Ben Sira were treated so differently from the Bible, as Segal and Lehmann claim, then the explanation for the attribution of these verses to Samuel may be different from that of the attributions of Ben Sira passages to rabbinic sages. Or, perhaps our assumptions about how well the sages knew biblical scripture in all its details overestimate the reality.

26. KEARNS, *Ecclesiasticus* (n. 19), p. 549. Kearns argues that the expanded text originated with the Essenes. See his unpublished Ph.D. thesis, *The Expanded Text of Ecclesiasticus: its Teaching on the Future Life as a Clue to its Origins*, Rome, Pontifical Biblical Commission, 1951.

27. See above, n. 10.

GEDANKEN ÜBER DEN THEMATISCHEN AUFBAU
DES BUCHES BEN SIRA

Das bisher noch nicht in der Ursprache, sondern nur im griechischen Text und danach folgenden Übersetzungen erhaltene Kapitel 24 des Buches Jesus Sirach (Ben Sira) mit seiner vermutlich später hinzugefügten Überschrift »Lob der Weisheit« bildet den gedanklichen Mittel- und Höhepunkt des ganzen Buches. Dies hat neben anderen Exegeten der Jubilar in einer frühen Studie in beeindruckender Weise mit vielen Einzelbeobachtungen neu unter Beweis gestellt und begründet[1]. Der überreiche Inhalt hat von jeher seine Leser begeistert. Dichterische Kraft, großartige Welt- und Naturkenntnisse und theologische Tiefe vereinigen sich zu einem unübertroffenen, imposanten Literaturwerk, das seinesgleichen sucht.

Viele Einzelbeobachtungen können diese Aussage stützen: Im Unterschied zu den Ausführungen in allen anderen Kapiteln des Buches läßt der Autor die Weisheit in einer autobiographischen Weise von sich reden. Dieser Stil wird vom Anfang bis zum Ende durchgehalten. In einem großen Bogen beschreitet der Inhalt einen Weg von der Erschaffung der Weisheit am Beginn der Schöpfung bis zur Gegenwart des Hörers. Ein kosmisches Geschehen rollt vor dem Auge des Lesers ab. Es spricht sich darin eine Erstaunen erregende Ganzheit des Denkens aus. Die Fülle der Geschichte leuchtet durch die Einzeletappen hindurch. Nicht in Einzelheiten verliert sich die gedankliche Explikation, so wichtig auch die vielen Details sind. Der Autor geht aber nicht in ihnen auf, sondern weiß sie einzuordnen in den großen Zusammenhang. In stringenter Weise läßt er seine reiche Kenntnis von Geschichte und Natur zur Geltung kommen, ohne das Ziel seiner Ausführungen je aus dem Auge zu verlieren. Wenn es ein Zeichen von besonderer Kraft des Denkens ist, große Zusammenhänge zu sehen und zu deuten, dann eignet diese Eigenschaft dem Autor in hohem Maße. Neben dieser formalen Beobachtung stehen viele Besonderheiten, die den Autor als ausgezeichneten Kenner der Geschichte des eigenen Volkes erweisen. Kenntnis der Weltgeschichte und der Vätergeschichte samt ihren Wanderungen verraten die Aussagen von v. 6 und v. 8. Der politische und religiöse Mittelpunkt auf dem Zion in Jerusalem ist der selbstverständliche Zielpunkt der geschichtlichen Ab-

---

1. M. GILBERT, *L'éloge de la Sagesse (Siracide 24)*, in *RTL* 5 (1974) 326-348.

folge (vv. 10f). Daß damit aber nicht eine gedankliche Engführung begründet wird, machen die Vergleiche deutlich, die das Wesen der Weisheit beschreiben. Hier verrät sich neben der Kenntis der Geschichte eine erstaunliche Begabung in der Beschreibung der Phänomene in der Natur. Die naturwissenschaftliche Erfahrung reicht von den stolzen Zedern im Libanon bis hin zu den Gewürzsträuchern der südlichen Länder. Schließlich ist auf die theologische Durchdringung dieser Phänomene immer schon aufmerksam gemacht worden. Die so umfassend beschriebene Weisheit ist in eins zu setzen mit dem Gesetz. Die Kühnheit dieses Gedankens gibt bis heute Rätsel auf und läßt die theologische Diskussion nicht zur Ruhe kommen. Aber auch diese Aussage verrät die denkerische Kraft des Autors, der dadurch sein Streben nach Erfassung der Zusammenhänge in einer ganzheitlichen Sicht erneut unter Beweis stellt.

Von dieser Mitte her können nun Überlegungen zu dem thematischen Aufbau des Buches Ben Sira angestellt werden, nach vorn bis zu Kapitel 1 und nach hinten bis zu Kapitel 51. Es wird sich erweisen, daß die angesprochene denkerische Kraft auch hier zu erkennen ist. Die großen Themen des Autors stehen in einem sinnvollen Bezug zueinander. Die reiche Fülle seiner Gedanken ist zu bewundern und läßt oft den Überblick verlieren oder verdunkelt ihn. Aber große Leitlinien lassen sich feststellen[2].

Das »Lob der Weisheit«, das in Kapitel 24 in Form eines Eigenlobs, also in der ersten Person, erklingt, wird im ersten Kapitel des Buches vorbereitet durch die Aussagen in der dritten Person. Hier wird in beschreibenden Worten das Wesen der Weisheit in umfassender Weise behandelt. Wie in Kapitel 24 beginnen die Aussagen beim Schöpfungsgeschehen. Noch ehe die Welt ins Dasein trat, war die Weisheit bereits existent (v. 1 und v. 4). Sie war beteiligt am Schöpfungsakt und ist daher auch in allen Schöpfungswerken präsent und über alle Werke ausgegossen (v. 9). Im besonderen erfüllt sie die Menschen, und hier wiederum die, die Gott fürchten (vv. 11-15). Sie aufzunehmen und ihr zu folgen, ist Vorrecht derer, die Gott fürchten. Damit sind wiederum die Glieder des Volkes Israel angesprochen; denn sie stehen in der Gemeinde der Erwählten. Hier hat die Weisheit ihren Ruheplatz gefunden. In Kapitel 24 wurde diese Mitte des Wirkens der Weisheit auf dem Zion gesucht. Diese Lokalisierung fehlt noch in Kapitel 1. Der Grund für die Auslas-

---

2. Zusammenfassend berichtet über die bisherigen Arbeiten zu der Frage nach der Struktur des Buches Ben Sira J. MARBÖCK, *Structure and Redaction History in the Book of Ben Sira. Review and Prospects*, in P.C. BEENTJES (ed.), *The Book of Ben Sira in Modern Research. Proceedings of the First International Ben Sira Conference, 28-31 July 1996* (BZAW, 255), Berlin-New York, de Gruyter, 1997, p. 61-79

sung einer topographischen Festlegung ist darin zu sehen, daß am Anfang der Darlegungen Ben Siras die Allgemeingültigkeit der folgenden Lebensregeln betont werden soll. Ein jeder soll sich angesprochen fühlen; so beziehen sich denn auch die kommenden Ratschläge auf das Leben des Individuums in seiner engeren Umgebung, in Familie und Haus. Das religiöse Zentrum, Jerusalem und der Zion, sind noch nicht im Blick. Hingegen wird auf das Gebot hingewiesen, das zu befolgen ist (v.26). Es handelt sich um das Gebot Gottes, von dem später gesagt werden wird, daß es mit dem Gesetz gleichzusetzen ist, das im Tempel von Jerusalem wohnt (Sir 24,23). Nach diesen grundlegenden Aussagen über die Weisheit beginnen die Einzelanweisungen, die sich nun dem Adressaten zuwenden, der im Mittelpunkt steht: dem Individuum in seiner Stellung zwischen der es umgebenden Welt und dem an es ergehenden Wort der Weisheit. Jede einzelne Person wird zur Entscheidung aufgerufen. Auf diesem Wege der Zuwendung zur Weisheit kann die Versuchung nicht ausbleiben. Davon spricht Kapitel 2.

Sprach Kapitel 1 in Form der Beschreibung in der dritten Person von der Großartigkeit der Weisheit, so redet in Kapitel 51 wiederum ein »Ich«, wie in Kapitel 24. Aber nun ist es das »Ich« des Autors. Er intendiert damit auch, die Stimme derer wiederzugeben, die seinem Wege gefolgt sind. Das Reden von der Weisheit bekommt nun einen bekenntnishaften Charakter. Vom allgemein gültigen Reden von der Weisheit in der dritten Person (Sir 1) spannt sich der Bogen über das Reden der Weisheit von sich selbst in der ersten Person bis hin zu dem Reden des Menschen in der ersten Person, der sich die Weisungen der Weisheit zu eigen gemacht hat und deshalb zum Bekenntnis geführt wird. Aber auch auf dem Wege des Bekenntnisses ist ein Werdeprozeß zu sehen: der Knabe irrt noch umher (v. 13), so wie die Weisheit viele Wege beschritt, ehe sie einen Ruheplatz finden konnte. Danach setzt die Phase des Suchens ein. Immer stärker wird das Verlangen und damit die Freude über die begehrenswerten Gaben der Weisheit. Diese Erkenntnis will der von der Weisheit Ergriffene aber nicht für sich behalten. Das Bekenntnis wird zum Anlaß, die gewonnene Lehre weiterzugeben: »lagert euch im Hause meiner Lehre!« (v. 23). Der, der den Reichtum der Weisheit (Sir 1) erkannt und die persönliche Anrede der Weisheit verstanden (Sir 24) und aufgenommen hat, wird nun selbst zum Weisheitslehrer (vv. 27-30). Mit diesem Schluß ist gleichzeitig ein neuer Anfang gewonnen. In der Form der Inclusio wird zurückgelenkt auf Kapitel 1. Die Lehre, von der der Autor in Kapitel 51 spricht, die er weiterzugeben gedenkt, nachdem er zur Weisheit gefunden hat, findet sich dort, wo man das Buch von Anfang an zu lesen beginnt.

Hat so das Buch in seiner Ganzheit einen in sich geschlossenen Rahmen gefunden, ist nun nach dem Inhalt und dem gedanklichen Aufbau der Zwischenteile zu fragen. Es lassen sich zwei große Gedankenblöcke deutlich voneinander abheben: Kapitel 2 bis Kapitel 23 auf der einen Seite als erster Teil, der von der in Kapitel 1 gegebenen Definition dessen, was Weisheit bedeutet, hinführt zu der Eigenaussage der Weisheit in Kapitel 24; sodann Kapitel 25 bis Kapitel 50 auf der anderen Seite als zweiter Teil, dem die Aufgabe zukommt, zurückzulenken von der Weite der Gedanken des Kapitels 24 zu der Wirklichkeit des Handelns im Kontext des persönlichen Lebens in der Gemeinschaft der Glieder des Volkes und schließlich zu der Einzelperson des Autors, dessen Bekenntnis am Ende alle Gedanken zusammenfaßt (Sir 51). Ein erster Versuch, Schwerpunkte in der Thematik der beiden Teile zu finden, ist früher schon gemacht worden. So ist vermutet worden, daß im ersten Teil Lehren aufgezeichnet sind, die das Leben des Einzelnen betreffen, während im zweiten Teil das Leben in der Öffentlichkeit im Vordergrund steht[3]. Von Wichtigkeit wird hierbei sein, die Übergänge vom großen Rahmen zu den Einzelausführungen richtig zu erfassen, also Kapitel 2 als Auftakt zu den folgenden Kapiteln 3-23 und Kapitel 50 als Schluß der Kapitelreihe 25-49 und Überleitung zu Kapitel 51. Dieser Frage ist nun nachzugehen.

Kapitel 2 hat durch Nuria Calduch-Benages[4] vor Kurzem eine eingehende Behandlung erfahren. Sie weist einerseits auf den programmatischen Charakter[5] des Kapitels hin und begründet andererseits den engen Zusammenhang zwischen den Kapiteln 1 und 2[6]. Ferner schlägt sie auch eine Brücke hin zu Kapitel 51,1-12, indem sie sagt: »Este último texto es una ilustración autobiográfica del tema del capítulo segundo«[7]. In all diesen Punkten ist der Argumentation voll zuzustimmen. Für die unter dem hier genannten Thema vorgetragene Beweisführung sind folgende Gesichtspunkte von Bedeutung:

3. G. SAUER, *Jesus Sirach (Ben Sira)*, in *JSHRZ*, t. III,5, 1981, p. 494, u. DERS., *Das Lob der Väter (Ben Sira 44–50) und die Wolke von Zeugen (Hebr. 11)*, W. PRATSCHER-G. SAUER (eds.), *Die Kirche als historische und eschatologische Größe, Festschrift für K. Niederwimmer zum 65. Geburtstag*, Frankfurt a.M. u.a., Lang, 1994, p. 126
4. N. CALDUCH-BENAGES, *En el crisol de la prueba. Estudio exegético de Sir 2,1-18*, Estella, Navarra, Editorial Verbo Divino, 1997 = Asociación Bíblica Espanola, 32; neuerdings: DIES., *Trial Motif in the Book of Ben Sira with Special Reference to Sir 2,1-6*, in *The Book of Ben Sira* (n. 2), pp. 135-151.
5. »Sir 2 es capítulo programático en la obra de Ben Sira«, *loc. cit.*, p.274.
6. Nach der Behandlung der Kriterien in Bezug auf das Vokabular und nach Hinweis auf formale Verwandtschaft kommt sie zu dem Schluß: »Todos estos elementos acercan indudublemente Sir 1 a Sir 2«, *loc. cit.*, p. 276.
7. *Loc. cit.*, p. 278.

Die Rede des Weisheitslehrers wendet sich an eine *Einzelperson*: »Mein Sohn!« in v. 1. Dieser wird ermahnt, am Anfang des Weges, der zur Erkenntnis der Weisheit führen soll, die Schwierigkeiten der Suche nach Weisheit zu bedenken und sich auf *Versuchung* vorzubereiten:

> 1b *So bereite dich vor auf Versuchung.*
> 2 *Mache dein Herz bereit und sei stark*
> *und errege dich nicht in der Zeit der Prüfung*[8].

Im Ablauf dieser Erfahrungen wird es nötig sein, *Geduld* zu beweisen:

> 4 *Alles, was auf dich zukommt, nimm an,*
> *und wenn sich dein Geschick zu deiner Erniedrigung wendet, so übe*
> *Geduld.*

Dabei kommt ihm zu Hilfe der Blick zurück in die *Geschichte*:

> 10 *Blickt auf frühere Geschlechter und seht:*
> *Wer vertraute auf den Herrn und wurde zuschanden?*
> *Oder wer blieb in seiner Furcht und wurde verlassen?*
> *Oder wer rief ihn an, und er übersah ihn?*

So weist der Lehrer darauf hin, eine tragfähige Grundposition einzunehmen. Diese wird in der *Furcht Gottes* gesehen:

> 17 *Die den Herrn fürchten, werden ihre Herzen vorbereiten,*
> *und vor ihm werden sie sich demütigen,*
> 18 *indem sie sagen:*
> *'Laßt uns fallen in die Hände des Herrn*
> *und nicht in die Hände der Menschen!*
> *Denn wie seine Größe,*
> *so ist auch sein Erbarmen'.*

Die Geschichte lehrt also, daß Gott durch die Not der Versuchung hindurchführt und Hilfe schafft. Am Ende des Weges steht das *Heil*:

> 3,1 *Das Gebot des Vaters hört, ihr Kinder,*
> *und handelt danach, damit ihr gerettet werdet.*

Diese Abfolge charakterisiert das Leben eines Menschen in seiner geschichtlichen Existenz. Dieses Leben begleiten nun die Lehren, die in den folgenden Kapiteln vorgetragen werden. Damit ist der Übergang gewonnen von der Deklaration dessen her, was Weisheit ist (Sir 1), zu den Einzelausführungen in den Kapiteln 3 bis 23, von deren Inhalt und Aufbau gleich noch mehr zu sagen sein wird. Kapitel 2 bereitet damit die

---

8. Dieses, wie auch alle folgenden Zitate aus Ben Sira werden wiedergegeben nach der Übersetzung von SAUER, *Jesus Sirach* (n. 2), jeweils z. St..

konkrete Anwendung der Erkenntnisse der Weisheit im Leben eines Individuums, des Schülers vor.

Eine Entsprechung zu dem, was eben zu Kapitel 2 gesagt werden
konnte, läßt sich auch bei dem Übergang von der Kapitelfolge 25 bis 50
nach Kapitel 51 hin aufweisen. Hier ist darauf zu achten, daß, wie gezeigt werden konnte, in Kapitel 51 wiederum von einem Individuum ge-
redet wird, und zwar in Form einer Selbstaussage in autobiographischer
Art. Es spricht der von der Suche nach Weisheit und von der Liebe zu
ihr ergriffene Autor, der als Suchender begann und damit gleichzeitig als
Lehrer erscheint, der sich nun nach der Erwerbung seiner Erfahrungen
als Lehrer fühlen darf. Auf diese Aussage bereitet Kapitel 50 unter einem doppelten Gesichtspunkt vor:

1.) Es wurde wiederholt darauf hingewiesen, daß Kapitel 50 den gedanklichen Schlußpunkt bildet in der Aussagereihe, die in 42,15 beginnt[9]. Die Geschichte des erwählten Volkes wird hier im Anschluß an
die Ermahnungen, die mit 42,14 rasch enden, in einem großen Zusammenhang von der Schöpfung angefangen geschildert[10]. In hymnischer
Weise wird die Größe der Schöpfungswerke gepriesen. Die Einzel-
themen müssen an dieser Stelle nicht benannt werden. Das Werk Gottes
in der Schöpfung vollendet sich da, wo aus der reichen Fülle der Ge-
schehnisse das Leben und Tun der Einzelpersonen unter dem Gesichtspunkt der ihnen erwiesenen Gnade erzählt wird. Es wird das »Lob der
Väter« besungen. Die Kapitel 44 bis 49 haben einen eigenen thematischen Aufbau, der keineswegs nur unter dem Gesichtspunkt der chrono-
logischen Folge steht. So ist bis heute ungeklärt, warum die Reihe der
Väter der Vorzeit mit Henoch begonnen wird (44,16) und nicht mit
Adam. Dieser steht vielmehr ganz am Ende (49,16).Ganz unmißver-
ständlich deutlich ist aber, daß die Geschichte abläuft in der Schilderung
der Taten einzelner Gestalten, deren Lebensweg im Rahmen des Volks-
ganzen sich hin und her bewegt zwischen Gefährdung und Rettung. Als
Höhepunkt und gleichzeitig als Schlußstein dieser Reihe sieht Ben Sira
das Wirken des Hohenpriesters Simon in Kapitel 50. Hier wird die Geschichte konkret in das Tun eines einzelnen Mannes zusammen-
gebündelt, der im Volke und für das Volk am Tempel handelt. Wie nun
nach Kapitel 24 Tempel und Weisheit zusammen gehören, so auch hier:

---

9. Vgl. dazu G. SAUER, *Die Abrahamgestalt im »Lob der Väter«. Auswahl und Intention*, in *Wiener Jahrbuch für Theologie* 1 (1996) 389-393.

10. Zur Fixierung des Neueinsatzes an dieser Stelle vgl. G. SAUER, *Das Lob der Väter
(Ben Sira 44-50) und die Wolke von Zeugen (Hebr 11)*, in W. PRATSCHER – G. SAUER
(eds.), *Die Kirche als historische und eschatologische Größe*, Festschrift für Kurt
Niederwimmer zum 65. Geburtstag, Frankfurt a. M. u.a., Lang, 1994, p. 126; dort auch
weitere Literatur.

die Einzelperson Simon am Tempel erfährt die in den Augen Ben Siras sachlich richtige Ergänzung durch den Hinweis auf die Einzelperson des Weisheitslehrers, der in Kapitel 51 spricht.

2.) Die Gedanken, die in Kapitel 2 von der Aussage über die grundlegende Bedeutung der Weisheit in Kapitel 1 überleiteten zu den konkreten Lehren in den Kapiteln 3–23 ließen sich zusammenfassen unter die Themen:»Einzelperson«, ferner »Versuchung«, »Geduld«, »Geschichte«, »Furcht Gottes« und »Heil«. In entsprechender Weise kehren diese Themen in Sir 42,15–50,29 wieder. Am Anfang steht im Rahmen der Schöpfung und im »Lob der Väter« die *Einzelperson*, bis hin zum Ende der Darstellung in der Person des Simon. Die ganze geschilderte Geschichte nimmt ständig Bezug auf die stetigen *Versuchungen*, die zu überwinden waren (z.B. Abraham; Sir 44,20). Auch Simons Amtszeit stand noch unter diesem Vorzeichen, indem er Tempel und Stadt befestigen muß (Sir 50,4). In den einzelnen Stadien der Geschichte wurde immer wieder in Treue *Geduld* geübt (z.B. Mose; Sir 45,4). So dient der Blick in die *Geschichte* dazu, in den Versuchungen zu bestehen. Der Schlußsatz in v. 29: »Denn die *Furcht* des Herrn bedeutet Leben«, kehrt zu der Grundaussage über den Ursprung der Weisheit zurück und weist gleichzeitig darauf hin, wo das *Heil* zu finden ist, nämlich in der Befolgung der Weisheitslehren ebenso wie im kultischen Handeln.

Ist auf diese Weise der große Rahmen gegeben, so ist nun auf die beiden Hauptteile in ihren Zusammengehörigkeiten und Entsprechungen einzugehen. Dabei fällt zuerst ins Auge, daß das Leben dessen, der eben in Sir 2,1 mit »mein Sohn« angeredet worden war, in seinem allerengsten Umkreis betrachtet wird. Es geht in Kapitel 3 um das Leben in der Familie, um die Erziehung der Kinder. »Das Gebot des Vaters hört, ihr Kinder!« Schritt um Schritt werden die Regeln des Zusammenlebens in der Familie erörtert. In der Familie werden die Grundlagen gelegt für das Leben in der Öffentlichkeit. So werden auch die außerhalb der Familie liegenden Gefahren benannt und die Warnung vor ihnen in die Erziehung mit einbezogen. Der vorsichtige Umgang mit dem Wort spielt eine große Rolle:

> 4,1 *Mein Sohn, spotte nicht über das Leben des Elenden,*

und ähnlich später.

Ebenso verhält es sich mit dem Gelde:

> 5,1 *Nicht sollst du dich stützen auf deinen Reichtum*
> *und nicht sollst du sprechen: 'Es steht in meiner Macht'.*

So wird das Kind vorbereitet auf seine Schritte in die Welt hinaus. Dort begegnet es Menschen, die ihm freundlich gesinnt sind und solchen, die ihm Böses antun. Für beide Lebensbezüge werden reichlich Beispiele beigebracht:

> 6,4 *Angenehme Rede vermehrt die Freundschaft,*
> *und anmutige Lippen entbieten freundlichen Gruß.*
> 7,1 *Nicht sollst du Böses tun,*
> *und nicht soll dich Böses treffen.*

In den Bereich der engen familiären Bezüge, aus denen der auf den Lehrer hörende junge Mensch kommt, gehören auch Betrachtungen über die Herkunft des Menschen, also über seine Geschöpflichkeit. Kapitel 17 geht darauf in grundlegenden Worten ein:

> 17,1 *Der Herr erschuf aus Erde den Menschen,*
> *und er läßt ihn wiederum zur Erde zurückkehren.*

Ben Sira verrät gute Kenntnisse der verstreuten Aussagen der kanonischen Schriften über das Leben und seine Dauer. Im besonderen aber wird bei der Bestimmung des Tuns des Menschen auf Gen 1 hingewiesen:

> 17,3 *So wie sich selbst umgab er sie mit Macht,*
> *und nach seinem Bilde schuf er sie.*
> 17,4 *Die Furcht vor ihm legte er auf alles Fleisch,*
> *daß er herrschte über Tiere und Vögel.*

Die Ermahnungen an das zu belehrende Kind enden in längeren Ausführungen über das Schuldigwerden in den Bezügen, in die das Kind hineingestellt ist:

> 21,1 *Mein Sohn, hast du eine Sünde begangen? Füge keine mehr hinzu!*
> *Und wegen deiner früheren (Sünden) bete!*

Als markanter Schluß steht in Sir 23,1-6 das persönliche Gebet um Bewahrung vor Sünde:

> 4 *Herr, Vater und Gott meines Lebens,*
> *den Blicken der Augen gib mich nicht hin!*
> 5 *Und Begierde wende ab von mir!*
> 6 *Die Begierde des Essens und die Lust mögen mich nicht ergreifen,*
> *und schändlicher Gier gib mich nicht preis!*

Ging der Weg der Gedanken in dem ersten Teil (Kapitel 3–23) von der kleinsten Zelle des menschlichen Zusammenlebens aus, nämlich von der Familie, so ist es in dem zweiten Teile des Buches Ben Sira in charakteristischer Weise umgekehrt. Hier setzt mit Kapitel 25 eine Thematik ein, die die volle Breite menschlicher Bezüge vor Augen hat:

> 25,1 *An drei Dingen habe ich Wohlgefallen,*
> *sie sind angenehm vor dem Herrn und vor Menschen:*

> *Eintracht unter Brüdern und Freundschaft unter Nächsten,*
> *und daß Frau und Mann miteinander gut auskommen.*

Das öffentliche Leben wird in seiner Vielfalt geschildert: Freunde und durch Zuneigung verbundene Menschen, auch die Ehe und Familie in dem Urteil der sie umgebenden Welt werden vorgeführt:

> 30,3 *Wer seinen Sohn unterrichtet, wird den Feind eifersüchtig machen,*
> *aber vor Freunden wird er über ihn frohlocken.*

Macht und Reichtum sind Gefahren, die dem Einzelnen drohen:

> 27,1 *Des Geldes wegen sündigten viele,*
> *und der, der es zu vermehren sucht, muß das Auge abwenden.*

Hier erweist sich die Standfestigkeit und gute Erziehung des Einzelnen:

> 27,3 *Wenn einer nicht an der Furcht des Herrn festhält,*
> *wird eilend in Kürze sein Haus zerstört werden.*

Die Gefahren, die hier drohen, sind besonders groß. In diesen Bereich gehört auch das rechte Benehmen in fremden Häusern, besonders beim Gastmahl:

> 31,12 *Mein Sohn, wenn du an einer großen Tafel sitzt,*
> *sollst du deinen Rachen über ihr nicht aufreißen;*
> *nicht sollst du sprechen:'Überfluß steht auf ihr'.*

Auch das Verhalten den religiösen Traditionen gegenüber wird angesprochen (Sir 35,1-20):

> 35,1 *Wer das Gesetz bewahrt, vermehrt die Opfer.*
> 2 *Es bringt Heilsopfer dar, wer sich an die Gebote hält.*
> 3 *Wer Liebe erweist, bringt Speiseopfer dar,*
> 4 *und wer mitleidvoll handelt, opfert ein Dankopfer.*

Den Höhepunkt der Worte, die das Eingebundensein des Einzelnen in die große Volksgemeinschaft zeigen, bildet das große Bittgebet in Kapitel 36. Danach wird in einem raschen Gefälle ein Weg beschritten, der in immer enger werdenden Bezügen schließlich wieder bei der Einzelperson und seinem Verhalten endet.

Es geht um die persönliche Beziehung zum Freund[11]:

> 37,1 *Ein jeder Freund spricht:'Ich bin dein Freund'.*
> *Es gibt aber einen Freund, der nur den Namen 'Freund' trägt.*

---

11. Siehe G. SAUER, *Freundschaft nach Ben Sira 37,1-6*, in F.V. REITERER (ed.), *Freundschaft bei Ben Sira. Beiträge des Symposions zu Ben Sira, Salzburg 1995* (BZAW, 244), Berlin-New York, 1996, pp. 123-131

Ferner geht es um das Gegenüber zum Arzt:

> 38,1 *Beweise Freundschaft dem Arzt, bevor du ihn brauchst;*
> *denn auch ihn hat Gott erschaffen!*

Der letzte Gedanke gibt Anlaß, an das Geschick des Todes zu denken, dem ein jeder entgegen geht. Die auf eine Einzelgestalt bezogenen Gedanken sind hier besonders deutlich (Sir 38,16-23):

> 38,16 *Mein Sohn, über einen Toten vergieße Tränen!*
> *Trauere und singe ein Klagelied!*
> *Wie es ihm zukommt, hülle ein seinen Leib!*
> *Und verbirg dich nicht bei seinem Verscheiden.*

Die Schilderung des Lebens und Tuns von Einzelpersonen setzt diese Reihe fort: der Künstler (Sir 38,27), der Schmied (Sir 38,28), der Töpfer (Sir 38,29f) und als Höhepunkt der Gesetzeslehrer (Sir 38,34).

Die Konzentrierung auf die Einzelperson wird in Kapitel 40,1-17 fortgesetzt durch eine nochmalige Behandlung des Themas der Geschöpflichkeit:

> 40,1 *Große Mühsal hat Gott zugeteilt,*
> *und ein schweres Joch (liegt) auf den Menschen*
> *von dem Tag an, an dem sie hervorgehen aus dem Schoß ihrer Mutter*
> *bis zu dem Tag, an dem sie zurückkehren zur Mutter alles Lebendigen.*

Im Unterschied zu Kapitel 17, wo ein Schwerpunkt auf der Betonung der Sünde und Vergänglichkeit lag, wird hier nun auf die vielen Möglichkeiten hingewiesen, bei denen ein Einzelner in seinem Leben in der Gemeinschaft Schwierigkeiten und damit seine Grenzen erfährt. So ist es auch zu verstehen, daß in diesem Zusammenhang noch einmal das Ende des menschlichen Lebens bedacht wird: sein Tod (Sir 41,1-4):

> 41,1 *Wehe, o Tod, wie bitter ist der Gedanke an dich*
> *für einen Menschen, dem es wohl ergeht in seinem Besitz;*
> *für einen zufriedenen Menschen und für einen, der in allen Dingen Erfolg hat,*
> *und der bei sich noch Lebenskraft hat, Freuden zu genießen!*
> 2 *Ach, o Tod, wahrlich, süß ist dein Gesetz*
> *für einen bedürftigen Menschen und für den, dem es an Kraft mangelt;*
> *für einen Menschen, der strauchelt und überall anstößt,*
> *der vergrämt ist und die Hoffnung verloren hat.*

Nun ist der Punkt erreicht, wo von der Schöpfung gesprochen wird (Sir 42,15ff):

> 42,15 *Gedenken will ich der Werke Gottes,*
> *und das, was ich erschaut habe, will ich erzählen,*

durch das Wort Gottes wurden seine Werke,
und ein Werk seines Wohlgefallens ist seine Lehre.

Dieses Tun erreicht in der Erschaffung des *Menschen* seinen Höhe- und Schlußpunkt (Sir 43,24-27).

Die folgende Geschichte wird in dem »Lob der Väter« in Form der Aufzählung der Einzelgestalten dargestellt, die als Repräsentanten des ganzen Volkes gelten. Damit ist die Konzentrierung auf das Individuum, von dem in Kapitel 2 der Ausgang genommen worden war, zum Abschluß gekommen. Der Kultdiener Simon und der Weisheitslehrer Ben Sira stehen am Ende.

Es ergibt sich damit folgender Aufbau in einem schematischen Überblick:

Präambel und Grundlegung; Rede von der Weisheit in der 3.Person:	Kapitel 1
Ausweitung und Themen	Kapitel 2
Lehren an die Einzelperson in Bezug auf das Individuum, die Familie und die Öffentlichkeit	Kapitel 3–23
Zentrum: Rede der Weisheit in der 1.Person	Kapitel 24
Lehren über das Verhalten in der Öffentlichkeit, in der Familie und für das Individuum	Kapitel 25,1–42,14
Themen und Konzentrierung auf das Individuum	Kapitel 42,15–50,29
Schlußbekenntnis; Rede des Weisheitslehrers in der 1.Person	Kapitel 51.

Rooseveltplatz 10/16
A-1090 Wien

Georg SAUER

STRATEGICAL SELF-REFERENCES IN BEN SIRA

INTRODUCTION

The problem of the structure of the book of Ben Sira has often been studied through a careful analysis of the socalled wisdom pericopes. Already for A Lapide (1567-1637)[1] the wisdom theme played an important role in his understanding of the composition of the book, although he understood wisdom only as an index of virtue, which constituted the real matter of content for him. With his hypothesis about the decalogue as structuring principle A Lapide introduced several noteworthy concepts. First he recognized that there were smaller, tightly constructed (thematic) units in the amalgam of the book, and, secondly, he proposed that there was a literary device at work by which these units had some meaningful relationship with eachother, viz. that there could be an organizing principle outside or behind the text of the book, according to which the author had moulded his material and which had left little or no trace of itself. Although A Lapide's methods and structural analysis are no longer accepted, still the most common approach to the problem of the structure of the book is to look for a linking factor between the socalled wisdom pericopes which would deceipher the order of the heterogeneous mass of the book. Particularly since Smend these wisdom sections and the exhortations to study Wisdom are seen as markers of the beginning of larger units[2]. Recently suggestions have been made that not all wisdom sections function in the same way (as markers of new units)[3], and that "literary and thematic structures are more plausible if more points of view are considered (text criticism, stylistics, poetics, vocabulary, thematic connections...)"[4].

1. Cornelius A LAPIDE, *In Ecclesiasticum*, in: A. Crampon (ed.), *Commentaria in Scripturam Sacram*, t. IX, Paris, L. Vivès, 1868 (Antwerpen, 1633-1643).
2. R. SMEND, *Die Weisheit des Jesus Sirach*. Berlin, G. Reimer, 1906, pp. XXX-XXXVI. But see also: J.G. EICHHORN, *Einleitung in den Apokryphen Schriften des Alten Testaments*, Leipzig, ¹1795, 1803, pp. 50-53. For a recent evaluation of the structure and redaction history, see: J. MARBÖCK, *Structure and Redaction History of the Book of Ben Sira. Review and Prospects*, in P.C. BEENTJES (ed.), *The Book of Ben Sira in Modern Research* (BZAW, 225), Berlin, de Gruyter, 1997, pp. 61-79.
3. H.-W. JÜNGLING, *Der Bauplan des Buches Jesus Sirach*, in J. HAINZ, H.-W. JÜNGLING, R. SEBOTT (eds.), *Den Armen eine frohe Botschaft*. FS F. Kamphaus, Frankfurt a. M., J. Knecht, 1997, p. 97: "Weisheitstexte, die sich gattungsmäßig auch unterscheiden".
4. J. MARBÖCK, *Structure and Redaction History of the Book of Ben Sira. Review and Prospects* (n. 2), p. 75.

One of the phenomena which always impressed itself on commentators of the Wisdom of Ben Sira and which recommends itself for an evaluation of possible structural implications, is that of the autobiographically coloured notes dispersed throughout the book. In these texts Ben Sira breaks away from his usual didactic patterns and adopts a personal tone. There is a notable increase of emphasis on the person of the author towards the end of the book[5]. In many instances, but not all, these texts are found attached to or near wisdom sections. Stylistically these texts seem well identifiable because of the first person that the author employs in them, sometimes in combination with direct speech (e.g. 24,31). Often, the understanding of these texts was indeed dominated by the search for order in the almost inscrutable structure of the book and they have engendered many hypotheses about the redaction history and structure[6]. In fact, it is generally accepted that "a purposeful literary redactional work is testified by the many autobiographical notes, as observed by many scholars, which announce that the work be continued after the sections on wisdom with 24,30-34; 33(30),16(25)-19(28); 39,12.32"[7]. The analyses by Roth, Harvey, and especially Jüngling, all make use, but in very different ways, of first person texts to discover a meaningful disposition in the book[8]. Jüngling noted correctly that one of the first person texts, viz. 16,24-25, usually is left out of consideration. He proposes to understand these verses as a subdivision of the first major part of the book (1,1–24,29) despite the resulting akward division of the theodicee section in 15,11–18,14 and without explaining the literary connections between Sir 23 and Sir 25, and between 24,23-29 and 24,30-34. He argues for a subdivision in the first person passage of 16,24-25 through a comparison with subdivisions which he distinguishes in other

---

5. J. HASPECKER, *Gottesfurcht bei Jesus Sirach* (AnBib, 30). Roma, PIB, 1967, p. 181, note 125. J.-L. PRATO, *Il problema della teodicea in Ben Sira* (AnBib, 65), Roma, PIB, 1975, p. 81.

6. The rather conspicuous use of the first-person has often gone underexposed and remained in the shadow of a narrow, diachronic approach of the speech of Lady Wisdom in Sir 24 in relation to such texts as Job 28; Prov 1–9 (esp. Prov 8); Bar 3,9–4,4; and Wisd 7–9. Especially Wisdom's equation with the law has attracted much attention and served often as a buoy toward which a reconstruction could be oriented. The outcome has been a variety of ingenious conjectures about the meaning of personified wisdom.

7. J. MARBÖCK, *Structure and Redaction History of the Book of Ben Sira.* (n. 2), pp. 76-77.

8. W. ROTH, *On the Gnomic-Discursive Wisdom of Jesus Ben Sirach*, in *Semeia* 17 (1980) 59-79. J.D. HARVEY, *Toward a Degree of Order in Ben Sira's Book*, in *ZAW* 105 (1993) 52-62. Roth and Harvey assume a structural function for both the wisdom texts and the first person passages. H.-W. JÜNGLING, *Der Bauplan des Buches Jesus Sirach*, p. 97, takes an opposite approach: "Nicht die Weisheitstexte, sondern die "Ich"-Passagen des "Authors" sind für die Struktur des Buches konstitutiv".

parts of the book. Starting at the end of the book and working back to the beginning he finds first person texts with a subdividing function in 44,1 and 33,16-18. All parts and subdivisions are marked by framing texts, of which the framing function is constituted by keywords and themes[9].

In his analyses Jüngling does not take into consideration all texts in which the sage employs the first person, nor does he distinguish between singular and plural first person texts. On the basis of keywords and syntagms (ἐκφαινεῖν παιδεῖαν, πληροῦν)[10], he distinguishes between different kinds of first person passages and singles out 16,24-25; 24,30-34; 33,16-18; 39,12; 42,15 as having a special structural significance. Some of these "I"-passages are connected to wisdom pericopes but this link is not evaluated. It seems therefor good to look at the first person texts again in order to evaluate anew their possible structural value.

SURVEY OF FIRST PERSON TEXTS IN BEN SIRA

A first person text is obviously constituted by the usage of the grammatical first person, but there are various ways in which this can be achieved: through independent personal pronouns, verbal forms, pronominal suffixes, and possessive pronouns. An overview of all these possible uses of the first person can provide the material for determining

---

9. H.-W. JÜNGLING, *Der Bauplan des Buches Jesus Sirach*, p. 103: "Wie die Unterteile Sir 39,12–43,33 und Sir 33,16–39,11 durch Rahmungen relativ feste Grenzen zeigten, läßt sich auch für Sir 16,24–24,29 eine feste Rahmung erkennen." Jüngling proposes as literary disposition (pp. 104-105):

Prologue

1st Part: 1,1–24,29	2nd Part: 24,30–39,11	3rd Part: 39,12–50,26
(1) 1,1–16,23	(1) 24,30–33,15	(1) 39,12–43,33
(2) 16,24–24,29	(2) 33,16–39,11	(2) 44,1–50,26

Epilogue: 50,27-29 (Sir 51)

One of the questions to be put to this disposition is: how can the division line between the 2nd and 3rd part be drawn after 39,11 when 38,24–39,11 has so many literary connections with the hymn of 39,12-35? (1) The verb διανοεῖσθαι, which occurs in 39,12a.32b without direct object, also is found in 39,7 with object. Likewise the objectless ἐκδιηγεῖσθαι in 39,12b occurs in 39,[2]10. (2) In the hymn the sage claims to 'be filled', 39,12, and the same is expressed in 39,6. (3) In the hymn the sage encourages his disciples to give thanks to the Lord and to praise Him, 39,14-15, and the same is found in 39,6. (4) Futhermore, there is some continuation in vocabulary (in Greek): ὄνομα (39,10.35) and αἴνειν (39,9.14-15). (5) Sir 39,4 speaks of 'good-and-evil' which is an important subject in the hymn, cf. 39,25.

A methodological point to be considered, is: If the Greek text is the basis for the structural analysis (since the Prologue is put as integral part of the "Bauplan"), why then the argumentation sometimes depends on the Hebrew text (as in 42,15 on p. 99, in 16,26 on p. 103)?

in what texts and how precisely the sage breaks away from his usual style in approaching the reader more personally. The results of such a survey can be classified in several categories, for even from a superficial reading it is immediately clear that Ben Sira employed the stylistic device of the first-person for more ends than speaking about himself. A criterium for distinguishing various uses of the first person could be whether the "I" is Ben Sira himself or someone else. It appears that Ben Sira used the "I" in several texts for other purposes than speaking about himself. There are notably Lady Wisdom and the fool, who both express themselves more than once in first person, and occasionally the householder (29,26-27) and even the dead (38,22) are presented as speaking in the first person. By using the first person in this way Ben Sira taps into a long sapiential tradition of personification, as a way of driving home his teaching. A very different usage of the first person is personal prayer which occupies a relatively prominent place in the Wisdom of Ben Sira[11], and which often, but not always nor exclusively, occurs in plural (e.g. 2,18; 36,1-17; 48,11; 50,22-24). First person utterances in hymn-like texts could also be grouped with Ben Sira's prayer language (24,23; 43,24b.27-28.32; 44,1).

A closer reading of the remaining first-person-singular texts reveals that not all self-references of Ben Sira have the same import. Only in some of the autobiographically tinged texts the readership is envisaged *directly* (and in some of these occurs the syntagm of ἐκφαινεῖν παιδείαν[12] as noted by Beentjes en Jüngling), while other personal remarks appear to be aimed at the readers only *indirectly*. As far as the person of the author is concerned, it seems possible to distinguish between self-references that testify to the educational strategy of Ben Sira towards his readership, and disclosures that speak rather of his inspiration. The distinctive criterium is the orientation of the subject matter. Ben Sira always speaks about wisdom in one way or another, but some first-person references are horizontally oriented towards the reader and deal with the mutual relationship of teacher and disciple and the kind of

---

10. H.-W. JÜNGLING, *Der Bauplan des Buches Jesus Sirach*, p. 97 n. 20: "Die genannten und so eng miteinander verzahnten "Ich"-Passagen [viz. 16,24-25; 24,30-34; 33,16-18; 39,12; 42,15] sind von anderen Ich-Stücken im Buch charakteristisch unterschieden ...".

11. The Book of Ben Sira stands out among wisdom books in that it contains a relatively high number of personal prayers; cf. M. GILBERT, *La prière des sages d'Israël*, in H. LIMET – J. RIES (eds.), *L'expérience de la prière dans les grandes religions* (Homo Religiosus, 5). Louvain-la-Neuve, 1980, pp. 227-243.

12. P.C. BEENTJES, *Profetie bij Jesus Sirach*, in B. BECKING – J. VAN DORP – A. VAN DER KOOIJ (eds.), *Door het oog van de profeten. Exegetische studies aangeboden aan prof. dr. C. van Leeuwen*. Utrecht, 1989, pp. 23-30.

dedication required for wisdom study. Other self-references display an extra vertically oriented dimension and speak about inspiration and religious motivation and about the author's relationship with God, the only Wise and the source of all wisdom.

In overview:

Personifications		Ben Sira		
The "fool"	Wisdom	As Teacher	About himself	prayer-language hymn-like texts
				2,18: *plural*
	4,15.17-19			
5,1.3-4.6		6,23		
7,9				8,5-7: *plural*
11,[19].23-24		12,12ef		
15,11-12		16,5		
16,17.20-22		16,24-25		
20,16				22,27–23,6
23,18	24,3-22	24,34	24,30-33	24,23: *plural*
		25,1-2.7.16: *numer.*		
		26,5.28: *numerical*		
		27,24: *numerical?*		
		33,19	33, 16-18	
		(: 30,27)	(: 36,16ᵃ+30,25-26)	
		31(34),10 (Hb only)		
		31(34),22		36,1-17: *plural*
		34(31),12-13		
37,[1].3?		39,13a	39,12.32	
[39,21.34]		41,16		
		42,15		43,24b: *plural*
				43,27-28.32: *plur.*
				44,1: *plural*
		49,13		48,11: *plural*
		50,25: *numerical*	50,27 (Gk only)	50,22-24: *plural*
			51,13-22.25.27	51,1-12
		51,23		

This survey[13] shows that the stylistic device of the first-person permeates the book, and even when not providing a (literary) structure it could be regarded as one of the author's tools for weaving networks of

---

13. The first person in the Gk of 3,1 is textcritically uncertain. Sir 8,5-7 is not a prayer nor a hymn, but its content matter (sin, old age, and death in reference to God) would seem to justify inclusion with the prayer language of Ben Sira. Despite its prosaic wording Sir 24,23 may also be counted among the hymn-like texts. Sir 31(34),10b1.b2.b3.b4 only occurs in Hb and appears to belong to the Hb II redaction: cf. J. LIESEN, *First-Person Passages in the Book of Ben Sira*, in C. O'CALLAGHAN (ed.), *Proceedings of the Irish Biblical Association*, 1998. Sir 50,27 employs the first person only in the Gk text.

centripedal forces in the book, which like magnets hold together apparently unconnected particles in an invisible field[14].

PERSONIFICATIONS

From a synchronic point of view the interventions in first person singular by a foolish person are, on the one hand, kept to a minimum. In case of the fool, the "I" is never developed outside its immediate context, and therefor there is hardly a real personification. This indicates the subordinate and ancillary nature of the category of the fool in the teaching of Ben Sira. On the other hand, the contexts in which the first person foolish utterances occur, display something of a pattern. It seems that (1) Ben Sira sometimes made use of "interventions" by an imaginary opponent, which trigger and focalize his own teaching[15]. Sir 14,20–18,14, e.g., is thus conceived as a unit, opening with a pericope on the pursuit of wisdom (14,20–15,10) followed by two interventions (15,11-12 and 16,17-22) which are each in turn refuted and corrected in two long treatises. In other instances (2) Ben Sira inserted the interventions as quotations in larger didactic discourses as a kind of contrapositions which serve to delineate his own position. The hymn of 39,12[16]-35, e.g., is structured with such a contraposition: 39,21.34.

The intervening function of statements by a foolish figure is an important part of the teaching and composition method of Ben Sira. Since the primary aim of such utterances is argumentation, they shed only little light on the foolish personage. In fact, one gets the impression that there is no person behind these utterances except the organizing mind of Ben Sira. Even the most fully developed intervention, which is 16,17-22, seems more attuned to the following refutation of it[16], than informative of the person(s) from whom it might have come. In 16,23 the first-person-singular reasoning of 16,17-22 is refered to as זאת, which is explained in Gk as μωρά, and is attributed to fools in general (/ חֲסַר לֵב / גֶּבֶר פּוֹתֶה, ἐλαττούμενος καρδίᾳ / ἀνὴρ ἄφρων). Haspecker suspects that fool-sayings in first-person-singular are more than a literary tech-

---

14. Differently: L. SCHRADER, *Leiden und Gerechtigkeit. Studien zu Theologie und Textgeschichte des Sirachbuches* (BET, 27). Frankfurt a.M., 1994, p. 67: "… nötigt auch der offensichtlich planvolle Aufbau des vorliegende Sirachbuches nicht dazu, Jesus Sirach als Urheber des Buchganzen Anzusehen".

15. J. HASPECKER, *Gottesfurcht bei Ben Sira*, pp. 142-144, esp. n. 45. Cf. PRATO, *Il problema della teodicea in Ben Sira*, p. 231.

16. J. HASPECKER, *Gottesfurcht bei Ben Sira*, pp. 148-149, n. 55: "die Entsprechungen sind zahlreich und unverkennbar"; especially 17,15-22 corresponds closely to 16,17-22.

nique and that they actually reflect different religious currents of the times of Ben Sira[17]. Debates with real adversaries, or perhaps inquisitive disciples, may well – and are indeed likely to – underlie some of the material of his teaching, but the book Ben Sira wrote, gives very little information about such opponents: apart from students (or sometimes rulers) no human being is formally addressed. If there are contrasting views which Ben Sira refuted, they have been absorbed in his didactic style almost without leaving clues to their origin[18.]

In the case of Lady Wisdom something of a coherent character is developed and maintained over several pericopes, indicating a special purpose for Wisdom. Since, however, this personification occurs only in the first half of the book (4,11-19; 6,18-31[37]; 14,20–15,8[10]; 24,1-22), and since its absence in the second half coincides with a noticable increase of emphasis of the author on himself, it seems likely that a link exists between the "I" of Wisdom and the "I" of Ben Sira. In other words: the "I" of Wisdom serves an educational purpose which is taken over explicitly by the "I" of Ben Sira in Sir 24[19].

BEN SIRA AS SELF-CONSCIOUS TEACHER

The first occurrences of Ben Sira employing the first-person as a reference to himself, do not come in the programmatic opening chapters, but in 6,23 in a brief invitatory call, in 12,12[ef] in concluding remark, in 16,5 in a notice about personal experience, more openly in 16,24-25 in an invitatory call with an explanatory note, with which he recommends his teaching, and in 22,25-26 in a remark on friendship. These first occurrences preceding the overtly personal ending of Sir 24 have in common that they are used side by side with the personification of Wisdom. In this paper these brief first person texts will be investigated in order to understand better the didactic strategy of Ben Sira.

---

17. *Ibid.*, p. 144, n. 45: "Mit dieser Formel ['sage nicht'] führt Sirach aktuelle Einwände ein". On possible opponents see also: B.G. WRIGHT III, *Fear the Lord and Honor the Priest*, in: P.C. BEENTJES (ed.), *The Book of Ben Sira in Modern Research* (BZAW, 225). Berlin, de Gruyter, 1997, pp. 218-220. Wright refers to an as yet unpublished study by Richard HORSLEY and Patrick TILLER, *Ben Sira and the Sociology of the Second Temple*.

18. It is remarkable that most of these "interventions" occur in the first half of the book of Ben Sira and that these are uniform: אל תאמר... . In the second half they are far less numerous, if present at all: in 37,1.3 only in Hebrew and in 39,21.34 in a different mode, not functioning as starting point for a treatise.This fact seems to corroborate the impression of most commentators that the book was not written all at once.

19. We believe that in Sir 24 Ben Sira oriented the personification of Wisdom so as to arrive at himself, by means of the Law; cf. J. LIESEN, *First-Person Passages in the Book of Ben Sira*.

Sir 6,23

When Ben Sira employs the first person as a teacher it is usually to appeal for attention or to state the value of his teaching. From the most conspicuous cases, i.e. 16,24-25; 24,30-34; 33H,16-19 [=36G,16ª+30G,25-27]; 39,12.32; 42,15, it has been deduced that in the Greek text such appeals or statements have their focal point in the syntagm παιδείαν ἐκφαινειν and in the verb πληρουν. When the first personal remark, 6,23, is considered in its context, a keyword is found which closely corresponds to παιδείαν ἐκφαινειν, viz. ἐπι/ἐκ-δέχομαι. Sir 6,23 is part of a unit, 6,18-37, in which the disciples are encouraged to strive for wisdom. The pericope of 6,18-37 is in fact an emphatical invitation to the disciples to listen and to be receptive in order to become wise. The pericope is structured in three strophes: 6,18-22, 6,23-31, and 6,32-37. Each of these strophes opens with the common wisdom address, τέκνον, and the verb ἐκ/ἐπιδέχομαι (6,18ª.23ª.33ª)[20]. The first strophe opens with the theme of the pericope: to achieve παιδεία and σοφία (6,18), and the last strophe emphasizes that the purpose is to be disciplined (παιδεύομαι, 6,32) and to become wise (σοφός, 6,33)[21]. The key to discipline and wisdom is a listening attitude, a readiness to accept and receive (cf. Solomon's prayer for wisdom in 1Kings 3,9: לֵב שֹׁמֵעַ).

The telling feature of the pericope is that there is a gradual development regarding to whom the disciple should be receptive to. In the first strophe the receptiveness required for discipline and wisdom regards personified wisdom (6,20ª, see also the personal and possessive pronouns in 6,19-21). In the middle strophe the receptive attitude a wisdom disciple should have, is for one verse unexpectedly concretized as listening to Ben Sira's opinions and advice (6,23), but the personification of wisdom is immediately resumed (6,24-31). In the last strophe the attention of the disciple is directed to a wise and intelligent person (6,34-36) and ultimately to the divine Law (6,37). This development is very revealing: the personification of Wisdom and the first person insertion by Ben Sira both serve the same purpose, viz. to instruct disciples in a certain way of life. Since the wisdom Ben Sira wants to inculcate is not a material knowledge to be passed on, but a way of life to be embraced, he can refer to himself and his own life as a point of reference for the wisdom

20. We accept the conjecture of Ziegler emendating επιλεξαι with επιδεξαι; cf. J. ZIEGLER, *Sapientia Iesu Filii Sirach* (Septuaginta, XII,2). Göttingen, Vandenhoeck & Ruprecht, ²1980, p. 152.

21. A direct object is lacking in 6,33a; the parallism with 6,32a suggests παιδείαν as in ms 548ᶜ; the Origenic recension and other mss (*O* L-694-743 542ᶜ) read συνεσιν, cf. Lat doctrinam; Anastasius Sinaita reads αὐτην referring to personified wisdom; the Hebrew of Ms A has only the verb תוּסָר.

disciples. What appears as the author's self-consciousness is therefor a fitting strategy of teaching wisdom.

The development of the wisdom pericope in 6,18-37 is reflected in Sir 24. The self praise of Wisdom (24,3-22) leads to the equation with the divine Law (24,23) which is described with images of its capacity to enable rich harvests (24,25-29; cf. esp. 24,27 ἐκφαίνειν παιδείαν), which in turn serve for describing the role of Ben Sira as a wisdom teacher (24,32 [παιδείαν] ἐκφαίνειν).

Sir 12,12ᵉᶠ and Sir 22,25-26

The self-reference in 12,12ᵉᶠ comes within the context of several pericopes which are more or less united by a common theme: care in selecting one's associates. In his teaching about one's associates Ben Sira suddenly refers to his own teaching: λόγοι μου, ῥήματα μου. Since wisdom and folly do not go together (cf. 4,18-19; 6,20-21), and since being a wisdom disciple involves close association with one's wisdom teacher (6,23.34-36), the warning for close contact with an enemy is fittingly concluded with a remark about the wisdom teacher. When the disciple disregards the teaching of Ben Sira, it effectively means that he dissociates himself from his teacher and his Law-abiding way of life. If this is the case and the disciple associates instead with sinners (12,14 ἀνὴρ ἁμαρτωλός), the disciple will realize too late (12,12ᵉ ἐπ' ἐσχάτων) the truth of Ben Sira's teaching[22].

The self-refences in 22,25-26 come in the context of sayings dealing with one's associates, specifically one's friends. True friendship, which is founded on the fear of God (6,16-17), may require to stay with a friend in times of distress, and Ben Sira expresses his willingness to do so, even to the point where he takes the evil on himself[23].

It is remarkable that the seemingly casual self-references of Ben Sira in 12,12ᵉᶠ and 22,25-26 both appear in contexts that deal with friendship and one's associates. The first friendship pericope, 6,5-17, comes just before the first wisdom pericope in which the first self-reference occurs. This state of affairs suggests that the themes of attaining wisdom and friendship on the one hand and the personification of wisdom and the self-references on the other hand are somehow connected for Ben Sira.

---

22. For the interpretation of the associate as professional rival, see L. SCHRADER, *Unzuverlässige Freundschaft und verläßliche Feindschaft. Überlegungen zu Sir 12,8-12*, in F.V. REITERER (ed.), *Freundschaft bei Ben Sira. Beiträge des Symposions zu Ben Sira, Salzburg 1995* (BZAW, 244). Berlin, de Gruyter, 1996, pp. 19-59.

23. Cf. J. MARBÖCK, *Gefährdung und Bewährung*, in F.V. REITERER (ed.), *Freundschaft bei Ben Sira* (n. 22), 1996, p. 96.

Wisdom is first presented as an associate on the road (4,11-19) and before presenting himself as a trustworthy associate on the road to discipline and wisdom (6,18-37), Ben Sira speaks of what defines a true friend, viz. fear of God (6,5-17).

Sir 16,5.24-25

The self-reference in 16,5 comes within the same context as the first person text of 16,24-25. In fact, Ben Sira's explicit call for attention (16,24-25), the provocative foolish statements (16,17-22) and Ben Sira's summary of such statements (16,23) are all part of a wider context, which is generally believed to span from (14,20) 15,11 to 18,14. There are several propositions regarding the composition of this didactic unit; the principal, interconnected issues are: whether 16,18-19 are to be attributed to the foolish interlocutor, and whether 16,17-23 go with the foregoing or the following.

FUSS considers 16,18-19 as a "Zusatz" which Ben Sira incorporated, even though it was not fully in keeping with his purposes. Fuß points out a keyword connection (לֵב in 16,23ᵃ.24ᵇ) and accepts only a "lediglich assoziative Beziehung" between the foolish utterances in 16,17-23 and the exposition in 16,24–17,14[24]. HASPECKER takes 14,20–15,10 as an introductory diptych (on the pursuit of wisdom) and identifies two expositions in 15,11–18,14 in which Ben Sira unfolds his teaching according to a certain pattern; 16,18-19 is attributed to Ben Sira[25]. In each exposition a foolish argument is first briefly denied (15,11ᵇ.12ᵇ and 16,18-19.23) and then systematicaly debilitated and shown to be untenable in a long treatise (15,13–16,14 and 16,24–18,14)[26]. SKEHAN-Di LELLA take 16,17-23 with the foregoing (as did Peters and Spicq) and consider 16,18-19 as an authorial parenthesis[27]. ARGALL regards 15,11–16,23 as a disputation speech, opening and closing with citations (15,11-12; 16,17ᵃ: each citation beginning in the same way with מֵאֵל, suggesting some relationship)[28]. Sir 16,18-19 are attributed to the sinful interlocutor. He distin-

24. W. FUSS, *Tradition und Kompostion im Buche Jesus Sirach* (unpublished dissertation). Tübingen, 1963, p.113.

25. J. HASPECKER, *Gottesfurcht bei Jesus Sirach*, pp. 142-149.

26. Prato basically follows Haspecker (also in his attribution of 16,18-19 to Ben Sira): G.-L. PRATO, *Il problema della teodicea in Ben Sira*, pp. 229-232.262. Differently: W. BAUMGARTNER, *Die literarische Gattungen in der weisheit des Jesus Sirach*, in *ZAW* 34 (1914) 176, 184.

27. P.W. SKEHAN – A.A. DI LELLA, *The Wisdom of Ben Sira* (AB, 39), New York, 1987, pp. 267-275.

28. R.A. ARGALL, *1Enoch and Sirach. A Comparative Literary and Conceptual Analysis of the Themes of Revelation, Creation and Judgement* (SBL Early Judaism and its Literature, 8). Atlanta, GA, 1995, pp. 226-232.

guishes two sections: 15,13-20, being an assertion of human responsibility, and 16,1-23, being a two-stanza exposition of the topic of the-many-versus-the-one (vv. 1-4) in view of judgment and individual retribution (vv. 5-14). Within the second stanza, 16,6-10 are of special importance: they list "stories from Jewish tradition to serve as examples of the exactitude of God's corporate judgment" (p. 229) and to demonstrate "the precision of God's use of the elements of creation to punish the many" (p. 230).

We follow the structural observations of Haspecker and consider all of 15,11–16,14 as a subunit on sin, human responsibility, and divine retribution, and 16,17–18,14 as dealing with the moral order in creation for which God himself is the model and the guarantee. In this large construct Ben Sira arranges his teaching as the refutation of some foolish statements. The first exposition answers the argument that God is to be held responsible for sin (15,11ᵃ.12ᵃ), and the second answers the position that God is unaware of the sinner and does not requite sin (16,17-22). We consider all of 16,17-22 going together as a thematic unit expressing the fool's thoughts. The main arguments for attributing 16,18-19 to the fool are: 1) the conjunction אַף in 16,19ᵃ, which demonstrates the unity of 16,18-19, and 2) the parallel construction of אֲלֵיהֶם in 16,19ᵇ and גַּם עָלַי in 16,20ᵃ, which ties 16,18-19 to the following. The identity, however, of the speaker of 16,18-19 and the structural function of 16,17-23 have been partially obscured by additions that belong to the secondary text-form: 16H,17ᵈ.18 (16S,17ᵈ; 16G,18ᶜ)²⁹.

The fact that Ben Sira organizes his teaching as refutations of foolish arguments implies a certain concept of what it takes to become wise. The disciple has to apply extreme care in choosing whom he listens to (16,24ᵇ) and whose outlook on life he is going to take as model. Against this background Ben Sira recommends his own teaching as based on much personal experience (16,5) and as being בְּמִשְׁקָל/ἐν σταθμῷ (16,25ᵃ by weight) and בְּהַצְנֵעַ/ἐν ἀκριβείᾳ (16,25ᵇ with accuracy [cf. 32,3ᵇ]). Given the midrashic nature of his argumentation in the second unit³⁰, the

---

29. The additional nature is evident from the added vocalization (עֲמוּדִים) and the length of the hemistichs in Ms A, which is not stichometrically arranged but indicates verse-endings with a sôp pāsûq: 16,18ab is written as if two verses instead of two hemistichs! Cf. *Facsimiles of the Fragments Hitherto Recovered of the Book of Ecclesiasticus in Hebrew*. London 1901; P.C. BEENTJES (ed.), *The Book of Ben Sira in Hebrew. A Text Edition of all Extant Hebrew Manuscripts & A Synopsis of All Parallel Hebrew Ben Sira Texts* (SVT, 68). Leiden, 1997, p.46.

30. J. DE FRAINE, *Het loflied op de menselijke waardigheid in Eccli 17,1-14*, in *Bijdragen* 11 (1950) 10-23. Cf. also: H. DUESBERG, *La dignité de l'homme, Sir 16,24-17,14*, in *Bible et Vie Chrétienne* 82 (1968) 15-21; L. ALONSO SCHÖKEL, *The Vision of Man in Sirach 16:24–17:14*, in J.G. GAMMIE e.a. (eds.), *Israelite Wisdom. Theological*

explicit recommendation in 16,24-25 may refer to the extensive scriptural knowledge of Ben Sira (cf. prologue, 6,37; 39,1-3+6-8). According to Ben Sira (personified) wisdom is found in the book of the covenant of the Most High, and as a wisdom teacher he is well versed in scripture knowing how to read and apply it. Ben Sira's scriptural allusions, quotations, and rereadings are a trustworthy guide for the uninstructed. As the disciples are invited to associate themselves with personified wisdom (4,12; 6,26) and carry her yoke (6,24-25), so they are invited to stay close to Ben Sira, to wear out his doorstep (6,36) and to carry his yoke (51,26).

As a student of Maurice Gilbert for many years it was a pleasure to wear out his doorstep and benefit from his profound knowlegde and wisdom.

Heyendahllaan 82   Jan LIESEN
NL–6464 EP Kerkrade

---

and Literary Essays in Honor of Samuel Terrien. New York, 1978, pp. 235-237. Since the foolish argumentation is based on the immediate perception of the visible world, Ben Sira goes back to the creational principles which underlie the tangible world; 16,26-31 and 17,1-14 are developed in correlation: the celestial people of God, the stars, serve as an example and background for the terrestrial people of God, the human beings.

THE CONCEPT OF 'BROTHER' IN THE BOOK OF BEN SIRA

A SEMANTICAL AND EXEGETICAL INVESTIGATION

It was an article on Psalm 133 in the Festschrift in honor of my teacher Rabbin Yehuda Aschkenazy[1] that first suggested the idea to me to investigate the concept of 'brother' as reflected in the Book of Ben Sira. A request to participate in the Festschrift in honor of Maurice Gilbert enabled me to make it my particular study[2].

Though the *Greek* translation[3] offers the most complete text of the Book of Ben Sira, and moreover the word ἀδελφός surprisingly shows up exactly *twelve* times in the grandson's version[4], it is nevertheless wished for to include in this investigation also the Hebrew[5] and Syriac[6] texts dealing with 'brother'[7].

1. B. HEMELSOET, *De broederschap bezongen: Psalm 133*, in I. ABRAHAM, L. BAKKER (eds.), *Tora met hart en ziel. Artikelen aangeboden aan Yehuda Aschkenazy bij zijn 65e verjaardag*, Hilversum, Gooi & Sticht, 1989, pp. 245-257.

2. O. WISCHMEYER, *Die Kultur des Buches Jesus Sirach* (BZNW, 77), Berlin, de Gruyter, 1995, has paid no attention at all to the concept of 'brother' in the first chapter of her stimulating study, dealing with 'family'. It is a pity that this monograph has no indexes whatsoever.

3. J. ZIEGLER, *Sapientia Iesu Filii Sirach* (Septuaginta ... Gottingensis, 12,2), Göttingen, Vandenhoeck & Ruprecht, 1965; J.H.A. HART, *Ecclesiasticus: the Greek Text of Codex 248*, Cambridge, 1909.

4. Not eleven, as given by F.V. REITERER, *Gelungene Freundschaft als tragende Säule einer Gesellschaft. Exegetische Untersuchung von Sir 25,1-11*, in ID. (ed.), *Freundschaft bei Ben Sira. Beiträge des Symposions zu Ben Sira, Salzburg 1995* (BZAW, 244), Berlin, de Gruyter, 1996, p. 143.

5. *Facsimiles of the Fragments Hitherto recovered of the Book of Ecclesiasticus in Hebrew*, Oxford-Cambridge, 1901; *The Book of Ben Sira*. Text, Concordance and an Analysis of the Vocabulary (The Historical Dictionary of the Hebrew Language), Jerusalem, The Academy of the Hebrew Language and the Shrine of the Book, 1973; P.C. BEENTJES, *The Book of Ben Sira in Hebrew*. A Text Edition of all Extant Hebrew Manuscripts & A Synopsis of all Parallel Hebrew Ben Sira Texts (SVT, 68), Leiden, Brill, 1997; P. BOCCACCIO – G. BERARDI, *Ecclesiasticus. Textus hebraeus secundum fragmenta reperta*, Rome, Biblical Institute, 1976; I. LÉVI, *The Hebrew Text of the Book of Ecclesiasticus* (Semitic Study Series, 3), Leiden, Brill, 1904, ³1969 (= Lévi, *Text*); S. SCHECHTER & C. TAYLOR, *The Wisdom of Ben Sira*, Cambridge, Cambridge University Press, 1899; M.Z. SEGAL, ספר בן־סירא השלם, Jerusalem, Bialik Institute, ²1958; H.L. STRACK, *Die Sprüche Jesus', des Sohnes Sirachs* (Schriften des Institutum Judaicum in Berlin, 31) Leipzig, Deichert, 1903; F. VATTIONI, *Ecclesiastico*. Testo ebraico con apparato critico e versioni greca, latina e siriaca (Testi 1), Naples, Istituto Orientale di Napoli, 1968; Y. YADIN, *The Ben Sira Scroll from Masada*, Jerusalem, Israel Exploration Society and the Shrine of the Book, 1965.

6. P. DE LAGARDE, *Libri Veteris Testamenti Apocryphi Syriace*, Leipzig/London, 1861 (Reproductio phototypica editionis, Osnabrück, 1972).

7. The noun 'sister' does not show up in the Book of Ben Sira, neither in Hebrew

In the following chart, all relevant data have been put together:

Nr.		Hebrew	MS	Greek	Syriac
1.	Sir 7,3	אח	A	—	—
2.	Sir 7,12	אח	A	ἀδελφός	ܐܚܐ
3.	Sir 7,18	אח	A	ἀδελφός	ܐܚܐ
4.	Sir 10,20	אח	A, B	ἀδελφός	ܐܚܐ
5.	Sir 14,14	אח	A	—	—
6.	Sir 14,16	אח	A	—	—
7.	Sir 25,1	—	—	ἀδελφός	ܐܚܐ
8.	Sir 29,10	—	—	ἀδελφός	ܐܚܐ
9.	Sir 29,27	—	—	ἀδελφός	ܐܚܝܐ
10.	Sir 33,20[8]	אהב[9]	—	ἀδελφός	ܐܚܐ
11.	Sir 33,31[10]	אח	E	ἀδελφός	ܐܚܐ
12.	Sir 38,12[11]	אח	Bm	—	—
13.	Sir 40,24	אח	B	ἀδελφός	ܐܚܐ
14.	Sir 45,6	—	B	ἀδελφός	—
15.	Sir 50,1[12]	אח	B	ἀδελφός	ܐܚܐ
16.	Sir 50,12a	אח	B	ἱερεύς	ܐܚܐ
17.	Sir 50,12c	בן	B	ἀδελφός	ܐܚܐ

I. BEN SIRA TEXTS IN WHICH אח IS TEXTCRITICALLY DISPUTED

There are four passages on this list (Nrs 1, 5, 6, 12) posing textual problems in such a way that it is very doubtful whether the noun אח at those places can be considered being authentic. These four texts (Sir 7,3; 14,14; 14,16; 38,12) will be discussed at first.

(אחות), nor in Greek (ἀδελφή). With respect to Ben Sira's view of women, see: C. CAMP, *Understanding a Patriarchy: Women in Second Century Jerusalem through the eyes of Ben Sira*, in A.-J. LEVINE (ed.), *"Women Like This". New Perspectives on Jewish Women in the Greco-Roman World* (SBL Early Judaism and Its Literature, 1) Atlanta, GA, Scholars Press, 1991, pp. 1-39; M. GILBERT, *Ben Sira et la femme*, in RTL 7 (1976) 428-442; W.C. TRENCHARD, *Ben Sira's View of Women. A Literary Analysis* (Brown Judaic Studies, 38), Chico, CA, Scholar Press, 1982.

8. Gr. 30,28.

9. In the 'Syrisch-hebräischer Index' of D. BARTHÉLEMY – O. RICKENBACHER, *Konkordanz zum hebräischen Sirach mit syrisch-hebräischem Index*, Göttingen, Vandenhoeck & Ruprecht, 1973, p. 2*, this word has erroneously been listed as אחב.

10. Gr. 30,39.

11. This occurrence has not been included in BARTHÉLEMY-RICKENBACHER, *Konkordanz* (n. 9), p. 12.

12. Gr. 49,15.

SɪR 7,3 (MS A):   אל תדע [13]חדושי על אה פן תקצרהו שבעתים

As far as the Hebrew text of Sir 7,3 is concerned, Ben Sira scholars till now have hardly paid attention to the special mark in MS's A right margin, viz. three dots in a triangle. Within MS A, such a special mark is found eleven times in the right margin[14], one time in the left margin (4,27), and one more time on top of a word that should be read differently and has been written in the right margin (16,13). The three dots in the right margin of Sir 7,3 are obviously a remark by the copyist that the Hebrew text was not in order. As the Greek and Syriac are nearly identical in their renderings ("Do not sow in the furrow(s) of injustice"), it is rather easily to see what failures in the Hebrew text the special mark is pointing at. Instead of תדע, the original Hebrew text most probably read תזרע. Then חדושי should be read הרושי as some text editions already emendated, and על must be restored to עֲוֵל. However precisely the noun אח remains problematic. The solution as proposed by Ginzberg not only is rather complicated, it also presupposes the Hebrew text of Sir 7,3a being a retroversion from Syriac[15]. His implicit presupposition however cannot be substantiated anyway.

It is more probable that אח has entered into the text when עויל was not longer considered a noun, but was erroneously read as a preposition (על) and required a noun. The striking resemblance with Sir 7,12a (אל תחרוש חמס על אח) has obviously caused the adoption of אח into Sir 7,3.

SɪR 14,14 (MS A):   אל תמנע מטובה יום
                  (1)   ובהלקח אח אל תעבר
                  (2)   וחמוד רע אל תחמוד

At first sight, Sir 14,14 seems to be a tristich. Among scholars however there is consensus of opinion that *tristichoi* are very seldom found in the Book of Ben Sira[16]. As far as Sir 14,14 is concerned, there is strong evidence that this verse is not to be characterized as a tristich. An

---

13. Though the copyist of MS A unequivocally wrote a *daleth*, some text editions however favour חרושי as the more correct reading; SEGAL, ספר (n. 5), p. 43; *The Book of Ben Sira* (n. 5), p. 8; N. PETERS, *Der jüngst wiederaufgefundene Hebräische Text des Buches Ecclesiasticus untersucht, herausgegeben, übersetzt und mit kritischen Noten versehen*, Freiburg i. Br., Herder, 1902, p. 133; BOCCACCIO-BERARDI (n. 5), p. 5. All of them have been guided more by the Greek (αὔλακας) and the Syriac (ܒܘ̈ܪ) than by the Hebrew characters of MS A itself. See e.g. the *daleth* as written in the word זדון in 7,6.
14. Sir 3,14; 4,26; 6,10; 7,3; 8,7; 10,1.11.16; 11,10; 13,22; 14,16.
15. L. GINZBERG, *Randglossen zum hebräischen Ben Sira*, in C. BEZOLD (ed.), *Orientalische Studien Th. Nöldeke gewidmet*, t. 2, Giessen, Töpelmann, 1906, pp. 609-625 (616).
16. O. RICKENBACHER, *Weisheitsperikopen bei Ben Sira* (OBO, 1), Göttingen, Vandenhoeck & Ruprecht, 1973, pp. 130-131.

analysis by H.-P. Rüger has brought out that Sir 14,14 is handing down an older (1) and a younger textual form (2) at the same time[17]. Greek and Latin follow the older textual form, whereas Syriac is rendering the younger one.

As a consequence of some clerical errors by which *he*, *ḥeth* and *taw* have been interchanged, ובהלקח אח in Sir 14,14 should be read as ובחלק תאוה, a reading that is confirmed by the Greek (καὶ μερὶς ἐπιθυμίας)[18]. Therefore, there is no question of a 'brother' in Sir 14,14 anymore.

SIR 14,16 (MS A) :   תן לאח ותין ופנק נפשך

Using a mark of three dots in the right margin of MS A, the copyist askes for the reader's attention, since to his belief there is something wrong in the main text. Text editions and commentaries hardly pay attention to such copyist's remarks[19]. As the *taw* of ותין has a small line on top of it, the marginal remark obviously refers to this word, indicating that it has to be removed from the text.

In respect of the topic of brotherhood in the Book of Ben Sira, attention must be paid to the opening words of Sir 14,16. Ben Sira scholars argue that לאח has to be corrected into וקח since it is required, in the first place, by the Greek (δὸς καὶ λάβε) and Syriac (ܣܒ ܘ ܗܒ)[20] and, in the second place, by the context of Sir 14,11-16 which emphasizes that one should enjoy the goods of life. Ginzberg argues that it was the interchange of *qoph* and *'aleph* in old Hebrew script that caused the reading as found here in MS A[21]. Since none of the extant Hebrew Ben Sira Manuscripts however has been handed down in old Hebrew script, it is difficult to adduce solid proof for such a view. And, moreover, are *'aleph* and *qoph* indeed so similar in shape in old Hebrew script?[22] The present author would not preclude another

17. H.-P. RÜGER, *Text und Textform im hebräischen Sirach* (BZAW, 112) Berlin, de Gruyter, 1970, pp. 19-20.

18. Recently, the emendation ובחלק תאוה has firmly been defended by M. GILBERT, *Qohélet et Ben Sira*, in A. SCHOORS (ed.), *Qohelet in the Context of Wisdom* (BETL, 136), Leuven, University Press and Peeters, 1998, pp. 161-179, esp. p. 176.

19. With respect of Sir 14,16, only SCHECHTER-TAYLOR, *Wisdom* (n. 5), p. (9), and BEENTJES, *Text edition* (n. 5), p. 43, have included this phenomenon in their presentation of the Hebrew text.

20. See e.g. I. LÉVI, *L'Ecclésiastique II* (Bibliothèque de l'École des Hautes Études, Sciences Religieuses, 10,1-2), Paris, Leroux, 1901, p. 104; PETERS, *Jüngst* (n. 13), p. 82; R. SMEND, *Die Weisheit des Jesus Sirach erklärt*, Berlin, Reimer, 1906, p. 135

21. GINZBERG, *Randglossen* (n. 15), p. 14.

22. The paleographic tables as provided by J. RENZ & W. RÖLLIG, *Handbuch der Althebräischen Epigraphik*, Band III (Texte und Tafeln, Section 'Tafeln zur Paläographie' 1-37), Darmstadt, Wissenschaftliche Buchhandlung, 1995, do not support Ginzberg's hypothesis.

possibilty, viz. that the transformation into לאה is the result of a dictation error[23].

SIR 38,12 (MS B):   ולא ימוש כי גם בו צורך

(Bm):   ואל ישמש מאח כ ג ב צרכיך[24]

The marginal reading of MS B as well as the Greek (καὶ μὴ ἀποστήτω σου) are textual evidence that the verbal form ימוש was originally accompanied by a prepositional element. Smend therefore seems to be right that the verb מוש used here should mean 'to keep aloof from'[25]. That a physician however should be called 'a brother' is not self-evident. It is more likely that מאח is a scribal error of מאתך ('from you')[26].

II. BEN SIRA ON BROTHERHOOD

Now time has come to meet the Ben Sira texts which really deal with 'brotherhood'.

SIR 7,12 (MS A):   אל תחרוש חמס על אח וכן על רע וחבר יחדו

Within Sir 7,1-17, being a section marked by a fourteenfold אל + prohibitive[27], Sir 7,12 functions as the heading of a new pericope (7,12-16)[28]. In fact, the noun אח in Sir 7,12 is the first real occurrence of this noun in the Book of Ben Sira, since אח in Sir 7,3 has been proved to be superfluous from a text critical point of view. It can hardly be an accident that precisely at this first mentioning in the Book of Ben Sira, אח is followed by a number of terms which cover a great deal of its semantic field: 1. רע ('neighbor'); 2. חבר ('companion'); 3. יהדו ('together').

(1) רֵעַ is one of Ben Sira's favourite words[29]. It is used 24 times in his book[30], which is a very high percentage as compared with 187 in-

---

23. Cf. P.C. BEENTJES, *Reading the Hebrew Ben Sira Manuscripts Synoptically: A New Hypothesis*, in ID. (ed), *The Book of Ben Sira in Modern Research* (BZAW, 255), Berlin, de Gruyter, 1997, pp. 95-111, esp. 104-110.

24. In BEENTJES, *Text edition* (n. 5), p. 66, this word has erroneously been printed as צוכיך.

25. "Übrigens scheint מוש hier (vgl. zu 40,10) nicht "weichen, fortgehen", sondern "fern bleiben" zu bedeuten"; SMEND, *Weisheit* (n. 20), p. 341.

26. SMEND, *Weisheit* (n. 20), p. 341; SCHECHTER-TAYLOR, *Wisdom* (n. 5), p. 61.

27. For an analysis of the structure of Sir 7,1-17, see P.C. BEENTJES, *Jesus Sirach 7:1-17. Kanttekeningen bij de structuur en de tekst van een verwaarloosde passage*, in *Bijdragen* 41 (1980) 251-259.

28. In MS A, the Hebrew text of Sir 7,15 is found between 7,8 and 7,10.

29. מרע occurs only in Sir 37,3, whereas it is used seven times in the Hebrew Bible (Gen 26,26; Judg 14,11.20; 15,2.6; 2 Sam 3,8; Prov 19,7).

30. Sir 5,12.14; 6,17; 7,12; 9,14; 10,6; 12,9 [2 x]; 13,21 [3 x]; 14,9; 15,5; 20,23; 25,18; 31[34],2.15.18.31; 33,20 [Gr. 30,28]; 37,2.3; 41,18.21.

stances in the Hebrew Bible[31]. In the Hebrew Book of Ben Sira, Sir 7,12 is the only occurrence that presents אח and רע as a couple. In the Hebrew Bible, these two nouns are found at least seven times as a parallel pair (2 Sam 3,8; Jer 9,3; Ps 35,14; 122,8; Prov 17,17; 19,7; Job 30,29)[32].

(2) The root חבר which in the Hebrew Bible shows up 27 times as a verb and 12 times as the noun חָבֵר, rather often has a pejorative and magical meaning[33]. A further observation is, that in the Hebrew Bible Wisdom Literature does not make much use of the root חבר. Unfortunately, Cazelles' article does not bear reference to the Book of Ben Sira. For the root חבר is not only met proportionally frequent in Ben Sira, viz. ten times as a verb (Sir 7,25; 12,13.14; 13,1.2 [3 x].16.17; 42,3) and four times as the noun חָבֵר (Sir 6,10; 7,12; 37,6; 41,18), it mostly has also a *positive* meaning: 'to join'. In Sir 7,25 (MS A), e.g., the meaning 'to marry' seems appropriate[34].

(3) As an adverb, יחדו occurs ninety times or more in the Hebrew Bible; an adverbial יחד is found forty or so times[35]. Within the Book of Ben Sira, יחדו is found four times (Sir 7,12; 31[34],11; 32[35],8; 50,17), and יחד two times (11,6; 25,24). Just as was the case with רֵע and חָבֵר, also the adverb יחד(ו) only in Sir 7,12 has a connection with 'brother' and its semantic field as is e.g. the case in Deut 25,5 and Ps 133,1.

A final question to be discussed with respect of Sir 7,12 is whether אח has been used here in its proper sense or as a synonym of רע and חבר. Since the second colon of Sir 7,12 opens with וכן ('and likewise'), we may infer that אח should be distinguished here from רע and חבר. It therefore seems to bear here a meaning that is rather strictly: a person's own brother or kinsman.

31. J. KÜHLEWEIN, רֵע / Nächster, in E. JENNI – Cl. WESTERMANN (eds.), *TWAT*, t. I, München, Kaiser, 1976, col. 786-791.

32. The reference to Job 6,15 as given by RINGGREN is not correct; H. RINGGREN, אָח, in G.J. BOTTERWECK – H. RINGGREN (eds.), *TDOT*, t. I, Grand Rapids, MI, Eerdmans, 1974, pp. 188-193 (191).

33. H. CAZELLES, חבר, in G.J. BOTTERWECK – H. RINGGREN (eds.), *TDOT*, t. IV, Grand Rapids, MI, Eerdmans, 1980, pp. 193-197 (196-197).

34. Sir 12,13 is the only occurrence in the Book of Ben Sira where the ancient magical meaning of the root חבר is found.

35. H.-J. FABRY, יָחַד, in G.J. BOTTERWECK – H. RINGGREN (eds.), *TDOT*, t. VI, Grand Rapids, MI, Eerdmans, 1990, pp. 40-48 (43) counts 96 occurrences; G. SAUER, אחד, in E. JENNI – Cl. WESTERMANN (eds), TWAT, I, München, Kaiser, 1976, col. 105 lists 94 passages; W. HOLLADAY, *A Concise Hebrew and Aramaic Lexicon of the Old Testament*, Grand Rapids, MI, Eerdmans, 1988, p. 132 has 90 instances, just as *BDB*, p. 403 and *HAL*³, p. 388. An adverbial יחד is found 43 times in the Hebrew Bible by Fabry, 44 times by Sauer, and 45 times by *BDB*.

Sir 7,18 (MS A):   אל תמיר אוהב במחיר ואח תלוי בזהב אופיר

The Book of Ben Sira has no less than *seven* paragraphs dealing with friendship (6,5-17; 12,8-12; 19,6-19; 22,19-26; 25,1-11; 27,16-21; 37,1-6)[36]. The *qal* active participle אוהב is found no less than 34 times in his work as against 65 times in the Hebrew Bible[37]. Nevertheless, Sir 7,18 is the *only* instance in Ben Sira's Book where אח is combined with אוהב.

Sir 7,18 has a marked rhyme pattern (*tamîr - bimḥîr - 'ôphîr*) and functions as the opening of a new paragraph (7,18-36)[38]. In the second colon, תלוי poses a serious problem, not in itself, but in its syntactical function. After the prohibitive אל תמיר ('Do not exchange'), Sir 7,18 offers a parallel structure: אוהב is parallel to אח, and במחיר has בזהב אופיר as corresponding item. This means that תלוי must be considered as a qualification of אח. But in what sense? The word תלוי as handed down by MS A is a *qal* active participle of תלה ('to hang') and is well known in the Hebrew Bible (Deut 21,23; 2 Sam 18,10; Cant 4,4; cf. Josh 10,26; Deut 28,66; Hos 11,7). However 'a hanged brother' does not make sense here. Ginzberg advances the opinion that the verb תלה in Sir 7,18 is used as referring to the fast rising of the weight of a balance. He therefore favours the rendering 'a brother who is weighted with gold of Ophir'[39]. However doing so, Ginzberg makes בזהב depend upon תלוי instead of linking it to the verb מור *hiph'il*, which is constructed with *beth* (cf. Jer 2,11): 'Do not exchange a friend for (ב) money, nor a brother ... for (ב) gold of Ophir'[40].

However what is the meaning and function of תלוי? Whereas the Syriac (ܐܚܐ ܕܐܝܬ ܠܗ) is of no help at all here, the Greek (ἀδελφὸν γνήσιον) is referring to one's 'own brother', a formula which by the way creates a perfect link and parallel to the expression 'the precious gold of Ophir'! Therefore, attention should be paid to Nöldeke's suggestion to read תלוי as תלים. He refers to אחין תלמין (Gen 49,5) in both Targum Pseudo-Jonathan and Fragmentary Targum, and to Samaritan in which תלים is the common word for 'brother' (Gen 4,2; 9,5; 19,7; 24,13; 49,5). In the Samaritan Targums, תלים a number of times has

---

36. All these pericopes have amply been studied in REITERER (ed.), *Freundschaft bei Ben Sira* (n. 4).

37. E. JENNI, אוהב, in *THAT*, t. I, col. 60-73 (61).

38. Cf. BEENTJES, *Kanttekeningen* (n. 27), p. 252.

39. 'Ein Bruder, der mit Ophirgold gewogen wird'; GINZBERG, *Randglossen* (n. 15), 617.

40. The combination of אוהב and מחיר is found in Sir 6,14, and 31,5.

been altered into אח[41]. Sir 7,18 therefore must be read and interpreted as offerering a climactic parallellism: 'friend – money' // 'own brother – gold of Ophir'. Just as in Sir 7,12, also in 7,18 the term אח therefore has it proper meaning.

SIR 10,20 (MS A):   [42][...בעו] בין אחים ראשם נכבד וירא אלהים בע
           (MS B):   בין אחים ראשם נכבד וירא אלהים נכבד ממנו

Sir 10,20 belongs to a pericope (Sir 10,19-11,6) which recently has been thoroughly investigated by several scholars[43]. The text of Sir 10,20 according to MS A has been characterized by H.-P. Rüger as the 'older' Hebrew text form, whereas 10,20 as found in MS B should be considered as the 'younger' one. Greek and Latin of Sir 10,20 are according to the 'older', Syriac agrees with the 'younger' textual form[44].

In respect of the lacuna in MS A, a great majority of Ben Sira scholars is favouring the reconstruction עיניו ('in his eyes')[45]. Within the structure of Sir 10,19-25, all second colae (cf. vv. 22b. 24b) [46] are explicitly related to God. We may infer therefore that *God* is also the antecedent of עיניו in 10,20b.

As can be inferred from 10,22a and 10,24a summing up social and political entities, אחים in 10,20a is obviously not referring to a relationship of full brothers, but is used in a metaphorical sense: members of the same nation.

---

41. The solution as given by SCHECHTER-TAYLOR, *Wisdom* (n. 5), p. 46 is a very complicated and unconvincing one.
42. VATTIONI, *Ecclesiastico* (n. 5), p. 53 has erroneously completed the lacuna of MS A as ממנו, in fact being the final word of MS B. However in MS A both a *beth* and some traces of an *'ayin* can be discerned.
43. A.A. DI LELLA, *Sirach 10:19-11:6: Textual Criticism, Poetic Analysis, and Exegesis*, in C.L. MEYERS & M. O'CONNOR (eds), *The Word of the Lord Shall Go Forth*. FS D.N. Freedman, Winona Lake IN, 1982, pp. 157-164; A. MINISSALE, *La Versione Greca del Siracide confronto con il Testo Ebraico alla luce dell' attività midrascica e del metodo targumico* (AnBib, 133), Rome, PIB, 1995, pp. 56-65; M. GILBERT, *Wisdom of the Poor: Ben Sira 10,19-11,6*, in BEENTJES (ed.), *The Book of Ben Sira in Modern Research* (n. 23), pp. 153-169. J. HASPECKER, *Gottesfurcht bei Jesus Sirach: Ihre religiöse Struktur und ihre literarische und doktrinäre Bedeutung* (AnBib, 30), Rome, Päpstliches Bibelinstitut, 1967, pp. 136-140.
44. RÜGER, *Text und Textform* (n. 17), p. 56.
45. Only Smend, and Di Lella are in favour of בעמו ('by his people'); R. SMEND, *Die Weisheit des Jesus Sirach Hebräisch und Deutsch*, Berlin, Reimer, 1902, p. 11; SMEND, *Weisheit* (n. 20), p. 97; A.A. DI LELLA, *The Recently Identified Leaves of Sirach in Hebrew*, in *Bib* 45 (1964) 153-167 (156).
46. Sir 10,21 is an expansion only to be found in Greek II. This verse has not been marked as such by VATTIONI, *Ecclesiastico* (n. 5), p. 52.

Sir 25,1c[47]:   ὁμόνοια ἀδελφῶν, καὶ φιλία τῶν πλησίον

To date, the Hebrew text of Sir. 16,26-30,11 has not been recovered except for some smaller portions[48]. With respect of Sir 25,1ab, this is the more disappointing, since the text as found in all Greek manuscripts is obviously corrupt, as has already been recognized by many commentators in the past[49]. Nowadays Ben Sira scholars unanimously follow Ziegler's conjectural emendation, which is based on Syriac and Old Latin[50].

Sir 25,1 is the start of a series of numerical sayings. Following the introductory formula 'There are three ...' (25,1ab), the first sight which warms the author's heart and is beautiful in the eyes of the Lord and of men is ὁμόνοια ἀδελφῶν, to which φιλία τῶν πλησίον[51] as the second element is a parallel couple, followed by the third example which mentions 'wife and man who share each others's company'[52]. In Sir 25,2, the author mentions three kinds of men who arouse his hatred and disgust him by their manner of life: 'a poor man who boasts, a rich man who lies, and an old fool who commits adultery' (REB).

It is striking that Ben Sira opens a new section of his book by mentioning precisely the ὁμόνοια ἀδελφῶν as his first delight[53].

Sir 29,10 :   ἀπόλεσον ἀργύριον δι' ἀδελφὸν καὶ φίλον

Sir 29,8-13 (giving alms) is the counterpart of 29,1-7 (making loans) and is followed by a section on going surety (29,14-20). The exhortation of Sir 29,10, viz. 'to lose money for a brother and a friend[54] rather than leave it to rust away under a stone', is surrounded by a twofold *inclusio*:

47. Sir 25,1-11 is amply commentated by REITERER, *Gelungene Freundschaft* (n. 4), pp. 133-169.
48. Sir. 18,30-32; 19,1-2; 20,4-6.13; 25,7-8.12.16-23; 26,1-3.13-17; 27,5-6.16.
49. O.F. FRITZSCHE, *Die Weisheit Jesus-Sirach's* (Kurzgefasstes exegetisches Handbuch zu den Apokryphen des Alten Testaments, 5), Leipzig, Hirzel, 1859, pp. 136-137; TRENCHARD, *Ben Sira's View* (n. 7), p. 209, n. 218.
50. Cf. ZIEGLER, *Sapientia* (n. 3), pp. 76-78. 242.
51. The same marked combination of plural and singular is found in 25,18b (ἀνὰ μέσον τῶν πλησίον). See the text critical notes in ZIEGLER, *Sapientia* (n. 3), pp. 242 and 244. Sir 25,18 has been recovered in Hebrew (MS C); πλησίον indeed corresponds to the plural form reïç.
52. Syriac: ܡܠܗ ܗܢܘܢ ܚܕ ('if they are peaceful').
53. 'Unter ἀδελφοι ... verstehe ich nicht Brüder im eigentlichen Sinne ..., sondern Stamm-, Volksgenossen'; FRITZSCHE, *Die Weisheit Jesus-Sirach's* (n. 49), p. 136.
54. The word combination ἀδελφός καὶ φίλος is found only one other time in the Book of Ben Sira, viz. Sir 30[33], 28[20]. True, in Sir 7,12 and 7,18 both words are used too, but not within one and the same colon.

29,8	ἐλεημοσύνη
29,9	ἐντολή
29,10	
29,11	ἐντολὰς ὑψίστου
29,12	ἐλεημοσύνη

It hardly can be accidental that 29,10 is the turning point of this passage: observing the commandments of the Most High and giving alms will ultimately appear to be of greater value than silver and gold.

SIR 29,27:   ἐπεξένωταί μοι ὁ ἀδελφός, χρεία τῆς οἰκίας

In 29,21-28, Ben Sira has apparently incorporated some of his own travelling experiences of which Sir 31[34], 9-13 is documentary evidence. N. Peters holds the view the author of Sir 29,21-28 has in mind the vicissitudes of Jewish merchants being abroad as opposed to people who under humble conditions live at home in Israel[55]. This is confirmed by the semantic wordplay between οἶκος (21b), οἰκία (24a. 24a. 27b) on the one hand and παροικεῖν (24b), πάροικας (26a. 27a), παροικία (23b. 28b)[56] on the other. Within this context, the word 'brother' is used by the author as opposed to the 'foreigner' (27a) who has to make away for that more important guest.

Instead of 'brother', the Syriac has ܐܪܚܐ ('traveller') which should not be preferred as a better reading. Because it is not just a traveller, but a special guest, viz. a brother—either someone's own brother or a relative—for whom the house is needed.

SIR 33,20 (MS E):   בן ואשה אהב ורע
    SIR 30,28 (Gr):   Υἱῷ καὶ γυναικί, ἀδελφῷ καὶ φίλῳ

Sir 33,20-24 [30,28-32 Gr] contains admonitions and maxims with respect of the independance of the *pater familias* to his family and friends till the day of his death. Whereas the notions 'son', 'wife', and 'friend' are present in the Hebrew text of 33,20, there is no word to be directly identified with 'brother', as is the case in both Greek (30,28) and Syriac (33,19). Instead of 'brother', the Hebrew reads אהב, a second term meaning 'friend' in this colon.

---

55. 'V. 25-28 schildern drastisch die Behandlung des Handelsjuden in der Fremde'; N. PETERS, *Das Buch Jesus Sirach oder Ecclesiasticus* (EHAT, 25), Münster, Aschendorff, 1913, p. 241; cf. A. EBERHARTER, *Das Buch Jesus Sirach oder Ecclesiasticus* (HSAT, VI/5), Bonn, Peter Hanstein, 1925, pp. 105-106.

56. There are text critical problems with respect of these two occurrences. See SMEND, *Weisheit* (n. 20), pp. 262-263; ZIEGLER, *Sapientia* (n. 3), pp. 263-264.

The participle אהב/אוהב is one of Ben Sira's favourite words. In the Hebrew Ben Sira text recovered so far it is found no less than 39 times. Usually it is rendered φίλος (21 x) or as some verbal form of ἀγαπάω (11 x). Sir 33,20 is the only occurrence where אהב/אוהב is rendered ἀδελφός. In the Septuagint too, one looks in vain for a similar case.

There are good reasons to assume that אהב in Sir 33,20 is a scribal error and should be read as אח. First, both Greek and Syriac obviously read אח. Secondly, אח is required by the content of this passage. Son, wife, brother, and friend 'are the significant others in the life of a Jewish adult male'[57]. Since אוהב and רע are synonymous[58], אח would be a more acceptable reading. Thirdly, since אוהב ורע is found a number of times in the Hebrew Bible as a fixed pair (cf. Ps 38,12; 88,19), a copyist who in fact had אח ורע in front of him could easily have misread this expression[59], having in mind the Biblical phrase אוהב ורע.

SIR 33,31 (MS E):   אחד עבדך כאח חשב[...]

The key word of the maxims in Sir 33,25-32 [30,33-40 Gr] undoubtedly is 'slave' (עבד: vv. 25b.26a.28a.30a.31a.31c). The last mentioned occurrences (vv. 31a.c) are very interesting, since they are addressed to a householder who has only *one* slave. He is adviced to treat such a slave with special care: 'let him be like yourself' (33,31a); 'consider him as a brother' (33,31c)[60]. Sir 33,31 reminds of the maxim as given earlier in the Book of Ben Sira: עבד מש[כי]ל אהוב כנפש (Sir 7,21; MS C)[61]. The latter's context has been made up of elements in family life identical to those amplified in Sir 33,20-32: 'friend', 'brother' (7,18), 'wife' (7,19), 'slave' (7,20-21). That a slave could have a privileged position within a family is documented e.g. in Prov 17,2: 'Where the son is a wastral, a prudent slave is master, and shares the inheritance with the brothers' (REB).

SIR 40,24 (MS B):   אח [..............] צרה

Unfortunately, the Hebrew text of Sir 40,22-24 (MS B) is heavily damaged as far as the opening words of each first colon are concerned.

---

57. P.W. SKEHAN & A.A. DI LELLA, *The Wisdom of Ben Sira* (AB, 39), New York, Doubleday, 1987, p. 405.

58. J. MARCUS, *A Fifth MS. of Ben Sira*, in *JQR* 21 (1930-1931), 234; I. LÉVI, *Un nouveau fragment de Ben Sira*, in *REJ* 92-93 (1932), 142.

59. Cf. Ps 122,8.

60. The order of the cola in Hebrew and Syriac (31a-b-c-d) is different from the sequence in Greek (31a-d-c-b); the order of Hebrew and Syriac should be considered more authentic.

61. In MSS A, B the synonymous verb חבב is used.

The Masada Scroll is of no help here, since precisely 40,22-27 has not been preserved.

Sir 40,18-26 is characterized by a series of ten proverbs, of which the final one is to be considered the climax, being a saying dealing with 'the fear of the Lord' (v. 26)[62]. All ten proverbs have an identical pattern. Each first colon consists of two nouns and a plural verbal form ('X and Y have ...'). Every second colon of 40,18-26 opens with משניהם ('but better than both of them is ...'), followed by a nominal clause.

However lacunal Sir 40,24a may be, from the overall pattern one may infer that the 'brother' – a word being preserved in MS B – gets a positive qualification related to the time of distress (צרה), the only other Hebrew word being preserved from this colon. Would it be coincidence to assume a direct link between Sir 40,24a and Prov 17,17b, where אח and צרה also form a couple, the more because עת – a commentator's unanimous conjecture for Sir 40,24a–is also found in Prov 17,17a (accompanied with the expression אהב הרע, 'the friend is loving')? Again in a Ben Sira passage, the notion 'brother' is found in a context dealing with 'friend', 'neighbour', and 'wife' (7,18-19; 25,1; 33,20).

SIR 45,6 (MS B):   וירם קדוש את אהרן למטה לוי

Ben Sira's extensive description of Aaron (45,6-22) – in fact being the largest passage of the *Laus Patrum* devoted to a single person – is characterized by a special literary device, which by D. Patte has been described as 'structural use of Scripture (or structural style)'[63]. It is a phenomenon to the effect that a passage in a (non-canonical Jewish) writing to a high degree is structured by elements from *one* or *two* Biblical texts. Sir 45,6-26 is no less than a key text, both to the structure and to the theology of the 'Hymn in praise of the Famous'. With the section on Aaron and Phinehas, Ben Sira wants to 'prove' that the succession of the Davidic dynasty has been transferred to the High priestly dynasty of Aaron and his descendants. That is why Ben Sira not only pays so much attention to Aaron (Sir 45,6-22), but also to Simon (Sir 50,1-24), the High Priest of his own days. Both texts on these two High Priests are expressely interrelated[64].

62. Cf. HASPECKER, *Gottesfurcht* (n. 43), pp. 113-118.

63. D. PATTE, *Early Jewish Hermeneutic in Palestine* (SBLDS, 22), Missoula, MO, 1975, pp. 171.189. The term 'structural use of Scripture (or structural style)' has to be preferred to the notion 'anthological style', as the latter could suggest a certain degree of arbitrariness, that is absolutely incorrect. See e.g. J.G. SNAITH, *Ben Sira's supposed love of liturgy*, in *VT* 25 (1975) 167-174, esp. 172-173.

64. More details in P.C. BEENTJES, *Jesus Sirach en Tenach*, Nieuwegein, Selbstverlag, 1981, pp. 175-199.

Sir 45,6-14 has been structured by explicit references to Exodus 28. This observation is reinforced by the fact that in Sir 45,6-14 there are no parallels whatsoever to the other two Biblical narratives (Exodus 39; Leviticus 8) in which the same subject is treated as in Exodus 28.

However there is one major difference between Exodus 28 and Sir 45,6-14. Whereas in Exodus 28 it is Moses who is the agent all the time, in Sir 45,6-14 he is not. And that precisely is the reason why the Hebrew text of 45,6 differs from the Greek. The opening words of Sir 45,6 according to the Hebrew text ('The Holy One raised up Aaron from the tribe of Levi') are very explicit as far as the agent of this sentence is concerned. I like to emphasize that from 44,21 onwards the 'he' who is the subject of all verbal forms is *God*. This feature is not only continued in 45,1-5, but as a matter of fact is applied to 45,6-14 too. The word קדוש as used in 45,6 without article has the value of a proper name. In the Hebrew Bible, it is found in that sense a number of times (Isa 40,25; 57,15; Hos 11,9; Hab 3,3; Job 6,10), as well as in Qumran literature (cf. 1QM XII,8). In 45,6, Ben Sira wants to emphasize that it is not Moses (as in Exodus 28), but the Holy One who is clothing Aaron in the High Priest's vestments, is putting the golden crown on his head, etc. It is not till Sir 45,15a that Aaron's installation as a High priest fits the Biblical account of Exodus 28. So we have an excellent pattern. Not only are 45,6-14 and 45,15-22 both openened with a proper name ('the Holy One, 45,6a; 'Moses', 45,15a)[65], but the two parts also have exactly the same number of stichoi, viz. sixteen.

However the Greek, probably influenced by Numb 16,5.7 and Ps 106,6, has connected קדוש with Aaron, resulting in a change of word order which looks rather artificial[66]. Nevertheless, all Ben Sira commentators prefer the Greek of Sir 45,6 to its Hebrew parent text[67]. The expression 'his brother' (45,6b Gr.) which has no equivalent in Hebrew nor in Syriac, can hardly be original, since in the Hebrew text of 45,6 such a possessive suffix should have a bearing on קדוש, which makes no sense.

SIR 50,1 (MS B):   גדול אחיו ותפארת עמו

In the Hebrew text, as well as in Syriac, this phrase opens a solemn praise of Simon, after Aaron (45,6-22) and Phinehas (45,23-25) being the third High Priest described by Ben Sira (50,1-21). In the Greek text

---

65. Just as the subsequent section will open with the proper name 'Phinehas'!
66. Ααρων ὕψωσεν ἅγιον ὅμοιον αὐτῷ ἀδελφὸν αὐτοῦ ἐκ φυλῆς Λευι.
67. I have registered just one exception: PETERS, *Jüngst* (n. 13), p. 237. However ten years later in his commentary, he favours the Greek; PETERS, *Das Buch Jesus Sirach* (n. 55), p. 387.

however, this colon is found in 49,15b and is applied to Joseph[68]. The expression תפארת עמו ('the splendor of his people') not only lays emphasis on the subsequent description of Simon whom Ben Sira undoubtedly has seen officiating his High Priestly duties, but functions also as a very strong link with the expression תפארת אדם at the end of Sir 49,16.

Maybe the words גדול אחיו are a reflexion of Lev 21,10 (הכהן הגדול מאחיו) which is also dealing with the High Priest. Ben Sira used the word אח here in a restrictive sense, viz. 'priest'. Doing so, the author created two 'circles'. For Simon is not only the most eminent priestly official ('the greatest among his brothers'), he also is the splendor of his people.These two 'functions' are elaborated in the subsequent paragraph. Sir 50,1cd deals with religious matters ('temple'), whereas in Sir 50,2-4 secular affairs, viz. the restoration of Jerusalem and its defences are mentioned[69].

SIR 50,12a (MS B):   בקבלו נתחים מיד אחיו

Since Sir 50,12a is a description of a typical priestly action dealing with special pieces of meat, the word אחיו can only be attributed the meaning 'priest', as was already the case in 50,1a. The Greek translator gave it an excellent rendering 'ad sensum': ἐκ χειρῶν ἱερέων.

SIR 50,12c (MS B):   סביב לו עטרת בנים

Both Greek (στέφανος ἀδελφῶν) and Syriac (ܐܚܘ̈ܗܝ ܟܠܝܠ) render 'a crown of brothers' which seems more authentic than 'a crown of sons' as handed down by MS B. The expression of the Hebrew text could have come into existence by its resemblance to either Ps 128,3b (בניך כשתלי זיתים סביב לשלחנך), especially caused by its Biblical *hapax* שתיל, or to Prov 17,6a (עטרת זקנים בני בנים).

CONCLUSION

After a text critical investigation of all Ben Sira texts in which the lexeme אח ('brother') is found, four occurrences (Sir 7,3; 14,14; 14,16; 38,12) turned out not to deal with this lexeme at all. In the remaining instances, the word 'brother' (אח / ἀδελφός / ܐܚܐ) is used in at least three different meanings. (1) In Sir 7,12; 7,18; 25,1; 33,20 [and 45,6

---

68. VATTIONI, *Ecclesiastico* (n. 5), p. 269 is completely wrong by giving this Hebrew colon its place in 49,15c.

69. One should notice the explicit mention of 'his people' in 50,4a.

(Gr.)], it appears in its proper sense, viz. a person's own brother or kins-men. (2) In Sir 10,20 and 25,1, 'brother' does not refer to a relationship of full brothers, but is used in a more or less metaphorical sense, viz. members of the same nation. (3) In Sir 50,1; 50,12a. 12c, אח is undoubt-edly used in a restricted sense which equates to 'priest'.

Katholieke Theologische Universiteit   Pancratius C. BEENTJES
P.O. Box 80101
NL-3508 TC Utrecht

DIE IMMATERIELLEN EBENEN DER SCHÖPFUNG
BEI BEN SIRA

Anregung für die folgende Untersuchung gab neben dem Interesse an der Bedeutsamkeit der Schöpfungsthematik für das Buch Ben Sira die Beobachtung, daß zwischen der Erschaffung der Schöpfung und jener der Weisheit unterschieden wird. Dieser Differenzierung nachzuspüren, ist Ziel der folgenden Untersuchung.

1. VORBEMERKUNGEN

(1) Mit vielen Themen zu Ben Sira hat sich der Jubilar beschäftigt, insbesondere sind es theologische. Das Zentrum stellt für ihn die Weisheit dar, wie die zahlreichen einschlägigen Beiträge kund tun. Es zeigt sich nun, daß sich bei Kernfragen über die Weisheit immer wieder Aussagen über die Schöpfung in den Mittelpunkt drängen. Sie besitzt für das Verständnis des Denkens Ben Siras ein großes Gewicht. Daher erhebt sich die Frage, welche Funktion die Schöpfung erfüllt. Wie ist sie einzuordnen? Hat sie vornehmlich theologische Relevanz, wie sie Gilbert für die Weisheit bis in die christliche Interpreation hin[1] nachzeichnet, oder ist es richtig, daß »this creation faith affirmed the ethical responsibility of the learners«?[2].

(2) Die Untersuchung wird dadurch erschwert, daß der hebräische Text nicht vollständig erhalten ist und bei Vorliegen von mehreren Rezensionen nicht selten erhebliche Abweichungen gegeben sind. Im folgenden wird ein erster Überblick geboten, wobei alle Stellen berücksichtigt werden, auch solche, bei denen man diskutieren kann, ob sie als ursprünglich anzusehen sind. Ziel ist eine repräsentative Auflistung der gesamten Textbasis.

---

1. »Peut-on donner, à la lumière de … faits toponymiques, une lecture chrétienne de *Sir* 24,10, qui respecte l'intention profonde du texte biblique?« (M. GILBERT, *Lecture mariale et ecclésiale de Siracide 24,10* [15], in *Marianum* 47 [1985] 536-542, p. 539). Und er fährt fort: »Pour le chrétien, la Révélation de Dieu ne s'achève pas avec la Bible hébraïque; elle culmine, – c'est notre foi, – dans la personne même de Jésus de Nazareth, reconnu comme Christ Messie, Parole même de Dieu faite chair et venue planter sa tente au milieu des siens, Emmanuel, Sagesse de Dieu jadis annoncée et enfin venue, comme le diront les Pères de l' Église, en poursuivant sur la lancée de saint Paul une théologie de Jésus-Sagesse de Dieu« (ebd. p. 540).

2. F.E. EAKIN, *Wisdom, Creation and Covenant*, in *PRSt* 4 (1977) 226-239, p. 230.

2. Das Belegmaterial

Für die nachfolgende Untersuchung wurden folgende Stellen herangezogen:

1,4a	κτίζειν, πάντα	18,26b (?)	πάντα	40,1a	חלק, κτίζειν
1,9a	κτίζειν	23,20a	κτίζειν	40,10a	ברא, κτίζειν
1,9c	ἔργον	24,8a	κτίστης ἅπαντα	40,15a	יצר
1,14b	συνκτίζειν	24,8b	κτίζειν		
3,16b	ברא	24,9a	κτίζειν	42,15a	מעשה, ἔργον
4,6b	ποιεῖν	33(36),1	כל, πάντα	42,15c	ἔργον
5,14c	ברא	34(31),13b	κτίζειν	42,16b	מעשה, ἔργον
7,15b	חלק, κτίζειν	34(31),13d	ברא	42,22a	מעשה, ἔργον
7,30a	עשה, ποιεῖν	34(31),13f	חלק	42,24b	עשה, ποιεῖν
10,12b	עשה, ποιεῖν	34(31),27d	יצר, κτίζειν	43,2b	מעשה, ἔργον
10,18a	κτίζειν	34(31),27f	חלק	43,5a	עשה, ποιεῖν
11,4c	מעשה, ἔργον	35(32),13a	עשה, ποιεῖν	43,11a	עשה, ποιεῖν
11,4d	ἔργον	36(33),10b	יצר, κτίζειν	43,14a	ברא
11,14b	מן	36(33),13a	יצר	43,25a	מעשה
11,15b	מן	36(33),13c	עשה, ποιεῖν	43,25b	κτίσις
11,15d	מן	36(33),15	ἔργον	43,26b	פעל
11,16a	יצר	36(33),15a	מעשה	43,28b	מעשה, ἔργον
		36,20a(14a)	κτίσμα		
11,16a	συνκτίζειν	37,3a	יצר	43,32b	מעשה, ἔργον
15,9b	חלק	38,1b	חלק, κτίζειν	43,33a	ποιεῖν, הכל, πάντα
15,11a	מן	38,4a	ברא, κτίζειν	44,2a	חלק, κτίζειν
15,11b	עשה, ποιεῖν	38,8b	מעשה, ἔργον	45,23c	כל
15,14a	ברא, ποιεῖν	38,12a	κτίζειν	46,1c	יצר
15,19a	מעשה	38,15a	עשה, ποιεῖν	46,13a	עשה
		38,34a(34c)	κτίσμα		
16,17d	κτίσις	39,5b	ποιεῖν	47,8c	עשה
16,26a	ברא, מעשה, ἔργον, κτίσις	39,14d	ἔργον	47,8d	ποιεῖν
16,26b	ποίησις			48,13b	ברא
16,27a	ἔργον	39,21b	κτίζειν	49,7b	יצר
17,1a	κτίζειν	39,25a	חלק, κτίζειν	49,14a	יצר, κτίζειν
17,3b	ποιεῖν	39,28a	κτίζειν	49,16b	κτίσις
17,8b	ἔργον	39,28d	ποιεῖν	50,15d	παμβασιλεύς
17,9(10b)	ἔργον	39,29b	ברא, κτίζειν	50,22a	πάντα
18,1a	κτίζειν, τὰ πάντα	39,30c	ברא	50,22d	עשה,
18,4a	ἔργον	39,33a	מעשה, ἔργον	51,12(4a)	הכל, יצר

(1) In 99 Kola[3] sind Schöpfungstermini belegt[4]. Wie sich aus der Häufigkeit des Vorkommens der verschiedenen Worte ablesen läßt, durchzieht das Thema der Schöpfung das gesamte Buch Ben Sira, wird es doch in 31 Kapiteln aufgenommen.

In keinem biblischen Buch spielt σοφία eine dermaßen herausragende Rolle wie bei Ben Sira: fast in jedem Kapitel wird das Wort verwendet und die 60-fache Erwähnung spricht allein aufgrund der Belege für sich. Wenn man deren Vorkommen mit dem der Schöpfungstermini vergleicht, tritt der überragende Stellenwert noch verdeutlicher hervor, übertrifft doch die *Schöpfung* (99) die *Weisheit* (60).

(2) Als terminologische Basis zeigen sich folgende Daten: ברא, עשׂה, חלק, יצר, מעשׂה, מן (von [Gott]), פעל, κτίζειν, ποιεῖν, ἔργον, (ἄ)παντα, παμβασιλεύς. Die syrischen Termini werden nur insofern berücksichtigt, als einschlägige Stellen ausführlicher behandelt werden.

3. Die Erschaffung der Weisheit und der übrigen Schöpfung

Sowohl im ersten wie im 24. Kapitel stößt man auf die Erwähnung der Schöpfung, wobei zwischen jener der Weisheit und der übrigen unterschieden wird. Diese Erscheinung veranlaßt dazu, die Texte unter einer Rubrik zu behandeln.

3.1. Gott – Weisheit – übrige Schöpfung

Bei dem häufigen Vorkommen der Themen Schöpfung und Weisheit ergibt sich automatisch die Frage nach dem Verhältnis untereinander. Man kann sich nicht nur mit dem Thema Schöpfung beschäftigen, sondern muß wohl auch zur Kernfrage nach der Weisheit vorstoßen: was ist die Weisheit, wie sie Sira meint, und wie ist ihre Rolle in der Schöpfung: »Current biblical scholarship has excelled in providing more her (= wisdom) pedigree than her identity«[5]. Eine Ausnahme bildet von

---

3. Terminologisch wird grundsätzlich folgende Differenzierung vorgenommen: als kleinste formal-poetische Einheit gilt das Kolon (ein Halbvers; vgl. dagegen z.B. 32,1.2.3.4.6.7 [ein Kolon bildet nach jeder Zählung einen Vers] = nach der Doppelzählung 35,1a.b. 2a.b. 4a.b); da diese meist paarweise vorkommen, wird vom Stichos gesprochen (diese Unterscheidung nimmt darauf Rücksicht, daß auch drei Kola einen Stichos bilden können). Die kleinen Buchstaben markieren die Kolonunterteilung (a.b.c.d. usw.). Acht zu geben ist auf f bzw. ff, das zumeist als traditionelle Bezeichnung für *folgend* bzw. *folgende* vorkommt, also in wenigen Fällen mißverständlich sein könnte.

4. Von den 46 Versangaben, die K.W. Burton, *Sirach and the Judaic Doctrine of Creation*, Glasgow, 1987, pp. 234f. aufreiht, sind 16,14 und 39,19 zu eliminieren, da dort von menschlichen Taten die Rede ist.

5. R.E. Murphy, *Wisdom and Creation*, in *JBL* 104 (1985) 3-11, p. 8.

Rad, der sich in seinem viel beachteten Buch mit der Schwierigkeit beschäftigt, die Weisheit zu greifen. Er sieht richtig, daß die Definitionen als Hypostase und Personifikation[6] einer Eigenschaft Gottes nicht wirklich angemessen sind[7]. Er tut sich auch schwer, den schöpfungsmäßigen Ort zu bestimmen. »Diese Weisheit ist irgendwo in der Welt zu suchen; sie ist da, aber nicht zu fassen .... Andererseits ist sie – und das ist freilich merkwürdig – auch wieder etwas von den Schöpfungswerken Abgehobenes. Diese ›Weisheit‹, ›Vernunft‹ muß also etwas wie den von Gott der Schöpfung eingesenkten ›Sinn‹, ihr göttliches Schöpfungsgeheimnis bedeuten, wobei nur zu bedenken ist, daß ... weniger an etwas Ideeles, sondern eher fast an etwas Dingliches«[8] zu denken ist. Ist es richtig, wenn Rad sie nachdrücklich als etwas Innerweltliches klassifiziert? Oder soll man Ziener folgen, wonach Weisheit eine Größe darstellt, »die alle Beziehungen zwischen Gott und dem Frommen umfaßt«?[9] – Ich frage mich, ob hier nicht die für das richtige Verständnis eigentlich entscheidende Frage zuwenig scharf in den Blickpunkt gestellt wird. Es zeigt sich innerhalb des sirazidischen Weisheitsverständnisses eine – wie in der Literatur mehr oder weniger durchwegs nicht vorgenommene – Unterscheidung zwischen zwei Präsenzformen der Weisheit: jener, wie sie der Schöpfung vorausgeht und sich dann als innere Ordnung in der Schöpfung zeigt, und jener, wie sie in praktischen

---

6. So z.B. K. HRUBY, *La Torah identifiée à la Sagesse et l'activité du 'Sage' dans la tradition rabbinique*, in *BVC* 76 (1967) 65-78, p. 65, Anm. 4; P. SCHOONENBERG, *A Sapiential Reading of John's Prologue: Some Reflections on View of Reginald Fuller and James Dunn*, in *ThD* 33 (1986) 403-421, p. 407.

7. Wenn man auch immer wieder dahingehende Äußerungen liest, wurde schon lange die Ablehnung laut: »Sie als eigene, personale ‚Hypostase' anzusprechen, geht zu weit«, V. HAMP, *Das Buch Sirach oder Ecclesiasticus*, in *Die Heilige Schrift in deutscher Übersetzung* (EB, IV), Würzburg, 1959, pp. 569-717 (p. 632); vgl. O.F. FRITZSCHE, *Die Weisheit Jesus-Sirach's. Erklärt und übersetzt* (KEHAT, 5), Leipzig, 1859, p. 125; O. ZÖCKLER, *Die Weisheit Jesus Sirachs*, in H. STRACK – O. ZÖCKLER (Hg.), *Die Apokryphen des Alten Testaments nebst einem Anhang über die Pseudepigraphenliteratur* (KK, 9), München, 1891, pp. 255-354, p. 301; G.H. BOX – W.O.E. OESTERLEY, *The Book of Sirach*, in R.H. CHARLES (Hg.), *The Apocrypha and Pseudepigrapha of the Old Testament in English*, t. I. *Apocrypha*, Oxford, 1913 (1976), pp. 268-517 (p. 307).

8. G. VON RAD, *Weisheit in Israel*, Neukirchen-Vluyn, 1970 (²1982), pp. 193f; wie nicht anders zu erwarten, hat sich auch J. MARBÖCK, *Weisheit im Wandel. Untersuchungen zur Weisheitstheologie bei Ben Sira* (BBB, 37), Bonn, 1971 (=[BZAW, 272], Berlin – New York, 1999), in seiner gewichtigen Untersuchung dazu geäußert, wenn er auch schreibt: »nach unserem Urteil (eine) durchaus nicht allzu wichtige Frage«; er hält fest: »Weisheit ist nach den vielfach wechselnden Bildern zu schließen eher [keine Hypostase, sondern] eher eine dichterische Personifikation für Gottes Nähe und Gottes Wirken und für Gottes persönlichen Anruf« (p. 130; vgl. pp. 62,66).

9. G. ZIENER, *Die theologische Begriffssprache im Buche der Weisheit* (BBB, 11), Bonn, 1956, p. 113.

Gegebenheiten anzutreffen ist, also »*die Weisheit von unten*«[10]. Noch deutlicher fühlt Hamp die Spannung, beschreibt richtig, findet aber keinen Ansatz, das ihn bedrängende Problem zu lösen: »Je aktiver, je persönlicher, je allmächtiger der Hauch, das Wort oder die Weisheit auftreten, um so mehr kann man beobachten, daß ihr ganzes Sein und Wirken mit der Person Gottes zusammenfällt«. Gerade eine weitere Befragung der Schöpfungsebenen im Buch Ben Sira kann weitere Punkte zur Klärung herbeischaffen und damit Zusammenhänge in der gesamten Schöpfung, also auch der Weisheit, erheben.

(1) Das erste Kapitel (1,1-30) stellt die Weisheit (σοφία; σύνεσις) und die Gottesfurcht (φόβος κυρίου) als zentrale Themen vor. In diesem Zusammenhang wird die Herleitung der *Weisheit* behandelt.

1,4a.b	προτέρα πάντων ἔκτισται σοφία	καὶ σύνεσις φρονήσεως ἐξ αἰῶνος
1,8a.b	εἷς ἐστιν σοφός, φοβερὸς σφόδρα	καθήμενος ἐπὶ τοῦ θρόνου αὐτοῦ
1,9a	(1) κύριος αὐτὸς ἔκτισεν αὐτὴν	
1,9b.c	(2) καὶ εἶδεν καὶ ἐξηρίθμησεν αὐτὴν	(3) καὶ ἐξέχεεν αὐτὴν ἐπὶ πάντα τὰ ἔργα αὐτοῦ.

(2) Nach 1,4a ist sie *vor allem* (προτέρα πάντων) geschaffen worden. Das Passivum erweist sich im Blick auf 1,8f als passivum divinum, wird dort doch ausdrücklich κύριος als Schöpfer angeführt.
Beachtenswert ist die Betonung des Monotheismus, der das Denken Ben Siras prägt. – Es besteht ein innerer Zusammenhang zwischen dem *einen* schlechthin Weisen, nämlich Gott selbst, und jener Weisheit, die Sira meint. Wie an anderen Stellen vorausgesetzt wird, daß Gott die Fülle des Lebens in sich trägt, er als Herr des Lebens dieses will und weitergibt, so ist er hier der Weise, gibt sein Weisesein in der Weisheit weiter und stellt den Herrn der Weisheit dar. Wenn damit die sirazidische Vorstellung von Weisheit auch noch keineswegs umfassend beschrieben ist, so zeigt sich schon, daß sie in keiner innerweltlichen Gegebenheit aufgehen kann. Hier deutet sich u.a. das Besondere der Weisheit an.

(3) In Verbindung mit V. 1 (πᾶσα σοφία παρὰ κυρίου καὶ μετ᾽ αὐτοῦ ἐστιν εἰς τὸν αἰῶνα) ergeben sich interessante Beobachtungen. Da der Übersetzer im Gebrauch der Satztypen weitgehend der hebräischen Vorlage folgt, ist anzunehmen, daß er Nominalsätze vor sich hatte, wie es auch in Syr der Fall ist: ܟܠ ܚܟܡܬܐ ܡܢ ܡܪܝܐ ܗܝ، ܘܥܡܗ ܗܝ ܠܥܠܡ. – Ein Nominalsatz beschreibt Fakten, Gegebenheiten, die unabhängig von Zeitkategorien existieren.

Es stellt sich nun die Frage, wie diese Feststellung zur in V. 9 erwähnten Schöpfung (κύριος αὐτὸς ἔκτισεν αὐτὴν) steht: ist anzunehmen,

---

10. MARBÖCK, *Weisheit*, p. 131.

daß die Weisheit im Rahmen der allgemeinen Schöpfung existiert und von jenem Moment an für immer gegeben ist? Dann hat man aber Probleme damit, daß der Autor schon mit Gott als dem Weisen (1,8a) rechnet, vor bzw. unabhängig von dem Faktum der Schöpfung der Weisheit und zudem ist diese προτέρα πάντων erschaffen.

Oder meint der Autor mit der Erwähnung des göttlichen *Schöpfungsaktes*, daß die im einzigen Gott, dem Weisen, – nach unserer Vorstellungsmöglichkeit – präexistente Weisheit durch den Schöpfungsakt für die übrige bzw. verglichen mit der Entstehung der übrigen Schöpfung[11] in eine *innerweltliche* Qualität übergeführt wird: Schöpfung ist in diesem Fall eine göttliche Transformation und keine Frage des Beginnes, denn der liegt ja seit je in Gott. Dann hat die Schöpfung, die auf alle Werke ausgegossen wird (πάντα τὰ ἔργα αὐτοῦ[12]), ihren bestimmten Platz und ihre Aufgabe. Der Platz der *geschaffenen Weisheit* ist die Vorordnung gegenüber der anderen Schöpfung: sie geht allem anderen voraus. Hier (προτέρα πάντων) wie in 24,8 (ἁπάντων) fungieren die Genetivobjekte als Schöpfungstermini zur allgemeinen Bezeichnung einer zu unterscheidenden Schöpfungsebene, eben jener der materiellen Welt.

3.2. Schöpfung der Weisheit und die übrige Schöpfung

(1) Sir 24,1-22 – in H nicht erhalten – stellt eine besondere Art eines Selbstlobes dar, welches die Weisheit über sich anstimmt. Dieses hymnische Gedicht ist sorgfältig durchkomponiert und gliedert sich in zwei größere Abschnitte: der erste beschreibt den Ausgangspunkt und die Wohnungssuche der Weisheit (Vv. 1-12). Hauptanlaß für den Preis ist die Herkunft der Weisheit, die aus Gottes Mund hervorging (ἐγὼ ἀπὸ στόματος ὑψίστου ἐξῆλθον; V. 3a), und ihre Überlegenheit über die kosmischen Gegebenheiten (καὶ ὡς ὁμίχλη κατεκάλυψα γῆν; V. 3b[13];

---

11. Diesen Bereich der Schöpfung verstehe ich im Sinne von MURPHY, *Wisdom*, p. 6: »By creation the Bible understands the whole range of existing things, from humans to ants, not excluding the abyss and Leviathan«.

12. Syr kann für den ganzen V. 9 der großen Abweichungen wegen nicht zu Rate gezogen werden, bestätigt aber doch das Vorkommen aller Schöpfungswerke:

ܚܘܬܩ ܚܘܝܫ ܚܘܝܣܘ ܚܘܪܣ ܚܘܪܣܘܡ (10a) ܚܠܘܦ ܚܘܕܝ ܠܩܕ ܚܬܒܘܣܗ,

13. H. CONZELMANN, *Die Mutter der Weisheit*, in E. DINKLER (Hg.), *Zeit und Geschichte*, FS R. Bultmann, Tübingen 1964, pp. 225-234 (= BEvT 65 [1974] 167-176) (= *The Mother of Wisdom*, in: J.M. ROBINSON [Hg.], *The Future of Our Religious Past*, New York, 1971, pp. 230-243), pp. 228f sieht hier Vorstellungen aus der ägyptischen Theo- und Kosmologie. Wenn F. CHRIST, *4. Kapitel: Sir 1; 5. Kapitel: Sir 24*, in Ders., *Jesus Sophia. Die Sophia-Christologie bei den Synoptikern* (ATANT, 57), Zürich, 1970, p. 34, auch nur eine kurze Anfrage stellt, ob hier eine Emanationsvorstellung vorliegt, so zeigt er, daß er Tiefendimensionen im Text spürt, die genauer erhoben werden sollten.

καὶ ὁ θρόνος μου ἐν στύλῳ νεφέλης; 4b; γῦρον οὐρανοῦ ἐκύκλωσα μόνη καὶ ἐν βάθει ἀβύσσων περιεπάτησα; 5)[14]. In den Versen 24,8-9 erreicht diese allumfassende Wirkung durch konzentrierte Schöpfungsaussagen ihren Höhepunkt:

24,8a.b	τότε ἐνετείλατό μοι ὁ κτίστης ἁπάντων	καὶ ὁ κτίσας με κατέπαυσεν τὴν σκηνήν μου
24,8c.d	καὶ εἶπεν Ἐν Ιακωβ κατασκήνωσον	καὶ ἐν Ισραηλ κατακληρονομήθητι
24,9a.b	πρὸ τοῦ αἰῶνος ἀπ᾽ ἀρχῆς ἔκτισέν με	καὶ ἕως αἰῶνος οὐ μὴ ἐκλίπω

ܘܗܘ ܕܒܪܝܢܝ ܘܐܫܪܝ ܡܫܟܢܝ	ܗܝܕܝܢ ܦܩܕܢܝ ܡܪܐ ܟܠ	24,8b.a
ܘܐܬܬܪܝܪܝ ܒܐܝܣܪܝܠ.	ܐܡܪ ܠܝ ܕܒܝܥܩܘܒ ܫܪܝ،	24,8d.c
ܘܠܥܠܡ ܥܠܡܝܢ ܠܐ ܢܒܛܠ ܕܘܟܪܢܝ	ܡܢ ܩܕܡ ܥܠܡܐ ܐܬܒܪܝܬ	24,9b.a

(2) Dreimal wird hier die Wurzel κτίζειν verwendet. Wie sich vielfältig zeigt, sind Dreier-Gruppen verschiedenster Art[15] für Sira – vgl. u.a. 4.1. (1); 5.2. (3) – bezeichnend. Mit diesem Stilmittel werden Schwerpunkte markiert. – Wenn man Syr befragt, sieht man sich bestätigt, da ὁ κτίσας με und ܕܒܪܝܢܝ wie ἔκτισέν und ܐܬܒܪܝܬ (passivum divinum) auf die gleiche Vorlage zurückgehen und die Entsprechung von ὁ κτίστης [ἁπάντων] mit verschiedenen Epitheta (ܡܪܐ [ܟܠ]) durchaus gängig ist[16].

(3) Zufolge V. 8 hat der Schöpfer (ὁ κτίστης) von allem (ἁπάντων = die gesamte sichtbare Schöpfung) auch die Weisheit geschaffen (ὁ κτίσας *με*). Entscheidender Nachdruck liegt also in 8a.b auf dem Fak-

Tatsächlich könnte man, wie der Grundtenor der gesamten Untersuchung deutlich macht, Sira in die angefragte Richtung mißverstehen: erst wenn man sieht, daß der Autor genau die Frage klären will, wie sich vor- bzw. immaterielle Schöpfungsgegebenheiten sowohl zum Schöpfer wie zur materiellen Schöpfung verhalten, beschreitet man den Lösungsweg.

14. Wenn die Weisheit als innerweltlich bestimmt wird und die Differenzierung zwischen materieller und immaterieller Schöpfungsebene nicht vorgenommen wird, stehen der Auslegung große Schwierigkeiten entgegen, wie sich selbst an einem Autor wie VON RAD (*Weisheit*, p. 209) zeigen läßt. »Daß sie wie ein Nebel die Erde bedeckte, muß man wohl als eine gewagte Exegese von 1 Mos 2,6 verstehen. Auf alle Fälle ist damit etwas über die enge Zugehörigkeit der Weisheit zur Erde gesagt. Spricht sie von einem Thron, so kann damit nichts Außergeschöpfliches gemeint sein«. Man fragt sich, warum wohl gerade der Nebel die innerweltliche Verbindung zwischen Weisheit und Geschaffenem zum Ausdruck bringen soll; der Autor verrät sich selbst mit seiner Qualifikation »gewagt«. Noch problematischer erscheint die Negation der Parallele zwischen dem Thron Gottes und jenem der Weisheit (vgl. 1,8 mit 24,4); vgl. auch das in 6.1.(5) Ausgeführte.

15. Vgl. F.V. REITERER, *Gelungene Freundschaft als tragende Säule einer Gesellschaft. Exegetische Untersuchung von Sir 25,1-11*, in DERS. (Hg.), *Freundschaft bei Ben Sira. Beiträge des Symposions zu Ben Sira – Salzburg 1995* (BZAW, 244), Berlin–New York, 1996, pp. 133-169 (pp. 138ff.).

16. Vgl. F.V. REITERER, *»Urtext« und Übersetzungen. Sprachstudie über Sir 44,16–45,26 als Beitrag zur Siraforschung* (ATSAT, 12), St. Ottilien, 1980, pp. 96f.

tum der Schöpfung an sich, wobei differenziert wird: jene der gewöhnlich als Schöpfungswerke bezeichneten Schöpfung und jene der Weisheit. Im Zusammenhang mit der Weisheit hat man nun weitere Dimensionen zu bedenken, welche das pure Faktum an sich übersteigen: *Vor dem Aion* (V. 9) – αἰών bezeichnet bei Sira retro- wie prospektiv die unbegrenzte Zeit – wurde die Weisheit geschaffen. Die Angabe αἰών gilt aber nur innerhalb der Schöpfung als Zeitangabe. Das bedeutet, daß die Weisheit schon vor der übrigen Schöpfung geschaffen wurde, letztere aber erst ab deren Entstehung benannt werden kann: ἀπ' ἀρχῆς[17].

(4) In Sira bezeichnet ἀρχή wie gewöhnlich in anderer Literatur *einen Beginn*, zumeist im Sinne *des allerersten Anfanges*, wobei vielfach immaterielle Gegebenheiten gemeint sind: Als Anfang (ἀρχή) des Hochmutes gilt der Trotz (10,12), die Verfehlung (10,13); er ist Ausgangspunkt (ἀρχή) für die Verfehlung die Frau.

Im Kontext von Schöpfungsaussagen allerdings geht es um den *ersten* Anfang von materieller Schöpfung: מראש מעשיו אל כברא bzw. ἐν κτίσει[18] κυρίου τὰ ἔργα αὐτοῦ ἀπ' ἀρχῆς (16,26). Festzuhalten ist, daß Gott (a) schuf und (b) dadurch ein radikaler Ausgangspunkt gesetzt ist, wie dies auch Syr gut zeigt: ܕܒ ܒܪܐ ܐܠܗܐ ܚܒܕܘܗܝ, ܡܢ ܠܥܘܠܡܝܢ.

Vom *Anfang* kann man also erst sprechen, wenn Gott die materielle Welt in actu setzt. In diesem Moment geschieht für das Funktionieren der Schöpfung Zentrales: Gott gibt die innere Ordnung mit: ἐκόσμησεν εἰς αἰῶνα τὰ ἔργα αὐτῶν καὶ τὰς ἀρχὰς αὐτῶν εἰς γενεὰς αὐτῶν (16,27). Gott hat die Anfänge (Plural wegen der Mehrzahl der Werke) für alle kommenden Zeiten (von innen) geordnet (τὰς ἀρχὰς αὐτῶν εἰς γενεὰς αὐτῶν)[19]. Hier erweist sich, daß Gott auch in Bereichen noch wirkt, die dem Menschen nicht mehr zugänglich sind,

---

17. Der syrische Übersetzer hat diese tiefsinnige Differenzierung nicht erkannt und eine einfache Verdoppelung gesehen und diese wie vielfach bei als Verdoppelung angesehenen Fällen weggelassen: ܡܢ ܡܪܡ ܥܠܡ.

18. RAHLFS: κρίσει.

19. Die Übersetzungen verraten nicht selten Ratlosigkeit: für ἐκόσμησεν εἰς αἰῶνα τὰ ἔργα αὐτῶν καὶ τὰς ἀρχὰς αὐτῶν εἰς γενεὰς bietet die Herderbibel: *Da ordnete er seine Werke für immer, von ihren Anfängen an bis zu ihrer fernen Zukunft.* Aus dem direkten Objekt zum Verb wird eine präpositionslose Zeitangabe. HAMP in der Einheitsübersetzung (*hat er ihre Aufgabe für immer festgelegt und ihren Machtbereich für alle Zeiten*) gibt für τὰς ἀρχὰς αὐτῶν als Bedeutung *ihren Machtbereich* an, was sich durch den sirazidischen Wortgebrauch keineswegs untermauern läßt. G. SAUER, *Jesus Sirach (Ben Sira)* (JSHRZ, III,5), Gütersloh, 1981, scheint diesem Verständnis zu folgen: *Er ordnete seine Werke für immer, und setzte ihre Bereiche auf Generationen hinaus fest.* Neben der nicht zu belegenden Bedeutung von τὰς ἀρχὰς für *Bereiche*, sieht sich der Übersetzer auch veranlaßt, ein Verb zu ergänzen. – Offensichtlich merken alle, daß man mit dem banalen *Anfang* nicht das Auslangen findet, jedoch wird die eigentliche Absicht, die dann keiner Veränderung bedarf, nicht erhoben.

weswegen dieser auch nicht versuchen sollte, jene Ebenen zu ergründen (3,20-23).

Ziel der Aussage ist also nicht nur das Faktum der Schöpfung, sondern die Mitteilung, daß der Beginn an sich inhaltlich entscheidend ist[20]: da werden die Regeln gegeben, die fürderhin den gelungenen Ablauf gewährleisten. *Anfang* ist also *nicht nur eine zeitliche*, sondern vor allem *eine qualitative* Aussage.

(5) Bestätigt wird diese Beobachtung durch 15,14, eine kompliziert formulierte Angabe: ברא אדם (H-B: מראש) אלהים מבראשית und ܐܠܗܐ ܒ݁ܪ݂ܐ ܗ݂ܘ ܢ݂ܫܐ ܒ݁ܢ݂[21] wie αὐτὸς ἐξ ἀρχῆς ἐποίησεν ἄνθρωπον. Die eigenartige Formulierung in H-A wird in H-B auf jene Phrase reduziert, wie man sie auch in den anderen Angaben über den Schöpfungsbeginn bei Sira findet (16,26; 36,20). Die Wortwahl ist offensichtlich dem Beginn der Bibel entnommen: בְּרֵאשִׁית בָּרָא אֱלֹהִים. Ihr folgt entsprechend H-A Syr. Sie dürfte auch in Γ vorauszusetzen sein, allerdings konnte Γ מן und ב nicht in der Art semitischer Sprachen kombinieren. Deutlich hebt 14a hervor, daß ein Ausgangspunkt (מן) gegeben ist, ab dem (ב) der Mensch als geschaffene Gegebenheit existiert, und daß es sich um einen Neueinsatz, einen Anfang (ראשית) im radikalen Sinne handelt. Daß zugleich qualitative Folgen damit verbunden sind, zeigt die Feststellung des freien Willens: וישתיהו ביד חותפו ויתנהו ביד יצרו.

Ein weiterer Beleg steht im Kontext des Bittgebetes 33(36),1-13a; 36,16b-22, nämlich in V. 20: Gott wird bestürmt, für seine Machwerke Zeugnis abzulegen. Gemeint ist ein konkreter, unterstützender Eingriff, wie man sich erzählt, daß ihn Gott in der Frühzeit vorgenommen hatte. Es liegt wieder eine schwierige *Zeitangabe* vor: למראש מעשיך; τοῖς ἐν ἀρχῇ κτίσμασίν σου. Als Partikel der Zuordnung fungiert ל, wobei das enklitische Pronomen ך- auf Gott zu beziehen ist. Gewichtiger für die Untersuchung ist aber die Angabe מראש, die sich mit 16,26 deckt. In Kurzform wird darin zusammengefaßt, daß die Mitglieder des Volkes Israels Schöpfungswerke sind, die von Gott den qualifizierten *Anfang* herleiten. Schöpfung wird dadurch zur Basis des Beistandes. – Syr durchschaute die Bezüge nicht und verdeutlichte den schwierigen Ausgangstext folgend: ܡܼܩܡ ܘܩܕܡ݂ܝ ܗ݂ܘܬ݂ܐ ܘ.ܩܒ݂ܠܬ݂ܐ. ܐܝܟ ܕ.ܡܢ ܪܝܫ[22].

---

20. Zurecht stößt man bei T.F. GLASSON, *Colossians 1,18.15 and Sirach 24*, in *JBL* 86 (1967) 214ff (= *NT* 11 [1969] 154ff), bei der Formulierung in Kol 1,18 (καὶ αὐτός ἐστιν ἡ κεφαλὴ τοῦ σώματος τῆς ἐκκλησίας· ὅς ἐστιν ἀρχή, πρωτότοκος ἐκ τῶν νεκρῶν, ἵνα γένηται ἐν πᾶσιν αὐτὸς πρωτεύων) auf Sir, wobei die obigen Ausführungen zeigen, daß die Diskussion um V. 6 kein vollständiges Bild ergibt. Der Gesamtbefund ist noch um vieles überzeugender.

21. Vgl. die Variante ܗܘ.

22. Vgl. die Variante ܡܕ.ܝܪ.

Syr geht es um Beistandszeugnisse, wie man sie schon seit langer Zeit
kennt, nicht – wie H und Γ meinen – um Implikationen am Schöpfungsbeginn.

Auf den ersten Blick scheint es sich im Unterschied zu den bisherigen
Beispielen in 39,25 um immaterielle Gegebenheiten zu handeln: לטוב
חלק מראש כן לרעים טוב ורע. Syr setzt H voraus: ܐܠܗܐ ܟܠ ܡܢ ܒܪܝܫܐ
ܐܬܒܪܝ. ܘܐܦ ܛܒܬܐ ܠܛܒܐ ܘܒܝܫܬܐ ܠ. Auch der Γ-
Text setzt H voraus, bringt aber eine ausgefeiltere Antithese, die dazu
führt, daß im zweiten Glied die Erwähnung des Guten weggelassen
wird: ἀγαθὰ τοῖς ἀγαθοῖς ἔκτισται ἀπ' ἀρχῆς οὕτως τοῖς ἁμαρτωλοῖς κακά. – Es geht nicht um die Schöpfung des Guten oder Bösen,
sondern um jene guter und böser Menschen, denen die Abstrakta zuge-
wiesen werden können. Es liegt also hinsichtlich der Fixierung des
Schöpfungsbeginns und seiner Gewichtung der gleiche Inhalt wie in
36,20 vor.

(6) Die Untersuchung des sirazidischen Wortgebrauches bestätigt,
daß die komplizierte Formulierung in 24,9 einen schwierigen Tatbestand
festhalten will. Marböck weist mehrfach darauf hin, daß es um die Feststellung des Alters der Weisheit geht[23], welches aber nur beiläufig für
die Argumentation Gewicht besitzt[24], in V. 9 aber eine der zentralen
Aussagen darstellt[25]. Zurecht verweist er zum Vergleich auf Aussagen in
verschiedenen Fassungen der Isis-Aretalogie, wo das Alter betont
wird[26]. Solche Gedichte und das Fluidum seiner geistigen Umwelt kannte Sira gut und geht auf diese Vorstellungen ein. Er konzentriert sich auf
diesem Hintergrund allerdings auf weitere Aspekte, die mit der Relation
zum Schöpfer in Verbindung zu bringen sind. Es ist richtig, wenn der
Autor festhält, daß in 1,4 und 24,9 »von der Existenz der Weisheit vor
der übrigen Schöpfung die Rede ist«[27]. Allerdings ist auch die
Präexistenz nicht das eigentliche Thema.

Da Marböck die Bedeutsamkeit der Dimensionen des *Anfanges* nicht
untersucht hat, ist ihm entgangen, daß es hier um einen Versuch geht,

23. Vgl. MARBÖCK, *Weisheit*, p. 73; DERS., *Gottes Weisheit unter uns. Sir 24 als Beitrag zur biblischen Theologie*, in Professorenkollegium der Philosophisch-Theologischen
Hochschule der Diözese St. Pölten (Hg.), *Verbum caro factum est*, FS A. Stöger, St.
Pölten–Wien, 1984, pp. 55-65, neu gedruckt in I. FISCHER (Hg.), *Gottes Weisheit unter
uns. Zur Theologie des Buches Sirach*, HBS, 6), Freiburg–Basel–Wien, 1995, pp. 73-87.

24. Vgl. MARBÖCK, *Weisheit*, p. 56.

25. Vgl. MARBÖCK, *Weisheit*, p. 64.

26. Vgl. MARBÖCK, *Weisheit*, p. 52; B. LANG, *Ist die Göttin Isis Vorbild der Weisheit? (Sir 24)*, in DERS., *Frau Weisheit. Deutung einer biblischen Gestalt*, Düsseldorf,
1975, pp. 152ff, bemüht sich um den Nachweis, wonach die Frau Weisheit und nicht die
Göttin Isis Vorbild für die Vorstellung Ben Siras ist.

27. MARBÖCK, *Weisheit*, p. 19.

die Abfolge des Schöpfungswirkens Gottes darzustellen. Wenn sich diese Phasen auch der korrekten Beschreibbarkeit entziehen, rechnet Sira mit einer Reihenfolge. Die göttliche Schöpfung beginnt vor jeglicher Zeitdimension: da wird die Weisheit – und vermutlich auch alle anderen Elemente, die die materielle Schöpfung von innen her durchwirken (vgl. u.a. 11,14-16 im Verein mit 16,27) – aktualisiert[28]. Darauf folgt die übrige Schöpfung. Ab da kann man dann von unbegrenzter Zeit sprechen, übrigens auch eine Vorstellung, die sich dem mentalen Zugriff letztlich entzieht.

Aufgrund dieser Beobachtungen wird man zwischen einer *immateriellen* und einer *materiellen Phase* der Schöpfung unterscheiden. Ab der zweiten kann man erst wirklich von einem *Anfang* sprechen, konkretisiert in greifbaren, Raum und Zeit konstituierenden Gegebenheiten. – In der Phase immaterieller Fakten (*Faktum* von *facere*) wird die Weisheit, von dem *Weisen* (Gott) stammend, als wichtigste weltumgreifende Gegebenheit[29] gebildet. Wenn man sie nach 24,3a (ἐγὼ ἀπὸ στόματος ὑψίστου ἐξῆλθον) als eine wie das Wort (Jes 55,9-11) aus dem Munde Gottes hervorgehende Realität (vgl. Jes 9,7; Jer 2,31; 23,29) versteht, ereignet sich in dieser Schöpfung anderes als in der übrigen: Gott wird partiell in der Weisheit eben als Weisheit präsent[30]. Dieses *Präsentwerden* ist eine *spezielle Form von Schöpfung*.

(7) Die Erwähnung des Schöpfers wie auch seiner Schöpfertätigkeit unterscheidet die zwei Ebenen. Einesteils bezieht sie sich auf das Gesamt der Schöpfung: ὁ κτίστης ἀπάντων (24,8a), andernteils auf jene der Weisheit: ὁ κτίσας με (24,8b). Sie ist die zentrale Gegebenheit für die übrige Schöpfung, aber besonders auf Israel (Zion bzw. Jerusalem)

---

28. Die Schwierigkeit, die Rolle der Weisheit zu fassen, wurde dahin gedeutet, daß sie eigentlich gar keine Bedeutung besitzt: »Ben Sira closely links Dame Wisdom with the creator and with the cosmos, but it is not clear that she has any specific role to play in the genesis of the cosmos«; J.F. ROGERS, *Wisdom and Creation in Sirach 24*, in *JNSL* 22/2 (1996) 141-156, p. 154.

29. Eine notierenswerte Anmerkung bietet M. CONTI, *Origine divina della Sapienza e i suoi rapporti col mondo, coll'uomo e col popolo dell'alleanza (Sir 24,3-22)*, in V. BATTAGLIA (Hg.), *L'uomo e il mondo alla luce di Cristo*, Vicenza, 1986, pp. 9-42 (p. 14), da er im Nebel (V. 3a) ein »segno visibile della potenza creatrice di Dio« sieht.

30. Unter diesem Gesichtspunkt ist die Zusammenfassung von G. SCHIMANOWSKI, *Weisheit und Messias. Die jüdischen Voraussetzungen der urchristlichen Präexistenzchristologie* (WUNT, 2/17), Tübingen 1985, »zum ersten Redeteil, der Ursprung und kosmische Funktion der Weisheit zum Thema hatte« (p. 53) von großem Interesse. Es ist festzuhalten, »daß ... der Ort der Weisheit in zwei Schritten beschrieben wird: 1. Vor der Schöpfung bei Gott, 2. Bei den Schöpfungswerken. Hier in Sir 24 sind beide Schritte weiter expliziert worden. Der Gedankenfortschritt liegt aber bei dem, was man das 'Wesen' der Weisheit nennen könnte, denn in Kap. 24 erhält man eine Antwort auf die Frage, was die Weisheit ist – der Epiphanieglanz, der göttliche כבוד. Konsequent wird in großer Zurückhaltung das weiter ausgefaltet, was in Ijob 28, Spr 8 und Sir 1 angelegt war«.

hingeordnet. Die enge Verbindung mit Israel zeigt, daß die Schöpfung der Weisheit auf Menschen ausgerichtet ist.

4. WEITERE IMMATERIELLE SCHÖPFUNGSGEGEBENHEITEN

Wenn man sich nach anderen Beispielen von Realitäten aus dem immateriellen Bereich umsieht, trifft man auf 11,14-16 und 34(31),16.

4.1. Sir 11,14-16

Im Abschnitt 11,10-19 beschäftigt sich Sira mit übereifrigen Bemühungen (modern: Manager-Syndrom), die letztlich auf keiner Ebene effektiv sind. Die Gefahr, die von solchen hektischen Aktivitäten ausgeht, besteht darin, in der Hast nicht nur nicht erfolgreich zu sein, sondern auch noch Unrecht zu begehen (Vv. 10-12). Im Gegensatz dazu wird der Rechtschaffene von Gott seinen Lohn erhalten, der in Reichtum und Ruhe besteht (Vv. 17-19).

(1) Im Übergang zwischen diesen Teilen wird Gottes Fürsorge beschrieben (11,13). Daran fügt sich eine ins allgemeine ausgedehnte grundsätzliche Feststellung an:

מייי הוא	טוב ורע חיים ומות ריש ועושר	14b.a (HS A)
מייי הוא	חכמה ושכל והבין דבר	15b.a
מייי הוא	חטא ודרכים ישרים	15d.c
ומרעים רעה עמם	שכלות וחושך לפשעים נוצרה	16b.a

Auf den ersten Blick zeigt sich, daß dieser Abschnitt – nur in der HS A erhalten – in einer wohl durchdachten metrischen Gestalt vorliegt:

– Von 14a zu 15a und 15c findet eine Steigerung statt, die durch akzelerierende Verkürzung gebildet wird. In 14a stehen 3 Hebungen: 1 (טוב ורע): 2 (חיים ומות) 3 (ריש ועושר).
– 15a besteht aus zwei Hebungen mit je zwei Worten: 1 (חכמה ושכל): 2 (והבין דבר).
– Darauf folgen in 15c drei Worte, die ihrerseits je eine Hebung bilden. Die Verschärfung rückt dieses Kolon in das Zentrum.

Der metrischen Konzentrierung entspricht eine inhaltliche Akzentsetzung: am positiven Höhepunkt (15a) geht es um Dimensionen der Weisheit. Die Setzung von ו spricht dafür, daß שכל und הבין דבר parallelisiert werden wollen. – Von der Verwendung der Substantiva aus gesehen, kann man den poetischen Weg der Akzentuierung weiter ausfalten: 6 Abstrakta in 14a, 4 Abstrakta in 15a und 3 Substantiva in 15a.

Als fixierender Halt steht der gleichbleibende Zweier מייי הוא in jedem Stichos dem ersten Kolon gegenüber. Da das erste Kolon immer verkürzt wird, verlängert sich relativ die Phrase מייי הוא, so daß diese an Gewicht gewinnt. Schrittweise, aber doch sehr nachdrücklich, tritt hervor, daß die immateriellen Gegebenheiten einzig und allein auf JHWH zurückzuführen sind. Endgültig unterstrichen wird die Schwerpunktsetzung durch das *drei*malige Vorkommen. Diese Beobachtungen weisen darauf hin, daß ein schon von Anfang an poetisch fein durchstrukturierter Abschnitt vorliegt.

In geradezu schriller Opposition steht V. 16 diesem Part gegenüber. Schon metrisch fehlt der Gleichklang (4:3) im Vergleich zum Vorangehenden. Es zeigt sich darin, daß der Autor die Vv. 14-15 als eine geschlossene – wenn auch antithetisch angeordnete – Gruppe sieht. Dieser stehen jene gegenüber (V. 16), die dann tatsächlich im Leben dafür sorgen, daß das Schlechte – sogar im Übermaß, wie die Länge und die Anhäufung potentiell negativer Termini: שכלות, חושך, פשעים, מרעים, רעה anzeigt – in Taten umgesetzt wird: das Schreckliche in den schlechten Taten ahmt der Autor auch poetisch meisterhaft nach[31]. Der Autor bleibt insofern konsequent, als er auch hier festhält, daß diese negativen Gegebenheiten geschaffen (יצר) wurden, wobei das Passivum (נוצרה) auf Gott verweist. – Es sei inhaltlich auf die Spannung innerhalb des Buches hingewiesen, die sich beim Vergleich mit 15,11-13 ergibt. – Für die vorliegende Untersuchung von großer Bedeutung ist, daß die Verwendung von יצר bekräftigt, daß es sich bei מייי הוא auch um Schöpfungsaussagen handelt.

(2) Der Syrer unterstützt in 11,14-15 alle Argumente zum H-A Text und bestätigt damit, daß er öfter gemeinsam mit jener Linie geht, zu der H-A gehört, als mit jener, die auch durch H-B, der Γ näher steht, repräsentiert wird. Auffällig ist, daß V. 16 in Syr nicht geboten wird. Dies kann darauf zurückgehen, daß Syr dort eine inhaltliche Wiederholung von 15c.d erkannte und sie daher weg ließ. Daß Syr – im Gegensatz zu Γ – nicht die gleiche Sorgfalt bei der Berücksichtigung der poetischen Feinheiten walten läßt, ist eine allgemeine Beobachtung.

ܩܕܡ ܐܠܗܐ ܫܩܝܢ ܐܢܘܢ	ܛܒܬܐ ܘܒܝܫܬܐ ܚܝ̈ܐ ܘܡܘܬܐ ܥܘܬܪܐ ܘܡܣܟܢܘܬܐ	14b.a
ܡܢ ܠܘܬ ܡܪܝܐ ܗܝ	ܚܟܡܬܐ ܘܣܘܟܠܬܐ ܘܐܘܪܚܬܐ ܕܢܡܘܣܐ	15b.a
ܡܢ ܠܘܬܗ ܐ̈ܢܝܢ	ܚܘܒܐ ܘܐܘܪܚܬܐ ܕܥܒ̈ܕܐ ܛܒ̈ܐ	15d.c

31. Da ich eine geschickte poetische Gestaltung entnehmen kann, vermag ich DI LELLA, *Wisdom*, p. 237, nicht zu folgen: »The uneven lengths of the Heb lines go to show that the two verses are an expansion of Ben Sira's text«.

Die Abweichungen in Γ sind gravierender als in Syr, da nur V. 14 in der älteren Version belegt ist, während die Vv. 15f durch ΓII repräsentiert werden.

14a.b ἀγαθὰ καὶ κακά ζωὴ καὶ θάνατος πτωχεία καὶ πλοῦτος παρὰ κυρίου ἐστίν
15a.b σοφία καὶ ἐπιστήμη καὶ γνῶσις νόμου   παρὰ κυρίου
15c.d ἀγάπησις καὶ ὁδοὶ καλῶν ἔργων   παρ' αὐτοῦ εἰσιν
16a.b πλάνη καὶ σκότος ἁμαρτωλοῖς συνέκτισαι   τοῖς δὲ γαυριῶσιν ἐπὶ κακίᾳ συγγηρᾳ κακία.

Das Drastische und Kompromißlose in den Aussagen werden veranlaßt haben, daß nur Teile davon in ΓI aufgenommen worden sind bzw. in der jüngeren Fassung von Γ [ΓII] doch wieder in einige Hss Eingang gefunden haben. Im großen und ganzen bestätigt Γ aber die H-Tradition. Ein bedeutender Unterschied ist in 15c gegeben, wo anstelle von חטא ודרכים ישרים ἀγάπησις καὶ ὁδοὶ καλῶν ἔργων zu lesen ist. Daß die Ausgangstexte einander nahe gestanden sind, wird daran erkennbar, daß דרכים ישרים und ὁδοὶ καλῶν ἔργων von gleichen Gegebenheiten handeln, wobei die griechische Version als eine Interpretation von H verstanden werden kann. Dagegen kann ἀγάπησις nicht auf חטא[32] oder eine ähnliche Vorlage zurückgeführt werden.

Aus poetischen wie innersirazidischen Beobachtungen wird man aber damit rechnen, daß Γ schon sehr früh gegeben war. Es entspricht Siras Argumentation, daß ἀγάπησις als ein inneres Bestimmungsziel zu sehen ist; vgl. 48,11. In 32,1-4 (= 35,1-2[33]) findet sich ein instruktives Beispiel subtiler Gewichtungen, wo Opfer, Gesetzeserfüllung und Liebestaten einander zugeordnet werden:

32,1 Ὁ συντηρῶν νόμον πλεονάζει προσφοράς
32,2 θυσιάζων σωτηρίου ὁ προσέχων ἐντολαῖς
32,3 ἀνταποδιδοὺς χάριν προσφέρων σεμίδαλιν
32,4 καὶ ὁ ποιῶν ἐλεημοσύνην θυσιάζων αἰνέσεως

In 32,1.2 zeigt die chiastische Konstruktion (Außenglieder: ὁ συντηρῶν νόμον und ὁ προσέχων ἐντολαῖς; Innenglieder: πλεονάζει

32. PETERS, Buch, p. 98, führt eine Reihe von Gründen an, weswegen seiner Meinung nach »die Stelle ... aber auch in ihrer ursprünglichen Form sekundär« ist. Besonders stört ihn aber חטא; er vermutet, daß es auf חִיבָה zurückgeht; dieses wurde zu חוב verlesen und dann in das gebräuchlichere חטא geändert. DI LELLA (Wisdom, p. 237) wiederum meint, daß ursprünglich אַהֲבָה gestanden hatte. Es verwundert, daß unbemerkt eine solche Malversation vorgenommen worden sein soll, die sich, obwohl sie theologische Probleme macht, auch noch durchgesetzt hat.

33. Zum Problem der Zählung im Buch Ben Sira vgl. F.V. REITERER, Overview of Recent Research on the Book of Ben Sira, in P.C. BEENTJES (Hg.), The Book of Ben Sira in Modern Research. Proceedings of the First International Ben Sira Conference 28-31 July 1996 Soesterberg, Netherlands (BZAW, 255), Berlin–New York, 1997, pp. 23-60 (pp. 34f).

προσφοράς und θυσιάζων σωτηρίου), daß die Opferdarbringung und die Gesetzeseinhaltung aufeinander hin geordnet sind und zugleich die erstere von der zweiten umschlossen wird. Wie die Steigerung in 32,3.4 zeigt, ist damit eine Akzentuierung gegeben. Das besagt, daß die Darbringung von Opfern nicht von solchem Gewicht ist, wie das Halten der göttlichen Vorschriften. Geht man nun zu 32,3f weiter, trifft man auf einen parallelen Aufbau. Die Liebestat wird zu dem in den Vv. 1-2 Bedeutsamen in Relation gesetzt: Danach gelten ἀνταποδιδοὺς χάριν und ὁ ποιῶν ἐλεημοσύνην als Überbietung von Opfern. Nun gehören χάρις und ἐλεημοσύνη zum gleichen Bereich wie ἀγάπησις. Man kann aus dem Vergleich vielleicht entnehmen, daß ἀγάπησις die abstrakte, immaterielle Vorgabe der Dimension Liebe ist, die sich in Liebestaten (χάρις, ἐλεημοσύνη) konkretisiert. – Wenn man also in 11,15c anstelle von Sünde von der Liebe liest, zeigt sich, daß ein für Sira zentrales Thema aufgenommen wurde. Es ist nicht auszuschließen, daß schon von Anfang an beide Versionen gegeben waren: das eine Mal geht die Argumentation antithetisch (in H erhalten), das andere Mal auf positiver Ebene steigernd vor (in Γ erhalten). Dann würde die Liebe auch noch die Weisheit überbieten, wenngleich nach 40,20 die Liebe zur Weisheit (ἀγάπησις σοφίας; vgl. aber H und Syr: Freundesliebe: אהבת דודים; ܪܚܡܘܬܐ ܕܪܚܡܐ) berauschende Festfreuden übertrifft, also selbst eine eigene Zielvorstellung in der Werthierarchie darstellt.

(3) Für die gegenständliche Fragestellung ist notierenswert, daß sich die Schöpfung hier auf immaterielle Gegebenheiten bezieht. In radikaler Art wird das in der weisheitlichen Argumentation Wesentliche so auf Gott zurückgeführt, wie es im Alten Testament kein zweites Mal vorkommt, wenngleich Jes 45,7 nahe heran reicht[34]. Man wird zwischen dem Faktum der Herkunft und dem Ziel dieser Schöpfungsgegebenheiten unterscheiden. – Für Sira bündeln sich die Fülle der Macht und Möglichkeiten Gottes in seiner *Schöpfertätigkeit*.

Von einem konsequenten monotheistischen Standpunkt aus ist die Position verständlich, daß die zentralen positiven und negativen Gegebenheiten auf immaterieller Ebene ausschließlich auf JHWH zurückgeführt werden. In die Augen sticht dabei, daß außergewöhnlich konsequent argumentiert wird. Für einen neuzeitlichen Leser sind die positiven Ebenen ohne Probleme mit Gott zu verbinden: Gutes, Leben, Reichtum, Weisheit, Einsicht, Verstehen des Wortes, Liebe (nach Γ; vgl. H) und das Schicksal der Rechtschaffenen. Geradezu schockierend kann dagegen die gleiche Konsequenz auf der negativen Ebene wirken: Übel, Tod,

---

34. Die Parallelität zum Wort hebt CONTI, *Origine*, pp. 11-14, hervor.

Armut, Sünde (vgl. Γ), Torheit, Finsternis, Schlechtes werden ebenso
auf Gott zurückgeführt.

Während man noch Übel, Tod, Finsternis wie in den Klagen der Beter
in den Verfügungsbereich Gottes stellt und diese von ihm zumindest insofern herleitet, als er der Souverän in der Handhabung bleibt, bereiten
Armut und Schlechtes – wohl als böse Tat zu verstehen – größere Probleme. Daß man Armut von Gott direkt herleitet, ist bei Sira so zu verstehen, daß sie eine selbstverständliche Existenzform darstellt, mit der
man einfach zu rechnen hat. Es kommt darauf an, was man damit
macht[35]: sie kann also als eine Aufgabe wie auch als eine Herausforderung von Gott her verstanden werden. Schlechtes und Sünde auf Gott
zurückzuführen, provoziert das religiöse Gefühl und man neigt dazu,
derartige Gedanken spontan abzulehnen. – Bei Sira ist dies eben anders.

(4) Bei der Frage nach der Intention der Schöpfungsaussagen ist zu
differenzieren. Einmal geht es um deren Funktion im Gedicht, das andere Mal um die Erhebung der Funktion im Denken Ben Siras.

Aus dem Kontext des Gedichts ergibt sich, daß die Allmacht Gottes
dem rastlosen Zielstreben der Menschen gegenüber gestellt wird. Ähnlich hatte schon Deuterojesaja im Zusammenhang mit der Rettung aus
dem Exil argumentiert: »Weißt du es nicht, hörst du es nicht? JHWH ist
ein ewiger Gott, der die weite Erde erschuf. Er wird nicht müde und
matt, unergründlich ist seine Einsicht. Er gibt dem Müden Kraft, dem
Kraftlosen verleiht er große Stärke. Die Jungen werden müde und matt,
junge Männer stolpern und stürzen. Die aber, die JHWH vertrauen,
schöpfen neue Kraft, sie bekommen Flügel wie Adler. Sie laufen und
werden nicht müde, sie gehen und werden nicht matt« (Jes 40,28-31).
Die dort in weltgeschichtlich-soteriologischem Kontext stehende Aussage wird von Sira auf das individuelle Bemühen angewandt und die gleiche Dynamik festgestellt.

Mit diesem Hinweis auf das schöpfungstheologische, prophetische
Argumentationsmodell verläßt man aber die Leistungsfähigkeit einer
einzelnen Einheit und stößt in den Bereich der Denkkategorien vor. Die
Schöpfungsaussagen stellen einen zentralen Zugang zu den Denkkategorien Ben Siras und seiner Art des Weltverständnisses dar. Die Basis für seine konkrete Argumentation im Kontext liegt in den von Gott
vorgegebenen Schöpfungszusammenhängen. Damit wird die Aussage
über die immateriellen Schöpfungsgegebenheiten zur Information über
die Ausrüstung der materiellen Schöpfung. Die immateriellen Vorgaben
gewährleisten das Funktionieren der materiellen Schöpfung.

---

35. Vgl. zur Thematik des Armen REITERER, *Freundschaft*, pp. 147-151.

Hauptziel der Schöpfungsaussagen ist es zu zeigen, daß Gott der Souverän in allen Bereichen vor dem und in dem menschlichen Leben ist und bleibt.

4.2. Sir 37,18 nach Syr

Im Kontext von 37,18 geht es um das rechte Wort und dessen Herkunftsort, nämlich nach H-B und Γ das menschliche Herz. Dieses wird wohl als Geburtsort des Wortes für so gewichtig gehalten, daß es nahezu auf die Ebene Gottes gestellt wird. Derartige Vorstellungen befremden, wenn man auch Sira nahezu alles zutraut. Wie der Syrer allerdings deutlich macht, geht er mutmaßlich, wie in 11,14f, auf H-A zurück. Dort nehmen טוב ורעה וחיים ומות natürlich von Gott den Ausgang. Oben wurde in einem Nominalsatz der Bezug zu Gott hergestellt (מייי הוא). Hier in 37,18 verwendet Syr den terminus technicus: ܒܪܐ. Die Berücksichtigung des ganzen Buches weist darauf hin, daß Syr die ältere Tradition bewahrt hat. In dieser Meinung kann man sich auch durch Γ bestätigt fühlen, da es zu einer Umstellung der Kola im Verhältnis zur in sich doch stark unterschiedlichen innersemitischen Belegung kommt.

37,18	טוב ורעה וחיים ומות	ומושלת בם כליל לשון
	ܡܢܗ ܒܪܝܐ ܟܠ ܛܒ ܘܒܝܫ ܚ̈ܝܐ ܘܡܘܬܐ	ܘܫܠܝܛ ܒܠܫܢܗ ܢܦܫܐ ܡܢ ܡܘܬܐ
37,18	τέσσαρα μέρη ἀνατέλλει καὶ ἡ κυριεύουσα ἐνδελεχῶς αὐτῶν γλῶσσά ἐστιν	ἀγαθὸν καὶ κακόν, ζωὴ καὶ θάνατος

Im Blick auf die Ausführungen zu 11,14-16 findet sich kein inhaltlich neuer Aspekt.

4.3. Das Übel in 34(31),13a

Wenn auch in 34(31),13a das böse Auge im Zentrum steht, ist doch ganz eindeutig, daß man nur so, wie in 13b.e gesagt, formulieren kann, wenn man auch Schlechtes von Gott geschaffen sieht.

13b.a	רע עין שונא אל	ורע ממנו לא ברא
13d.c	כי זה מפני כל דבר תזוע עין	ומפנים דמעה תדמע
13f.e	רע מעין לא חלק אל	על כן מפני כל נס לחה
13d.c	ܡܛܠ ܕܒܝܫܘܬ ܥܝܢܐ ܣܢܐ ܐܠܗܐ	ܘܕܒܝܫ ܡܢܗ ܠܐ ܒܪܐ
13d.c 13f.e	ܡܛܠ ܗܢܐ ܡܢ ܩܕܡ ܟܠܡܕܡ ܕܚܙܐ ܥܝܢܐ	ܘܡܢ ܐܦ̈ܐ ܕܡܥܐ ܕܡܕܡܥܐ
13a.b	μνήσθητι ὅτι κακὸν ὀφθαλμὸς πονηρός	πονηρότερον ὀφθαλμοῦ τί ἔκτισται
13c		διὰ τοῦτο ἀπὸ παντὸς προσώπου δακρύει

Trotz der schwierigen Lage der Textüberlieferung ist ersichtlich, daß der Autor nicht die geringste Berührungsangst hat, wenn es darum geht, auch das Böse auf die Schöpferkraft Gottes zurückzuführen.

Weil Gott das Böse geschaffen hat, ist er auch in der Lage, darüber Autorität auszuüben, so daß es keine unkontrollierbare Eigenwirkung entwickeln kann.

5. Abfolge in der immateriellen und materiellen Schöpfung

In 15,11-20 beschäftigt sich Sira mit dem Thema der Verantwortung des Menschen. Den Ausgangspunkt der Argumentation bildet die Ausrede, wonach auch das menschliche Fehlverhalten auf Gott zurückzuführen und von ihm zu verantworten ist. Da er der Schöpfer ist, ist er somit selbst für das Geschaffene und die davon ausgehenden Folgen verantwortlich. Nicht verwundern wird es daher, daß in diesem Kontext Gewichtiges über die Schöpfungsthematik zu erheben ist. – Zwei Stufen sind zu unterscheiden: die immaterielle Ebene (Vv. 11ff) und die materielle (V. 14), die sich hier auf den Menschen konzentrieren.

5.1. Sir 15,11ff

אל תאמר מאל פשעי כי את אשר שנא לא עשה

ܠܐ ܬܐܡܪ ܕܡܢ ܡܪܝܐ ܐܢܐ ܐܣܛܝܬ ܡܛܠ ܕܡܕܡ ܕܣܢܐ ܠܐ ܥܒܕ.

μὴ εἴπῃς ὅτι Διὰ κύριον ἀπέστην ἃ γὰρ ἐμίσησεν οὐ ποιήσει. (15,11)

(1) Gleich eingangs (15,11a) weist der Autor eine vorgeschobene Entschuldigung zurück, die die Eigenverantwortlichkeit ausschließen würde. Die Formulierung מאל, also מן + GN, fungiert bei Sira, wie schon im Zusammenhang von 11,14f gesehen, als nominale Schöpfungsaussage.

(2) Vergleicht man Syr mit H, stellt sich die Frage ob מן und ܡܢ ܡܕܡ gleich zu verstehen sind, hat man doch den Eindruck, daß ܡܕܡ – als *vor* eingefügt – den Inhalt stark verändert: denn die Relationen stellen sich ganz anders dar, wenn ich *vor Gott sündige* oder *von Gott her* sündige. Wenn es auch nur wenige Vergleichstexte (מן + GN) gibt, in denen zumindest formal vergleichbare Bezüge vorkommen, zeigt der Übersetzungsusus, daß Syr H folgt. In Ps 37,39 scheint von H aus gesehen die nächst verwandte Stelle zu stehen: וּתְשׁוּעַת צַדִּיקִים מֵיְהוָה. Allerdings läßt Syr die Rettung nicht von Gott ausgehen, sondern nennt JHWH *selbst* als Rettung: ܦܘܪܩܢܐ ܕܙܕܝܩܐ ܡܢ ܡܪܝܐ, verändert also die grammatischen Bezüge, so daß *von* wegfällt. Die Überprüfung der Ausdrucksweise mag dies untermauern: In Ijob 32,2 steht: »Wegen des sich

selbst Gerecht-Haltens gegenüber Gott«. Der sehr *wörtlichen* Übertra-
gung liegt zugrunde: עַל־צִדְקוֹ נַפְשׁוֹ מֵאֱלֹהִים. In Syr steht: ܗܘܢ ܠܚ
ܘܢܦܫ ܠܟ ܡܢ ܐܠܗܐ. In der Bedeutung von *gegenüber, im Verhältnis, gemessen an* steht also in Ijob 32,2 für מִן ܡܢ. In Ijob 35,2 geht: »du
hast gesagt: meine Gerechtigkeit gegenüber Gott« auf אָמַרְתָּ צִדְקִי מֵאֵל
zurück und wird übersetzt mit ܐܟܬܒ ܗܘ ܡܢ ܐܠܗܐ. Es ver-
bleibt noch Ijob 20,29: זֶה חֵלֶק־אָדָם רָשָׁע מֵאֱלֹהִים וְנַחֲלַת אִמְרוֹ מֵאֵל. Hier
nun findet man die gleiche Präposition wie in Sir 15,11: ܘܡܢ ܗܘ,
ܗܢܘ. ܘܡܢܐ ܕܣܢܐܬ ܡܢ ܗܘ ܡܪܡ ܐܠܗܐ. Es ergibt sich also, daß
Syr und H in diesem Punkt gleich zu verstehen sind: »von Gott her«. –
Die griechische Version hebt noch stärker als Syr Gott als Verursacher
der Verfehlung hervor: διὰ κύριον.

(3) Deutlich ist, daß sowohl Vergehen, als auch Gott und Mensch
durch diese Argumentationsweise in engen Zusammenhang gebracht
werden. Es gilt nun zu klären, wie dies zu verstehen ist. Der Nominalsatz in H ist am klarsten: מֵאֵל פִּשְׁעִי. Es ist und bleibt des Menschen Vergehen, wie das enklitische Possessivpronomen deutlich zeigt. מֵאֵל kann
also nicht im Sinne des direkten Verursachers (= Γ) gemeint sein, denn
dann müßte es zu *seinen*, nämlich Gottes, Vergehen werden, also ungefähr: פִּשְׁעוּ עֲלֵי.

(4) Wenn auch der Inhalt im Allgemeinen verbleibt, ergibt sich soviel, daß die Verwirklichung der Sünde als Einzeltat von Gott *gehaßt*
(אֶת אֲשֶׁר שָׂנֵא) wird. – Deutlich ist, daß Sira damit rechnet, daß es sich bei
פֶּשַׁע um eine Realität handelt, die Gott im Sinne der Möglichkeit in der
Schöpfung *grundgelegt hat*: Darauf gestoßen wird man durch die Verwendung von עשׂה (11b), dem auch ܥܒܕ wie ποιεῖν entsprechen, welches hier das Schaffen Gottes bezeichnet. Allgemeines *Tätigen* scheint
schon von da her auszuschließen, daß man Gott nicht so naiv gezeichnet
sieht, daß er etwas bewerkstelligt, was er selbst ablehnt. Der Blick auf
die Wortverwendung z.B. in 7,30 (עוֹשֶׂךָ; τὸν ποιήσαντά σε; ܥܒܕ),
38,15 (עוֹשֵׂהוּ; τοῦ ποιήσαντος αὐτόν; ܐܠܗܐ), 42,24 (עשׂה;
ἐποίησεν; ܥܒܕ), und 43,5 (עוֹשֵׂהוּ; ὁ ποιήσας αὐτόν; ܘܥܒܕܗ), zeigt,
daß es sich um Schöpfungstermini handelt, wobei bei H und Γ die Wortwahl gleich bleibt, während Syr je eigene Akzente setzt und so zu Erkennen gibt, daß für ihn *Gott*, der *Schöpfer* und der *Machende* aus-
tauschbar sind. – Danach ist klar, daß פֶּשַׁע nicht von Gott selbst als
schlechte Tat begangen wird: er ist der Schöpfer der Potenz zur Sünde,
aber nicht der, der sie konkret begeht.

(5) Bevor noch die Fragestellung über die Herkunft von פִּשְׁעִי aufgrund von weiteren Bezügen innerhalb des Buches in den Mittelpunkt
rückt, soll der weitere Kontext innerhalb der Perikope dargestellt werden. Es wird eine Meinung zitiert, welche Gott subtil unterstellt, daß ja

er den Menschen verführt habe, wenn Gewalttaten geschehen: פן תאמר
באנשי חמס (H-B חפץ; H-A) הוא התקילני כי אין צורך (V 12) und dagegen
(H-B אלהים; H-A רעה ותועבה שנא ייי) (V 13a). Es geht also um ganz
konkrete verbrecherische Taten, die aber nicht mehr direkt mit Gottes
Schöpfungshandeln in Verbindung gebracht werden können: Täter ist
der Mensch und daher ist er für die konkrete Tat allein verantwortlich.

(6) Die Frage läßt sich nicht umgehen, wie sich diese Worte zu
11,14a.15c verhalten, wo טוב ורע und חטא direkt auf Gott zurückgeführt
werden (מייי). Kann man denn annehmen, daß weder der Autor, noch der
Redaktor diese Spannung bemerkt haben sollten? – Unbestritten, eine
Schwierigkeit, zumindest eine Möglichkeit, verkürzt zu argumentieren,
bleibt, auch wenn man folgend argumentiert: Wenn Gott die Potenz zum
Schlechten geschaffen hat, dann relativiert sich der Gegensatz. Das Problem liegt dann gerade darin, daß trotzdem nicht gesagt werden kann, daß
die konkrete böse Tat von Gott vollzogen wird: wenn sie nicht geschieht,
ist das eine positive Bewältigung der Herausforderung, welche ihrerseits
tatsächlich von Gott ausgeht; vgl. ähnlich die Rolle von Satan im
Ijobprolog. – Für dieses Verständnis spricht auch der zitierte Vorwurf –
zugleich eine Ausrede –, der im erwirkenden Kausativum (15,12a) enthalten ist und wodurch die Spannung noch erhöht wird: התקילני – *er erwirkte*
[im Sinne von: *vollbrachte*] *das mich Stolpern, Versuchen.* Also vollzieht
nach dieser vorgeschobenen Argumentation nicht der Mensch, sondern
Gott selbst die schlechte Tat, während der Mensch – wehrloses – Werkzeug ist. Es ist oben gezeigt worden, daß Sira damit rechnet, daß Gott die
Potenz zum Schlechten in der Schöpfung anlegte. Richtig wäre also der
Satz im Qal, wodurch Grundgegebenheiten in Sprache gefaßt werden: es
existiert faktisch die durch Gott bewerkstelligte Vorgabe zum Stolpern/
Versuchen, die sich als eine Herausforderung erweist. Abzulehnen ist nur
die Formulierung der Gegner im Kausativ, die Gott die praktische Umset-
zung des Scheiterns unterschiebt und sich gleichzeitig aus der Eigenver-
antwortung des Menschen stiehlt. Richtig ist, daß Gott solche Rahmenbe-
dingungen gesetzt hat, daß der Mensch Übel erfahren (vgl. auch die
Schreckensbotschaften im Prolog des Ijob-Buches) und im Falle des falschen Verhaltens auch selbst Übel vollbringen *kann*. Noch herausfordern-
der wird dieses Thema am Schluß des Herrengebetes formuliert: καὶ μὴ
εἰσενέγκῃς ἡμᾶς εἰς πειρασμόν, ἀλλὰ ῥῦσαι ἡμᾶς ἀπὸ τοῦ πονηροῦ
(Mt 6,13) und καὶ μὴ εἰσενέγκῃς ἡμᾶς εἰς πειρασμόν (Lk 11,4b).

Interessanterweise wird dieses Thema abgehandelt, bevor Sira – jetzt
nachträglich begründend – von der Menschenschöpfung spricht. Dies
kann als Hinweis verstanden werden, daß der Autor zwischen der immateriellen und der materiellen Phase unterscheidet, wie dies in 1,4.9 und
24,8f gezeigt werden konnte.

5.2. *Sir 15,14-20*

»We now have before us a third crucial aspect of what might well be called Sirach's triune theology: God, wisdom and man«, faßt Burton[36] zusammen und hebt damit die Probleme wie die Bedeutung gleicherweise hervor. In 15,14 bietet Sira die schöpfungstheologische Begründung, weswegen es nicht möglich ist, mit dem Argument des Geschaffenseins die Verantwortung für Vergehen auf Gott abzuschieben. Auffallend ist die poetische Gestaltung als Trikolon, in dem das erste Element herausgehoben wird und die anderen beiden – einen Parallelismus bildend – erläuternd und zugleich konstitutiv in der Aussage folgen:

(1)		אלהים מבראשית ברא אדם	14a
ויתנהו ביד יצרו		וישתיהו ביד חותפו	14c.b
ותבונה לעשות רצונו		אם תחפץ תשמר מצוה	15b.a
גם אתה תחיה		אם תאמין בו	15d.c

(2) H-B bestätigt den vorliegenden Text aus H-A, hat aber folgende Abweichungen. In 14a setzt der Text ein: הוא מראש. Im Verhältnis zu H-A handelt es sich bei מראש um eine Glättung, die eine ungewöhnliche Formulierung leichter macht und zudem innerhalb des Buches eine Übereinstimmung vornimmt, so daß die – trotz der ungewöhnlichen Formulierung – gegebene Verständlichkeit für H-A spricht. Daß man in 15b eine Constructus-Verbindung (רצון אל) anstelle eines Pronominalausdruckes (רצונו) findet, ist die Folge des unterschiedlichen Einsatzes in 14a: הוא steht anstelle von אלהים. Die Veränderung dient der aufgrund des Fehlens des Gottesnamens notwendig gewordenen Klarstellung, daß es sich in 15b nicht um den Willen des Menschen handelt, von dem in 14c (יצרו) die Rede war.

Zu beachten ist der parallele Aufbau von 14b.c: Narrativ – Präpositionalausdruck – davon abhängiges Objekt, je mit einem enklitischen Possessivpronomen so versehen, daß eine Assonanz entsteht. Zudem strafft der Präpositionalausdruck ביד die Verhältnisgleichheit. Das Metrum 3:3 ist die bei Sira vorherrschende Verteilung der Hebungen und rückt im Verhältnis zu den vier Hebungen in 14a in das zweite Glied, obwohl im Trikolon von V. 14 dem ersten Kolon (14a) zwei in 14b.c gegenüberstehen.

Hinzuweisen ist, daß 14b nicht selten als ein Zusatz aufgefaßt wird, der nach Di Lella »makes flagrant nonsense in this place«[37]. Die Beurteilung dieser Frage führt schon weit in die Deutung hinein. Unter חותף (Räuber) sieht Peters eine später eingefügte Erwähnung des Teufels[38]. – Derlei Interpretation scheint ausgeschlossen: das würde bedeuten, daß

---

36. Vgl. BURTON, *Sirach*, p. 194.
37. DI LELLA, *Book*, p. 269.
38. Vgl. PETERS, *Buch*, p. 130: »Gemeint ist in der Glosse der Teufel«.

die Schöpfung des Menschen dafür geschehen war, daß der Geschaffene unter den Teufel gestellt wird, – eine absurde Interpretation: sie paßt einfach nicht zur monotheistischen Argumentation Ben Siras. Aber man kann sich auch nicht vorstellen, wer einen solchen Gedanken hätte eintragen wollen. – Wenn man allerdings die Folgen von negativen Entscheidungen (vgl. die dramatischen Bilder in 16-17: Feuer und Tod als wählbare[39] Alternativen zu Wasser und Leben) vor Augen hat, dann sieht man schon, daß in der Fähigkeit zur negativen Entscheidung auch die Potenz zur Lebensberaubung enthalten ist. – Versteht man nun das Kolon in diesem Sinne, paßt es ausgezeichnet zum Kontext.

(3) Vom poetischen Standpunkt aus gesehen, bedient sich Sira bei der Verwerdung eines Trikolons gehobener Stilistik, die auch andernorts für die Vermittlung gewichtiger Inhalte eingesetzt wird: In Ps 29 kann man zeigen, wie die Verwendung poetischer Mittel das Lied strukturiert: durch die drei Trikola in den Vv. 3 und 7-9 zeigt der Poet die Schwerpunkte an[40]. Ähnlich stellt sich Ps 24,7-10 dar, wo durch מֶלֶךְ הַכָּבוֹד die Gewichtungen innerhalb der Kola vorgenommen werden: auf diese Weise wird in den Vv. 7 und 9 je das dritte Kolon, in den Vv. 8 und 10 das erste Kolon herausgehoben:

(II) וְהִנָּשְׂאוּ פִּתְחֵי עוֹלָם		שְׂאוּ שְׁעָרִים רָאשֵׁיכֶם (I) 7
	(III) וְיָבוֹא מֶלֶךְ הַכָּבוֹד:	
	(I) 8 מִי זֶה מֶלֶךְ הַכָּבוֹד	
(III) יְהוָה גִּבּוֹר מִלְחָמָה:		יְהוָה עִזּוּז וְגִבּוֹר (II)
(II) וְהִנָּשְׂאוּ פִּתְחֵי עוֹלָם		שְׂאוּ שְׁעָרִים רָאשֵׁיכֶם (I) 9
	(III) וְיָבֹא מֶלֶךְ הַכָּבוֹד:	
	(I) 10 מִי הוּא זֶה מֶלֶךְ הַכָּבוֹד	
(III) הוּא מֶלֶךְ הַכָּבוֹד		יְהוָה צְבָאוֹת (II)

39. Das Element der Wahl findet sich auch in Dtn 30,15.19; Jos 24,15.

40. Es wird hier keine weitere Behandlung der poetischen Feinstruktur (wie z.B. Vorkommen gleicher Worte, Wechsel vom Grundstamm zum D-Stamm, metrische Verkürzung als Steigerungsmittel) geboten, sondern nur der gegliederte Text:

הָבוּ לַיהוָה כָּבוֹד וָעֹז:	הָבוּ לַיהוָה בְּנֵי אֵלִים	(1)
הִשְׁתַּחֲווּ לַיהוָה בְּהַדְרַת־קֹדֶשׁ:	הָבוּ לַיהוָה כְּבוֹד שְׁמוֹ	(2)
אֵל־הַכָּבוֹד הִרְעִים	קוֹל יְהוָה עַל־הַמָּיִם	(3)
	יְהוָה עַל־מַיִם רַבִּים:	
קוֹל־יְהוָה בֶּהָדָר:	קוֹל־יְהוָה בַּכֹּחַ	(4)
וַיְשַׁבֵּר יְהוָה אֶת־אַרְזֵי הַלְּבָנוֹן:	קוֹל יְהוָה שֹׁבֵר אֲרָזִים	(5)
וְשִׂרְיֹן כְּמוֹ בֶן־רְאֵמִים	וַיַּרְקִידֵם כְּמוֹ־עֵגֶל לְבָנוֹן	(6)
קוֹל יְהוָה יָחִיל מִדְבָּר (8)	קוֹל־יְהוָה חֹצֵב לַהֲבוֹת אֵשׁ:	(7)
	יָחִיל יְהוָה מִדְבַּר קָדֵשׁ	
וַיֶּחֱשֹׂף־יְעָרוֹת	קוֹל יְהוָה יְחוֹלֵל אַיָּלוֹת	(9)
	וּבְהֵיכָלוֹ כֻּלּוֹ אֹמֵר כָּבוֹד	
וַיֵּשֶׁב יְהוָה מֶלֶךְ לְעוֹלָם	יְהוָה לַמַּבּוּל יָשָׁב	(10)
יְהוָה יְבָרֵךְ אֶת־עַמּוֹ בַשָּׁלוֹם	יְהוָה עֹז לְעַמּוֹ יִתֵּן	(11)

Sira greift diese Art der Akzentuierung auf. Die kunstvolle Gestaltung gibt nun auch die Abfolge der Interpretation vor: Kolon 14a wird man als These nehmen und die Kola 14b.c als eine parallel strukturierte weitere Information.

(4) Die alten Versionen weisen beträchtliche poetische Abweichung auf und scheinen aber doch untereinander Querverbindungen zu besitzen, zumindest eine sehr ähnliche Vorlage. Da man kaum annehmen kann, daß es einem späteren Überarbeiter eingefallen wäre, nachträglich aus V. 14 ein Trikolon, aus V. 15 zwei Parallelismen zu machen, wird man den Grundbestand in H für ursprünglich annehmen. – Es fällt auf, daß H-B (הוא) und Γ (αὐτός) gleich beginnen und diese Version durch den jüngeren Beleg in Syr (ܗܘ) unterstützt wird. In diesem Kontext sei einmal in Erinnerung gerufen, daß die griechischen Handschriften die ältesten sind, die syrische Version in den HSS ab dem 7. Jhdt. bezeugt ist, was wohl darauf hinweist, daß beide auf alte Zeugnisse zurückgehen, innerhalb Syr ܗܘ allerdings von Γ beeinflußt ist. H-A dagegen stammt aus dem 11., H-B vermutlich aus dem 12. Jhdt; beide Zeugen sind also deutlich jünger als Γ und Syr.

| | 15,14.b.a |
| | 15b.a |

14a.b αὐτὸς ἐξ ἀρχῆς ἐποίησεν ἄνθρωπον καὶ ἀφῆκεν αὐτὸν ἐν χειρὶ διαβουλίου αὐτοῦ
15a.b ἐὰν θέλῃς συντηρήσεις ἐντολὰς καὶ πίστιν ποιῆσαι εὐδοκίας

(5) Über die Aussagen hinsichtlich der *Schöpfungsphasen* wurde diese Stelle oben schon befragt: Jetzt geht es um weitere Aspekte. In 14a – durch die in einem Trikolon unterstrichene Position angezeigt – wird nachdrücklich die *Schöpfung* des *Menschen* durch *Gott* hervorgehoben מבראשית ברא (ἐποίησεν) אלהים אדם (Gott hat – beginnend mit dem Anfang – den Menschen erschaffen)[41]. Diese Formulierung erinnert stark an Gen 1,1 (בְּרֵאשִׁית בָּרָא אֱלֹהִים אֵת הַשָּׁמַיִם וְאֵת הָאָרֶץ) in Verbindung mit Gen 1,27 (וַיִּבְרָא אֱלֹהִים אֶת־הָאָדָם)[42]. Es zeigt sich darin, daß Sira den

41. In seinem Beitrag beschäftigt sich J.B. BAUER, *Der priesterliche Schöpfungshymnus in Gen 1*, in *ThZ* 20 (1964) 1-9 [vgl. DERS., *Sir. 15,14 et Gen. 1,1*, in *VD* 41 (1963) 243f (= BAUER, *Schola biblica et patristica*, Graz 1972, pp. 19f.)] sowohl philologisch wie thematisch mit diesem Text. Wenn ich dem auch nicht folgen kann, daß es sich in H-A ausschließlich um eine Übernahme aus dem syrischen Bereich handelt (2), ist seine Sensibilität für die Absicht richtig. Wenn er gesehen hat, daß es eine Schöpfungsphase vor der materiellen Welt gibt, kann man mit Einschränkungen folgen: »Von da an, da Er den Menschen schuf ...« (3).
42. Ich halte es auch für keinen Zufall, daß Gen 1,27 wie ein Trikolon gestaltet ist:

בְּצַלְמוֹ	אֶת־הָאָדָם	אֱלֹהִים	וַיִּבְרָא	a
אֹתוֹ	בָּרָא	אֱלֹהִים	בְּצֶלֶם	b
אֹתָם	בָּרָא	וּנְקֵבָה	זָכָר	c

Inbegriff von *Schöpfung* in der des Menschen sieht[43]. Mit ihr kann man die irdische Zeitrechnung beginnen lassen; vgl. oben 3.2. (4).(5). Es ergibt sich daraus, daß die Periodisierung des Schöpfungsgeschehens wesentlich eine qualitative und weniger eine temporale Untergliederung darstellt.

(6) Im nächsten Schritt geht es um die Klärung, welches Ziel der Schöpfungsakt für den Menschen beinhaltet. Dieses wird in den Verben von 14b.c (ויתנהו; וישתיהו) und den davon abhängigen Präpositionalausdrücken (ביד יצרו; ביד חותפו) mitgeteilt[44].

Während die Phrase שית ביד nie belegt ist, ist נתן ביד häufig bezeugt. Der Präpositionalausdruck beschreibt in wenigen Fällen einen Überlieferungs- oder Vermittlungsprozeß (z.B. »weitergeben durch Mose...« [נָתַן ... בְּיַד־מֹשֶׁה])[45]. Viel wichtiger ist der militärische Verwendungsbereich, wonach jemand in die Gewalt eines anderen gegeben wird, wobei auf Seiten des Unterlegenen ein hohes Maß an Hilflosigkeit eingeschlossen ist. Ein eindrückliches Beispiel dafür stellt Jer 44,30 dar: »So spricht der JHWH: Seht, ich liefere den Pharao Hofra, den König von Ägypten, in die Hand seiner Gegner (אֹיְבָיו) und Todfeinde (מְבַקְשֵׁי נַפְשׁוֹ) aus (נֹתֵן ... בְּיַד), wie ich Zidkija, den König von Juda, in die Hand Nebukadnezzars, des Königs von Babel, seines Gegners (אֹיְבוֹ) und Todfeindes (מְבַקְשֵׁי נַפְשׁוֹ), ausgeliefert habe (נָתַתִּי ... בְּיַד)«[46].

Wie der Vergleich des Raubenden mit einer Prostituierten (Spr 23,28) zeigt, ahnt man zwar nicht, wo man auf den Räuber trifft, man kann ihm zwar schwer, aber doch entkommen. חותף ist kein Räuber, der unwiderstehlich zuschlägt, wie dies bei räuberischen Horden angenommen wird.

Es sticht die dreimalige Verwendung von ברא hervor, der die Erwähnung von אֱלֹהִים (in c im Verb enthalten) und אָדָם (in b und c je im enklitischen Pronomen enthalten) entspricht.

43. Die herausragende Bedeutung der Menschenschöpfung läßt die Vermutung laut werden, daß derart wichtige Passagen auch für die Buchstruktur Bedeutung besitzen; allerdings wird man Zweifel anmelden, ob eine Stelle wie 16,24-17,20, wie SMITH annimmt, nur eine Überleitung von 16,18-20 zu 17,21-18,14 sein will; vgl. M. SMITH, *In Praise of Creation. Sir 16:24-23:27*, in L. JOHNSTON – M. SMITH (Hg.), *Psalms and Wisdom* (SDC, 6), London, 1972, pp. 196-201 (p. 196).

44. In diesem Kontext ist zu notieren, daß auch an anderen Stellen »Ben Sira offers us a deep reflection on man – or upon the position of man in creation« (L. ALONSO SCHÖKEL, *The Vision of Man in Sirach 16,24-17,14*, in J.G. GAMMIE – W.A. BRUEGGEMANN – W.L. HUMPHREYS u.a. [Hg.], *Israelite Wisdom. Theological and Literary Essays*, FS S. TERRIEN, Missoula, 1978, pp. 235-245 [pp. 235]); wenn der Autor darlegt, daß in seiner untersuchten Stelle allgemein Gültiges für die Menschen an sich formuliert ist (ebd. pp. 242f.), dann müßte man ergänzen, daß das sirazidische Bild erst vollständig ist, wenn man alle bedeutenden Stellen zur Kennzeichnung heranzieht.

45. Lev 16,21 (בְּיַד אִישׁ); vgl. 26,46; 1Chr 16,7; 2Chr 29,25; 34,16, Dan 9,10.

46. Vgl. 1Sam 14,12; 2Sam 10,10; 1Kön 18,9; 22,12.15; 2Kön 18,30; 19,10; 1Chr 19,11; 2Chr 18,11; 28,5; Jes 36,15; 37,10; Jer 21,10; 29,21; 32,3.4.28; 34,2; 37,17; 38,3; 39,17.

Ist die Beobachtung richtig, dann fügt sich der Stichos geschmeidig in den Kontext: Potentiell kann das Böse immer seine verheerende Wirkung hervorbringen; allerdings gibt es keine regelhafte Dynamik, daß die negativen Folgen eintreffen müssen. Dazu gehört mehr, nämlich die willentliche Zustimmung, wie 15,14c dann sagt. Gott ist es, der vom Menschen diese Entscheidung herausfordert: man kann ihr an sich nicht entrinnen, dem Negativen muß man aber nicht erliegen. Es ist auch beobachtbar, daß der Mensch seine Entscheidungsmöglichkeit weithin dazu mißbraucht, sich selbst – zumindest indirekt – zu schädigen. »Il male è una consequenza dell'abuso di libertà da parte dell'uomo«[47].

In der Bibel gibt es keinen Terminus für Selbstzerstörung, ein Wort, welches man heute immer wieder hört. Die Sache aber, daß man sich selbst schädigt, scheint es zumindest zur Zeit der hellenistischen Herausforderung massiv gegeben zu haben.

Unter dieser Voraussetzung hält V. 15,14 fest, daß der Mensch ebenso, wie schon früher die Potenz zum Bösen, von Gott geschaffen ist. Darin inkludiert ist der unentrinnbare Auftrag, seine Entscheidungsfähigkeit (יצר) so zu steuern, daß man sich nicht – wie allzuhäufig – selbst beraubt (חותף), was wohl als Lebensminderung zu verstehen ist. Sira wird sowohl aufgrund der negativen Erfahrungen im alltäglichen Leben, als auch vor allem aufgrund der allgemeinen Verunsicherung im Rahmen der beginnenden politischen Wirren unter den Seleukiden die Phrase »dem eigenen Willen ausgeliefert sein« gewählt haben. Er sieht einerseits die Faktizität, andererseits das große Risiko, welches damit verbunden ist.

Wenn – also nach vorausgehender willentlicher Zustimmung – man sich nach dem *Auftrag* Gottes und sich nach *dessen Willen* ausrichtet, was ist dann? – Nun fehlt der eigentliche Inhalt, wenn man, wie z.B. Peters und Di Lella, 15c.d als von Hab 2,4 veranlaßtes (הִנֵּה עֻפְּלָה לֹא־יָשְׁרָה נַפְשׁוֹ בּוֹ וְצַדִּיק בֶּאֱמוּנָתוֹ יִחְיֶה) Addendum ansieht. Im Habakuk-Text wird moralisches Verhalten Grundlage für die Lebenserhaltung: Im weiteren Sinne mag dies auch für Sira zutreffen. Im engeren Sinne geht es aber um viel weiter Reichendes: שמר מצוה meint die Achtsamkeit auf all das, was Gott angeordnet hat – Gebotserfüllung ist für Sira keine oberste Norm (vgl. oben 4.1. (2)) –, und zwar bezogen auf die Regeln, die der Schöpfung zugrunde liegen. Das paßt gut dazu, daß man Gottes Willen als ganzen einhalten sollte (עשות רצון), also auch schon vor der konkreten Tat hellhörig zu sein hat.

In Hab 2,4 geht es wie in Sir 15,15c.d um Existenzgefährdung: solche Thematik findet man auch in Jes 7,9: אִם לֹא תַאֲמִינוּ כִּי לֹא תֵאָמֵנוּ. – Allen

---

[47]. F. FESTORAZZI, *La creazione nella storia della salvezza*, in *La Scuola Cattolica* 90 (1962) 3-27, p. 18.

Stellen eignet ein gemeinsamer Kern: das *sich selbst Festmachen* (Kausativ von אמן) in Gott, gewöhnlich einfach mit *Glauben* umschrieben. So bleibt Gott die innere Mitte, nicht das menschliche Verhalten, wobei die aktive Mitwirkung des Menschen (vgl. wiederum das Kausativ) konstitutiv ist. Das auf Gott Vertrauen, sich an ihn Klammern führt zum bzw. erhält das Leben (אתה תחיה). – Das konkrete menschliche Verhalten ist zwar bedeutsam, tritt aber hinter Gott zurück: Gottes Lebenswille für den Menschen und nicht des Menschen gutes Verhalten sind letztlich entscheidend. Der Vergleich in den Vv. 16-17 formuliert auf neue Weise den gleichen Inhalt.

(7) Gleichsam als Zusammenfassung dienen 15,19f: Gott kennt seine Werke und befiehlt niemandem, zu sündigen. Aus dem vorher Ausgeführten wird die Intention der Worte klar, daß er um alle seine Werke Bescheid weiß: Gott ist und bleibt Souverän, ist er doch mit seinen Augen überall: עיני אל יראו מעשיו והו יכיר עֶל כל מפעל איש (19); vgl. so auch ܪܚܒܼ. ܗܠܡܘܕ̈ܝܢ ܗܘ̇ ܐܠܟ̈ܬܐ ܚܠܡܝ ܡܘܣܟܙ ܣܘܒ ܚܢܘܣ̈ܗܘ. ܐܒܟ. Gottes Werke meint keineswegs den Menschen oder seine Taten allein, sondern all das Geschaffene. Es muß sich nicht auf die für Menschen sichtbare Schöpfung beschränken.

Angemerkt sei, daß Γ auf der Ebene der Ethik verbleibt und sich so als Interpretation erweist: καὶ οἱ ὀφθαλμοὶ αὐτοῦ ἐπὶ τοὺς φοβουμένους αὐτόν καὶ αὐτὸς ἐπιγνώσεται πᾶν ἔργον ἀνθρώπου. Allerdings zählt die Gottesfurcht, die auch die grundlegende, die Einzeltat bei weitem übersteigende positive Haltung zu Gott bedeutet, zu den großen Themen Ben Siras, so daß die Deutung dem Geist des Buches entspricht.

5.3. Summe

Die Schöpfung bezieht sich in V. 11 auf die Sünde, in V. 19 (vgl. dagegen V. 14) auf nicht näher fixierbare, wahrscheinlich materielle Gegebenheiten. Die Aussage dient dem Ziel, den freien Willen wie das Versagen des Menschen und die in jeder Lebensphase (von der Erstschöpfung bis zur Lebensgestaltung) anwesende Gegenwart des Schöpfers zu verbinden. Seit Beginn untersteht der Mensch dem Schöpfer. Dies bedeutet keine personale Vergewaltigung durch den Schöpfer, sodaß in Gottes Präsenz die individuelle Verantwortlichkeit aufgehoben würde. Schlechte Handlungen kann man nicht auf Gott zurückführen. Dieser wollte die Freiheit des Menschen, der sich der Mensch oft sogar *ausgeliefert* weiß. Trotzdem bleiben Verhalten und deren Folgen unter der Aufsicht und Obhut des Schöpfers. Wenn auch nicht näher bestimmbare Gegebenheiten unter Schöpfungstaten subsumiert werden, ist der Bezug zum Menschen immer gegeben.

6. Immaterielle Elemente der Weltausstattung

Die zentrale Begründung, weswegen 7,15 und 40,1.10 gemeinsam behandelt werden, liegt darin, daß je das Verb חלק vorkommt. 40,1.10 werden deswegen vorgezogen, weil sich dort die Zusammenhänge sehr deutlich zeigen.

6.1. Sir 40,1.10

In 40,1-11 spricht Sira von der großen Mühsal, die das menschliche Leben auszeichnet. Sie beginnt beim Verlassen des Mutterschoßes und endet, wenn der Mensch zur Erde zurückkehrt. Die für die Untersuchung wichtigsten Verse lauten:

(1)

ועול כבד על בני אדם	(Bm עליון) עסק גדול חלק אל	40,1b.a
עד יום שובו אל אם כל חי	מיום צאתו מרחם אמו	40,1d.c
ובעבור תמוש כלה	[.]ל רשע נבראה רעה	40,10b.a
ואשר ממרום אל מרום	כל מארץ אל ארץ ישוב	40,11b.a

Aus dem Vergleich dieser beiden Verse ergibt sich, daß חלק und ברא grundsätzlich die gleiche Aufgabe erfüllen: sie sagen, was Gott für Menschen geschaffen hat. Die unterschiedlich Wortwahl weist allerdings auf Nuancierungen hin.

(2) Die Übersetzungen bieten hier schon von vorneherein Schöpfungsaussagen. In Syr ist jedoch V. 10 nicht überliefert:

ܘܢܝܪܐ ܬܩܝܠܐ ܥܠ ܒܢ̈ܝ ܐܢܫܐ	ܨ̈ܒܘܬܐ ܪܘܪܒܬܐ ܒܪܐ ܐܠܗܐ	40,1b.a
ܘܥܕܡܐ ܕܗܦܟܝܢ ܠܐܪܥܐ ܕܚܝ̈ܐ	ܡܢ ܝܘܡܐ ܕܢܦܩܘ ܡܢ ܟܪܣܐ ܕܐܡܗܘܢ	40,1d.c
ܘܕܡܢ ܪܘܡܐ ܠܪܘܡܐ	ܟܠ ܡܕܡ ܕܡܢ ܐܪܥܐ ܗܘ ܠܐܪܥܐ ܗܦܟ	40,11b.a

40,1a.b	᾿Ασχολία μεγάλη ἔκτισται παντὶ ἀνθρώπῳ	καὶ ζυγὸς βαρὺς ἐπὶ υἱοὺς Αδαμ
40,1c.d	ἀφ᾿ ἡμέρας ἐξόδου ἐκ γαστρὸς μητρὸς αὐτῶν	ἕως ἡμέρας ἐπιστροφῆς εἰς μητέρα πάντων
40,10a.b	ἐπὶ τοὺς ἀνόμους ἐκτίσθη ταῦτα πάντα	καὶ δι᾿ αὐτοὺς ἐγένετο ὁ κατακλυσμός
40,11a.b	πάντα ὅσα ἀπὸ γῆς εἰς γῆν ἀναστρέφει	καὶ ἀπὸ ὑδάτων εἰς θάλασσαν ἀνακάμπτει

Auf den ersten Blick fällt auf, daß Γ stärker praktisch argumentiert und vermutlich auch naturphilosophische Argumente in 11b vor Augen hat. Erde und Wasser sind zudem eine gebräuchliche Opposition.

(3) Der Einleitungssatz verwendet חלק, einen Terminus für qualifiziertes Schaffen: die Zuweisung des Geschicks ist damit gemeint[48].

48. Vgl. F.V. Reiterer, *Deutung und Wertung des Todes durch Ben Sira*, in J. Zmijewski (Hg.), *Die alttestamentliche Botschaft als Wegweisung*, FS H. Reinelt, Stuttgart, 1990, pp. 203-236 (pp. 223f.).

Wenn man sich an der obigen Untersuchung orientiert, erscheint es einsichtig, daß der sehr sensibel differenzierende Autor verschiedene Phasen mitteilen will: jetzt geht es nicht um die Voraussetzung der materiellen Schöpfung – Menschenschöpfung als Zentrum der Schöpfungstat wurde schon herausgestellt – sondern um deren Ausstattung. Diese geschieht ganz am Anfang, noch vor, spätestens bei der Geburt: ab dieser treten die Wirkungen voll in Kraft. – In den Augen der Übersetzer (ἔκτισται und ܪܒ) fallen diese beiden Ebenen zusammen.

(4) Beispielhaft werden als erste Lasten das Dahinsinnieren und die innere Verunsicherung (τοὺς διαλογισμοὺς αὐτῶν καὶ φόβον καρδίας und ܒ ܐܘܒ ܐ ܘܐܪ ܐܘ (40,2 [der Vers ist in H nicht erhalten]) angeführt: man kommt nie zur Ruhe. Man erinnert sich an das Gilgameschepos[49], wo sich der Held auf den Weg macht, um die Pflanze gegen die innere Unruhe zu finden. Dieses Kraut, das Kraut des Lebens findet der Heros zwar, doch raubt ihm dieses wiederum eine Schlange. Daraufhin erklärt ihm die Göttin Schenkin: »Gilgamesch, wo läufst du hin? Das Leben, das du suchst, wirst du nicht finden! Als die Götter die Menschheit erschufen, teilten den Tod sie der Menschheit zu, nahmen das Leben für sich in die Hand«[50].

Hier trifft man also auch bei Sira auf das quer durch alle Kulturen und Zeiten zentrale Problem: Wie kann man das Leben gewinnen und vor allem so sichern, daß es nicht mehr gefährdet ist? Nicht umsonst wird als letzte und wohl auch größte Bedrohung in 9b der Tod (מות) genannt[51]. Daneben werden von 5-9 verschiedene Schrecknisse (Eifersucht, Sorge, Furcht, Todesangst, Zank, Streit, Alpträume, Pest, Blutvergießen, Glut, Dürre, Verderben, Hunger, Böses) aufgeführt.

In V. 10 wird nun begründet, welchen Sinn diese bedrohlichen Erscheinungen haben. Sie sind für die Bösen geschaffen: על רשע נבראה רעה (vgl. ἐπὶ τοὺς ἀνόμους ἐκτίσθη ταῦτα πάντα). Es handelt sich also um einen Schöpfungsakt, welcher sich auf eine negativ qualifizierte Gruppe von Menschen richtet. Im Kontext geht es aber nicht um Konstituentia des Menschseins, sondern um eine Reihe von Sanktionsmitteln, um die Bösen zur Ordnung zu rufen. Geschaffen werden durch-

---

49. Hier wie in 6.2.(3) verstehe ich die Parallelität zu mythischen Texten nicht als eine direkte Aufnahme desselben. Vielmehr zeigt es sich, daß Mythen für die Sinnfindung zentrale Themen so darstellten, daß die dort vertretene Position Kultur prägend wurde und auch dort erhalten ist, wo man möglicherweise die einschlägigen Mythen überhaupt nicht mehr kannte.

50. A. HECKER, Das Gilgamesch-Epos. Meissner-Millard-Tafel Kol. III, 1-14 (TUAT, III/4), Gütersloh, 1994, pp. 665f.

51. Γ hat diese Pointe nicht recht verstanden und beginnt V. 9, anstelle daß er damit endet, mit: θάνατος καὶ αἷμα. Aber auch am Kolonende würde αἷμα die Spitze verändern.

wegs immaterielle Gegebenheiten, die das Leben entscheidend erschweren und z.T. unmöglich machen können.

(5) Zum Schluß ist noch auf die zeitlichen Perspektiven der Schöpfung hinzuweisen. Alles von der Erde Stammende kehrt zu ihr[52] und das aus der Höhe Stammende dorthin zurück. Hier spricht Sira auf den ersten Blick leicht verständlich und doch zugleich verhüllend. Was kehrt wohin zurück? Die verdunkelnde Formulierung drängt den Leser dazu, weiterzufragen und innerhalb der Schöpfungsebenen Differenzierungen vorzunehmen[53]. Das materiell Geschaffene bleibt innerhalb dieser Dimension. Was zur immateriellen Schöpfung zählt, hat auch nach der innerweltlichen Funktion dort ihren Platz. – Nur, was gehört zu dieser Ebene? Sicher scheint, daß *hier* der Bereich (מרום) Gottes[54] der geschaffenen Welt gegenüber steht. Weiters zählt für Sira z.b. die Weisheit nicht einfachhin zur irdenen (מארץ) Schöpfung, ja das gilt auch für Ausstattungselemente, wie עסק und was sonst noch in dieser Perikope angeführt wurde. Wo sind z.B. Leben einerseits (vgl. in 11,14a unter den immateriellen Gegebenheiten, in 15,15d ein Ziel des Gotteswillens) und Tod (in 11,14a unter den immateriellen Gegebenheiten, in 40,10 ein Ausstattungselement) einzureihen, die auch nicht zum Irdenen gerechnet werden können? – Von dieser Stelle ausgehend kann man keine Rückschlüsse über Endlichkeit oder Unendlichkeit ziehen, sondern nur die Zuordnungen vornehmen.

6.2. *Sir 7,15b*

(1) Der Teil 7,1-17 besteht aus Ratschlägen (z.T. in Verbotsform) für die Zuhörer bzw. Schüler über Bereiche, von denen man sich klugerweise fernhalten soll. Innerhalb dieser Anleitungen wird festgehalten, daß man sich nicht der Mühe der Arbeit entziehen darf. Als Begründung wird angeführt:

7,15b.a אל תאיץ בצבא מלאכת עבדה   הי כאל נחלקה

---

52. Vgl. den Hinweis auf den Mythos der Mutter Erde bei F.V. REITERER, *Das Verhältnis Ijobs und Ben Siras*, in W.A.M. BEUKEN (Hg.), *The Book of Job* (BETL, 114), Löwen, 1994, pp. 405-429 (pp. 423f.).

53. R.A. ARGALL, *Reflections on 1 Enoch and Sirach: A Comparative Literary and Conceptual Analysis of the Themes of Revelation, Creation and Judgement*, in *SBLSP* 34 (1995) 337-351 (p. 345), unterscheidet in Sira analog 1 Henoch zwischen einer »upper« und einer »lower world«.

54. Daß man mit מרום den Bereich Gottes meint, die Höhe (Mi 6,6) in der Gott – im Gegensatz zu den Menschen – auch wohnt (Jes 33,5; 57,15), ist vielfach belegt; vgl. Ps 10,5; 71,19; 92,9; Jes 40,26; Jer 17,12; 51,53; Ez 20,40. Allerdings wird nicht überall מרום im gleichen Sinn gebraucht. Man liest z.B. davon, daß – Himmel und Erde wie bei Sira in Opposition – Gott gegenüber nicht unendlich sind: »Die Erde (הָאָרֶץ) welkt, sie verwelkt, die Welt (תֵּבֵל) zerfällt, sie verwelkt, die Höhe (מָרוֹם) und Erde (הָאָרֶץ) zerfallen« (Jes 24,4).

Da die textlichen Probleme gravierend sind[55], kann man jene Autoren verstehen, die sich gleich Γ zuwenden, zumal Syr auch nicht gegeben ist. Soviel sei aufgenommen[56]: Die Arbeit wird als Mühsal gesehen, was sie aber nicht abwertet. Die Begründung liegt wohl darin, daß sie Gott zugeteilt hat (נחלקה).

(2) Der Grieche rechnet offensichtlich mit der inneren Ablehnung der anstrengenden Ackerarbeit; inzwischen wurde nämlich die allgemeine עבדה konkretisiert: μὴ μισήσῃς ἐπίπονον ἐργασίαν καὶ γεωργίαν ὑπὸ ὑψίστου ἐκτισμένην. Allerdings verschärft er die Problematik, da er sie auf einen Schöpfungsakt zurückführt. So wird, das geht aus der Begründung hervor, nicht nur die Ackerarbeit an sich, sondern auch der Schöpfer dieser negiert.

(3) Peters geht an der Absicht des Texte vorbei, wenn er erstens davon ausgeht, daß, weil »der Ackerbau … in der ganzen antiken Welt als die ehrenhafteste Arbeit beurteilt« wurde, sich die »Spitze gegen den Handelsgeist der Juden«[57] richten soll. »Die Hochschätzung der körperlichen Arbeit«[58] läßt sich bei Sira gut belegen. Man kann allerdings nicht behaupten, daß sie immer als besonders faszinierend dargestellt wird. Die Sprecherin im Hohen Lied sieht nämlich darin das Ideal, eben nicht auf dem Feld arbeiten zu müssen; obwohl sie dazu gezwungen ist und das auch an ihrem Teint erkennbar ist, hält sie sich trotzdem für schön und anziehend (vgl. Hld 1,5). Aber es geht hier überhaupt nicht vordringlich um die Arbeit, sondern um deren Einordnung in das Schöpfungsganze[59].

Wiederum wird man an frühe altorientalische Vorstellungen erinnert, nach denen die Menschen *dazu geschaffen* wurden, um die Götter zu entlasten. Diese haben an deren Stelle den Tragkorb zu schleppen: »Eure schwere Mühsal habe ich (damit) abgeschafft; euren Tragkorb legte ich dem Menschen auf«[60]. – Bei Sira spürt man nichts von den fa-

---

55. P.C. BEENTJES, *The Book of Ben Sira in Hebrew. A Text Edition of All Extant Hebrew Manuscripts and a Synopsis of All Parallel Hebrew Ben Sira Texts* (SVT, 68), Leiden, 1997, p. 30, ordnet den Stichos zwischen 7,8 und 7,10 ein.

56. Vgl. F.V. REITERER, *Die Stellung Ben Siras zur »Arbeit«. Notizen zu einem kaum berücksichtigten Thema sirazidischer Lehre*, in Ders., *Ein Gott – eine Offenbarung*, FS N. Füglister, Würzburg, 1991, pp. 257-289 (pp. 282f.).

57. PETERS, *Buch*, p. 68.

58. REITERER, *Stellung*, p. 277.

59. Nach L.G. PERDUE, *»I Covered the Earth Like a Mist«. Cosmos and History in Ben Sira*, in Ders., *Wisdom and Creation. The Theology of Wisdom Literature*, Nashville, 1994, pp. 243-290, dient diese Stelle neben 5,14 dazu, »to point to providence as the continuation of originating acts of creation« (ebd., pp. 255f); unter dem Aspekt der Vorsehung sieht er auch die ganze Geschichte Israels (ebd., pp. 284f); vgl. S. GAON, *Creation in Ben Sira*, in *Milltown Studies* 36 (1995) 75-85, p. 83.

60. Entnommen aus W. VON SODEN, *Die erste Tafel des altbabylonischen Atramḫasīs-*

talistischen Aspekten des Mythos, doch scheint er sich trotz all der positiven Konnotationen mit der Arbeit den altorientalischen Denkkategorien nicht zu entziehen.

6.3. Sir 44,2

Der folgende Beleg dient als Zeugnis dafür, daß Ben Sira eine Vorliebe für Termini aus dem Schöpfungskontext hatte. Er verwendet sie auch dann, wenn er Vorgänge, die schöpfungsähnlich verstanden werden können, meint. In der Wortwahl (חלק) zeigt er an, daß er eine abgeschwächte, vielleicht analoge Form des Schöpfungsaktes zur Sprache bringen will. Der Syrer hat das richtig erkannt und nimmt ein Verb, das nur noch für *Handeln* gebraucht wird:

ונדלה מי		רב כבוד חלק עליון	Ma 44,2b.a
ונדלו מימות עולם		רב כבוד חלק עליון	B

ܪ̈ܒܠܐ ܕܐܝܬ ܠܗ ܘܗܝ ܕܐܗܘܘ ܡܢܗܘܢ   ܠܗܘܢ ܥܒܕ ܐܠܗܐ ܡܢ

πολλὴν δόξαν ἔκτισεν ὁ κύριος   τὴν μεγαλωσύνην αὐτοῦ ἀπ᾽ αἰῶνος.

Wenn es sich hier, wie gesagt, auch nicht um die Schöpfung im eigentlichen Sinne handelt, wird doch die Aktivität Gottes scharf herausgekehrt. Die Herrlichkeit der Vorväter, auf die die Israeliten mit Stolz blicken, war nicht deren Eigenleistung, sondern wurde durch Gott verliehen und war von ihm selbst initiiert worden.

7. ZUSAMMENFASSUNG

Wenn man von Schöpfung bei Ben Sira spricht, muß man sich in Acht nehmen, daß es nicht zu unzulässigen Verallgemeinerungen kommt. Der weisheitliche Autor differenziert wie auch sonst in dieser Frage besonders feinsinnig. Daher wird man versuchen, behutsam die Mehrdimensionalität der Schöpfung darzustellen.

7.1. Da es auf dem beschränkten Raum einfach nicht möglich ist, die Fülle des Materials intensiv zu untersuchen, seien wichtige Aspekte in summarischer Form zusammengetragen.

Mythus. 'Haupttext' und Parallelversionen, in ZA 68 (1978) 50-94; vgl. Tafel VI,26: »Aus seinem Blute mischte (?) er die Menschen, Legte ihnen auf die Dienste der Götter, die Götter ließ er frei. Als die Menschen geschaffen waren, rettete (?) *Ea* (die Götter). Den Dienst der Götter legten sie ihm auf«, in H. SCHÄFER, *Babylonisch-Assyrische Texte. Das babylonische Weltschöpfungslied »Als droben«*, in H. GRESSMANN (Hg.), *Altorientalische Texte zum alten Testament*, Berlin – Leipzig ²1970 [= ²1926], pp. 108-129); G. PETTINATO, *»Enki und Ninmah«-Mythos*, pp. 6-38, in *Das altorientalische Menschenbild und die sumerischen und akkadischen Schöpfungsmythen*, Heidelberg, 1971, pp. 69-73; DERS., *Nr. 2: KAR 4-Mythos*, in *Das altorientalische Menschenbild und die sumerischen und die akkadischen Schöpfungsmythen*, Heidelberg, 1971, pp. 74-81.

(1) Sira setzt, wie an einigen Stellen aufgrund der antithetischen Beispiele belegbar ist, einen entschiedenen Monotheismus voraus. Es findet
sich – eine rhetorische Anspielung ausgenommen (18,2b) – keine Abhe-
bung gegenüber polytheistischen Glaubensformen, auch spielt ein etwai-
ger Einfluß des Glaubens an viele Götter keine argumentative Rolle;
dies ist wohl auch deswegen verwunderlich, weil zu Siras Zeit – Übergang von der ptolemäischen zur seleukidischen Regierung – diese Fragen ein Politikum darstellten. – Für Sira ist diese Position dermaßen
klar, daß es auch zu keinen indirekten Anspielungen kommt, daß durch
die Schöpfertätigkeit der Einfluß, die Anerkennung oder gar die Existenz Gottes erst abgesichert werden muß, wie dies z.B. bei den Argu-
mentationen von Dt.-Jes der Fall war.

Daher fällt die Antwort darauf, wer der Schöpfer ist, auch sehr klar aus:
Es ist demnach durchwegs JHWH anzunehmen (בורא in 3,16b; 39,29b;
עושה in 7,30a; 10,12b; 35(32),13a; 36(33),13c; 38,15a; 43,5a.11a;
46,13a; 47,8c; יוצר 51,12(4a); ὁ κτίστης 24,8). Sira vermeidet die Nen-
nung des klassischen Namens und umschreibt ihn mittels ייי (11,4.
12.14.15[2mal].17; 36,8.11; 42,16b.17; 43,2b.5; 46,3.6.13.17.19.20;
47,11; 50,22; 51,12) bzw. אל (38,4; 42,15a); אלהים (15,14); עליון (43,2
Ma; 44,2a); vgl. צור (4,6b). In der griechischen Version dominiert
κύριος (z.B. 1,8f; vgl. aber auch ὕψιστος in 7,15b).

An vielen Stellen wird durch die passive Umschreibung (passivum
divinum) indirekt auf Gott Bezug genommen, dies gilt für ברא N in
39,28a(Γ).29b.30c; 40,10a und 48,13b; יצר N in 11,16a, 34(31),27d;
36(33),10b; 37,3a; 39,28a; 40,15a; 46,1c; 49,7b.14a; חלק N in 7,15b;
15,9b; 34(31),27f; von עשה gibt es keinen N-Beleg.

Auch die Verbverwendung im Rahmen der Schöpfungsaussagen ist
notierenswert: Es fällt auf, daß bei finiten Verbformen (act. wie pass.;
nie der Imp.) fast durchwegs die Grundform in der SK gewählt wurde:
ברא (von 10 Belegen 6 Vorkommen im N-Stamm); יצר (9 Belege; nur
pass.); חלק (von 7 Belegen 3 Vorkommen im N-Stamm); עשה (3 Belege; nur act.), in 50,22d steht der Narr (ויעשהו) parallel zum H-Ptz von
גדל (22c). Die einzige sichere PK steht in 43,26b: יפעל. – Dieser Über-
hang perfektivischer bzw. perfektischer Aspekte unterstützt die Argumentation, daß für Sira JHWH der einzige und alleinige Souverän der
Schöpfung ist. Gottes Sonderstellung ist ein Faktum, das zwar bis zur
Gegenwart weiterwirkt, aber im Prinzip schon abgeschlossen ist, d.h.
nicht mehr dergestalt in Frage steht, daß jemand die göttliche Position
anzweifelt oder gar bedroht. – Die Wirksamkeit für die Gegenwart wird
besonders durch den häufigen Gebrauch des Ptz, vor allem von עשה,
deutlich.

Auf die Frage, auf welchem Weg die Schöpfung vollzogen wird, kann man mit 42,15c antworten, daß sie באמר אדני (durch das Wort des Herrn) realisiert wird.

(2) Nicht an allen Stellen sind die Objekte des Schöpfungsaktes zu präzisieren. In 50,22 wird allgemein von »Wunderbarem« gesprochen, das Gott »nach seinem Willen (כרצונו)« geschaffen hat. Noch unbestimmter ist das Ergebnis des (göttlichen) Willens in 43,26, wo nur die Schöpfertätigkeit festgehalten wird.

Auch der Verweis auf die Schöpfung als ganzes bleibt im Allgemeinen: 18,1a; 23,20a; 24,8 (τὰ πάντα); 39,21b (vgl. H: הכל; aber kein Verb für schaffen); 43,33a; הכל 51,12(4a).

Daß es sich um realistische Erscheinungen handelt, bringt der immer noch allgemeine Verweis auf das Werk (11,4e), die Schöpfungswerke (11,16; 16,26; 17,8; 18,4a; 42,15a.c.16b; 43,2b) oder alle Schöpfungswerke (1,9c; 36[33],15a (כל מעשה); 39,14d.16a.33a; 42,22a.24; 43,25) zur Sprache.

(3) Das wichtigste Konkretum, das Sira nennt, ist der Mensch. Daß Gott אדם geschaffen hat, steht in 15,14a; 36(33),10b.13c; 50,22c.d; ἄνθρωπος 17,1.3. – Aus dem Kontext, im Regelfall durch ein ePP angezeigt, sind es Menschen, die besonderes Anliegen Siras sind. So ist es in 4,6b der sozial Bedürftige[61]; in 7,30a der die Priester Ehrende; in 48,13b (נברא N!)[62] ein ehemals Toter.

Besonders ist darauf hinzuweisen, daß auch Personen mit negativen Verhaltensweisen in diese Kategorie fallen: in 3,16b ist es jener, der Gott ärgert; in 10,12b der protzend Hochmütige; in 35(32),13a der (in Verärgerung oder betrunken) ein Gastmahl Verlassende; in 38,15a der Arztkritiker/ -besucher.

Etwas präziser sind die folgenden Angaben: Gott schafft nach 38,1.12a (Γ) den Arzt, nach 39,5b (ποιεῖν) den Weisen. Antithetisch dazu kann der böse Mensch (רָע) in 37,3a genannt werden.

Andere Stellen listen aus der Geschichte bekannte und bedeutende Einzelpersönlichkeiten auf: angeführt wird in 46,1c Josua; in 46,13a Samuel; in 49,7b Jeremia als Prophet; in 49,14a Henoch; indirekt (ePP) in 47,8c David, der seinen Schöpfer preist. Unter diesen ist kein Negativbeispiel anzutreffen.

(4) Menschliche Körperorgane als Ergebnis der Schöpfung sind zu nennen: Mund, Zunge, Augen, Ohren und das Herz (17,6); Auge 34(31),13c.

(5) Es gibt keine allgemeine Notiz wie z.B in Gen 2, daß neben dem Menschen auch Tiere von Gott geschaffen werden. Die Erwähnungen

---

61. Vgl. so auch in Spr den Armen (14,31; 17,5) bzw. Reiche und Arme (22,2).
62. Vgl. 2Kön 13,21.

sind vielmehr in den Kontext eingebunden und als Beispiele zu verstehen. Für die Größe Gottes spricht nach 43,25, daß er Meeresgeschöpfe
und mächtige Wasserlebewesen geschaffen hat. In relativem Gegensatz
dazu ist auf 39,30a zu verweisen, wo reißende Tiere, Skorpione, Ottern
als Plagen für die Menschen genannt werden.

(6) Gegebenheiten aus der unbelebten Natur als Ergebnis der Schöpfung sind in 43,2a die Sonne; in 43,14 der Speicher (ברא) für Blitz und
Donner; in 39,28a Stürme.

Als Leben erhaltende Gegebenheit ist der Wein in 34(31),27d zu er-
wähnen. In 38,4 werden Heilmittel (nach Bm »wohlriechende Heilmittel« mit ברא als Objekt regierendem Verb) erwähnt.

Weiters werden lebensbedrohende Gegebenheiten angeführt. Nach
39,29 zählen Feuer, Hagel, Hunger und Pest dazu; in 39,30b ist es das
Racheschwert.

7.2 Neben den eben genannten Realitäten spricht Sira von der Erschaffung von nicht sicht-, hör- oder greifbaren Ebenen, die aber sehr
wohl erfahrbar sind, ja noch mehr: *ohne diese gibt es keine* Schöpfung,
zumindest trifft dies für die belebte, insbesondere menschliche Existenz
zu: man denke an Leben und Tod.

(1) Innerhalb dieser immateriellen Ebenen spielt die Weisheit eine
besondere Rolle. Es ist nicht leicht, deren Rolle und Erscheinungsform
zu umschreiben: sie geht der materiellen Schöpfung voraus, kommt aber
nach dem Schöpfer. Sie strukturiert die Schöpfung, indem sie bei allen
weiteren Schöpfungsakten eine besondere Rolle durch ihre Anwesenheit
spielt, wobei sie in diesem Fall ähnlich präsent wie Gott selbst beschrieben wird. »Die Beschreibung der Präexistenzvorstellung der Weisheit ist
… ohne zeitliche Kategorien ausgekommen. Trotzdem ist es Sirach ge-
lungen, die präkosmische Existenz der Weisheit herauszustellen. Sie
wird durch eine durchgängige Bewegung zum Ausdruck gebracht: aus
dem Munde Gottes kommend, erfüllt sie alle transzendenten und imma-
nenten Bereiche, jeden Raum und jede Zeit«[63].

(2) Nahe an unser Ergebnis kommen die Ausführungen von Barbour.
»Wisdom … formed a bridge between a transcendent God and the world
of human affairs precisely because it could be conceived both as an
aspect of God's being and power and as a characteristic of men without
blurring the distinction between the two, and at the same time could be

---

63. SCHIMANOWSKI, *Weisheit*, p. 59. Die Thematik der Präexistenz kennzeichnet den
Autor (vgl. u.a. pp. 38, 58); da man mit dem Fachausdruck aber – wenn auch unbestimm-
te – Zeitkategorien unterlegt, fragt es sich, ob die beste terminologische Wahl getroffen
worden ist.

personified in a manner which gave it living reality«[64]. – Man wird aber doch dahin verschärfen müssen, daß die Brückenfunktion zu wenig entsprechend ist. Denn die Weisheit setzt die Weisheit des Einen, des einen Weisen *präsent*. So wird klar, daß diese *Weisheit eine für die Schöpfung konzentrierte Präsenzform Gottes* ist. Die Berührung mit der menschlichen Ebene ist nicht konstitutiv, sondern eine Adaption in der und an die materielle Schöpfung: Gott ist mehr als die Weisheit, die Weisheit übersteigt die gewöhnliche Schöpfung, deren innere Strukturierung aber von jener ausgeht. – Die Weisheit wird zu Recht mit Tätigkeiten verbunden, die in der unbelebten Natur nicht vorkommen. Allerdings bleibt die Qualifizierung als Personifikation nur ein Annäherungswert und ist immer unzureichend.

(3) Innerhalb der immateriellen Ebenen werden ohne Scheu auch die negativen Potenzen der Schöpfung angeführt, wie z.B. das Übel, das Böse. Das bedeutet offensichtlich nicht, daß hier auch die konkrete böse Tat inkludiert ist. Diese Ebenen sind vor allem auf den menschlichen Bereich hingeordnet. Sie stellen eine Herausforderung durch Gott dar: mit Hilfe des freien Willens kann der Mensch den Plan Gottes realisieren und sich dem Guten gegen das Böse zuwenden.

(4) Auch im Gefolge der materiellen Schöpfungsgegebenheiten setzt Gott *Realitäten*, die die Schöpfung *begleiten*: so z.B. die Mühsal, die Ehrenstellung usw. Hier handelt es sich nicht um eine Schöpfung im gleichen Sinne wie zuvor dargestellt. Zum Ausdruck kommt, daß Gott und nicht der Mensch der Souverän über die Schöpfung ist und bleibt.

7.3. Die das Denken strukturierende Funktion der Schöpfung

Wenn man sich intensiv mit dem Buch Ben Sira beschäftigt, sieht man nicht nur, daß Hinweise auf den Schöpfer das ganze Buch durchziehen. »The doctrine of creation is developed as an intricate part of Sirach's message. It can be said that Sirach has a distinct doctrine of creation running throughout his whole text ... The whole of Sirach's text is a well planned symphony, every note, every movement is part of the whole. There are subleties and allusions throughout which must be seen as notes which give fullness and harmony to his message«[65]. Diesem Ergebnis kann man aufgrund folgender Beobachtungen grundsätzlich zustimmen. Es ist sogar eine weitere Präsizierung möglich: das Verständnis der Schöpfung steuert das Denken Ben Siras und beeinflußt seine Darstellungsweise.

---

64. R.S. BARBOUR, *Creation, Wisdom and Christ*, in R.W.A. MCKINNEY (Hg.), *Creation, Christ and Culture*, FS T.F. Torrance, Edinburgh, 1976, pp. 22-42 (p. 36); vgl. auch die interessanten christologischen Konnotationen ebd., p. 34, wobei besonders die Notizen zu Christ as *arche* of creation im Blick auf 3.2 (4) von großem Interesse sind.

65. BURTON, *Sirach*, pp. 219.222.

(1) Es fällt auf, daß Sira bei wichtigen Themen Dreiergruppen wählt, seien das drei auf der gleichen Ebene befindliche Gegebenheiten, seien das drei Kola, seien dies Strophen, die in einem Gedicht aufeinander hingeordnet sind.

(2) Dieser Dreierschritt scheint von seiner Sicht der Schöpfung beeinflußt zu sein: Gott – immaterielle und materielle Ebenen.

(3) Wenn in einer Zusammenfassung auch nur Schlagworte stehen, so sei doch darauf hingewiesen, daß man diesen Dreier-Rhythmus im ganzen Buch verfolgen kann: die Beschäftigung mit der Weisheit als Schöpfungsgegebenheit findet sich nur zwischen den Kap. 1–24.

Im zweiten Buchteil (Kap. 25–43) trifft man auf konkrete Lebensfragen. Das Thema Schöpfung scheint zurückzutreten: Mitnichten! Der längste Text über die unbelebten Schöpfungsgegebenheiten steht in 42,15–43,33[66].

Im dritten Buchabschnitt folgt die *Personwerdung* der in der Schöpfung grundgelegten, auf den Menschen (15,14-20; 16,24–17,10) hingeordneten Ansätze, insbesondere die Weisheit des Schöpfungshandelns, paradigmatisch dargestellt in der Geschichte Israels. Es fällt auf, daß in den Kapiteln 1–43 im Rahmen der vielfältigen Notizen zur Schöpfung nur einmal ein konkreter Name genannt wird: ab Kapitel 44 ist das anders. In den großen Ahnen Israels wird jetzt greifbar, was schon in 24,8 gesagt war: »Da gab der Schöpfer des Alls mir Befehl; er, der mich schuf, wußte für mein Zelt eine Ruhestätte. Er sprach: In Jakob sollst du wohnen, in Israel sollst du deinen Erbbesitz haben«.
Es gibt demnach folgende Phasen der Schöpfung, die sich an der Weisheit darstellen lassen:

  (a) Der nachgöttliche und vormaterielle Abschnitt,
      in dem die immateriellen Fakten anzusiedeln sind.
  (b) Die materielle Phase der Schöpfung,
      die sich wiederum unterteilen läßt in die natürlichen wie auch kosmischen und die allgemeinen weisheitlichen Gegebenheiten. Im letzteren Bereich sind als erstes die bei der Schöpfung von Gott mitgeteilte Ausstattung, als zweites die Ergebnisse des Wirkens und des Verhaltens aufgrund der Weisheit zu nennen.
  (c) Zum Schluß folgt noch die personalisierte Phase.
      Hier geht es um konkrete, historische Personen, die in ihrem Leben und ihrem Verhalten zu Repräsentanten der Weisheit werden.

---

66. Es ist interessant, daß man aufgrund der Untersuchung dieser Stelle – vor allem unter dem Gesichtspunkt der Herrlichkeit – und im Blick auf das ganze Buch zur Überzeugung kommt, daß Sira die priesterliche Theologie, obwohl er kein Priester war, beschreibt, aber weil er Philosoph ist, sie neben seine Weisheitstheologie stellt, die Schöpfung aber höchstens eine untergeordnete Rolle spielt: so W. ROTH, *The Lord's Glory Fills Creation. A Study of Sirach's Praise of God's Words (42:15–50:24)*, in *Explor* 6 (1981) 85-95, pp. 93f.

(4) Wie immer wieder zu beobachten, waren *drei* Ebenen anzuführen. Ich halte diese Periodisierung in Dreierschritten im Buch Ben Sira nicht für einen Ausfluß eines stilistischen Systems. Vielmehr argumentiert Sira auf die ihm eigene Weise, weil er grundsätzlich in Kategorien der Schöpfung denkt und natürlich auch in die Schöpfung nachempfindenden Dreierschritten formuliert.

Universitätsplatz 1   Friedrich Vinzenz REITERER
A-5020 Salzburg

GUT UND BÖSE

ANTITHETISCHES DENKEN IM NEUEN TESTAMENT UND BEI JESUS SIRACH

I

Die urchristlichen Schriftsteller kennen das Gegensatzpaar »Gut und Böse« unter verschiedenen semantischen Oppositionen:

ἀγαθός und πονηρός[1],
ἀγαθός und κακός[2],
καλός und πονηρός[3],
καλός und κακός[4].

Das Gute und das Böse als ethische Orientierungs- und Zielangaben für das Leben der Christen sind in den synoptischen Evangelien und in der Briefliteratur selbstverständliche Grössen. Sie werden weder hergeleitet noch diskutiert, sondern vorausgesetzt und theologisch angewendet. Das Q-Gleichnis Mt 12,33-35 setzt die metaphorisch gewählten Qualitätsbegriffe von guten und verfaulten Früchten in ethische Begriffe um: ἀγαθὰ καὶ πονηρά (12,34f.). Paulus formuliert im 1. Thessalonicherbrief τὸ ἀγαθόν[5] klar als Zielgrösse[6] und warnt zugleich vor dem πονηρόν (5,15.21f). In Röm 12, 9-21 ist die usuelle Paränese[7] von Hinweisen auf die Gut-Böse-Thematik durchzogen:

> 9   *Die Liebe (sei) ungeheuchelt. Verabscheut das Böse, schliesst euch dem Guten an.*
> 17 *Gebt niemandem Böses für Böses zurück, seid auf Gutes allen Menschen gegenüber bedacht.*
> 21 *Lass dich nicht vom Bösen besiegen, sondern besiege das Böse mit dem Guten[8].*

---

1. 15 relevante Belege: Mt 5,45; 7,11.17.18; 12,34.35 (3 mal); 20,15;22,10; Lk 6,45 (3 mal); 11,13; Röm 12,9.
2. 19 relevante Belege: Mk 3,4; Lk 6,9; 16,25; Röm 3,8; 7,19; 12,21; 13,3 (2 mal).4; 16,19; 1Thess 5,15; 1Petr 2,14.15; 3,10.11.13.17; 3Joh 11 (2 mal).
3. 6 relevante Belege: Mt 7,17.18.19; 13,38: 1Thess 5,21; Jak 4,17.
4. 8 relevante Belege: Röm 7,18.21; 12,17; 14,21; 2Kor 13,7; 2Thess 3,13; Hebr 5,14; 1Petr 2,12.
5. T. HOLTZ, *Der erste Brief an die Thessalonicher* (EKK, XIII), Zürich–Einsiedeln–Köln. 1986, p. 256, weist auf die Weite des Begriffs τὸ ἀγαθόν hin.
6. Zielgrösse: διώκειν; cf. HOLTZ, *1. Thessalonicher* (n. 5), pp. 255f.
7. Vgl. dazu W. POPKES, *Paränese und Neues Testament* (SBS, 168), Stuttgart, 1996, esp. pp. 13-52.
8. Die stark theologisch interpretierende Auslegung des Guten bei U. WILCKENS, *Der Brief an die Römer* (EKK, VI/3), Zürich–Einsiedeln–Köln, 1982, pp. 17f. (Liebe als Kriterium des Guten) wird der Weite und Allgemeinheit der Begriffe nicht ganz gerecht.

Eine bedeutende Rolle spielt die Gut-Böse-Thematik in Röm 13,1-7. Das Gemeinwesen ist auf die ethischen Richtgrössen Gut und Böse verpflichtet. Daher darf es das Gute fordern und das Böse strafen (13,4). Der römische Staat kommt also von seiner juridischen Funktion her in den Blick, die Paulus zugleich in ihren religiösen und ethischen Dimensionen darlegt[9]. Die christlichen Gemeinden sollen sich an derselben Struktur wie das römische Reich orientieren: »weise zum Guten, unzugänglich für das Böse« (Röm 15,19). Dasselbe gilt für die Gemeinde des 1. Petrusbriefes, die ganz allgemein auf das Gute und gegen das Böse verpflichtet wird (3,11.13). Wieder ist das Gute eine Zielangabe wie 1Thess 5,15 (1Petr 3,13: ζηλωταὶ τοῦ ἀγαθοῦ). Schliesslich heisst es lapidar im 3. Johannesbrief 11: μὴ μιμοῦ τὸ κακὸν ἀλλὰ τὸ ἀγαθόν. Die latente Struktur des Guten und Bösen wird in der Welt manifest: in den ἔργα oder metaphorisch καρποί des Guten und des Bösen. Von den Äusserungen, ja den Produkten der beiden Grössen kann auf diese selbst zurückgeschlossen werden. Die Warnung vor den falschen Propheten und Aposteln in Mt 7,15-23[10] fasst diese Erfahrung in das Gleichnis von den guten und schlechten Früchten, an denen man die Qualität der jeweiligen Bäume erkennen kann[11].

Eine eher ethische Metaphorik liegt in dem Ausdruck »gute/böse Werke« vor (Röm 13,3; 1Petr 2,12), in Mt 12,35 par. ist sie psychologisch vertieft (ἀγαθὸς/πονηρὸς θησαυρός des Herzens). In den Früchten bzw. in den Werken des Menschen kommt das Tun der Menschen zum Ausdruck. Auf das ποιεῖν bzw. πράσσειν hin werden die Menschen verpflichtet, ja abgefragt: so dramatisch in Mk 3,1-6par. Gutes bzw. Böses tun ist hier mit Leben retten (σῶσαι) bzw. Töten verbunden. Auch 2Kor 13,7; Röm 3,8; 13,3.4; 1Petr 3,11; Jak 4,17 verstehen verantwortliches Handeln in dieser Grundalternative.

Entsprechend dazu kennt das Neue Testament Täter des Guten und des Bösen: 2Thess 3,13; 1Petr 2,12.15; 3,17; 3Joh 11 (καλοποιοῦντες, κακοποιοῦντες, ἀγαθοποιοῦντες).

Die Täter des Guten und des Bösen können auch als gute oder böse Menschen (Mt 12,35) oder abgekürzt als die Guten und die Bösen bezeichnet werden. Mt 5,45 spricht in der sechsten Antithese ganz lapidar

9. Religiös: die ἐξουσία ist Gottes Dienerin. Ethisch: das Motiv der συνείδησις in v. 5. Dass der römische Staat hier von der Seite der Rechtsprechung und der Rechtsgarantie her in den Blick genommen wird, wie es für Provinzialrömer selbstverständlich war, ist in der Auslegung von Röm 13,1-7 nicht genügend berücksichtigt; vgl. nur WILCKENS, *Römer* (n. 8) 28-66, bes. zur Auslegungsgeschichte.

10. Vgl. U. LUZ, *Das Evangelium nach Matthäus* (EKK, I/1), Zürich–Einsiedeln–Köln, 1985, pp. 400-410.

11. Der Bezugsrahmen ist apokalyptisch-juridisch: v.19.

von Guten und Bösen, die Gott erhält. Dass hier nicht autonome ethische Sprache, sondern wieder die auf Gott bezogene Bedeutungsgebung leitend ist, zeigt die parallele Wendung »Gerechte und Ungerechte«[12]. Mt 13,38 formuliert auf dieser Grundlage im Rahmen eines Gleichnisses so etwas wie ein dualistisches Prinzip:

> *Der Acker aber ist die Welt (κόσμος), der gute Samen aber sind die Söhne des Reiches, das Unkraut aber sind die Söhne des Bösen[13].*

Der Rahmen ist deutlicher als in Mt 7 apokalyptisch-juridisch. Die »Guten« sind die Gerechten, die gerettet werden, die Bösen, die die Ungerechtigkeit tun (v. 41),dagegen die Verdammten. Ethisches Verhalten und endzeitliches Geschick sind in einer logisch schwer zu bestimmenden Weise in dem dualistischen Gefüge von Gut und Böse miteinander verbunden. Die Deutung des Gleichnisses (13,24-30) bleibt dem Gleichnis selbst insoweit verbunden, als die Deutung weder einen Kausalnexus noch einen durchgehaltenen Dualismus bietet. Der Menschensohn und der Teufel verursachen nicht die guten und bösen Taten der Menschen. Und weiter: Weder sind der Menschensohn und der Teufel einander gleichgeordnet, noch stehen den »Kindern des Reiches«, die Jesu Gottesreichbotschaft annehmen, die »Kinder des Teufels bzw. des Bösen« gegenüber, die das Reich ablehnen. Ebensowenig ist der Licht-Finsternis-Dualismus ausgeführt[14], d.h. das duale Prinzip von Gut und Böse im Kosmos beschränkt sich auf die Beschreibung des Geschickes des Gottesreiches in der Welt, ohne es dualistisch zu erklären.

Ähnlich steht es mit 3Joh 11:

> *Geliebter, ahme nicht das Böse nach, sondern das Gute. Wer Gutes tut, ist aus Gott. Wer Böses tut, hat Gott nicht gesehen.*

Auch hier verfestigt sich die duale, zur Abstraktion tendierende Wahrnehmung des Menschen, der Gutes und dessen, der Böses tut, nicht zu einer dualistischen Erklärung. Der Böses tut, ist nicht »aus dem Satan« zu erklären, sondern von Gott getrennt.

Die Strukturen von Gut und Böse sind erkennbar: zunächst als Nützliches bzw. als Schädliches (Röm 14,20f.). Im ersten Thessalonicherbrief spricht Paulus die Gemeinde auf ihr ethisches Urteilsvermögen an (5,22):

> *Alles aber prüft, das Gute behaltet, von jedem Schein des Bösen haltet euch fern.*

---

12. Vgl. auch Mt 7,11: ihr, die ihr böse seid (πονηροί!)
13. Dazu U. Luz, *Das Evangelium nach Matthäus* (EKK, II/1), Zürich–Einsiedeln–Köln, 1990, pp. 337f. Luz betont den universalen Aspekt, ohne auf die Frage eines möglichen Dualismus einzugehen.
14. Die Lichtmetaphorik klingt nur in v.45 an.

Derselbe Verweis begegnet am Schluss des Römerbriefs. Röm 16,19 appelliert Paulus in seiner Schlussparänese grundsätzlich an das Unterscheidungsvermögen der römischen Christen:

θέλω δὲ ὑμᾶς σοφοὺς εἶναι εἰς τὸ ἀγαθόν, ἀκεραίους δὲ εἰς τὸ κακόν.

Hebr 5,14 vertieft diesen Aspekt in einem kurzen interkommunikativen Abschnitt (5,11-6,3). Der Verfasser des Hebräerbriefes unterscheidet zwischen dem Anfangsunterricht für Christen und dem λόγος δικαιοσύνης, in dem die Vollkommenen gelehrt werden, τῶν διὰ τὴν ἕξιν τὰ αἰσθητήρια γεγυμνασμένα ἐχόντων πρὸς διάκρισιν καλοῦ τε καὶ κακοῦ (5,14). Hierbei ist mehr im Spiel als die Genesiszitation (Gen 2,17). Denn im Zusammenhang geht es um τελειότης (6,1) im Sinne jener höheren christlichen Belehrung, wie sie der Verfasser des Hebräerbriefes seiner Gemeinde zuteil werden lässt: um theologisch-christologische Erkenntnisfähigkeit im Sinne »kritischen« Verstehens des λόγος θεοῦ[15].

Der Hebräerbrief benutzt also die noetische Komponente des Begriffspaares – und zwar in dieser Deutlichkeit als einzige neutestamentliche Schrift[16]. Die diakritische Funktion der christlichen Belehrung bzw. des christlichen Verstehens der Vollkommenen (5,14) entspricht dem diakritischen Vermögen des λόγος θεοῦ in 4,12-13.

Die neutestamentlichen Schriftsteller verwenden das Begriffspaar »das Gute und das Böse« fast durchgehend im Sinne ethischer Grundorientierung, d.h. sie setzen es zum Handeln und Sich-Verhalten der Menschen in Beziehung. Weder ein rein qualitatives Verständnis noch eine kosmologische Strukturbildung im Zusammenhang mit dem Begriffspaar sind Themen der neutestamentlichen Schriftsteller. Das Verständnis der ethischen Größen ist überwiegend sehr konkret, d.h. folgen- bzw. erfolgsorientiert: Früchte, Werke, usw.

Den weiteren semantischen Bezugsrahmen bilden einerseits das dikanisch-forensisch-eschatologische Begriffspaar δικαιοσύνη und ἀδικία, andererseits die Steigerung des Guten, das Vollkommene, und die Beziehung des Guten zu Gott. Kaum im Blick ist eine explizite Herleitung des Guten aus Gott (3Joh 11). Die Theodizeefrage kommt im Zusammenhang mit dem Begriffspaar nicht zur Sprache. Damit ist das Begriffspaar in die Wirklichkeit und Wirksamkeit Gottes und Jesu Christi eingebunden.

---

15. Zu αἰσθητήρια τῆς καρδίας Jer 4,19 im Sinne des geistlichen Unterscheidungsvermögens vgl. O. MICHEL, *Der Brief an die Hebräer* (KEK, XIII), Göttingen, [12]1966, p. 237. Auf verwandten stoischen Sprachgebrauch weist E. GRÄSSER, *An die Hebräer* (EKK, XVII/1), Zürich–Einsiedeln–Köln, 1990, pp. 330f. hin.

16. Ähnlich GRÄSSER, *Hebräer* (n. 15) p. 331: »Hebr ist auf dem besten Wege, das theoretische und moralische Element in den theologischen Darlegungen zu entdecken und für seine Argumentation fruchtbar zu machen. Theologie wird zum Regulativ christlichen Lebens«. Dies ist eine ntl. Grenzposition.

Eine entscheidende Rolle in der neutestamentlichen Ethik, d.h. in der
Lebensführung der urchristlichen Gemeinden (περιπατεῖν, πολιτεύεσ-
θαι) und in der Belehrung über die Lebensführung (διδαχή, παράκλη-
σις, Paränese)[17] spielt das Gegensatzpaar nicht. Denn die Basis neutesta-
mentlicher ethischer Wirklichkeit und Belehrung bzw. Ermahnung ist
die nachösterliche Ermöglichung eines Lebens »in Christus« mit ihren
vielfältigen Aspekten. Und die Realisierung dieses Lebens erfolgt in den
Spielarten der ἀγάπη bzw. des ἀγαπᾶν. Das Leben in der Liebe aber
schliesst das Böse aus (1Kor 13,5; Röm 13,10). So kann die Liebe auch
lapidar als Tun des Guten und als Ablehnung des Bösen verstanden werden: ἡ ἀγάπη ἀνυπόκριτος ἀποστυργοῦντες τὸ πονηρόν, κολλώ-
μενοι τῷ ἀγαθῷ (Röm 12,9).

II

Im gesamten Alten Testament ist die Gut-Böse-Opposition fest veran-
kert[18]. Bedeutungsaspekte sind

1. gut und schlecht im geschmacklichen Qualitätssinn
2. heilbringend und unheilbringend
3. gut und böse im ethischen Sinn
4. gut und böse im noetisch-urteilenden Sinn.

Dtn 30, 15-30 und Am 5,14 verbinden Gutes und Böses mit Recht und
Ethos und stellen beide Grössen in den Rahmen von gewonnenem und
verlorenem Leben[19]. Gen 2 und 3 fassen die Gut-Böse-Erkenntnis sehr
allgemein, mindestens in Gen 3,5 enthält das Gegensatzpaar eine noetische Konnotation.

In den weisheitlichen Schriften finden sich die meisten Belege für den
Gut-Böse-Merismus in den Sprüchen, bei Kohälät und in Jesus Sirach.
Das Begriffspaar wird üblicherweise grundsätzlich ehtisch verstanden
(Spr 15,3 »Die Augen des Herrn…schauen auf Gutes und Böses«). Da-
bei ergibt sich eine Doppelstruktur von gut-gerecht-fromm-weise einer-
seits und böse-ungerecht-unfromm-töricht andererseits.

Wie stellt sich dem Siraziden diese Struktur dar? Zunächst kennt er
dieselben Bedeutungsbereiche von Gut und Böse wie die anderen
weisheitlichen Schriftsteller. Sirach kennt gute und schlechte Menschen

---

17. Vgl. dazu zuletzt POPKES, *Paränese* (n. 7), esp. pp. 13-52.

18. Vgl. H.-J. STOEBE, Art. טוב, in; THWAT t. I, München, 1971, cc. 652-664, esp.
cc. 658f.; I. HÖVER-JOHAG, Art טוב, TWAT t. III, Stuttgart u.a., 1977, cc. 315-339, esp. cc.
329-331.

19. Vgl. dazu U. LUCK, *Das Gute und das Böse in Römer 7*, in H. MERKLEIN (ed.)
Neues Testament und Ethik, FS R. Schnackenburg, Freiburg, Wien, 1989, pp. 220-237.

bzw. Gute und Schlechte, die als εὐσεβεῖς καὶ ἁμαρτολοί (39,27) bezeichnet werden. Aber diese Unterscheidung ist dem Siraziden nicht so wichtig wie jene andere zwischen Weisen und Tora- oder Gottesfürchtigen bzw. Frommen und Sündern.

Wichtiger ist bei Sirach die sehr grundsätzliche blosse Struktur des Guten und Bösen:

> ἀγαθὰ καὶ κακά, ζωὴ καὶ θάνατος... παρὰ κυρίου ἐστιν (11,14).
> ἐπιστήμην συνέσεως ἐνέπλησεν αὐτοὺς καὶ ἀγαθὰ καὶ κακὰ ὑπέδειξεν αὐτοῖς (17,7).

So fragt der Sirazide auch in 18,8:

> τί ἄνθρωπος, καὶ τί ἡ χρῆσις αὐτοῦ; τί τὸ ἀγαθὸν αὐτοῦ, καὶ τί τὸ κακὸν αὐτοῦ;

Der Weise erforscht

> ἀγαθὰ γὰρ καὶ κακὰ ἐν ἀνθρώποις (39,4).

Im Einzelnen differenziert und wertet der Weise zwischen guten und schlechten Frauen (26,1)[20], guten und schlechten Zeiten (11,25) und guten und schlechten Umständen (12,9). Über die Herkunft des Guten und Bösen lehrt Sirach einerseits:

> [Gott] ἀγαθὰ τοῖς ἀγαθοῖς ἔκτισται ἀπ᾽ ἀρχῆς, οὕτως τοῖς ἁμαρτωλοῖς κακά (39,25).

Und:

> *Für die Guten wendet sich alles zum Guten so für die Sünder zum Bösen (39,27).*

Auf der anderen Seite gilt auch:

> *Aus dem Herzen kommen ἀγαθὸν καὶ κακόν, ζωὴ καὶ θάνατος (37,18).*

Tiefer sieht er im Rahmen einer grossen Abhandlung über die Erschaffung des Menschen durch Gott (16,24–18,14):

> ἐπιστήμην συνέσεως ἐνέπλησεν αὐτοὺς καὶ ἀγαθὰ καὶ κακὰ ὑπέδειξει αὐτοῖς (17,7)[21].

Durch 17,11 wird deutlich, dass Sirach sich hier auf Gen 2 und 3 bezieht:

> προσέθηκεν αὐτοῖς ἐπιστήμην καὶ νόμον ζωῆς ἐκληροδότησεν αὐτοῖς.

Im Rahmen dieser Schöpfungsanthropologie legt Sirach zunächst grössten Wert auf die Darstellung der noetischen und kritischen Fähig-

---

20. Vgl. die Wertung zwischen Mann und Frau 42,14.
21. Vgl. zu diesem Abschnitt P.W. SKEHAN und A.A. DI LELLA, *The Wisdom of Ben Sira* (AB, 39), New York, 1987, pp. 276ff.

keiten des Menschen, weiterhin auf ihre ethische Kompetenz, d.h. auf angemessenes Verhalten gegenüber dem Gesetz (17,12-24).

Nun ist Sirach wieder nicht weiter an den Früchten des Guten und Bösen interessiert, wie es sich anbieten könnte, sondern sein eigenes Denken geht einen eher theoretischen Weg in 32,14–33,18. Dieser grosse Abschnitt über das Böse und die Schöpfung Gottes[22] arbeitet nicht nur mit den traditionellen Metaphern des Töpfers, der Wege, der Werke Gottes und der Zuordnung von Gutem/Leben und Bösem/Tod. Vielmehr versucht der Weise[23], ein Gesetz des göttlichen Schöpfungshandelns zu erkennen und zu formulieren.

33,14: ἀπέναντι τοῦ κακοῦ τὸ ἀγαθόν, καὶ ἀπέναντι τοῦ θανάτου ἡ ζωή, οὕτως ἀπέναντι εὐσεβοῦς ἁμαρτωλός[24]
15: καὶ οὕτως ἔμβλεψον εἰς πάντα τὰ ἔργα τοῦ ὑψίστου, δύο δύο, ἓν κατέναντι τοῦ ἑνός[25].

Den letzten Halbvers scheint der Sirazide für die höchste ihm zugängliche Erkenntnis über Gottes Schöpfungswerk zu halten. Er fasst sie in eine geschliffene Sentenz, die zugleich als Pointe wie als Ergebnis den Abschluss des Abschnitts über die Schöpfung Gottes darstellt. Dieselbe Einsicht formuliert Sirach ein zweites Mal im Zug der grossen Schöpfungsdarstellung am Ende des ersten Teils seines Werkes 42,15–43,33[26]: Gott schuf

πάντα δισσά[27], ἓν κατέναντι τοῦ ἑνός.

Sirachs Einsichten betreffen zwei Aspekte:

1. die Zweiheit der Schöpfungsstruktur (δύο δύο, δισσά)
2. die Gegenständigkeit/wechselseitige Bezogenheit der Schöpfungsstruktur (ἓν κατέναντι τοῦ ἑνός).

Sirach ist hier über die Einsichten und Formulierungsmöglichkeiten Kohäläts hinausgelangt. Koh 7,13 bleibt bei der Aussage stehen, Gott habe böse wie gute Tage gemacht. Aus dieser schöpfungsbezogenen Glaubensaussage formuliert er aber gerade kein Gesetz und verbindet seine Aussage auch nicht mit Erkenntnis. Im Gegenteil: Gott hat beide Tage geschaffen, »damit der Mensch *nicht wissen* soll, was künftig ist«

---

22. Vgl. SKEHAN – DI LELLA, *Ben Sira* (n. 22), pp. 393ff. Monographisch: G.L. PRATO, *Il Problema della teodicea in Ben Sira* (AnBib, 65), Rom, 1975, esp. pp. 13-61.

23. Sirach betont hier besonders seine weisheitliche Kompetenz und Begabung: 32,14f.; 33,16-18.

24. MS E fügt das Begriffspaar Licht und Finsternis hinzu.

25. LXX übersetzt den hebräischen Text wörtlich: כולם שנים שנים.

26. Vgl. SKEHAN, DI LELLA, *Ben Sira* (n. 22) pp. 484ff.

27. δισσά übersetzt zwei/doppelt: stilistisch besser als δύο δύο. Die Erwägungen in P. WINTER, *Ben Sira and the teaching of »Two ways«*, in *VT* 5 (1955) 315-318, p. 317, zu δισσά sind sprachlich nicht notwendig.

(7,14)[28]. Sirach dagegen *erkennt* das Grundgesetz der Schöpfung Gottes und wagt es, dies als abstraktes Zahlenverhältnis zu formulieren: Gott schafft nach einem *dualen Prinzip*. Damit steht Sirach an theologischer Erkenntnis sowohl über der blossen Beschreibung von Wirklichkeit, wie sie Kohälät leistet, als auch über der Zwei-Geister- bzw. Zwei-Wege-Lehre anderer frühjüdischer Schriften[29], der die als Ordnungsprozess verstandene Dualität der Schöpfung in einen mythologischen Dualismus verwandelt. Ausserdem bleibt die Dualität der göttlichen Schöpfungswerke bei Sirach in seine schöpfungstheologisch-hymnische Ästhetik einbezogen[30], ohne sich als gleichsam metaphysische Rede zu verselbständigen.

III

Der theologische Vorstoss Sirachs in die Erkenntnis der Struktur des göttlichen Schöpfungshandelns, wie er sie der dualen Anordnung von Schöpfungswerken entnehmen wollte, ist von den neutestamentlichen Schriftstellern nicht wiederholt worden. Bei ihnen bleibt »Gut und Böse« eine ethische Orientierungsbestimmung mit einer noetischen Komponente wie in den übrigen atl. Schriften. Allerdings verlor diese ethische Oppositionsbildung an ethisch-theologischer Bedeutung, da die ntl. Ethik eine Antwort auf die Realität des in Jesus Christus gekommenen Heils darstellt: das »Wandeln im Geist«. Gut und Böse wird in diesem Rahmen zu einer unter vielen möglichen Orientierungshilfen.

Einblicke in die Schöpfungsvorgänge werden im NT nur mit Hilfe von Vorformen einer Logos- bzw. Sophia-Christologie ermöglicht. Die Öffnung, die der Sirazide um 220 v.Chr. in Richtung auf eine Schöpfungstheologie hin vollzog, wurde von Philo gesehen und aufgenommen. Die neutestamentlichen Schriftsteller dagegen griffen diese schöpfungstheologische Möglichkeit dualen Denkens nicht auf, da sie christologisch dachten.

Theologisches Seminar   Oda WISCHMEYER
    der Universität Erlangen
Kochstrasse 4
D-91054 Erlangen

---

28. SKEHAN–DI LELLA, *Ben Sira* (n. 22), p. 401, schreiben unzutreffend zu Sir 33,15: »The thought expressed here is similar to that of Qoh 7:13-14«.

29. Vgl. J. DUCHESNE-GUILLEMIN; H. DÖRRIE, Art. *Dualismus*, RAC IV, 1959, 334-350. Vgl. weiter P. WINTER, *Ben Sira* (n. 28). Winter vergleicht Sir 33, Text Ass 1,3–5,2 (δύο ὁδοί) und 1QS 3,13-4,26 (Gott schuf zwei Geister und zwei Wege).

30. Kap. 42f. Vgl. zur Ästhetik Sirachs O. WISCHMEYER, *Die Kultur des Buches Jesus Sirach* (BZNW, 77), Berlin–New York, 1995, pp. 155ff.

BEN SIRA AND HISTORY

It is a commonplace that Ben Sira was the first Jewish wisdom writer to concern himself with historical events and persons. That he did in fact do so, and that that concern is more than a peripheral one in his work is clear: more than one tenth of his book, the so-called Hymn of the Fathers, chapters 44–49(50), is devoted entirely to accounts of the achievements of famous men of the past. Besides this, the whole work with its emphasis on the centrality of the Jewish Torah promotes a historically based Jewish theology quite unlike the unspecific teaching of the book of Proverbs, which is generally supposed to be representative of Israel's "early wisdom". History for Ben Sira is not an eccentric appendage to his teaching; it is part and parcel of his conception of "wisdom theology"[1].

Various theories have been put forward to account for this departure from so-called "traditional wisdom writing". Most of these have one common feature: they are conceived in developmental terms. In other words, they are based on the recognition that as all literature is affected by political, social and intellectual forces, wisdom and its literature are no exception to the rule. It was inevitable that Ben Sira's ideas, being those of a man of the second century B.C., should mark advancement on those of an earlier age.

Some scholars have argued that the new factor in Ben Sira's writing was his concept of scripture. He was familiar with virtually all those books that would eventually form the canon of the Old Testament, and held them in reverence as holy scripture[2]. Although he remained essen-

---

1. J. MARBÖCK, *Weisheit im Wandel. Zur Weisheitstheologie bei Ben Sira* (BBB, 37), Bonn, Hanstein, 1971, p. 68, is emphatic in his claim that Ben Sira was the first author who positively and systematically developed the notion of a close connection between wisdom and Israel. H.H. SCHMID, *Wesen und Geschichte der Weisheit* (BZAW, 101), Berlin, Töpelmann, 1966, maintained that the wisdom of Israel and its neighbours was concerned with history, but he seems to have confused history *in* the wisdom literature with the historical development *of* the wisdom literature.

2. E. JACOB, *L'histoire d'Israël vue par Ben Sira*, in *Mélanges bibliques en l'honneur de André Robert*, Paris, Bloud & Gay, 1957, pp. 288-296 argued that Ben Sira took his stand on the entire biblical canon as his norm. G. VON RAD, *Weisheit in Israel*, Neukirchen-Vluyn, Neukirchener Verlag, 1970, pp. 309-336, held that it was principally from the Torah with its concern for order that Ben Sira's concern for history was derived, while M. HENGEL, *Judentum und Hellenismus*, Tübingen, Mohr, 1969, p. 247 (ET *Judaism and Hellenism*, t. I, London, SCM, 1974, p. 135) speaks also of the historical and prophetical books as his source. Similarly, P.W. SKEHAN and A.A. DI LELLA, *The Wisdom of Ben Sira* (AB, 39), regard him as having used the sacred writers to create a "new synthesis" to serve the needs and interests of the Jewish community of his time.

tially a wisdom writer he found it natural to make use in his teaching of examples taken from that collection of books many of which are historical in character. Other developments in Jewish life have been invoked to account for Ben Sira's interest in history. These include a change in the concept of the scribal profession of which he was a member, which led him to compose a wisdom book more in keeping with the age[3]; a growing nationalism already making itself felt prior to the outbreak of the Jewish Revolt[4]; Ben Sira's espousal of the priestly outlook which was supposedly especially concerned with the created order and consequently with the course of historical events[5]. But the most persuasive of these arguments was that which stressed the influence of Jewish Hellenism on Jewish life, an influence from which Ben Sira as a writer was certainly by no means free[6].

However, as far as Ben Sira's use of history is concerned, the Hellenistic (i.e., Greek) argument is not as conclusive as it is sometimes believed to be. That Ben Sira as a cultured man of his time was thoroughly familiar with Hellenistic culture and literature is undoubted (cf., e.g., 39,1-4); on the other hand there is strong evidence that his book was written to warn Jewish readers *against* the wholesale acceptance of Greek ideas to the detriment of their faith. The question to what extent his teaching was influenced either in form or content by Greek literary forms or intellectual notions remains disputed.

3. HENGEL, *Judaism and Hellenism* (n. 2), p. 135 speaks of "an inner" transformation of the *sōpēr* in which "'the wisdom teacher' becomes the man learned in the scriptures". Cf. J.L. CRENSHAW, *Old Testament Wisdom. An Introduction*, Atlanta, John Knox, 1981, pp. 151-152.

4. E.g. E. JACOB, *L'histoire d'Israël vue par Ben Sira* (n. 2), p. 289, and *Sagesse et Religion chez Ben Sira*, in E. JACOB (ed.), *Sagesses et Religion. Colloque de Strasbourg*, Paris, PUF, 1979, pp. 88-90; J.G. SNAITH, *Ecclesiasticus* (CBC), Cambridge, CUP, 1976, p. 216.

5. HENGEL, *Judaism and Hellenism* (n. 3), suggests that "Perhaps those conservative and nationalist circles which became dominant under the high priesthood of Simon the Just awakened interest in the prophetic and historical traditions of Israel" (p. 135). MARBÖCK, *Weisheit im Wandel* (n. 1) pointed to Ben Sira's close affinities with the priesthood, and in particular to 45,25-26 and 50,23 as showing that he associated Israel's future with the covenant with Aaron. L.G. PERDUE, *Wisdom and Cult*, Missoula, Scholars Press, 1977, pp. 188-211, in a detailed study of Ben Sira's devotion to the Temple and Israelite cult, maintained that for him cosmological wisdom was identical with the cult as well as with the Torah, and that the concern to assert the perpetuity of the inheritance of Aaron as on a par with that of the kings of Israel was an important motive for the composition of the Hymn of the Fathers.

6. A recent proponent of a significant Hellenistic influence on Ben Sira was T. MIDDENDORP, *Die Stellung Jesus ben Sira zwischen Judentum und Hellenismus*, Leiden, Brill, 1973. But see the recent discussion by O. KAISER, *Judentum und Hellenismus. Ein Beitrag zur Frage nach dem hellenistischen Einfluss auf Kohelet und Jesus Sirach* (BZAW, 161), Berlin, de Gruyter, pp. 146-153.

It has often been suggested that the Hymn of the Fathers bears marks of Greek historiography[7]. In support of this view it has been pointed out that this passage consists entirely of portraits of named personalities, a feature that is wholly absent from both Proverbs and Job; and it is undeniable that Greek histories are much concerned with the lives and deeds of great men. On the other hand, it has been pointed out that there is no attempt by Ben Sira to write a continuous history. The Hymn of the Fathers consists of a series of unconnected episodes each listing what Ben Sira considered to be the principal activity of a particular individual. There is no continuity here, no sense of cause and effect, no feeling of a history moving towards a recognizable goal. This is not historiography in any true sense, Greek, Jewish or other, and it would be hard to find any Greek example with which it could be compared. It may – perhaps – owe something to Greek historiography in its predilection for the use of proper names as pegs on which to hang the narrative; but the "historical books" of the Old Testament could just have easily provided a model in this respect. If Ben Sira thought it important to include a "historiographical" section in his wisdom book, he had no need for Greek or Hellenistic models.

The assertion that the inclusion of a "historical" section in Ben Sira's book was a complete departure from "traditional" wisdom writing calls for definitions of history and historiography; it equally invites definitions of wisdom and wisdom literature. It is also relevant to question the meanings of "tradition" and "traditional". What in fact in Israelite terms *is* the "wisdom tradition"? In the Hebrew canon only three books are universally agreed to be "wisdom books". These constitute an extremely small and inadequate sample for a basis for the definition of a genre, especially in view of the fact that they differ so greatly among themselves. How can it be known whether they are typical representatives of the genre, if such a genre exists? The only one of them that can be regarded as a precursor of Ben Sira is the book of Proverbs. This is a book with which Ben Sira was clearly familiar, and parts of his own

---

7. A.A. DI LELLA, *Conservative and Progressive Theology: Sirach and Wisdom*, in *CBQ* 38 (1966) 142, considered that its intention was to "convince Jews and well disposed Gentiles that true wisdom is to be found in Jerusalem, not in Athens". So also HENGEL, *Judaism and Hellenism* (no, 2), pp. 141-142, and JACOB, *L'histoire d'Israël vue par Ben Sira* (n. 2), p. 289. MARBÖCK, *Weisheit im Wandel* (n. 1), pp. 72-73, simply remarks that Ben Sira's concern with history was necessary if Israel was to take its place in the Hellenistic world. On the other hand, VON RAD, *Wisdom in Israel* (no. 2), and J.D. MARTIN, *Ben Sira – A Child of His Time*, in J.D. MARTIN and P.R. DAVIES (eds.), *A Word in Season. Essays in Honour of William McKane* (JSOTSS, 42), Sheffield, JSOT Press, 1986, pp. 141-161, attributes the Hymn of the Fathers to Jewish rather than Greek tradition.

book come close to being paraphrases or expansions of the earlier work. But can we be sure that Proverbs is not a rather eccentric and untypical example of Hebrew "wisdom literature"? While it is true that it has a number of affinities with foreign, especially Egyptian, works that have been labelled "wisdom books" and which are quite "unhistorical" in the same sense, its dissimilarity to the other Old Testament wisdom books puts it into a class by itself. Can we, then, be sure that Ben Sira's introduction of a historical element into a wisdom book was the innovation that it has been claimed to be? In other words, can we be certain that there were no earlier wisdom books, no longer extant, written in Israel, which included a historical theme?

There is, then, a possibility that the presence of a historical theme in Ben Sira is not entirely unprecedented. It is not even correct to say that it is absent from the book of Proverbs. Ben Sira was no doubt aware of wisdom's claim in Prov 8,15 that

> By me kings reign
> and rulers decree what is just,

and that text may well have served as the inspiration for his eulogies of particular kings in Israel. Further, the number of references elsewhere in Proverbs to the role of monarchs as dependent on the will of God would have confirmed him in his intention to offer examples, both positive and negative, in support of that claim[8].

Ben Sira's treatment of history in the Hymn of the Fathers in terms of outstanding individuals is in keeping with earlier wisdom also in another important respect: that it is concerned with the individuals rather than with society as a whole. In Proverbs human nature at its best is depicted in the portraits of the wise man (ḥākām) and the righteous man (yāšār, ṣaddîq) – two figures who are not clearly differentiated. These figures dominate the whole book from chapter 10 onwards: ḥākām occurs forty-one times, yāšār twenty and ṣaddîq sixty-two times in the course of twenty-two chapters. Whom did the authors of these Proverbs have in mind? They were certainly not making an abstract philosophical enquiry in the Socratic manner about the nature of the good or of wisdom. They were observing and commenting on the influence on the communities in which they lived of the good and the wise; and it is difficult to believe that when these proverbs were first composed they did not have actual

---

8. S. L. HARRIS, *Proverbs 1–9. A Study of Inner-Biblical Interpretation*, Atlanta, Scholars Press, 1995, finds in Proverbs "an attempt preceding Sirach which links traditions in Proverbs with traditions in Israel's history" (p. 27). However, his claim to have discovered direct allusions to passages from Genesis and Jeremiah in those chapters lacks plausibility.

individuals in mind. The names of those good and wise men are unknown to us. We may presume that they were among these of whom
Ben Sira wrote with regret:

> *of others there is no memory;*
> *they have perished as though they had never been,*
> *they and their children after them (44,8-9).*

These men were unknown to later generations because the authors of
Proverbs (and subsequent writers) failed to name them. They did not, for
whatever reason, think it appropriate to personalize their observations in
this way. The famous men whom Ben Sira commemorates did not, of
course, need his mention of them to secure their fame; nevertheless it is
his contribution to the wisdom genre that he, unlike the authors of Proverbs, believed that those who were particularly worthy of mention as
wise and good *should* be named in a wisdom book. If this constituted a
new departure it was not a particularly startling one. The Hymn to the
Fathers is not an eccentric phenomenon but remains well within the
norms of the older wisdom as far as those can be known.

The question whether some Old Testament books or parts of books
apart from Proverbs, Job and Ecclesiastes may be considered, at least to
some extent, to be redolent of wisdom thought has frequently been discussed. The divergence of critical views on this subject is due to the
above-mentioned difficulty of defining wisdom. Some years ago there
was a tendency to widen the term to such an extent that virtually the
whole of the Old Testament would merit inclusion in that category. That
tendency had now abated; but on the other hand it is now generally recognised that wisdom is not a formal literary genre but may assume a
number of different literary forms. Among these is narrative. Even in
Proverbs, narrative is occasionally used for didactic purposes (Prov 7,6-
27; 24,30-34). These are brief fictional moral lessons in narrative form.
But besides this there is reason to suppose that there is a wisdom compo-
nent in several more extended narrative passages elsewhere in the Old
Testament which come under the heading not of fiction but of
historiography- passages intended to give instruction through the medium of a narrative that their authors believed to be basically historical.
Such "wisdom" narratives may well be seen as precedents for Ben
Sira's Hymn of the Fathers. At any rate, they demonstrate that before his
time wisdom writing was already a flexible medium that could be
adapted to the genre of historical narrative.

One comparatively short work that is widely considered to qualify as
wisdom literature is Psalm 78. In the introduction to this psalm (vv. 1-4)
the author states his intention to recount the history of Yahweh's glori-

ous deeds performed on Israel's behalf. This history has been handed
down from previous generations and is now to be taught to the next generation so that the knowledge of it be not lost. But this historiographer
specifically claims to be a wisdom teacher. The admonition to "incline
the ear" (*haṭṭû 'oznĕkem*), v. 1a is almost identical with the admonition
of a father to his son in Prov 4,20; 5,1; the phrase "my teaching"
(*tôrātî*) in the parallel line v. 1b occurs in a similar instruction in Prov
3,1; 4,2; 7,2. *māšāl*, "proverb" (v. 2a) is a characteristic wisdom term
(Prov 1,6; 10,1; 25,1), and *ḥîdâ* (v. 1b), "riddle, obscure saying" (?),
occurs in Prov 1,6 where it denotes a particular kind of wisdom saying
and is parallel with "words of the wise". In sum, these opening verses of
Ps 78 are a typical introduction to a piece of wisdom teaching such as is
found in the series of instructions by a human teacher in Prov 1–7.

Ps 78 resembles Ben Sira's Hymn of the Fathers in that both texts take
the form of surveys of Israel's history (Ben Sira also includes the pre-Israel-
ite patriarchs) up to the respective times of the writers. Both claim to be
wisdom literature, and both are concerned to teach moral and religious lessons by commenting on the events that they narrate. The lessons that they
inculcate are naturally different since the circumstances of their respective
readers also differed widely. One important feature of Ben Sira's poem that
is lacking in Ps 78 is that the latter prefers a corporate approach and avoids
mentioning proper names: the nation is simply referred to as "they", and
their leaders are not named. However, it is evident that more than one approach was available to these writers, for Ps 105 offers a quite different survey of Israelite history in which several names are mentioned: Abraham,
Isaac, Jacob, Moses. Ps 105 makes no claim to be a wisdom psalm, but like
the Hymn of the Fathers it has the character of a psalm of thanksgiving.
There are other surveys of Israelite history in the Old Testament (e.g. Neh
9,6-37); these attest to a wide variety of possible approaches to it. At any
rate, Ben Sira's Hymn of the Fathers fits into a recognized category of wisdom psalms/hymns of praise of a historical character.

There are other Old Testament texts which have a historiographical
flavour and in which wisdom plays a significant role. The story of
Joseph (Gen 37–50) was believed by VON RAD to be a narrative depic-
tion of wisdom in the person of Joseph, whom he saw as a living paradigm of the wise man and an exemplification of the ideal inculcated in
the book of Proverbs[9]. VON RAD's thesis has been severely criticized,

---

9. G. VON RAD, *Josephsgeschichte und ältere Chokma*, in *Congress Volume, Copen-
hagen* (SVT, 1), Leiden, Brill, 1953, pp. 120-127 (ET *The Joseph Narrative and Ancient
Wisdom*, in *The Problem of the Hexateuch and Other Essays*, Edinburgh and London,
Oliver & Boyd, 1966, pp. 291-300).

probably with reason; but it is undeniable that Joseph, who is presented in Genesis as being the "discerning and wise" (*nābôn wĕḥākām*) person that he himself had recommended to be overseer of the land of Egypt (Gen 41,33) corresponds in many respects to the ideal wise man who according to Proverbs will achieve power and great wealth. Although Joseph is not one of the great men selected by Ben Sira in the Hymn of the Fathers, Genesis presents him as the wise man *par excellence* who through his wisdom played a crucial role in establishing the fortunes of the future people of Israel. The Joseph story is thus an example of early historiographical wisdom.

Another "historical" narrative with important wisdom features is one that was actually used by Ben Sira as the basis for one of his figures in his catalogue of famous men. This is the history of the reign of Solomon (1 Kings 3–11; Sir 47,12-22). Ben Sira's use of this text is particularly significant because it shows how he was consciously imitating an already established practice of using historical narrative as a basis for sapiential comment and moral lessons. He faithfully follows the text of Kings (not that of Chronicles) in his references to the main features of its narrative – Solomon's peaceful reign due to David's earlier achievements, his building of the temple and his wealth – but especially in the contrast that he makes between the wise young king renowned internationally for his wisdom and the same monarch's foolish behaviour which led to the disastrous division of his kingdom. In fact Ben Sira brings out this contrast more clearly than does the author of Kings in that he specifically characterizes Solomon's behaviour as folly, and that when he deals in the next section with Solomon's successor Rehoboam he categorizes him as "foolish and lacking sense", so pointing out a further contrast, one between the once wise Solomon and the foolish Rehoboam, a contrast that is only indirectly implied in Kings. In this way Ben Sira contrived to make even clearer the moral lesson inculcated in the narrative of Kings.

Deut 32 is also a wisdom text giving an account of the history of Israel together with a cautionary moral. Like Ps 78, it has an introduction (vv. 1-3) in which the author sets out his claim to be a wisdom teacher. His use of admonitions to hear and pay attention to his teaching, though addressed here to heaven and earth rather than to a human audience, echoes Ps 78,1. As in Ps 78 he used the expression "the words of my mouth" (*'imĕrê-pî*). In v. 2 he describes his teaching as *leqaḥ*, a rare word almost exclusive to Proverbs (Prov 1,5; 4,2; 9,9; 16,21.23). Israel is castigated first for having abandoned the true God who had chosen and nurtured them (vv. 8-9) and then for their stupidity in failing to recognize the source of the punishments that he had inflicted. The author concludes that

> *They are a nation void of sense,*
> *There is no understanding in them.*
> *If they were wise they would understand this;*
> *they would comprehend their fate (vv. 28-29).*

Deut 4,5-8 similarly but more positively stresses that Israel has been given the opportunity to behave wisely if it chooses to do so. There Moses tells the people that if they obey the Torah they will be envied by other nations. This notion, that the Torah can be the source of Israel's greatness, is very close to Ben Sira's outlook, of which it is indeed the very essence.

This is summed up in Sir 24, where in vv. 3-22 a personified Wisdom addresses the "assembly of the Most High", and once more in a "historical" narrative recounts her origins and history. In a speech which is partly based on wisdom's speech in Prov 8 she speaks first of her primordial origin as a creature of God dwelling in the heavens (vv. 3-7), but then departs significantly from her prototype in Proverbs. In v. 7 she claims that although she held sway over all peoples, she desired to settle in one place, and that the Creator chose a dwelling-place for her, commanding her to make Israel her home (v. 8). She then describes how she found rest and became established in Jerusalem (vv. 10-11), where she grew tall and scattered her fragrance (vv. 13-17).

Wisdom's appeal (vv. 19-22), based on prototypes in Proverbs, is addressed to all and sundry. There is still a place for the Gentiles, who have already been acquainted with her (v. 6), to share the benefits that she has to offer. Ben Sira's concern with history is here seen not to be rigidly restrictive. V. 6, indeed, suggests that the nations outside Judaism are not entirely without a share in wisdom. To this v. 23, apparently in prose, appears to come as a douche of cold water: "All this"(that is, Wisdom's benefits) is identified with the Law of Moses that was given to Jews alone, "as an inheritance for the sons of Jacob". Yet for Ben Sira this Law, the "Book of the Covenant", now appears (vv. 25-27) not to be static and unmovable. He pictures it as a river which overflows it banks to fertilize the surrounding country. Ben Sira here reverts to human beginnings – to the Garden of Eden and the first man (vv. 28-29) – and confesses that wisdom is beyond human wits to fathom. In this way he attempts to embrace all human history in his scope while holding firmly to the belief that true wisdom is indissoluble from the Torah. Whether he succeeds in resolving this paradox is a matter of debate.

It is both a privilege and a pleasure to make a contribution to this volume honouring Maurice Gilbert, a distinguished member of a group of scholars who, amidst onerous administrative and other pre-occupations has made notable contributions to the study of the wisdom literature of ancient Israel, especially in the rediscovery of its theological importance.

Faculty of Divinity   † R. N. WHYBRAY
University of Cambridge

DE LA CRÉATION À L'ALLIANCE SINAÏTIQUE

LA LOGIQUE DE SI 16,26–17,14

«En Si XVI,24-XVII,14, [...] les derniers versets font allusion
à l'alliance sinaïtique dans un contexte de création: c'est dire
non seulement le rapport entre histoire et création, mais aussi
la portée de l'histoire biblique pour tout être humain.»
M. Gilbert[1]

Dans sa méditation sur la création et sur la place que l'être humain est
invité à y tenir (16,26–17,14), Ben Sira renvoie clairement son lecteur
aux premières pages de la Genèse. Dans les strophes initiales du moins.
Car à partir de 17,6, malgré une allusion plutôt paradoxale à Gn 2,17
(«bien et mal il leur montra», Si 17,7b), au lieu d'évoquer la faute pri-
mordiale, le sage passe à un développement plus personnel sur ce qui
ouvre l'homme à la louange; il multiplie ensuite les références au récit
du don de la Loi dans le cadre de la théophanie du Sinaï (Ex 19–20).
Pourtant, comme Maurice Gilbert le suggère avec d'autres[2], jusqu'au
bout, l'horizon reste universel et c'est toujours de l'être humain qu'il
s'agit. Comme l'écrit John J. Collins, «Sirach allows no interval
between the creation and the giving of the Torah. Rather, he implies that
the law was given to humanity from the beginning[3]».

La question que je voudrais explorer dans ces pages concerne les as-
sociations qui ont pu amener Ben Sira à ce glissement inattendu à partir
du texte de la Genèse, pour tenter d'en saisir la logique. Autrement dit,
quelle lecture de Gn 1 et 2 est à même de supporter la surprenante application de la loi mosaïque à tout humain? S'agit-il seulement d'associa-
tions libres, sans lien structurel avec la dynamique des deux premiers
chapitres du Livre? Ou le développement de Ben Sira suit-il une logique

---

1. M. GILBERT, Art. *Siracide*, dans *DBS*, t. XII, Paris, 1996, col. 1389-1437, voir
col. 1432.
2. J. DE FRAINE, *Het loflied op de menselijke waardigheid in Eccli 17,1-14*, in
Bijdragen 11 (1950) 10-22, pp. 20-21; L. ALONSO SCHÖKEL, *The Vision of Man in Sirach
16:24–17:14*, in J.G. GAMMIE (ed.), *Israelite Wisdom. Theological and Literary Essays in
Honor of S. Terrien*, New York, 1978, pp. 235-245, voir pp. 242-243; J.J. COLLINS, *Seers,
Sybils and Sages in Hellenistic-Roman Judaism* (JSJS, 54), Leiden, Brill, 1997,
pp. 375-376. J.G. SNAITH, *Ecclesiasticus or the Wisdom of Jesus Son of Sirach* (CBC),
Cambridge, University Press, 1974, p. 88, ne partage pas cet avis.
3. COLLINS, *Seers, Sybils and Sages*, p. 376.

cachée de ces récits, sa lecture implicite permettant dès lors de la reconnaître et de la mettre en lumière? Ne peut-on étendre à toute la péricope ce que Luis Alonso Schökel dit des versets sur l'homme mortel en Si 17,1-2a, à savoir que loin de changer la doctrine de la Genèse, il se pourrait que le sage interprète la Genèse avec davantage de rigueur que des traditions postérieures[4]?

Après une invitation à écouter (Si 16,24-25), la méditation du Siracide se développe en quatre strophes. La première évoque en quatre distiques la fondation de l'univers et des astres (16,26-28). Plus longue de deux distiques, la deuxième s'attache au monde terrestre où l'humain est situé (16,29–17,4). Les deux dernières, en quatre distiques chacune, traitent de ce qui relie les humains à Dieu[5]: la faculté de comprendre le monde et de louer le créateur (17,6-10) et une loi de vie qui ouvre à l'alliance avec lui (17,11-14)[6]. Au vu d'une telle structure, la question qui se pose est de savoir si le lien entre les deux dernières strophes et les premières relève ou non d'une exégèse, même tacite, de Gn 1–2.

> 16, 26 Quand le Seigneur créa[7] ses œuvres au commencement,
>   dès qu'il les fit, il sépara leurs parties;
>   27 il ordonna pour toujours leurs œuvres (= tâches)[8]
>   et leurs commandements pour leurs générations;
>   elles n'ont pas faim ni ne se fatiguent,
>   ni ne délaissent leurs œuvres (= tâches).
>   28 Aucune n'écrase sa voisine (= son prochain)
>   et jusqu'à toujours, elles ne failliront pas à sa parole.

---

4. ALONSO SCHÖKEL, *The Vision of Man*, pp. 236-237.

5. Dans ce texte, pour lequel nous ne possédons de fragment hébreu que pour 16,26a, certains manuscrits grecs enregistrent quelques ajouts remontant sans doute à la deuxième édition de la traduction grecque: 17,5. 8c et 11c. J. ZIEGLER, *Sapientia Iesu Filii Sirach* (Septuaginta, XII, 2), Göttingen, Vandenhoeck & Ruprecht, 1965, les reprend en plus petit. Avec la majorité des commentateurs, je n'en tiens pas compte directement.

6. On peut discuter la place de 16,29-30 où est évoquée l'œuvre d'ornementation de la terre – sans doute les végétaux (v. 29) et les animaux (v. 30), selon H. DUESBERG, *La dignité de l'homme. Siracide 16,24–17,14*, dans BVC 82 (1968) 15-21, p. 16, et SNAITH, *Ecclesiasticus*, pp. 87-86. Avec d'autres, G.L. PRATO, *Il problema della teodicea in Ben Sira* (AnBib, 65), Roma, Biblical Institute Press, 1975, pp. 266-267, préfère lier les vv. 29-30 à la strophe qui précède, ce qui a le mérite de situer l'humain à part de la «création du ciel et de la terre»; ce découpage peut trouver un appui littéraire dans la ressemblance du début des deux premières strophes: 16,26: ἐν κτίσει κυρίου (voir note 7), et 17,1: κύριος ἔκτισεν. Mais, avec SNAITH, *Ecclesiasticus*, p. 85, par exemple, on peut être davantage sensible aux liens internes entre 16,29-30 et 17,1-4: Si y parle de la terre (γῆ) et de son peuplement mortel (ἀποστροφή – ἀποστρέφω), l'humain ayant autorité sur tout le terrestre, en particulier les animaux (16,30 et 17,2b-4).

7. En lisant κτίσει avec l'édition de Ziegler qui adopte une correction de Smend en s'appuyant sur l'arménien et l'hébreu (כברא). Les mss grecs ont κρίσει.

8. τὰ ἔργα αὐτῶν: leçon retenue par Ziegler suivant quelques mss appuyés par les versions latines et syriaques; la majorité des témoins grecs a τὰ ἔργα αὐτοῦ.

29 Et après cela, le Seigneur regarda vers la terre
et la remplit de ses biens:
30 du souffle de tout vivant, il a couvert sa face
et vers elle, ils retournent.
17,1 Le Seigneur créa de terre l'humain
et de nouveau l'y fit retourner.
2 Des jours comptés et un temps fixé il leur donna,
il leur donna aussi autorité sur les choses de la terre.
3 Selon ce qu'il est, il les revêtit de force
et selon son image il les fit.
4 Il mit sa crainte en toute chair
et[9] qu'il soit seigneur des fauves et des oiseaux.

6 Le conseil, la langue et les yeux
les oreilles et le cœur, il les leur donna pour réfléchir.
7 Du savoir d'intelligence il les remplit;
bien et mal, il leur montra.
8 Il mit son œil[10] en leurs cœurs
pour leur montrer la grandeur de ses œuvres.
10 Et ils loueront son saint nom
(9) afin de raconter la grandeur de ses œuvres.

11 Il ajouta[11] pour eux le savoir
et d'une loi de vie il les fit héritiers.
12 Il établit avec eux une alliance de toujours,
et il leur montra ses jugements.
13 Leurs yeux virent la grandeur de sa gloire,
et leur oreille entendit la gloire de sa voix.
14 Et il leur dit: «gardez-vous de toute injustice[12]»,
leur donnant à chacun des ordres au sujet du voisin [prochain].

I

Il est courant de dire que la première strophe (16,26-28), si fortement
liée à Gn 1, concerne essentiellement la création des astres avec leurs

---

9. Le καί manque dans certains témoins. Beaucoup de traductions actuelles l'omet-
tent, comprenant l'infinitif qui suit (κατακυριεύειν) dans un sens final: voir par exemple
la *Bible de la Pléiade* (J. Hadot), Osty, la *TOB* et la *BJ*.

10. J'opte pour la *lectio difficilior* τὸν ὀφθαλμὸν αὐτοῦ avec la plupart des mss grecs
que suit l'édition de Rahlfs, alors que Ziegler retient la leçon faiblement attestée τὸν
φόβον αὐτοῦ.

11. Ou «il mit devant eux», si l'on suit la correction adoptée par Ziegler qui a
προέθηκεν à la place du προσέθηκεν attesté par les mss et les versions.

12. En grec, le génitif ἀδίκου peut être masculin ou neutre. On peut donc traduire
aussi: «gardez-vous de tout (homme) injuste». Voir plus loin.

13. C'est vrai en tout cas des vv. 27-28: voir p. ex. ALONSO SCHÖKEL, *The Vision of
Man*, pp. 235-236, ou encore P.W. SKEHAN & A.A. DI LELLA, *The Wisdom of Ben Sira*
(AB, 39), New York, Doubleday, 1987, p. 281.

fonctions particulières[13]. Sans vouloir contester cette position, je me demande si elle n'est pas trop restrictive. Si, comme le note Gian-Luigi Prato, le nom des astres ne figure pas dans le poème[14], c'est peut-être que le sage n'entend pas limiter aux seuls corps célestes ce qu'il affirme dans ces lignes[15]. Pour Ben Sira, qui suit l'auteur du chapitre 1 de la Genèse, l'œuvre créatrice consiste essentiellement en des séparations permettant une mise en ordre. Ainsi, l'ἀρχή, le commencement – ou le principe – de la création, ce sont des ἀρχαί, des commandements par lesquels le Seigneur ordonne (κοσμεῖν) les parties de l'univers en leur assignant une place singulière où elles remplissent une tâche propre[16]. Elles gardent ainsi sans faillir la parole divine qui assure l'ordre du «cosmos»: lumière et ténèbre (cf. Gn 1,3-5), cieux, terre et mers (cf. vv. 6-10), et bien sûr les corps célestes (cf. vv. 14-18).

Une question se pose à propos de cette strophe. D'aucuns ont souligné avec raison que ce développement à propos de la création constitue une réponse à l'objection d'un insensé qui s'égare (Si 16,23): cet homme prétend que, perdu dans la masse, il échappe au regard de Dieu, comme s'il n'avait pas dans la création une place où Dieu puisse le voir (Si 16,17). L'objection se prolonge aux vv. 21-22 Héb. où le même insensé conclut qu'il est donc indifférent de mener une vie droite et de chercher à faire son devoir[17]. Dans ce cadre, on peut se demander pourquoi le Siracide, au lieu de préciser d'emblée la place propre de l'être humain dans l'univers, commence par évoquer la mise en ordre par séparations du cadre de vie où celui-ci est situé.

Un parallélisme mis en évidence par Luis Alonso Schökel constitue sans doute une bonne clé pour saisir la logique du début du poème. «As the celestial beings have a dominion, a function, a mandate and companions, so does man have dominion, function, law and companions» – affirmation qu'il illustre par une série de contacts thématiques et verbaux entre Si 16,27-28 et 16,30-17,14[18]. Selon lui, l'intention de Ben Sira est d'exalter la position de l'homme. Mais si la fonction du

14. PRATO, *Il problema della teodicea*, p. 269, pour qui les vv. 27-28 visent seulement les astres.

15. C'est en se sens inclusif que j'entends le «par exemple» de M. GILBERT, Art. *Siracide*, col. 1433: «L'homme (…) est créé libre et responsable de ses actes dans un ensemble ordonné où les astres, *par exemple*, obéissent parfaitement (XVI,26-29)» (je souligne).

16. En réalité, en 16,27b, ἀρχαί vise les «commandements» par lesquels les deux luminaires président au jour et à la nuit (cf. Gn 1,16). Mais ceux-ci obéissent ainsi à un commandement du Seigneur.

17. Voir en particulier PRATO, *Il problema della teodicea*, pp. 262-279, *passim*, ou encore SNAITH, *Ecclesiasticus*, p. 85.

18. ALONSO SCHÖKEL, *The Vision of Man*, pp. 235-236.

19. Selon le titre de l'article de DE FRAINE, *Het loflied op de menselijke waardigheid*.

poème est moins de célébrer la valeur de celui-ci[19] que de répondre à l'objection de l'insensé, le parallèle entre les parties du cosmos et l'humain peut avoir une autre portée. Au fond, que dit la première strophe, sinon que l'ordre du monde est assuré parce que chaque élément séparé par le Créateur occupe sa place sans prendre celle de l'autre, conformément à la parole divine (v. 28)? Dès lors, si l'humain leur ressemble par sa maîtrise (Si 17,2-3), sa fonction (vv. 4.10) et la loi reçue de Dieu touchant aux relations avec autrui (vv. 7.11-12.14), c'est en tenant sa place propre qu'il contribuera à assurer le maintien de l'ordre cosmique. Ainsi apparaît le danger de la position de l'insensé: nier que l'humain ait une place à occuper, une tâche à remplir, c'est risquer de mettre en péril l'ordre de la création[20].

Mais quelle est cette place de l'humain dans l'univers? Ce qu'en dit le Siracide rejoint-il le premier chapitre de la Genèse?

II

À l'instar de tous les vivants de l'univers terrestre (Si 16,30), l'être humain occupe tout d'abord une place non seulement limitée, mais aussi transitoire. Son existence est un être-pour-la-mort (Si 17,1) dont les jours sont comptés (v. 2a). En cela, Ben Sira ne contredit pas la Genèse. Le poème sacerdotal ne dit rien de la mort, en effet. Quant au récit dit jahviste, même si, à première vue, il fait de la mort le salaire du péché, il envisage aussi le retour à la terre comme le terme normal de la vie (Gn 3,19, voir 2,7)[21]. Dès lors, la «mort», salaire de la faute, n'est pas le trépas. C'est cette mort, bien plus radicale, qui empêche les humains de naître à leur existence propre dans des justes relations avec autrui, ce qu'illustre la seconde partie du chapitre 3[22].

Si donc, pour ce qui est du don de la vie avec sa limite, les humains sont

---

20. En ce sens PRATO, *Il problema della teodicea*, p. 270, suggère que «l'ordine fissato per le stelle deve valere anche per la terra e gli uomini: la disubbidienza assumerebbe dimensioni catastrofiche». Voir aussi pp. 276.279.

21. Si 17,1 reprend l'expression de Gn 2,7 et 3,19 LXX, ἀποστρέφω εἰς τὴν γῆν. Sur ce point, voir par exemple SKEHAN – DI LELLA, *The Wisdom of Ben Sira*, p. 281.

22. Comme l'écrit P. BEAUCHAMP, *L'un et l'autre Testament. Essai de lecture* (Parole de Dieu), Paris, Seuil, 1976, p. 199: «La vraie mort n'est pas le terme de la vie; elle est ce qui, dès le début, empêche de naître». Je développe cette lecture de Gn 2,17 dans A. WÉNIN, *Pas seulement de pain... Violence et alliance dans la Bible* (LD, 171), Paris, Cerf, 1998, pp. 41-47 et 65-71. Voir aussi en un sens analogue, DUESBERG, *La dignité de l'homme*, p. 17, ou ALONSO SCHÖKEL, *The Vision of Man*, pp. 236-237. Ceci dit, plusieurs soulignent que Si ne parle pas de la faute: ainsi, par exemple, T. MIDDENDORP, *Die Stellung Jesu ben Sira zwischen Judentum und Hellenismus*, Leiden, Brill, 1978, p. 53; COLLINS, *Seers, Sybils and Sages*, p. 375.

semblables aux vivants avec qui ils partagent leur espace vital, il est un autre don de Dieu qui les distingue: l'autorité sur le monde terrestre (Si 17,2b-4). Ici, Ben Sira suit très exactement les affirmations de la Genèse (Gn 1,26-28). Créée le même jour que les bêtes peuplant la terre – et avec le même procédé, ajoutera le second récit (Gn 2,7 et 19) –, l'humanité occupe le même espace qu'eux. Aussi doit-elle se rendre maître de la gent animale pour pouvoir fructifier et se multiplier, selon l'invitation divine.

Ici, Ben Sira introduit l'idée que l'humain est à l'image du «Seigneur» (Si 1,1: κύριος): revêtu de force (v. 3) pour dominer la terre (v. 2b) et être seigneur (κατακυριεύειν) des animaux (v. 4, voir aussi Gn 9,2). Loin d'amalgamer indûment deux éléments distincts de Gn 1,26-28, comme le dit Prato[23], le Siracide en propose au contraire une lecture pertinente. En effet, en Gn 1,26, la maîtrise que les humains doivent exercer sur les animaux et la terre est intimement liée au projet de les faire à l'image et à la ressemblance de Dieu. Cela n'est guère étonnant, vu l'image de Dieu que cette page dessine: un Dieu qui déploie sa maîtrise pour organiser le monde par la parole, en s'imposant à ce qui pourrait en menacer l'ordre. N'y a-t-il pas là une belle image de la vocation de l'humanité, appelée à organiser son monde par la parole en y maîtrisant toute animalité[24]? Car lorsque l'auteur sacerdotal dit que l'humain est à l'image de Dieu, je ne pense pas qu'il veuille se livrer à une description de l'humain. C'est plutôt une tâche qu'il énonce, tâche que Dieu explicite par deux fois: lorsqu'il forme le projet (Gn 1,26), puis lorsqu'il parle aux humains dès leur création (Gn 1,28)[25]. C'est cette même tâche que Ben Sira rappelle lorsqu'il précise: «qu'il soit seigneur des fauves et des oiseaux» (Si 17,4b). Ainsi, si l'être humain a une fonction à remplir sur terre, c'est de se rendre maître de l'animalité.

III

Ici, le discours de Ben Sira semble prendre ses distances vis-à-vis de

---

23. PRATO, *Il problema della teodicea*, p. 274. Voir aussi ALONSO SCHÖKEL, *The Vision of Man*, pp. 237-238; SKEHAN – DI LELLA, *The Wisdom of Ben Sira*, p. 281, pour qui être à l'image de Dieu et dominer les animaux sont deux choses différentes. Selon DE FRAINE, *Het loflied op de menselijke waardigheid*, p. 18; J. Hadot, dans É. DHORME, *La Bible. Ancien Testament*, t. II, (La Pléiade), Paris, Gallimard, 1959, p. 1762, le lien entre les deux est un rapport de cause à effet: parce qu'il est l'image de Dieu, l'homme est à même de maîtriser l'animal.

24. Dans ce cadre, on comprend mieux l'addition du v. 5 dans la seconde édition du grec. Après avoir cité les cinq sens que les humains partagent avec les animaux supérieurs, elle ajoute les deux dons distinctifs de l'humain: l'intelligence (νοῦς) et surtout la parole (λόγος), septième don qui permet à l'humanité de maîtriser comme Dieu.

25. À ce sujet, voir mon développement en WÉNIN, *Pas seulement de pain...*, pp. 26-28.

la Genèse. En effet, il évoque les dons divins permettant à l'humain de réfléchir, de comprendre bien et mal et d'admirer la grandeur des œuvres divines (Si 17,6-10), là où l'auteur sacerdotal parle d'un autre don de Dieu: la nourriture de l'humain et des animaux (Gn 1,29-30). En outre, si le sage pense à la Genèse, c'est plutôt au second chapitre, qu'il évoque en Si 17,7b. Mais il le fait non seulement avec d'autres mots, mais encore à rebours. Car il dit que Dieu leur a montré bien et mal (καὶ ἀγαθὰ καὶ κακὰ ὑπέδειξεν αὐτοῖς), alors qu'en Gn 2,17, au moment où il lui donne sa nourriture, le Seigneur-Dieu interdit à l'humain la jouissance de l'arbre du connaître bien et mal (LXX: γινώσκειν καλὸν καὶ πονηρόν)[26].

C'est d'ailleurs là un point étonnant, parce que commun aux deux récits ouvrant la Genèse: le don d'une nourriture – végétale – par une parole où Dieu pose la nécessité d'une limite, d'un en-moins: tous les végétaux, donc implicitement pas les animaux (Gn 1,29); tous les arbres du jardin, mais pas celui du connaître (Gn 2,16-17). La nourriture devient ainsi pour l'humain le lieu d'une option à prendre face à la parole de Dieu. Selon le récit jahviste, ce choix est crucial puisqu'il engage la vie et la mort. Pour «vivre» au sens fort d'épanouir son humanité, il ne suffit donc pas de manger; il faut encore écouter la parole. Mais lorsqu'il prévient l'homme de ce qui peut le couper de la vie authentique, Dieu ne lui «montre»-t-il pas bien et mal, selon l'expression de Si 17,7b[27]?

Dans le récit sacerdotal également, la parole sur la nourriture est, comme le dit Paul Beauchamp, «la racine cachée d'une loi»[28]. En effet, donner une nourriture végétale à l'humain immédiatement après lui avoir commandé de maîtriser les animaux revient à suggérer que, pour se réaliser à l'image de Dieu, l'humain devra déployer cette maîtrise avec douceur. «Ce qui qualifie l'image n'est pas seulement la suprématie mais, tout autant, la manière dont cette domination s'exerce. Or c'est

---

26. J. HADOT, *Penchant mauvais et volonté libre dans la sagesse de Ben Sira (l'Ecclésiastique)*, Bruxelles, Presses Universitaires, 1970, pp. 108-111, insiste sur cette opposition. Voir aussi, p. ex. DE FRAINE, *Het loflied op de menselijke waardigheid*, p. 18. PRATO, *Il problema della teodicea*, p. 278, s'étonne avec d'autres de l'écart manifeste et se demande si Ben Sira a réellement voulu suivre le récit des origines.

27. Donner une loi revient à indiquer le bien et le mal: les mots ἀγαθὰ καὶ κακά du v. 7b font penser à Dt 30,15 où ces mots sont employés au singulier avec l'article (LXX) à propos du don de la Loi qui ébauche un chemin de vie.

28. P. BEAUCHAMP, *Création et fondation de la loi en Gn 1,1–2,4a. Le don de la nourriture végétale en Gn 1,29s.*, in L. DEROUSSEAUX (ed.), *La Création dans l'Orient ancien* (LD, 127), Paris, Cerf, 1987, pp. 139-182, voir p. 140. Tout cet article peut illustrer mon propos, mais surtout les pp. 149-153 et 178-181. Voir en ce sens aussi WÉNIN, *Pas seulement de pain...*, pp. 26-38.

le régime alimentaire qui suppose une forme pacifique de cet exercice»[29]. Ainsi, à nouveau, la parole divine met l'humain en situation de liberté tout en éclairant son choix. Car elle donne à penser que la douceur qui consiste à maîtriser sa force dans le respect de la vie d'autrui permet à l'humain de réaliser sa vocation propre, tandis que la violence est un mal qui, si on lui donne prise, conduira l'homme à l'animalité (voir Gn 4,7-8) et ramènera le monde au chaos (voir Gn 6,5-13). Ainsi, que l'être humain tienne sa place de maître et qu'il le fasse avec douceur a pour enjeu non seulement son propre achèvement à l'image de Dieu, mais aussi le maintien actif de l'ordre de la création.

Au début de sa troisième strophe, Ben Sira s'écarte-t-il beaucoup d'une telle lecture (Si 17,6-10)? Après avoir situé la vocation de l'humain à maîtriser l'animalité, il ajoute que le Seigneur l'a doté de ce qui est nécessaire pour aller vers la sagesse: la capacité d'incliner sa liberté vers bien ou mal[30]; une langue pour parler, certes, mais aussi pour manger; des yeux pour voir ce qu'il est possible de manger (cf. Gn 3,6); des oreilles pour entendre la Parole qui oriente le choix; enfin, un cœur pour réfléchir et se décider. Mais au fond, dans le récit de la Genèse, les premières paroles adressées à l'humain au sujet de la nourriture – c'est-à-dire ce qui lui est nécessaire pour vivre –, ne jouent-elles pas ce rôle d'éveil de l'homme à la faculté de penser et d'opter avec liberté, de se déterminer en bien ou en mal? Ces paroles ne peuvent-elles être lues en quelque sorte comme la version narrative du don que Ben Sira thématise en Si 17,6-7?

Mais en même temps, ces paroles révèlent à qui peut les entendre que le désir de Dieu pour le monde et pour l'homme est la vie et la paix. En ce sens, elles donnent de voir les choses avec le regard même de Dieu (Si 17,8a) et de découvrir dans le monde la grandeur de son projet et de ses œuvres. Car Dieu ne se contente pas d'ordonner l'univers. Il crée encore l'être humain avec sa limite mais aussi avec sa responsabilité de maîtrise, lui offrant une parole qui suscite sa liberté et l'invite à occuper sa place de maître de l'univers terrestre, en exerçant cette ἐξουσία (Si 17,2) de telle sorte qu'il promeuve la vie, à l'image

29. BEAUCHAMP, *Création et fondation de la loi*, p. 152.
30. Comme premier don de Dieu, le texte grec mentionne le διαβούλιον, le «conseil» au sens de capacité de se déterminer librement entre différentes possibilites offertes. Voir HADOT, *Penchant mauvais et volonté libre*, pp. 97-103 et 106-111, à propos de notre texte. Comme, en 15,14, διαβούλιον rend l'hébreu יֵצֶר, «penchant», bon ou mauvais sans doute (voir 15,15-17), on peut penser qu'en hébreu, 17,6 commençait par וִיצֶר. Appuyés par la version syriaque qui traduit par *br'*, d'aucuns préfèrent donc lirent le verbe au Wayyiqtol («et il forma...»): ainsi DE FRAINE, *Het loflied op de menselijke waardigheid*, p. 13; PRATO, *Il problema della teodicea*, p. 277 et la note 158. Mais peut-on rejoindre ce dernier quand il voit là une «faute»? N'est-ce pas plutôt une option de traduction recevable autant que l'autre? SKEHAN – DI LELLA, *The Wisdom of Ben Sira*, p. 282, montrent bien la logique d'une telle interprétation.

de son Seigneur.

En Gn 1,31, la création s'achève dans l'émerveillement: «Et Dieu vit tout ce qu'il avait fait, et voici, c'est très bien!». La finale de la troisième strophe du poème de Ben Sira (Si 17,8.10) ne pourrait-elle être une réminiscence – fût-ce inconsciente – de ce texte? L'œil de Dieu placé au cœur de l'être humain pour qu'il puisse découvrir la grandeur de ses œuvres (v. 8) ne rappelle-t-il pas en effet le regard divin contemplant tout ce qu'il avait fait? Et la louange qui jaillit de ce voir et se prolonge en récit (v. 10), n'est-elle pas l'écho en l'homme du והנה־טוב מאד de la louange divine – reprise en apothéose du כי־טוב six fois répété? Si en se réalisant à l'image de Dieu, l'être humain peut partager le regard de celui-ci, est-il étonnant qu'il se joigne aussi à la louange divine, tout en célébrant son Nom de sainteté?

IV

À propos du Nom, on pourrait se demander pourquoi Ben Sira le qualifie ici de «saint» (ὄνομα ἁγιασμοῦ)? Serait-ce par association avec le Dieu qui sanctifie le sabbat en Gn 2,3? Car le poème sacerdotal a pour point culminant le sabbat de Dieu au septième jour (Gn 2,1-3). À ce point, le sage ne semble pas faire allusion, préférant parler de la loi de vie et de l'alliance, en lien avec le récit des événements du Sinaï en Ex 19–24. Or, dans la théologie sacerdotale, un fil caché unit sainteté de Dieu, sabbat, loi et alliance perpétuelle. En Ex 31,13-17, en effet, en lien explicite avec la fin du premier récit de création (v. 17), le sabbat fait l'objet d'une loi où il est qualifié d'alliance perpétuelle (v. 16: TM ברית עולם; LXX διαθήκη αἰώνιος). Saint pour le Seigneur (v. 15), ce jour est saint aussi pour Israël (v. 14), signe que ce peuple participe de la sainteté de son Dieu (v. 13).

Il est possible, je crois, de comprendre la logique implicite qui unit les deux textes sacerdotaux, Gn 1 et Ex 31, une logique que peut refléter implicitement l'enchaînement du Siracide. Lorsque Dieu achève la création le septième jour, il met un terme au déploiement de sa puissance, se montrant ainsi plus fort que sa force, maître de sa propre maîtrise, au point que celle-ci se révèle authentique douceur[31]. Ce faisant, lui aussi prend sa place: renonçant à tout remplir, il assume une limite, de sorte que l'on a pu dire que «seul l'homme, l'homme humain, *par* sa limite,

---

31. Ce point a été bien mis en évidence par P. BEAUCHAMP. Voir, par exemple, *Au commencement Dieu parle, ou les sept jours de la création*, dans *Études* 365 (1986) 105-116, p. 113.

32. P. BEAUCHAMP, *La loi du Décalogue et l'image de Dieu*, dans *Croire aujourd'hui* 186 (1987) 397-406, p. 404. Je souligne.

est l'image de ce que Dieu est»[32]. Or, en se retirant ainsi, Dieu fait-il autre chose que signifier sa «sainteté», marquer sa différence à la fois vis-à-vis de la toute-puissance que l'homme lui prête spontanément et vis-à-vis des autres dieux dont la surpuissance écrase? Mais aussi, au moment même où il prend sa place, comme à distance, il accepte d'être «tenu en respect» par l'autre à qui il ouvre un espace d'autonomie. C'est ainsi qu'il prépare le terrain pour l'alliance qui suppose des partenaires distincts et libres. À cette alliance, Israël adhèrera dans la mesure où il acceptera lui aussi sa limite en entrant dans une dynamique sabbatique[33].

Au demeurant, si le sabbat trouve son fondement dans le repos de Dieu qui achève l'œuvre créatrice (Gn 2,1-3), c'est au Sinaï qu'il est donné comme loi au cœur de la Loi (Ex 20,8-11)[34], une loi dont le Deutéronome ne cesse de répéter qu'elle est pour la vie (voir en particulier Dt 30,15-20). D'où les allusions de Ben Sira aux circonstances du don de la Loi de vie, en Si 17,12-13. Reste qu'en situant la réflexion dans le prolongement de sa lecture du chapitre 1 de la Genèse, il élargit à l'humanité entière la proposition d'alliance de Dieu. D'ailleurs, en un sens, on pourrait dire qu'en faisant sabbat, en assumant une limite qui offre à autrui un espace de vie, Dieu «met devant»[35] les humains un exemple de sagesse, d'ἐπιστήμη authentique, et lui «lègue» ainsi, dans l'acte même de se retirer, une «loi de vie».

Celle-ci consiste, comme le rappelle Si 17,14, à se garder de tout ce qui est injuste et à se situer vis-à-vis du prochain. Or, au cœur des dix Paroles, le précepte du sabbat peut certainement receler de telles harmoniques. En effet, en Dt 5,11-15, le sabbat est non seulement le jour où l'Israélite ne travaille pas, mais aussi le jour où il ne fait pas travailler ceux qui, d'ordinaire, œuvrent pour lui, qu'ils soient fils ou immigrés. De cette façon, il proclame concrètement l'égalité de tous – ce jour-là, même serviteur et domestique sont «comme toi» – et il se montre juste

---

33. En ce sens, on peut comprendre l'ajout postérieur du v. 11c: «une loi de vie... pour penser que c'est en tant que mortels qu'ils existent maintenant». La loi de vie permet à l'homme de consentir à sa limite, et donc à sa mort. Noter que, selon Ex 31, la pratique du sabbat est tellement essentielle que celui qui la transgresse s'exclut du peuple de l'alliance (vv. 14-15).

34. Le sabbat est au cœur des deux versions du décalogue. Il trône au centre de la structure littéraire: voir R. MEYNET, *Les dix commandements, loi de liberté. Analyse rhétorique d'Ex 20,2-17 et de Dt 5,6-21*, dans *Mélanges de l'Université de Beyrouth* 50 (1984) 405-421 et A. WÉNIN, *Le décalogue, révélation de Dieu et chemin de bonheur*, dans *RTL* 25 (1994) 145-182, pp. 154-164. Il est également central quant au sens: voir par exemple P. BEAUCHAMP, *Au cœur de la Loi, le décalogue*, dans *Croire aujourd'hui* 184 (1987) 259-570, pp. 267-270.

35. Voir ci-dessus, note 11.

en refusant de faire de sa maison un lieu de servitude.

De plus, si, comme le disent certains commentateurs[36], l'injuste dont il faut se garder n'est autre que l'idole, on se rapproche peut-être davantage encore du cœur de la loi du sabbat. En effet, comme l'écrit superbement Paul Beauchamp, «s'il n'y avait pas le remède du sabbat, le travail n'arriverait pas à se dégager de la pente de l'idolâtrie[37]». C'est que, dans le travail, il en va de l'image de Dieu qui est la vocation de l'être humain. Qui ne met pas de limite à son travail, ne montre-t-il pas de quel Dieu il se veut l'image: un Dieu imaginaire dont la puissance n'a pas de limite? Et tandis qu'un tel homme croit être son propre maître, il est en réalité l'esclave de lui-même, de son travail et de ce qu'il procure: profit et pouvoir.

Enfin, dans cette dernière strophe du poème de Ben Sira, il y a peut-être aussi, plus largement, un écho discret à la «loi» que cache, en Gn 1,29-30, le don de la nourriture – loi de vie s'il en est –, ainsi qu'à son prolongement explicite dans la première parole adressée à l'adam dans le second récit en Gn 2,16-17. En effet, sous le don du régime végétal, ne peut-on lire l'invitation à se garder de l'injustice que contient toute violence, comme on l'a vu plus haut? N'est-ce pas là un commandement indirect à propos d'un prochain à ne pas heurter, à ne pas opprimer ou écraser (ἐκθλίβειν), à l'instar des astres qui, obéissant à l'ordre de Dieu, respectent la place l'un de l'autre (voir Si 16,28)? Quant à la parole qui pose une limite à la possession du don de Dieu en Gn 2,16-17, elle aussi avertit d'un danger qui menace la relation à l'autre. Car ce serait un manque de justice – de justesse – que vivre sa vie dans le déni de la limite qu'impose la présence d'autrui, ou dans une prétention à tout savoir qui ruinerait les chances d'une relation vraie avec lui.

On le voit, ces deux paroles divines ont une portée relationnelle: au fond, elles définissent les conditions fondamentales pour que l'humain puisse entrer dans une dynamique d'alliance qui est pour la vie. Dès lors, ces paroles ne révèlent-elles pas quelque chose de la gloire et de la grandeur de Celui qui les énonce (cf. Si 17,13)? Or, s'il y a révélation, elle

---

36. DE FRAINE, *Het loflied op de menselijke waardigheid*, p. 19, ou ALONSO SCHÖKEL, *The Vision of Man*, p. 241, qui pense que le ἀδίκου du grec renvoie à un original hébreu כזב désignant l'idole (voir sa traduction dans *Proverbios y Eclesiástico* [Los libros sagrados], Madrid, Cristiandad, 1968, p. 202. DUESBERG, *La dignité de l'homme*, p. 19-20, traduit «apostasie».

37. P. BEAUCHAMP, *La loi du Décalogue*, p. 398. Voir aussi le développement aux pp. 399-401, ou A. WÉNIN, *Le Sabbat. Histoire et théologie* (Horizons de la Foi, 70), Bruxelles, Connaître la Bible, 1996, pp. 21-25.

est bien dans la manière du Dieu du Sinaï qui se montre en se cachant, se voile en se dévoilant, comme le suggère la symbolique de la nuée[38]. Car ces paroles qui énoncent une loi de vie le font de manière indirecte, comme pour susciter la liberté et l'intelligence de l'humain invité à s'accomplir à l'image de Dieu. Ainsi, derrière les apparences d'un discours banal parlant de manger, une parole bien plus profonde dissimule le désir de vie et de liberté qui anime le Créateur à l'égard de tout homme.

C'est peut-être ce dont le Siracide a l'intuition lorsque, en prolongeant son discours sur la création, il en vient à dire que la gloire de Dieu n'éclate vraiment que lorsqu'il offre à l'homme le savoir et qu'il l'invite à l'alliance en lui léguant une loi de vie. Et si la chose devient claire pour Israël au Sinaï, elle est déjà présente en germe dans la création, lorsque Dieu donne à l'homme l'exemple du sabbat et qu'il lui donne sa nourriture. Car il lui suggère, avec la discrétion que suppose le respect de sa liberté, que seule une vie vécue en esprit d'alliance permet qu'il tienne sa juste place dans le monde, se gardant ainsi de l'injustice qui risque toujours de mener celui-ci au chaos. C'est un même dessein qui anime la création et l'histoire d'Israël, signe d'une continuité profonde dans l'œuvre d'un Dieu qui ne se résigne pas à l'échec lorsque la faute de l'humain la menace. Le mérite de Ben Sira est de le souligner à sa manière, avec une profonde intelligence des choses de Dieu.

Boulevard du Nord 56/10   André WÉNIN
B-5000 Namur

---

38. Voir, par exemple, M. GIRARD, *Les symboles dans la Bible. Essai de théologie biblique enracinée dans l'expérience humaine universelle* (Recherches, N.S. 26), Montréal-Paris, Bellarmin-Cerf, 1991, pp. 455-456. — Je remercie mon collègue Jean-Marie Auwers pour ses avis stimulants.

SIRACH 22,9-15
"THE LIFE OF THE FOOL IS WORSE THAN DEATH"

That Ben Sira has much to say about the wise and wisdom should come as no surprise[1]. Indeed, wisdom together with fear of the Lord[2] is the principal concern of the book. Nor is it unexpected that the sage throughout his work likewise makes many remarks about the fool and folly, the opposite of wisdom, precisely because it is, in his theology, the result of willful ignorance and moral deficiency. Scholars have written extensively about the wise and wisdom in Ben Sira; few studies, however, have appeared that deal with the fool and folly. The present article is an attempt at analyzing one of the sage's major poems on the subject. Unfortunately, the text of 22,9-15 is not extant in Hebrew; so I will base my analysis on a critical study of the Greek text, utilizing of course also the Syriac and Latin witnesses[3]. In this poem Ben Sira expresses his ut-

1. In the book, including the grandson's prologue, the number of occurrences of the words "wisdom" and "wise" is instructive. In Gk I, one of the complete forms of the book, the root σοφ-, as the noun "wisdom", as the adjective "wise", or noun "the wise", and as the verb "to be wise", occurs a total of 90 times; Gk II has a few more occurrences. In the *NAB*, which was based on the Cairo Geniza MSS and other Hebrew fragments of the book, the word "wisdom" occurs 66 times, and "wise" or "the wise" 38 times for a total of 104 times. For the concordance work of the MT, LXX (RAHLFS' text comprises the data base, which gives Gk I, but not Gk II, of Sirach), Latin, Greek NT, and *NAB* I used the elegant computer programs found in *Accordance CD-ROM Library 2 with Accordance 3.0: Bible Study Software for the Macintosh*, Vancouver, WA = Altamonte Springs, FL: Gramcord Institute/OakTree Software Specialists, 1997 (for my abstract of these programs see *OTA* 21 [1998] #1193).

2. The expression "fear the Lord or God" or equivalent recurs some 55 to 60 times in the book; so J. HASPECKER *Gottesfurcht bei Jesus Sirach. Ihre religiöse Structur und ihre literarische und doktrinäre Bedeutung* (AnBib, 30), Rome, Biblical Institute, 1967, p. 82.

3. I will cite the chapter- and verse-numbers in Ben Sira as given in their proper order in J. ZIEGLER, *Sapientia Jesu Filii Sirach* (Septuaginta 12/2), Göttingen, Vandenhoeck & Ruprecht, 1966, which I used for the Greek textual criticism of the poem. For the Syriac, since there is no critical edition of Sirach available yet, I consulted the facsimile of A. M. CERIANI (ed.), *Translatio Syra Pescitto Veteris Testamenti ex codice Ambrosiano sec. fere VI photolithographice edita*, Milan, Pogliani, 1876-1883; P.A. DE LAGARDE, *Libri Veteris Testamenti apocryphi Syriace*, Leipzig-London, F.A. Brockhaus-Williams & Norgate, 1861, a diplomatic edition of a VIth-century codex, British Library 12142; *Biblia sacra juxta versionem simplicem quae dicitur Pschitta*, Beirut, Imprimerie Catholique, 1951; and B. WALTON, *Biblia sacra polyglotta*, 4, London, Thomas Roycroft, 1657. For the Latin, I used *Biblia sacra iuxta Latinam vulgatam versionem*, 12: *Sapientia Salomonis, Liber Hiesu filii Sirach*, Rome, Typis Polyglottis Vaticanis, 1964. For the Hebrew fragments I used R. SMEND, *Die Weisheit des Jesus Sirach, hebräisch und deutsch*, Berlin, Reimer, 1906, the best edition of the Geniza MSS available at that time; *The Book of Ben Sira: Text, Concordance and an Analysis of the Vocabulary*, Jerusalem: The Academy of

ter contempt for the fool. The reason is that the fool embodies the exact opposite of what the sage teaches about wisdom, which together with fear of the Lord, is the primary theme of his book[4].

TEXT AND TEXTUAL CRITICISM

Part A

I

22,9   συγκολλῶν[5] ὄστρακον[6] ὁ[7] διδάσκων μωρόν,
        ἐξεγείρων[8] καθεύδοντα[9] ἐκ βαθέος ὕπνου.
22,10 διηγούμενος[10] νυστάζοντι ὁ διηγούμενος μωρῷ,
        καὶ ἐπὶ συντελείᾳ ἐρεῖ Τί[11] ἐστιν[12];

II

22,11 ἐπὶ νεκρῷ κλαῦσον, ἐξέλιπεν γὰρ φῶς,
        καὶ ἐπὶ μωρῷ κλαῦσον, ἐξέλιπεν γὰρ σύνεσις[13].
        ἥδιον κλαῦσον ἐπὶ νεκρῷ, ὅτι ἀνεπαύσατο,
        τοῦ δὲ[14] μωροῦ ὑπὲρ θάνατον ἡ ζωὴ πονηρά[15].

the Hebrew Language and the Shrine of the Book, 1973; and A.A. DI LELLA, *The Newly Discovered Sixth Manuscript [MS F] of Ben Sira from the Cairo Geniza*, in *Bib* 69 (1988) 226-238. All translations of Ben Sira are my own; other biblical translations, except where otherwise noted, are taken from the *NAB*.
    4. There is discussion regarding the primary theme of Ben Sira. J. HASPECKER (*Gottesfurcht bei Jesus Sirach* [n. 2], pp. 87-105) holds that fear of God is the total theme. But G. VON RAD (*Wisdom in Israel*, Nashville, Abingdon, 1972, p. 242) and J. MARBÖCK (*Weisheit im Wandel. Untersuchungen zur Weisheitstheologie bei Ben Sira* [BBB, 37], Bonn, Hanstein, 1971) insist that wisdom is the fundamental theme. My own view is that Ben Sira's primary theme is wisdom as fear of the Lord; see P.W. SKEHAN and A.A. DI LELLA, *The Wisdom of Ben Sira* (AB, 39), New York, Doubleday, 1987, pp. 75-76.
    5. Pr. ὡς ὁ 575, Syr, Lat, Coptic, Armenian.
    6. ὄστρακα O-V, Syr (see exegesis); *testam ad testam* Sahidic.
    7. Pr. οὕτως 575, Lat, Syr, Armenian.
    8. Pr. ὡς ὁ Antonius Melissa, Lat; pr. *et quasi*, Syr, Coptic.
    9. καθεύδοντας many MSS, Antonius Melissa, Syr.
    10. Pr. καὶ ὡς 575 (cf. Syr); pr. ὡς ὁ 697, Coptic, Ethiopic.
    11. τίς 253 *c* 429 743, most Lat witnesses.
    12. For this verse Syr reads: "And like one who eats bread when he is not hungry, so is the one who teaches a fool. And when your words are finished, he says to you: What did you say"?
    13. So B[c] *L*´-672-743 *b* and many other cursives, Lat, some Church Fathers, and some other versions; σύνεσις καὶ σοφία 575; φρόνεσις (-σης) 534; σύνεσιν (preferred by RAHLFS and ZIEGLER) the rest; Syr has "wisdom".
    14. γάρ S* A O-V *L*-315´-743 and other cursives (see Lat and Syr); > C and some cursives.
    15. For this verse Syr reads: "For the dead you should weep because he is deprived of the light, but for the fool because he is deprived of wisdom; you should not weep for the dead because he is at rest; indeed, worse than death is an evil life".

22,12 πένθος νεκροῦ ἑπτὰ ἡμέραι,
μωροῦ δὲ καὶ ἀσεβοῦς[16] πᾶσαι αἱ ἡμέραι τῆς ζωῆς αὐτοῦ[17].

Part B

III

22,13 μετὰ ἄφρονος μὴ πληθύνῃς λόγον
καὶ πρὸς ἀσύνετον[18] μὴ πορεύου[19].
φύλαξαι ἀπ᾽ αὐτοῦ, ἵνα μὴ κόπον ἔχῃς
καὶ οὐ μὴ μολυνθῇς ἐν τῷ ἐντιναγμῷ αὐτοῦ.
ἔκκλινον ἀπ᾽ αὐτοῦ καὶ εὑρήσεις ἀνάπαυσιν
καὶ οὐ μὴ ἀκηδιάσῃς ἐν τῇ ἀπονοίᾳ αὐτοῦ[20].

IV

22,14 ὑπὲρ μόλιβον[21] τί βαρυνθήσεται;
καὶ τί αὐτῷ ὄνομα ἀλλ᾽ ἢ μωρός;
22,15 ἄμμον καὶ ἅλα καὶ βῶλον σιδήρου
εὔκοπον[22] ὑπενεγκεῖν ἢ ἄνθρωπον ἀσύνετον[23].

I

22,9 Whoever teaches a fool is (like) one who glues potsherds together,
(or) rouses a sleeper from deep slumber.

---

16. Because Syr omits καὶ ἀσεβοῦς, N. PETERS *Das Buch Jesus Sirach oder Ecclesiasticus übersetzt und erklärt* (HAT), Münster in W., Aschendorffsche Verlagsbuchhandlung, 1913, p. 180, considers the words a doublet. Aug. Gn q 172 also omits the words. See exegesis below.

17. The reading found in most witnesses and chosen also by RAHLFS and ZIEGLER; αὐτῶν A 311 575, Lat, and some other versions. See exegesis.

18. Syr has "pig", most likely the original reading that suits the context of the the verse better than ἀσύνετον, which probably was imported from v. 15b to soften the harshness of the image. The Syr reading is also preferred by R. SMEND, *Die Weisheit des Jesus Sirach erklärt*, Berlin, Reimer, p. 199; G.H. BOX and W.O.E. OESTERLEY, *Sirach*, in R.H. CHARLES (ed.), *The Apocrypha and Pseudepigrapha of the Old Testament in English*, Oxford, Clarendon, 1913, vol. 1, p. 391; N. PETERS, *Das Buch Jesus Sirach* (n. 16), pp. 180-181; and H. DUESBERG and I. FRANSEN, *Ecclesiastico* (La Sacra Bibbia... di S. Garofalo; Antico Testamento, ed. G. RINALDI), Turin, Marietti, 1966, p. 188.

19. Gk II (*L´*-672, Antonius Melissa) adds a colon: ἀναισθητῶν γὰρ ἐξουθενήσει σου τὰ πάντα, "for having no sense, he will treat with contempt everything about you". Instead of σου τὰ πάντα, 493-637 read σε.

20. For this verse Syr reads: "With the fool do not have pleasant conversations, and with a pig do not walk on the road; keep away from him lest he grieve you and lest he pollute you when he shakes himself off. Keep away from him and you will find rest, and he will not weary you by the abundance of his conversations".

21. The MSS spell this word in various ways: μόλιβδον, μόλυβδον, μόλυβον; the same variety is found in 47,18d.

22. εὐκοπώτερον many MSS and Lat (*facilius est*).

23. For the last three words Syr reads: "than to dwell with a foolish man". For the last two words Lat reads: *hominem inprudentem et fatuum et impium*, "an imprudent and foolish and godless person".

22,10 Whoever speaks with a fool speaks with a drowsy person;
       and when it is over, he will say, "What is that"?

II

22,11 Weep for the dead, for (his) light has failed;
       but weep for the fool, for (his) sense has failed.
       Weep less bitterly for the dead, for he is at rest;
       but the life of the fool is worse than death.
22,12 Mourning for the dead (lasts) seven days,
       but for the fool, the ungodly, all the days of his life.

III

22,13 With the stupid do not prolong talk,
       with a pig do not walk.
       Stay clear of him lest you have trouble
       and be spattered when he shakes himself off.
       Turn away from him and you will find rest
       and never be wearied by his loss of all sense.

IV

22,14 What is heavier than lead?
       And what is its name but "Fool"?
22,15 Sand and salt and a lump of iron
       are easier to bear than a senseless person.

COMMENTARY

Limits of the Poem and Strophic Structure

For the following reasons I consider 22,9-15 as a discrete poem[24]: (1)
the key word μωρός, "the fool" (recurring six times), and its synonyms
ἄφρονος, "the stupid" (22,13a), and ἀσύνετος, "the senseless"
(22,15b), comprise the obvious subject matter; (2) this subject matter is
different from that in 22,1-8 (vv. 7-8 are found only in Gk II) and in
22,16-18; and (3) the rather precise strophic structure.

The poem has clearly marked strophes divided into two parts: Part A
with two strophes (22,9-10 and 22,11-12); and Part B also with two strophes (22,13 and 22,14-15). Interestingly, each part has about the same
number of words: 62 in Part A, and 61 in Part B. Moreover, strophes I
and IV have 21 and 22 words, and strophes II and III have 41 and 39,
respectively, thus providing a symmetical word balance between the two
parts. Each strophe has a distinctive theme: strophe I stresses the futility
of teaching or talking with a fool; strophe II contrasts mourning for the

---

24. ZIEGLER in his edition (n. 3) also sets these verses apart as a unit.

dead with mourning for the fool; strophe III adds more daring images in resuming the theme of strophe I; and strophe IV concludes scornfully that lead, sand, salt, and iron (four classic images) are easier to bear than the fool. The key word μῶρος appears in each of the five bicola of Part A, and again, by way of *inclusio*, in the first bicolon (22,14b) of the last strophe.

Exegesis

Strophe I (22,9-10)

If you do not instruct and correct a child while he is still young (see Sir 7,23), he will become, as he grows older, a fool lacking in intelligence and good judgment. Later in his life it is useless for you to try to teach him, for he is already set in his ways, as Ben Sira clearly explains in 6,18-22; 25,3; and 30,7-13. Since the fool rejects discipline he will never have the ethical sense to fear the Lord (see Sir 32,16-33,2). The fool will, therefore, never attain wisdom, which is a gift of the Lord (Sir 1,6.8-10).

The opening verse (22,9) gives Ben Sira's overall view of the matter: teaching a fool is as pointless and futile as gluing together pieces of broken pottery, for just as the glued pot will fall apart when used again, so the fool obtains no benefit at all from what you are trying to teach him. In fact, the phrase in Syriac 22,9a, *mĕdabbeq ḥespē'*, "gluing potsherds together", became a proverb for "wasting labor"[25]. Ben Sira created this imagery, for it appears nowhere else in the OT. He expresses a similar thought in 21,14, not extant in Hebrew: ἔγκατα [a hapax in the LXX] μωροῦ ὡς ἀγγεῖον[26] συντετριμμένον καὶ πᾶσαν γνῶσιν οὐ κρατήσει, "The inner parts [=mind] of a fool are like a broken cistern; indeed, he can hold no knowledge at all"; see Jer 2,13 for the imagery. As regards the futility of trying to teach a fool, see Prov 1,22; 23,9; and 24,7.

In the grandson's translation (Gk I), μωρός occurs 26 times (6 times in our poem); in the rest of the Greek OT, the word appears only 9 other times: 4 times in Isaiah (19,11; 32,5; 32,6 [*bis*]); once each in Deut 32,6, Ps 93,8, Job 16,7, Jer 5,21, Dan 13,48[27]. Curiously, μωρός never occurs in the LXX of Proverbs, Ben Sira's favorite book. In a more ex-

---

25. J. PAYNE SMITH (ed.), *A Compendious Syriac Dictionary*, Oxford, Clarendon, 1903, p. 82.

26. Read "cistern" with Syriac.

27. In the NT, μωρός occurs 12 times: 6 times in Matthew and 4 times in 1 Corinthinans, and once in 2 Tim 2,23 and in Tit 3,9.

tensive poem, 22,13-26, which contrasts the wise and the fool, the grandson uses μωρός also 6 times; apparently, this is his favorite word for "fool". The vocabulary for "fool" is of course varied both in Hebrew and in Greek. In our poem, for example, the grandson likewise employs the synonyms ἄφρων, "stupid" (22,13a)[28], and ἀσύνετος, "senseless" (22, 13b [but see the textual note: the reading of Syriac, which has "pig", is to be preferred] and 22,15b), another word never found in LXX Proverbs. Whatever the vocabulary for "fool", however, Ben Sira considers such an individual lacking not only in intelligence (or theoretical wisdom) but also in morality (or practical wisdom)[29], by equating, as 22,12b shows, the fool and the ungodly; see also Prov 1,7; 27,22.

The sage now uses the familiar, though in this context quite uncomplimentary, image of rousing a sleeper from deep slumber (22,9b) to emphasize how futile it is to try to teach a fool. A sleepyhead will never learn. Instead of being on the watch to acquire wisdom, as Ben Sira urges his students (see, e.g., 6,18-37), the fool prefers to be in the "deep slumber" of his ignorance and ethical indifference (see 15,7-8). The graphic image continues in 22,10 where the poet describes speaking with the fool as speaking with "a drowsy person", νυστάζοντι, who is so inattentive and unmotivated to learn that he fails to get the point you are making and so blurts out, "What is that"? Ben Sira may have derived the imagery here from Prov 24,30-34, which aims its barbs at the lazy person: "I passed by the field of the sluggard, by the vineyard of the man without sense;/ And behold! it was all overgrown with thistles; its surface was covered with nettles, and its stone wall broken down./ And as I gazed at it, I reflected; I saw and learned the lesson:/ A little sleep [LXX ὀλίγον νυστάζω], a little slumber, a little folding of the arms to rest—/Then will poverty come upon you like a highwayman, and want like an armed man" (see also Prov 6,4-11).

Strophe II (22,11-12)

Ben Sira's language now becomes funereal. In these two verses the fool, μωρός, and the dead, νεκρός, recur together[30] the emphatic number of three times. In this strophe Ben Sira compares and contrasts

28. This is the favorite word for "fool" in LXX Proverbs where it recurs 74 times (and only 59 times in the rest of the LXX). For a study of words for fools and folly in the Jewish Bible and Ben Sira, see M.V. Fox, *Words for Folly*, in *ZAH* 10 (1997) 4-15.
29. See A.A. DI LELLA, *The Meaning of Wisdom in Ben Sira*, in L.G. PERDUE et al. (eds.), *In Search of Wisdom*. FS John G. Gammie, Louisville, KY, Westminster/John Knox, 1993, pp. 133-148.
30. Nowhere else in the LXX do νεκρός and μωρός occur in the same verse.

the two major tragedies of life, viz., death and folly; of the two, folly is by far the worse, for unlike death, it could have been avoided. You should mourn and weep for the dead, Ben Sira urges (22,11a), for at the moment of death "the light", φῶς, is gone out forever, nor is there life or hope of any kind in Sheol (Sir 14,16-17; 17,27-28; Job 14,12), which was thought to be the abode of all the dead – the saint and the sinner alike. The imagery here probably derives from Prov 20,27a: "The breath of a person is the lamp from Yahweh" (my translation of the MT); LXX, φῶς κυρίου πνοὴ ἀνθρώπων, "The breath of human beings is the light from the Lord"; cf. Prov 20,20. Ben Sira may employ the image of light also to refer to the light of day that has gone out for the dead. In Qoh 12,6 there are four other images of death: "The silver cord is snapped and the golden bowl is broken, and the pitcher is shattered at the spring, and the broken pulley falls into the well". You should also weep for the fool, because his "sense, or understanding", σύνεσις, has abandoned him (22,11b). In Bar 3,14, σύνεσις and φῶς also appear together: "Learn where prudence is, where strength, where understanding [σύνεσις];/ That you may know also where are length of days, and life, where light [φῶς] of the eyes, and peace".

Then Ben Sira makes two astounding statements, which I paraphrase: Weep less for the dead, for after all he is at rest and free from the aches and pains and sorrows that are inevitable parts of anyone's life (22,11c); for the idea of the dead being "at rest", see Job 3,11-19 and Qoh 4,1-2. But even though the text does not say so, the structure and balance of the verse clearly imply that you should "weep more for the fool", for as Ben Sira explicitly states, "the life of the fool is worse than death" (22,11d). Such an implied clause provides the contrast to 22,11c. By employing a deliberate ellipsis or aposiopesis[31], Ben Sira dramatizes the tragedy of a fool's life. Indeed, lacking wisdom, the fool was never in touch with the mystery of his own existence. The Lord, source of all wisdom (Sir 1,1), "has lavished her upon all who love[32] him" (Sir 1,10b); but the fool, despising discipline and education and ignoring the Law (Sir 21,6.18-

---

31. Other examples of the literary device of aposiopesis are found in the OT. In Deut 30,19, Moses says, "I call heaven and earth today to witness against you: I have set before you life and death, the blessing and the curse. Choose life, then, that you and your descendants may live"; in the context of Deut 30,15-20, we would expect the converse exhortation, "and do not choose death lest you and your descendants die". In Tob 14,11, Tobit says, "My children, note well what almsgiving does, and also what wickedness does—it kills"; after the clause, "what almsgiving does", there is an ellipsis of the words, "it gives life", which we would expect since this clause is the converse of the phrase, "it kills". See A.A. DI LELLA, *The Deuteronomic Background of the Farewell Discourse in Tob 14:3-11*, in *CBQ* 41 (1979) 380-389, pp. 386-387.

32. So most witnesses; the *l*-group and Syr read "fear".

19; 32,15.17-18; 33,2 in MS B), will never possess the divine gift of wisdom that alone makes life worth living. The point of 22,11 is that the loss of light at the moment of death is not so great a calamity as the loss of sense in the fool. Indeed, death is inevitable; folly is not.

The period of mourning for the dead lasted "seven days" (22,12a; see also Gen 50,10; Jdt 16,24), called שִׁבְעָה to this day among orthodox Jews. Ben Sira now identifies the fool with "the ungodly", καὶ ἀσεβοῦς, which is epexegetical to μωροῦ; hence, I judge this expression to be essential in the poem (see the critical note), for it describes exactly the one who has no fear of the Lord. Mourning for such a person should last "all the days of his life", πᾶσαι αἱ ἡμέραι τῆς ζωῆς αὐτοῦ (22,12b; I read the singular pronoun because the expressions "the fool" and "the ungodly" refer to the same individual; see the critical note) since he is worse off than the dead, as 22,11 argues. We should contrast what Ben Sira states here with the admonition he gives in 38,16-23, where he urges moderation in mourning for the dead, "a day or two" (38,17c) presumably of the more intense wailing and weeping that were traditional (see Jer 9,16-19), since the full period of more subdued mourning was seven days, as already noted. Mourning for the fool, however, has no such limits.

Strophe III (22,13)

This strophe amplifies what Ben Sira speaks of in the first strophe. Not only is teaching a fool a waste of time and talking with him like talking with a sleepy person (22,9-10), you should not waste your words on the fool (22,13a), now called "the stupid", ἄφρων, the favorite word for "fool" in LXX Proverbs, as noted above. Then the sage employs the contemptuous epithet, "pig", to describe the fool (22,13b, see the textual note). The pig was viewed as an unclean animal, which one was forbidden to eat and whose dead body one was not allowed to touch (Lev 11,6-8; Deut 14,8). You should keep your distance from the fool to avoid trouble as well as the defilement of his nonsense and stupidity when he, like a pig after emerging from the muck it has wallowed in, "shakes himself off" (22,13cd). The fool must be avoided, the sage implies mockingly, because he is unclean like the pig. The particular repugnance the Jews felt for the pig was exactly the sentiment Ben Sira felt for the fool. Compare Matt 7,6: "Do not give what is holy to dogs, or throw your pearls before swine, lest they trample them underfoot, and turn and tear you to pieces". Background for Sir 22,13ab may have come from Prov 17,12, "Face a bear robbed of her cubs, but never a fool in his folly"!

In 27,12a, Ben Sira exhorts you to "limit the time you spend among the senseless [ἀσύνετοι]". But keeping away from the fool altogether is the sure way to find "rest", ἀνάπαυσις (22,13e; see 6,28), secure in your own sound judgment and good sense (see 51,17 Greek). Then you will never be worn out by his "loss of all sense", ἀπονοία (21,13f), which can also signify "madness", perhaps the meaning implied here in view of the harshness of the language in this poem. You will also be spared the fool's senseless chatter, as Ben Sira teaches elsewhere: "The mind of fools is in their mouth" (21,26a); the fool speaks without thinking. "The mind of a fool is like a fast cart-wheel, and his thoughts like a turning axle" (33,5 MS F; see also 27,11), changing all the time, with no convictions or considered opinions. The fool fails to grasp the ironic truth found in Prov 17,28: "Even a fool, if he keeps silent, is considered wise; if he closes his lips, intelligent". The ideas in Sir 22,13 are echoes from Proverbs: "The mouth of a fool is imminent ruin" (Prov 10,14b); "The just man's lips nourish many, but fools die for want of sense" (Prov 10,21); "A shrewd man conceals his knowledge, but the hearts of fools gush forth folly" (Prov 12,23); "Walk with wise men and you will become wise, but the companion of fools will fare badly" (Prov 13,20); see also Prov 15,2; 18,7; 26,11 (v. 11a is quoted in 2 Pet 2,22).

Strophe IV (22,14-15)

In the concluding strophe Ben Sira summarizes his total exasperation and disgust with the fool, by asking "what is heavier than lead?" and then answering his own question with a biting rhetorical question, "And what is its name but 'Fool'"? (22,14b). The image of the heaviness of lead here may have been borrowed from Exod 15,10: "When your wind blew, the sea covered them [the pursuing Egyptians]; like lead they sank in the mighty waters".

The sage echoes the imagery of "sand" as a heavy load, which is, however, easier to bear than the fool's behavior (22,15a), from Prov 27,3: "Stone is heavy, and sand a burden, but a fool's provocation is heavier than both" (see also Job 6,2-3). The mention of "salt" in the same context as "lead" and between obviously heavy items like sand and iron is curious. Perhaps the sage had in mind the text of Ahiqar ii,45 (Syriac version): "My son, I have carried salt and removed lead: and I have not seen anything heavier than that a man should pay back a debt that he did not borrow"[33]. In 39,26ab, Ben Sira mentions among the necessities of life "water and fire and iron and salt". Harder to bear, for all

---

33. Cited in BOX and OESTERLEY, *Sirach* (n. 16), p. 296.

the reasons described in the poem, "than sand and salt and iron" is "a senseless person", ἄνθρωπον ἀσύνετον (22,15b). The Latin (see the critical note) emphatically expands that Greek expression, describing such a person as being likewise "imprudent" and "godless", for indeed in Ben Sira's theology that is precisely what the fool happens to be.

CONCLUSION

In view of Ben Sira's primary thesis that true wisdom consists in fear of the Lord, it is not surprising that he speaks so caustically about fools who lack intellectual ability (22,11b,13) as well as essential righteousness (22,12b; 34,1). In addition to our text, he devotes another more extensive composition to the fool (21,13-26). In that poem the sage makes many other scathing comments: "A fool's chatter is like a load on a journey" (21,16a; see 22,15). "Like a house in ruins is wisdom to a fool, and the knowledge of the senseless person is talk without sense [lit., unexamined words]" (21,18). "Education is like fetters on the feet of the unintelligent, and like manacles on the right hand" (21,19). But in our brief poem Ben Sira employs especially stark images to express his most scathing observations concerning the fool. Small wonder he makes that astounding statement in 22,11d: "The life of the fool is worse than death".

The Catholic University   Alexander A. DI LELLA, O.F.M.
    of America
Washington, DC
USA

LA PARABOLE DE LA VEUVE
DE BEN SIRA 35,11-24 À LUC 18,1-8

Le livre de Ben Sira peut être considéré comme un fruit tardif de la tradition biblique. A l'époque où s'ébauche le Judaïsme, il offre un florilège des grands thèmes contenus dans les textes sacrés antérieurs (cf. Si 33,16-18) et repris par la littérature rabbinique. Moins de deux siècles plus tard, Jésus de Nazareth et, à sa suite, les premiers auteurs chrétiens ont bénéficié du même patrimoine culturel et religieux que Ben Sira; comment s'étonner, dès lors, que beaucoup d'expressions ou d'images présentées par cet auteur soient utilisées dans l'Evangile? Aucune citation explicite n'autorise à parler d'emprunt direct au Siracide dans le Nouveau Testament, bien que la plupart des textes chrétiens inspirés aient été écrits avant que ne soit fixé le canon juif des Ecritures et que Ben Sira soit exclu du nombre des livres saints. L'Ecclésiastique est néanmoins l'un des derniers maillons d'une tradition à laquelle le Christ puise, comme un «scribe avisé», ajoutant à cet ancien «trésor» la nouveauté propre à l'Evangile. Un exemple de cette continuité entre les paroles de Jésus, fils de Sira, et celles de Jésus, Fils de Dieu, peut être trouvé dans deux petits textes, concernant une veuve et son juge: Si 35,12(14)-24(26)[1] et Lc 18,1-8. La similitude entre les deux passages a été souvent remarquée, rarement étudiée en détail[2].

---

1. Pour les citations du texte grec, nous emploierons ici la numérotation de A. Rahlfs, utilisée par la Bible de Jérusalem. Lorsqu'une citation est prise dans le texte hébreu, le chiffre entre parenthèses renvoie à la numération de la Vulgate, utilisée pour le manuscrit B du Caire, dans P. BOCCACCIO – G. BERARDI, *Ecclesiasticus, textus hebraeus secundum fragmenta reperta*, Roma, Pontificio Istituto Biblico, 1986, cf aussi A.A. DI LELLA, *The Hebrew Text of Sirach, A Text-Critical and Historical Study*, The Hague, 1966. Pour un état de la question: M. GILBERT, *L'Ecclésiastique: quel texte? quelle autorité?* in *RB* 94 (1987) 233-250, et *Jérôme et l'oeuvre de Ben Sira*, in *Le Muséon* 100 (1987) 109-120.

2. Même W.O.E. OESTERLEY, *The Gospel Parables in the Light of Their Jewish Background*, London, 1936, pp. 202 et 222, ne s'arrête pas sur le texte de Ben Sira et C. SPICQ, *La parabole de la veuve obstinée et du juge aux décisions impromptues (Lc XVIII,1-8)*, in *RB* 68 (1961) 68-90, lui accorde peu d'importance. Plus récemment, G. ROSSÉ, *Il vangelo di Luca*, Roma, 1992, p. 687 se contente de noter le parallèle entre les versets Lc 18,7 et Si 35,17-20. W. GRUNDMANN, *Das Evangelium nach Lukas*, Berlin, 1969, p. 348 suppose dans Lc 18,7-8 une glose due à l'influence de Si; déjà D. BUZY, *Le juge inique (Luc XVIII,1-8)*, in *RB* 39 (1930) 388, critiquait une position similaire de A. Jülicher. L'étude effectuée par K.E. BAILEY, *Through Peasant Eyes*, Grand Rapids, MI, 1983, pp. 127-138, est assez approfondie et l'auteur conclut: «There is a clearly identifiable literary background… in this case our prototype is Ben Sira». Cf aussi C. G. MONTEFIORE, *The Synoptic Gospels*, London, 1909 p. 552.

Dans l'Ancien Testament, la figure de la veuve est le type même d'une faiblesse qui n'a que Dieu pour recours: *Dieu est le justicier des veuves* (Ps 68,6)[3]. Parler de *veuve* évoque Tamar, ancêtre de la tribu de Juda, Noémi et Ruth, aïeules de David, Judith, *«qui a enlevé sa robe de deuil pour relever les affligés d'Israël»*[4] ou la fausse veuve de Teqoa (2 S 14), envoyée à David par Joab et présentant sa situation comme une parabole du peuple en détresse. Jérusalem en ruines est identifiée à une veuve en Jr 51,5, dans les premiers versets des Lamentations ou le quatrième chapitre de Baruch[5]. La veuve personifie donc souvent la tribu de Juda, Jérusalem ou le Peuple Saint dans l'épreuve[6]. Cette allégorie est présente à l'esprit de Ben Sira, puisque dans la finale apocalyptique du chapitre 35, c'est le *peuple* du Seigneur qui bénéficie de la justice et de la miséricorde divine (Si 35,23), à l'instar de la veuve (Si 35,15-18)[7].

Luc est le seul évangéliste (hormis Mc 12,40ss dans le passage parallèle à Lc 21,2ss) à utiliser cette figure traditionnelle. La parenté de la parabole de Lc 18 avec l'allégorie de Si 35 constitue ainsi un exemple précieux de l'insertion du témoignage spécifique à Luc sur Jésus dans le judaïsme contemporain, même si le sujet a été élaboré avec le talent propre à cet évangéliste[8].

Dans le troisième évangile, en effet, l'image de la veuve en prière demeure un exemple de la persévérance des justes d'Israël, telle Anne au Temple (Lc 2,37), mais elle prend une dimension universelle, par le rappel de la veuve de Sarepta en 4,25-26[9]; elle est le type des pauvres, ob-

---

3. F.C. FENSHAM, *Widow, Orphan and the Poor in Ancient Near Eastern Literature.* in J. CRENSHAW (ed.), *Studies in Ancient Israelite Wisdom*, New York, 1976, 161-174 et C. VAN LEEUWEN, *Le développement du sens social en Israël avant l'Ere chrétienne*, Assen, 1955, pp. 26-28. Sur 72 occurrences de אלמנה (χήρα), seules 17 sont au pluriel. Comme dans le reste de l'Orient Ancien, le terme est souvent associé à *orphelin* et *étranger*, en particulier dans la littérature deutéronomique et prophétique, mais aussi en Jb, Ps, Tb, 2 M. Dans la littérature de Sagesse: Pr 15,25; 23,10; Sg 2,10; Si 4,10. Sur la législation concernant les veuves, voir A. TOSATO, *Il matrimonio israelitico, una teoria generale*, Roma, 1982, pp. 148ss, et E. NEUFELD, *Ancient Hebrew Mariage Laws*, London, 1944, p. 243.

4. J. ALONSO-SCHÖKEL, *Judit, Rut* (Libros Sagrados, 8), Madrid, 1973, pp. 108-109.

5. C. COHEN, *The Widowed City*, in *JANES* (1973) 75-81.

6. J.F. CRAGHAN, *Ester, Judith and Ruth, Paradigms of Human Liberation* in *Bibl Theol Bull.* (1982) 11-19. Le thème est antique: dans la littérature extra-biblique, le premier texte à mentionner Israël, la stèle de Merneptah (env. 1230 av. J.-C.) affirme: *«Israël est restée dévastée, sa race n'est plus, Hurru (la Grande Palestine) est devenue une veuve pour l'Egypte»* (ANET, p. 378).

7. C. SPICQ, *L'Ecclésiastique* (La Sainte Bible, éd. Pirot-Clamer, t. VI), Paris, 1946, p. 743, reprenant R. SMEND, *Die Weisheit des Jesus Sirach*, Berlin, 1906 et N. PETERS, *Ecclesiasticus Ebraice*, Munster, 1913. P.W. SKEHAN – A.A. DI LELLA, *The Wisdom of Ben Sira* (AB, 39) New York, 1987, pp. 419-420.

8. *«La langue propre à Luc est en contraste avec le caractère sémitique de la parabole»*, SPICQ, *La parabole* (n. 2), p. 68.

9. La lecture universaliste du thème de la veuve s'accorde avec la tradition de l'An-

jets de la miséricorde toute-puissante du Christ, comme la veuve de Naïm (Lc 7,12); elle offre aux disciples le modèle du sacrifice, comme celle qui verse tout son nécessaire vital dans le trésor du temple (Lc 21,2-3). Bref, elle représente les humbles, peuple des élus sauvé par le Christ[10].

Le genre littéraire des deux textes est sensiblement différent: alors que Luc met en scène une parabole, le texte du Siracide prend simplement la veuve en exemple. Mais il convient de souligner que Lc 18,1-8 est, comme Si 35, un texte sapientiel. L'utilisation du genre parabolique n'est pas le seul indice qui permet de l'affirmer. L'invitation à écouter: «Écoutez ce que dit ce juge inique!» (v. 6), unique chez Luc, reprend une technique fréquente dans les écrits de sagesse et surtout le Siracide (Si 3,1; 6,23; 16,24; 23,7; 31,22; 33,19; 39,13...). L'apostrophe est ici paradoxale: il s'agit d'écouter un juge inique pour comprendre a fortiori l'attitude du juste Juge. La finale interrogative: «Le Fils de l'homme, quand il viendra trouvera-t-il la foi sur la terre?» est aussi un procédé didactique que l'on trouve plusieurs fois chez Ben Sira, par exemple en Si 33,33 et 34,26.

Les deux textes font de la veuve un modèle de persévérance dans la prière, mais le Siracide met davantage en relief la puissance de la supplication des humbles, en contraste avec l'inefficacité d'un sacrifice injuste, tandis que Luc souligne la nécessité de prier sans se décourager. Cette divergence de but[11] – clairement rédactionnelle chez Luc[12] – s'explique par les deux modes de prière auxquels les auteurs font habituellement référence: pour Luc, la prière permanente, typique de l'esprit paulinien, est fondamentale (Lc 11,5-13), pour Ben Sira, c'est la sincérité du culte qui est examinée[13]: il s'agit de ne pas chercher à corrompre Dieu par un sacrifice qui voudrait couvrir l'injustice. Il n'est pas surprenant de voir ici le sacrifice injuste supplanté par la plainte des malheureux: cette spiritualisation du culte a été préparée par deux passages de même facture concernant les sacrifices (Si 34,18-35,10)[14];

---

cien Testament: la veuve de Sarepta est habitante de Sidon, Tamar est Cananéenne, Ruth Moabite. L'insistance de Luc sur le veuvage de cette femme en fait une figure de l'Israël universel, cf L. SABOURIN, L'Évangile de Luc, Roma, 1985.

10. M.-J. LAGRANGE, Évangile selon saint Luc, Paris, 1921, s'oppose à l'interprétation de la veuve comme figure de l'Église en Luc 18,1-8 en contraste avec la tradition (Augustin, Raban Maur, S. de Sacy) cf. SPICQ, L'Ecclésiastique (n. 7), p. 743.

11. BAYLEY (n. 2), p.128.

12. C'est Luc lui-même qui intervient pour expliquer l'intention de la parabole en Lc 18,1.

13. Si 45 et 50. Ce passage montre que le judaïsme de Si s'inscrit dans la ligne des prophètes (Jr 6,20; 7,21ss, Is 1,11; Am 5,21ss etc): la pratique de la Loi assume elle-même la valeur de culte.

14. Si 35,3: «Ce qui plaît au Seigneur, c'est qu'on se détourne du mal, c'est offrir un sacrifice expiatoire que de fuir l'injustice».

elle correspond à une manière propre au sage de traiter le thème de la prière[15].

Ainsi s'explique l'application de la parabole aux «élus»[16], chez Luc, plutôt qu'à «celui qui rend un culte» (à l'autel), chez Ben Sira. Mais il faut ajouter qu'en Si 35,16, «celui qui rend le culte de tout son coeur» (BJ) ou «celui qui sert de façon agréable à Dieu» (v. 16: θεραπεύων ἐν εὐδοκίᾳ) est mis en parallèle avec «l'humble» du v. 17 et désigne le pauvre, l'opprimé, l'orphelin et la veuve des vv. 13-15. Or, tout au long de l'évangile de Luc, les «élus» en détresse sont justement ces «serviteurs» agréables à Dieu[17], les humbles, les pauvres, les opprimés, les veuves (cf. Lc 21,3: «cette veuve qui est pauvre a mis plus qu'eux tous» et les Béatitudes en 6,20-23).

Au-delà de cette nuance dans l'intention des auteurs, l'image de la veuve est utilisée dans les deux cas pour exhorter à la confiance: le jugement est inéluctable (Si 35,19; Lc 18,7). La place accordée à la dimension apocalyptique de ce jugement semble plus importante en Si que chez Luc, mais ce n'est qu'une apparence: la parabole de la veuve fait suite à la petite apocalypse de Lc 17,22-37[18]. La mension des *élus* et la référence finale au *Fils de l'Homme quand il viendra* relient Lc 18,8 aux quatre annonces du *Jour du Fils de l'Homme* situées dans le discours précédent où est exprimé le jugement des nations au temps de Noé ou de Sodome.

Ainsi, malgré de réelles différences, les deux textes concernant la veuve présentent des affinités en de qui concerne le genre littéraire et l'intention: ils sont didactiques, ayant pour but l'enseignement de la prière au moyen d'un même exemple et ont une portée eschatologique.

On constate aussi une certaine similitude dans la structure des passages qui peuvent être divisés en quatre temps:

1. *Le but du texte* est présenté par une courte phrase en tête des deux écrits: il faut prier sans cesse et ne pas se décourager (Lc 18,1), N'es-

---

15. Voir les grandes prières de Si 22,27-23,6; 36,1-22; 51,1-12.

16. A. GEORGE, *La parabole du juge qui fait attendre le jugement*, in *Assemblées du Seigneur* (II) 60 (1975) 68-79, note que ce terme n'est employé qu'ici par Luc pour désigner des hommes et qu'il a toujours une portée eschatologique dans les synoptiques (Mt 24,22-31 et Mc 13,20-27). Ce qui rapproche Lc 18,7b de Ap 6,10-11.

17. Εὐδοκία, utilisé en Si 35,16, signifie en Lc 2,14 et 10,21 l'élection des humbles par Dieu. L'interprétation du verset hébreu est difficile: «l'affliction est une amertume bien accueillie» (Levi) ou la plainte apportée de façon droite est un «bien acceptable» (Smend).

18. C.E.B. CRANFIELD, *The Parable of the Unjust Judge and the Escatology of Luke-Acts* in *ScotJT* 16 (1963) 297-301.

saye pas de le corrompre par des présents, il les refuse, ne t'appuie pas sur un sacrifice injuste (Si 35,11)[19].

2. *L'exemple proprement dit* se déroule de façon similaire dans les deux cas. Le lecteur assiste d'abord à l'entrée en scène des personnages: après la présentation du juge (Lc 18,2; Si 35,12), vient celle de la veuve (Lc 18,3a). Elle est accompagnée, en Si, des autres «humbles»: le pauvre, l'opprimé et l'orphelin, mais l'accent est mis sur sa plainte (Si 35,13-14). La situation dramatique est ensuite décrite: la veuve vient sans cesse (Lc 18,4-5a) et les larmes redoublent (Si 35,15a)[20]. Finalement l'auteur annonce la résolution du conflit: la puissance d'intercession des humbles, dont la veuve est le type, suscite la sentence car les larmes de la veuve molestent le juge ou risquent de le mettre en disgrâce auprès des gens de la ville selon Lc 18,5b[21]; ses larmes deviennent un cri qui accuse celui qui les provoque en Si 35,15b.

3. *L'application de cet exemple* aux élus (Lc 18,7a) ou aux serviteurs (Si 35,16) met en relief leur persévérance (Lc 18,7b – Si,35,17-18) et assure l'intervention rapide de Dieu, en réponse à leur prière (Lc 18,7c-8a – Si 35,19).

4. *Une finale apocalyptique* clôture les deux passages[22]: la venue du Fils de l'homme sur la terre est annoncée chez Lc (18,8bc), tandis que le jugement impitoyable des nations est évoqué en Si 35,20-24 dans une formulation apparentée aux textes prophétiques contre les nations (cf. Is 25,2-5) et mis en contraste avec la justice et la miséricorde salvatrice[23] rendue à Israël.

Le dicton final de Si 35,24[24] tombe aussi abruptement que l'interrogation de Lc 18,8. La *tribulation* et les *nuées* dont il est question en Si appartiennent au vocabulaire apocalyptique lié au Fils de l'homme (Dn 7,13; 12,1; Mt 24,29), et utilisé par Lc dans un autre texte (21,23-28).

---

19. En Si 35,11, comme en Lc 18,1, l'introduction de la parabole est nettement séparée du reste du texte. Si 35,11 constitue un impératif que justifie le long développement de 35,12-23.

20. Le verbe ירד est utilisé en 46,6 pour la grêle. SMEND (n. 2), p. 314, s'appuie sur le syriaque pour défendre la valeur intensive du verbe.

21. J.D.M. DERRETT, *Law in the New Testament: The Parable of the Unjust Judge*, in *NTS* 18 (1971-72) 178-191.

22. Le lien entre les deux finales est souligné par Ph. BOSSUYT et J. RADERMAKERS, *Jésus Parole de la Grâce selon saint Luc,* Bruxelles, 1984, p. 399.

23. En Si 35,23(25) la *miséricorde* du grec (ἐν τῷ ἐλέει αὐτου) correspond en hébreu au *salut* (בישועתו).

24. Le verset 24 constitue soit un ajout d'un copiste ancien, soit un proverbe introduit là dans le texte initial en raison du mot-crochet miséricorde. Le texte hébreu n'est pas d'un grand secours car le premier stique est corrompu, mais il confirme l'antiquité de ce verset. E. LEVI, *L'Ecclésiastique*, Paris, 1898, p. 167.

Chez les deux auteurs, la conclusion de la parabole, la «morale» pourrait-on dire, consiste en un jeu d'oppositions, qui met en relief la certitude de l'intervention du «Seigneur», maître de l'univers, face au doute qu'engendre la souffrance des justes. Sur le plan littéraire, cet effet est rendu chez le Siracide par le contraste entre la prière de l'humble et la réponse décisive du Seigneur (répétition de «Et il ne...pas jusqu'à ce que»); chez Luc, l'opposition est exprimée par la question réthorique que Jésus pose au nom des disciples (interrogatif négatif) et sa réponse décisive (affirmatif positif)[25].

La prière de l'humble pénètre les nuées:

> *b) jusqu'à ce qu'elle parvienne à son but,*
> *a) elle ne se console pas (ne s'arrête pas, hé),*
> *a) et elle ne cesse pas*
> *b) jusqu'à ce que le Très-haut regarde*
> *et juge en faveur des justes*
> *et accomplisse le jugement*

> *a') et le Seigneur ne tarde pas*
> *et il ne se contiendra pas envers eux*
> *b') jusqu'à ce qu'il ait brisé les reins des sans-pitié*
> *et accompli envers les nations la revanche... (Si 35,19-20)*

> *b) Et Dieu n'accomplirait pas la revanche*
> *a) de ses élus qui crient vers lui jour et nuit*
> *a') alors qu'il se contient envers eux?*

> *je vous dis*
> *b') qu'il réalisera leur revanche avec rapidité (Lc 18,7-8a)*

Le contraste est basé sur l'opposition apparente entre l'insistance de l'homme et l'apparente non réponse de Dieu, d'un côté, et la certitude de l'accomplissement de la justice divine, «la revanche», de l'autre. Donc entre la réalité présente et l'attente[26]. Mais il existe une différence importante entre les deux manières de concevoir le «jugement». Chez Luc, la «revanche» est un rétablissement de la justice en faveur des élus et l'accent est mis sur la rapidité de la réponse divine; aucun châtiment des adversaires n'est évoqué: Luc ne s'intéresse pas directement au jugement des nations ou des «impies», bien que Sodome soit évoquée dans la péricope précédente (17,22-37). Le Siracide, lui, est plus dualiste: l'opposition entre la justice rendue aux justes (v. 19) et la punition des nations (35,20-21) est suivie par une affirmation du principe de rétribu-

---

25. «Je vous dis» (v. 8) reprend «Le Seigneur dit» du v. 6.
26. BAYLEY (n. 2), p. 130 constate la structure concentrique de ces versets, en fonction du temps des verbes: futur-présent-futur.

tion: «Tant qu'il n'aura rendu à chacun selon ses oeuvres et jugé les actions humaines selon les coeurs» (35,22), avant que le texte ne se conclue par deux versets chantant la miséricorde de Dieu pour son peuple (35,23-24).

Mais c'est surtout la convergence de vocabulaire qui souligne la parenté entre Luc et Si. Les termes communs aux deux textes abondent, à commencer par les noms des acteurs principaux: la veuve, le juge et Dieu.

La «veuve» (χήρα), mentionnée deux fois par le Si grec (35,14.15), ne l'est qu'une fois en hébreu (35,14 (17); chez Luc, elle intervient à deux reprises (18,3.5). Le «Juge» (κριτής), cité en Si 35,12 dans le texte grec, n'apparaît qu'en 35,18(22) dans l'hébreu; il se retrouve en Lc 18,2.6. Ce personnage est Dieu dans Si, il est une image confrontée à Dieu en Luc. Tout en tenant compte de cette opposition, la similitude des expressions employées est frappante: le «juge ne craignant pas Dieu» (Lc 18,2) appelle «Dieu est un Juge» de Si 35,12gr ou «il est le Dieu du jugement» dans le texte hébreu (Si 35,12[15]) et le «juge d'injustice» (Lc 18,6) évoque le «Très haut, Juge pour les justes» (Si 35,18 gr) ou le «Dieu et Juge juste qui établit le droit» (Si 35,18[22] hé). «Dieu», dans le Siracide grec, est appelé «Seigneur» (35,12.19) puis «le Très-Haut» (35,18). En hébreu, seul le mot «Dieu»[27] est employé (35,12[15]. 19[22]); chez Lc, Jésus reçoit le titre de «Seigneur» (18,6), alors qu'il donne au Père le nom de Dieu (18, 2.4.7). Ainsi κύριος κριτής ἐστιν, le Seigneur est juge, de Si 35,12gr («Il est le Dieu du jugement» dans le Si hébreu), correspond chez Lc à θεὸς...ποιήσει τὴν ἐκδίκησιν, «Dieu réalisera leur revanche».

La similitude de vocabulaire la plus notable réside dans l'expression utilisée pour désigner la patience de Dieu:

καὶ ὁ κύριος ...οὐδὲ μὴ μακροθυμήσῃ ἐπ' αὐτοῖς (Si 35,19)
Le Seigneur n'aura pas de patience à leur égard (BJ)
ὁ δὲ θεὸς... καὶ μακροθυμεῖ ἐπ' αὐτοῖς (Lc 18,7)
Et Dieu ... tandis qu'il patiente à leur sujet! (BJ)

L'interprétation de ces deux sentences est problématique[28]: celle de Luc est généralement considérée comme interrogative ou exclamative,

---

27. En fait, κύριος et θεὸς sont employés indifféremment dans l'ensemble de Si gr pour rendre אל ou יהוה.

28. A. WIFSTRAND, *Lukas XVIII,7*, in *NTS* 11 (1964), H. RIESENFELD, *Zu μακροθυμει (Lk. 18,7)*, in J. BLINZLER (ed.), *Neutestamentliche Aufsätze*, FS Joseph Schmid, Regensburg, Putset, 1963, pp. 214-217, M.-J. LAGRANGE, *Évangile selon saint Luc.* 471, SPICQ, *La parabole*, p. 77; H. LJUNGVIK, *Zur Erklärung einer Lukasstelle (Luk XVIII,7)*, in *NTS* 10 (1963-64) 289-294; R. DESCHRYVER, *La parabole du juge malveillant (Lc 18,1-8)*, in *RHPR* 48 (1968), 362-365. La difficulté d'interprétation de Si se reflète dans l'apparition de variantes: μακροθυμήσει (B et pc), μακροθυμήσῃ (textus receptus).

pour lui donner le sens d'une négation (comme dans Si): «Et Dieu pa-
tienterait?». Mais, dans la plupart des traductions, l'objet de la patience
divine, en Si et chez Lc, est différent: le αὐτοῖς dont il est question dans
les deux cas ne peut désigner que les élus chez Luc, tandis qu'on le réfère aux impies dans le texte de Ben Sira.

Ainsi, alors que seul le temps du verbe change et que la négation est
remplacée par une interrogation dubitative, la difficulté d'interprétation
fait aboutir, pour une même expression, à des traduction nettement dis-
semblables, par exemple dans la *TOB*:

> *Il n'aura pas de patience envers eux* (Si 35,19)
> *Et il les ferait attendre?* (Lc 18,7, avec en note: *«alors qu'il est patient en-
> vers eux»*).

Le sens ordinaire de μακροθυμέω est «patienter» ou «être persévé-
rant». La *Bible de Jérusalem*, jouant sur l'idée de patience souligne la
parenté des deux textes. Si, avec la *TOB*, on veut traduire en Lc 18,7
«faire attendre (les élus)», ce qui est difficilement admissible, rien
n'autorise à traduire différemment en Si 35,19(22), et cela implique que
l'objet soit du même ordre: Dieu ne peut pas faire attendre les nations et
les orgueilleux! Il serait plus plausible de référer le αὐτοῖς aux «justes»
du verset précédent plutôt qu'aux nations citées par la suite. Pour rester
conséquent, il conviendrait de traduire alors «Il ne les (les justes) fera
pas attendre» (Si), «Et il les (les élus) ferait attendre?» (Lc).

Le texte hébreu permet cependant d'oser une troisième interprétation
qui laisse la possibilité de référer αὐτοῖς aux impies. Le verbe grec
μακροθυμέω correspond en hébreu à אפק. A la lumière des emplois de
ce terme en Is 63,15, 64,11 et Gn 45,1, on peut le traduire par «contenir
ses sentiments» (de miséricorde ou de fureur)[29] ou «se contenir». Ceci
ne trahit pas le sens classique de μακροθυμέω, et reste proche du sens
étymologique: θύμος signifie en effet «sentiment, coeur, colère». Il
n'est alors plus indispensable de faire porter l'interrogation de Lc 18,7
sur ce verbe: «Il ne contiendra pas ses sentiments envers eux[30] (hé:
comme un héros)». (Si); «Il contient ses sentiments envers eux» (Lc).
On obtient ainsi pour Lc 18,7: «Quant à Dieu, il ne ferait pas du tout la
revanche de ses élus, eux qui crient vers lui jour et nuit alors qu'il contient ses sentiments envers eux? Je vous dis qu'il accomplira leur revan-

---

29. En accord avec T.W. MANSON, *The Sayings of Jesus,* Grand Rapids, MI, 1979
(1957), p. 307: *Dieu retient sa colère.* Cependant Manson pense que Dieu retient sa colère envers les oppresseurs des élus, mais ils ne sont pas mentionnés par Luc et αὐτοῖς se
réfère obligatoirement aux élus, par conséquent c'est plutôt son émotion d'amour que
Dieu contient envers les élus.

30. SPICQ, *L'Écclésiastique* (n. 7), p. 744: «comme un guerrier qui ne se contient
pas».

che promptement». Et pour Si 35,19: «Le Seigneur ne tarde pas, il ne contiendra pas ses sentiments envers eux (gr; héb: comme un héros), jusqu'à ce qu'il ait brisé les reins des sans-miséricorde...»

On peut encore constater que le jugement est présenté, chez les deux auteurs, comme une vengeance ou une revanche[31] qui appartient de droit aux élus (génitif) chez Luc, et qui est rendue contre les nations (datif) en Si: τοῖς ἔθνεσιν ἀνταποδώσει ἐκδίκησιν (Si 35,20), «Il réalisera la revanche envers les nations»; ὁ δὲ θεὸς οὐ μὴ ποιήσῃ τὴν ἐκδίκησιν τῶν ἐκλεκτῶν αὐτοῦ (Lc18,7), «Le Seigneur ne ferait pas (du tout) la revanche de ses élus...?»

D'autres expressions des deux passages diffèrent dans leur vocabulaire mais offrent une signification identique.

En premier lieu se trouvent les deux sentences consécutives aux précédentes:

ποιήσει τὴν ἐκδίκησιν αὐτῶν	ἐν τάχει.	Lc 18,8
Il fera leur revanche	*rapidement*	
ποιήσει κρίσιν.	καὶ ὁ κύριος οὐ μὴ βραδύνῃ	Si 35,18-19
Il fera le jugement	*et le Seigneur ne tarde pas*	

Les deux phrases soulignent de façon identique l'idée d'un jugement accompli par Dieu et la rapidité de sa réponse[32] comme conséquence du cri des justes.

La présentation du juge, chez les deux auteurs, revêt aussi un aspect similaire, sous un vocabulaire et dans un but différents: il ne se soucie pas de l'opinion publique[33]:

Un juge auprès duquel il n'y a aucune acception de personne
et qui ne regarde personne au détriment du pauvre (Si 35,12-13)
Un juge ne craignant pas Dieu
et ne considérant pas l'homme (Lc 18,2)

D'autres parallélismes de vocabulaire peuvent être notés, concernant la prière: προσεύχεσθαι (prier, Lc 18,1) suggère προσευχὴ ταπεινοῦ («la prière de l'humble», Si 35,17) et βοώντων (ceux qui crient, Lc

---

31. Le terme de vengeance est un sémitisme (OESTERLEY, *The Gospel,* 224) qui signifie la manifestation de la justice concernant la cause de l'opprimé, entraînant la confusion de l'oppresseur. Ap 6,10-11 exprime la même idée. H. ZIMMERMANN, *Das Gleichnis vom Richter und der Witwe (Lk 18, 1-8),* in R. SCHNACKENBURG (ed.), *Die Kirche des Anfangs,* Leipzig 1977, p. 83

32. Contrairement à Spicq, *La parabole* (n. 2), pp. 81-84 et en accord avec LAGRANGE, dans sa note 8a à 18, 8, c'est la notion de rapidité qui semble primer ici, en raison du lien avec le v. 4: ἐπὶ χρόνον. L'idée de violence, défendue par Spicq ne ferait qu'accentuer le lien avec Si 35,19(22) où le Seigneur agit «comme un preux».

33. Si 35, 12(15) hé va aussi en ce sens, on peut traduire: «auprès de lui la fausseté du visage n'existe pas». LEVI (n. 24): «Il ne se laisse pas gagner». Contrairement à SMEND (n. 2), p. 315: «Gr traduit mal».

18,7) évoque ἡ δέησις («la supplication», Si 35,16). La persistance de cette prière est pareillement soulignée: οὐ μὴ παρακληθῇ καὶ οὐ μὴ ἀποστῇ («il ne se console pas et il n'a de cesse», Si 35,17-18; héb: il ne s'arrête pas) correspond à μὴ ἐγκακεῖν (ne pas se décourager, Lc 18,1). L'accomplissement de la supplication est envisagé de manière identique: ἕως συνεγγίσῃ,... ἕως ἐπισκέψηται («jusqu'à ce que soit arrivée, ... jusqu'à ce qu'Il regarde», Si 35,17-18) suggère la même idée que εἰς τέλος («jusqu'à la fin») en Lc 18,5.

Finalement, la différence la plus notable entre les deux textes réside dans le fait que le Christ emploie la figure du juge comme un exemple négatif assurant a fortiori la réponse de Dieu à ses élus, alors que Ben Sira l'emploie en sens positif[34]. Pour Jésus, la justice de Dieu dépasse infiniment celle des hommes et on ne saurait la comparer à celle des juges de la terre, dont les juifs devaient avoir des exemples peu édifiants[35]. Selon Ben Sira, la justice finira par triompher quand Dieu donnera libre cours à ses sentiments et anéantira les impies. Chez Luc, le fait de «patienter» ou «contenir ses sentiments» manifeste, à l'opposé, que la tendresse de Dieu envers les humbles, ses élus, est inséparable de sa justice absolue. En conséquence, la vengeance de Dieu, dont il est question dans les deux textes, est présentée chez Luc comme un fruit de son amour: c'est la manifestation de la justice qui appartient aux élus et non une vengeance contre les nations impies. La parabole annonce ainsi l'accomplissement de la justice dans la miséricorde par la Croix: «Pour nous c'est justice, nous payons nos actes, mais lui n'a rien fait de mal... Jésus, souviens-toi de moi quand tu viendras avec ton royaume... aujourd'hui tu seras avec moi...» (Lc 23,41). Seule la Foi persévérante (Lc 18,1 et 8b) permet d'accueillir ce paradoxe et de hâter la manifestation de la justice (Lc 18,5 et 8a).

Mise à part cette différence de fond, propre à l'excellence du Nouveau Testament sur l'Ancien, les points de contact entre les textes du Siracide et de Luc sont nombreux: le thème choisi, le vocabulaire employé et la structure de la parabole offerte par le Christ rappellent l'Ecclesiastique.

---

34. Augustin, *Quaest. Ev. 1145* Sermo 115,1: «Hic ergo iniquus judex non ex similitudine sed ex dissimilitudine adhibitus est ut ostenderet Dominus quanto citiores esse debeant qui Deum perseveranter rogant». (Ce juge inique est utilisé non pour sa ressemblance mais pour sa différence, pour que le Seigneur montre combien ceux qui prient Dieu avec persévérance doivent être plus pressants).

35. Cf. Dn 13,5 et So 3,3.

Cette constatation invite à voir dans l'enseignement de Ben Sira un pont non négligeable entre l'Ancien et le Nouveau Testament, un point de référence pour comprendre la prédication du Christ. Or il faut bien reconnaître que cet «enfant terrible» en ce qui concerne la critique textuelle demeure actuellement l'un des «parents pauvres» de l'exégèse et de l'étude théologique...

Séminaire Catholique de Russie   Pierre DUMOULIN
«Marie, Reine des Apôtres»
1 Krasnoarmeiskaia, 11
198005 Saint-Petersbourg
Russie

L'ÉLOGE DES PÈRES DANS LE SIRACIDE (SI 44–50)
ET LE CANON DE L'ANCIEN TESTAMENT

Dans son excellent article sur le Siracide dans le *Supplément au Dictionnaire de la Bible*, M. Gilbert signale les différents problèmes qui ont trait à la section du Siracide communément appelée «éloge des pères» (Si 44–50)[1]. La discussion porte avant tout sur la composition et le genre littéraire et les travaux les plus importants sont ceux de B.L. Mack[2], Th.L. Lee[3] et R. Petraglio[4]. Une seconde question a retenu l'attention de nombreux exégètes depuis quelques années: les rapports entre cette fresque historique du Siracide et la formation du canon hébraïque des Écritures[5]. La plupart des auteurs pensent que la Tora (*tôrâ*) avait déjà un statut canonique – pour autant que l'on puisse employer ce terme – à l'époque de Ben Sira. En outre, il serait possible de trouver, précisément dans l'éloge des pères, une des première attestation de l'existence d'un canon des prophètes (*nᵉbî'îm*). La troisième partie du canon hébreu de l'Ancien Testament (*kᵉtûbîm* ou «écrits») pose de grosses difficultés, comme on le sait, et le texte du Si 44–50 ne fournit guère d'éléments qui puissent clarifier la situation. C'est surtout des «Prophètes» que l'on discute ces derniers temps. Deux positions opposées s'affrontent. D'un côté, O.H. Steck affirme que le Siracide connaît déjà un «canon» des livres prophétiques[6]. De l'autre, plusieurs exégètes de langue anglaise hé-

1. M. GILBERT, art. *Siracide*, in *DBS*, t. XII, facs. 71, Paris, Letouzey et Ané, 1996, col. 1389-1437, spéc. col. 1431-1433. Genre littéraire: col. 1422. L'article contient une bibliographie complète sur Si 44–55. Voir aussi F.V. REITERER, *Review of Recent Research on the Book of Ben Sira (1980-1996)*, in P.C. BEENTJES (ed.), *The Book of Ben Sira in Modern Research* (BZAW, 255), Berlin – New York, de Gruyter, 1997, pp. 23-60, spéc. 55-57.

2. B.L. MACK, *The Wisdom and Hebrew Epic. Ben Sira's Hymn in Praise of the Fathers* (Chicago Studies in the History of Judaism), Chicago – London, The University of Chicago Press, 1985.

3. Th.R. LEE, *Studies in the Form of Sirach 44-50* (SBLDS, 75), Atlanta, GA, Scholars Press, 1986.

4. R. PETRAGLIO, *Il libro che contamina le mani. Ben Sira rilegge il libro e la storia d'Israele* (Teologia, 4), Palermo, Augustinus, 1993.

5. Sur ce problème, voir GILBERT, *Siracide* (n. 1), col. 1423-1424 ("Ben Sira et l'Ancien Testament"), avec bibliographie (col. 1424). Cf. J.L. KOOLE, *Die Bibel des Ben Sira*, in *OTS* 14 (1965) 374-396, qui affirme que le Siracide connaissait déjà les trois parties du canon hébraïque, loi, prophètes et écrits. Il fut critiqué par J.G. SNAITH, *Biblical Quotations in the Hebrew of Ecclesiasticus*, in *JTS*, N.S. 18 (1967) 1-12. M. Gilbert doute que le Siracide ait eu une idée de «canon des Écritures» (*Siracide*, col. 1423).

6. O.H. STECK, *Der Abschluß der Prophetie im Alten Testament. Ein Versuch zur Frage der Vorgeschichte des Kanons* (Biblisch-Theologische Studien, 17), Neukirchen-

sitent à dire que les livres autres que ceux de la Tora aient pu former à une date aussi haute un «canon» définitif. Selon ces auteurs, les «Prophètes» désigneraient seulement une série de livres qui ne font pas partie de la Tora, mais appartiennent au patrimoine religieux de la communauté postexilique. Cette liste serait encore «ouverte» à l'époque du Siracide[7].

Dans cette brève contribution qui voudrait rendre hommage à l'un de mes tout premiers initiateurs aux méthodes exégétiques, je tenterai d'apporter quelques éléments supplémentaires à cette discussion sur la formation du canon hébraïque. Plus concrètement, la question sera de savoir s'il est possible de découvrir quelques convergences entre les principes qui ont présidé à la composition de l'éloge des pères du Siracide et la structure du canon hébraïque, du moins dans ses deux premières parties.

Un premier paragraphe examinera les arguments des deux positions en présence (I). Le second cherchera à préciser quel est le but du Siracide dans son «éloge des pères» (II). Le dernier tirera les conclusions de l'analyse du texte de Si 44–50 (III).

I. LES DEUX POSITIONS EN PRÉSENCE

O.H. Steck s'appuie surtout sur des indices littéraires pour prouver qu'à l'époque de Ben Sira (180 av. J.-C. environ) existait déjà une «unité littéraire» comprenant les trois grands et les douze petits prophètes:

1. Si 48,22–49,10 cite les trois grands prophètes dans l'ordre qui est celui du canon hébraïque. En outre, il fait allusion à un certain nombre de textes qui appartiennent aux livres canoniques attribués à ces prophètes[8].

Vluyn, Neukirchener Verlag, 1991, pp. 136-144; ID., *Die Prophetenbücher und ihr theologisches Zeugnis. Wege der Nachfrage und Fährten zur Antwort*, Tübingen, Mohr, 1996, p. 130. Cette opinion est assez répandue. Cf. par ex. R. BECKWITH, *The Old Testament Canon and the New Testament Church and its Background in Early Judaism*, Grand Rapids, MI, W.B. Eerdmans, 1985, pp. 72-73.

7. J. BARTON, *Oracles of God: Perceptions of Ancient Prophecy in Israel after the Exile*, London, Darton, Longman & Todd, 1986, p. 48, suivi par D.M. CARR, *Canonization in the Context of Community: An Outline of the Formation of the Tanakh and the Christian Bible*, in R.D. WEIS – D.M. CARR (eds.), *A Gift of God in Due Season. Essays on Scripture and Community in Honor of James A. Sanders* (JSOTSS, 225), Sheffield, Academic Press, 1996, 22-64, spéc. 38-39.

8. Pour Isaïe: Is 10,32; 22,9-11; 36,1-22; 40,1-2; 42,9; 49,8-13; 61,1-3. Ben Sira connaît donc les trois parties d'Isaïe et, pour lui, elles forment un seul livre. Pour Jérémie: Jr 1,5.10 (citations littérales); 11,19; 18,7; 20,1-2; 31,28; 37,11-16; 38,4-13. Pour Ézéchiel: Ez 1 et 10; 14,14.20. Pour plus de détails, voir les commentaires, entre autres P.W. SKEHAN – A.A. DI LELLA, *The Wisdom of Ben Sira* (AB, 39), New York,

2. Si 49,10 contient la première mention connue des «douze prophètes». Pour O.H. Steck, il ne peut s'agir que d'un seul livre contenant les écrits des douze petits prophètes. En effet, le Siracide les cite en bloc après avoir parlé d'Ézéchiel, sans faire aucune distinction entre eux. Pour ces douze petits prophètes, il ne suit pas l'ordre chronologique. Amos, par exemple, ne précède pas Isaïe. De plus, à propos de Zorobabel (49,11), il mentionne un oracle d'Aggée (2,23), ce qui suppose à nouveau qu'existait dès cette époque un texte écrit attribué à ce prophète[9].

3. Selon Si 48,22–49,10, il existerait donc quatre rouleaux prophétiques dans l'ordre du canon hébraïque: Isaïe, Jérémie, Ézéchiel et les douze petits prophètes.

4. Dans l'éloge des pères, les mots «prophète» et «prophétie» et le verbe «prophétiser» apparaissent uniquement dans la section 46,1–49,10. Le premier personnage à propos duquel on parle de «prophétie» est Josué, le successeur de Moïse «dans la prophétie», «dans la fonction prophétique». Sur ce point Si innove, car aucun livre biblique ne fait de Josué un «prophète». Les autres «prophètes» sont Samuel (46,13.15.20), Natan (47,1), Élie (48,1) et Élisée (48,8 H; 48,13 G). Ben Sira connaîtrait donc un corpus qui comprendrait les prophètes antérieurs (de Josué à 2 Rois) et les prophètes postérieurs, c'est-à-dire la partie du canon hébraïque appelée *n^e bî'îm*.

À cette argumentation qui, à première vue, est sans faille, D. Carr a fait quelques objections qui l'ont conduit à rejeter l'hypothèse[10]:

1. L'éloge des pères de Ben Sira contient de nombreuses allusions aux livres des Chroniques qui font partie des «Écrits» et non pas des «Prophètes». Il ne distingue donc pas les deux dernières parties du canon hébraïque.

2. Cet éloge ne se termine pas par les douze petits prophètes, mais continue par le mention de Zorobabel, Josué, Néhémie (49,11-13), puis ajoute quelques figures appartenant aux origines comme Enoch, Joseph, Shem, Seth et Adam (49,14-16) et finit par l'éloge du prêtre Simon (50,1-21). Comment intégrer ces éléments dans un «canon prophétique»?

Doubleday, 1987, pp. 538-539; 543-544; P.C. BEENTJES, *Jesus Sirach en Tenach. Een onderzoek naar en een classificatie van parallellen, met bijzondere aandacht voor hun functie in Sirach 45:6-26*, Niewegein, 1981; H.P. RÜGER, *Le Siracide: un livre à la frontière du canon*, in J.-D. KAESTLI – O. WERMELINGER (eds.), *Le canon de l'Ancien Testament. Sa formation et son histoire* (Le Monde de la Bible), Genève, Labor et Fides, 1984, pp. 47-69, spéc. pp. 60-65.
9. Voir aussi 48,10 qui cite littéralement Ml 3,24.
10. CARR, *Canonization* (n. 7), p. 39.

3. Certes, Si n'emploie pas le mot «prophète» après 49,10; toutefois, il n'est pas toujours logique dans sa façon de procéder puisque plusieurs personnages de la section 46,1–49,10 ne sont pas appelés prophètes (Caleb, les Juges, les rois…).

4. Par conséquent, il faut dire que Si trace une sorte d'histoire d'Israël qui va de la création jusqu'à la reconstruction du temple en utilisant librement un certain nombre d'écrits jouissant d'une autorité reconnue au sein de sa communauté. Parmi les livres cités qui n'appartiennent pas à la Tora, certains se retrouvent dans la seconde section du canon hébraïque (les «Prophètes»), d'autres n'en font pas partie. On ne peut donc pas conclure que Ben Sira ait connu un «canon» des Prophètes.

D. Carr a-t-il réussi à renverser l'hypothèse de O.H. Steck? À mon avis, ses objections n'atteignent pas toutes leur but. Il suffira de noter quelques points plus importants.

1. L'étude du texte de Ben Sira montrera à suffisance que l'éloge des pères comprend non pas deux, mais trois parties: 44,1–45,28 (de Noé à Pinhas), 46,1–49,10 (de Josué aux douze petits prophètes) et 49,11–50,21 (la reconstruction du temple)[11]. Ben Sira distingue bien la période des prophètes de celle qui suit. Il peut certes citer les Chroniques, entre autres à propos de David et de Salomon, mais il ne confond pas les différentes périodes de l'histoire d'Israël. D'autre part, il dépend plus de l'histoire deutéronomiste que des Chroniques.

2. Le Siracide est très logique quant à l'emploi du mot «prophète». Il est réservé à certains personnages qui font partie de la période qui va de la conquête de la terre jusqu'à l'exil (de Josué jusqu'aux douze petits prophètes). La seconde partie du canon hébraïque couvre la même période. Il y a donc de claires analogies entre l'éloge des pères du Siracide et le canon hébraïque des «Prophètes».

Ces observations enlèvent de leur force aux objections de D. Carr. Néanmoins, il reste vrai que Si 44–50 entend d'abord écrire une histoire

---

11. L'éloge des pères est parfois divisé en deux parties principales: 44,16–45,25 (le temps des alliances) et 45,26–50,24 (de Josué au prêtre Simon). Cf. Beentjes, cité par GILBERT, *Siracide* (n. 1), col. 1431-1432. MACK, *Wisdom* (n. 2), pp. 37-64 (schéma p. 67), divise l'hymne en trois grandes parties: les ancêtres et les alliances (44,17–45,25); les prophètes et les rois (46,13–49,10); l'éloge de Simon (50). Ces trois parties sont reliées par des passages de transition: la conquête, œuvre de Josué, Caleb et des Juges (46,1-12) et la restauration due aux initiatives de Josué, Zorobabel et Néhémie (49,11-13). La seconde solution paraît mieux tenir compte des éléments textuels. Cependant, on peut se demander s'il ne faut pas supprimer les périodes intermédiaires pour mieux respecter les conceptions théologiques du Siracide.

et non parcourir une «bibliothèque sacrée». Tous les commentateurs du texte en sont conscients, et O.H. Steck ne fait pas exception[12]. D'autre part, personne ne nie que le Siracide ait utilisé des textes connus pour composer sa galerie de portraits. Le problème est donc de savoir quel est le rapport entre l'histoire d'Israël, telle que la présente le Siracide, et le canon des Écritures. Pour faire un pas de plus, il est nécessaire de retourner au texte pour en étudier certains éléments de structure et certains principes de composition. Il faudra en particulier s'interroger sur la théologie de l'éloge des pères.

II. SI 44–50 ET LA PÉRIODISATION DE L'HISTOIRE D'ISRAËL

Mon but n'est pas d'étudier la structure du passage comme tel. D'autres l'ont fait et il n'est pas nécessaire de revenir sur la question. Je voudrais plutôt montrer que le Siracide entend présenter une histoire d'Israël en trois parties et que cette structure tripartite correspond en gros à celle du canon hébraïque. La chose est plus claire pour les deux premières parties et beaucoup moins pour la dernière. Cela ne surprendra d'ailleurs personne, car on sait que le canon des «Écrits» n'a été fixé que très tard. Mon propos sera donc avant tout de comprendre comment le Siracide structure l'histoire d'Israël.

1. Le prologue (Si 44,1-15)

Il n'est pas inutile de relire le prologue pour clarifier l'intention du Siracide lorsqu'il entreprend de faire éloge des pères. C'est en effet là qu'il nous dit pourquoi il a choisi certains personnages et en a écarté d'autres.

Dans un premier paragraphe (44,1-7), le Siracide fait la liste des «hommes pieux» (H: 'nšy ḥsd) ou des «hommes illustres» (G: andras ekdoxous). Cette liste comprend douze catégories de héros qui ont été célèbres de leur temps (44,3-6.7)[13]. Mais la raison principale du choix du Siracide est expliquée dans le paragraphe suivant (44,8-15), où il oppose «ceux qui ont laissé un nom» (44,8) à «ceux dont il ne reste pas de souvenir» (44,9). Il va évidemment s'occuper uniquement des premiers (44,10-15). En mots plus simples, le Siracide veut faire l'éloge des personnages dont on se souvient encore à son époque. L'idée de continuité et de survie est essentielle dans cette perspective[14]. Bien des hommes ont

---

12. Steck, *Abschluß* (n. 6), p. 136.
13. Voir entre autres Skehan – Di Lella, *Ben Sira* (n. 8), p. 500.
14. Mack, *Wisdom* (n. 2), pp. 41-48, insiste beaucoup sur l'importance de l'idée de succession dans l'éloge des pères.

péri comme s'ils n'avaient jamais existé (44,9). D'autres ont survécu en raison de leur renommée (44,8.10.14.15) ou de leur postérité (44,12.13). Dans chacune des sections qui vont suivre, le Siracide illustre cette perspective de façon différente.

2. *La Tora (Si 44,16-23a)*[15]

Les premiers ancêtres de l'Israël postexilique sont les patriarches. Cette première partie pourrait s'intituler: «la période des alliances»[16]. Le mot *b^erît* y apparaît sept fois, au moins dans le texte hébreu: 44,12 (prologue); 44,17 (Noé); 44,20 (Abraham); 44,22 (Jacob); 45,15 (Aaron); 45,24 (Pinhas); 45,25 (David). Le mot réapparaît dans la dernière section lorsque, dans une prière pour Simon, le Siracide demande à Dieu qu'il «maintienne pour lui l'alliance conclue avec Pinhas» (50,24 H). Ces alliances ont pour but de sauvegarder l'existence de l'univers (Noé; cf. Gn 9,9), celle d'Israël (Abraham; cf. Gn 17) ou du sacerdoce (Aaron et Pinhas). À Abraham, Dieu promet une nombreuse descendance (44,21), tandis qu'à Jacob, il promet la terre en patrimoine (44,23). Ces deux promesses traversent les récits patriarcaux tels que nous les trouvons actuellement dans la Genèse.

Ces alliances concernent en général la postérité des personnages en question et illustrent donc le thème qui avait été annoncé par le prologue[17]. Cela apparaît plus clairement pour Noé (44,18), Abraham (44,20-21), Aaron (44,15) et Pinhas (44,24-25). Pour ce dernier, le Siracide montre la supériorité de l'alliance avec Aaron sur celle avec David précisément sur ce point: celle de David passe à un seul de ses fils, tandis que l'alliance avec Aaron passe à tous ses descendants. Le Siracide oppose donc la succession individuelle à la succession collective.

---

15. Sur cette partie, voir J. MARBÖCK, *Die "Geschichte Israels" als "Bundesgeschichte" nach dem Sirachbuch*, in E. ZENGER (Hrsg.), *Der Neue Bund im Alten. Zur Bundestheologie der beiden Testamente* (QD, 146), Freiburg i.Br., Herder, 1993, pp. 177-197.

16. MACK, *Wisdom* (n. 2), p. 39; MARBÖCK, *Geschichte* (n. 15), p. 183-192.

17. C'est sans doute la raison pour laquelle il n'a pas d'alliance avec Moïse, du moins dans le texte hébreu de Si 45,1-5. Nulle part il n'est question des descendants de Moïse. Cf. MACK, *Wisdom* (n. 2), p. 39. MARBÖCK, *Geschichte* (n. 15)., 186, propose une solution assez proche. Il reprend une idée de A. JAUBERT, *La notion d'Alliance dans le judaïsme aux abords de l'ère chrétienne* (Patristica Sorboniensia, 6), Paris, Le Seuil, 1963, p. 217, n. 361, qui montrer que le Siracide privilégie une idée d'alliance proche de l'écrit sacerdotal. Pour P comme pour Si, l'alliance est avant tout un pacte unilatéral par lequel Dieu garantit une faveur. Pour P, il n'y a que deux alliances, l'une avec Noé, pour tout l'univers (Gn 9,1-17), et une autre avec Abraham et les patriarches, concernant Israël (Gn 17; cf. Ex 2,24; 6,4-5). P et le Si ne parlent pas d'alliance lorsque le pacte est bilatéral et requiert l'observance d'une loi de la part d'un des partenaires. C'est pourquoi il ne parle pas de l'alliance du Sinaï.

Par ailleurs, ce passage souligne le rôle capital de Moïse dans cette première partie de l'histoire de l'univers et d'Israël[18]. En général, les auteurs soulignent l'importance d'Aaron (45,6-22) qui est avec Simon (50,1-21) le personnage qui reçoit le traitement le plus développé. Toutefois, même si Moïse est traité avec moins d'honneurs (18 stiques, 44,23c–45,5), il occupe un rang supérieur à Aaron[19]. Ce dernier est «semblable à Moïse» (45,6), non l'inverse. C'est Moïse qui lui confère l'investiture (45,15). Aaron reçoit un pouvoir législatif (44,17), mais il est subordonné à celui de Moise, puisque la loi (tôrâ) est donnée à Moïse, non à Aaron (45,5). Le mot tôrâ n'apparaît d'ailleurs que deux fois dans toute cette section (45,5; 49,4). La première fois, le Siracide dit qu'elle est confiée à Moïse et la seconde, qu'elle a été abandonnée par les rois. À propos d'Aaron, il n'est jamais question de tôrâ. Enfin, Moïse a fait l'objet d'une élection toute particulière (44,4), il est le seul à avoir pu voir quelque chose de la gloire de Dieu (45,3) et à avoir entendu sa voix (45,5); enfin, il a «reçu les commandements face à face» (45,5)[20]. Aaron est donc un héritier privilégié, mais il n'est pas un fondateur ou un pionnier. Ce rôle revient exclusivement à Moïse.

La loi est essentielle, parce que c'est elle qui va permettre à Israël de survivre et c'est pourquoi le Siracide l'appelle «loi de vie et d'intelligence» (45,5). Après les alliances avec les patriarches, il s'agit donc de l'un des fondements de la vie du peuple d'Israël. Ses premiers gardiens seront Aaron et Pinhas, c'est-à-dire les prêtres. C'est à eux qu'ils revient en premier de transmettre aux générations futures l'héritage mosaïque (45,15.24).

Aaron reçoit, comme on l'a vu, la mission d'enseigner la loi et de la faire appliquer (45,17)[21]. Pinhas, quant à lui, fait la transition entre la première et la seconde partie de Si 44–50. Il résiste à un peuple rebelle et obtient son pardon (45,23). De ce fait, il est un premier exemple de fidélité à la loi, un thème qui va réapparaître dans la seconde partie (46,1–49,10)[22]. Le thème de la postérité, élément central de la première partie, est mentionné une dernière fois dans la première partie à propos de Pinhas (45,24-25). La section suivante, qui parle de chefs, de prophètes et de rois, ne parle plus d'ancêtres et ne s'occupe donc peu de leur postérité. Les seules exceptions sont Caleb (46,9) qui lègue à sa descen-

---

18. Voir MACK, *Wisdom* (n. 2), p. 39.

19. Par exemple LEE, *Studies* (n. 3), p. 12, n. 51 et p. 207 (avec bibliographie).

20. Pour le «face à face» de Dieu et Moïse, voir Ex 33,11; Dt 34,10; cf. l'expression «bouche à bouche» de Nb 12,8.

21. Sur le rôle d'Aaron et de Pinhas dans l'éloge des pères et sa signification pour le Siracide, voir MARBÖCK, *Geschichte* (n. 15), pp. 187-188.

22. Voir 46,7.11.15; 48,22; 49,3; pour l'infidélité, voir 47,20.23-25; 48,15-16; 49,4.

dance la terre qu'il a obtenue par sa fidélité (46,10), David (45,25; cf. 46,11) et Salomon (47,22). Mais pour les descendants de David, le Siracide ajoute quelques nuances importantes, comme on l'a vu plus haut (cf. 45,25) et, en fait, les rois disparaissent de la scène (48,16; 49,4). Les patriarches et les prêtres sont donc les seuls qui ont laissé une postérité durable.

En ce qui concerne le «canon», quatre observations s'imposent à propos de cette première section de l'éloge des pères. (1) La première période ou «temps des alliances» correspond à la période couverte par le Pentateuque. (2) Ben Sira divise cette période en trois moments: l'histoire universelle ou temps des origines, c'est-à-dire l'époque de Noé; l'époque des promesses patriarcales (Abraham, Isaac et Jacob; le Siracide connaît donc déjà cette généalogie, mais il ne mentionne pas Joseph à cet endroit[23]); la loi et le sacerdoce liés à Moïse, Aaron et Pinhas[24]. Les personnages forment donc trois groupes selon le schéma 1+3+3. (3) Enfin, le Siracide ne connaît pas la division en cinq livres ou ne s'y intéresse pas. La structure qu'il propose correspond plutôt à une division entre temps des origines (Gn 1–11 ou même Gn 6–9); temps des patriarches (Gn 12–36); époque de Moïse (Ex–Dt ou Ex–Nb). (4) En dernier lieu, le Siracide reconnaît une place prépondérante à Moïse, tout en soulignant le rôle décisif du sacerdoce dans la vie d'Israël[25]. Or, c'est le même principe qui a déterminé la formation du Pentateuque. Celui-ci se conclut par la mort de Moïse parce qu'avec la disparition du plus grand des prophètes (Dt 34,10) se conclut la phase la plus importante de la révélation de Dieu à Israël[26].

3. Le temps des prophètes ou la période de la fidélité et de l'infidélité (Si 46,1–49,10)

À partir de Si 46,1, le ton est donné par le mot «prophète» et les termes apparentés (46,1.13.20; 48,1.8; 49,7.9.10). Ici encore, le prologue avait annoncé le thème (44,3). Deux personnages sont à la fois chefs politiques et prophètes, Josué (46,1) et Samuel (46,13-14). À partir de

23. Cf. 49,15, mais ce texte est suspect pour certains exégètes.
24. Le texte souligne les liens entre ces trois personnages. Voir 45,1; 45,6 (Aaron est un «saint semblable à Moïse»); 45,23 (Pinhas est «le troisième en gloire»).
25. Sur le sacerdoce dans Si, voir S.M. OLYAN, *Ben Sira's Relationship to the Priesthood*, in *HThR* 80 (1987) 261-286.
26. Cf. l'exégèse récente de Dt 34,10-12 par Ch. DOHMEN in Ch. DOHMEN – M. OEMING, *Biblischer Kanon, warum und wozu? Eine Kanontheologie* (QD, 136), Freiburg i.Br., Herder, 1992, pp. 54-68; R. Lux, *Der Tod des Mose als "besprochene und erzählte Welt"*, in *ZTK* 84 (1987) 395-425; N. LOHFINK, *Moses Tod, die Tora und die alttestamentliche Sonntagslesung*, in *TP* 71 (1996) 481-494.

Natan (47,1) et de l'instauration de la monarchie, le pouvoir politique est distingué de la mission prophétique.

Du point de vue de la formation du canon, il faut noter que dans cette section le Siracide suit davantage l'histoire deutéronomiste que celle du Chroniste. Ceci va à l'encontre de l'opinion de ceux qui insistent sur les affinités entre Si et 1–2 Ch[27]. En effet, plusieurs indices montrent clairement que Ben Sira emprunte l'essentiel de sa présentation et de ses idées à l'histoire deutéronomiste. Ses contacts avec le Chroniste sont beaucoup plus ponctuels[28].

Tout d'abord, le Siracide mentionne plusieurs personnages qui n'apparaissent pas dans le Chroniste, comme Josué, Caleb, les Juges, Samuel, Élie et Élisée[29]. Or, ces personnages se retrouvent dans l'ordre dans l'histoire deutéronomiste (Jos, Jg, 1–2 S, 1–2 R).

Si l'évocation de David contient quelques éléments liturgiques qui rappellent la description du règne de ce roi par le Chroniste (1 Ch 16; 21–29), celle de Salomon est totalement différente. Les critiques que le Siracide adresse au successeur de David sont absentes des Chroniques et elles sont même impensables dans cette œuvre. Le Siracide s'inspire au contraire des descriptions peu favorables à Salomon que l'on trouve en 1 R 10–11.

Il est étonnant que les seuls rois qui échappent à la critique ne soient que trois: David, Ézéchias et Josias (49,4). Le Chroniste ajoute deux rois à cette série, Asa (2 Ch 14–16) et Josaphat (2 Ch 17–20), et il leur accorde beaucoup de place dans son œuvre. Ici encore, Ben Sirach est proche de l'histoire deutéronomiste qui ne réserve à Asa et Josaphat aucune attention particulière. Certains auteurs ont pu objecter que ces deux rois n'échappent pas entièrement à la critique dans les Chroniques (2 Ch 16,7-12; 19,2; 20,35-37) et que le Siracide les aurait écarté pour cette raison[30]. Mais le Chroniste blâme aussi Ézéchias (2 Ch 32,25.31) et Jo-

---

27. Voir CARR, *Canonization* (n. 7), p. 39.

28. Cf. Si 47,9-10 et 1 Ch 16. Sur les rapports entre l'éloge des pères et le Chroniste, voir MACK, *Wisdom* (n. 2), pp. 117-118. Selon cet auteur, le Siracide et le Chroniste auraient quatre éléments en commun: (1) la distinction entre les rois acceptables et les rois qui ne le sont pas; (2) les liens entre David et le culte; (3) les deux racontent une histoire qui finit à leur époque; (4) ils racontent tous deux l'histoire pour justifier les institutions cultuelles de la communauté postexilique. Les éléments (1) et (3) ne paraissent guère caractéristiques ni du Siracide ni du Chroniste. On peut en dire autant de l'historien deutéronomiste. Les points (2) et (4) sont plus intéressants, mais ils apparaissent seulement dans la description du règne de David (47,9-10) et dans celle de l'époque postexilique (49,11–50,24) dont l'historien deutéronomiste ne parle pas. Mack note aussi les différences essentielles entre Si et 1–2 Ch.

29. Isaïe est mentionné par le Chroniste (2 Ch 32,20), mais il occupe une place beaucoup moins importante que dans 2 R 19–20. Les autres prophètes sont absents de l'histoire deutéronomiste comme des Chroniques.

30. SKEHAN–DI LELLA, *Ben Sira* (n. 8), p. 543.

sias (2 Ch 35,22). Le choix du Siracide ne dépend donc pas entièrement des jugements du Chroniste sur les rois.

Enfin, Si ne parle pas des lévites, alors qu'ils occupent une place centrale dans les Chroniques[31]. En réalité, le Siracide parle du sacerdoce d'Aaron, non pas du sacerdoce lévitique, et il l'évoque durant la première et la dernière période de sa reconstruction historique (44,6-22.23-26 et 50,1-21). Les prêtres sont absents de la seconde période, en particulier durant toute la période qui va de la construction du temple de Salomon (47,13) jusqu'à la destruction de Jérusalem (49,6). Le culte authentique inauguré par Aaron et Pinhas sera rétabli après l'exil. Le Chroniste fait au contraire de l'époque de David et Salomon un «âge d'or», et les lévites participent à tous les moments de gloire de la monarchie. La différence entre le Siracide et le Chroniste est par conséquent considérable.

En ce qui concerne les prophètes comme tels, il faut ajouter une chose. Le Siracide parle d'une période «prophétique» qui va de Josué jusqu'à l'exil de Juda, et il montre clairement que les prophètes sont les personnages clés de cette période. Sur ce point, il y a plus d'une convergence entre le Siracide et la ligne adoptée par le canon hébraïque en ce qui concerne les «Prophètes». En premier lieu, l'histoire de la monarchie est une faillite pour le Siracide comme pour l'histoire deutéronomiste. En second lieu, les prophètes sont présentés comme critiques vis-à-vis de la royauté (cf. les cycles d'Élie et d'Élisée; 2 R 20,12-19; 17,13)[32]. Enfin, les douze petits prophètes annoncent avant tout la restauration d'Israël: «Ils ont guéri Jacob[33] et ils l'ont délivré par la fidélité de l'espérance» (49,19). Ce message de consolation se retrouve dans les chapitres finaux de presque tous les petits prophètes: Os 14,2-9, Jl 4,4.18-21, Am 9,13-15, Ab 19-21; Mi 7,8-20; Ha 3,1-19; So 3,14-20; Za 14,1-21; Ml 3,22-24[34], sans compter d'autres oracles à l'intérieur des livres. Le phénomène comme tel est frappant et mériterait

31. Cf. MACK, *Wisdom* (n. 2), p. 118; OLYAN, *Ben Sira's Relationship to the Priesthood* (n. 25), pp. 261-286.

32. MACK, *Wisdom* (n. 2), p. 120, affirme que le Siracide "constructed his hymn without recourse to a Deuteronomistic view of Israel's history". Au vu des observations faites dans ces pages, il conviendrait de nuancer cette conclusion. Pour une autre vue, plus proche de celle défendue ici, voir J. MARBÖCK, *Weisheit im Wandel. Untersuchungen zur Weisheitstheologie bei Ben Sira* (BBB, 37), Bonn, Hanstein 1971, pp. 73, 95-96, 176-177; G.T. SHEPPARD, *Wisdom as Hermeneutical Construct* (BZAW, 151), Berlin – New York, de Gruyter, 1980, pp. 63-71; M. FISHBANE, *From Scribalism to Rabbinism: Perspective on the Emergence of Classical Judaism*, in *The Garments of the Torah*, Bloomington and Indianapolis, IN, Indiana University Press, 1989, pp. 64-78.

33. Selon l'hébreu.

34. Ml 3,24 est cité textuellement en Si 48,10.

sans doute d'être étudié de plus près[35]. Ces passages sont pour la plupart des additions postérieures et le Siracide serait donc le témoin de cette relecture des douze petits prophètes qui en fait des hérauts du salut à venir.

4. Le temps de la reconstruction (49,11–50,24)

La dernière partie se distingue de la précédente sur trois points. (1) Il n'est plus question de prophètes. (2) Il n'existe plus d'opposition entre figures positives et figures négatives. Comme dans la première partie, toutes les figures sont positives. (3) Le Siracide s'intéresse uniquement à la reconstruction du temple (49,12) et de Jérusalem (49,13). La description du prêtre Simon commence elle aussi par la mention de ses travaux en faveur du Temple et de la ville sainte (50,1-3).

La présence, dans cette section, de quelques personnages étrangers à l'histoire de cette époque (Hénok, Joseph, Sem, Seth et Adam; 49,14-16) pose un problème particulier. Pour quelques auteurs, ces versets formeraient une addition qui pourrait provenir de la main du Siracide lui-même ou de l'un de ses disciples. Le raisonnement, cependant, ne peut s'appuyer que sur des raisons internes. Ces personnages ne sont pas à leur place dans cette fresque. Ils devraient tous apparaître plus tôt, dans la première section de l'éloge des pères. Ils ne jouent pas de rôle particulier dans l'histoire d'Israël, sauf peut-être Joseph, «soutien de son peuple» (49,15), et peu de choses dans leur destinée correspondent aux intérêts majeurs du Siracide. Sans doute Ben Sira ou l'un de ses éditeurs a-t-il voulu insérer ici, juste avant la dernière partie qui traite du prêtre Simon, une série de personnages célèbres à cette époque en raison de leur origine ou de leur sort particulier[36]. Quoi qu'il en soit, il est difficile de tirer argument d'un passage quelque peu problématique.

Dans cette dernière partie de son éloge, le Siracide résume à très grands traits le contenu des livres d'Esdras et de Néhémie pour y ajouter la figure du prêtre Simon. Il est évident qu'il faut expliquer pourquoi il ne parle pas d'Esdras. Pour certains, le livre d'Esdras est plus tardif que le Siracide[37]. Pour d'autres, le Siracide aurait éliminé Esdras à cause de

---

35. Sur ce point, voir STECK, Abschluß (n. 6), passim; pour plus de détails, voir B.A. JONES, The Formation of the Book of the Twelve: A Study in Text and Canon (SBLDS, 149), Atlanta, GA, Scholars Press, 1995. Sur les oracles de salut dans les livres prophétiques, voir C. WESTERMANN, Prophetische Heilsworte im Alten Testament (FRLANT, 145), Göttingen, Vandenhoeck & Ruprecht, 1985 (liste de textes pp. 78-80).

36. Sur ce point, voir MACK, Wisdom, 201-203.

37. G. GARBINI, Storia e ideologia nell'Israele antico, Brescia, Paideia, 1986, pp. 208-235.

ses liens trop étroits avec les lévites[38]. La troisième solution est sans doute préférable parce qu'elle tient mieux compte de l'intention de Ben Sira. Il aurait centré sa dernière partie sur la reconstruction du Temple et de Jérusalem. Or, Esdras n'y a pas participé aussi directement que Zorobabel, Josué, Néhémie et Simon, les personnages qui figurent dans cette dernière partie de l'éloge des pères. Esdras est davantage l'homme de la Loi de Moïse que celui du culte et du Temple et, pour cette raison, il n'intéressait pas le Siracide[39].

Les différences entre le canon hébraïque et l'éloge des pères sont évidentes. Il suffit de noter que le Siracide s'intéresse uniquement à la reconstruction de Jérusalem et à la restauration du culte du Temple. Bien sûr, quelques textes, surtout dans Esdras-Néhémie, font allusion aux mêmes événements. Mais il tout aussi clair que le Siracide n'a aucunement en vue les « Écrits » dans leur totalité sous leur forme canonique. Cela peut être confirmé par le prologue du traducteur, le petit-fils du Siracide, qui emploie des expressions fixes pour parler de la Tora et des Prophètes, mais reste très vague lorsqu'il parle de la troisième partie du canon: «les autres [livres] qui suivent [la Loi et les Prophètes]» (2); «les autres livres de nos pères» (10); «les autres livres» (25). Le Siracide lui-même parle de la Loi, des Prophètes et de la « sagesse de tous les anciens» en 39,1. La dernière expression est certainement plus vague que les deux autres[40]. Il existe donc bien une troisième catégorie de livres à côté de la Loi et des Prophètes, mais ils ne forment pas encore une collection aux contours et au profil bien définis[41].

---

38. P. HÖFFKEN, *Warum schweigt Ben Sirach über Esra?*, in *ZAW* 87 (1975) 184-201.

39. C. BEGG, *Ben Sirach No-Mention of Esra*, in *BN* 42 (1988) 14-18. Plus d'autres solutions, voir LEE, *Studies* (n. 3), pp. 209-210 (avec bibliographie). Il relève trois explications principales: (1) Le Siracide aurait trouvé la législation d'Esdras sur les mariages mixtes trop sévère. (2) Esdras est un scribe qui ne s'occupe que de l'interprétation de la loi de Moïse. Pour le Siracide, un scribe doit être versé dans toute la sagesse et donc Esdras n'est pas un modèle. (3) La troisième explication est politique. Ben Sira préférait la vision politique solide de Simon II au quiétisme d'Onias III, son fils, qui sur ce point était trop semblable à Esdras. Le Siracide a préféré ne pas mentionner Esdras dans son éloge des pères pour ne pas encourager Onias III dans sa conduite. Ces raisons sont un peu recherchées, à mon avis. Le Siracide ne mentionne que les personnages qui l'intéressent. MACK, *Wisdom* (n. 2), p. 119 (cf. p. 229, n. 10), reprend la théorie de Höffken (n. 38) sur l'aversion du Siracide pour les lévites et Esdras qui a partie liée avec eux.

40. RÜGER, *Le Siracide* (n. 8), pp. 65-66; même avis chez BARTON, *Oracles* (n. 7), p. 280, n. 31.

41. RÜGER, *Le Siracide* (n. 8), p. 68: "On dira qu'à l'époque de Jésus Sira comme à celle de son petit-fils, la Loi et les Prophètes étaient déjà disponibles à titre de collections closes, mais que la troisième partie du canon, qu'on nomme les Écrits, était encore entièrement ouverte." L'analyse du texte faite ici confirme ces vues. Sur les Écrits, voir aussi D.F. MORGAN, *Between Text and Community. The "Writings" in Canonical Interpretation*, Minneapolis, MN, Augsburg Fortress Press, 1990.

III. Quelques conclusions

Ce bref parcours permet de tirer quelques conclusions provisoires. Le Siracide n'est guère intéressé par les livres bibliques en tant que tels. Son premier but était de parcourir l'histoire de son peuple pour mettre en évidence les personnages qui lui ont permis de survivre aux vicissitudes de son histoire tourmentée. Cependant, Ben Sira introduit dans cette reconstruction un principe de périodisation qui se retrouvera, en grande partie, dans les deux premières parties du canon hébraïque. À l'encontre de ceux qui ont pu émettre des doutes à ce sujet, il est donc légitime d'affirmer que dès l'époque du Siracide des collections de rouleaux jouissaient d'une autorité particulière dans les milieux cultivés et les élites religieuses d'Israël. Cela vaut pour la Tora, mais aussi pour les «Prophètes». Quant aux «Écrits», ils n'atteindront leur forme canonique que plus tard[42].

Pontificio Istituto Biblico   Jean Louis SKA
Via della Pilotta, 25
I-00187 Roma

---

42. Je tiens à remercier H.-W. Jüngling et S. Pisano pour leurs judicieuses remarques durant la rédaction de cet article.

POURQUOI FALLAIT-IL ÉDIFIER DES REMPARTS?
LE SIRACIDE ET NÉHÉMIE

Dans sa galerie des grands ancêtres (chap. 44–50), le Siracide n'accorde qu'un seul verset (49,13) au personnage de Néhémie. Sauf erreur, cette notice n'a jamais fait l'objet d'une étude particulière[1]. Et pourtant elle est remarquable, à plus d'un titre: Néhémie est, avec Zorobabel et le grand-prêtre Josué, le seul personnage de l'époque perse à être cité; bien plus, il occupe la dernière place de la liste, juste avant la récapitulation générale des vv. 14-16 et le portrait idéalisé du grand-prêtre Simon (50,1-21). D'autre part, le livre de Néhémie semble porter la marque d'un rédacteur proche, à maints égards, du Siracide. Il vaut donc la peine de s'interroger sur les rapports qui unissent le Siracide et le milieu dont il est représentatif avec Néhémie (le personnage et surtout le livre qui porte son nom).

Je dédie cette étude au Père Maurice Gilbert, qui fut promoteur de ma thèse de doctorat, puis de ma thèse de maîtrise en théologie à l'Université Catholique de Louvain, en lui exprimant à la fois toute ma reconnaissance et mon admiration pour la qualité de sa recherche exégétique.

I. Néhémie dans le livre du Siracide

Si 49,13 figure dans un seul des manuscrits hébreux retrouvés jusqu'ici, le «manuscrit B»[2]. Le texte est court et assez simple:

נחמיה יאדר זכרו	Néhémie: il est éclatant, son souvenir,
המקים את חרבתינו	lui qui (re)dressa nos ruines,
וירפא את הריסתינו	et il répara nos [murs?] détruits,
ויצב דלתים גבריח	et il plaça des portes à verrou[3].

---

1. Malgré son titre, l'article de A. BENTZEN, *Sirach, der Chronist und Nehemia*, dans *Studia Theologica* 3 (1949) 158-161, ne consacre que quelques lignes à la question. L'auteur explique que le Siracide s'inscrit, avec 2 M (cf. 1,18-36; 2,13), dans la ligne d'un courant qui exalte Néhémie et ignore Esdras. L'étude la plus minutieuse est, à ma connaissance, celle d'U. KELLERMANN, *Nehemia. Quellen, Überlieferung und Geschichte* (BZAW, 102), Berlin, Töpelmann, 1967, pp. 112-115.

2. Première édition par S. SCHECHTER et C. TAYLOR, *The Wisdom of Ben Sira*, Cambridge, 1896. Je suis le texte transcrit par P.C. BEENTJES, *The Book of Ben Sira in Hebrew* (SVT, 58), Leiden, Brill, 1997, p. 88.

3. גבריח est un mot impossible. Il faut sans doute lire ובריח, avec la LXX.

L'auteur ne retient de l'histoire de Néhémie qu'un seul élément: la reconstruction des remparts avec ses portes et leur système de fermeture. Ce motif est utilisé, avec grande insistance, en Ne 3, où l'on retrouve les mêmes mots דלת (vv. 1,3,6,13,14,15) et בריח (vv. 3,6,13,14,15); le motif des portes (דלת) figure aussi en 7,1,3 et 13,19 et le verbe חרב en 2,3,17. Il faut cependant constater que l'auteur utilise le pluriel דלתים, alors que Ne a constamment la forme דלתות; d'autre part, plusieurs des mots qu'il emploie (les verbes רפא, הריס et יצב, par exemple) ne figurent même pas dans cet ouvrage. De ce rapide examen, il ressort que Si 49,13 ne cite pas le livre de Néhémie: il reprend seulement – avec liberté – le motif de la reconstruction des murailles avec leurs portes, qui figure dans les «mémoires de Néhémie».

Envisageons à présent le texte grec:

καὶ Νεεμιου ἐπι πολὺ τὸ μνημόσυνον	Et Néhémie: au-dessus de beaucoup son souvenir,
τοῦ ἐγείραντος ἡμῖν τείχη πεπτωκότα	lui qui éleva pour nous des remparts écroulés
καὶ στήσαντος πύλας καὶ μοχλοὺς	et qui plaça portes et verrous,
καὶ ἀνεγείραντος τὰ οἰκόπεδα ἡμῶν	et qui releva nos bâtiments.

La différence la plus saillante entre l'hébreu et le grec réside dans le déplacement du deuxième membre, mis en finale de l'ensemble. Cette inversion paraît former système avec des différences plus minimes, si bien que le grec peut s'expliquer comme une interprétation de l'hébreu. Dans le «manuscrit B», Néhémie est, semble-t-il, crédité d'une seule œuvre majeure: la réparation des remparts de Jérusalem, avec ses portes fortifiées. Le texte grec, en revanche, distingue deux œuvres: la reconstruction des murailles écroulées (τείχη πεπτωκότα, interprétation de הריסתינו) avec ses portes, et celle de la ville elle-même (τὰ οἰκόπεδα ἡμῶν, interprétation de חרבתינו, «nos ruines»)[4]. Ce deuxième acte n'est pas mentionné dans le livre de Néhémie[5] et peut être considéré comme un élargissement de la louange faite au personnage.

La construction des murs est la seule œuvre dont le Siracide (texte hébreu) fait mention lorsqu'il parle de Néhémie. Il emploie le même motif de la fortification de Jérusalem en tête de sa notice sur Ézéchias (יחזקיהו חזק עירו, 48,17), alors que les textes bibliques antérieurs (livres des Rois, d'Isaïe et des Chroniques) n'en disent pas un mot[6]; on le retrouve à pro-

---

4. Dans la LXX, οἰκόπεδον traduit toujours חרבה.

5. Ne 7,4 parle de la nécessité de rebâtir des בתים, mais le contexte montre que le mot בית doit y être compris dans le sens de «famille».

6. 2 R 20,20 et 2 Ch 32,30 rapportent le percement d'un canal pour amener de l'eau

pos du grand-prêtre Simon (ומחזק עירו מצר, 50,4; voir déjà les vv. 1-2). L'importance symbolique de ce thème ne doit pas être sous-estimée: Néhémie, qui se réduit à sa fonction d'«homme des murailles», est le dernier personnage de la galerie des ancêtres éminents, et le grand-prêtre Simon, qui incarne son idéal, apparaît comme un «nouveau Néhémie». Cette importance symbolique ressort d'autant plus que l'édification des remparts n'est motivée par un danger précis ni à propos de Néhémie, ni à propos de Simon («pour le cas de siège»); à propos d'Ézéchias, suivant les récits de 2 R 36–37 et d'Is 18–19, l'auteur rapporte ensuite l'expédition de Sennachérib, qui «leva la main contre Sion, dans l'insolence de son orgueil».

Pourquoi le Siracide met-il ainsi Néhémie et le motif de la construction des murailles en évidence? Je pense que ce choix s'inscrit – consciemment ou non, peu importe – dans le contexte plus général de la visée polémique du livre, et qu'il doit donc avoir rapport avec les craintes de l'auteur. Pour le Siracide, il est essentiel de se prémunir contre des dangers mortels, et l'ouvrage comprend nombre de mises en garde: il s'agit de ne pas pratiquer la crainte de YHWH avec un cœur double (1,28-30), de ne pas se laisser entraîner au temps de l'adversité (2,2)[7], etc. Le lecteur est donc menacé par une série de dangers: orgueil, mauvaises fréquentations, convoitise, mépris de la tradition, séduction des femmes (et en particulier de la femme étrangère)…; c'est pour repousser ces menaces qu'il doit édifier des murs symboliques.

Au-delà de ces recommandations multiples et souvent assez floues, que vise le Siracide? Où se trouve l'ennemi? Nulle part, le livre ne donne réponse explicite à cette question. La clé pourrait cependant se trouver en 50,25-26: «En deux nations s'irrite mon âme, et la troisième n'est pas un peuple: les habitants de Sé'îr[8] et la Philistie et la nation stupide résidant à Sichem». Le Siracide n'a donc pas moins de trois ennemis: les Édomites, les Philistins et les Samaritains! On explique souvent: Édom a collaboré avec Nabuchodonosor et a pillé Juda à l'époque babylonienne, ce qui les a fait détester[9]; les Philistins sont les ennemis

---

dans la ville. Le «tunnel d'Ézéchias» fait partie des mesures prises par le roi en prévision d'une attaque de Jérusalem par Sennachérib, mais il faut remarquer qu'aucun texte ne parle d'un renforcement des murailles.

7. En suivant le Grec. Ces deux passages ne figurent pas dans les manuscrits hébreux qui sont aujourd'hui à notre disposition.

8. Le Grec propose: «la montagne de Samarie», mais cette lecture ne peut être retenue, car les Samaritains forment précisément la troisième nation.

9. L'hostilité à l'égard d'Édom s'exprime à travers bon nombre de textes bibliques qu'il faut dater, pour la plupart au moins, au début de la période perse; voir à ce sujet B. Dicou, *Edom, Israel's Brother and Antagonist. The Role of Edom in Biblical Prophecy and Story* (JSOTSS, 169), Sheffield, JSOT Press, 1994.

traditionnels du temps des débuts de la monarchie; les Samaritains, enfin, ont rompu depuis un certain temps avec les Juifs. La haine que le
Siracide manifeste à l'égard des Samaritains est compréhensible, car le
conflit est virulent à son époque. Mais comment expliquer ce qu'il dit
des Édomites et des Philistins, qui ont disparu depuis longtemps en tant
que nations ou groupes distincts? Serviraient-ils uniquement de faire-va-
loir pour les Samaritains, les plus détestés de tous? Cela reviendrait à
dire que les mises en garde de l'ensemble du livre devraient être lues
dans la ligne d'une polémique anti-samaritaine. Est-ce plausible? Je
pense qu'une autre réponse est possible, et que l'auteur pourrait viser
une double menace bien réelle à son époque: l'expansion des Nabatéens
(qui occupent l'ancienne Édom) et surtout l'attrait grandissant pour
l'hellénisme, représenté par les Philistins. Cette double supposition me
paraît trouver confirmation dans le livre de Néhémie. Cela nous amène à
la deuxième partie de cet article.

II. Le livre de Néhémie et l'esprit du Siracide

La reconstruction des murailles de Jérusalem fait l'objet des chap. 1–7
du livre de Néhémie. On y apprend que ce personnage, muni d'une autorisation officielle du pouvoir perse, quitte Suse lors de la vingtième année d'Artaxerxès (446-445) pour reconstruire les murailles de la ville,
restée sans protection depuis le temps de Nabuchodonosor (587). Il se
heurte à l'opposition de Sanballât le Horonite, de Tobiyya l'Ammonite
et de Géshem l'Arabe, qui se moquent des Juifs et se mettent en colère,
puis décident d'attaquer Jérusalem (4,2,5); cependant l'assaut n'a pas
lieu, et la réfection des remparts est achevée au bout de 52 jours de travail, puis la ville est repeuplée par une population descendante des fa-
milles déportées. À ma connaissance, l'historicité du récit n'a pas fait,
jusqu'ici, l'objet de contestations fondamentales, si ce n'est celle de David J.A. Clines[10]; on considère, en effet, que Ne 1–7 appartient, pour
l'essentiel au moins, aux «Mémoires de Néhémie», document autobiographique comportant en outre des sections importantes des chap. 10–
13[11]. De fait, rien ne permet de mettre en doute la reconstruction des

---

10. D.J.A. Clines, *The Nehemiah Memoir: The Perils of Autobiography*, dans Id.,
What Does Eve to Help? And Other Readerly Questions to the Old Testament (JSOTSS,
94), Sheffield, Academic Press, 1990, pp. 124-172, a montré que, sur une série de points
tout au moins, il n'est pas raisonnable de faire confiance à Néhémie comme historien.

11. Pour un bref état de la question, voir par exemple O. Kaiser, *Einleitung in das
Alte Testament*, Gütersloh, Mohn, ⁵1985, pp. 182-184. D.J.A. Clines, *Ezra, Nehemiah,
Esther* (NCBC), Grand Rapids, MI, Eerdmans, et London, Marshall, Morgan and Scott,
1984, p. 4, exprime l'opinion générale des commentateurs en déclarant: «It has been

remparts de Jérusalem par Néhémie en l'an 445. Je crois cependant pouvoir montrer que l'opposition de Sanballât, Tobiyya et Géshem est un élément introduit dans le récit par le rédacteur final du livre, qui interprète celui-ci dans l'esprit du Siracide et projette sur l'histoire du Ve siècle une problématique bien plus tardive[12].

1. Des invraisemblances historiques

En dehors du livre de Néhémie lui-même, nous ne disposons d'aucune source de renseignement à propos des circonstances entourant la reconstruction des remparts. Faut-il pour autant faire aveuglément confiance au narrateur?[13] S'ils ne peuvent être considérés comme des preuves formelles d'une contradiction avec les faits historiques, plusieurs éléments du récit sont néanmoins troublants:

- L'entreprise de Néhémie n'est pas motivée par un danger militaire immédiat. La situation de Jérusalem est décrite en 1,3: «Ceux qui sont restés de la captivité, là, dans la province, sont dans une grande détresse et dans la honte, et le rempart de Jérusalem a des brèches, et ses portes ont été incendiées». La ville est donc sans défense, ouverte aux pillards comme à d'autres assaillants, mais il n'est pas question d'une menace précise. Les ennemis ne décident d'attaquer Jérusalem qu'au moment où la réparation des remparts est déjà bien lancée (4,1-2,5), et cette décision n'est pas exécutée. Jamais on ne parle d'une armée rassemblée, et la crise ne débouche ni sur une victoire militaire ni sur un quelconque accord de paix.
- La coalition des ennemis de Jérusalem («nos ennemis», 4,5,9; cf. 5,9; 6,1) ne manque pas d'intriguer, d'autant plus qu'elle apparaît «à géométrie variable». Lors de leur première mention (2,10), il est question de «Sanballât le Horonite et Tobiyya le serviteur ammonite». On retrouve ces deux mêmes personnages en 3,33-35. Dans d'autres passages, cependant, la liste est étoffée: le narrateur y adjoint

subject to practically no editorial revision». De même, en dehors de quelques gloses, U. KELLERMANN, *Nehemia* (n. 1), pp. 8-26,55-56, tient le récit de la reconstruction des murailles pour homogène, œuvre autobiographique de Néhémie en personne.

12. Je ne puis traiter ici les problèmes posés par Esd 4,6-23, où il est question d'une autre tentative de restaurer le rempart de Jérusalem.

13. Telle est l'attitude presque générale des commentateurs, qui s'appuient sur le caractère autobiographique des «Mémoires de Néhémie». L'auteur, témoin oculaire des événements qu'il raconte, serait nécessairement crédible. En réalité, le témoignage en «je» ne garantit pas l'historicité des faits rapportés! Néhémie a pu écrire l'histoire en s'écartant des faits pour justifier sa propre conduite, et d'autres que lui ont pu se mettre à sa place (pour l'ensemble du récit ou pour certaines sections), le «je» devenant pseudépigraphique.

Géshem l'Arabe en 2,19 et 6,1-2 (voir aussi «les Arabes», 4,1; «Gashmu», 6,6); en 4,1, il est aussi question des Ashdodites; 6,1 mentionne «nos autres ennemis»; 6,17-19, enfin, parle de complicités parmi les notables de Jérusalem. Comment tous ces gens se rencontrent-ils? Qu'est-ce qui les réunit, alors qu'une telle alliance n'est attestée nulle part ailleurs? Pourquoi s'opposent-ils ensemble à la reconstruction du rempart[14], comme si cette entreprise menaçait leurs intérêts vitaux? Autant de questions sans réponse!

– À une exception près (6,11-19, où Tobiyya agit seul[15]), Sanballât est toujours cité en tête de la liste; le gouverneur de Samarie apparaît ainsi comme le leader de la coalition ennemie. Mais si l'hostilité de Samarie envers Jérusalem a déjà atteint en 445 un tel paroxysme qu'il est question d'attaque militaire et d'une volonté de massacre (4,5), comment expliquer les lettres d'Éléphantine datées des années 407-406, lettres qui semblent tout ignorer du conflit?[16] Et comment expliquer l'adoption du Pentateuque – qui suppose à tout le moins l'action d'Esdras, sans doute postérieure à celle de Néhémie – par les Samaritains? On peut admettre sans difficulté une certaine tension entre Samarie et Jérusalem assez tôt à l'époque perse, mais la rupture n'est intervenue que plus tard, à l'époque hellénistique.

– Plusieurs autres textes bibliques de l'époque perse (Ps 51; Is 27,4; 49,13-17; 60,10-11; Am 9,11-12; Mi 7,11-13; cf. Jr 1,18-19; 15,20-21; 31,38-40) évoquent l'érection des murailles: ils parlent de l'œuvre de Néhémie ou répondent à l'espoir d'avoir une ville fortifiée; aucun d'entre eux, cependant, ne mentionne Sanballât, Tobiyya ou Géshem, et aucun d'entre eux ne fait allusion à la menace d'une attaque militaire.

Bref, il y a lieu de se demander si la coalition ennemie est un fait historique ou si l'œuvre de Néhémie n'a pas été motivée par une insécurité

---

14. Les villes fortifiées sont peu nombreuses, il est vrai, dans la Palestine du Vᵉ siècle, comme le montre l'archéologie; cf. K.G. HOGLUND, *Achaemenid Imperial Administration in Syria-Palestine and the Missions of Ezra and Nehemiah* (SBLDS, 125), Atlanta, GA, Scholars Press, 1992, pp. 210-211. À elle seule, cependant, la réparation des remparts ne peut être interprétée comme une revendication d'indépendance nationale (accusation proférée par Sanballât et Gashmu en 6,6-7), d'autant plus qu'elle a lieu avec l'autorisation explicite d'Artaxerxès (2,1-9).

15. Aux vv. 12 et 14, la LXX – qui reflète sans doute ici le texte primitif – ne parle que de Tobiyya, tandis que le TM lui adjoint Sanballât.

16. Voir P. GRELOT, *Documents araméens d'Égypte* (LAPO, 5), Paris, Cerf, 1972, pp. 406-417: la lettre 102 adressée à Bagôhî, gouverneur de Judée, et parlant d'une autre lettre envoyée à Dalayah et Šèlèmyah, fils de Sin'uballit (Sanballât), et la lettre 103, qui rapporte la réponse commune de Bagôhî et Dalayah. Ces lettres montrent que le judaïsme de cette époque comprend deux pôles de référence, Jérusalem et Samarie, mais aussi que les relations entre les deux groupes étaient assez bonnes pour donner une réponse commune à une demande extérieure.

plus générale, Jérusalem étant la proie facile de bandes de pillards ou souhaitant simplement se doter d'une muraille pour faire face à tout imprévu. Dans ce dernier cas, les passages qui parlent de Sanballât et de ses alliés devraient se révéler secondaires dans le texte de Ne 1–7, et il faudrait pouvoir déterminer pourquoi ces figures ont été introduites dans le récit. C'est ce que je voudrais établir à présent.

2. *Des difficultés littéraires*

Dans le récit de Ne 1–7, les coalisés interviennent tellement souvent qu'on pourrait penser leur action indissociable de la trame fondamentale du texte. En fait, celui-ci présente une succession de scènes où Sanballât et les ennemis de Jérusalem sont alternativement absents et présents:

- À Suse, Néhémie apprend la détresse de Jérusalem, prend le deuil et implore YHWH (chap. 1).
- Muni de l'autorisation royale, il se met en route avec une escorte (2,1-9).
    Informés, Sanballât et Tobiyya sont contrariés (2,10).
- Arrivé à Jérusalem, Néhémie inspecte secrètement les remparts (2,11-16), puis il fait son rapport aux notables de la ville, qui prennent la décision de les reconstruire (2,17-18).
    Informés, Sanballât, Tobiyya et Géshem se moquent des Juifs, entraînant une vive réplique de Néhémie (2,19-20).
- Les habitants de Jérusalem sont mobilisés pour reconstruire le rempart, section par section (3,1-32); notons que Néhémie n'apparaît pas dans ce long texte, qui reproduit sans doute une pièce d'archives.
    Informés, Sanballât et Tobiyya se mettent en colère et se moquent à nouveau des Juifs, puis une voix anonyme appelle Dieu à la vengeance (3,33-37).
- Le rempart est réparé jusqu'à mi-hauteur (3,38).
    Informés, Sanballât et ses alliés se mettent en colère et décident d'attaquer Jérusalem. Les gens de la ville («nous») invoquent Dieu et établissent une garde de jour et de nuit (4,1-3).
- Cependant les Judéens sont découragés par l'ampleur de la tâche (4,4), tandis que leurs ennemis se préparent à les attaquer par surprise (4,5). Avertis de ces projets, les hommes de Jérusalem prennent des mesures de défense militaire, et les ennemis renoncent à leur entreprise (4,6-9). Les travaux reprennent, mais avec les armes à portée de main (4,10-17). [Le chap. 5 suppose une situation postérieure de douze ans et ne fait pas partie des «Mémoires de Néhémie» dans leur forme originelle].

Informés de l'état d'avancement des travaux (le rempart est réparé, mais les portes ne sont pas encore munies d'un verrou), Sanballât et Géshem convoquent Néhémie à Ha-Kephirim, pour lui tendre un piège. Comme celui-ci refuse de quitter Jérusalem, ils lui font parvenir un message qui l'accuse de briguer la royauté. Encore une fois, Néhémie déjoue ce piège destiné à l'effrayer (6,1-9).

— Un certain Shemaya annonce à Néhémie qu'on cherche à le tuer et l'enjoint à se réfugier à l'intérieur du sanctuaire, mais il refuse (6,10-11); peut-être le gouverneur craint-il de commettre un péché en pénétrant dans une zone réservée aux prêtres[17].

Néhémie déclare que Shemaya a été soudoyé par Tobiyya, qui cherchait à l'effrayer et à l'entraîner à pécher. Il prie Dieu d'agir contre Tobiyya et les autres prophètes qui ont voulu l'effrayer (6,12-14)

— Le rempart est enfin achevé, et les ennemis reconnaissent que ce travail a été accompli grâce au Dieu des Juifs (6,15-16).

Parmi les notables judéens, beaucoup sont en correspondance avec Tobiyya et s'avèrent être ses alliés. Tobiyya cherche encore à effrayer Néhémie par ses lettres (6,17-19).

— Néhémie décide que les portes de la ville devront être fermées la nuit, et qu'une garde devra être organisée avec les habitants (7,1-3).

— Jérusalem est repeuplée par une population revenue de l'exil; l'auteur utilise ici un recensement généalogique (7,4-72).

Il est probable que les «Mémoires de Néhémie» comportaient aussi, en finale, certains éléments des chap. 11–13; en réalité cela importe peu ici, car Sanballât et ses alliés n'y jouent plus de rôle actif en relation avec les murailles de Jérusalem[18].

Quoi qu'il en soit de ce dernier point, il suffit de lire le texte en omettant les différents passages où Sanballât ou Tobiyya interviennent (voir les résumés en retrait, ci-dessus) pour s'en rendre compte: le récit y gagne en cohérence[19]. Dans le texte actuel, par exemple, la décision d'atta-

---

17. Voir par exemple H.G.M. WILLIAMSON, *Ezra, Nehemiah* (WBC, 16), Waco, TX, Word, 1985, p. 259.

18. Le nom de Tobiyya revient encore en 13,4,7,8, mais il faut remarquer que le personnage n'y joue plus aucun rôle actif: le narrateur parle seulement du prêtre Élyashib (cf. 3,1), qu'il déclare lié à Tobiyya. Ajoutons que le chap. 13 ne parle pas de la construction des murailles.

19. En crédibilité aussi! D.J.A. CLINES, *The Nehemiah Memoir* (n. 10), pp. 135-152, demande, avec raison, comment Néhémie, censé écrire ses propres souvenirs, a pu connaître les pensées et intentions de ses adversaires. L'examen des textes montre que ceux-ci sont rédigés du point de vue judéen, même lorsqu'il s'agit de propos tenus par Sanballât ou Tobiyya; en 2,10, par exemple, ils n'auraient pas parlé d'«Israélites», mais de «Judéens» (p. 137).

quer Jérusalem est prise une première fois par Sanballât et ses complices (4,2), puis une deuxième fois par des ennemis anonymes (4,5), de même que les mesures prises en 4,3 font double emploi avec celles du v. 7 et surtout du v. 16. De même encore, le découragement évoqué en 4,4 forme la suite logique de 3,38, et la section 4,1-3 complique le déroulement narratif. Autre exemple: en 2,18, les notables de Jérusalem déclarent: «Levons-nous et construisons!»; cette décision est aussitôt mise en pratique: «Élyashib le grand prêtre et ses frères les prêtres se levèrent et construisirent...» (3,1); les réactions de Sanballât, Tobiyya et Géshem ainsi que la réplique de Néhémie (2,19-20) brisent cet enchaînement. Un dernier exemple: en 6,1, Néhémie dit qu'il n'a pas encore fixé les battants aux portes, ce qui contredit 3,1,3,6,13,14,15.

Si l'on met donc entre parenthèses les interventions de Sanballât et de ses alliés (2,10,19-20; 3,33-37; 4,1-3; 6,1-9,12-14,17-19), ainsi que le chap. 5, le récit de la reconstruction des remparts gagne donc en cohérence. Encore faut-il comprendre selon quels procédés et dans quel but les additions ont été introduites. Commençons par les procédés littéraires. Les additions sont liées entre elles. On observera une gradation dans les réactions de Sanballât et de ses alliés (contrariété, moquerie, décision de passer à l'offensive, piège tendu à Néhémie en personne)[20]. Les cinq premières additions ont quelque chose de stéréotypé, avec la reprise d'un même schéma: 1° les opposants sont informés (on ne dit jamais par quel canal!); 2° ils réagissent (avec une violence croissante); 3° Néhémie et ses alliés réagissent à leur attaque. Les deux dernières additions (6,12-14,17-19) ne mettent pas en œuvre ce schéma et ne parlent plus que de Tobiyya, sans référence à Sanballât; cependant on y rencontre le motif commun de la volonté d'effrayer Néhémie, comme en 6,9. D'autre part, chacune des additions emprunte certains éléments à son contexte immédiat:

– La première addition (2,10) dit la forte contrariété de Sanballât et de Tobiyya, lorsqu'ils apprennent qu'un hommes est venu travailler «au bien (טובה) des fils d'Israël». Cette expression semble avoir été inspirée par le v. 8b, où Néhémie déclare que «la main bienveillante (הטובה) de Dieu est sur lui (voir aussi 2,18). Notons que l'irritation de Sanballât et de Tobiyya, inattendue dans le cours du récit, n'est pas motivée par le projet de reconstruire les murs, mais par la volonté générale de nuire aux Israélites.

– L'addition de 2,19-20 reprend mot pour mot (v. 20a) l'expression נקום ובנינו, «nous nous lèverons et nous bâtirons» (v. 18). Le motif des mo-

---

20. Cf. M.A. THRONTVEIT, *Ezra-Nehemiah* (Interpretation), Louisville, KY, Knox, 1992, p. 60.

queries pourrait avoir été suggéré par la finale du v. 17, mais il faut reconnaître que la formulation est différente.

- Au début de la troisième addition (3,33-37), l'expression אנחנו בונים את־החומה, «nous bâtissons le mur», paraît calquée sur ce qui suit immédiatement dans le texte de base présumé: ונבנה את־החומה, «nous bâtissions le mur» (v. 38).
- L'addition suivante (4,1-3) attribue aux coalisés la décision d'attaquer Jérusalem, ce qui anticipe ce que le narrateur disait de «nos ennemis» au v. 5; le rédacteur introduit en outre le projet de confondre Néhémie personnellement (v. 2). De même, les mesures défensives prises au v. 3 anticipent celles qui seront prises au v. 16 (même mot משמר, «garde»; même mention du jour et de la nuit).
- De la même manière, l'épisode du piège tendu à Néhémie par Sanballât et Tobiyya (6,1-9) transpose sur ces personnages le projet d'attentat contre le gouverneur révélé par Shemaya (v. 10), avec le même refus de se déplacer (vv. 3-4,11).
- Toujours au chap. 6, les vv. 12-14 se greffent évidemment sur les vv. 10-11, dont ils donnent une interprétation: c'est sur l'ordre de Tobiyya que Shemaya a parlé, et son but est de faire pécher Néhémie. Notons que l'invocation finale (v. 14) est parallèle à celle de 5,19.
- La dernière addition (6,17-19) est liée à la précédente par le même motif de la volonté d'effrayer Néhémie (vv. 13a,14b,19b), ainsi que par le motif des lettres (vv. 5,17,19). On notera la même forme consonantique מרבים en 6,17 et 7,2.

Bref, tout se passe comme si un rédacteur avait systématiquement retravaillé le texte primitif des «Mémoires de Néhémie». Dans quel but? Il nous faut ici nous interroger sur l'identité des coalisés.

3. *Sanballât, Tobiyya, Géshem et leurs complices*

Qui sont les coalisés, aux yeux de l'historien et dans le projet du rédacteur? Tentons de rassembler les données disponibles.

Commençons par l'homme présenté comme l'opposant principal à Néhémie et l'âme de la coalition: Sanballât. Ce personnage est probablement gouverneur de Samarie, comme en témoigne Ne 3,33-34. Ne serait-ce pas de lui qu'il est question dans une lettre écrite par Yédonyah, chef de la communauté juive d'Éléphantine, le 26 novembre 407 et adressée à Bagôhî, gouverneur de Judée?[21] En effet, Yédonyah écrit: «Nous avons envoyé une lettre en notre propre nom à Dalayah et Šèlèmyah, les fils de Sinuballit, le gouverneur de Samarie». P. Grelot

---

21. Voir P. GRELOT, *Documents araméens d'Égypte*, pp. 408-415.

commente: «Les Juifs d'Éléphantine savent que Sinuballit est mort; mais ils semblent ignorer lequel de ses fils lui a succédé dans la charge de gouverneur de Samarie»[22]. Cette interprétation est plausible, même si elle n'est pas totalement assurée. Mais elle pose une question difficile: si Sinuballit/Sanballât est mort peu avant l'an 407, pouvait-il être déjà gouverneur quelque 38 ans plus tôt? Quoi qu'il en soit, le livre de Néhémie ne lui donne jamais ce titre, mais il l'appelle «le Horonite». On considère souvent que ce nom fait référence au village de Beth-Horon-le-Bas ou Beth-Horon-le-Haut, proches de la vallée d'Ayyalôn[23]. Mais peut-être vaut-il mieux y lire une allusion à la cité moabite de Horonaïm (cf. Is 15,5; Jr 48,3)[24]; dans ce cas, le rédacteur soulignerait l'origine païenne de Sanballât ou tout au moins son lien avec un peuple particulièrement détesté. En d'autres termes, cette manière de parler renforcerait la portée anti-samaritaine du texte; on peut reconnaître la même tendance en Si 47,21,24; 50,25-26. Il n'est pas moins intéressant d'apprendre par Flavius Josèphe[25] que le temple du Garizim a été édifié au temps d'Alexandre le Grand par un autre Sanballât, lui aussi gouverneur de Samarie. Sans marquer la rupture définitive entre Juifs et Samaritains[26], cet acte a dû être une étape significative du conflit entre les deux groupes. Josèphe ajoute que Sanballât avait accordé la main de sa fille Nicaso au prêtre Manassé, frère d'un grand-prêtre de Jérusalem; Manassé ayant été expulsé de sa charge, Sanballât lui a confié le sacerdoce suprême du nouveau temple. Encore une fois, le rapprochement avec le Sanballât du livre de Néhémie s'impose: un de ses gendres – anonyme – n'est autre qu'un prêtre de Jérusalem, petit-fils du grand-prêtre Élyashib, et lui aussi est expulsé de la ville sainte (13,28). La coïncidence est étonnante, et d'autant plus que la Bible hébraïque ne connaît pas d'autre cas d'expulsion d'un prêtre! Comme la Bible ne parle pas de l'érection du temple du Garizim, plusieurs auteurs[27] ont mis en doute l'historicité des

22. *Ibidem*, note i, pp. 412-413. Je pense cependant que le fait d'avoir adressé la lettre à Dalayah et Šèlèmyah n'implique pas que l'un des deux est gouverneur: si Yédonyah ignore qui a succédé à Sanballât/Sinuballit, il est logique qu'il s'adresse aux fils de celui-ci, car il les connaît.

23. Voir Ph. ABADIE, art. *Sanballat*, dans *DBS*, t. XI, Paris, Letouzey et Ané, 1991, col. 1098-1104 (col. 1098).

24. Cf. D.J.A. CLINES, *Ezra, Nehemiah, Esther* (n. 11), p. 144.

25. *Antiquités juives*, XI, 302-325.

26. Rappelons l'existence du temple juif de Léontopolis, dans le delta du Nil: l'unicité du Temple de Jérusalem n'était pas absolue. Le schisme samaritain a fait l'objet de nombreuses hypothèses contradictoires; voir en particulier J.D. PURVIS, *The Samaritans*, dans W.D. DAVIES et L. FINKELSTEIN, *The Cambridge History of Judaism*, t. II, *The Hellenistic Age*, Cambridge, 1989, pp. 591-613; É. NODET, *Essai sur les origines du Judaïsme*, Paris, Cerf, 1992, pp. 94-163.

27. Par exemple J. BRIGHT, *A History of Israel*, London, SCM, [2]1972, p. 412.

faits rapportés par Josèphe, qui aurait confondu les deux Sanballât; ces faits sont cependant aujourd'hui confirmés par l'archéologie et par la découverte des «papyri de Samarie», datés des années 375-335, qui mentionnent un troisième Sanballât[28]. Faut-il dès lors penser que des événements identiques (expulsion d'un prêtre de Jérusalem, gendre d'un gouverneur de Samarie appelé Sanballât) se sont produits deux fois à quelques générations d'intervalle?[29] Il serait tentant de croire que le doublet provient plutôt du rédacteur du livre de Néhémie, qui projetterait au milieu du Ve siècle la figure détestée de Sanballât, devenue symbole du schisme samaritain. Un tel travail d'écriture s'inscrirait au mieux alors que l'hostilité entre Jérusalem et Samarie avait atteint un niveau important; or les premiers incidents graves ont eu lieu, d'après Josèphe, aux alentours de l'an 200[30]. Cela nous mène à une époque voisine de la rédaction du Siracide.

Le deuxième grand personnage de la coalition hostile à Jérusalem est «Tobiyya, le serviteur (עבד) ammonite». Le mot עבד est expliqué de deux manières. Pour les uns[31], il désigne Tobiyya comme un auxiliaire ammonite de Sanballât; pour d'autres[32], ce serait plutôt un titre de haute fonction (gouverneur?) en Ammon. En tout cas, la qualité d'Ammonite est tout aussi mal vue que celle de Moabite, à laquelle elle est d'ailleurs associée: «L'Ammonite et le Moabite ne seront pas admis à l'assemblée de YHWH; même leurs descendants à la dixième génération ne seront pas admis à l'assemblée de YHWH, et cela pour toujours» (Dt 23,4); précisément, cette phrase est citée, d'une manière un peu simplifiée, en Ne 13,1[33]. En dehors du livre de Néhémie, aucun Tobiyya n'est connu au Ve siècle[34]. En revanche, le personnage peut être rapproché de Joseph fils de Tobias, qui intervient sur la scène politique de Jérusalem à partir de l'an 230 environ[35]: cet homme originaire du pays d'Ammon va deve-

---

28. Les principales pièces du dossier sont rassemblées par J.D. PURVIS, *The Samaritans* (n. 26), pp. 598-599. Sur les papyri de Samarie et leur apport au débat, voir Ph. ABADIE, art. *Sanballat* (n. 23), col. 1103.

29. Telle est la solution retenue par J.D. PURVIS, *The Samaritans* (n. 26), p. 598.

30. *Antiquités juives*, XII, 154-156; cf. J.D. PURVIS, *The Samaritans* (n. 26), pp. 602-603.

31. Ainsi, W. RUDOLPH, *Esra und Nehemia* (HAT, I,20), Tübingen, Mohr, 1949, p. 109; A.H.J. GUNNEWEG, *Nehemia* (KAT, XIX/2), Gütersloh, Mohn, 1987, p. 56.

32. Par exemple B. MAZAR, *The Tobiads*, dans *IEJ* 7 (1957) 137-145,229-238 (p. 144); H.G.M. WILLIAMSON, *Ezra, Nehemiah* (n. 17), pp. 183-184; J. BLENKINSOPP, *Ezra-Nehemiah* (OTL), London, SCM, 1989, p. 218.

33. Notons que les Ammonites et les Moabites sont encore associés, conjointement aux Ashdodites, en Ne 13,23.

34. Deux inscriptions araméennes טוביה ont été retrouvées à Iraq el-Emir (Transjordanie); la paléographie invite à les dater au IIIe siècle environ; voir J. NAVEH, *The Development of the Aramaic Script*, Jérusalem, The Israel Academy of Sciences and Humanities, 1970, pp. 62-64.

35. La date exacte est controversée, et notamment parce que le récit de Flavius JOSÈPHE, *Antiquités Juives*, XII,160-224; 228-234, n'est pas fiable en ce qui concerne la chronolo-

nir «représentant du peuple» (προστάτης); levant des impôts exorbitants pour le compte de Ptolémée III, il fera preuve d'une grande brutalité et travaillera à l'hellénisation du pays. La famille des Tobiades sera d'ailleurs, pendant une cinquantaine d'années, la championne du mouvement d'hellénisation, qui touche en particulier les milieux les plus aisés de Jérusalem. Or précisément, Tobiyya cherche à entraîner Néhémie dans le péché (Ne 6,13), et il a des alliés parmi les hommes importants de la ville (6,17-19). S'il est vrai que les sections du livre de Néhémie où Sanballât et ses alliés interviennent font partie d'une strate secondaire de l'ouvrage, l'hypothèse d'une réécriture aux alentours de l'an 200 dans un sens hostile à l'hellénisme est plausible.

Moins important, à première vue, que les deux premiers, Géshem l'Arabe ou Gashmu est le troisième homme de la coalition. Ce nom a été rapproché d'une inscription gravée en araméen sur un bol en argent trouvé à Tell el-Maskhouta, dans la région de l'actuelle Ismaïlia: זי קינו בר גשם מלך קדר קרב להנאלת, soit «Ce que Qaïnu fils de Géshem, roi de Qédar, a offert à Han-Ilat»[36]. L'archéologie et la paléographie permettent de dater cette inscription aux alentours de l'an 400[37], ce qui est compatible avec le règne de Géshem lui-même vers 445. À l'époque perse, le royaume arabe s'étend sur une large zone semi-désertique, qui va de l'extrémité orientale du delta du Nil jusqu'en Transjordanie en passant par le Négueb et la Arabah[38]; en d'autres termes, il occupe toute la région qui se trouve au Sud de la province de Judée, à l'exception possible de l'Idumée. À vrai dire, on ne sait pas quand cette province, qui avait Marésha pour capitale, a été créée; elle est seulement mentionnée dans les archives de Zénon en 259[39]. Dans l'hypothèse d'une rédaction du texte aux alentours de l'an 200, l'évocation de Géshem l'Arabe pourrait se référer aux Nabatéens[40], qui ont remplacé les Qedarites vers la fin de

---

gie. Ainsi, J.A. GOLDSTEIN, *The Tale of the Tobiads*, dans *Christianity, Judaism and Other Greco-Roman Cults*. FS M. Smith, t. III, Leiden, Brill, 1975, pp. 85-123 (spéc. pp. 97,101), situe la nomination de Joseph fils de Tobias comme fermier des impôts de Cœlé-Syrie dans les années 227-224; Christiane SAULNIER, *Histoire d'Israël*, t. III, *De la conquête d'Alexandre à la destruction du Temple*, Paris, Cerf, 1985, pp. 451-454, date de même événement de l'an 248. Les archives de Zénon montrent en tout cas que Tobias lui-même vivait en 259.

36. Traduction selon A. LEMAIRE, *Populations et territoires de la Palestine à l'époque perse*, dans *Transeuphratène* 3 (1990) 31-74, p. 47. Cet article a été reproduit, avec des modifications non négligeables, sous le titre *Histoire et administration de la Palestine à l'époque perse*, dans E.-M. LAPERROUSAZ (éd.), *La Palestine à l'époque perse*, Paris, Cerf, 1994, pp. 11-53 (p. 26).

37. *Ibidem.*

38. A. LEMAIRE, *Populations et territoires de la Palestine à l'époque perse* (n. 36), p. 25.

39. Cf. *ibidem*, p. 28.

40. Sur ces derniers, voir A. NEGEV, *The Nabateans and the Provincia Arabia*, dans *ANRW*, t. II/8, *Politische Geschichte (Provinzen und Randvölker: Syrien, Palästina, Arabien)*, Berlin-New York, de Gruyter, 1977, pp. 520-686.

l'époque perse[41]. Mais cela n'est qu'une hypothèse, d'autant plus que nous ne sommes guère renseignés sur les rapports entre Nabatéens et Judéens à cette époque[42]. Notons que dans le second livre des Chroniques, les Arabes – ignorés dans l'histoire deutéronomiste – sont plusieurs fois mentionnés comme peuple ennemi de Juda, se livrant au pillage (22,1) en compagnie des Philistins (21,16; 26,7; cf. 17,11); on les retrouve associés aux Méûnites (26,7), eux-mêmes cités avec les Moabites et les Ammonites (20,1). Nous constatons ainsi des liens qui font penser à la coalition de Géshem l'Arabe avec Sanballât le Horonite (allusion possible à une origine moabite) et Tobiyya l'Ammonite. La mention des Méûnites est intéressante: elle paraît désigner une population située à l'Est de Pétra[43], et le récit de 2 Ch 20 les appelle aussi «les montagnards de Sé'ir» (vv. 10,22,23); ceci fait penser aux «habitants de la montage de Sé'ir» dont parle Si 50,26 à côté des Philistins et des Samaritains.

Aux côtés de Sanballât et Tobiyya, Ne 4,1 parle de la présence de trois groupes parmi les ennemis de Jérusalem: les Arabes, les Ammonites et les Ashdodites. Les deux premiers sont liés à Géshem et à Tobiyya, respectivement. Mais qu'en est-il du troisième? Ashdod, qui fut une des cinq cités philistines, est ensuite devenue capitale d'une province assyrienne, qui correspondait à l'ancien pays des Philistins. Cette province a probablement survécu comme entité administrative sous les régimes babylonien et perse; la ville sera encore un centre important à l'époque hellénistique. Ne 13,23-24 parle des Juifs qui ont épousé des femmes ashdodites et dont les enfants ne parlent pas «judéen» mais la langue d'Ashdod. On explique en général que l'auteur fait référence à un dialecte local[44]. Je crois cependant qu'une autre hypothèse doit être envisagée: l'auteur parlerait en fait de la langue grecque. La présence grecque sur plusieurs sites de la côte palestinienne dès l'époque perse est

---

41. «Les Arabes sont devenus des Nabatéens», *ibidem*, p. 28.

42. 1 M 9,35-42 rapporte que des Amraï, apparentés aux Nabatéens, ont tué Jean, frère de Judas Maccabée, trahissant ainsi l'alliance qui unissait les deux groupes. Les sources manquent pour la période antérieure à cet épisode.

43. Telle est l'opinion de la plupart des commentateurs, qui mettent les Méûnites en relation avec la localité actuelle de Ma'an. Voir par exemple H.G.M. WILLIAMSON, *1 and 2 Chronicles* (NCBC), Grand Rapids, MI, Eerdmans, et London, Marshall, Morgan and Scott, 1982, pp. 293-294; R.B. DILLARD, *2 Chronicles* (WBC, 15), Waco, TX, 1987, pp. 155-156.

44. Pour A. LEMAIRE, *Histoire et administration de la Palestine à l'époque perse*, p. 31, l'ashdodite serait plutôt «un nouvel état de langue du dialecte cananéen parlé en pays philistin au Fer II, dialecte qui semble avoir été proche du phénicien et de l'hébreu». D'autres auteurs pensent à l'ancienne langue philistine, ou encore à un langage incompréhensible pour les Judéens, sans autre précision.

aujourd'hui bien établie[45], et la région d'Ashdod a sans doute été un des foyers les plus anciens d'hellénisation de la région palestinienne[46]. Ce qui paraît visé, c'est l'adoption de la culture grecque: il y a là, aux yeux de l'auteur, un vrai scandale[47].

Ne 6,17-19 parle d'un dernier groupe d'adversaires de Néhémie: il s'agit des alliés de Tobiyya parmi l'élite sociale de Jérusalem. Ces gens font publiquement l'éloge de l'Ammonite et lui rapportent les paroles du gouverneur lui-même. Plus loin (13,4-9), on apprend que le grand prêtre Élyashib, ami de Tobiyya, avait aménagé à son usage une salle du Temple, puis qu'il était lui-même apparenté à Sanballât (13,28). Tout cela suscite la colère de Néhémie. S'il est vrai que Tobiyya représente ici la famille des Tobiades, partisans zélés de l'hellénisation du pays, ces textes doivent être rapprochés de 1 M 1,10-15 et 2 M 4,7-17, qui évoquent l'adoption de l'hellénisme par les prêtres et les notables de Jérusalem au temps d'Antiochos Épiphane; il est certain, cependant, que la nouvelle culture avait déjà touché la ville sainte depuis plusieurs générations.

De cette petite enquête, il ressort qu'il faut, une fois de plus, distinguer les faits historiques et les faits littéraires. Aux yeux de l'historien, la royauté d'un certain Géshem, roi de Qédar dans la seconde moitié du Ve siècle est probable, de même que l'existence, vers la même époque, d'un gouverneur de Samarie appelé Sinuballit ou Sanballât, même s'il est douteux qu'il exerçait déjà sa charge en 445. En revanche, on n'a pas trouvé trace d'un Tobiyya l'Ammonite avant la seconde moitié du IIIe siècle. C'est un rédacteur écrivant aux alentours de l'an 200 qui imagine ces trois personnages comme s'opposant à Néhémie et à son entreprise, projetant sur le Ve siècle des conflits qui lui sont contemporains; sans doute songe-t-il respectivement aux Samaritains (Sanballât), aux Juifs hellénisés (Tobiyya) et aux Nabatéens (Géshem). Ces groupes sont présentés comme liés les uns aux autres, et non comme trois forces isolées. Samaritains et Nabatéens seraient-ils perçus comme influencés par la

---

45. Cf. Josette ELAYI, *Présence grecque sur la côte palestinienne*, dans E.-M. LAPERROUSAZ (éd.), *La Palestine à l'époque perse*, pp. 245-260.

46. S'il est vrai que l'auteur écrit un peu avant ou un peu après l'an 200, l'ensemble de la Palestine est déjà très hellénisée, comme en témoignent les inscriptions; voir J. BARR, *Hebrew, Aramaic and Greek in the Hellenistic Age*, dans W.D. DAVIES et L. FINKELSTEIN, *The Cambridge History of Judaism*, t. II, *The Hellenistic Age*, pp. 79-114 (spéc. p. 102); voir aussi M. HENGEL, *The Interpenetration of Judaism and Hellenism in the pre-Maccabean Period*, ibidem, pp. 167-228. Parler du grec comme «langue d'Ashdod» garde cependant sa pertinence, car cette expression fait référence au premier foyer d'hellénisation du pays.

47. Dans son commentaire de Si 50,25-26, A.A. DI LELLA, *The Wisdom of Ben Sira* (AB, 39), New York, Doubleday, 1987, p. 558, explique dans le même sens: «The Philistine (…) stand here for those who have accepted paganism and Hellenization».

culture hellénistique? Ce n'est pas impossible[48]. De toute manière, les éléments hostiles à Néhémie représentent les différentes forces qui menacent de l'intérieur comme de l'extérieur la communauté juive de Jérusalem aux alentours de l'an 200. Dans ce contexte, la déclaration de Néhémie en 2,20 («Quant à vous, vous n'avez ni part, ni droit, ni souvenir dans Jérusalem») prend un sens très concret: il s'agit de refuser tout pouvoir aux Juifs hellénisés et à ceux qui sont considérés comme leurs alliés. On sait ce qu'il en est advenu sous Antiochos IV.

4. *Une rédaction du livre de Néhémie dans l'esprit du Siracide*[49]

La réécriture du récit de la reconstruction des murailles n'est pas un phénomène isolé. C'est l'ensemble du livre de Néhémie qui a fait l'objet d'une nouvelle édition dans l'esprit du Siracide. À défaut d'un examen complet de la rédaction de l'ouvrage, tâche qui ne peut être entreprise dans les limites de cet article, je me contenterai de noter deux indices d'une telle édition.

Au chap. 5, qui interrompt le fil du récit et apparaît ainsi comme un élément ajouté[50], Néhémie appelle les notables de Jérusalem à la «crainte de Dieu» (יראת אלהים, v. 9), qualité qu'il revendique pour lui-même (v. 15). On trouvait déjà le même souci dans la prière de Ne 1,5-11 (au v. 11), et le thème reviendra encore en 7,2; ces deux textes forment, eux aussi, des éléments secondaires dans les «Mémoires de Néhémie»)[51]. Le plaidoyer pour la «crainte de Dieu» dans le sens de «fidélité à la Loi» est, précisément, un des thèmes les plus insistants et les plus caractéristiques du Siracide (Si 1,11,12,13,14,16,18,20,27,28,30; etc.)[52]. D'autre part, le livre de Néhémie condamne les mariages mixtes (13,23-

---

48. Sur l'hellénisation de Samarie, voir M. BAILLET, art. *Samaritains*, dans *DBS*, t. XI, Paris, Letouzey et Ané, 1991, col. 773-1047 (col. 986).

49. Voir déjà J. VERMEYLEN, *Le Dieu de la promesse et le Dieu de l'Alliance* (LD, 126), Paris, Cerf, 1986, pp. 281-282, avec une argumentation qui restait encore très fragmentaire.

50. Dans ce chapitre, l'attitude de Néhémie correspond à celle d'Onias II, qui refusa d'acquitter les taxes annuelles à Ptolémée III; c'est à la suite de ce refus que le pouvoir effectif sur Jérusalem fut confié à Joseph fils de Tobias, qui n'hésita pas à augmenter considérablement l'impôt.

51. L'appartenance de la prière au texte originel des «Mémoires de Néhémie» est discutée depuis longtemps; voir par exemple A.H.J. GUNNEWEG, *Nehemia* (n. 31), p. 50. D.J.A. CLINES, *The Nehemiah Memoir* (n. 10), pp. 129-132, a montré qu'on ne peut la considérer comme la mise par écrit d'une prière effectivement prononcée par Néhémie. Au chap. 7, le discours du v. 3 s'adresse aux portiers installés par Néhémie au v. 1; le v. 2 brise la continuité naturelle du récit et forme un élément ajouté.

52. Voir notamment J. HASPECKER, *Gottesfurcht bei Jesus Sirach* (AnBib, 30), Roma, 1967; W.H. IRWIN, *Fear of God, the Analogy of Friendship and Ben Sira's Theodicy*, dans *Bib* 76 (1995) 551-559.

29), c'est-à-dire l'union de Juifs avec «des femmes ashdodites, ammonites ou moabites» (v. 23)[53]. Cette section du livre fait référence à
Sanballât le Horonite (v. 28) et paraît donc liée aux additions déjà relevées aux chap. 1–7; son caractère secondaire[54] est confirmé par la formule finale en «souviens-toi» (v. 29b), à rapprocher de 5,19 et 6,14[55]. Si
cet aspect des réformes de Néhémie n'appartient pas au texte primitif
des «Mémoires», il y a lieu de penser que ces versets ont été inspirés
par les mesures rapportées en Esd 9–10, d'autant plus que le vocabulaire
est largement commun[56]. D'autre part, on notera une différence d'accent
entre les deux textes. Dans le livre d'Esdras, la symbolique dominante
est celle de la souillure avec les peuples des pays (voir en particulier
9,11): il s'agit de maintenir la distance entre Israël comme peuple séparé
et les nations païennes (Cananéens, Hittites, Perizzites, Jébuséens, Ammonites, Moabites, Égyptiens, Amorites, 9,1); dans cette optique, on
comprend la nécessité de renvoyer les femmes étrangères (10,3-
5,11,14,17,19,44). En Ne 13,23-31, la symbolique de la souillure et la
nécessité de renvoyer les femmes étrangères n'apparaissent pas, mais
l'auteur attire l'attention sur l'emploi de la langue ashdodienne (v. 24),
dont nous avons vu qu'elle renvoie sans doute à la culture grecque. On
retrouve à peu près la même chose dans le Siracide, qui déconseille la
fréquentation de la femme étrangère (9,1-9); ainsi que le suggèrent les
parallèles du livre des Proverbes, cette mise en garde vise probablement
la culture hellénistique[57]. Il faut sans doute encore lire dans la même li-

53. Il est possible, cependant, que la mention des Ammonites et des Moabites soit secondaire; cf. H.G.M. WILLIAMSON, *Ezra, Nehemiah* (n. 17), p. 397.

54. C. PICHON, *La prohibition des mariages mixtes par Néhémie (XIII 23-31)*, dans *VT*
47 (1997) 168-199, estime que l'interdiction des mariages mixtes en Ne 13 n'appartient
pas au texte primitif des «Mémoires de Néhémie», mais dérive d'Esd 9–10; l'auteur aurait
cependant utilisé des matériaux anciens: une controverse sur l'usage de la langue judéenne
et l'expulsion d'un petit- fils d'Élyashib par Néhémie. Il est possible, en effet, que la
péricope ait connu une certaine histoire littéraire; il faudrait cependant examiner si les tensions relevées par Ch. Pichon ne sont pas explicables par le fait que l'auteur de la péricope
voulait à la fois transférer à l'époque de Néhémie la réforme d'Esd 9–10 et l'interpréter
dans un sens nouveau, anti-hellénistique (d'où le motif de la langue ashdodienne).

55. Des phrases semblables apparaissent encore en 13,22,31, qui appartiennent à la
même strate littéraire. On retrouve en Si 49,13 le même verbe זכר en rapport avec Néhémie: serait-ce une simple coïncidence? On considère en général que la formule du «Souviens-toi, mon Dieu» est une des marques les plus caractéristiques des «Mémoires de Néhémie»; je pense, au contraire, qu'elle provient d'une rédaction secondaire.

56. Cf. A.H.J. GUNNEWEG, *Nehemia* (n. 31), p. 172.

57. Cf. J. VERMEYLEN, *La femme étrangère dans le livre des Proverbes*, dans Th. RÖ-
MER (éd.), *Lectio difficilior probabilior?* FS F. Smyth-Florentin (DBAT, Beiheft 12),
Heidelberg, 1991, pp. 221-235. Le livre des Proverbes a connu, lui aussi, une importante
édition dans l'esprit du Siracide; c'est ainsi que le portrait de la femme parfaite (31,10-
31; cf. Si 26,1-4) représente la crainte de YHWH comme sagesse véritable, par opposition à la fausse sagesse proposée par la nouvelle culture.

gne la mise en valeur de Pinḥas (45,23-26), l'homme qui avait appliqué d'une manière exemplaire l'interdit des mariages mixtes en frappant de sa lance un Juif et une Madianite en pleins ébats amoureux (Nb 25,6-8). Ces observations en témoignent: le livre de Néhémie a connu une importante édition – sans doute son édition définitive – à la fin du IIIᵉ ou au début du IIᵉ siècle; le rédacteur exprime des préoccupations qui sont aussi celles du Siracide: la crainte de YHWH (au sens de fidélité à la Loi) et, par opposition, le refus de la culture hellénistique, symbolisée par la femme étrangère. C'est dans ce cadre que le récit de la reconstruction des murailles a été complété par les différents épisodes où Sanballât et ses alliés interviennent.

CONCLUSION

Le Siracide met en valeur Néhémie, l'homme des murailles, dernier héros de sa galerie des ancêtres d'Israël avant le grand prêtre Simon (49,13). Il représente la nécessité pour la communauté juive de se protéger contre des dangers mortels. Quels dangers? La réponse paraît se trouver en 50,25-26, où l'auteur désigne comme objets de sa haine «les habitants de la montagne de Sé'ir, les Philistins et le peuple stupide résidant à Sichem». Cette liste est elle-même énigmatique, d'autant plus qu'Édomites et Philistins ont disparu depuis longtemps en tant que tels. Elle s'éclaire cependant à la lecture du livre de Néhémie.

Néhémie, gouverneur de Jérusalem à partir de l'an 445, a rebâti les murailles écroulées et a ainsi doté la ville d'une défense bien nécessaire en des temps d'insécurité. C'est ce dont témoignent les «Mémoires» autobiographiques qui forment le squelette du livre qui porte son nom. Contrairement à l'opinion générale des commentateurs, cependant, il apparaît que ce texte n'est pas homogène: il porte la marque d'un important travail de réécriture à une époque voisine du Siracide et dans le même esprit. Parmi les additions relevant de cette rédaction, il faut compter en particulier les passages où le projet de Néhémie se heurte à l'hostilité de Sanballât le Horonite, Tobiyya l'Ammonite et Géshem l'Arabe. Nous rencontrons donc, comme en Si 50,25-26, trois ennemis. Sanballât, adversaire principal de Néhémie et gouverneur de Samarie, correspond au «peuple stupide résidant à Sichem»: il représente les Samaritains; sa qualité de «Horonite» pourrait en outre faire allusion à Moab. Tobiyya évoque pour le lecteur la famille des Tobiades, grands promoteurs de l'hellénisme à Jérusalem; il est lui-même lié aux Ashdodites et correspond donc aux Philistins de Si 50,26. Géshem l'Arabe, enfin, paraît représenter les Nabatéens, ce qui correspond aux habitants de la montagne de Sé'ir. Les trois adversaires sont liés. Ensemble, ils représentent la menace idéologique et culturelle qui plane sur la communauté juive: si Jérusalem adopte la culture hellénistique (cf. Ne 13,24), si elle se laisse contaminer par le schisme samaritain ou par d'autres déviations, elle est perdue! Il lui faut donc un solide rempart. En définitive, celui-ci n'est autre que la Torah, qui suscite la crainte de YHWH. Peut-être n'est-ce pas par hasard que la lecture de la Loi et l'engagement solennel du peuple de s'y conformer (Ne 8–10) figurent entre le récit de l'édification des murailles (chap. 1–7) et celui de leur dédicace (12,27-43). Dans le Siracide également, on peut lire que les rois de Juda, hormis David, Ézéchias (qui «fortifia sa ville», 48,17) et Josias, ont abandonné la Loi du Très-Haut, «car ils livrèrent leur vigueur à d'autres, leur gloire à une nation étrangère» (49,5): ne pas faire barrage à ce qui vient du dehors conduit à abandonner la Torah et, avec elle, l'identité juive.

Il est des jours où la situation exige des mesures de défense. La reconstruction des remparts était sans doute nécessaire, de même que les mises en garde du Siracide à l'encontre des dangers qui menaçaient la fidélité à la tradition israélite. Au-delà de la lecture du Siracide et du livre de Néhémie, une question demeure cependant, et elle est toujours actuelle: pourquoi les bâtisseurs de murs – les champions du nationalisme, les porte-drapeau d'une identité idéologique excluante – sont-ils si souvent mis à l'honneur dans nos sociétés, nos États, nos Églises, alors que les bâtisseurs de ponts le sont plus rarement? L'histoire enseigne pourtant que les murailles les plus puissantes finissent toutes, un jour, par être percées…

Avenue H. Conscience 156   Jacques VERMEYLEN
B-1140 Bruxelles

DER HOHEPRIESTER SIMON IN SIR 50

EIN BEITRAG ZUR BEDEUTUNG VON PRIESTERTUM UND KULT IM SIRACHBUCH

Maurice Gilbert hat mit seiner Studie zum Psalm in Sir 51,1-12[1], den er als Danksagung für das Bestehen der in Sir 2 angekündigten Prüfungen versteht, einen bedeutungsvollen Vorschlag zur Gesamtstruktur des Buches gemacht. Die folgende Skizze zu Sir 50,1-24 gilt einem weiteren Text vom Schluß des Buches, der bis vor kurzem fast nur im Rahmen von Sirachkommentaren oder in Studien zum Väterlob[2] Beachtung gefunden hat. Abgesehen vom Beitrag von O'Fearghail[3] ist erst in jüngster Zeit das Interesse an der Gestalt des Hohepriesters Simon in diesem Kapitel neu erwacht[4]. Hayward, der sich mit Sir 50 am ausführlichsten beschäftigt hat, ist sogar der Meinung: »It is difficult to overestimate this chapter's importance«[5]. Im folgenden sollen einige Themen und Linien hervorgehoben werden, die über das Väterlob hinaus auf das Ganze des Buches verweisen, als kleiner Beitrag zur Bedeutung von Priestertum und Kult in der Weisheit des Jesus Sirach.

1. Sir 50,1-24 im Kontext

In der noch nicht abgeschlossenen Diskussion um Aufbau und Gliederung des Buches[6] mag hier die Frage offen bleiben, ob als Schluß des

---

1. M. GILBERT, *L'action de grace de Ben Sira (Sir 51,1-12)*, in R. KUNTZMANN (ed.), *Ce Dieu qui vient. Mélanges offerts à B. Renaud* (LD, 159), Paris, 1995, pp. 231-242.

2. Cf. zuletzt B.L. MACK, *Wisdom and the Hebrew Epic. Ben Sira's Hymn in Praise of the Fathers*, Chicago, 1985; Th. R. LEE, *Studies in the Form of Sirach 44–50* (SBLDS, 75), Atlanta, GA, 1986; R. PETRAGLIO, *Il libro che contamina le mani: Ben Sirac rilegge il libro e la storia d'Israele*, Palermo, 1993.

3. F. Ó FEARGHAIL, *Sir 50,5-21: Yom Kippur or the Daily Whole-Offering?*, in *Bib* 59 (1978) 301-316.

4. J.C. VANDERKAM, *Simon the Just: Simon I or Simon II?*, in D.P. WRIGHT et al. (eds.), *Pomegranates and Golden Bells. Studies in Biblical, Jewish, and Near Eastern Ritual, Law, and Literature in Honor of J. Milgrom*, Winona Lake, IN, 1995, pp. 303-318.

5. C.T.R. HAYWARD, *Behind the Dead Sea Scrolls: The Sons of Zadok, the Priest, and Their Priestly Ideology*, in *Toronto Journal of Theology* 13 (1997) 7-21, p. 10; cf. ferner C.T.R. HAYWARD, *Sacrifice and World Order: Some Observations on Ben Sira's Attitude on the Temple Service*, in S. W. SYKES (ed.), *Sacrifice and Redemption* (Durham Essays in Theology), Cambridge, 1991, pp. 22-34; C.T.R. HAYWARD, *The Jewish Temple. A Non-Biblical Sourcebook*, London, 1996 [pp. 38-72: The Wisdom of Jesus Ben Sira in Hebrew; pp. 73-84: The Wisdom of Jesus Ben Sira in Greek].

6. Cf. J. MARBÖCK, *Structure and Redaction History of the Book of Ben Sira. Review*

Buches ein großes Diptychon über die Werke Gottes in der Schöpfung
(Sir 42,15–43,33) und in den Gestalten der Geschichte Israels (Sir 44–
50) beabsichtigt bzw. anzunehmen ist, wie es m.E. durchaus plausibel
scheint[7], oder ob das Väterlob K. 44–50 eher für sich allein zu sehen ist[8].
Kein Zweifel dürfte darüber bestehen, daß die Schilderung des Hohepriesters Simon in K. 50 nicht von K. 44–49 isoliert werden darf. Auf
die Zusammengehörigkeit verweisen, wie noch verdeutlicht wird, sowohl strukturelle Gemeinsamkeiten zwischen Sir 50 und der Darstellung
Aarons Sir 45,6-26, mit der das Väterlob einen ersten Abschluß erreicht,
als auch mehrfache thematische Verklammerungen[9]. Von daher darf bereits vermutet werden, daß die Stellung von Sir 50 am Schluß der großen
Geschichtsschau und am Schluß des Buches nicht bloß formales, sondern auch sachlich-inhaltliches Gewicht haben wird, das gewiß noch
größer ist, wenn man ein Schlußdiptychon von 42,15–50,24 akzeptiert.

2. SIR 45,6-26 UND 50,1-24:

GRUNDLEGUNG UND GEGENWÄRTIGER VOLLZUG

Die unverkennbaren wechselseitigen Bezüge[10] der umfangreichen
Darstellungen Aarons und Simons an Schlüsselstellen von Sir 44–50
sind für das Verständnis von Sir 50,1-24 höchst bedeutsam; sie betreffen
sowohl Struktur als auch wesentliche Themen beider Texte.

Der Text über *Aaron*[11] spricht von dessen Erwählung (45,6-7a), der
Ausstattung mit Herrlichkeit in der Kleidung (45,7b-13ab), den Aufgaben des priesterlichen Dienstes in Opferdarbringung und Lehre

---

and Prospects, in P.C. BEENTJES (ed.), *The Book of Ben Sira in Modern Research*
(BZAW, 255), Berlin, 1997, pp. 62-79 sowie J. MARBÖCK, *Das Buch Jesus Sirach*, in
E. ZENGER et al., *Einleitung in das Alte Testament*, Stuttgart, [3]1998, pp. 363-370, bes.
pp. 364-367. Ein sehr beachtenswerter Vorschlag zum Aufbau des Buches findet sich bei
H.-W. JÜNGLING, *Der Bauplan des Buches Jesus Sirach*, in J. HAINZ et al. (eds.), *»Den
Armen eine frohe Botschaft«. FS Franz Kamphaus*, Frankfurt a.M., 1997, pp. 89-105.

7. Eine Zusammenstellung formaler und inhaltlicher Berührungspunkte zwischen Sir
42,15-43,33 und 44-50 s. bei P.C. BEENTJES, *The »Praise of the Famous« and its Prologue. Some Observations on Ben Sira 44:1-15 and the Question on Enoch in 44:16*, in
Bijdragen 45 (1984) 374-383; cf. auch LEE, *Studies* (n. 2), pp. 3-10; MACK, *Wisdom*
(n. 2), pp. 189-193. – Auch ein Vergleich mit Sir 17 und 24 könnte dies nahelegen.

8. JÜNGLING, *Bauplan* (n. 6), pp. 97.99.105; J.L. CRENSHAW, *The Book of Sirach*, in
The New Interpreter's Bible 5, Nashville, 1997, pp. 630-633.

9. Neben dem in n. 7 genannten Aufsatz von BEENTJES, *Praise*, p. 379f. s. J. MARBÖCK,
Die »Geschichte Israels« als »Bundesgeschichte« nach dem Sirachbuch, in J. MARBÖCK,
Gottes Weisheit unter uns. Zur Theologie des Buches Sirach. Hg. von I. FISCHER (HBS,
6), Freiburg–Basel–Wien, 1995, pp. 103-123, bes. pp. 107f.

10. LEE, *Studies* (n. 2), pp. 12-15.

11. Cf. die Darstellung zentraler Themen von Sir 45,6-22 in HAYWARD, *Temple* (n. 2),
pp. 63-71.

(45,13cd-17), von der Bestrafung angemaßter Kompetenzen (45,18f), vom priesterlichen Erbteil (45,20-22). Den Abschluß bilden die Erzählung von Bund und Hohepriesteramt für Pinhas (45,23-25d) sowie Lobpreis (45,25ef) und Bitte um Weisheit des Herzens (45,26). Das Kapitel über *Simon* beginnt mit der rühmenden Vorstellung Simons (50,1ab), erzählt von dessen Sorge für Tempel und Stadt (50,1c-4) und beschreibt in 50,5-21 Simons Herrlichkeit beim Vollzug der Liturgie: das Hervortreten aus dem Zelt (50,5), das Anlegen der Gewänder und das Hinaufsteigen zum Altar (50,11), die Opferriten (50,12-16), die erste Reaktion des Volkes (50,17-19), das Herabsteigen zum Segen und die zweite Reaktion des Volkes (50,20-21).

Am Schluß stehen wiederum die Aufforderung zum Lobpreis (50,22), sowie nach dem hebräischen Text von Ms[B12] die Bitte um Weisheit des Herzens, Frieden und Beständigkeit der Huld Gottes und des Pinhasbundes für Simon und seine Nachkommen (50,23f).

Die offenkundigste Strukturparallele zwischen beiden Texten ist der jeweilige Abschluß der Darstellung mit Aufruf zum Lobpreis (45,25ef/ 50,22) und der Bitte um Weisheit des Herzens (45,26a/50,23) sowie die Erwähnung des Bundes mit Pinhas (45,24/50,24). Der Unterschied liegt vor allem in der Perspektive der Darstellung: der Text über Aaron erzählt von der Erwählung durch Gott, vom Handeln Gottes bei der Ausstattung und Festsetzung seiner priesterlichen Aufgaben. K. 50 hingegen macht Leser und Leserinnen in V. 5-21 zu Betrachtern der Gestalt Simons, zu Zeugen des liturgischen Vollzuges mit seinem hohen ästhetischen Charakter[13]. Der Aspekt des Enkomiums[14] ist unübersehbar. Man darf die beiden Sichtweisen wohl als göttliche Grundlegung des Priestertums in Aaron und Pinhas und als ideale Realisierung in der Gestalt und Funktion Simons bezeichnen, die zugleich als Wunschbild für die Zukunft gilt.

Der Blick auf gemeinsame Motive und Themen der zwei Texte wie Bund, Herrlichkeit, Kleidung Aarons/Simons, Opferdarbringung, Segen und Lobpreis dürfte diese Perspektive einer Zuordnung eindrücklich bestätigen.

---

12. Das Fehlen des Pinhasbundes in Gr, Syr, Lat von 50,24 könnte bereits den Bruch in der legitimen Nachfolge der zadokidischen Hohepriester nach Onias III andeuten: cf. MARBÖCK, *Geschichte* (n. 9), p. 117.

13. O. WISCHMEYER, *Die Kultur des Buches Jesus Sirach* (BZNW, 77), Berlin, 1995, pp. 261-265, hat mit Recht erstmals auf die Bedeutung der ästhetischen Dimension des Gottesdienstes in Sir 45 und 50 aufmerksam gemacht.

14. So vor allem LEE, *Studies* (n. 2), pp. 234-237. Mit LEE das Ganze des Väterlobes von K. 44–50 nur als Enkomium auf Simon zu verstehen, scheint mir jedoch die Gewichte ungebührlich zu verschieben. Auch Ch. A. ROLLSTON, *The Non-Encomiastic Features of Ben Sira 44–50* (MA thesis), Johnson City, 1992 lehnt die Sicht als Enkomium nachdrücklich ab.

Darüber hinaus soll die Skizzierung einiger Züge des Bildes Simons in K. 50 etwas von der fundamentalen Bedeutung des Kultes in der Weisheit des Jesus Sirach überhaupt zur Sprache bringen.

3. THEMEN VON SIR 50,1-24

Mehr als es auf den ersten Blick scheint, laufen in Sir 50,1-24, darin K. 24 vergleichbar, Linien des gesamten Buches zusammen, sodaß der Vollzug der Liturgie durch Simon geradezu als Illustration des Axioms »Lex orandi – lex credendi« durch den Autor verstanden werden könnte. Aus der Fülle der Motive und Fragen, angefangen von den Differenzen zwischen der hebräischen und griechischen Version, werden hier nur einige für das Bild Simons und das Ganze des Buches wichtig erscheinende Züge skizziert[15], die vielleicht die Studien von Hayward[16] noch etwas weiterführen.

1. Simons Sorge für Heiligtum und Stadt

Für eine Identifikation des in Sir 50 genannten Simon mit dem Hohenpriester Simon II, einem Sohn Onias II, sprechen gegen die jüngst von VanderKam geäußerte Skepsis[17] immer noch eine Reihe von Argumenten: dies ist nicht bloß die in 50,1b-4 gerühmte Bautätigkeit für Tempel und Stadt, sondern m.E. vor allem der Unterschied zwischen der Erzählung über die Grundlegung der priesterlichen Funktionen in Aaron und der Beschreibung des Vollzuges, die Erfahrungen des Autors und der Adressaten spiegeln dürften.

Auch eine Reihe weiterer Motive aus Sir 44–49, insbesondere der Herrlichkeit Adams (49,16), die in der Gestalt Simons konvergieren, legen die Aktualisierung an einer Gestalt der Gegenwart nahe. D.h. die scheinbar profanen Tätigkeiten verweisen bereits auf theologische Anliegen.

15. Über die Sirachkommentare und die Materialsammlung bei PETRAGLIO, *Libro* (n. 2), pp. 115-147 (zu Sir 45,6-25) und pp. 380-415 (zu Sir 49,16–50,24) hinaus bietet HAYWARD, *Temple* (n. 5), pp. 38-63.73-84 m.E. die bisher beste theologische Würdigung der Konzeptionen des hebräischen bzw. griechischen Textes von Sir 49,15–50,26. Sir 50 würde zweifellos eine Monographie verdienen.

16. Cf. die n. 5 und 15 genannten Arbeiten.

17. J.C. VANDERKAM, *Simon* (n. 4) hält es gegen die dort p. 312 dokumentierte opinio communis genausogut für möglich, die von Sir 50,1-4 erwähnte Bautätigkeit trotz des von Josephus, *Ant.* XII, §139.141 erwähnten Briefes Antiochus III über die Beseitigung von Kriegsschäden in der Stadt und am Heiligtum mit Simon I zur Zeit Ptolemaios I Soter um 300 v. Chr. zu verbinden.

Der *Tempel* ist eines der wichtigen Themen Sirachs. Simons Tätigkeit für das Heiligtum (50,1-2 nach Gr; in Ms[B] 50,1 u. 3)[18] wird durch das Verb פקד (50,1c) mit Gottes besonderer Sorge für Gestalten der Anfänge (49,16), insbesondere für den Leichnam Josefs (49,15; cf. Gen 50,25; Ex 13,19) verbunden. Er schließt aber auch an das Werk der unmittelbar zuvor (49,11-12) genannten Gestalten, des Statthalters Serubbabel und des Priesters Joschua beim Bau des zweiten Tempels an, der nach 49,12d für ewige Herrlichkeit bestimmt ist. Die königliche Note, die Erinnerung an Salomo als Erbauer des ersten Tempels (47,13), ist ebenfalls gegenwärtig[19]. Die vom Tempel nicht trennbare Bausorge für die Stadt in 50,3-4 setzt die Tätigkeit Nehemias fort, die in 49,13b als »Aufrichten unserer Ruinen« (cf. Jes 44,26; 51,3; 61,4) und in 49,13c als »Heilen unserer Trümmer« (cf. Am 9,11; Jes 49,19), d.h. als Erfüllung prophetischer Verheißungen verstanden wird. Das 50,3 zweifach genannte Wasserreservoir (Ms[B] 50,2) verbindet Simon auch mit dem Tun König Hiskijas in 48,17 (cf. 2 Kön 20,20; Jes 22,11). Diese an erster Stelle genannten Stichworte Stadt und Tempel bedeuten mehr als königlich-priesterliche Bautätigkeit. Simon sorgt damit für den in Sir 24 an zentraler Stelle genannten Ruheort bzw. für das Ziel des Weges der Weisheit, die in 24,10 von sich sagt:

Im heiligen Zelt tat ich Dienst vor ihm und so wurde ich auf Zion eingesetzt.

Sir 50,6-8 wird diese Beziehung des Hohepriesters Simon zur Weisheit von K. 24 noch deutlicher. So hat m.E. in diesem Kontext des Buches auch das leidenschaftliche Gebet Sir 36 mit der Bitte für Stadt und Tempel (36,13-14: Ms[B]; 36,18-19: Gr) durchaus seinen Platz[20]:

Erbarme dich deiner heiligen Stadt,
über Jerusalem, den Ort deiner Wohnung!
Erfülle Zion mit deiner Pracht
und deinen Tempel mit deiner Herrlichkeit!

18. G.J. WIGHTMAN, *Ben Sira 50:2 and the Hellenistic Temple Enclosure in Jerusalem*, in S. BOURKE et al. (eds.), *Trade, Contact and the Movement of People in the Eastern Mediterranean. Studies in Honor of J. Basil Hennessy* (Mediterranean Archaeology. Suppl. 3). Sydney, 1995, pp. 275-283 versucht eine archäologische Konkretisierung der hebräischen und griechischen Angaben von Sir 50,1-3: Simon II hätte die Fundamente für eine große Umfassungsmauer über das Areal der Tempelhöfe der Perser- und Ptolemäerzeit hinaus gelegt. – Cf. auch die Diskussion von Ms[B] und Gr zu Sir 50,1-4 bei HAYWARD, *Temple* (n. 5), pp. 47-49.77-78 sowie die Kommentare.

19. Auch an die Arbeiten am Tempel unter Joschija könnte erinnert sein: cf. das Partizip מפקדים 2 Kön 22,5; 2 Chron 34,10.

20. Cf. R. HAYWARD, *The New Jerusalem in the Wisdom of Jesus Ben Sira*, in *SJOT* 6 (1992) 123-138, pp. 131-137. Nach Hayward, der die Authentizität des Textes voraussetzt, entspricht das Jerusalem der Gegenwart Sirachs dem prophetischen Ideal; es fehlt nur noch die Sammlung der Exilierten.

2. Herrlichkeit

Erstes Wort über den Priester (Gr: Hohepriester) Simon ist nach der Anordnung von Ms[B] neben dem Herausragen über seine Brüder תפארת עמו, Ruhm, Herrlichkeit, Zierde seines Volkes. תפארת begegnet nicht nur an Eckpunkten des Väterlobes, die Wurzel פאר/תפארה/תפארת nimmt im gesamten Buch eine gewichtige Rolle ein[21], vielfach parallel zu כבד/כבוד, vielleicht mit dem Unterschied, daß תפארת bei Sirach nie im Zusammenhang der Herrlichkeit Gottes in der Natur, sondern als dem Menschen vorbehaltene Kategorie von Herrlichkeit begegnet, die auf Gott verweist. Sie ist gegenüber angemaßtem Rühmen (47,4d: Goliat; 38,25 mit dem Stachel des Treibers) Zeichen und Lohn gottesfürchtigen Verhaltens, das sich durch Reichtum nicht vom rechten Weg abbringen läßt[22]. Ja, Gottesfurcht selber ist Ruhm, Herrlichkeit des Menschen (9,16), auch des Fremden, des Ausländers und Armen (10,22). תפארת ist höchste Qualität der religiösen Gestalten der Geschichte (44,7; cf. auch כבוד 44,2). Sie ist am ersten Höhepunkt des Väterlobes höchster von Gott verliehener Glanz der priesterlichen Gewänder Aarons (45,8; cf. 45,7 כבוד/הוד). In 6,31 ist es die Weisheit, die geradezu kultisch ihre Schüler mit Gewändern von כבוד kleidet und mit תפארת krönt. Am Schluß des Väterlobes 49,16b steht »die Herrlichkeit Adams über alles Lebendige«; d.h. Israels in den Gestalten seiner Geschichte entfaltete Herrlichkeit war bereits seinem ersten Vorfahren geschenkt[23]. Sir 50,1a schlägt von diesen Anfängen mit תפארת auch die Brücke zur Gegenwart; 50,11b und 20d begegnet die Wurzel nochmals. Der Hohepriester Simon als letzte (gegenwärtige) Gestalt von 44-50 sammelt und verwirklicht alle genannten Dimensionen: die Herrlichkeit Adams, Gottesfurcht und Weisheit, vor allem den priesterlichen Glanz von Aarons Kleidern (cf. 45,7.8 und 50,11); Vollendung ist der Segen über das Volk, der ihn an der Herrlichkeit des göttlichen Namens teilnehmen läßt (50,20cd). Der in den Begriffen von הדר (50,5.11) und כבוד auch angedeutete kosmische Glanz Simons (cf. 43,1.9.11; 42,16.17; 43,11.12) wird noch zur Sprache kommen.

21. Cf. HAYWARD, *Temple* (n. 5), pp. 44-47; MACK, *Wisdom* (n. 2), pp. 167-171.

22. Innerhalb der drei Bezeugungen von תפארת in 31,10 (Ms[B]) begegnet sogar einmal die (göttliche) Zusage לתפארת אהיה לך, ebenso in einer Randlesart.

23. Daß mit dieser Herrlichkeit Adams, wie HAYWARD, *Dead Sea Scrolls* (n. 5), pp. 11-12 meint, bei Sirach bereits, wie kurz darauf im Jubiläenbuch 3,27, die priesterliche Kleidung Adams als erster Priester angedeutet sei, scheint nicht völlig auszuschließen. J.R. LEVISON, *Portraits of Adam in Early Judaism. From Sirach to 2 Baruch* (JSPS, 1), Sheffield, 1988, pp. 44-45 sieht allerdings in seiner Diskussion von Sir 49,16 kein Zeugnis einer speziellen Adamstradition: Adam werde, wenn auch hervorgehoben, in die Geschichte Israels eingeordnet.

3. Liturgie als Verwirklichung Israels

Das zwischen dem Hervorblicken vom Zelt, dem Hervortreten aus dem Haus des Vorhanges in 50,5[24] und dem Segen in 50,20f beschlossene liturgische Geschehen, das nach der Studie von Ó Fearghail dem Ritus des zweimaligen täglichen Ganzopfers nach Tamid VI,3-VII,3 am nächsten steht[25], reicht weit über die Vergegenwärtigung göttlicher Herrlichkeit in der Person Simons hinaus. Der Vollzug der in 45,6-22.23-25 grundgelegten Funktionen Aarons im Bild der Liturgie Simons ist zugleich höchste Verwirklichung Israels vor Gott. Dieser sich immer wieder ausweitende Horizont prägt nach der Schilderung Simons in 50,5-10 das Geschehen zwischen Hinaufsteigen (50,11c) und Herabsteigen (50,20a) vom Altar. Simon inmitten seiner Brüder und seines Volkes (50,1) bestimmt die Ordnung des Feueropfers: seine Brüder (12a), der Kranz seiner Söhne rings um ihn (12c), alle Söhne Aarons (13a), und in 13c die Gegenwart der ganzen Gemeinde Israels - כל קהל ישראל. Die Gegenwart ganz Israels wird besonders intensiv in Musik, Anbetung und Segen 50,16-21 erfahrbar: die Söhne Aarons, die Priester[26], blasen die Trompeten (V. 16); auch das Lied von 18a ist ihre Aufgabe; dazwischen steht als Reaktion des Volkes (כל בשר) Niederfallen und Anbeten vor dem Heiligen Israels (V. 17), in V. 19 wieder der Jubel des ganzen Volkes des Landes כל עם הארץ. 50,20 erhebt Simon seine Hände zum Segen על כל קהל ישראל (cf. 13c), über die ganze Gemeinde Israels, die nach V. 21 ein zweites Mal zur Anbetung niederfällt. Der Auftrag Gottes an Aaron, sein Volk in/mit seinem Namen zu segnen (45,15f),

---

24. Zelt und »Haus des Vorhanges« verstehe ich mit HAYWARD, *Temple* (n. 5), p. 50 und P.W. SKEHAN – A.A. DI LELLA, *The Wisdom of Ben Sira* (AB, 39), New York, 1987, pp. 551-552, vom Tempelgebäude.

25. Cf. n. 3 – Mit Ó FEARGHAIL auch SKEHAN – DI LELLA, *Wisdom* (n. 24), pp. 550-552 und HAYWARD, *Temple* (n. 5), pp. 50-61. – Nach CRENSHAW, *The Book of Sirach* (n. 8), p. 859 ist die Deutung des traditionell vom Yom Kippur verstandenen Ritus von Sir 50,5-21 allerdings offen. HAYWARD, *Dead Sea Scrolls* (n. 5), pp. 16-18 hält auch eine Beschreibung von Sukkot für denkbar (cf. Sir 50,10 – Neh 8,15; Sir 50,12 – Lev 23,40). – Die tatsächlich gegenüber dem Mischnatraktat Tamid bestehenden Differenzen, vor allem die Stellung des Segens am Abschluß in Sir 50,20 sowie das Fehlen des Rauchopfers, werden verschieden erklärt: mit Anlehnung an das Schema von 45,15 (SKEHAN – DI LELLA), mit Entwicklung seit der Zeit Sirachs oder auch damit, daß der Autor es mit der Beschreibung von Einzelheiten nicht so genau nahm: cf. M.Z. SEGAL, ספר בן סירא השלם, Jerusalem, 1958, pp. 346-347, in seinem Vergleich mit dem Gottesdienst Hiskijas von 2 Chron 29,20-30.

26. Gegenüber der Aufgabe der Leviten für Musik und Gesang des zweiten Tempels in den Chronikbüchern ist ihr Fehlen bzw. die Ersetzung durch die Söhne Aarons in 50,16 bemerkenswert: cf. zuletzt M. KLEER, »*Der liebliche Sänger der Psalmen Israels*«. *Untersuchungen zu David als Dichter und Beter der Psalmen* (BBB, 108), Bodenheim, 1996, p. 186 n. 3; cf. auch S.M. OLYAN, *Ben Sira's Relationship to the Priesthood*, in *HThR* 80 (1987) 261-286, bes. pp. 273-276, wonach bei Sirach sowohl die Leviten als auch die Zadokiden aufgrund seiner panaaronidischen Tendenz ignoriert würden.

kommt ausdrücklich zur Erfüllung. Wie schon in 45,25ef die Grundlegung des aaronidischen Priestertums, wird in 50,22 die Schilderung
der gefeierten Liturgie als Verwirklichung ganz Israels nun auch für die
angesprochenen Adressaten dieses Textes Aufruf zum Anschluß an dieses Israel, als Ziel der Lehre von K. 44–50[27]. Wie sehr der Gottesdienst
des Hohepriesters Israel vor Gott vergegenwärtigt, zeigt auch die Wurzel
זכר: die Trompeten der Aaronssöhne (V. 16) dienen dieser Erinnerung
Israels vor dem Höchsten wie bereits Num 10,9. Sir 50,9 dürfte im Bild
vom Weihrauch die Gedächtnisfunktion אזכרה des Speiseopfers (Lev
2,1-2; 6,8) andeuten. Bereits bei Aaron hat diese »Erinnerung« ihr Gewicht[28]. Das Gebet des Volkes vor dem Barmherzigen – רחום (19c) bestätigt diesen Horizont, der auch K. 17, vor allem K. 24 sowie in der
Bitte um das Erbarmen für Volk, Stadt und Heiligtum im Gebet 36,12f,
Gr 36,17f gegenwärtig ist. Die Bedeutung der ästhetischen Dimension
der Ordnungen des liturgischen Vollzuges (cf. 50,12b.14b.18b Ms^B.19d)
und der Ordnung Israels (Hohepriester – Söhne Aarons – Volk), für
Identität und Selbstbewußtsein Israels, dessen Herrlichkeit als Epiphanie
Gottes zu sehen (50,5-20) und auch zu hören ist (50,16.18.19), wäre
ebenfalls ausführlicher zu würdigen[29].

4. Kult im Horizont der Schöpfung

Wenn zum Unterschied von 50,13.20 (כל קהל ישראל) in 50,17 gesagt
ist, daß sich כל בשר, alles Fleisch, beeilt, niederzufallen zur Anbetung,
ist es kaum von der Hand zu weisen, daß die kultische Versammlung um
den Hohenpriester als Repräsentantin der Menschheit, ja vielleicht sogar
der Schöpfung, dargestellt wird. Damit ist ein weiterer Aspekt genannt,
der im Väterlob wie im Sirachbuch mehrfach anklingt und in K. 50
nochmals zur Sprache kommt: die universale, ja kosmische Bedeutung
von Kult und Weisheit.

50,17 erinnert an das Ziel des Noachbundes am Ende der Flut, daß
nicht mehr »alles Fleisch« vernichtet wird (Sir 44,18)[30]. Dieser Bund

27. Cf. MACK, Wisdom (n. 2), pp. 78.80-87: The Assembly as the Place of Praise. –
Auch wenn in einer Vorgeschichte des Textes die Söhne Aarons angesprochen gewesen
wären, im gegenwärtigen Text ist es das ganze Gottesvolk; cf. F. BÖHMISCH, Die Text-
formen des Sirachbuches und ihre Zielgruppen, in Protokolle zur Bibel 6 (1997) 87-122
(bes. pp. 96-98.108-110).
28. Cf. die Funktion der Erinnerung an Israel für Glöckchen und Granatäpfel am Or-
nat Aarons in 45,9c, sowie für die kostbaren Steine in 45,11c, ferner das Gedächtnisopfer
in 45,16.
29. N. 13 wurde bereits auf die Studie von WISCHMEYER, Kultur, pp. 261-265 hingewiesen, wo die Autorin die Formung einer sakralen Ästhetik durch Ben Sira hervorhebt,
wie sie im Aristeasbrief und bei Philo weitergeführt wurde.
30. Cf. KLEER, Sänger (n. 26), p. 189. – Vielleicht ist כל עם הארץ in 50,19 dem כל

klingt bereits in 50,7b erstmals an, wenn dort das Hervortreten Simons zur Liturgie mit dem Bogen verglichen wird, der in der Wolke als Zeichen des Bundes sichtbar wird (cf. Gen 9,13.14.16); d.h. in Simon wird das Zeichen der Zusage Gottes zur Bewahrung der Schöpfung und der Stabilisierung ihrer Ordnung sichtbar (cf. auch bereits den Preis des Bogens in 43,11). Neben der Verklammerung mit der Herrlichkeit Adams (49,16), der Menschheit, die der Hohepriester nach 50,1 repräsentiert, ist in diesem Kontext eine weitere Brücke zum Beginn des Väterlobes denkbar: der große Segen Simons in 50,20 ist nicht nur Erfüllung des Auftrages an Aaron zum Segen über das Volk (45,15), auch die Perspektive des Abrahamsegens für die Völker von 44,21 kann zum Ziel kommen[31]. Übrigens war auch Aaron erwählt מכל חי – aus allen Lebenden (45,16; cf. auch 45,1 von Mose, 49,16 von Adam). Schließlich gilt das Weiterwirken des gottesdienstlichen Lobes in 50,22 dem universalen Schöpferwirken des Gottes Israels auf Erden, jedem Menschen.

Der universale, kosmische Aspekt der hohepriesterlichen Liturgie Simons in K. 50 erfährt eine gewichtige Bestätigung durch eindeutige Bezüge des Textes zur großen Aretalogie der Weisheit Sir 24. Der Vergleich der Pracht der Erscheinung Simons in 50,6-12 mit Bäumen und Pflanzen aus ganz Israel sowie kultischen Ingredienzen entsprechen in vielen Details der Gestalt der von Gott ausgehenden universalen Weisheit, ihrer Gegenwart im Kult auf dem Zion und ihrem Wachsen und Blühen in Israel nach Sir 24,10-15[32].

So begegnen für Simon die Bilder von der »Blume von Rosen« (50,8a; cf. 24,14: Rosenpflanzung)[33], von den sprossenden Pflanzen bzw. sprossenden Zedern des Libanon (50,8c.12d; cf. 24,13a: Zeder des Libanon), vom grünenden Ölbaum (50,10a; cf. 24,14c), von einer Zypresse, erhöht in den Wolken (50,10b; cf. 24,13b: Zypresse auf dem Hermongebirge), vom Kreis von Stämmen von Palmen um ihn (50,12e; cf. 24,14a). Der Vergleich mit dem Feuer des Weihrauchs 50,9 verbindet mit explizit kultischen Bildern der Weisheit von K. 24: mit Galbanum,

---

בשר von K. 17 zwar nicht gleichzusetzen, wie KLEER meint, aber bewußt ambivalent, offen auf eine universale Gottesdienstgemeinde.

31. KLEER, *Sänger* (n. 26), pp. 184.188-189.

32. Cf. J. MARBÖCK, *Weisheit im Wandel. Untersuchungen zur Weisheitstheologie bei Ben Sira* (BZAW, 272), Berlin, ²1999, p. 74, sowie die Gegenüberstellung bei HAYWARD, *Sacrifice* (n. 5), p. 24 sowie HAYWARD, *Temple* (n. 5), pp. 52 u. 78.

33. Da für Sir 24 der griechische Text die älteste Version darstellt, verwende ich für den Vergleich auch für K. 50 Gr. Daß die griechische Fassung von Sir 50 stark von K. 24 geprägt wurde, geht aus den Differenzen von Ms^B z.B. in 50,8a.10b.12c deutlich hervor. – Beachtenswert ist auf jeden Fall, daß Zeder, Zypresse, Ölbaum, Palme, Libanon im griechischen Sirach nur in diesen beiden Perikopen begegnen. [Für eine Diskussion der Versionen sei auf die Kommentare verwiesen].

Onyx und Stakte als Bestandteilen des Weihrauchs 24,15cd (cf. Ex 30,34)[34].

Der zweimal genannte liturgische Dienst Simons (cf. λειτουργεῖν bzw. λειτουργία 50,14a.19d) entspricht dem Dienst (ἐλειτούργησα) der Weisheit im heiligen Zelt (24,10a). Das bedeutet, der Hohepriester vollzieht und entfaltet auch das Werk der Weisheit bzw. der Kult spiegelt die göttliche Ordnung des Kosmos. Übrigens hat, allerdings kaum irgendwo beachtet, bereits das Gedicht Sir 4,11-19 diese Beziehung zwischen Kult und Weisheit angedeutet: Die ihr dienen, dienen (משרתי λειτουργήσουσιν) dem Heiligen (dem Heiligtum? Ms[A] קדש) (4,14a). Zweimal führt im Sirachbuch die Bewegung von der universalen Gabe der Weisheit von der Schöpfung ausdrücklich zu Israel, in K. 17,1-17 und in K. 24. Das kultische Geschehen in K. 50,5-21 ist nochmals Verdichtung und Reflex von Israels Weisheit und Tora[35].

5. Sir 50 und die Wirklichkeit von »Bund«

Wohl nicht von ungefähr schließt der letzte Text des Väterlobes in Sir 50,24 mit einem Wort zum Thema Bund; damit steht der Begriff, der den ersten Teil 44,1-45,26 strukturiert[36], auch am Ende von Teil zwei, sodaß Hayward die Gestalt Simons als Hohepriester als »Focal Point of Covenants«[37] bezeichnen kann, in der die Fundamente der sieben Bundesschlüsse der Anfänge ihre höchste, bleibende Verwirklichung finden sollen. Die Bewegung hin zum Höhepunkt in 50,24 beginnt mit der schon erwähnten Erinnerung an die Fundamente der Bewahrung der kosmischen Ordnung im Noachbund (cf. 50,7b.17a)[38].

Der Schlußwunsch 50,24 Ms[B] lautet

יאמן עם שמעון חסדו
ויקם לו ברית פינחס
אשר לא יכרת לו ולזרעו
כימי שמים

und führt damit zurück zur Begründung des Priestertums in K. 45. »Wie die Tage des Himmels« V. 24c erinnert an bereits beim ewigen Bund

34. Sir 24,15ab bezieht in die Bilder für die Weisheit auch die Bestandteile des heiligen Salböls nach Ex 30,23 ein. – Zur Textdiskussion cf. HAYWARD, Sacrifice (n. 5), p. 33 n. 11.

35. HAYWARD, Sacrifice (n. 5), pp. 24-26, verweist von jüdischen Traditionen zu den Motiven von Weihrauch und Libanon auf weitere denkbare Beziehungen zwischen Kult, Weisheit und Tora auch für Sir 50.

36. Cf. MARBÖCK, Geschichte Israels (n. 9), pp. 103-123; zu Sir 50,24, cf. pp. 116-118.

37. HAYWARD, Dead Sea Scrolls (n. 5), p. 14.

38. HAYWARD verweist im n. 37 genannten Artikel auch auf die Bilder von Gestirnen, Mond und Sonne Sir 50,6-7 für Simon als Zeichen der Beständigkeit wie in Ps 148,3.

mit Aaron 45,15c durchscheinende, im Davidsbild 47,1-11 fehlende (!)
davidisch-königliche Züge (cf. Ps 89,30b, auch Sir 45,12 u. Ps 21,4)[39].
Die Wurzel אמן Sir 50,24a läßt auch die Natansverheißung anklingen (2
Sam 7,16; cf. Ps 89,29)[40]. Von höchstem Interesse und Gewicht ist die
Bindung Simons an den Pinhasbund, der bereits 45,24b als ברית שלום
für dessen Dienst im Heiligtum begegnet ist und als Steigerung des
Aaronsbundes sowie als Höhepunkt der Bundessetzungen bei Sirach
überhaupt zu sehen ist[41]. Sir 45,24d spricht ja gegenüber dem Friedens-
bund und dem Bund ewigen Priestertums für Pinhas von Num 25,12f
erweiternd von der ewigen Hohepriesterwürde - כהונה גדולה für Pinhas
und seine Nachkommenschaft. Der Wunsch nach Dauer dieses
Pinhasbundes für Simon ist Wunsch nach der vielleicht bereits gefährde-
ten bleibenden Verwirklichung der Fundamente Israels in Amt und
Funktion des Hohepriesters[42].
Mit der Bitte 50,24 mag auch eine Klammer zur Bezeichnung Simons
als גדול אחיו in 50,1a im Blick auf seine Stellung unter den Söhnen Aarons, seinen Brüdern (cf. auch 50,12a), geschlossen sein. Vor allem
aber: der Bestand des Pinhasbundes verbürgt und vergegenwärtigt die
Wirksamkeit aller vorausgehenden Bundesschlüsse bis zurück zu deren
Beginn mit Noach, d.h. für die Schöpfung.

4. DER GRIECHISCHE TEXT VON SIR 50,1-24 – REFLEX EINES WANDELS

Ein Blick auf einige Akzente der griechischen Übersetzung, die
Hayward sehr schön herausgestellt hat[43], zeigt Anliegen und Tendenzen
der Stunde des Enkels Ben Siras, wohl der Spätzeit der Regierung von
Johannes Hyrkan I (135-104 v. Chr.). Dies ist vorerst die in Gr angedeu-

39. MARBÖCK, *Geschichte Israels* (n. 9), pp. 113-114.
40. Die Zuordnung davidischer Prärogative und Verheißungen kommt noch deutlicher
in Sir 45,24-25 zum Ausdruck, wo der Bund mit David dem Bund mit Pinhas ein- bzw.
untergeordnet wird, wie der Text ohne Emendationen wohl zu verstehen ist: cf.
MARBÖCK, *Geschichte Israels* (n. 9), pp. 114-115. – Nach OLYAN, *Relationship* (n. 26),
pp. 270.276, versucht Ben Sira in 45,24f. im Interesse aller Aaroniden Exklusivansprüche
der Zadokiden abzuwehren, so auch B.G. WRIGHT, *»Fear the Lord and Honor the
Priest«. Ben Sira as Defender of the Jerusalem Priesthood*, in P. C. BEENTJES (ed.), *Book
of Ben Sira* (n. 6), pp. 189-222; bes. pp. 192-196. Mit dieser Position gegen den bisherigen Konsens der Sirachauslegung muß OLYAN allerdings gegen die Plausibilität der text-
geschichtlichen Entwicklung die griechische Version mit dem Fehlen von Simon und
Pinhasbund in 50,24 als ursprünglich und den hebräischen Text von Ms[B] als Erweiterung
betrachten.
41. J. MARBÖCK, *Geschichte Israels* (n. 9), pp. 116-118.
42. Cf. die Präzisierungen von KLEER, *Sänger* (n. 26), pp. 186-188.
43. HAYWARD, *Temple* (n. 5), bietet pp. 73-75 eine Übersetzung des griechischen Textes und anschließend pp. 75-84 eine Darstellung der darin erkennbaren Tendenzen; cf.
auch PETRAGLIO, *Libro* (n. 2), pp. 408-413.

tete neue Situation unter der politischen und religiösen Führung der Hasmonäer, angefangen vom Titel ἱερεὺς ὁ μέγας (50,1a).

Hatte der griechische Text bereits 45,24 bei Pinhas die Vorsteherrolle für das Heiligtum (bzw. die Heiligen) und sein Volk betont, wird, wie schon erwähnt, in 50,24 nach dem Ende der zadokidischen Linie der Hohepriester die Erinnerung von Ms^B an den Pinhasbund für Simon bzw. seine Nachkommen getilgt, als Dokumentation der Loyalität des Übersetzers gegenüber den Hasmonäern, die 1 Makk 2,23-26.54 in Pinhas ein Vorbild ihres Handelns sahen[44]; statt dessen erbittet 50,24 Gr allgemein Erbarmen und Befreiung für die Gegenwart, vielleicht eine Andeutung von Problemen unter Johannes Hyrkan[45]. Zu den spezifisch theologischen Akzenten der griechischen Fassung im hellenistischen Kontext gehören die Betonung der Universalität des Gottes Israels z.B. durch die Vermehrung des Gottestitels »Höchster« in 50,7(.15?).19.21 über den hebräischen Text hinaus, durch das Hapax παμβασιλεύς im Vers 15, der in Ms^B fehlt, die Ergänzung παντοκράτωρ in 50,14b.17d sowie θεὸς πάντων 50,22a, πάντῃ 22b (cf. Gott des Alls in Ms^B 36,1; 45,23). Die Bedeutung des kultischen Dienstes des Hohepriesters für die Welt wird damit unterstrichen; dies geschieht auch in der Verdeutlichung der Ordnung der Opfer (50,12.14.19) durch κόσμος/κοσμεῖν mit der vielschichtigen Bedeutung von κόσμος als Welt, Ordnung, Schmuck, Schönheit... Die hier angedeutete Beziehung der Ordnung (und Schönheit) des täglichen Kultes zur Ordnung und Vollendung der Welt (cf. LXX Gen 2,1)[46] ist Ansatz und Beispiel einer Theologie der Liturgie.

In eine ähnliche Richtung weisen auch die bereits genannten[47] Ausweitungen der Bilder der in Israel blühenden Weisheit aus Sir 24,13-15 für den Vergleich mit der Erscheinung Simons in 50,8-12 Gr gegenüber der hebräischen Fassung.

5. Sir 50 und die Dimensionen des Kultes im Sirachbuch

Gestalt und Liturgie Simons in K. 50 können als gewichtiger Endpunkt einer Bewegung betrachtet werden, die im Bogen 42,15 – K. 50

---

44. Neben SKEHAN – DI LELLA, Wisdom (n. 24), p. 554, HAYWARD, Temple (n. 5), pp. 81-82 sieht neuerdings auch CRENSHAW, The Book of Sirach (n. 8), p. 859 in 50,24 Gr den Reflex einer gewandelten religions-politischen Situation. Gerade die von HAYWARD überzeugend entfaltete Gesamtsicht von Gr 50,1-24 und 45,6-26 spricht m.E. stark gegen die von OLYAN (n. 26) vertretene Priorität der griechischen Version.

45. Cf. PETRAGLIO, Libro (n. 2), pp. 412-413. Nach HAYWARD, Temple (n. 5), p. 78, könnte auch die Ersetzung von Seir (Ms^B) durch Samaria in 50,25 Gr ein solcher Hinweis sein.

46. Cf. HAYWARD, Temple (n. 5), pp. 79-80.83.

47. Cf. n. 33.

vom Preis der Schöpfungswerke über die Gestalten und Setzungen der Geschichte in die Gegenwart reicht, ja als Ziel des mit K. 1 einsetzenden Wirkens der Weisheit im ganzen Buch.

Der Vielschichtigkeit des Buches entsprechender ist vielleicht die Sicht als ein Brennpunkt, in dem komplementär zum großen Text über die Weisheit in 24,1-29 der dort ebenfalls bedeutsame kultische Aspekt nun selbständig und groß entfaltet wird. Zu dieser für eine Weisheitsschrift unerwarteten Betonung und Hochschätzung von Priestertum und Kult im Sirachbuch, die einer umfassenden Studie wert wäre, sollen abschließend kursorisch noch die Texte aufgelistet werden, die zeigen, wie mit der Atmosphäre und dem Odor der Weisheit in Israel zugleich Atmosphäre und Odor des Kultes bei Sirach gegenwärtig sind[48].

Dies beginnt in K. 3 mit Aussagen über die kultische, sündentilgende Wirkung der Erfüllung des Elterngebots Sir 3,14f und der Wohltätigkeit in 3,30[49]. In den Weisheitsperikopen 4,11-19 und 6,18-37 begegnet der Dienst an der Weisheit als kultischer Dienst für den Heiligen (4,14a), das Mühen um Weisheit wird Mühen um Gott selber als Erfüllung des Hauptgebotes (6,26); Lohn und Gegenwart der Weisheit tragen priesterlichen Charakter (6,30b: Purpurbänder für den Brustschild der Priester; cf. auch 6,31b die Krone, 45,12 vom Diadem Aarons, sowie 50,12 Krone/Kranz der Söhne Aarons). Sir 7,29-31 wird die Sorge für die Priester und ihren Anteil durch die sprachliche Parallele zur Formulierung des Hauptgebotes (Gott fürchten/lieben) hervorgehoben[50]. In 23,9-11 warnt der Sirazide vor dem Mißbrauch des Namens des Heiligen. Kultische Ästhetik begegnet auch nach den Aussagen von K. 24,8-15 über Gegenwart und Dienst der Weisheit im Heiligtum und in Israel: die Lampe auf dem heiligen Leuchter (26,17) und goldene Säulen auf silberner Basis (26,18) geben der Schönheit der Ehefrau ihre Würde (cf. auch das kosmische Bild von der Sonne 26,16a und 50,7a vom Hohepriester). Sir 33 (Gr 36),8-9 sprechen von einer weisheitlich-kultischen Ordnung der Schöpfung bzw. der Zeit durch Festtage, die gesegnet und geheiligt sind (cf. auch Gr II 18,3bc die Trennung des Heiligen vom Profanen). Die schon in 3,14f.30 angeklungene Thematik der kultischen Bedeutung und Wirksamkeit des Ethos wird 34 (Gr 31),21-35 ausführlich und leiden-

---

48. Cf. neben den bereits mehrfach genannten Beiträgen von HAYWARD, MACK, OLYAN vor allem H. STADELMANN, *Ben Sira als Schriftgelehrter. Eine Untersuchung zum Berufsbild des vor-makkabäischen Sofer unter Berücksichtigung seines Verhältnisses zu Priester-, Propheten- und Weisheitslehrertum* (WUNT, 6), Tübingen, 1980.

49. Cf. J. MARBÖCK, *Sündenvergebung bei Jesus Sirach*, in J. MARBÖCK, *Weisheit* (n. 9), pp. 176-184, bes. pp. 178-179.

50. Cf. STADELMANN, *Schriftgelehrter* (n. 48), pp. 55-68.

schaftlich in einer Auseinandersetzung um den rechten, Gott wohlgefälligen Opfergottesdienst entfaltet[51]. So gehört auch in der Arztperikope 38,1-15 im Krankheitsfall beides zur Erfüllung der Ordnung Gottes: das Beiziehen des Arztes (38,1-7.12-13), aber genauso Gebet, Reinigung des Herzens, Gedächtnisopfer und Gaben (38,9-11). Im Väterlob ist neben Aaron, Pinhas und Simon vor allem die Gestalt Davids mit seiner Sorge für den Kult durch Musik, Gesang und Festfeier (47,8-10) auch umfangmäßig (47,1-11) hervorgehoben[52]. Samuel begegnet 47,13cd (Ms[B]) auch in priesterlicher Funktion und bringt Opfer dar (47,16c). Joschija, der die Götzengreuel beseitigt hat (49,2), wird durch die Aura des Weihrauchs charakterisiert (49,1). So beschließen nicht zufällig Serubbabel und Joschua als Wiedererbauer des Tempels in 49,11-12 die nachexilische Geschichte vor Simon.

Die Vergegenwärtigung der Liturgie Simons für die Adressaten des Sirachbuches enthält bedenkenswerte Ansätze für eine Theologie des Gottesdienstes. Dazu gehört die Dimension des Ästhetischen, etwas vom Glanz (תפארת) des Göttlichen; Kult ist ja Gottesdienst der Weisheit, ein Stück Offenbarung kosmischer Ordnung in Israel, die untrennbar ist von der Ordnung des Ethos. Im Kult verwirklicht sich ganz Israel als Repräsentant der Menschheit und erfährt feiernd die Beständigkeit der Huld Gottes durch die Vergegenwärtigung der von Gott geschenkten Fundamente. Auch über das Scheitern der Erwartungen Sirachs durch das Ende der Oniaden hinaus hat das Bild der Tempelliturgie von Sir 50 noch an die zweihundert Jahre das Leben Israels geprägt. Es dürfte schließlich nicht zuletzt auch Reflexionen des Siraziden zu verdanken sein, daß selbst nach dem Ende von Priestertum und Opferkult mit der Zerstörung des zweiten Tempels eine wesentliche Dimension des Fundamentes der עבודה, des Gottesdienstes[53], lebendig geblieben bzw. zentral geworden ist, das Gebet als Bitte vor

---

51. HAYWARD, *Sacrifice* (n. 5), pp. 30-31, betont zu Recht, daß für Sirach sowohl die kultisch-liturgischen Gebote (Opfer) als auch die ethischen Vorschriften von der einen Tora kommen. Der gottesfürchtige Weise erfüllt in Übereinstimmung mit der göttlichen Weltordnung beide. – Cf. auch STADELMANN, *Schriftgelehrter* (n. 48), pp. 68-138.

52. J. MARBÖCK, *Davids Erbe in gewandelter Zeit (Sir 47,1-11)*, in MARBÖCK, *Weisheit* (n. 9), pp. 124-132. Cf. auch KLEER, *Sänger* (n. 26), pp. 129-202. – Eine Gesamtdarstellung zum Gebet im Sirachbuch wäre wünschenswert: cf. die kurze Zusammenfassung J.L. CRENSHAW, *The Restraints of Reason, the Humility of Prayer*, in J.L. CRENSHAW, *Urgent Advice and Probing Questions. Collected Writings on Old Testament Wisdom*, Macon, GA, 1995, pp. 206-221.

53. Cf. Mischna, Abot I, 2: »Auf drei Dingen steht die Welt: auf der Tora, auf dem Kultus und auf der Liebestätigkeit.« Text nach: Die Mischna IV.9: Abot (Väter), Gießen, 1927, pp. 7-8; die Herausgeber des Traktates K. MARTI und G. BEER verweisen dort auch auf die nach der Zerstörung des Tempels in den Pirqe de-Rabbi Eliezer K. 16 begegnende Bezeichnung des Gebetes als עבודה.

dem Barmherzigen (50,19b) und als Lobpreis des Schöpfers (50,22). Lobpreis ist vor allem bei Sirach die Lehre des Weisen, des Schriftgelehrten geworden[54].

Karl-Franzens-Universität Graz   J. MARBÖCK
Institut für atl. Bibelwissenschaft
A-8010 Graz

---

54. J. MARBÖCK, *Sir 15,9f – Ansätze zu einer Theologie des Gotteslobes bei Jesus Sirach,* in MARBÖCK, *Weisheit* (n. 9), pp. 167-175. An Texten wäre vor allem auf Sir 15,9f; 39,12-15.32-35 und 42,15; 43,30 zu verweisen.

UN CHIARIMENTO DI STORIA LINGUISTICA
A SIR 50,26

L'attuale emergere della cultura dei Filistei[1] richiede qualche osservazione di commento a Siracide 50,26 perchè in tale versetto degli scritti biblici ebraici i Filistei sono menzionati per l'ultima volta[2].

Partendo dal testo[3], si può fare una prima osservazione circa la denominazione attribuita a questa popolazione palestinese. Comparando testo greco[4] ed ebraico[5], emerge in quest'ultimo la denominazione *yšby plšt*, tradotta in greco con φυλιστιιμ e non con quello abituale nella LXX di ἀλλόφυλοι[6]. Tale denominazione è presente nella Bibbia ebraica solo in Es 15,14. Il termine *plšt*, poi appare isolato in Is 14,29,31 e Ps 60,10; 83,8; 87,4 e 108,10 indicando una regione geografica e non una popolazione. Il medesimo termine φυλιστιιμ apparirà poco dopo la morte di Ben Sira[7] in 1 Macc 3,24. Circa due secoli dopo Flavio Giuseppe[8] farà uso corrente della denominazione Παλαιστινοι analogamente a quanto si riscontra presso degli storici quali Erodoto, Polibio, Plinio e Plutarco nel definire la costa meridionale del paese di Canaan[9].

1. Cf. dopo la classica sintesi archeologica di T. DOTHAN, *The Philistines and Their Material Culture*, Jerusalem, 1982. Cf. le seguenti opere che tengono conto delle recenti aquisizioni: T. and M. DOTHAN, *People of the Sea. The Search of the Philistines*, New York, 1992; C.S. EHRLICH, *The Philistines in Transition. A History from ca. 1000-730 B.C.E.* (Studies in the History and Culture of the Ancient Near East, 10), Leiden, 1996; G. GARBINI, *I Filistei. Gli antagonisti di Israele*, Milano, 1997.

2. Altre menzioni dei Filistei in Sir 46,18 e 47,7. Il testo ebraico impiega ovunque il termine *plštym*.

3. Per il testo, cf. la pratica edizione di F. VATTIONI, *Ecclesiastico. Testo ebraico con apparato critico e versioni greca, latina e siriaca*, Napoli, 1968, nonchè quella sinottica dei testi ebraici di P.C. BEENTJES, *The Book of Ben Sira in Hebrew. A Text Edition of All Extant Hebrew Manuscripts and a Synopsis of All Parallel Hebrew Ben Sira Texts* (SVT, 68), Leiden, 1997.

4. Ἐν δυσὶν ἔθνεσιν προσώχθισεν ἡ ψυχή μου, καὶ τὸ τρίτον οὐκ ἔστιν ἔθνος· οἱ καθήμενοι ἐν ὄρει Σαμαρείας καὶ Φυλιστιιμ καὶ ὁ λαὸς ὁ μωρὸς ὁ κατοικῶν ἐν Σικιμοις.

5. *bšny gwym qṣh npšy wh lyšyt 'ynnw 'm ywšby š'yr wplšt wgwy nbl hdr bškm.*

6. Su tale denominazione cf. l'analisi di R. DE VAUX, *Les Philistins dans la Septante*, in J. SCHREINER (ed.), *Wort, Lied und Gottesspruch. Beiträge zur Septuaginta*. FS J. Ziegler (FzB, 1), Würzburg, 1972, pp. 185-194.

7. Ci siamo serviti della magistrale sintesi di M. GILBERT, art. *Siracide*, in *DBS*, t. XII, Paris, 1996, col. 1398-1438; cf. in particolare sulla figura dell'A. col. 1402-1407 ed in particolare col. 1402-1403.

8. Per Flavio Giuseppe e le sue fonti, cf. Z. SAFRAI, *The Description of the Land of Israel in Josephus' Works*, in L.H. FELDMAN – G. HETA (eds.), *Josephus and the Bible and History*, Detroit, 1989, pp. 295-324 (p. 299).

9. H.G. FELDMAN, *Some Observation on the Name of Palestine*, in *HUCA* 61 (1990)

Il nostro versetto si riferisce ai consueti nemici dei Giudei associando tra di loro Samaritani e Filistei e soltanto nel testo ebraico gli Edomiti che vengono chiamati con il nome più antico di Seir[10]. Per quanto concerne i Samaritani J. D. Purvis[11] ha sottolineato come il versetto sia la prima fonte d'epoca preromana che testimoni relazioni tese di questo gruppo con i Giudei ma non è il caso di soffermarsi su questa questione in questa sede. Per quanto concerne l'associazione di Filistei ed Edomiti è noto come già in epoca preesilica sia Edomiti sia Filistei erano concomitatamente entrati in contrasto con il regno di Giuda[12] e quindi questa menzione alla luce della rivisitazione della storia ebraica di Ben Sira – cf. Sir 44,1–49,13 – è ben comprensibile. Inoltre non si può dimenticare che questa associazione dei nemici di Israele è gia comparsa in Es 15,14-15 e Ps 60,8,11 (// Ps 108,8-11) e che apparirà anche in testi posteriori come è il caso di Giubilei 24,29[13] e 37,5-10 e Henoch 89,10-16[14], 89,42,47 e 90 nonchè 1QH 1,2 dove appare il termine *plšt* come sostantivo retto di un reggente purtroppo quest'ultimo assente per lacuna del testo. All'epoca della composizione del Siracide sappiamo che le città della pianura costiera erano già ellenizzate[15] ma tuttavia persisteva ancora la memoria dell'antica presenza filistea come risulta da 1 Macc 3,24 dove si viene menzionato il paese dei Filistei γῆ φυλιστιιμ.

1-23, ripreso in H.G. FELDMAN, *Studies in Hellenistic Judaism*, Leiden, 1996, pp. 553-576; cf. in particolare p. 3 per Erodoto, pp. 6-7 per Polibio, pp. 8-9 per Plinio, p. 9 per Plutarco.

10. Per il valore storico-geografico del termine, cf. Diana V. EDELMAN, *Edom: A Historical Geography*, in D.V. EDELMAN, *You Shall not Abhor an Edomite for He Is Your Brother. Edom and Seir in History and Tradition* (Archaeology and Biblical Studies, 3), Atlanta, GA, 1995, pp. 1-11 (pp. 7-10).

11. J.D. PURVIS, *Ben Sira and the Foolish People of Shechem*, in *JNES* 24 (1965) 89-94, p. 89; sul passo, cf. sempre GILBERT, art. *Siracide* (n. 7), col. 1403-1404, nonchè M. HENGEL, *Judaism and Hellenism. Studies in Their Encounter in Palestine during the Early Hellenistic Period*, t. I-II, London, 1974 (t. I, p. 153).

12. Per una storia degli Edomiti, cf. J.R. BARTLETT, *Edom and the Edomites* (JSOTSS, 77), Sheffield, 1989. Per delle relazioni contemporaneamente ostili tra Giuda, Filistei e Edomiti, cf. 2 Cron 28,16-21 et Ez 25, per gli oracoli contro Ammon, Moab, Edom e i Filistei.

13. Per un'analisi storica del passo, cf. D. MENDELS, *The Land of Israel as a Political Concept in Hasmonean Literature. Recourse to History in Second Century B.C. Claims to the Holy Land* (Texte und Studien zum Antiken Judentum, 157), Tübingen, 1987, pp. 68-69.

14. Risulta utile per esplicitare la presenza dei Filistei la versione amarica segnalata da L. FUSELLA in P. SACCHI, *Apocrifi dell'Antico Testamento*, Torino, 1981, pp. 611 e 625.

15. Cf. ad esempio A. KASHER, *Jews and Hellenistic Cities during the Second Temple Period (332-70 CE)* (Texte und Studien zum Antiken Judentum, 21), Tübingen, 1990, p. 51. Per la storia delle singole città ce si è fondati su E. SCHÜRER, *Storia del popolo giudaico al tempo di Gesù Cristo (175 a.C. – 135 d.C.)*, ed. italiana a cura di B. CHIESA, t. II (Paideia Collezione di Storia e Storiografia dei Tempi Biblici, 6), Brescia, 1987, pp. 119-233 §23.

In questa sede lo scrivente desidera soffermarsi su uno di quegli elementi che più concorrono a definire l'identità di un gruppo sociale: la lingua che assieme ai costumi ed alla religione costituisce gli elementi costitutivi dell'etnicità. Se per questi ultimi due elementi si era relativamente informati essendo ben noto che i Filistei avevano fama di essere incirconcisi[16] e di venerare delle proprie divinità locali[17], sulla loro a lingua fino al verificarsi di importanti scoperte epigrafiche ci si trovava in una situazione di indeterminatezza lamentata non solo all'inizio del secolo R. A. Macalister[18] ma anche più recentemente da J. F. Brug[19] e dai coniugi T. e M. Dothan[20]. Va ricordato che basandosi sulla menzione nella Bibbia ebraica in Neemia 13,24 del dialetto ashdodita 'ašdôdît, contrapposto all'ebraico di Giuda denominato nello stesso versetto yᵉhûdît[21], era legittimo aspettarsi di ritrovare una qualche peculiarità linguisticamente distintiva nell'area. Le testimonianze epigrafiche ed onomastiche della regione da noi precedentemente raccolte[22] lasciavano intuire un processo di acculturazione dei Filistei alla cultura cananea in quanto il dato onomastico lasciava supporre che nella regione si parlasse un dialetto cananeo, ma nel suo insieme il dato epigrafico era privo di tratti morfologici o lessicali specifici fatta eccezione per un grafito di Ashdod[23] che attestava il termine aramaico

16. Cf. in merito P. ARATA MANTOVANI, *Circoncisi ed incirconcisi*, in *Henoch* 10 (1988) 51-68, in particolare p. 67.

17. Per la religione dei Filistei, cf. da ultimo G. GARBINI, *I Filistei* (n. 1), pp. 165-203. Per le singole divinita, cf. ad esempio J.F. HEALEY, art. *Dagon*, in *DDD*, pp. 407-413, e W. HERRMANN, art. *Baal Zebub*, in *DDD*, pp. 293-295.

18. Analisi della documentazione indiretta allora disponibile in R.A.S. MACALISTER, *The Philistines. Their History and Civilisation* (The Schweich Lectures 1911), London, 1913, pp. 78-87, cf. in particolare p. 78.

19. J. F. BRUG, *A Literary and Archaeological Study of the Philistines* (BAR International Series, 265), Oxford, 1985: analisi della documentazione disponibile, pp. 193-200, nonchè cf. pp. 193, 196 e 200 in particolare.

20. T. and M. DOTHAN, *People of the Sea* (n. 1), pp. 258-259.

21. Per le diverse interpretazioni del passo, cf. A. LEMAIRE, *Ashdodien et Judéen à l'époque perse: Ne 13,24*, in K. VAN LERBERGHE – A. SCHOORS (eds.), *Immigration and Emigration within the Ancient Near East*. FS E. Lipinski, Leuven, 1995, pp. 153-163 (pp. 158-161). Segnaliamo che quella di J. BLENKINSOPP discussa da LEMAIRE (pp. 160-161) di fatto viene a coincidere con la nostra.

22. F. ISRAEL, *Note di onomastica semitica 7/1. Rassegna critico bibliografica et epigrafica su alcune onomastiche palestinesi: Israele e Giuda, la regione filistea*, in *Studi Epigrafici e Linguistici* 8 (1991) 119-140 (pp. 134-140), e F. ISRAEL, *Note di onomastica semitica 8. L'onomastica della regione filistea et alcune sue possibili sopravvivenza nell'onomastica fenicio-punica*, in M. PITTAU – M. NEGRI – F. ASPESI – P. FILIGHEDDU, *Circolazioni culturali nel Mediterraneo antico. Atti del I Convegno Internazionale di Linguistica dell'area mediterranea*, Sassari 24-27 aprile 1991, Cagliari, 1994, pp. 127-188.

23. Editio princeps: M. DOTHAN – D.N. FREEDMAN, *Ashdod I, The First Season of Excavations 1962*, Jerusalem, 1967, pp. 84-85; fotografia '*Atiqot* VII, 1967, tav. XV, fig. 8. Sull'iscrizione, cf. F. ISRAEL, *Note di onomastica semitica 8* (n. 22), p. 151.

pḥr «vasaio»[24] al posto del termine canaico *yoṣer* documentato in ugaritico[25], in fenicio[26] ed in ebraico[27].

L'attuale progresso degli scavi archeologici ha permesso di accrescere l'inventario[28] delle iscrizioni della regione filistea soprattutto grazie alla pubblicazione di un ostracon da Ashkelon[29] e delle iscrizioni di Ekron: queste comprendono nel loro insieme sia delle iscrizioni di natura amministrativa e sacra[30] che un'iscrizione di natura storica[31] parzialmente conservata come è abituale nel contesto palestinese[32]. Questi nuovi testi rivelano putroppo pochi dati utilizzabili a fini linguistici ma essi, una volta sottoposti ad analisi, consentono di percepire l'identità linguistica della regione filistea differenziandola da quella geograficamente contigua della Giudea. I tratti fonetici e morfologici distintivi che emergono concernono la contrazione dei dittonghi *'ay bt*[33] «tempio» e

24. Cf. per esempio C. BROCKELMANN, *Lexicon Syriacum*, Halle, 1928[2], p. 563.

25. C.H. GORDON, *Ugaritic Textbook* (AnOr, 38), Roma, 1961, p. 414, n° 1142.

26. J. HOFTIJZER – K. JONGELING, *Dictionary of the Northwest Semitic Inscriptions* (Handbuch der Orientalistik, 21/1-2), Leiden, 1995, p. 466, s.v. *y ṣ r*.

27. HAL, p. 410.

28. Precedentemente F. ISRAEL, *Note di onomastica semitica 8* (n. 22), completato con la nuova documentazione ed inclusione di materiali da noi omessi da G. GARBINI, *I Filistei* (n. 1), pp. 245-268.

29. Editio princeps: F. M. CROSS, *A Philistine Ostracon from Ashkelon*, in *BAR* 22/1 (1996) 64-65; fotografia ibid., p. 64.

30. Edizione provvisoria per le iscrizioni n° 1-5: cf. S. GITIN, *Seventh Century B.C.E. Cultic Elements at Ekron*, in *Biblical Archaeology Today. Proceedings of the Second International Congress on Biblical Archaeology, Jerusalem June-July 1990*, Jerusalem, 1993, pp. 243-258; fotografie: *ibid.*, p. 251, fig. 2a, 2b, 3, 3a. Per l'iscrizione n° 6, cf. S. GITIN, *Tel Miqne-Eqron in the 7th Century B.C.E. The Impact of Economic Innovation and Foreign Cultural Influences on a Neo-Assyrian Vassal City-State*, in S. GITIN (ed.), *Recent Excavations in Israel. A View to the West. Reports on Kabri, Nami, Miqne-Ekron, Dor and Ashkelon* (Archaeological Institute of America, Colloquia and Conference Papers, 1), Dubuque Iowa, 1995, pp. 61-79; fotografia *ibid.*, p. 74, fig. 4.19; cf. G. GARBINI, *I Filistei* (n. 1), pp. 259-260, n° 31-37.

31. Editio princeps: S. GITIN – T. DOTHAN – J. NAVEH, *A Royal Dedicatory Inscription from Ekron*, in *IEJ* 47 (1997) 1-16; fotografia: *ibid.*, p. 10, fig. 5; facsimile: *ibid.*, p. 10, fig. 6. Sull'iscrizione, cf. D. BETZ – B. EGO – J. KAMLAH – A. LANGE – D. RÖMHELD, *Dokumentation neuer Texte*, in *ZAH* 11 (1998) 109-124 (pp. 110-111); Ch. SCHÄFER-LICHTENBERGER, *PTGJH – Göttin und Herrin von Ekron*, in *BN* 91 (1998) 64-76; M. GÖRG, *Die Göttin der Ekron-Inschrift*, in *BN* 93 (1998) 9-10; A. DEMSKY, *The Name of the Godess of Ekron. A New Reading*, in *JANES* 95 (1998) 1-5; J. NAVEH, *Achish-Ikausu in the Light of the Ekron Dedication*, in *BASOR* 310 (1998) 35-37.

32. Si rimanda ai seguenti esempi di iscrizioni storiche frammentariamente conservate: nell'epigrafia ebraica, cf. a) frammento di Samaria, cf. da ultimo J. RENZ – W. RÖLLIG, *Handbuch der althebräischen Epigraphik*, t. III, *Texte und Tafeln*, Darmstadt, 1995, p. 135 (facsimile: *ibid.*, tav. XII,4); b) frammento dell'Ophel, cf. *ibid.*, pp. 266-267 (facsimile: *ibid.*, tav. XXXI,3); c) citta di Davide, cf. *ibid.*, pp. 190-191 (fotografia mai publicata). Nell'epigrafia moabita, cf. l'iscrizione di Kerak, per cui cf. S. TIMM, *Moab zwischen den Mächten. Studien zur historischen Denkmälern und Texten* (ÄAT, 17), Wiesbaden, 1989, pp. 269-277.

33. Iscrizione storica di Ekron, linea 1, cf. sopra n. 31.

'*aw ymh*[34] «i suoi giorni», il femminile singolare -*at*[35], -'*šrt*, il pronome relativo *š*[36], il pronome suffisso 3ᵃ p.s. m. -*h*, nonchè una forma verbale alla 3ᵃ p.s. m del pf. di verbo *tertiae jod*, *bn*[37].

Questi tratti fonetici e morfologici, seppure minimi, sono rilevanti per definire il dialetto adoperato nella regione filistea. Nella fonetica esso si allineava nella'evoluzione dei dittonghi con l'ortografia fenicia[38] e israelitica ma non con quella giudea[39]. Nella morfologia esso si differenziava dall'ebraico epigrafico[40] di Samaria e di Giuda – unitario rispetto alla variegata presenza di dialetti nella Bibbia ebraica[41] – proprio nelle forme del femminile singolare e nell'ortografia della 3ᵃ p.s. del perfetto nei verbi *tertiae jod*[42]. Esso divergeva dal fenicio standard[43] nei settori

34. Iscrizione storica di Ekron, linea 4, cf. sopra n. 31.
35. Iscrizioni di Ekron n° 1, n° 2 = G. GARBINI, *I Filistei* (n. 1), p. 259, n° 31; cf. sopra n. 30.
36. Ostracon di Ashkelon, linea 1, cf. sopra n. 29.
37. Iscrizione storica di Ekron, linea 1, cf. sopra n. 31.
38. Sugli esiti dei dittonghi nel semitico siro-palestinese, cf. R.W. GARR, *Dialect Geography of Syria Palestina 1000-586 BCE*, Philadelphia, 1985, pp. 35-40, §8 (in particolare pp. 35-36 per il fenicio).
39. F. ISRAEL, *Studi di lessico ebraico epigrafico I: I materiali del Nord*, in *Langues Orientales Anciennes, Philologie et Linguistique* 2 (1989) 36-67, pp. 47-48.
40. Per il femminile singolare, cf. F. ISRAEL, *Studi di lessico ebraico epigrafico I* (n. 39), pp. 49-50. Per il pronome relativo '*šr*, cf. *ibid.*, p. 51. Per il pron. Suffisso, cf. *ibid.*, pp. 50-51 et p. 51, n. 102. Per le sue attestazioni nel sud, per i verbi *tertiae yod* le uniche forme che qui ci concernono direttamente sono *hṭh* (cf. J. RENZ – W. RÖLLIG, *Handbuch der althebräischen Epigraphik*, t. II/1, *Zusammenfassenden Erörterungen Paläographie und Glossar*, Darmstadt, 1995, p. 227, s.v. *nṭh*), *nsh* (cf. *ibid.*, p. 227, s.v. *nsh*), '*šh* (cf. *ibid.*, p. 229, s.v. '*šh*), *rṣh* (cf. *ibid.*, p. 232, s.v. *rṣh*).
41. Per un'analisi dei vari dialetti fondamentale I. YOUNG, *Diversity in Pre-Exilic Hebrew* (FAT, 5), Tübingen, 1993. Cf. *ibid.* p. 168, per l'unitarietà dell'ebraico epigrafico sorta in epoca della monarchia unita. Questa unitarietà era stata da noi segnalata in ISRAEL, *Studi di lessico ebraico epigrafico I* (n. 39), p. 33, n. 5, a proposito della notazione simbolica delle cifre e sullo stesso problema indipendentemente da noi anche per le unità ponderali e per i termini relativi alla scrittura dobbiamo rimandare a F. ISRAEL, *Studi fenici 3: Parole di origine fenicia o costiera nel lessico di Canaan?*, in E. ACQUARO (ed.), *Alle soglie della Classicità. Il Mediterraneo tra tradizione e innovazione*. FS S. Moscati, Pisa, 1996, pp. 1161-1177 (p. 1177), e C.H.J. DE GEUS, *Reflections on the Continuity of Egyptian Influence on the Administration and the Material Culture of Pre-Exilic Israel*, in M. WEIPPERT – S. TIMM (eds.), *Meilenstein. FS Herbert Donner* (ÄAT, 30), Wiesbaden, 1995, pp. 44-51 (pp. 46-47).
42. Per la grafia dei verbi *tertiae yod* a Biblos, cf. M.G. AMADASI GUZZO, *Lingua e scittura a Biblo*, in COLL., *Biblo. Una città e la sua cultura. Atti del Colloquio Internazionale (Roma, 5-7 dicembre 1990)*, Roma, 1994, pp. 179-194 (p. 182). Per questo dato morfologico nell'iscrizione di Kilamuwa (KAI 24) che cronologicamente rappresenta la data di stabilizzazione grafica dell'evoluzione fonetica in questione, cf. J. TROPPER, *Die Inschriften von Zincirli. Neue Edition und vergleichende Grammatik der phönizischen sam'alischen und aramäischen Textkorpus* (Abhandlungen zur Literatur Alt-Syrien-Palästinas, 6), Münster i.W., 1993, p. 224.
43. Per il pronome relativo nei dialetti fenici, cf. dapprima G. GARBINI, *I dialetti del fenicio*, in *AION* 47b (1977) 283-294 (p. 286). Per il dialetto giblita sul quale cf. la

del pronome relativo e del pronome suffisso. In questi due settori la comparazione proposta dagli editori[44] dell'iscrizione storica di Ekron con il dialetto giblita, magistralmente studiato da M. G. Amadasi Guzzo[45], non è proponibile. Dobbiamo ricordare che le grafie del pronome suffisso restano uno dei punti più controversi quanto a interpretazione della morfologia fenicio-punica[46] e che le diverse grafie presenti nel dialetto giblita non si prestano ad una comparazione diretta con l'iscrizione di Ekron perchè esse corrispondono a due fasi di attestazione non coeve alla nostra iscrizione. In queste due fasi di attestazione le differenze sono il prodotto di uno sviluppo fonetico verificatosi per elisione di *h* intervocalica come provano gli esempi presi dall'iscrizione di Ahirom (= KAI 1) e di Yehimilk (= KAI 4), Elibaal (= KAI 6), Sphitbaal (= KAI 7) In Ahirom si veda annesso al caso indiretto *'bh* (l. 1), *mlkh* (l. 2), *mšpṭh* (l. 2) come oggetto ad una forma verbale *šth* (l. 1) mentre in epoca posteriore si ritrovano ad esempio i termini *'dtw* (Elibaal l. 2, Shipitbaal 4) al singolare sempre annesso al caso indiretto e *šntw* annesso al caso diretto ma plurale in Yehimilk l. 5, Elibaal l. 3 e Shipitbaal l. 5. Restano significative poi le attestazioni del pronome femminile *mspnth* (Yahwmilk [= KAI 10] l. 6) e *'mdh* (Yahwmilk l. 14) che provano essere stata conservata in Byblos la forma semitica nordoccidentale comune. Nell'iscrizione di Ekron il pronome suffisso *-h* appare annesso al caso indiretto -*'dth*[47], oppure al caso diretto *ymh*[48], *'rsh*[49] oppure ad un verbo *tbrkh*[50], *tšmrh*[51]. Ci si deve pertanto limitare a rilevare la diversa ortografia[52] sia dal dialetto giblita che dal fenicio standard[53]. Le forme del fenicio standard debbono essere interpretate come il

---

successiva sintesi di AMADASI GUZZO, *Lingua e scittura a Biblo* (n. 42), pp. 182,186. Per il dialetto di Tiro, cf. *ibid.*, pp. 287-288, et di Sidone, p. 288. Per il punico, cf. *ibid.*, p. 291.

44. S. GITIN – T. DOTHAN – J. NAVEH, *A Royal Dedicatory Inscription from Ekron* (n. 31), in particolare p. 12.

45. AMADASI GUZZO, *Lingua e scittura a Biblo* (n. 42): p. 182 per Ahirom; pp. 182-183 per il periodo successivo; p. 184 per l'epoca persiana ed ellenistica.

46. Per una storia degli studi, cf. parzialmente F. ISRAEL, *Rassegna critica sugli studi di lingua fenicia*, in V. BRUGNATELLI, *Sem, Cain, Iafet. Atti della 7a Giornata di Studi Camito-Semitici en Indeuropei*, Milano 13 giugno 1993 (Studi Camito-Semitici, 1), Milano, 1994, pp. 95-97.

47. Iscrizione storica di Ekron, linea 3, cf. sopra n. 31.

48. *Ibidem*, linea 4.

49. *Ibidem*, linea 5.

50. *Ibidem*, linea 3.

51. *Ibidem*, linea 3-4.

52. Per una spiegazione che tenga conto della comparazione semitica, cf. J. HUEH-NERGARD, *The Development of the Third Person Suffixes on Phoenician*, in *Maarav* 7 (1991) 183-194.

53. Si usa questa difinizione seguendo R.W. GARR, *Dialect Geography of Syria Palestina 1000-586 BCE* (n. 38), p. 13.

prodotto dell'elisione di -*h* intervocalica che in caso di annessione al caso indiretto produceva la grafia -*y* | *yu* | < maschile **iyu* < **ihu* oppure | *ya* | < femminile **iya* < **iha* mentre in caso di annessione al caso diretto si produceva la grafia Ø.

Per quanto concerne poi il pronome relativo la forma attestata nell'ostracon di Ashkelon[54] essa differisce dalla forma *'š* attestata nei tre dialetti fenici della madrepatria[55] – giblita, tirio e sidonio – ma si accosta al punico che accanto alla forma *'š* attesta anche la forma *š*. Questo accostamento resta storicamente rilevante per due motivi: in primo luogo conferma l'origine levantina della forma peraltro ipotizzabile per la norma dell'area coloniale della geografia linguistica di M. Bartoli. In secondo luogo mostra il legame del dialetto di Ashkelon con una forma pronominale ben nota sia nell'ebraico biblico settentrionale[56] che in quello tardivo come è il caso dell'ebraico mishnaico[57] e qumranico[58]. Per quanto poi concerne quest'ultima varietà di ebraico le forme attestate in 4QMMT rivelano un'evoluzione parallela al punico[59].

Il confronto fin qui condotto tra il dialetto cananeo impiegato nella regione filistea con il fenicio e l'ebraico ci obbliga in conclusione a definirne la posizione rispetto ai due termini di comparazione. Nel nostro procedere non è possibile attenersi aile coordinate storico-politiche[60] come precedentemente abbiamo fatto per gli altri dialetti del paese di Canaan e della Transgiordania, perchè la regione filistea è rimasta continuatrice del sistema delle città stato del secondo millennio e non innovatrice essendovi assenti gli stati etnici o nazionali[61]. La

54. Cf. sopra, n. 29 e 36.

55. Cf. sopra, n. 43.

56. Cf. Giud 5,7 e 2 Re 6,11.

57. M.H. SEGAL, *A Grammar of Mishnaic Hebrew*, Oxford, 1927.

58. Si rimanda al dettagliato studio di S.E. FASSBERG, *The Orthography of the Relative Pronoun –hv in the Second Temple and Mishnaic Period*, in H.M. COTTON – J.J. PRICE – D.J. WASSERSTEIN, *Studies in Memory of A. Wasserstein = Scripta Classica Israelica* 15 (1996) 240-250, dove le varie fonti sono indicate e le diverse vocalizzazioni analizzate.

59. Cf. le note introduttive di E. QIMRON, in E. QIMRON – J. STRUGNELL, *Qumran Cave 4. V. Miqṣat ma'aśé ha-torah* (DJD, 10), Oxford, 1984, p. 68, §3.1.4.4, dove sono analizzate le diverse vocalizzazioni e l'accurata analisi di M. Sznycer del dialogo plautino per le grafie *sy* (vv. 930, 933, 1023), *si* (vv. 930, 935), *se* (v. 944) e *us* (v. 948): M. SZNYCER, *Les passages puniques en transcription latine dans le «Poenulus» de Plaute* (Études et Commentaires, 65), Paris, 1967, pp. 52, 71-72, 88, 127, 128, 144.

60. F. ISRAEL, *L'épigraphie et le lexique politique des sociétés en Palestine ancienne*, dans *Semitica* 43-44 (1995) 37-52.

61. Per queste due denominazioni, cf. M. LIVERANI, *Dal «piccolo regno» alla «città stato»*, in E. ACQUARO (ed.), *Alle soglie della Classicità* (n. 41), pp. 249-259 (pp. 254, 256), e I. FINKELSTEIN, *Toward a New Periodization and Nomenclature of the Archaeology of the Southern Levant*, in J.S. COOPER – G.M. SCHWARZ, *The Study of the Ancient Near East in the Twenty-First Century. The W.-F. Albright Centennial Conference*, Winona Lake, IN, 1996, pp. 103-123 (pp. 119-123, con tabella a p. 123).

denominazione del dialetto in essa usato dovrà quindi ancorarsi alle coordinate geografiche ma purtroppo la denominazione «filisteo» avrebbe il difetto di essere troppo generica ed ambigua. Ugualmente ambigua sarebbe una definizione del tipo «fenicio meridionale»[62] perchè essa pur rispettando la locazione geografica del dialetto in questione non lo sarebbe da un punto di vista strettamente epigrafico, vista la presenza di diverse scritture nella regione sottolineata correttamente da G. Garbini[63]. Per rispettare sia il dato linguistico sia le coordinate geografiche l'unica denominazione del dialetto cananeo della regione filistea possibile a proporre sia, tenendo in parte conto di alcune osservazioni di J. Tropper[64], quella di «cananeo costiero meridionale» contrapposto al fenicio da definire per locazione gegrafica «cananeo costiero settentrionale».

Lo scrivente spera con queste linee di avere illuminato da un punto di vista che gli è proprio – la filologia semitica nordoccidentale – un passaggio di un libro biblico tra i più cari al p. Gilbert S.J., antico Rettore del Pontificio Istituto Biblico. Presso questa istituzione chi scrive, come molti orientalisti italiani, ha avuto modo di completare prima la propria formazione di studente e poi sistematicamente grazie alla liberalità con cui la sua splendida biblioteca è ecumenicamente aperta a tutti gli studiosi, ha potuto continuare le proprie ricerche.

Via Lazzaretto Vecchio, 13   Felice ISRAEL
I-34123 Trieste

---

62. Per una definizione della Fenicia meridionale, cf. la segnazione di J.F. SALLES, *Phénicie*, in V. KRINGS (ed.), *La civilisation phénicienne et punique. Manuel de recherche* (Handbuch der Orientalistik, 21), Leiden, 1995, pp. 553-582 (pp. 563-564). Per la definizione di «fenicio», cf. la sintesi di S. MOSCATI, *Chi furono i Fenici. Identità storica e culturale di un popolo protagonista dell'antico mondo mediterraneo*, Torino, 1992, pp. 15-44.

63. G. GARBINI, *I Filistei* (n. 1), pp. 231-244.

64. Cf. J. TROPPER, *Is Ugarit a Canaanite Language?*, in G.J. BROOKE – A.W. CURTIS – J.F. HEALEY (ed.), *Ugarit and the Bible. Proceedings of the International Symposium on Ugarit and the Bible, Manchester, September 1992*, Münster i.W., 1994, pp. 343-353 (p. 352), che definisce il fenicio «coastal canaanite» et l'ebraico e i dialetti transgiordanici «inlands dialects». Non concordo invece con il collega tedesco nella sua definizione dell'ugaritico, che a mio parere è stata definita al meglio da W. VON SODEN, *Introduzione all'orientalistica antica* (Studi sul Vicino Oriente antico), Brescia, 1989, p. 38, come lingua siriana con superstrati cananei.

THE BOOK OF WISDOM

SANITAS COME TRADUZIONE LATINA DI *ΣΩΤΗΡΙΑ*

Nella Vetus Latina, traduzione africana della Sapientia Salomonis, appare *sanitas* in 6,26 e 18,7 come corrispondente di σωτηρία con valore più o meno escatologico, e in 10,4 troviamo *sanare* per σῴζειν. Noi, in questa breve nota, che desidereremmo ben più importante per onorare degnamente l'amico stimatissimo p. M. Gilbert, vorremmo ricercare se gli autori classici latini (intendiamo quelli del tutto lontani e indipendenti da influenze ebraiche o ebraico-cristiane) abbiano mai usato *sanare* e *sanitas* nel senso del greco σωτηρία. E, trascurato l'ordine cronologico, cominciamo con Seneca.

Fedra è in preda a furore amoroso e non vuole sentire ragione di rinsavire, gettando in ansiosa preoccupazione la vecchia nutrice, la quale la implora con queste parole (*Phaedra* 246-249):

> *Per has senectae splendidas supplex comas*
> *fessum curis pectus et cara ubera*
> *precor, furorem siste teque ipsa adiuva,*
> *pars sanitatis velle sanari fuit.*

> Per questi candidi capelli della mia vecchiaia,
> per questo cuore stanco di preoccuparsi e per il mio seno a te caro,
> ti prego, frena la follia e soccorri te stessa,
> gran parte della *sanitas* è *velle sanari*.

Il perfetto *fuit* è certamente gnomico: «fu sempre ed è ancora». La sentenza senecana ci ricorda da vicino quella celebre di Agostino: *qui creavit te sine te, non salvabit te sine te*, «colui che ti ha creato senza di te, non ti salverà senza di te», cioè per la «salvezza» ci vuole irrinunciabilmente la partecipazione di colui che intende salvarsi. La nutrice sembra alludere a questo principio: *teque ipsa adiuva*, «devi essere tu ad aiutare te stessa». In questo gioco delle parti il significato immediato è: se vorrai applicare quello che in te è il dispositivo di sicurezza, ti salverai; questo dispositivo si chiama: ragione. Se la ragione non funzionerà per qualunque motivo, la disfatta è assicurata. Il perfetto *fuit*, come dicevamo, è gnomico ed è più che probabile che il modo proverbiale abbia origine medicale, ma qui, cioè in Seneca, l'accento posto sulla volontà risponde a un principio ascetico. C'è un altro proverbio che qui qualche commentatore ricorda: *dimidium facti qui bene coepit, habet* (Hor. *epist.* 1,2,40), cioè il difficile è cominciare, il resto viene da sé; altri ricorda Ovidio, *rem.* 91: *principiis obsta; sero medicina paratur / cum mala per longas convaluere moras*; ma la frase della *Fedra* ha valore diverso: è quello che, anche altrove, Seneca enuncia con lo stesso modulo, e*pist.* 34,3: *pars magna bonitatis est velle fieri bonum* ed *epist.* 71,36: *magna pars est profectus velle proficere.* Anche per Fedra si tratta di una salvezza morale, se non escatologica[1].

In queste frasi peso determinante ha il verbo *velle* che è sempre presente, come abbiamo visto: è, come dice M. Bellincioni (*Educazione alla Sapienza in Seneca*, pp. 60 ss.), «caratteristica distintiva del pensiero morale di Seneca: la volontà concepita come valore essenziale dell'uomo»; il Pohlenz (*Kl. Schriften*, t. I, pp. 440 ss.) riteneva questa caratteristica introdotta nel pensiero stoico da Seneca con sensibilità tutta romana. Comunque, ci sembra che il *velle* debba considerarsi in un quadro più generale: una salvezza che l'uomo, come ogni animale, cerca sistematicamente, spinto dalla volontà di sopravvivenza; così nella vita fisica come in quella morale.

La nutrice è indignata davanti alla pertinacia di Fedra nel suo furore amoroso e la implora dicendole: *furorem siste*, una frase che meritava una nota dai recenti commentatori della *Fedra*. Il verbo *sistere* è usato per «fermare» l'irrompere violento di cose disordinate, come una fuga (Liv. 6,29,3: *ab effuso cursu*) o l'acqua di un fiume (Verg. *Aen.* 4,489: *sistere aquam fluviis*; Ov. *met.* 7,154: *concita flumina*). Anche la nutrice di Medea la supplica con le stesse parole (*Med.* 157): *siste furialem impetum, alumna*; quel *furialis* che è variato con *furibundus* proprio ancora nella *Medea* 263: *siste furibundum impetum.* È, in sostanza, un verbo caro a Seneca per queste situazioni, usato prevalentemente nelle opere teatrali[2].

Seneca mette in bocca alla nutrice di Fedra le parole della saggezza, ma sono parole talmente comuni nella problematica della salvezza che Seneca avrebbe potuto – in poesia – far ripetere alla nutrice quelle frasi che – in prosa – scrive in una delle sue lettere (*epist.* 59,9):

> *hoc quaeram quod saepe mecum dispicio, quid ita nos stultitia tam pertinaciter teneat? primo quia non fortiter illam repellimus nec toto ad salutem impetu nitimur...*

---

1. Per la nutrice, Fedra, la figlia (*alumna*) diletta, è degna di vivere, cioè di salvarsi, perché si crede degna di meritare la morte per il suo *furor*: *dignam ob hoc vita reor / quod esse temet autumas dignam nece* (vv. 256-257); essa è pienamente consapevole del male, le manca la volontà di salvarsi.

2. Per *furor* in generale, v. *La scrittura del* furor: *temi e forme della drammaturgia senecana* in G. PETRONE, *La scrittura tragica dell'irrazionale*, Palermo, Palumbo, 1984, pp. 11 ss. e, sul motivo del *furor*, v. ancora F. GIANCOTTI, *Poesia e filosofia in Seneca tragico: La Fedra*, Torino, Celid, 1986, pp. 13 ss.

questa cosa mi chiederò su cui spesso rifletto: perché la stoltezza ci tenga in suo possesso così tenacemente. Primo perché non la respingiamo con forza e non ci impegnamo con tutte le nostre forze verso la salvezza.

Anche qui la *stultitia* è l'ostacolo maggiore per raggiungere la *salus*, come il *furor* per la *sanitas* e la volontà tesa al massimo sforzo (*toto... impetu nitimur*) è anche qui messa come condizione, anche se un amico può sempre darci una mano, ma nulla più (*epist.* 29,4):

> *Marcellinum nostrum ego nondum despero; etiamnunc servari potest, sed si cito illi manus porrigitur.*

Io non ho perso le speranze per il nostro Marcellino; può ancora salvarsi, ma bisogna dargli subito una mano.

C'è un testo di Seneca, meno citato di quanto meriterebbe il suo significato, che ci parla appunto della «salute», anzi senz'altro della «salvezza» totale e unica per l'uomo se non vuol cadere nelle spire del capriccio, nel vortice dell'irrazionalità. Ci dice, dunque, Seneca (*epist.* 119,15):

> *id actum est ab illo mundi conditore qui nobis vivendi iura descripsit, ut salvi essemus non ut delicati: ad salutem omnia parata sunt et in promptu, delicis omnia misere ac sollicite conparantur*

quel (grande) autore del mondo, che scrisse per noi le leggi del vivere, si preoccupò della nostra sopravvivenza (salvezza) e non delle nostre voluttà: tutto ciò che riguarda la nostra esistenza è pronto e a portata di mano, per i nostri piaceri tutto costa affanno e preoccupazione.

Il testo, avulso dal resto della *Lettera 119*, potrebbe nella sua prima parte, essere messo in bocca a un padre della Chiesa, soprattutto per la frase *ab illo mundi conditore*, che assomiglia fin troppo al «creatore del mondo» ed è, invece, semplicemente «l'ordinatore del *chaos*» e non il creatore *ex nihilo* dei cristiani[3]: il *conditor* stoico trae il cosmo dall'ἀταξία.

3. Il passo ricorda *prov.* 5,8: *ille ipse conditor et rector scripsit quidem fata, sed sequitur; semper paret, semel iussit*, è «l'ordinatore», come si dice *conditor legis* il νομοθέτης; ma *mundi conditor* merita doppia osservazione, prima per *mundus* che sta assumendo il valore che poi rimarrà fisso nelle lingue romanze, ma che nei cristiani sarà per lo più evitato per le connotazioni negative che poteva avere (come, del resto, il greco κόσμος) per preferire *orbis terrarum*; per gli autori latini *mundus* è usuale in Marziale (cf., per es., 7,7,5: *te, summe mundi rector et parens orbis*, significativa la sinonimia); l'altra osservazione va a *conditor*: è termine che con questo specifico significato di Dio «creatore», negli autori latini profani è usato solo in poesia (Iuv. 15,147-148; Stat. *Theb.* 3,483; Man. *astr.* 2,701: *mundi conditor ille*); l'unico prosatore è Seneca, dal quale – noi crediamo – passa agli scrittori africani, come Tertulliano, cfr., per es., *praescr.* 13,2: *mundi conditorem*; *adv. Iud.* 2,1: *universitatis conditor*; *adv. Prax.* 1,1; *virg. vel.* 1,3; nella *Vulgata* latina è del tutto assente e Girolamo sceglie costantemente *creator* (*conditor* solo in Hebr. 11,10); v. Braun, *Deus chr.*, 356-357 e A.P. Orbán, *Les dénominations du monde chez les premiers auteurs chrétiens*, Nijmegen, Dekker & Van De Vegt, 1976, pp. 214 ss.

L'espressione *ut salvi essemus* rimanda a quella salvezza immessa, come dicevamo, nell'uomo come istinto alla sopravvivenza. Ciò verrebbe confermato anche da Musonio Rufo se il testo suggerito dal Braun (p. 490, nr. 4) è l'esatta corrispondenza del nostro testo (Hense, p. 103): θεὸς ὁ ποιήσας τὸν ἄνθρωπον τοῦ σῴζεσθαι χάριν, οὐχὶ τοῦ ἥδεσθαι, «quel Dio che ha fatto l'uomo in modo che si salvasse (pensasse a sopravvivere), non a godere», dove σῴζειν è *salvare* ed ἥδεσθαι è *in deliciis esse* ed è pensiero topico, cfr. Cic. *nat. deor.* 3,87.

Che valore daremo a *salvus* in Hor. *epist.* 1,2,10? Paride viene additato al disprezzo del «saggio» Omero, quel Paride che porta alla rovina la patria per seguire la propria passione: egli fugge dalla battaglia per giacere con Elena, per di più di giorno, debolezza ignota ai combattenti omerici che di giorno non s'accostavano nemmeno alla propria moglie, ma Paride

> *ut salvus regnet vivatque beatus*
> *cogi posse negat*

dice che nessuno può obbligarlo a starsene al sicuro e felice nel suo regno, cioè a «salvarsi», restituendo Elena: è quella «salvezza» finale che significa riacquistare la ragione e pensare alla propria «sopravvivenza», altrimenti si arriva dritti alla distruzione e Paride rivendica pazzamente proprio questa libertà.

La storia di *sanitas* è strettamente unita a quella di *salus* e noi, anche a giustificazione della presente nota linguistica, cominciamo dall'uso dei testi cristiani di *salus* e dalle convinzioni correnti, non sempre pienamente esatte. Scrive V. Loi nel suo commento a Novaziano (*La Trinità*, Torino, SEI, 1975, pp. 237-238): «Il termine *salus* ricorre nel *De Trinitate* sia con il significato di 'salvezza spirituale', sia con quelli di 'salvezza eterna'; queste accezioni sono acquisite al termine *salus* fin dalle prime testimonianze letterarie cristiane, nelle quali appare quale equivalente del greco σωτηρία, arricchitosi, a sua volta, di profonda novità di contenuto religioso in riferimento alla salvezza dal peccato e dalla morte operata dal Cristo». Molto più sfumato uno studioso di valore, il Braun (*Deus christianorum*, Paris, Ét. Augustiniennes, ²1977) che esaminando il termine *salus* in Tertulliano, ne percorre meticolosamente le tappe profane e nomina Seneca e Apuleio, come gli autori nei quali il termine si era particolarmente spiritualizzato[4].

Noi vogliamo rintracciare il valore metaforico di *salus* nel periodo anteriore a Seneca e in Seneca stesso, prima che il termine si caricasse di valenze cristiane.

---

4. Nel BRAUN si trova la bibliografia utile per la storia delle traduzioni latine bibliche di σῴζειν e σωτηρία, prima del THIELE, che citiamo più avanti.

Un uso tutto particolare molto interessante perché non figura nelle opere filosofiche, ricorre in Cicerone nell'epistolario, quindi, in un tipo di lingua corrente. Nelle lettere dall'esilio[5], *salus* è costantemente chiamato il «ritorno» e la frase presente come un ritornello è: *spes reciperandae salutis* (cf. *fam.* 14,4,5), cfr., per es., *ad Q. fr.* 1,3,10: *reliqua ita mihi salus aliqua detur potestasque in patria moriendi...* («una qualche possibilità di ritorno»); ma in queste lettere appare anche *sanare*, cfr. *Att.* 3,12,2: *id, si putas me posse sanari, cures velim, sin plane perii, minus laboro*, «occupati per favore della questione, se ritieni che si possa trovare una soluzione al mio ritorno, se, invece, sono già del tutto spacciato, non mi preoccupo piú»; qui la metafora è resa evidente dal contrapposto con *perire*[6].

Salus è la «vita» politica di un cittadino, restituirgliela significava «salvarlo», come diceva Cic. *pro Mil.* 100:

> *vos obsecro, iudices, ut vestra beneficia quae in me contulistis, aut in huius salute augeatis, aut in eiusdem exitio occasura esse videatis*
>
> vi scongiuro, o giudici, voi che mi avete accordato i vostri benefici, di accrescerli ancora salvando Milone o di considerarli perduti con la sua condanna.

Anche nella *Pro Caelio* 22, la *salus* dell'imputato è la restituzione alla dignità civile, cioè la «salvezza» politica; Cicerone chiama P. Lentulo *restitutor salutis meae*, «autore della mia salvezza» (*pro Mil.* 39), colui, cioè, che lo aveva aiutato a ritornare alla vita politica.

Lo stesso valore ha *salus* anche in Seneca; Caligola negò la grazia a un padre che pregava affinché suo figlio tenuto in prigione venisse liberato, anzi, fece mandare a morte immediatamente il figlio; il testo latino suona, *ira* 2,33,3: *rogante patre ut salutem sibi fili concederet*; *salus* cioè σωτηρία, la salvezza, la grazia. Quanto *salus* significasse politicamente e civilmente «salvezza», lo dimostra anche un passo di Tacito che vale la pena di citare, *ann.* 13,44:

> *Octavius (Sagitta plebei tribunus) contra modo conqueri, modo minitari, famam perditam, pecuniam exhaustam obtestans, denique salutem quae sola reliqua esset, arbitrio eius permittens*
>
> Ottavio d'altra parte ora si lamentava, ora minacciava, protestando che la sua reputazione era perduta, la sua fortuna esaurita, infine egli affidava alla discrezione di Ponzia la sua stessa vita (la salvezza), l'unica cosa che ancora gli rimaneva.

---

5. Raccolte ora in comoda edizione, con traduzione italiana e buon commento da R. DEGL'INNOCENTI PIERINI (M. Tullio Cicerone, *Lettere dall'esilio*, Firenze, 1996).

6. L'opposizione è stata sempre sentita, fin da Plauto (con *salvus*), cf. *Aul.* 207: *Di me servant, salva res est* («tutto va bene»)... *Salvom est, si quid non perit*.

E Seneca nell'*Oedipus* (108-109):

> *una iam superest salus*
> *si quam salutis Phoebus ostendat viam*
> ormai resta una sola possibilità di salvezza
> se una qualche via di salvezza vuol mostrarci Febo.

Come si vede, anche *salus* non è traducibile con «salute», quando il suo uso è metaforico.

E ora dopo *salvare* e *servare* veniamo a *sanare* e a *sanitas*.

Anche l'italiano «sanare» ha un'ampia applicazione metaforica, più o meno vicina al senso fisico; diciamo «sanare i crediti in sofferenza», dove la sofferenza ci riporta nell'ambito della malattia e «sanare il deficit di bilancio»; diciamo «sanare le paludi», ma diciamo anche «sanare una contesa», «sanare un passo disperato», quando un testo non corre e «risanamento» è passato quasi esclusivamente al senso metaforico. Così giova ricordare che in latino *insanus* vale, ovviamente «non sano» ma non è mai usato in senso fisico, come, del resto, ha significato metaforico *insania*.

In italiano «insania» ha perso ormai il suo rapporto con *sanus*, per vivere una sua vita indipendente, ma sorprende che ai tempi di Cicerone tale percorso fosse già arrivato al capolinea:

> *nomen insaniae* – dice Cicerone, *Tusc.* 3,8 – *significat mentis aegrota-*
> *tionem et morbum, id est insanitatem et aegrotum animum quam*
> *appellarunt insaniam,*
>
> la parola *insania* significa malessere e malattia della mente, cioè la mancanza di salute e un'anima ammalata cui diedero il nome di *insania*[7].

Così – ci diceva già Cicerone, *Tusc.* 3,10 – la *sapientia* è la *sanitas animi*, la *insipientia* è, per così dire, la *insanitas*, cioè la *insania*, cioè la *dementia*. Siamo, come si vede, in clima stoico, di una scuola, cioè, che considerava le passioni come malattie dell'animo, come espressamente si dice ancora in Cic. *Tusc.* 4,23: anche l'anima ha le sue malattie; la passione *sanitate spoliat animum morbisque perturbat*, «toglie all'anima la *sanitas*, il lume della ragione» come pensavano gli Stoici, seguendo Crisippo. Seneca ne è convinto anche per Fedra. Arrivare all'*insania*, alla perdita della *sanitas*, è facile e veloce come si dice in *ira* 2,36,5: *nulla celerior ad insaniam via est... (irati) irasci se negant non*

---

7. Cicerone deve spiegare anche *aegrotatio* perché il termine è un suo conio, anche se forse era in uso senza avere ottenuto cittadinanza letteraria: *morbum appellant totius corporis corruptionem aegrotationem morbum cum imbecillitate...* (*Tusc.* 4,28), «chiamano *morbus* (malattia) l'alterazione dell'intero corpo, infermità (*aegrotatio*) chiamano la malattia unita alla debolezza».

minus quam insanire furiosi, ..., «come i furiosi (i pazzi) dicono di non essere pazzi», cioè *insani*[8].

Ritorniamo ora alla *Fedra*. Pare impossibile – dice la nutrice – che ogni volta che una donna di Creta è presa da furore amoroso, il mondo udrà *prodigia insueta* e vedrà le sue leggi calpestate o violate. Ma Fedra risponde che il *furor* amoroso la costringe (*cogit*) a seguire il male, anzi il peggio (*peiora*); la sua anima sa di correre verso la rovina (*in praeceps*) e invano si appella a sani consigli (*sana consilia*) (vv. 174 ss.), cioè propositi di «salvezza».

Anzi, Fedra vuol seguire Ippolito ovunque, anche tra il fuoco e per il mare «insano», ma questo *mare insanum* (v. 703), pur reminiscenza degli *insani fluctus* di Virgilio (*ecl.* 9,43), è inquadrato in un contesto amoroso; è un mare»furioso» come i flutti di Virgilio che feriscono (*feriant*) le coste; è un «mare in tempesta» (come bene traduce il Traina), com'è in tempesta l'animo degli innamorati pazzi; «dovunque volgerai i tuoi passi – dice Fedra a Ippolito (v. 705) – là la mia pazzia mi trascinerà»: *amens agar* con *amens* che insiste sull'assenza della *ratio*. In questa «tempesta», in questo conflitto, a Fedra sembra soluzione unica il morire fra le braccia di Ippolito, uccisa da lui *salvo pudore*; «orsù – implora Fedra – così tu salvi una pazza (*sanas furentem*)»; e ritorna *sanare* per una soluzione radicale e finale; altra «salvezza» Fedra non vede al suo *furor*.

Seneca usa *sanare* anche in contesti lontani dall'opposizione col *furor* e in contesti non esplicitamente legati alla *ratio*, più vicini, diremmo, alla «salvezza» morale quale troveremo nei testi biblici di cui parleremo. Così, per es., in *benef.* 1,4,6: *at ingenia sanare et fidem in rebus humanis retinere, memoriam officiorum incidere animis volunt: serio loquantur et magnis viribus agant*, «ma essi vogliono salvare l'anima e mantenere la fedeltà nei rapporti umani e incidere nel cuore il ricordo dei benefici»: (allora) parlino seriamente, lasciando (come dice sopra) le futilità ai poeti... Così *ingenia sanare* significa, press'a poco, «portare l'anima alla virtú»; un *sanare* tutto simile al σῷζειν dei Greci.

La *sanitas* opposta al *furor* ricorre anche in *epist.* 18,15: *ingentis irae exitus furor est et ideo ira vitanda est non moderationis causa sed*

---

8. È utile, forse, ricordare che Seneca usa indifferentemente i termini *insania*, *dementia* e *furor*, mentre in Cicerone *furor* è riservato alla pazzia patologica, *Tusc.* 3,11: *hanc insaniam, quae iuncta stultitiae patet latius, a furore distinguimus* e *Tusc.* 3,9: *omnium insipientium animi in morbo sunt: omnes insipientes igitur insaniunt*; per Cicerone rimandiamo alle note precise di N. MARINONE, commento al terzo libro delle *Tusculanae*, Firenze, La Nuova Italia, 1966, pp. 16 ss. e v. M. BELLINCIONI, L. Anneo Seneca, *Lettere a Lucilio (94 e 95)*, Brescia, Paideia, 1979, pp. 150-151. E ci piace ricordare anche Hor. *carm.* 1,34,2-3: *insanientis dum sapientiae consultus erro*, «mentre mi aggiro nell'errore, esperto in una filosofia pazza (l'epicurea)».

sanitatis, tradotto da una studiosa moderna: «... ma anche per mantenersi sani»; meglio il Noblot: «pour sauvegarder notre raison»; Seneca vuol dire che non si tratta di «moderazione», cioè di misura, ma della salute dell'anima, cioè della ragione, la quale, altrimenti, è preda dell'insania. «Potresti chiamare 'sano' uno che è schiavo d'un delirio furioso?» dice Seneca in *ira* 3,3,3: *sanum hunc aliquis vocat qui... furenti malo servit?*, «sano» cioè «ragionevole»[9]. Anche in Ovidio *sanus* è usato con questo significato (*met.* 7,10 ss.) e il *furor* si oppone alla *ratio*:... *postquam ratione furorem / vincere non poterat* (Medea)... *si possem sanior essem... video meliora proboque / deteriora sequor*[10].

Quirino appare in sogno a Orazio, *post mediam noctem visus, cum somnia vera* (*sat.* 1,10,31-35) per proibirgli di fare versi in greco, perché la Grecia non aveva bisogno di queste aggiunte al suo già ricco patrimonio di poesia: *in silvam non ligna feras insanius*, «non potresti essere più pazzo se ti mettessi a portare legname in un bosco».

Anche Plinio il Giovane conosce quest'uso di *sanitas* e di *sanus* (*epist.* 6,15,3); in una lettera al suo amico Romano racconta un fatto che lo ha indignato: Passeno Paolo aveva cominciato la sua lettura così: *Prisce, iubes*, «Prisco, tu vuoi...» quando uno dal pubblico (Iavoleno Prisco) lo interruppe dicendo: *ego vero non iubeo*, suscitando uno scroscio di risate e mandando a male tutta la recitazione. Plinio commenta: *est omnino Priscus dubiae sanitatis*, «Prisco è assolutamente di dubbio equilibrio» e chiude la lettera con questo consiglio: *tam sollicite recitaturis providendum est non solum ut sint ipsi sani, verum etiam ut sanos adhibeant*, «chi si appresta a fare una lettura pubblica deve non essere matto e anche procurarsi un pubblico non matto».

Né va trascurato un uso politico del termine *sanitas*, già in Cicerone, col significato accentuato di «equilibrio», mancanza di *amentia*; è «saggezza» più che «salvezza», cf. Liv. 2,29,6: *nihilo plus sanitatis in curia quam in foro esse*; il libro terzo delle Favole di Fedro si chiude con questo verso: *dum sanitas constabit, pulchre meminero*, cioè che un plebeo non può lagnarsi ad alta voce: «lo ricorderò bene, finché avrò la testa a posto».

Questo uso latino, anzi questa impostazione filosofica è rimasta viva in italiano dove si dice «insano» l'amore incestuoso fra fratelli o fra padri e figlie, ecc.: un amore contro la ragione, la virtù, la religione. Potremmo dire con Platone, cioè con tutta la tradizione classica, che la

---

9. Pieno d'interessanti confronti e notizie è P. MASTANDREA, *Lettori cristiani di Seneca filosofo*, Brescia, Paideia, 1988, pp. 12 ss.

10. Cf. Rainier JAKOBI, *Der Einfluß Ovids auf den Tragiker Seneca*, Berlin, de Gruyter, 1988, pp. 69 ss.

«virtú non sarebbe altro che la salute (ὑγίεια), la bellezza e il benessere dell'anima e il vizio la malattia (νόσος), la bruttezza e la debolezza della stessa (*rep.* 444d)».

Del termine *salus* ci è stato facile cogliere in Cicerone e in Seneca il significato metaforico sempre corrente, ma decisamente religioso è *salus* in Apuleio che nelle *Metamorfosi* descrive una vicenda tipicamente religiosa: colpa, punizione, salvezza. Ora l'ultimo libro, l'undecimo, racconta la miracolosa riassunzione della forma umana da parte dell'asino-Lucio e descrive anche l'iniziazione di Lucio ai misteri. L'una e l'altra trasformazione è qualificata come *salus*, «salvezza», con queste parole (*met.* 11,12,1): *ecce praesentissimi numinis promissa nobis accedunt beneficia et fata salutemque ipsam meam gerens sacerdos adpropinquat...*, «ecco a me venire i benefici e i fati promessi della dea soccorritrice e la sacerdotessa che in sua mano tiene la mia stessa salvezza s'avvicina...». Come bene osserva il Pesce[11], la salute qui è opera esclusiva della dea. Per l'iniziazione le parole son queste (*met.* 11,21,2-7):

> *nec minus in dies mihi magis magisque accipiendorum sacrorum cupido gliscebat, summisque precibus primarium sacerdotem saepissime conveneram petens ut me noctis sacratae tandem arcanis initiaret,*
>
> «così, di giorno in giorno, s'accresceva in me il desiderio di ricevere la consacrazione ed ero andato a trovare il gran sacerdote frequentemente per supplicarlo con preghiere pressanti di iniziarmi finalmente ai misteri della santa notte».

Con l'iniziazione si rinasce ad una vita spirituale prima negata: arrivare a questa nuova vita è arrivare alla *salus*[12].

Anche se un po' tarda rispetto ai traduttori biblici dei quali parleremo, ci sembra molto significativa una testimonianza di Arnobio 2,46: *ille salus rerum deus, omnium virtutum caput*, cioè σωτηρία κόσμου (v. avanti citazione da *Sap.* 6,26), «quel Dio salvatore dell'universo». Questo passo di Arnobio potrebbe rivelarci che nel latino africano dei cristiani *salus* per σωτηρία era corrente anche al tempo di Arnobio.

Apuleio col suo contesto iniziatico potrebbe offrire il fianco all'obiezione di chi esprime un certo scetticismo per un Seneca spiegato con i misteri e le iniziazioni, alla quale noi rispondiamo con qualche citazione, *nat. 1 praef.* 12: (*homo*) *velut vinculis liberatus in originem*

---

11. Cf. D. PESCE, *La nozione della salvezza nell'antichità classica*, in *Il problema della salvezza*, Centro di Studi filosofici di Gallarate, Padova, 1979, ora in D. PESCE, *Studi platonici*, Parma, Zara, 1988, pp. 233-242.

12. Su questa parte delle *Metamorfosi* rimando alle pagine informate di un libro dimenticato, P. SCAZZOSO, *Le Metamorfosi di Apuleio*, Milano, Renon, 1951, pp. 117 ss.

redit; *vit. b.* 15,7: *deo servire summa libertas est*, al quale risponde
Apuleio, *met.* 11,15,5: *nam cum coeperis deae* (cioè Iside) *servire, tunc
magis senties fructum tuae libertatis*; *Herc. f.* 681: *neve remeandi
amplius pateat facultas*, con *remeare* tecnico per il «ritorno» al mondo
astrale, e cfr. Apuleio, *de deo S.* 155: *at ubi vita edita remeandum est*, o
per «ritornare» alla σωτηρία come in *Phaedr.* 180 (già citato sopra).[13]

D'altra parte in ambiente egiziano, nel quale Seneca aveva trascorso
qualche tempo, la letteratura misterica era molto vivace tanto che Seneca
sembra aver scritto un'opera sull'argomento (*de situ et de sacris
Aegyptiorum*) e questo può spiegare due cose: sia alcune predilezioni di
Seneca (come il nostro *sanitas* per σωτηρία), sia la persistenza degli
stessi termini in ambiente africano[14].

Abbiamo lasciato per ultimo un riscontro che da solo vale cento altri.
Seneca in *epist.* 28,9 manda a Lucilio la *diurna mercedula*, il dono di
una massima filosofica da meditare e tradurre in alimento vitale; eccola,
presa da Epicuro: «*initium est salutis notitia peccati*». *Egregie mihi hoc
dixisse videtur Epicurus, nam qui peccare se nescit corrigi non vult.*
Dichiaratamente qui abbiamo un Seneca traduttore dal greco. Il Grilli[15]
crede di trovare il testo greco di Epicuro in una citazione dataci
dall'abate Nilo: ἀρχὴ σωτηρίας ἡ ἑαυτοῦ κατάγνωσις, «inizio della
salvezza è la condanna di se stessi», cioè della propria colpa. Non so se
questa fosse proprio *verbatim* la sentenza di Epicuro, ma ha ragione il
Grilli nel ritenerlo molto probabile perché nel commento che segue
Seneca insiste sulla partecipazione che ognuno deve prestare: *accusa-
toris primum partibus fungere, deinde iudicis, novissime deprecatoris*;
solo alla fine tu devi assumere il ruolo d'intercessore, ma comincia con
l'accusarti, perché la ἀρχή della salvezza è la κατάγνωσις, la condanna
della propria colpa.

Questa frase di Seneca (*initium salutis*) ci porta a ricordare
un'affermazione preziosa di Cicerone, la quale segna una tappa
ineliminabile nella storia di *salus*; dice, dunque, Cicerone (*Verr.*
2,63,154): *itaque eum* (sc. *Verrem*) *non solum patronum illius insulae,
sed etiam* Σωτῆρα *inscriptum vidi Syracusis. Hoc quantum est? ita
magnum ut Latine uno verbo exprimi non possit. Is es nimirum* σωτήρ,
qui salutem dedit; non si può con una sola parola esprimere in latino
il greco σωτήρ, cioè «il salvatore», colui che diede la salvezza alla
città.

---

13. Per il valore nuovo di questo *remeare* basterebbe confrontarlo con l'uso fattone da
Orazio in *sat.* 1,6,94.

14. Larga informazione in proposito in P. GRIMAL, *Sénèque ou la conscience de l'Em-
pire*, Paris, Hachette, 1978, pp. 66 ss.

15. A. GRILLI, *Seneca ed Epicuro, fr. 522 Us.*, in *Paideia* 12 (1957) 337-338.

Nell'interpretare un testo antico non è certo utile, vocabolario e concordanze alla mano, capire a modo proprio un passo, quanto piuttosto chiedersi cosa capiva il lettore contemporaneo al quale lo scrittore si rivolgeva.

In altre parole, in *sanare*, in *sanitas* e in *salus* era sentita l'idea di «salvezza»? Sicuramente sì, se le traduzioni bibliche usano questi termini latini per rendere i termini greci σῴζειν e σωτηρία. E così veniamo ai passi della *Sapientia* latina, passi che era nostra intenzione illuminare un po' da vicino:

> Sap 6,26: *multitudo autem sapientium sanitas est orbis terrarum*, gr.: πλῆθος δὲ σοφῶν σωτηρία κόσμου, «la moltitudine dei saggi è la salvezza del mondo»;

> Sap 18,7: *sanitas quidem iustorum, iniustorum autem exterminatio*, gr.: σωτηρία δικαίων, ἐχθρῶν δὲ ἀπώλεια, «salvezza dei giusti, ma sterminio degli ingiusti»[16].

Come nella *Fedra* di Seneca la salvezza veniva dal *logos*, così nella nostra Sapientia Salomonis (10,4) la salvezza viene dalla *sapientia*, dono di Dio: *iterum sanavit sapientia*, gr.: πάλιν ἔσωσεν σοφία[17].

Nella Sapientia Salomonis sono inoltre da notare:

1,14	sanabilis gr.	σωτήριος
6,26	sanitas	σωτηρία
9,18	sanare	σῴζειν
10,4	sanare	(δια)σῴζειν
14,4	sanare	σῴζειν
16,7	sanare	σῴζειν
18,7	sanitas	σωτηρία

L'antica versione latina della *Lettera di Barnaba* traduce più volte σῴζειν con *sanare* (4,1; 5,10; 8,6); in Is 49,6 il testo della Vulgata suona: *dedi te in lucem gentium ut sis salus mea usque ad extremum terrae* (gr.: εἰς σωτηρίαν), ma questa citazione, ripetuta alla lettera dai LXX, nella *Lettera di Barnaba* (14,8) suona nell'antica versione latina *sanitas mea* e, in una citazione di Cipriano, *salvatio*[18].

---

16. Cf., fra i molti testi, Lc 19,10: σῶσαι τὸ ἀπολωλός; Iac 4,12: ὁ δυνάμενος σῶσαι καὶ ἀπολέσαι.

17. A proposito di *sanare* per σῴζειν l'unica informazione che D. DE BRUYNE sa darci è che *sanare* è un «mot nouveau» (non sappiamo in che senso), a p. 127 del suo art. *Étude sur le texte latin de la Sagesse*, in *Revue Bénédictine* 41 (1929) 101 ss.

18. Cf. W. THIELE, *Die lateinischen Texte des 1. Petrusbriefes*, Freiburg i. Br., Herder, 1965, pp. 200, e J.M. HEER, *Die Versio Latina des Barnabasbriefes und ihr Verhältnis zur altlateinischer Bibel*, Freiburg i.Br., Herder, 1908.

Per molte altre testimonianze bibliche rimando a W. Thiele, pp. 195 ss.; ma molte testimonianze possono essere scomparse per la sostituzione con *salvare*, cf. Ps 97,1: *salvabit sibi dextera eius*, dove Agostino ci dà *sanavit*[19]. Il Libro della Sapienza col suo traduttore africano, con Agostino (ecc.) può farci pensare a particolarità di quei luoghi e può anche essere vero, ma resta il problema di sapere donde tale uso venga ai traduttori africani, e ad orientarci potrebbe essere un passo di Cipriano, *epist.* 51,1: *exultanter excepimus Maximum presbyterum et Urbanum confessorem... haeretico furore deserto, unitatis ac veritatis domicilium fideli sanitate repetisse*: essi hanno abbandonato il *furor* dell'eresia, per ritornare con fedele salvezza (conversione) alla casa della unità e della verità; il passo di Cipriano ha come polo opposto alla salvezza dell'anima il *furor* dell'eresia, come Fedra era fuorviata dal *furor* dell'amore, cioè dall'irrazionalità.

Tertulliano è contemporaneo al traduttore della Sapientia Salomonis, ambedue africani. Di Tertulliano si è ripetuta fino alla nausea la frase del *de anima* (20,1): *Seneca saepe noster* e certamente *noster* non allude alla lingua (latina), ma al contenuto morale e filosofico degli scritti di Seneca, mentre noi vogliamo richiamare l'attenzione sulla lingua[20]. Tertulliano ha letto per conto suo Seneca? certamente, ma prima lo ha letto e studiato a scuola, nella scuola di Cartagine dove si studiava anche il greco, ma che era tutta orgogliosamente romana e tale da produrre scrittori latini come Apuleio e poi Cipriano. Seneca fu autore esemplare per Tertulliano anche nella concezione e nella pratica della retorica. Quindi, Seneca fu oggetto di uno studio attento, ma la nostra conclusione riguarda solo relativamente Tertulliano, quanto piuttosto un Seneca autore di scuola, amato dai giovani africani[21], del quale si leggeva anche il teatro[22].

Prova ne potrebbe essere anche il testo citato di Cipriano, dove l'accostamento di *furor* e *sanitas* è tanto sorprendente da non poter essere messo in conto a casualità. Noi crediamo – ma l'argomento è

---

19. Di queste sostituzioni o alternanze gli esempi sono numerosissimi e una viene registrata, per es., dal VACCARI, *Studi critici sopra le antiche versioni latine del Vecchio Testamento*, Roma, Pontificio Istituto Biblico, 1914, p. 27, per Abacuc 3,8: *adaequatio tua salus* che nei codd. appare anche come *equitatio tua salus* e nella maggioranza dei codd.: *equitatus tuus sanitas*.

20. Una disamina precisa del valore della frase ci offre J.-Cl. FREDOUILLE, «*Seneca saepe noster*», in *Présence de Sénèque*, Paris, 1991, pp. 127-142.

21. Cf. J.-Cl. FREDOUILLE, *Tertullien et la conversion de la culture antique*, Paris, 1972, pp. 32 ss.

22. Cf. l'*Introduction*, pp. 46-47, all'ed. del *de anima* di J.H. WASZINK, Amsterdam, 1947. Da Tertulliano sappiamo per l'Africa ciò che per Roma sappiamo (dopo Quintiliano) da fonti dirette come Aulo Gellio e Frontone che cioè gli *adulescentuli* romani amavano leggere Seneca; cfr. I. LANA, *I giovani e Seneca*, in *Seneca e i giovani* (a c. di I. LANA), Venosa, Osanna, 1997, pp. 197 ss.

stato studiato solo parzialmente – che Cipriano, come il nostro traduttore, avesse letto Seneca nelle scuole e che Seneca fosse molto amato e letto dai giovani in Africa come a Roma.

Così, vorremmo aggiungere un altro passo della Sapientia Salomonis dove senso fisico e senso figurato si assommano, Sap 16,12: ἀλλὰ ὁ σός, κύριε, λόγος ὁ πάντας ἰώμενος, tradotto: sed tuus, Domine, sermo qui sanat omnia (su di un testo greco che aveva πάντα, non πάντας), dove, inoltre, si vede come anche la lingua greca conoscesse un uso metaforico di ἰᾶσϑαι, soprattutto nel greco biblico, cfr. Sir. 3,28: ἐπαγωγῇ ὑπερηφάνου οὐκ ἔστιν ἴασις, tradotto, forse, dallo stesso studioso che ha tradotto la Sapienza: synagogae superborum non est sanitas[23].

Ritornando, quindi, al testo di Seneca dal quale siamo partiti, confortati anche dal latino biblico tradurremo: «parte della salvezza (sanitatis) è volersi salvare (sanari)», più che sicuri che così intendeva il lettore sia a Roma, sia nell'Africa romana, tanto che il traduttore della Sapientia per σωτηρία ha scelto, senza esitazione, sanitas come corrispondente latino.

Conclusione: in una serie di articoli, di cui questo è il primo, vorremmo elencare le sorprendenti coincidenze tra il lessico di Seneca e il lessico dei traduttori africani della Bibbia, per dimostrare che questi conoscevano Seneca e vanno accomunati, in questo aspetto della loro cultura, a Tertulliano e a Cipriano (e ad Apuleio).

I cristiani insoddisfatti di sanitas e di salus (e dei loro derivati) insisteranno su salvare e salvator, termini che non erano latini ma ai quali i cristiani fecero concedere piena cittadinanza, come affermò Agostino con le celebri parole del Sermo 299,6: salvare et salvator non fuerunt haec Latina antequam veniret Salvator. Quando ad Latinos venit et haec Latina fecit[24].

via Emilia, 8
I-25125 Brescia

Giuseppe Scarpat

---

23. Un testo gnostico è esplicito: ἰασάμενος αὐτὸν τῆς νόσου, τουτέστιν τῶν ἁμαρτιῶν, «guarendo dalla malattia, cioè dai peccati» (Origene, in Io. 13,60).

24. Su salvus e i suoi derivati salvare, salvator, buona esposizione, con particolare riguardo a Tertulliano, e molta documentazione, in R. BRAUN, Deus christianorum, pp. 490 ss. F. HAHN, Christologische Hoheitstitel, Göttingen, Vandenhoeck, ⁵1995, p. 45 n. 6, si augurava che si intraprendesse una nuova fondamentale ricerca su σῴζειν, σωτηρία e σωτήρ; noi vorremmo aver portato un piccolo contributo alla sua storia (o preistoria) in ambiente classico.

PROVERBS AS A SOURCE FOR WISDOM OF SOLOMON

It is widely recognized that Wisdom of Solomon is a remarkable blending of ancestral Hebrew literature and Hellenistic Greek philosophy and rhetoric. Chs. 7–9 develop the picture of wisdom in Job 28, Prov 1–9, and Sir 24. Ch. 10 reshapes the history of Israel in the Pentateuch and Deuteronomistic History into a sequence of great individuals who were guided by wisdom. Chs. 11–19 is an exposition of the exodus in the Pentateuch and the Psalms in the form of seven great comparisons. In every case, the traditions were shaped by an erudite and skilled author.

Less widely recognized is the substantial borrowing from one biblical book: Proverbs. One reason this borrowing has largely gone unnoticed is that Proverbs and Wisdom of Solomon, though both "wisdom literature", have been judged to be utterly different. Proverbs is often regarded as conventional advice to individuals. Wisdom of Solomon, on the other hand, is judged to be a call to Jews to remain faithful and recognize the wisdom and validity of their national traditions. Small wonder that commentators have not generally thought of one book as an important source for the other. In the following pages, we will attempt to show, many commentators notwithstanding, that Wisdom of Solomon found in Proverbs the seeds of some of its core teachings. Wisdom of Solomon in fact can be regarded as an early interpretation of Proverbs.

It is a pleasure to pay homage to Professor Maurice Gilbert, S.J., who has done so much to bring wisdom literature, especially Wisdom of Solomon, from the margin to the center of biblical studies. He combines careful attention to details with an interest in synthesis, showing in his scholarship erudition, superb judgment, and expository skill.

Of all the biblical books, Proverbs has exercised the greatest influence upon Wisdom of Solomon. The exodus from Egypt, which dominates Wis 11 + 16–19, is not derived exclusively from the *book* of Exodus, for the Psalms and other Jewish literature have made their contribution. P. W. Skehan many years ago demonstrated in detail that Proverbs was an important source for Wisdom of Solomon.[1] Both books begin with a

---

1. SKEHAN studied the topic in his dissertation in the 1930s and updated his findings in *The Literary Relationship of the Book of Wisdom to Earlier Wisdom Writings*, in *Studies in Israelite Poetry and Wisdom* (CBQMS, 1), Washington, Catholic Biblical Association, 1971, pp. 173-191. Translations of Proverbs are my own. Translations of Wisdom of Solomon are from *NRSV*.

speech by the wicked expressing their philosophy of life (Prov 1,11-14 and Wis 2,1-20). Both books early on warn against "folly" and show its destructive effects (Prov 1; Wis 1–5) before showing positively the value and fruits of wisdom and virtue (Prov 2, 8, 9 and Wis 6-9). Only after unmasking evil do the books introduce reified wisdom and show her as a dispenser of divine knowledge, witness to God's work, and protector of the righteous.

Skehan followed these general observations with detailed arguments to show that Wisdom of Solomon borrowed from the Hebrew rather than the Greek text of Proverbs (though he allowed the latter possibility). An example of borrowing from the Hebrew text is the application to Wisdom of the title τεχνῖτις in Wis 7,22 and 14,2. Wisdom of Solomon interpreted אָמוֹן in Prov 8,30 אָמוֹן אֶצְלוֹ וָאֶהְיֶה, "and I was beside him (as) an אָמוֹן", like Ct 7,2 אָמָן, "artisan", but did not use the LXX translation of אָמוֹן, ἁρμόζουσά, "joiner; artisan", which would have been apposite[2]. Skehan provides other persuasive examples of borrowing from the Hebrew text of Proverbs and possible borrowings from LXX. In many cases, he recognizes that a definitive judgment is impossible because both books use a "hakamic" style.

It is possible to extend Skehan's observations about the dependence of Wisdom of Solomon on Proverbs to dependence regarding important themes. The borrowing of one theme—reified wisdom—no one doubts[3], but there are at least five others: 1. the righteous person as the *locus* where divine action becomes visible; 2. God as a father who teaches his son by a process involving correction and even punishment (παιδεία = מוּסָר); 3. the wise king; 4. life and death as more-than-biological realities; 5. the world (κόσμος) protecting the righteous and punishing the wicked.

The righteous person is the occasion for the revelation of divine action. In Proverbs, the righteous person (often singular) appears frequently, often as an antithesis to the wicked (often plural)[4]. This antithesis, and the related antithesis of the wise *versus* the fool, are very important to the argument of Proverbs[5]. Modern commentators generally

---

2. *The Literary Relationship*, pp. 175-76. C. LARCHER also lists verses that may have been borrowed, in *Études sur le Livre de la Sagesse*, Paris, Gabalda, 1969, pp. 97-98;.

3. E.g., D. WINSTON, *The Wisdom of Solomon* (AB, 43), New York, Doubleday, 1969, pp. 34-36; A. SCHMITT, *Weisheit* (NEchtB), Würzburg, Echter Verlag, 1989, pp. 39-49.

4. For a recent discussion of the types, see J. HAUSMANN, *Studien zum Menschenbild der alteren Weisheit* (FAT, 7), Tübingen, Mohr, pp. 37-56.

5. The contrast seems to have originated with Proverbs. It is not found in Egyptian wisdom literature, which, when it does use contrast, contrasts the hothead and the "cool" person. The seventh-century Aramaic work *Ahiqar* contains two pairs of verses that may be relevant. One verse speaks about the wicked and the other speaks about the wicked,

interpret the Proverbs antitheses as devices to affirm (divine) retribution in the world. By describing the behavior and especially the fates of the types, Proverbs shows that good and bad actions have good and bad consequences, thus demonstrating that the world is ruled by justice. Implementation of the justice can be expressed directly as when Yahweh is named as the agent, or indirectly by the use of passive verbs, the so-called. divine passive. In any event, the cosmos in Proverbs is "self-righting", inherently frustrating the unjust and foolish, rewarding the righteous and wise.

Wisdom of Solomon develops Proverbs' teaching that justice is inherent in the world through the categories of Middle Platonism[6]. Wisdom of Solomon presents two worlds[7]. The "real world" is the world ruled by God; it is immortal though not yet visible in any permanent way. Its opposite is the *Erscheinungswelt*, the world of appearances, which is marked by death. Each world has its citizens or "party" (μερίς, 2,16; 2,24) who belong to it – the righteous or the wicked. The citizens of the visible world, the world of appearances, are unaware that it is temporary and marked by corruption. The real world becomes visible or real, however, through the righteous, when they act justly. It is especially when they are persecuted or killed by the wicked that one can expect God to bring that world to visibility. As in Proverbs, the workings of the world are illustrated by anonymous types, the righteous person (usually singular) and the wicked (usually plural)[8].

The above remarks can be illustrated by Wis 1–5: 1,16 (cf. 2,23) states that the ungodly belong to the party of death, they have invited death by the error of their ways. The way of the righteous person offends them, especially his claim to be a child (παῖς, 2,13) of God who is his father (2,16). They therefore plot to kill him (2,19-20). The death of the righteous is only apparent (3,1-9), however, and leads to the punishment of the wicked (3,10-13). In the judgment scene (4,20–5,23), the right-

but this is hardly comparable to the massive Proverbs use. See J. DAY, *Foreign Semitic influences on the wisdom of Israel and its appropriation in the book of Proverbs*, in J. DAY, R.P. GORDON, & H.G.M. WILLIAMSON (eds.), *Wisdom in Ancient Israel*, FS J.A. Emerton, Cambridge, Cambridge University Press, 1995, p. 63.

6. For a concise and up-to-date review of the philosophical background of Wisdom of Solomon, see J.J. COLLINS, *Wisdom and Cosmos*, in *Jewish Wisdom and the Hellenistic Age*, Louisville, KY, Westminster John Knox, 1997, pp. 196-221.

7. Our treatment owes much to D. GEORGI, *Der vorpaulinische Hymnus Phil 2, 6-11*, in E. DINKLER (ed.), *Zeit und Geschichte*, FS R. Bultmann, Tübingen, Mohr, 1964, pp. 262-93.

8. The contrast between the righteous person in the singular and the wicked in the plural seems to be borrowed from Proverbs. The variation in grammatical number maximizes the contrast.

eous person rises up with confidence before the wicked, who now recognize their error and confess that they have not understood the nature of reality. The false world is shown to be characterized by corruption and death. The enduring world is revealed by the actions of the righteous person.

D. Georgi points out that the drama in Wis 2 is about two basic types representing different realms[9]. Their actions show forth or actualize their respective realms. In Wisdom 1–5, the instrument of revelation is the righteous person ("Das göttliche Werkzeug ist in der Sapientia der Gerechte")[10]. In chs. 6–9, the instrument of revelation is the wise man *par excellence*, the wise king (Solomon). In 11,1-14 + chs. 16–19, the instrument is the holy people, God's "son" (18,13).

Wisdom of Solomon regarded the actions of the Proverbs types as revealing the immortal world and unmasking the world ruled by Gentile kings. In fact, this is a correct interpretation of Proverbs, for there the fate of the righteous (and the wicked) reveal the underlying character of the word.

> *When the storm has passed, a wicked person is no more,*
> *but a righteous person has a lasting foundation (10,25).*
> *Righteousness leads to life,*
> *but who pursues evil heads toward his death (11,19).*

Already in Proverbs, then, the respective fates of the two types disclose divine actions. Wisdom of Solomon goes further, "ontologizing" the ethical dimension of Proverbs.

Within this immortal but not-yet-disclosed world, wisdom guides and protects the just. The theme of wisdom protecting the righteous is especially clear in Prov 2. Those who seek wisdom will be protected by the same wisdom.

> *[5]then you will understand the revering of Yahweh,*
> *you will find knowledge of God;*
> *[6]for Yahweh gives wisdom,*
> *from his mouth come knowledge and insight;*
> *[7]he stores up resourcefulness for the upright*
> *and is a shield for those who walk in integrity;*
> *[8]he protects the paths of justice,*
> *safeguards the way of those loyal to him.*
> *[11]prudence will safeguard you,*
> *insight will protect you.*

9. GEORGI, *Der vorpaulinische Hymnus*, p. 270.
10. GEORGI, *Der vorpaulinische Hymnus*, p. 271. Later on, in the seven comparisons in chs. 11–19, the righteous person is identified as the holy people (cf. 18,13). In the plagues, the people are differentiated from the wicked and reveal God's justice.

Proverbs goes on to say that wisdom will save her disciples from deceptive men (vv. 12-15) and the deceptive woman (vv. 16-19), making them "walk on the way of the good" and "dwell on the land"; the wicked will be cut off from it. In Wisdom of Solomon Wisdom similarly protects the just, for example, guiding the seven righteous heroes in ch. 10. In the immediately preceding chapter, Solomon prays that wisdom will guide his actions (9,11). The chief difference between wisdom's guidance in the two books is that in Wisdom of Solomon wisdom has a wider reference, being almost akin to divine energy.

A second major theme adapted from Proverbs is the father who teaches his son to live wisely through a process the book calls παιδεία. In Proverbs, especially in chs. 1–9, the biological father[11] instructs his son to live in accord with wisdom:

> *[11]My son, do not reject the discipline of Yahweh,*
> *do not disdain his correction,*
> *[12]for anyone he loves he reproves,*
> *like a father the son whom he favors* (3,11-12).

Wisdom of Solomon does not present itself as a father's instruction to his son like Prov 1–9 and other ancient Near Eastern instruction. Its genre is different[12]. Rather, it applies to God the father's role in teaching or reproving his son. The righteous person (a wisdom type) boasts that God is his father in 2,16 ("he boasts that God is his father"). The primary meaning of "father" here is not begetter but teacher as is shown by the context of 2,12-20. The entire passage is about the divine *teaching* the righteous man lives by. The language is that of learning and putting into practice what one knows. The righteous person reproaches the wicked, accusing them of sins against their training (παιδεία 2,12). Sins against παιδεία presuppose that the wicked were given instruction but chose to ignore it. In Proverbs, the life style or "way" of the righteous person is an implicit rebuke to the "way" of the wicked.

> *A scoffer does not like being corrected;*
> *he never visits the wise.* (15,12)
> *A fool spurns the discipline of his father,*
> *but one who attends to reproof grows wise.* (15,5)
> *Do not correct a scoffer, for he will become your enemy*
> *correct a wise person and he will become your friend.* (9,8)

The references to the righteous person as a child of the Lord (παῖδα κυρίου, 2,13) who calls God his father (2,16) and is known as a son of

---

11. The mother is also mentioned in 1,8 and 6,20.

12. For a judicious discussion of the much vexed question of the genre, see M. GILBERT, art. *Sagesse de Salomon*, in *DBS*, t. 11, Paris Letouzey et Ané, 1991, col. 77-87.

God (υἱὸς θεοῦ, 2,18), are often interpreted as allusions to lament psalms (e.g., Ps 22,9) or to the servant song in Isa 52,13–53,12[13]. Though possibly influenced by Psalms and Isaiah, the more obvious source is the genre of instruction as it appears in Proverbs 1–9. The father instructs his son to live according to wisdom; the son's decision to live in accord with the father's instructions sets him apart from the wicked and the foolish. The outcome or end of each type (Wis 2,16.17) reveals which of the two ways was valid. In Proverbs the outcome or end similarly allows one to judge the validity of the acts leading up to it, for example, "There is a road that seems straight to a person, but its end is the path to death" (14,12). In the context of Wis 2, to boast of God as one's father is to be proud of his teachings and live up to them. The most obvious background of Wis 2 and 5 is the Proverbs theme of the father instructing his son.

The first excursus (Wis 11,15–12,27), which describes God correcting the Egyptians (11,15–12,2,23-27) and the Canaanites (12,3-22), is a good portrayal of God as a teacher who corrects and only reluctantly punishes those who persist in their sins. Sin is "folly", not knowing God; it consists in being led astray (12,24) and not knowing the true God (11,15; 12,27). God intends that sinners "learn" (11,15), "repent" (11,23; 12,10; 12,19-20), and change their ways. Punishment is inflicted only after a process of correcting (παιδεία). God carries out the process of correcting even when there is no hope of conversion, as with the Canaanites (12,10-11). God wishes to teach them but is forced to punish them by their disobedience. Rejecting the violent means always available to an all-powerful God, God prefers to reprove rather than destroy, which is the nuance of the Hebrew verb יוֹכִיחַ that lies behind this passage. The manner of education in this excursus is that of Proverbs. Its goal is learning rather than punishment: "so that they may be freed from wickedness and put their trust in you, O Lord" (Wis 12,2).

Excursus II (chs. 13–15) is about knowledge of God. The three groups, the philosophers ("foolish", 13,1-9), image venerators ("miserable", 13,10–15,13), and worshipers of animals ("most foolish", 15,14-19) fail to recognize God or construct images of him. Their vice is ignorance, which is portrayed in three stages of increasing culpability for failure to recognize God as the true God of the universe.

---

13. The allusion to the Isaian servant is widely though not universally accepted. See, among others, D. GEORGI, *Der vorpaulinische Hymnus*, p. 271, G.E. NICKELSBURG, *Resurrection, Immortality, and Eternal Life in Intertestamental Judaism* (HThS, 26), Cambridge, MA, Harvard University Press, 1972, pp. 48-92, and, with appropriate qualifications, M. GILBERT, art. *Sagesse de Salomon*, col. 94.

In sum, adapting Proverbs' description of God as father-teacher, Wisdom of Solomon presents a full-scale portrayal of the One who teaches his sons, and malicious fools as well, how to live wisely.

A third theme borrowed from Proverbs and transformed is that of the wise king. Proverbs presents itself as almost entirely the work of King Solomon in 1,1 (cf. 10,1 and 25,1)[14]. The king is mentioned as a functioning institutional figure approximately twenty-three times in Proverbs, every mention recognizing unquestioningly his exalted status[15]. He has a central role in the governance of the universe including the administration of justice.

A king sitting upon a throne of justice
scatters evil by a mere glance. (20,8)
It is the glory of God to conceal a matter;
and the glory of a king to search out a matter.
Like the heavens in their height and the earth in its depth,
the mind of a king cannot be searched out. (25,2-3)

To understand the role of the king in Proverbs, one needs to recall that wisdom in the ancient Near East was concieved quite differently than in the modern West: it was hierarchized and institutionalized. Belonging by right to the gods, it was graciously transmitted to human beings through an orderly process involving divine or semi-divine culture-bringers (in Mesopotamia called *apkallu* or *ummānu*), ending finally in earthly *institutions* such as kings, scribes, literature, schools, and heads of families[16]. In Proverbs, the institutions that mediate wisdom to human beings are the king, wisdom writings (cf. 1,2.6), and the father.

Wisdom of Solomon uses two of the three mediating institutions of Proverbs but alters them significantly. Writings are not mentioned as a means to wisdom. The institution of the the father who, as head of the family, is the teacher of his son, is transposed to God the father who teaches his children, as noted under number 2. The institution of the king is complex. On the one hand, kings, rulers, or judges rule this world and, albeit unwittingly[17], are subject to divine control and admonition (1,1-5; 6,1-11). On the other hand, the wise king Solomon (not named in accord

---

14. The only exceptions to Solomon's authorship are 22,17-24,22 and its appendix 24,23-34, which are from "the wise", and all or part of chs. 30–31, which are from Agur and the mother of Lemuel.

15. The nearest thing to a critical remark about kingship is 14:28, which may suggest that a king's glory depends on the number of his people.

16. See C. WILCKE, *Göttliche und menschliche Weisheit im Alten Orient*, in A. ASSMANN (ed.), *Weisheit: Archäologie der literarischen Kommunikation III*, München, Fink, 1991, pp. 259-270.

17. Pagan kings elsewhere in the Bible are unaware they are under divine control: Ps 2, Isa 10,5-7 and 45,4-5.

with the typifying convention of wisdom literature) dominates the middle chapters (Wis 7–9). He is the ideal king, the antithesis to the ignorant office holders in Wis 1 and 6. He is everything a king should be; he loves righteousness and seeks the Lord. Solomon does what Woman Wisdom in Proverbs asks her clients to do, preferring her to silver and gold (Wis 7,9) and praying that God give wisdom to him. He is thus the model seeker of wisdom.

A fourth borrowing from Proverbs is life and death as more-than-biological realities. The blessings that accrue to a righteous or wise person in Proverbs are entirely this-worldly – reputation, enjoyment, security, long and healthy life, children, wealth. All these can be included under "life", a summarizing that is clearest in Prov 3,13-10, where wisdom is a "tree of life". Life thus means human life lived with an abundance of good things. The contrast to life, death, also has a metaphorical dimension. Death in this sense seems to be premature death and diminishment inflicted in retribution. In Proverbs, death can be loss of reputation (Prov 12,8), health (14,30), and wealth (Prov 15,6). Wisdom of Solomon transposes the ethical dualism to an ontological level, making use of the Platonic tradition to do so. Wis 1,12.16 develop the Proverbs view that death comes from evil conduct:

> Do not invite death by the error of your life,
>   or bring on destruction by the work of your hands...
> But the ungodly by their words and deeds summoned death...

Though commentators commonly interpret the verse as an allusion to Isa 28,15 ("We have made a covenant with death"), Proverbs is more likely as an influence. That death results from wickedness is so common a sentiment in Proverbs that it need only be illustrated by one example.

> Righteousness leads to life,
>   but who pursues evil heads toward his death. (11,19)

Wisdom of Solomon puts matters in only a slightly different way: the wicked by the fact of their wickedness have already chosen death.

The fifth and final borrowing from Proverbs that will be mentioned is its portrayal of the world (ὁ κόσμος) as on the side of the righteous person and against the wicked[18]. The idea appears in all three of the main

---

18. The phenomenon has been noticed by many scholars as a distinctive feature of Wisdom of Solomon, e.g., J.J. COLLINS, *Cosmos and Salvation: Jewish Wisdom and Apocalypticism in the Hellenistic Age*, in *HThR* 17 (1977)121-142; M. KOLARCIK, *Creation and Salvation in the Book of Wisdom*, in R.J. CLIFFORD and J.J. COLLINS (eds.), *Creation in the Biblical Traditions* (CBQMS, 24), Washington, Catholic Biblical Association, 1992, pp. 97-107.

sections of Wisdom of Solomon. In the trial that vindicates the righteous person (ch. 5), God arms all creation (5,17) to fight with him against the perverse (5,20). The second part of the book (6,22–10,21) declares that God created the world through wisdom that guides it at every moment, safeguarding those who seek wisdom. In the third section (chs. 11–19), God protects the righteous (the holy people Israel) by orchestrating the elements of the world into a new harmony that protects the child of God, the holy people. The exodus plagues are presented as seven comparison in which the elements of the plagues are altered so that they reward the righteous and punish the wicked.

> *For creation, serving you who made it,*
> *exerts itself to punish the unrighteous,*
> *and in kindness relaxes on behalf of those who trust in you.* (16,24)
> *For the elements changed places with one another,*
> *as on a harp the notes vary the nature of the rhythm,*
> *while each note remains the same.* (19,18)

Obviously, Proverbs is not the only source for the idea. The arming of the κόσμος adapts Isa 59,17-19, and the enduring world seems to be derived from Middle Platonism. But the conviction that the world protects the righteous and punishes the wicked is found already in Proverbs, where the world is self-righting. The conviction is a logical conclusion of God's creating the world through wisdom.

> *Yahweh by wisdom founded the earth,*
> *established the heavens by understanding.* (3,18)

Hence, the universe works for the righteous and against the wicked.

Innumerable proverbs states the κόσμος is active, rewarding and punishing people.

> *Righteousness protects the one whose way is right,*
> *but wickedness overturns the sinner.* (13,6)
> *Poverty and disgrace come to one letting go of discipline,*
> *but who holds on to correction will be honored.* (13,18)

In conclusion, despite their obvious differences, Wisdom of Solomon drew from the book of Proverbs not only for its outline, pace of presentation, and some sayings, but for several important themes. The adaptation, needless to say, was profoundly original and engaging.

Weston Jesuit School of Theology   Richard J. CLIFFORD, S.J.
Cambridge, MA 02138
USA

A PROPOSITO DI MISERICORDIA:
E' IPOTIZZABILE UN RAPPORTO TRA SAPIENZA E I PROFETI?

La misericordia di Dio, non solo verso Israele ma anche verso i pagani, affiora qua e là nella terza parte del libro della Sapienza, cc. 10–19, nella rilettura delle vicende dell'Esodo, nel confronto continuo tra la sorte di Israele e quella dei suoi nemici.

Pur non essendo un tema principale, si impone proprio per la sua atipicità nell'ambito della riflessione sapienziale, come è stato magistralmente messo in luce dagli studi di p. M. Gilbert, al quale mi è caro offrire queste pagine. Niente pare possibile aggiungere alle sue intuizioni e conclusioni, soltanto partire da esse per un'eventuale acquisizione di altri dati.

L'autore sacro riveste di condiscendente indulgenza la grande potenza egiziana, ponendosi dall'alto dell'onnipotenza divina. Legge la misteriosità delle vie di Dio come pervasa da un sentimento di compassione, radicato sul valore della vita che rende preziosa agli occhi di Dio l'intera creazione: è il suo amore che chiama all'esistenza e dona a tutto ciò che esiste la possibilità di mantenersi in vita. La potenza creatrice si presenta intrisa di amore per ogni realtà esistente a motivo dello spirito di Dio che tutto pervade[1].

I testi più significativi si trovano all'interno del primo dei cosiddetti *sette dittici* sull'Esodo (11,6-14); nella *prima* (11,15–12,27) e *seconda digressione* (13–15) al primo dittico, secondo lo schema suggerito dallo stesso M. Gilbert[2].

Mentre l'interpretazione dell'agire misericordioso di Dio verso il popolo ebraico si fonda sulla teologia della elezione di Israele e dell'alleanza, la misericordia verso i pagani sfocia nelle considerazioni sulla moderazione con cui il Signore li ha puniti quando si sono scontrati con le vicende di Israele[3].

---

1. M. GILBERT, *Les raisons de la modération divine (Sg 11,21-12,2)*, in A. CAQUOT – M. DELCOR (eds.), *Mélanges bibliques et orientaux en l'honneur de M. Henri Cazelles* (AOAT, 212), Neukirchen-Vluyn, 1981, pp. 159-160 e C. LARCHER, *Le livre de la Sagesse ou la Sagesse de Salomon* (EB, n. s. 5), t. III, Paris, 1985, pp. 699-701, presentano in modo completo i dati per una esatta interpretazione di questo πνεῦμα dalle connotazioni culturali greche, ma rigorosamente adattato alle più autentiche tradizioni bibliche.

2. M. GILBERT, *Sagesse de Salomon (ou Livre de la Sagesse)*, in *DBS*, t. XI, Paris, 1986, cc. 58-119.

3. Tale problematica è compiutamente affrontata in M. GILBERT, *Les raisons de la modération divine (Sg 11,21–12,2)* (n. 1), pp. 149-162.

La misericordia si trova al centro dell'unità strutturale della pericope che comprende da 11,16 a 12,1, in un rapporto stretto con i temi dell'onnipotenza divina e del cammino di fede di tutti i peccatori[4]. La riflessione su Dio, che attenua la severità dei castighi connessi alla sua giustizia per spingere alla conversione (11,23), determina anche la riconsiderazione delle misure punitive adoperate con le popolazioni di Canaan (12,2-18), secondo un modo di agire che dovrebbe fungere da esempio per gli stessi Israeliti (12,19-22)[5]. Poi l'attenzione torna nuovamente sugli Egiziani (12,23-27)[6].

Il contesto di questi passi è la rilettura dei fatti dell'Esodo, in una dinamica che ha a che fare con un dato storico e la sua ermeneutica. Le vicende relative all'uscita dall'Egitto e alla conquista sono ritenute le sole adatte a veicolare ed esaurire il senso pieno di tutta quanta la storia di Israele. Così si rivestono di valore *tipico*, ricco della possibilità intrinseca di interpretare anche l'insieme delle altre tappe della vita di questo popolo, alla fine della sua visibilità storica come nazione[7].

E' lecito allora chiedersi se esiste un rapporto, ed eventualmente quale, con altre precedenti teologie della storia nell'Antico Testamento, visto che anche l'autore di Sapienza azzarda, a suo modo, una teologia della storia. Si serve, infatti, di moduli letterari tipici del genere sapienziale, filtrandoli attraverso tecniche rabbiniche, per mettere a punto la sua personale valutazione dell'opera della sapienza, nel dispiegarsi dell'esistenza di Israele.

Non è peregrino né arbitrario operare un confronto con le tradizioni profetiche.Volendo poi rispettare il valore assoluto attribuito all'Esodo, l'indagine può limitarsi a Geremia e al Deutero-Isaia.

Il libro di Geremia più di tutti presenta la storia di Israele secondo un movimento contrario a quello dell'Esodo, intendendola come giudizio e punizione di Dio, annientamento del processo di salvezza e di liberazione partito dall'Egitto e riproposta di schiavitù e oppressione sotto la potenza babilonese[8].

---

4. M. GILBERT, *Ibid.*, pp. 149-162, esp. 150.

5. M. GILBERT, *La conjecture μετριοτητι en Sg 12,22a*, in *Bib* 57 (1976) 550-553; = ID., *On est puni par où l'on pèche (Sg 11,16)*, in A. CAQUOT – S. LÉGASSE – M. TARDIEU (eds.), *Mélanges bibliques et orientaux en l'honneur de M. Mathias Delcor* (AOAT, 215), Neukirchen-Vluyn, 1985, pp. 183-191. Al riguardo è importante anche A. VANHOYE, *Mesure ou démesure en Sag. XII,22?*, in *RSR* 50 (1962) 530-537, la cui ipotesi di lettura viene accettata da Gilbert.

6. M. GILBERT, *La critique des dieux dans le livre de la Sagesse (Sg 13–15)* (AB, 53), Rome, 1973, pp. XVI-XIX.

7. La seconda metà del primo secolo a.C. come data di composizione del libro della Sapienza non pare oggi più posta seriamente in discussione. Per riferimenti sul dibattito in merito rimandiamo a J. VILCHEZ-LINDEZ, *Sabiduría*, Estella, Navarra, 1990, pp. 59-69.

8. Tale prospettiva è presente in B.S. CHILDS, *The Book of Exodus. A Critical,*

Il Deutero-Isaia, al contrario, riprende al positivo la categoria interpretativa dell'Esodo, annunciando il ritorno nella terra promessa secondo le modalità di un nuovo Esodo[9].

Può l'autore di Sapienza, un israelita sicuramente consapevole del proprio patrimonio tradizionale, per quanto in dialogo con la cultura del suo tempo, aver azzerato tali prospettive presentando la propria? Soprattutto, è possibile che venga disattesa completamente, in una lettura tipica della storia di Israele, la catastrofe storica dell'esilio a Babilonia con le sue interpretazioni di stampo profetico?[10]

Forse proprio il tema della misericordia costituisce la possibilità di un raccordo tra le due linee interpretative, diversamente inconciliabili.

I

Alcuni temi richiamano in particolare l'attenzione: il castigo; l'idolatria, la mancata conoscenza di Dio.

1. Il castigo

Il termine παιδεύω è un dato prezioso. Con esso Sap 3,5 mette a confronto la brevità della pena delle prove dei giusti per rapporto all'abbondanza dei loro benefici.

A parte Sap 6, che lo usa in altro modo e contesto, il verbo si trova in Sap 11,9 e 12,22, brani significativi per la lettura della storia del nostro autore, che coincidono con il suo parlare di misericordia.

Sap 11,9 lo adopera in riferimento ad una delle prove del popolo nel deserto: la sete. Il testo intende sottolineare la misericordia di Dio nel provare il suo popolo, contrapponendola alla sua severità precedente nei confronti degli Egiziani. La prima è considerata frutto dell'atteggiamento paterno di Dio verso Israele; la seconda, conseguenza del dispiegarsi del dominio divino universale e della sua giustizia.

Theological Commentary, Philadelphia, 1974, pp. 53-60, ed è stata approfondita da L. ALONSO SCHOEKEL, *Jeremías como anti-Moisés*, in M. CARREZ – J. DORÉ – P. GRELOT (eds.), *De la Tôrah au Messie*. FS H. Cazelles, Paris, 1981, pp. 245-254.

9. Concordiamo al riguardo con l'opinione della maggioranza degli studiosi. Tra i tanti, cf. J. BLENKINSOPP, *La tradition de l'Exode dans le Second Isaïe*, in *Concilium* 20 (1966) 41-48; P.E. BONNARD, *Le Second Isaïe* (EB), Paris, 1972, p. 113. Invece ci pare debole la posizione di H. SIMIAN YOFRE, *Exodo in Deuteroisaías*, in *Bib* 61 (1980) 530-553; = ID., *La teodicea del Deuteroisaías*, in *Bib* 62 (1981) 55-72, che nega la tematica di un nuovo esodo.

10. Nella presentazione dei personaggi significativi di Israele, in Sir 44–49, letti alla luce dell'agire della sapienza nella storia, si trovano qua e là riferimenti ad una realtà che non fu indenne da peccati e colpe.

In Sap 12,22 παιδεύω denota come correzione l'agire di Dio verso il solo Israele. Contro i nemici del popolo il Signore pone in atto altri tipi di castighi e punizioni, anche se con misura e moderazione.

Negli oracoli geremiani il termine indica il castigare gravi deviazioni: l'apostasia da YHWH (cf. 2,19); l'iniquità che pervade la città di Gerusalemme (cf. 6,8); una punizione meritata che pur si auspica misurata nella supplica del profeta (cf. Ger 10,24; 46 gr.(26 ebr.),28); il castigo che riassume in senso complessivo le dure lezioni di YHWH (cf. 38 gr.(31 ebr.),18).

Sia Sapienza che Geremia conoscono allora lo stesso impiego del verbo παιδεύω per parlare dei castighi di Dio come correttivi della condotta iniqua del suo popolo Israele. Per la punizione verso i nemici vengono usati altri verbi.

Si può ipotizzare con buona dose di probabilità che l'autore di Sapienza ha presente Geremia ed ha assimilato da lui[11] questa sfumatura di linguaggio che si serve di παιδεύω soltanto in merito ai castighi di Dio su Israele, di altri termini per esprimere la diversità delle punizioni inflitte ai nemici di Israele[12].

Quasi del tutto assente la radice e i suoi derivati nel Deutero-Isaia[13].

2. *L'idolatria*

Colpisce indubbiamente la foga appassionata con cui l'autore di Sapienza stigmatizza il grande peccato degli Egiziani: l'idolatria. Soprattutto stupisce. Infatti, la più diffusa spiegazione dei profeti per tutte le punizioni-correzioni di Dio al suo popolo è appunto l'idolatria.

Al tempo di Sapienza non era più di certo tale l'atteggiamento di Israele verso il suo Dio. Il crogiuolo dell'esilio aveva purificato dall'idolatria, considerato peccato originario e continuamente riproposto nel tempo, ed aveva aperto ad una nuova comprensione del rapporto di *conoscenza* tra YHWH e il suo popolo[14].

---

11. Anche Os 7,12.15; 10,10 propone lo stesso linguaggio col medesimo significato, ma nell'insieme sembra piuttosto che Sapienza lo tragga dalle pagine geremiane, a loro volta eredi di Osea.

12. Occorre sottolineare che Geremia conosce di più l'uso del sostantivo corrispondente παιδεία e sempre in merito alla incapacità e alla mancata volontà di Israele di accettare e comprendere la lezione che le vicende della sua storia insegnano (cf. Ger 2,30; 5,3; 7,28; 17,23; 37[30],14; 39[32],33; 42[35],13). Anche questa volta il profeta pare debitore a un suo immediato predecessore: Sofonia (cf. 3,2.7), ma l'impiego di Geremia risulta particolare perché si adatta in senso negativo al processo dell'Esodo.

13. L'unica ricorrenza della radice verbale è Is 46,3. Quanto al sostantivo corrispondente παιδεία si trova anche in Is 50,4.5; 53,5. Il significato è sempre ben lontano dal riferimento alla comprensione degli eventi storici, come in Geremia.

14. M. GILBERT, *La critique des dieux* (n. 6), p. 182.

Tuttavia, se si considera la grande polemica contro l'idolatria, che attraversa in modo precipuo Sap 13–15 con un crescendo che si dispiega in tre tempi e che sostiene il successivo approfondimento del *midrash* sull'Esodo[15], è facile osservare che alcune pericopi hanno il loro sostrato proprio in alcuni oracoli profetici, rispettivamente di Geremia e del Deutero-Isaia.

In Geremia l'idolatria è tra i temi centrali, a partire dal capitolo iniziale e in modo continuo per tutto il libro, nelle sue diverse articolazioni e redazioni. Ampie sono le sue sfumature di senso. La grande sezione che abbraccia i capitoli da 1 a 10 ne mostra la varietà: dalla classica idolatria cultuale (cf. Ger 1,16; 2,5-35; 3,1-13; 7,16-20.29-32); a quella politica, che si esplica nel cercare accordi di potere non permessi da Dio (cf. Ger 2,18.36-37); a quella morale, che si attua in una condotta iniqua che non tiene conto delle esigenze della fedeltà all'alleanza nei rapporti fraterni e civili (cf. Ger 5,1-9.25-29; 6,6-7.13-15; 7,1-15.21-28; 9,1-8); a quella più sottile che concerne lo stravolgimento di senso dell'esercizio stesso dell'autorità in Israele (cf. Ger 2,8; 5,30-31; 8,8-9).

Ma nel libro di Geremia si trova anche una pericope dal tenore particolare, Ger 10,1-16, che non differisce molto per forma e contenuto da Sap 13,10-19. In essa l'autore sacro – Geremia?[16] – pare aver dimenticato tutte le accuse precedenti mosse ad Israele e Giuda e si proietta verso i popoli pagani e i loro dèi inutili ed inefficaci ad operare nella storia. Il linguaggio è solenne e ieratico in riferimento a YHWH, derisorio quanto agli idoli e alle genti che li adorano. Implicitamente si afferma che la supremazia di YHWH si manifesterà nello sconvolgimento storico delle nazioni legate a dèi che nulla possono[17].

Di sicuro l'autore di Sapienza conosce questa pagina di Geremia, che ha probabilmente influito anche sulla satira di Is 40,19-20 e Is 44,9-20, per limitarci ai profeti[18]. In ogni caso la polemica di Geremia e del

---

15. M. GILBERT, *La connaissance de Dieu selon le Livre de la Sagessse*, in J. COPPENS (ed.), *La notion biblique de Dieu. Le Dieu de la Bible et le Dieu des philosophes* (BETL, 41), Leuven, 1976, pp. 200-210.

16. L'autenticità geremiana di questa pericope è discussa, ma è fuori dell'interesse di questo studio perché il libro della Sapienza conosce il libro di Geremia nella sua forma redazionale di cui, in ogni caso, Ger10,1-16 fa parte integrante. L. HOLLADAY, *Jeremiah 1* (Hermeneia), Philadelphia, 1986, pp. 324-326, offre una panoramica esaustiva del dibattito in corso sull'argomento.

17. Cf. *Ibid.*, pp. 321-337.

18. Molto valida la disamina compiuta al riguardo da C. LARCHER, *Le livre de la Sagesse* (n. 1), p. 775, che evidenzia il sostrato eminemente biblico della polemica antiidolatrica di Sap 13,10-19 e il suo rapporto con le categorie culturali del mondo greco dell'autore sacro.

Deutero-Isaia ha una motivazione squisitamente teologica: serve a rafforzare la fede nell'onnipotenza e nella sovreminenza della sovranità di YHWH. Si è dunque ben lontani dall'uso cui l'ha piegato il libro della Sapienza.

3. La conoscenza

Non intendiamo riprendere l'argomentare sulla conoscenza di Dio in tutto il libro della Sapienza[19].Queste pagine si interessano alla conoscenza di Dio solo nella misura in cui il tema si riconnette ad una comprensione interna all'agire stesso di Dio, secondo modalità diffuse nella Scrittura. Non a caso questo avviene nella terza sezione del libro, oggetto della presente indagine.

La conoscenza attraverso la storia nel libro della Sapienza

L'idea che gli eventi hanno la capacità di far comprendere la presenza di Dio all'opera, e che testimoniano la sua pedagogia nel cercare di attrarre a sé i popoli peccatori, pervade la riflessione sulla storia che si snoda a partire da Sap 11[20]. In Sap 16,16a, diventa il principio basilare che mette in luce il peccato degli Egiziani e giustifica il dispiegarsi dei prodigi divini, finalizzati pur sempre alla vera conoscenza di Dio e al rendimento di grazie[21]. Il tocco finale di Sap 17,1 sintetizza in breve che l'insieme dei castighi abbattutisi sui nemici di Israele rivela la loro incapacità a comprendere nel suo giusto valore la lezione della storia, causa del loro continuo indurimento del cuore. Solo Israele è stato in grado di penetrare il senso misterioso degli eventi e di percepirvi la grandezza e l'amore gratuito del proprio Dio[22].

E' Sap 15,1-6 che chiarifica il punto di vista dell'autore riguardo l'atteggiamento di Israele e la consapevolezza del particolare legame che lo unisce al Signore. Il brano sembra offrire una sintesi perfetta di tutti i temi di nostro interesse: la pazienza di Dio che si esprime nella sua misericordia; la sua onnipotenza e sovranità cosmica; l'idolatria generale non condivisa dal popolo eletto. Il tutto pare avere la sua radice nell'esperienza della conoscenza di Dio, una conoscenza della sua potenza, che però si riferisce all'esperienza concreta che Israele ne ha fatto nella sua esistenza.

19. Per l'approfondimento di tale problematica cf. M. GILBERT, *La critique des dieux* (n. 6), pp. 1-52; = ID., *La connaissance de Dieu selon le Livre de la Sagesse* (n. 15), pp. 191-200, e la bibliografia ivi contenuta.
20. Cf. in particolare M. GILBERT, *La connaissance de Dieu* (n.15), pp. 208-210.
21. Così P. DUMOULIN, *Entre la manne et l'Eucharistie. Étude de Sg 16,15-17,1a* (AnBib, 132), Roma, 1994, p. 26.
22. Cf. M. GILBERT, *La connaissance de Dieu* (n. 15), pp. 208-209.

E' facile constatare che tali affermazioni riconducono ad una teologia dell'alleanza, sia per il triplice insistere sul rapporto di mutua appartenenza (*nostro Dio – siamo tuoi – ti apparteniamo*, tipico del rinvio alla formula classica di alleanza *Io sono il vostro Dio – voi siete il mio popolo*); sia per gli attributi di *bontà e fedeltà* che indubbiamente rimandano al Dio dell'alleanza; sia ancora per la confessione della magnanimità e della misericordia che ripropongono una delle più belle definizioni di Dio, in Ex 34,6-7[23].

Di più. La perfetta conoscenza che di Dio ha Israele si ricollega anche alla sua accettazione della sovranità divina, che necessita di essere riconosciuta nella fedeltà all'alleanza e alle sue implicazioni concrete, secondo la migliore tradizione sia di Osea che di Geremia. Ma nella pericope in questione tutto ciò ha il sapore della realtà presente, per cui con ragione si deve ritenere che l'autore vanta quella conoscenza piena, preannunciata nell'oracolo geremiano della Nuova Alleanza (cf. Ger 31,31-34), che adesso pare realizzata. A questo rinviano le due espressioni che fanno riferimento al peccato come una eventualità che tuttavia non si realizzerà[24]:

> *Anche se pecchiamo siamo tuoi, conoscendo la tua potenza sovrana,*
> *ma non peccheremo, sapendo che ti apparteniamo* (Sap 15,2).

La conoscenza in Geremia 9,22-23

Il notevole sostrato veterotestamentario, e in particolare geremiano, induce a riflettere non tanto sulla compiutezza dell'oracolo della Nuova Alleanza, che l'autore sembra prediligere come attuato, bensì su una pericope di Geremia anch'essa visibilmente presente nel tessuto tradizionale di Sap 15,1-3.

Si tratta di Ger 9,22-23, che in greco recita così:

> *Così dice il Signore:*
> *Non si vanti il saggio della sua saggezza*
> *e non si vanti il forte della sua forza,*
> *e non si vanti il ricco della sua ricchezza,*
> *ma di questo si vanti chi si vanta,*
> *di comprendere e di sapere (conoscere)*
> *che io sono il Signore che realizza*
> *misericordia e diritto e giustizia sulla terra,*
> *perché in queste cose (o in questi "uomini"?)*
> *è la mia volontà, dice il Signore.*

---

23. M. GILBERT rileva con attenzione i riferimenti veterotestamentari in *La critique des dieux* (n. 6), pp. 174-182. Ugualmente C. LARCHER, *Le livre de la Sagesse* (n. 1), pp. 847-850.

24. M. GILBERT, *La critique des dieux* (n. 6), p. 183.

Tale oracolo profetico, pur con leggere varianti testuali tra ebraico e greco che in questa sede non sono decisive, riflette una espressione specifica del messaggio geremiano e si presenta come una critica della ideologia regale[25]. Saggezza, forza e ricchezza si contrappongono nelle parole del profeta alla conoscenza di Dio. All'ebraico che porta, come complemento oggetto del *conoscere*, un *me* riferito a YHWH, il greco sostituisce un'intera frase che centra l'attenzione sulla sovranità di Dio, arricchita delle caratteristiche tipiche della sua rivelazione nell'alleanza: misericordia, diritto, giustizia[26].

I contatti con Sap 15,1-3 sembrano evidenti, pur con le sottolineature personali dell'autore dovute alle esigenze della sua composizione letteraria. In modo particolare colpisce in entrambi i passi il riferimento alla sovranità di YHWH, alla quale sono rapportate la misericordia e la giustizia[27], come nella precedente pericope di Sapienza.

Si può concludere che l'autore di Sapienza conosce a fondo la profezia di Geremia, che adatta di volta in volta alla propria sensibilità culturale e al proprio contesto, senza tuttavia snaturarla.

Ma sorge spontanea a questo punto una domanda: se conosce e si appropria di questa pagina, deve pur ben conoscere le pagine di tenore differente che l'hanno preceduta. Infatti in Geremia la conoscenza non è mai di carattere intellettuale ma sempre esistenziale e fa sempre riferimento all'attuazione dell'alleanza. Proprio la mancanza di conoscenza di Dio e delle sue vie è ciò che il profeta continuamente rimprovera ai suoi connazionali, servendosi anche di paragoni di stampo sapienziale, tratti dalla sfera del dominio cosmico ed universale di YHWH:

> *Anche la cicogna nel cielo conosce il suo tempo,*
> *la tortora e la rondinella, la gru*
> *osservano i tempi del loro migrare,*
> *ma il mio popolo non conosce gli ordini del Signore* (Ger 8,7).

O ancora:

> *...Poiché i capi del mio popolo non mi hanno conosciuto;*
> *sono figli stolti e non intelligenti;*
> *sono sapienti nell'agire male,*
> *ma non sanno agire bene* (Ger 4,22).

---

25. In tal senso orienta ormai la convincente posizione di W.A. BRUEGGEMANN, *The Epistemological Crisis of Israel's Two Histories (Jer 9:22-23)*, in J.G. GAMMIE (ed.), *Israelite Wisdom, Theological and Literary Essays in Honor of Samuel Terrien*, Missoula, 1978, pp. 85-105.

26. Per un'esauriente impostazione dello studio di questa pericope rinviamo a W.L. HOLLADAY, *Jeremiah 1* (n. 16), pp. 316-318.

27. Concordiamo al riguardo con M. GILBERT, *La critique des dieux* (n. 6), pp. 189-190; = ID., *La connaissance de Dieu* (n. 15), pp. 207-208, e C. LARCHER, *Le livre de la Sagesse* (n. 1), pp. 852-853.

E:

...non conoscono la via del Signore e il diritto di Dio (Ger 5,4.5),
riferito ugualmente ai piccoli e ai potenti tra il popolo di Israele.

In Geremia il contrasto è stridente sia con la sapienza iscritta
nell'ordine naturale dell'universo, sia con una sapienza connessa alla
comprensione autentica del rapporto con il Signore.

In sintesi, Geremia, come già si evinceva per il peccato di idolatria,
rimprovera ad Israele esattamente quanto l'autore di Sapienza rimprovera ai nemici di Israele.

Ma proprio su un nuovo tipo di conoscenza è basata la promessa di
un'alleanza nuova, in Ger 31,31-34, resa possibile dal dono di un cuore
nuovo. Poiché l'Israele del post-esilio testimonia a più riprese il suo
nuovo orientamento verso Dio, non stupiscono le affermazioni di Sap
15,1-3[28].

II

Se la fiducia nella realizzazione della Nuova Alleanza può costituire
una solida base per comprendere la virata dell'autore di Sapienza
riguardo alla fedeltà di Israele e alla sua capacità di comprendere la
storia, rimane sempre un grosso interrogativo circa il diverso atteggiamento misericordioso di Dio verso Israele e i pagani.

1. Le tradizioni dell'Esodo

Infatti, nelle tradizioni antiche sull'esodo, il deserto e la conquista nel
Pentateuco, non emergono riflessioni su una eventuale misericordia di
Dio verso i nemici di Israele: anzi, su di essi incombe un linguaggio
duro e minaccioso che si traduce in gesti ed eventi negativi. Se la
tradizione sacerdotale in Ex 14, ed in altri singoli versi qua e là, può
avallare un orientamento vago alla conoscenza del Signore[29], niente del
genere affiora sul tema della misericordia.

---

28. E' quanto ha messo ben in evidenza M. Gilbert, *La critique des dieux* (n. 6), pp.
183-184.

29. Cf. Ex 14,4b.18 che sfocia in 14,25b nella confessione-ammissione degli
Egiziani: *Fuggiamo davanti a Israele perché il Signore combatte per loro contro gli
Egiziani*. In sintesi, anche Gs 4,24; 5,1b possono designare l'atteggiamento dei popoli
cananei. Per una stimolante presentazione di Ex 14 cf. la pregevole opera di J.-L. Ska, *Le
passage de la mer. Étude de la construction, du style et de la symbolique d'Ex 14,1-31*
(AnBib, 109), Roma, 1986. Per i nessi con la tradizione profetica è interessante J.-L. Ska,
La sortie d'Égypte (Ex 7–14) dans le récit sacerdotal (P^S) et la tradition prophétique, in
Bib 60 (1979) 191-215.

Per restare alle tradizioni profetiche, e a Geremia in particolare, se il
cuore di Dio si manifesta sempre disponibile ad attuare il suo amore
verso Israele perdonandolo e riprendendo il rapporto di alleanza, pure un
severo giudizio sovrasta il popolo, in forma uguale e contraria alla
benevolenza abitualmente sperimentata. Così le potenze ostili, l'Assiria
prima e Babilonia poi, hanno il sopravvento rispettivamente sul regno di
Israele e su quello di Giuda. Il Signore consegna ai pagani il suo popolo
come punizione per la rottura della alleanza: conseguenza della idolatria
e della mancata conoscenza. E' un movimento esattamente contrario a
quello dell'Esodo, un *anti-esodo* che parte dalla terra promessa ai padri e
conduce via in un'altra terra, in condizione di schiavitù.

Nessuna differenza tra la punizione di Israele e quella delle nazioni
idolatre, perché di fatto uguale ne è l'atteggiamento di fondo.

Ma la storia di Israele non finisce così. Sia Geremia che Ezechiele, e
soprattutto il Deutero-Isaia, lasciano intravedere un futuro diverso, che
riprende le caratteristiche della vicenda esodiale, stavolta al positivo,
come un *nuovo esodo*[30].

Ancora, sia nei racconti esodiali delle cosiddette *piaghe*, sia nel
passaggio del mare, sia in seguito in tutti gli eventi del deserto e della
conquista, YHWH manifesta un potere che, se è di salvezza storica per
Israele e di punizione concreta per gli Egiziani, è radicato sulla sua
signoria sugli elementi della natura che si piegano ai suoi fini.

Il legame tra salvezza e creazione è forte nelle tradizioni del Pentateuco, ma lo è altrettanto in quelle profetiche. Ger 4,23-26 interpreta la
distruzione di Gerusalemme e la fine del popolo quasi come un ritorno al
caos iniziale, prima della creazione.

Nel Deutero-Isaia la grandezza di Dio creatore è il fondamento stesso
della sua capacità di ridonare al popolo la salvezza[31]. Inoltre, diventa la
motivazione di fondo dell'appello alla conversione rivolto alle stesse
nazioni pagane[32].

L'autore di Sapienza trova dunque nei profeti la chiave di volta per
poter a sua volta assumere l'intero arco delle vicende relative all'Esodo
come *tipo* di ogni tappa della storia del suo popolo.

Deve probabilmente anche a loro la base per una comprensione
diversa della misericordia di Dio a partire dalla creazione, che poi le sue
più sviluppate categorie sapienziali gli consentiranno di maturare e di
presentare in modo nuovo.

---

30. Non entriamo nel merito del dibattito sulla rilettura deuteronomistica, sia del
Deuteronomio che del libro di Geremia o di altri libri, solo ci permettiamo di ricordare
che al riguardo essa è debitrice delle categorie profetiche e in particolare degli oracoli
autentici di Geremia.
31. Cf. Is 40,12-28; 42,1-9; 44,24-28; 45,9-13 etc.
32. Cf. Is 45,20-24; 51,4-6.

2. *Un anello mancante?*

Non è allora azzardato affermare che, meditando sulla storia della sua gente alla luce dei profeti, l'autore di Sapienza giunge a percepire che Dio guida sempre gli eventi del suo popolo con misericordia, anche quando appare come punizione.

Ma nella lettura della storia in Geremia e nel Deutero-Isaia emerge un dato assolutamente nuovo ed inquietante per Israele: il Signore chiama a compiere il suo progetto sul suo popolo alcuni dei più eminenti personaggi stranieri dell'antichità: Nabucodonosor di Babilonia e Ciro di Persia.

Per la prima volta la volontà di YHWH si realizza nell'assoggettare (δουλεύειν) la terra, compreso il piccolo regno di Giuda, al potere di un capo pagano, Nabucodonosor[33].

Quanto a Ciro, in Is 45,1a il Signore gli si rivolge con il titolo incredibile ed inaudito di *mio unto*, τῷ χριστῷ μου, e l'intera pericope 45,1-7 testimonia il particolare favore che YHWH accorda a questo potente pagano che la promessa: *Io camminerò davanti a te* (Is 45,2a) riassume efficacemente.

E' anche vero che, nelle loro redazioni finali, le sole conosciute dall'autore di Sapienza, sia il libro di Geremia (cc. 27-28 gr.[50-51 ebr.])[34] che il libro di Isaia (cc. 13; 14; 21; 46; 47)[35] annunziano la caduta di Babilonia e di Nabucodonosor. Il motivo è lo smisurato orgoglio e l'arroganza che hanno ecceduto lo spirito con cui Dio se ne era servito per i suoi scopi. Il loro rigetto è dunque determinato dal peccato. Come era avvenuto per lo stesso Israele.

IPOTESI CONCLUSIVA

L'analisi compiuta induce a ritenere che l'autore del libro della Sapienza abbia tenuto in gran conto il patrimonio delle tradizioni

---

33. Mentre il TM legge a proposito di Nabucodonosor il titolo *'abdî* "mio servo", la LXX porta la finalità dell'azione con δουλεύειν αὐτῷ. Anche se la discussione è molto vivace tra gli studiosi, la lezione greca sembra da preferire, con W.E. LEMKE, *Nebuchadnezzar, my Servant*, in *CBQ* 28 (1966) 45-50, e J.G. JANZEN, *Studies in the Text of Jeremiah*, Cambridge, 1973, pp. 54-57. Le differenze testuali non sono talmente rilevanti da richiedere una nostra presa di posizione perché entrambe non alterano il procedimento del nostro argomentare.

34. Quanto all'autenticità geremiana di tali capitoli (ebr. 50–51), un'ampia e documentata discussione si trova in W.L. HOLLADAY, *Jeremiah 2* (Hermeneia), Minneapolis, 1989, pp. 401-415.

35. M.A. SWEENEY, *Isaiah 1–39. With an Introduction to Prophetic Literature*, Grand Rapids/Cambridge, 1996, pp. 213-238; 277-283, offre un'illuminante disamina della formazione redazionale del testo sacro di Isaia e dell'effettiva attribuzione a Babilonia di Is 13,2-22; 14,2-23; 21,1-10.

profetiche, in particolare Geremia e per altro verso il Deutero-Isaia, entrambi, anche se in maniera diversa, legati ad una interpretazione della storia di Israele sulla base dell'Esodo.

Molti sono i contatti che consentono di ipotizzare tale sostrato, ma rimane problematica l'apertura alla misericordia, seppure appena accennata, verso i nemici di Israele. Non si tratta di sguardo positivo verso i pagani, che è talvolta presente in qualche oracolo profetico per quanto tardivo, ma di estendere ai nemici di Israele la stessa sovranità dell'unico Dio e portarla fino alle estreme conseguenze, implicandovi appunto la misericordia, che nelle tradizioni profetiche sembra esclusivamente qualificare il rapporto tra YHWH e il suo popolo.

Poiché l'autore del libro della Sapienza attribuisce ai pagani le stesse colpe che i profeti, soprattutto Geremia, rimproverano a Israele, riteniamo che l'ampliarsi della prospettiva della misericordia abbia anche al suo fondamento una attenta meditazione degli oracoli dei profeti e una seria valutazione della storia stessa di Israele.

Se l'esperienza dell'esilio ingenera in Israele la consapevolezza della conversione, di una conoscenza rinnovata e di una alleanza nuova col Signore, se le vicende dell'esodo e della conquista diventano agli occhi dell'autore di Sapienza capaci di esprimere la totalità del senso della storia del suo popolo, è però vero che solo l'intervento degli stranieri come strumenti della giustizia di Dio può avere determinato un profondo ripensamento delle tradizioni esodiali, con l'inserimento del tema della misericordia per tutti: se Dio si è servito di essi è perché anch'essi gli appartengono, pur se in modo diverso da Israele.

Inoltre, Sapienza si manifesta abituata ad una interpretazione *tipica* della storia. Ora, perché non dovrebbe leggere nel suo peccato di idolatria e di mancata conoscenza di Dio la *tipicità* del peccato di tutti gli altri popoli? Solo la tracotanza allontana le nazioni nemiche dal rapporto con il vero Dio. In questo gli Egiziani e i Cananei anticipano gli Assiri, i Babilonesi e tutti i popoli ostili ad Israele. Ma questo, in fondo, era già avvenuto ad Israele stesso.

Se allora Dio regna anche sui pagani, se essi ripropongono le stesse dinamiche di colpevolezza che Israele ben conosce, non infondatamente l'autore di Sapienza può aver percepito all'opera nella storia delle genti una dinamica di misericordia divina non uguale a quella attuata verso Israele, ma analoga. In tal modo avrà compreso la necessità di ampliare verso orizzonti più universalistici il *proprium* di Israele, pur senza sminuirne la singolarità.

Da qui quella nuova rilettura dell'Esodo capace di discernere, dove non esistevano, tracce di misericordia divina nei confronti dei nemici ed aprire timidamente ad una compassione più universale, anche se solo accennata e non compiutamente sviluppata.

Di certo, questo è possibile all'autore di Sapienza per l'apporto di una più articolata teologia sapienziale della creazione ad una formazione squisitamente biblica e per l'assimilazione di categorie culturali del mondo greco, in grado di offrire i mezzi idonei per approfondire il valore della vita. Proprio la vita, dono che proviene sempre dal Creatore, esprime la presenza dello spirito di Dio e determina l'appartenergli per il solo fatto di esistere.

L'amore di Dio per tutte quante le sue creature è, in queste pagine della Sapienza, la gemma più preziosa sull' *unica* pianta dell'Antico Testamento, preludio allo sbocciare della pienezza dell'Amore nel Nuovo Testamento.

Facoltà Teologica di Sicilia   Silvana MANFREDI
Corso Vittorio Emanuele 463
I-90134 Palermo

LA LUZ EN EL LIBRO DE LA SABIDURÍA

Es muy frecuente el uso que el autor del libro de la Sabiduría hace de la naturaleza: la tierra, el mar, el cielo; de los fenómenos que ocurren en la naturaleza, como son los atmosféricos relacionados con el agua: la humedad, las nubes, la niebla, la tormenta o tempestad, la lluvia, el rayo, el trueno, las chispas, el fuego, el hielo, el granizo o pedrisco, la nieve, la escarcha, el rocío; relacionados con el viento: el vendaval, el huracán, la brisa, etc. En este breve estudio nos vamos a detener en el ámbito celeste, a saber, en el fenómeno de la luz, como aparece en el libro de la Sabiduría; de modo secundario tocaremos también el fenómeno de la oscuridad o tinieblas; pero subordinado totalmente al de la luz.

LA LUZ DEL DÍA, DON DE LA NATURALEZA

La luz o claridad por la que vemos los objetos que nos rodean, cercanos o lejanos, es uno de los dones más apreciados de la naturaleza, como pueden serlo el aire, el agua, el calor, la tierra, el alimento, etc. Todos estos son dones elementales y necesarios que nos mantienen en la vida y nos la hacen agradable. El autor del libro de la Sabiduría se vale literariamente del fenómeno natural de la luz como de un valor sobresaliente en sí mismo, pero siempre en un contexto determinado moral o religioso. Antes que él otros autores, profanos y sagrados, hicieron de la luz el mismo uso. El sabio Qohélet opina que es preferible "la luz a las tinieblas" (Qoh 2,13) y que "realmente es dulce la luz y agradable a los ojos ver el sol" (Qoh 11,7)[1].

Sab 17,1–18,4 es el lugar en que el autor desarrolla más ampliamente la antítesis luz-tinieblas. En este momento prestamos atención al primer término de la antítesis, a la luz; más adelante nos fijaremos en el segundo, en las tinieblas. El pasaje se basa fundamentalmente en la descripción que Ex 10,21-23 hace de la plaga de las tinieblas en Egipto. En Ex 10,23 leemos que los egipcios "no se veían unos a otros ni se movieron de su sitio durante tres días, mientras que todos los israelitas

---

1. Ver, además, *Gilgamés*, X: "¡Deja que mis ojos contemplen el sol, a fin de que me sacie de luz!" (ANET, 89b); TEOGNIS 569: una vez muerto, "abandonaré la hermosa luz del sol"; EURÍPIDES: "Pues es agradable contemplar la luz" (*Ifigenia en Aulide*, 1218s).

tenían luz en sus poblados". Esta "luz en sus poblados" es la luz natural
del día, que en Sab 17,20 se la denomina "una luz radiante" y en 18,1
"una luz magnífica", en contraposición a la oscuridad y "noche
agobiante" (Sab 17,21a). La luz del día es causa de alegría y de alivio,
doblemente subrayada por el autor: primero por la disposición al trabajo
diario de los israelitas: "El mundo entero, iluminado por una luz radiante, se entregaba sin trabas a sus tareas" (Sab 17,20); después por la
dificultad natural que entraña la oscuridad o falta de luz, al llegar la
"noche agobiante" sobre los egipcios. La naturaleza vegetal y animal
también despierta a la vida con la nueva luz del amanecer; lo mismo que
el israelita piadoso que madruga "más que el sol para darte gracias y
salir a tu encuentro hacia el nacimiento de la luz del día" (Sab 16,28).
Tan apreciada por el autor de Sab es la luz del sol que es punto de
referencia para ensalzar el valor de la Sabiduría: "Ella es más bella que
el sol y que todas las constelaciones; comparada a la luz es más
brillante" (7,29).

EL SOL Y LAS ESTRELLAS SON FUENTES DE LUZ

En Sab 7,29 el autor de Sab acaba de hablar de la fuente principal de
la luz, es decir, del sol. Según Gén 1,16 "hizo Dios las dos lumbreras
(φωστῆρας) grandes: la lumbrera mayor para regir el día, la lumbrera
menor para regir la noche, y las estrellas (τοὺς ἀστέρας)". De las tres
fuentes de luz de que habla el Génesis: la lumbrera mayor o sol (ἥλιος),
la lumbrera menor o luna (σελήνη) y las estrellas (ἀστέρες), en el libro
de la Sabiduría explícitamente no se habla de la luna, pero sí de las otras
dos.

Del sol, como manantial principal de luz, Sab es un testimonio
magnífico. Seis veces aparece ἥλιος en Sab. En cuatro de ellas se
entiende en su sentido físico más propio, como cuerpo celeste que emite
luz y calor. *Sol* simplemente en 7,29: la Sabiduría "es más bella que el
sol" y en 16,28: "es preciso madrugar más que el sol"; *rayo de sol* en
2,4e y 16,27b. Una vez compara el autor *la columna de fuego* del Exodo
a "un sol inofensivo" (18,3c), que ilumina a los israelitas de noche, pero
no abrasa como el del desierto (cf. Ex 13,21-23). Otra vez se aplica el
fenómeno natural de *la salida del sol* al orden moral: se supone que los
impíos reflexionan sobre su vida en el más allá y constatan tristemente
que "no nos iluminó la luz de la justicia, para nosotros no salía el sol"
(5,6bc).

A las estrellas o constelaciones (ἀστέρες) las considera el autor
cuerpos celestes luminosos, pero fijos y lejanos en el cielo nocturno;

ellas siempre han sido objeto de admiración por su belleza fría y serena. Entre los conocimientos astronómicos de Salomón se cuenta el de "la posición de las estrellas" (7,19b). Estos cuerpos celestes maravillosos llegaron a ser también venerados como seres divinos, según testifica Sab 13,2: "Tuvieron por dioses... a las órbitas astrales (κύκλον ἀστρῶν)", y en contra de la tradición bien arraigada en Israel (cf. Dt 4,19). En sentido metafórico se dice de la Sabiduría que fue para los israelitas "resplandor de astros por la noche" (10,17), identificando a la Sabiduría con "la columna de fuego" (cf.18,3).

EL FUEGO, FUENTE DE LUZ Y DE CALOR

El fuego (πῦρ) es, sin duda, fuente de luz y de calor. En el libro de la Sabiduría predomina el uso literario del fuego, como fuente de calor destructivo. La inmensa fuerza expresiva del fuego devorador es una imagen que los autores sagrados han utilizado frecuentemente, al hablar del rechazo incondicional de Dios a la maldad y la injusticia, y de la eficacia de ese rechazo en la historia y metahistoria de los hombres. Sab 10,6: "Cuando la aniquilación de los impíos, ella puso a salvo al justo [Lot] fugitivo del fuego llovido de la pentápolis", hace referencia al relato de Gén 19,15-29 sobre la destrucción de Sodoma y Gomorra – de sus habitantes y sus campos – por el fuego que Dios envió desde el cielo, imagen plástica y terrible del enojo de Dios por sus maldades.

LOS RAYOS EN LAS TORMENTAS

El autor de Sab trata ampliamente del fuego que se produce espontáneamente en las tormentas, de los rayos. Este fuego puede ser destructivo, benéfico o ambivalente, según los casos. En un pasaje, inequívocamente escatológico de Sab, el autor expone uno de sus temas preferidos: "El universo peleará junto a Dios en contra de los insensatos" (Sab 5,20; cf. v. 17). Como la impiedad de los impíos invade todo el ámbito humano: la creación o cosmos, la lucha contra la maldad es también universal (cf. 5,23), en ella debe intervenir la creación que es buena (cf.1,14; Gén 1) y está de parte de Dios (cf. Rom 8,19-22)[2]. El autor de Sab prosigue en 5,21: "Saldrán certeras ráfagas de rayos y del

---

2. Cf. J. VÍLCHEZ, *Sabiduría*, Estella, 1990, p. 220. El comentario añade: "Esta reflexión del autor sobre la función de la creación o cosmos es un elemento sapiencial nuevo y muy coherente en el libro de la Sabiduría. Se anuncia un tema que será ampliamente desarrollado en la tercera parte (cf. 16,17c.24; 19,6.18-21)".

arco bien tenso de las nubes volarán hacia el blanco". Imaginativamente el autor nos introduce así en el seno de una gran tormenta y se vale de ella metafóricamente para explicarnos la actuación de Dios en medio de la historia, actuación que los autores llaman punitiva. La creación en uno de sus fenómenos más imponentes, la tormenta, aparece como aliada del Señor en el combate cósmico contra sus enemigos; pone al rayo -el fuego de la tormenta- a las órdenes de su Señor, como en las grandes teofanías (cf. Ex 19,16; Sal 18,12-15; 97,3-4). Los negros y densos nubarrones son el gigantesco arco, curvado y tenso de donde son lanzados como dardos los rayos incendiarios (cf. Hab 3,11; Zac 9,14) contra la maldad de la tierra y de sus habitantes.

En Sab 19,13 también son mencionados *los rayos*, aunque no como castigo, sino como precursores de lo que van a sufrir los egipcios en el paso del Mar Rojo: "Y a los pecadores [los egipcios] les sobrevinieron los castigos no sin el previo aviso de violentos rayos (κεραυνοί)". Ex 14,22ss, que narra el paso del Mar Rojo, no hace mención alguna de tormenta con aparato eléctrico; sin embargo, en Sal 77,17-20 leemos: "Te vio el mar, oh Dios, te vio el mar y tembló; las olas se estremecieron, las nubes descargaban sus aguas, retumbaban los nubarrones, tus saetas zigzagueaban; rodaba el estruendo de tu trueno, los relámpagos (ἀστραπαί) deslumbraban el orbe, la tierra retembló estremecida: tú te abriste camino por las aguas, un vado por las aguas caudalosas, y no quedaba rastro de tus huellas"[3].

Sab 16,15-23 forma parte del cuarto díptico, el central, en la tercera parte del libro de la Sabiduría: *Plaga de los elementos atmosféricos – don del cielo, el maná*. En este momento sólo nos interesa subrayar de esta perícopa cuál es la función del fuego. El autor tiene delante el pasaje de Ex 9,18-35 sobre la plaga del granizo. Leemos en el relato del Exodo que "Moisés extendió su bastón hacia el cielo, y el Señor lanzó truenos, granizo y rayos (πῦρ) zigzagueando hacia la tierra... Vino el granizo, con rayos (πῦρ) que se formaban entre el granizo... El granizo hizo destrozos en todo el territorio egipcio: hirió a todo lo que se encontraba en el campo, hombres y animales, destrozó la hierba..." (Ex 9,23-25). Sab 16,16 interpreta el mismo hecho de la siguiente manera: "A los impíos que no querían conocerte, los azotaste con tu brazo vigoroso: los perseguían lluvias insólitas, y pedrisco y tormentas impla-

---

3. Tradiciones semejantes de una gran tormenta al cruzar el Mar Rojo encontramos en FILÓN (cf. *De vita Mosis*, I, 176), FLAVIO JOSEFO (cf. *Antiq.*, II [16,3], 343-344) y Targum Neoph. I a Ex 14,24: "Y era el tiempo de la mañana cuando Yahvé observó con cólera los campamentos de los egipcios y arrojó sobre ellos nafta, fuego, piedras de granizo".

cables, y el fuego los devoró". El relato del Exodo nos habla del fuego que en una tormenta son los rayos. Lo que no nos dice Exodo es que los egipcios fueran destrozados, "devorados" por el fuego de los rayos, si bien se puede deducir de Ex 9,25.

Los fenómenos atmosféricos, especialmente los extraordinarios, son manifestación del poder soberano de Dios.

AMBIVALENCIA DEL FUEGO

En Sab 16,17 se admira el autor de algo extraordinario: "Lo más sorprendente (παραδοξότατον): en el agua, que todo lo apaga, ardía más el fuego". ¿En qué consiste este hecho tan *paradójico*? En que el agua, en vez de apagar el fuego, lo avivaba más; en que la llama o fuego encendido por los egipcios o por la tormenta (los rayos), se mitigaba (Sab 16,18) o superaba su propia virtud (Sab 16,19) contra toda expectativa. La intención del autor de Sab es abiertamente teológica: intenta probar que "el cosmos es paladín de los justos" (Sab 16,17); y para ello se vale de la interpretación teológica de unos hechos extra-ordinarios de Ex 9,18-25, apoyándose en las teorías físicas, vigentes en su tiempo[4]. Tan convencido está el autor de Sab de haber encontrado la clave físico-teológica para explicarse a sí mismo y a sus lectores los sucesos extraordinarios de las plagas de Egipto, que la aplica también a lo ocurrido con el maná en el desierto. El autor funde tiempos diferen-tes – el de Egipto y el del desierto – con un punto de referencia común: *el fuego*. Uno el suscitado por la tormenta (los rayos), descrita en Sab 16,16; otro el fuego común de la cocina en el desierto. Uno y otro tienen efectos diferentes, que el autor interpreta ingeniosamente, aplicando la teoría de la transmutación de los elementos. En el desierto el fuego de la cocina no derretía *la nieve y el hielo*, es decir, el maná[5]: "*Nieve y hielo* aguantaban el fuego sin derretirse" (Sab 16,22; cf. Ex 16,23; Núm 11,8), olvidando así "su propia virtud" (Sab 16,23). Por el contrario, el fuego de la tormenta arde "en medio de la granizada" y centellea "entre chubascos", con el resultado destructivo de "los frutos de los enemigos" (Sab 16,22; cf. 16,16). La voluntad del Señor domina a placer las fuerzas ocultas y los elementos de la naturaleza para dirigir la actividad benéfica (Sab 16,23) o destructora (16,22) del fuego.

4. Acerca de la doctrina sobre los elementos constitutivos de la naturaleza y de sus virtudes, de sus contrastes y armonía, cf. J. VíLCHEZ, *El libro de la Sabiduría y la teoría de la transmutación de los elementos. Miscelánea A. Segovia*, Granada, 1986, pp. 37-49.
5. Ex 16,14 LXX dice del maná que era "como hielo"; Núm 11,7 LXX que tenía "el aspecto del hielo", "del cristal" (cf. Sab 19,21).

VOCABULARIO RELACIONADO CON LA LUZ

Según Sab la luz depende del sol y del fuego, pero existe, además, un rico vocabulario que está relacionado con la luz en su sentido etimológico y metafórico.

La gloria. La fama entre los hombres pertenece al ámbito de la gloria – δόξα – y de la luz. Los que la poseen, personas o cosas, se llaman gloriosos, preclaros, ilustres. El pseudo-Salomón canta a la Sabiduría y confiesa: "gracias a ella tendré gloria (δόξα) entre la muchedumbre" (8,10a), es decir, prestigio, honor, renombre. De José se dice otro tanto: la sabiduría "le concedió gloria perenne" (10,14f), como correspondía al segundo después del rey de Egipto (cf. Gén 41,40-44; Sal 105,21). En la historia de Israel los doce patriarcas gozan de una fama imperecedera; sus nombres son los "nombres ilustres" (δόξαι) por antonomasia (Sab 18,24b). Pero cuando la δόξα adquiere el máximo esplendor es en aquellos pasajes, donde el autor habla de la δόξα divina. Salomón pide la Sabiduría al Señor en estos términos: "Envíala desde el cielo sagrado, mándala desde el trono de tu gloria" (9,10ab). El cielo es sagrado porque se considera la morada de Dios (cf. Dt 26,15; Sal 115,3.16), el trono de Dios: "El cielo es mi trono y la tierra el estrado de mis pies" (Is 61,1). Pero es un trono glorioso, porque lo envuelve la gloria de Dios que está presente. La gloria de Dios en la Escritura se expresa también por medio de la metáfora de la luz (cf. 7,25b), por eso los que participan de su presencia brillan como la luz. En Sab 7,25b la δόξα es estrictamente divina, pues es "la gloria del Omnipotente". De ella se deriva la Sabiduría, como el agua del manantial. Esta Sabiduría participa de los atributos divinos; por eso se le aplica el vocabulario de la luz, como a Dios mismo y a su gloria.

Radiante. "Radiante e inmarcesible es la Sabiduría" (6,12a): los adjetivos realzan la luminosidad y belleza de la Sabiduría. *Radiante* – λαμπρά – y luminosa, como el resplandor de los astros (cf. 17,20), es la Sabiduría, como la luz que ha de brillar sobre Jerusalén: "¡Levántate, brilla, que llega tu luz; la gloria del Señor amanece sobre ti! Mira: las tinieblas cubren la tierra, la oscuridad los pueblos; pero sobre ti amanecerá el Señor, su gloria aparecerá sobre ti; y acudirán los pueblos a tu luz, los reyes al resplandor de tu aurora" (Is 60,1-3). Como la luz también la Sabiduría es imperecedera. En la profecía sobre la Jerusalén futura, escatológica, el tercer Isaías se atreve a hablar de Dios como de su única luz inextinguible con estas palabras: "Ya no será el sol tu luz en el día, ni te alumbrará la claridad de la luna; será el Señor tu luz perpetua, y tu Dios será tu esplendor; tu sol ya no se pondrá ni menguará tu luna, porque el Señor será tu luz perpetua y se habrán cumplido los días de tu luto" (Is 60,19-20)[6].

Reflejo. De la Sabiduría se nos dice en 7,26a que es "reflejo (ἀπαύγασμα) de la luz eterna", destello, reverbero de Dios, luz de luz[7]. Por esto también leemos que "su resplandor (φέγγος) no tiene ocaso" (7,10c), pues participa plenamente de la naturaleza divina.

LAS TINIEBLAS, ANTÍTESIS DE LA LUZ

Sabemos que en Sab 17,1-18,4 el autor trata la antítesis luz-tinieblas a propósito de la plaga de las tinieblas en Egipto, según nos narra Ex 10,21-23. Hasta el presente hemos hablado del primer término de la antítesis, de la luz; digamos ahora una palabra del segundo término de la antítesis, de las tinieblas (τὸ σκότος), para realzar el valor de la Sabiduría por vía del contraste. La experiencia de las tinieblas u oscuridad es una experiencia primaria. La oscuridad o carencia de luz natural para los seres que gozan del sentido de la vista es totalmente negativa.

La noche. La noche (νύξ) es el verdadero reino de las tinieblas, el momento apto para las grandes desgracias (cf. Sab 18,14). La oscuridad de la noche se debe entender primeramente en su más estricto sentido literal; así, de hecho, lo entiende el autor de Ex 10,21-23, que habla de "una oscuridad palpable", de "una densa oscuridad", por causa de la cual "no se veían unos a otros". Por el contrario, "los israelitas tenían luz en sus poblados". El autor de Sab, que reflexiona sobre los datos del Éxodo, parte del sentido físico de las tinieblas, pero con facilidad pasa a un sentido metafórico. A los tres días, convertidos en "una larga noche" (17,2b) por la densa oscuridad que cayó sobre Egipto, el autor de Sab los llama "noche siniestra" (17,5c), "noche impotente" (17,14a), "noche agobiante" (17,21a). Por esto aquella noche, a juicio del autor, se convirtió para los egipcios en un inmenso "calabozo" (17,2b) y "las tinieblas" en las rejas y los lazos que los retenían aprisionados (cf. 18,4b), como si todo Egipto fuera ya anticipadamente el lugar tenebroso

---

6. La metáfora de la luz tendrá éxito en el Nuevo Testamento, y se aplicará también a Dios (cf. 1 Jn 1,5; Ap 21,23 y 22,5).

7. Este último título fue aplicado a Jesucristo en el *Símbolo* de Nicea (DS 125).

o seol, adonde se encaminan los muertos (cf. 17,14.21). La noche adquiere, pues, un trágico valor negativo, que sólo afecta a aquellos que actúan en contra de la voluntad del Señor, al pueblo egipcio que, con el faraón al frente, se opone al plan del Señor para liberar a su pueblo. Para los que están con el Señor o el Señor protege, la noche no es amenaza de nada, sino todo lo contrario (cf. Sab 10,17; 18,6), como lo fue la primera noche de Pascua en que "el Señor hirió de muerte a todos los primogénitos de Egipto" (Ex 12,29), y a su pueblo le dio la salvación. Sab 18,6-9 acumula en una noche – *aquella noche* – recuerdos nostálgicos que acompañarán al pueblo hebreo a lo largo de su atormentada historia, para alivio de sus penas. El autor tiene conciencia de que *aquella noche* fue trascendental para Israel. Desde entonces Israel comienza a ser un pueblo libre, pero consagrado al Señor. La liturgia pascual había hecho de ella el centro de la vida religiosa y cultual[8].

Las tinieblas u oscuridad en sentido figurado simbolizan el estado de ceguera moral de todos los que practican a sabiendas la maldad y la injusticia, representados en el libro de la Sabiduría por los egipcios, que "yacían prisioneros de las tinieblas en el calabozo de una larga noche..., prófugos de la eterna providencia" (17,2; cf. 18,4b). A la imagen del prisionero encerrado en la oscuridad del calabozo se añade la del prisionero encadenado: "a todos amarraba la misma cadena de tinieblas" (17,18a). La conciencia moral acusa y paraliza y se convierte en "noche agobiante, imagen de las tinieblas que iban a acogerlos" definitivamente en el lugar de los muertos (17,21).

LA LUZ EN SENTIDO METAFÓRICO

El uso literario de la luz es frecuente en el libro de la Sabiduría, como lo es en todo el Antiguo Testamento. De la luz del día, como realidad envolvente, se salta con toda normalidad a la luz en el orden intelectual y moral, a la luz en sentido metafórico. En Sab se aplica la metáfora de la luz a dos categorías centrales y ligadas entre sí: a la Sabiduría y a la Ley o Torá.

La Sabiduría es luz. La Sabiduría es luz porque ilumina y guía al que la posee o, mejor, es poseído por ella. Los "insensatos" y necios son aquellos que no tienen nada en común con la Sabiduría. "La Sabiduría

---

8. Los cristianos hemos heredado la tradición judía. La liturgia de la Vigilia Pascual canta las glorias de aquella noche. Ver, en especial, el himno *Exultet* y el Prefacio de la bendición del cirio pascual.

no entra en alma de mala ley ni habita en cuerpo deudor del pecado"
(1,4). Alma y cuerpo designan aquí al hombre que maquina el mal con
malas artes y está privado de su dignidad y libertad por su relación
directa con el pecado; es igual que el hombre pecador con sus dos caras
o facetas, íntimamente relacionadas: la interior y la exterior. Por esto el
insensato – el que no tiene Sabiduría – se sale del camino de la verdad y
no tiene la luz de la justicia (cf. 5,6). Por el contrario, la Sabiduría, al
entrar en las almas buenas, hace de ellas "amigos de Dios y profetas"
(7,27bc). La Sabiduría entra, se comunica, penetra en los justos y los
transforma en amigos de Dios. El que obra el mal no posee la Sabiduría
ni convive con ella; es enemigo de sí mismo y de Dios (cf. Sab 1,3-6).
El que posee la Sabiduría es guiado por ella y puede hablar en su nombre.

La Sabiduría es más que la luz, "pues a la luz del día la releva la
noche, mientras que a la Sabiduría no la puede el mal" (7,30). La
naturaleza y el origen de la Sabiduría son divinos (cf. 7,22ss), por lo que
es impensable que la maldad pueda prevalecer sobre la Sabiduría. Todo
ser humano necesita de la Sabiduría, por esto los educadores, pedagogos
y maestros de todos los tiempos han recomendado a sus discípulos la
búsqueda de la Sabiduría. Salomón, el sabio arquetipo de los libros
sapienciales del Antiguo Testamento y protagonista escondido en el
libro de la Sabiduría, tiene plena conciencia de ello y confiesa en primera persona: "La quise [a la Sabiduría] más que a la salud y la belleza
y me propuse tenerla por luz" (7,10ab), como guía suprema e interna. La
luminosidad de la Sabiduría no es como la del sol o las estrellas; es
interior al hombre, y pertenece al orden moral y divino: "Su resplandor
no tiene ocaso" (7,10c), pues participa de la fuente originaria del bien y
de la luz que es Dios mismo (cf. Is 60,19-20), del que es "reflejo",
"espejo nítido", "e imagen de su bondad" (Sab 7,26).

La Ley es luz. Los gobernantes tienen motivos para pedirla al Señor,
como hace Salomón: "Dame la Sabiduría que comparte tu trono" (9,4a),
"envíala..., mándala desde tu trono glorioso, para que esté a mi lado y
trabaje conmigo, enseñándome lo que te agrada" (9,10). La manifestación de la voluntad de Dios la tenemos plasmada en su Ley o Torá,
que en Sab es llamada también luz. El autor, dialogando con el Señor,
habla de "la luz incorruptible de tu ley" (18,4c). Según la venerable
tradición del antiguo y del nuevo Israel la Ley fue dada por Dios al
pueblo elegido por medio de Moisés en el Sinaí (cf. Ex 19,3–34,8; Jn
1,17; Gál 3,19). Esta Ley del Señor es *luz* (cf. Sal 19,9; 119,105; Bar
4,1-2), no sólo para Israel, sino para todas las naciones (cf. Is 2,3; 51,4;

Miq 4,2). "Los cristianos creemos que el cumplimiento perfecto de este sueño universalista se ha realizado con la venida de nuestro Señor Jesucristo. El es ya el único mediador entre Dios y los hombres (cf. 1 Tim 2,5; Heb 8,6; 9,15; 12,24). El vino "no para destruir la ley, sino para dar cumplimiento" (Mt 5,17). Del siervo del Señor se dijo que sería "luz de las naciones" (Is 49,6), y de Jesús se dice que es "luz para iluminación de los gentiles" (Lc 2,32). Jesús, en efecto, es la luz del mundo (cf. Jn 1,4.9; 3,19; 8,12; 9,5; 12,46). Su doctrina es la nueva ley de la nueva economía de salvación (cf. Mt 5,21.27-28.33.34.38-39.43.44); esta doctrina se transmitirá de generación en generación por medio de sus discípulos, que son luz del mundo (cf. Mt 5,14)"[9].

Facultad de Teología   José VÍLCHEZ S.J.
Apdo. 2002
E-18080 Granada

---

9. J. VÍLCHEZ, *Sabiduría*, p. 440.

UNIVERSALISM AND JUSTICE
IN THE WISDOM OF SOLOMON

A religious world-view based on a theology of creation tends to be universalistic in its basic orientation. This can be explained by the simple fact that images of creation are in themselves universalistic, that is, open to the view and scrutiny of all. Ever since it was noticed that the Sapiential Literature of Israel is prone to a universalistic stance, the corollary idea of its creation based theology has been noted as well[1]. The wisdom literature of Israel is built on a theology of creation. The Lord is the creator of the universe; therefore the universe matters and speaks of God. The structures of the created world and the myriad experiences of human beings constitute a locus for discovering the word of God. There is still always room in this religious world-view for a particular or unique revelation and encounter between Israel and God. But, often enough, God is understood to employ the ordinary structures of the universe and the various movements of the human heart to speak a divine word.

Notice how the key personage of the book of Job is not even described as an Israelite, but rather as a wise man of the East. When God finally speaks to Job through the whirlwind, it is more to direct Job's attention to the universe itself rather than to God's covenants or to Israel's salvation history. The figure of personified wisdom in Proverbs who is present at the creation of the world shares her knowledge with all who care to listen in the open market place. Similarly, the terse ruminations of Qoheleth rely more on practical and common sense reflections, available to everyone with an open mind, rather than on authoritative statements of belief. The Song of Songs expresses an exuberance for life through various songs of love between lovers without ever even mentioning the God of Israel. Sirach, though admittedly with a more con-

---

1. Very early on in his scholarly work, Walther ZIMMERLI noticed the creational and universalistic stances of Israel's Sapiential tradition, *The Place and Limit of the Wisdom in the Framework of the Old Testament Theology*, in *ScotJT* 17 (1964) 146-158. Inspired by Zimmerli's observation of the importance of creation in Wisdom theology, Leo Perdue goes so far as to speak of creation's centrality in wisdom. "I would go a step further by suggesting that creation is truly at the"center "of wisdom theology, meaning that creation integrates all other dimensions of God-talk as well as anthropology, community, ethics, epistemology (both reason and revelation), and society" (Leo G. PERDUE, *Wisdom & Creation: The Theology of Wisdom Literature*, Nashville, Abingdon, 1994, p. 35).

servative view, accepts the essential thrust of creation theology through the genre of the teaching of a father to his son and through the personification of Wisdom present at creation[2]. Finally, the Wisdom of Solomon bases the benevolent and just spirit of God in history to be rooted in the very beginning of creation, when God made all things by his word, and formed human beings through wisdom (Wis 9,1-2).

This brings me to the problem of the spirit of universalism and the particular expressions of Israelite faith in the Wisdom of Solomon. Though the Wisdom of Solomon continues the universalistic thrust of Israelite Wisdom Literature, in the third part of the book, namely the midrashic treatment of the exodus (Wis 11–19), we discern a strong tendency to defend and to highlight the particular aspects of God's salvific deeds toward Israel in history. This is an interesting problem that requires some explanation. How do the spirit of universalism and the particular tenants of Israelite faith stand side by side in the text without devouring one another?

Recently, in the presidential address at the Catholic Biblical Association General Meeting, John Collins spoke of the inherent tension between natural theology and divine revelation that the Wisdom of Solomon exhibits[3]. His contention is that although much of the religious view exemplified in the book is consistent with a "natural theology," under social oppression, the author falls back upon the unique revelation between God and Israel. God has entered into the turmoil of Israelite history to defend the righteous against their enemies. The midrashic treatment of the exodus in the third part of the book embodies this inherent tension between "natural theology" and "divine revelation"[4].

My question is more specific than the problematic issue of the relationship of natural theology and divine revelation. Does the author of the Wisdom of Solomon betray the universalistic spirit that abounds in the

2. A.A. DI LELLA, *Conservative and Progressive Theology: Sirach and Wisdom*, in *CBQ* 28 (1966) 139-154, also in J.L. CRENSHAW (ed.), *Studies in Ancient Israelite Wisdom*, New York, Ktav, 1976, pp. 401-416.

3. John J. COLLINS, *Natural Theology and Biblical Tradition: The Case of Hellenistic Judaism*, in *CBQ* 60 (1998) 1-15. The address itself and a discussion with Professor Collins regarding the "difficulty" for many students to harmonize pluralistic and universalistic values in the third part of the Book of Wisdom, inspired the focus of this particular paper. For an earlier treatment of the issue of natural theology, see *The Biblical Precedent for Natural Theology*, in *JAAR* 45/1 Supp. B (1977) 35-67.

4. The tension between natural theology and divine revelation is already present in Solomon's prayer for wisdom. Although Solomon describes himself as being naturally endowed with insight (Wis 8,21), he recognizes that wisdom is a unique gift given by God. Similarly, though wisdom is described throughout the eulogic sections as permeating the entire universe (e.g. Wis 7,27-30), at the moment of prayer, wisdom resides in the holy heavens by the throne of God (Wis 9,10).

first two parts of the book and is equally present in sections of the third? Is universalism sacrificed in the face of polemics arising from a need for defense against the oppression of the Jewish community in the diaspora, such as the persecutions in Alexandria under Roman rule[5]? It is one thing to have a generous and universalistic spirit in times of strength. It is quite another to maintain a universalistic spirit of openness in times of oppression or weakness. My contention is that, in the final part of the book, the spirit of universalism is expressed through an adherence to the value of justice. In times of oppression or weakness, the author applies the universal category of justice to defend the faithful in their need. Even in polemics, the author does not abandon the spirit of universalism but maintains a defense for the faithful by recalling the unexpected strength of justice. The midrashic treatment of the exodus is viewed essentially from the lens of justice.

The Spirit of Universalism

The universalistic spirit of the work is present in all three major parts of the book[6]. In the first part (Wis 1-6), it is God's relationship to the cosmos that guarantees the positive and optimistic spirit associated with a theology of creation. All the forces of creation are described as wholesome,

> For he created all things so that they might exist;
> the generative forces of the world are wholesome,
> and there is no destructive poison in them,
> and the dominion of Hades is not on earth (Wis 1,14).

The author is clearly attacking a gnostic dualism that would attribute to the forces of creation themselves a sinister and evil power. For the author of Wisdom, such a power exists not in the forces of the created world but rather in the concrete choices of human beings (cf. Wis 1,12,16; 2,21-24). The realm of the human will is the forum where

5. See how John Collins addresses the problem of universalism and particularism arising from the Wisdom of Solomon (John J. COLLINS, *Jewish Wisdom in the Hellenistic Age*, Louisville, KY, Westminster John Knox Press, 1997, pp. 218-221). The author's intentions were indeed universalistic. But under pressure stemming from persecution and relying on traditional theology, the author draws firm lines between the holy people and the enemies.

6. For a study on the presence of a creational perspective in all three parts of the work see M. KOLARCIK, *Creation and Salvation in the Book of Wisdom*, in R.J. CLIFFORD – J.J. COLLINS (eds.), *Creation in the Biblical Traditions* (CBQMS, 24), Washington, DC, The Catholic Biblical Association of America, 1992, pp. 97-107; also W. VOGELS, *The God Who Creates Is the God Who Saves: The Book of Wisdom's Reversal of the Biblical Pattern*, in *EeT*, 22 (1991) 315-335.

choices are made for virtue which brings eternal life or for injustice which brings death. This fundamental assertion at the beginning of the work characterizes the essential ethical thrust of the entire book.

Interestingly, it is the cosmos itself which comes to the aid of those who practice a life of virtue and spurn a life of injustice. This nuanced understanding of the cosmos is a rather novel idea in the biblical world. It exemplifies the positive, universalistic spirit of a theology of creation for which the Wisdom of Solomon is such a good example. Though the idea is novel, it is quite consistent with the positive portrayal of creation in Genesis 1, and God's lordship over the universe in the prophetic works, primarily Isaiah. Borrowing the metaphor of the hoplite to convey divine attributes from Isa 59,17-19, the Wisdom author transforms it radically by attributing to the cosmos a prime role in divine judgment (Wis 5,17-23). The forces of creation are bound up with God's royal task to exercise divine judgment and to restore justice. God is said to arm creation as a defense for the virtuous against the perpetrators of injustice. It is precisely this quasi-philosophical principle that will govern the midrashic treatment of the exodus events in the third part of the book.

In the second part of the book (Wis 6,22–10,21), the spirit of universalism is conveyed primarily through the open discourse of the unnamed figure of Solomon and the description of personified wisdom. Solomon shares his insights on wisdom very much like the figure of wisdom in Prov 8. Personified wisdom teaches her insights publicly and without deceit, on the heights, beside the way, at the crossroads, beside the gates and at the entrance of the portals (Prov 8,2-3). Solomon likewise dispenses his insights regarding wisdom unreservedly (cf. Wis 7,13).

> *I will tell you what wisdom is and how she came to be,*
> *and I will hide no secrets from you,*
> *but I will trace her course from the beginning of creation,*
> *and make knowledge of her clear,*
> *and I will not pass by the truth;*
> *nor will I travel in the company of sickly envy,*
> *for envy does not associate with wisdom* (Wis 6,22-23).

Solomon claims to have received the wisdom of God not because of elitism or privileged status. On the contrary, Solomon emphasizes his commonality with all human beings in his pursuit of wisdom.

> *And when I was born, I began to breathe the common air,*
> *and fell upon the kindred earth;*
> *my first sound was a cry, as is true of all.*

I was nursed with care in swaddling cloths.
For no king has had a different beginning of existence;
there is for all one entrance into life, and one way out (Wis 7,3-4).

The wisdom that comes from God is open to all who desire it. The only condition for the reception of wisdom is freedom from deceit and envy (Wis 1,4; 6,23). The wisdom of God is inimical to injustice.

Personified wisdom which is praised throughout the second part of the book is described as pervading the entire universe. The author joins together the sapiential description of personified wisdom from Proverbs and Sirach to the descriptions of the goddess Isis who was particularly popular in Alexandria[7]. Similarly, the Stoic presentations of *pneuma* and *logos* are especially evident in the eulegic praise of wisdom (Wis 6,22–8,1). The use of source material from Greek philosophy and even from the diffused Isis cult of Ptolemaic Egypt do not occasion polemics in the book's portrayal of wisdom, but rather point to a cultural openness not unlike that of Philo. The author makes allusions to current philosophical explanations and religious ideas in order to "make the figure of Wisdom intelligible by depicting it in terms that were familiar and well respected in the Hellenistic world"[8].

Because the wisdom of God was present at the creation of the world, she provides a mediating role between people and God (Wis 9,9). She makes human beings "friends of God and prophets" (Wis 7,27). Wisdom is an effective mediator because she was present at the creation of the cosmos and she has intimate knowledge of God (Wis 9,1,9). An illustration of wisdom's salvific role for righteous human beings is drawn up in Wisdom 10 from a number of the main personages of Genesis (Adam, Noah, Abraham, Lot, Jacob, Joseph and finally Israel with Moses). Wisdom has come to the aid of all because of their righteousness (except in the case of the first-formed father of the world, who is delivered from his transgression, Wis 10,1). On the other hand, the wicked

7. For a thorough study of the borrowing from the cult of Isis to the description of personified wisdom in Wis 6–9 see J.S. KLOPPENBORG, *Isis and Sophia in the Book of Wisdom*, in *HThR* 75 (1982) 57-84.

8. John J. COLLINS, *Jewish Wisdom in the Hellenistic Age*, Louisville, KY, Westminster John Knox, 1997, p. 204. Collins rightly points out that many of the attributes of wisdom described in the book are general enough to point to both an Israelite and Greek origin. Three clusters of images in the book do in fact point to a borrowing from the descriptions of Isis: a) the feminine identity of wisdom which abides both with God and Solomon corresponds to the identity of Isis as the wife of the god Osiris and also as the spouse of the reigning king; b) the motif of kingship that runs through the book including that of Solomon is consistent with the role of Isis as nurse and counselor of the king; c) wisdom's particular role as savior, rather unique in Israel's sapiential literature, echoes the saving role of Isis (pp. 203-204).

have no success. It is interesting to note the dominance of wisdom's salvific role extended to the righteous. It is not wisdom who punishes the wicked in the contrasts. Only in the case of Joseph does wisdom take an active role regarding the wicked, but even here it is simply to reveal their false accusations against Joseph. The emphasis is clearly on wisdom standing by the righteous to protect them and bring them to prosperity. In the midrashic treatment of the exodus which follows the illustrations, it is God who employs the forces of the cosmos in an active role both to save the just and to counter the wicked.

The active role of God to save the just and to punish the wicked by means of the cosmos permeates the third part of the book. But before we turn to the polemic nature of this section, it will be helpful to note the universalistic passages that the author took pains to insert even within a heavily polemic text.

With regards to injustice, God is described as showing mercy to all for the sake of their conversion. In a concluding reflection to the first plague which explains why the plagues against Egypt were progressive in nature and not one single show of strength, God's universal mercy is extolled.

> *For it is always in your power to show great strength,*
> *and who can withstand the might of your arm...*
> *But you are merciful to all, for you can do all things,*
> *and you overlook people's sins so that they may repent* (Wis 11,21,23; cf.
> 12,1-2).

The universal care that God extends over the entire created world is reasserted in continuity with the first part of the Book of Wisdom (Wis 1,14).

> *For you love all things that exist, and detest none of the things that you*
> *have made...*
> *You spare all things, for they are yours, O Lord, you who love the living.*
> *For your immortal spirit is in all things* (Wis 11,24,26;12,1).
>
> *For neither is there any god besides you, whose care is for all people*
> *(things)...* (Wis 12,13)
>
> *You are righteous and you rule all things righteously,*
> *deeming it alien to your power to condemn anyone who does*
> *does not deserve to be punished.*
> *For your strength is the source of righteousness,*
> *and your sovereignty over all causes you to spare all* (Wis 12,15-16).

The author even draws a lesson for the righteous from the way God is seen to deal with the enemies of Israel. Just as God is kind, in that even those who are unjust are given the possibility of conversion and repentance, so too are the righteous to exercise this sort of kindness. When the righteous are in a position to exercise judgment, they should remember the goodness of God.

> *Through such works you have taught your people*
> *that the righteous must be kind (φιλάνθρωπον),*
> *and you have filled your children with good hope,*
> *because you give repentance for sins* (Wis 12,19)
> *... so that when we judge, we may meditate upon your goodness,*
> *and when we are judged we may expect mercy* (Wis 12,22).

POLEMICS IN THE THIRD PART OF THE BOOK OF WISDOM

These expressions of a universalistic and open spirit in the third part of the book are consistent with expressions in the first and second parts. However, another spirit emerges even more forcefully because of the polemical nature of the midrashic exposition of the exodus events. The author offers a lengthy critique of the Egyptians and adds a polemic against idolatry which includes Greeks, Canaanites and Egyptians (Wis 13–15). Moreover, the universalistic spirit of the work appears to waver under the weight of the identity of Israel as the righteous and the enemies as the wicked. Are there restrictions that the author places on the polemic, or must we admit that the spirit in the work has turned into an unbridled nationalism?

As can be expected in a reflection on the exodus events, it is the Egyptians who are most severely critiqued, then come the Canaanites (Wis 12,3-11; 13,10-19) and then only to some degree the Greeks (Wis 13,1-9)[9]. As has been the case throughout the book, proper names of persons or peoples are not identified. Yet from the illustrations used from Exodus and Numbers and within the polemic against idolatry we can identify with relative ease the Israelites as the just, and the Egyptians, the Canaanites and even the Greeks as oppressors and false worshippers.

The types of phrases that manifest a markedly antagonistic stance can be grouped into two groups: a) phrases where the enemy of Israel is poignantly condemned, b) phrases where God is presented as showing greater favour to Israel than to her enemies. Although it is true that in each context the author mitigates the criticism somewhat through an ex-

---

9. This progression of critique from those of the least guilty, namely the Greeks, to the Canaanites and then finally to the Egyptians is especially noticeable in the very literary structure of the polemic against idolatry; see Maurice GILBERT, *La critique des dieux dans le livre de la Sagesse* (AnBib, 53), Rome, Pontifical Biblical Institute, 1973, p. 254.

planation that God gave people opportunities to repent, the declarative condemnation is very striking.

DECLARATIVE CONDEMNATION

The author is unflinching in condemning the social practises of the Canaanites, especially that of child sacrifice.

> *Those who lived long ago in your holy land*
> *you hated for their detestable practices...* (Wis 12,3-4).

> *... you were not unaware that their origin was evil*
> *and their wickedness inborn, and that their way of thinking*
> *would never change.*
> *For they were an accursed race from the beginning*
> *and it was not through fear of anyone that you left*
> *them unpunished for their sins* (Wis 12,10-11).

For the manner in which they lead people astray to worship false gods, even the idols themselves are severely condemned (Wis 14,8-11). The idol makers receive particular disdain.

> *Their heart is ashes, their hope is cheaper than dirt,*
> *and their lives are of less worth than clay...* (Wis 15,10).

The author appears to be at a total loss to explain the origins of animal worship and as a result condemns most severely both the animals and their worshippers.

> *But most foolish, and more miserable than an infant,*
> *are all the enemies who oppressed your people...*
> *Moreover, they worship even the most hateful animals,*
> *which are worse than all others*
> *when judged by their lack of intelligence;*
> *and even as animals they are not so beautiful in appearance*
> *that one would desire them,*
> *but they have escaped both the praise of God and his blessing* (Wis 15,14-19).

COMPARATIVE CONDEMNATION

What appears even more perplexing from the point of view of the author's universalistic spirit are the several comparative condemnations of Israel's enemies. The author recognizes that Israel also receives the stern judgment of God, but not so harshly as the enemies.

> *For you tested them (the righteous) as a parent does in warning,*
> *but you examined the ungodly as a stern king does in condemnation*
> (Wis 11,10).

So while chastening us you scourge our enemies ten thousand times more
so that, when we judge, we may meditate upon your goodness, and when
we are judged, we may expect mercy (Wis 12,22).

For even if we sin we are yours, knowing your power;
but we will not sin, because we know that you acknowledge us as yours
(Wis 15,2).

I believe it is fair to say that the author has been carried away by the
rhetoric of polemics to state the condemnation of Israel's enemies in the
harshest manner possible. This leads to contradictory assertions. God
loves all things that exist (Wis 11,23-26). Yet, certain animals have es-
caped the blessing and praise of God. Idols made of elements from
God's created world are condemned. Certain people are considered an
accursed race from the beginning[10]. However, the context of the
midrashic treatment of the exodus and the context of the entire book provide a perspective on justice that does not allow the universalistic spirit
of the work to be undermined.

THE PRINCIPLE OF JUSTICE

The over-arching principle that governs the author's rhetoric in the
midrashic treatment of the exodus is that of justice (δικαιοσύνη). The
notion of justice does not refer simply to social justice, but rather to justice in the three primordial relationships of human beings: to God, to
others and with regards to self. God protects the righteous in their need
and punishes the unrighteous through the cosmos itself[11]. The plagues
against Egypt and the polemics against false worship are continuously
guided by the principle of justice.

---

10. A similar contradiction appears in the author's argumentation in the first part of
the book. The text clearly states that the wicked bring on their own destruction through
their words and deeds (Wis 1,16). Yet, in the diptych contrasting the childlessness of the
just and the 'prolific brood of the ungodly', it appears on the surface that the children suffer the condemnation due to the parents (Wis 4,1-6). In this case, however, the prolific
brood of the ungodly is a metaphor for the unjust profits the ungodly have acquired
through their injustice. As if they were their own children, the fruit of their labours, these
very profits will accuse them to their face in the day of reckoning. See, M. KOLARCIK, *The
Ambiguity of Death in the Book of Wisdom (1–6), A Study of Literary Structure and Interpretation* (AnBib, 127), Rome, Pontifical Biblical Institute, 1991, pp. 88-94.

11. It is interesting to notice in the commentary normally attributed to Bonaventure in
the XIIIth century, how the theme of justice was the key for interpreting the first section of
Wisdom. Justice remains critical for interpreting the third part as well (*Commentarius in
librum Sapientiae*, in *Opera Omnia* 1-10, circa 1270, ed. QUARACCHI, 1893, pp. 139-171),
see M. KOLARCIK, *Ambiguity*, pp. 3-4. After considerable neglect of this theme for understanding the Book of Wisdom, B. Celada reintroduces justice as a key principle for following the Wisdom author's argumentation (B. CELADA, *El libro de la Sabiduría,
recuperado para la causa de la justicia*, in *CuBíbl* 37 [1980] 43-55).

There are two principles stated by the author that give shape to the midrashic treatment of the exodus (Wis 11–19). Both principles are derived from a perspective of justice. The first principle explains how the unrighteous receive punishment according to the manner in which they sinned (Wis 11,16, cf. 3,10). The second principle illustrates how creation itself uses the same means of the cosmos to thwart injustice and to help the just (Wis 11,5,13).

The plagues against Egypt are not seen simply as a show of might against injustice, but are understood as having their own internal logic. The very root of injustice brings forth its eventual fruit. Deeds of injustice come to haunt their perpetrators at a later time.

THE FIVE DIPTYCHS

1) The Pharaoh ordered the Hebrew males to be thrown into the Nile; the Nile becomes polluted as if by blood (Wis 11,6-14).
2) The Egyptians worshipped animals; animals come to consume their livelihood (Wis 11,15–16,14).
3) The Egyptians failed to recognize God of the heavens; the heavens shower down disaster in the form of hail, lightening and storms (Wis 16,15-29).
4) The Egyptians enslaved the Hebrews; they become enslaved by frightening darkness (Wis 17,1–18,4).
5) The male children of the Hebrews were killed by decree; the first born in Egypt are slain (Wis 18,5-19,21).

This attempt to interpret the plagues as the eventual results of Egypt's injustice toward the Hebrews is rather unique in the biblical tradition[12].

It is interesting to note as well the two references that the author makes to the righteous being punished by God through the plague of serpents and the experience of death in the desert (Wis 16,5-14; 18,20-25). Though one could say that the interpretation of the author favours the comparative preference of Israel, the issue of justice remains the guiding principle in the argumentation. Since the author illustrated the plagues as an expression of Egypt's injustice, the same can be said for the plagues which struck Israel as well.

Injustice wherever it occurs, among the enemies of Israel or among the Israelites themselves, is met with the resistance of God. The author

---

12. A reference to the same idea in an extra biblical source can be seen in *The Twelve Patriarchs*, "For by whatever capacity anyone transgresses, by that also is he chastised" (*The Twelve Patriarchs, Gad, the ninth son*, 5,10).

feels compelled to explain how the righteous also experienced suffering and death in their roaming through the desert. The two episodes of punishment the author refers to are taken from Num 21,6-9 (the brazen serpent) and Num 16,1-50 (the rebellion of Korah). In both cases the people received an affliction of death due to their rebellion against God. Through the intercession of Moses in the first case and through the priestly action of Aaron in the second case, the plagues did not destroy them to the end. The author recalls these incidents to point to the strength of their intercessors who act as a sign of their conversion from rebellion. But the overall point is clear even within this polemic against Israel's oppressors. Injustice carries with it the seeds of its own destruction whether among other nations or among the chosen people. In light of these two references to death which strikes the righteous as well for injustice, the author is not simply fostering a pro-Israelite stance that could be envisaged apart from the exigencies of justice itself. Even within a text which is polemic against Israel's enemies, the righteous are subtly reminded that the integrity of their own lives lies under the scrutiny of God and creation. Justice applies to the holy people who stand under God's special favour as well as to the enemies of Israel.

With respect to the wicked, the plagues are understood as the result of their own injustice and folly. From the perspective of God, the plagues are a final attempt elicit conversion and to restore justice. Despite the instances of strong rhetoric against Israel's traditional enemies, the plagues are placed in a context of God's desire for conversion and even mercy. Two of the clearest expositions of God's desire for repentance occur at the beginning of the illustration of the plagues.

> *For you are merciful to all, for you can do all things,*
> *and you overlook people's sins, so that they may repent* (Wis 11,23).

> *For your immortal spirit is in all things.*
> *Therefore you correct little by little those who trespass,*
> *and you remind and warn them of the things through which they sin,*
> *so that they may be freed from wickedness and put their trust in you,*
> *O Lord* (Wis 12,1-2; cf. 12,8-10,19,26; 15,1; 16,6,11,18; 19,4,13).

The other principle of interpretation also guides the illustration of the plagues episodes through the function of the cosmos. By the very means by which the unjust meet resistance, do the righteous experience salvation.

> *For through the very things by which their enemies were punished,*
> *they themselves received benefit in their need* (Wis 11,5).

The cosmos itself plays a key role in resisting injustice and promoting the just. It is not difficult to see how the plague narratives of the exodus provided rich soil indeed to the author for exploring God's use of creation itself to thwart injustice.

THE SEVEN ANTITHESES FOR THE UNRIGHTEOUS AND THE JUST

1) the water of the Nile is non drinkable — water in the desert, Wis 11,6-14
2) animals suppress the appetite — delicious animals in the desert, Wis 16,1-4
3) animals kill — the brazen serpent saves, Wis 16,5-14
4) rain, hail, fire destroy, lack of food — manna resists burning by fire, Wis 16,15-29
5) captivity by darkness — pillar of fire in darkness, Wis 17,1–18,4
6) death of the firstborn — a blameless one stops the destroyer, Wis 18,5-25
7) drowning in the sea — the righteous pass through the sea, Wis 19,1-9

In this way, through two principles of interpretation, the author places the entire illustration of plagues against Egypt into an over-all perspective of justice: justice both for the unrighteous and for the just.

The context of the entire book also provides an explanation as to why the author uses the principle of justice to interpret the events of the exodus. The first section of the book attempts to assert the strength of justice and the weakness of injustice despite all appearances to the contrary. The book opens with an exhortation 'to love justice'. But the apparent strength of injustice is portrayed through the very reasoning of the wicked (Wis 2). The wicked set forth their program of unbridled luxury, oppression of all who are weak and finally the death of the just one who opposes them. With the death of the just the wicked rest their case. In three diptychs, the author dismantles the arguments of the wicked. The author champions the case of the just one who has been unjustly killed, the case of the just who have no outward signs of their labours and the case of the premature death of a just youth (Wis 3–4). The author is likely speaking for a persecuted Jewish community of Alexandria under Roman rule. All three categories refer to a community under siege. The author rests the argument on behalf of the just on the day of judgment when the just are vindicated through God's royal decree.

To live a life of justice even under difficult circumstances where there seems to be no immediate or outward benefit is more fitting than a life of injustice. But what basis does the author have to support such a day of judgment? Precisely in the midrashic treatment of the exodus, the author envisages a concrete example of God's vindication of the just and the re-dressing of injustice. The author tries to uphold the strength of justice despite all appearances to the contrary, and similarly the utter weakness of injustice despite all the advantages that a way of injustice seems to offer. To confirm this strategy, the author refers to the foundational story of Israel's existence. In the past, a small righteous group, despite all odds, won the favour of God and the cosmos itself. On the contrary, the powerful, with all the advantages at their disposal, suffered calamity as a result of their injustice. This theme of justice is one that a persecuted community or group can easily identify with. Adhering unswervingly to justice is a theme of a universalistic community in persecution. When the perspective of justice remains a value under which all live, one's enemies and one's own group, then the tendency to particularism is bound by the restriction of justice itself.

It is clear that the author is speaking for a community persecuted and under siege. It is equally clear that the author could have recoiled from universalistic language and embraced unbridled nationalism. But this is not the case. The author maintains a universalistic spirit sympathetic to what is eminently reasonable in Hellenism. At the same time, the book challenges all forms of injustice, primarily the injustice inflicted on the Jewish community, but equally all forms of injustice. The spirit of universalism which is inspired by creation theology, maintains itself through a respect for justice in times of persecution. Not simply a justice for one's enemy, but a justice for all. Justice is a value that is inherent in the entire universe. According to the reasoning of the entire book, it is the universe itself that in the long run resists those who perpetrate injustice and comes to the aid of those who practice a life of justice. The opening words of the book find their echo all through the midrashic treatment of the exodus, "Love righteousness, you rulers of the earth…".

Regis College   Michael KOLARCIK, S.J.
Toronto

LA THÉMATIQUE ESCHATOLOGIQUE
DANS LE LIVRE DE LA SAGESSE
EN RELATION AVEC L'APOCALYPTIQUE

Dans cette étude, nous ne tenterons pas de définir l'apocalyptique. En effet, des définitions multiples ont déjà été proposées, à partir de points de vue divers, sans qu'aucune n'apparaisse comme satisfaisante[1]. À l'exception de quelques auteurs comme P. Sacchi, on s'accorde cependant pour reconnaître comme «apocalyptique» un type de littérature biblique et extrabiblique (ou intertestamentaire) présentant quelques caractéristiques communes.

1. Ces œuvres proposent une conception particulière de l'*histoire*, qu'elles embrassent d'un seul coup d'œil. Elles regardent le passé à partir du présent; s'appuyant sur l'exactitude manifeste des faits «annoncés», elles peuvent ensuite décrire le futur proche, avec la «visite» (*pāqad*) eschatologique de Dieu, le Jugement du monde et l'instauration d'un nouvel αἰών. Une réalité inédite adviendra, à la fois d'ordre cosmique et socio-institutionnel. Dans ce monde nouveau ou nouvel «Éden», toutes les institutions d'Israël seront renouvelées: la Royauté davidique, le Temple, l'Alliance, le Sacerdoce (Is 65,17; 66; Jr 31,31-34; Ez 36,25-27.35; 37,24-28). Ces textes ne disent jamais clairement si la nouvelle réalité sera terrestre ou céleste, s'il faut ou non la comprendre comme l'irruption définitive de la transcendance divine dans le domaine humain. Des thèmes comme celui du Fils de l'homme (Daniel, 1 Hénoch), celui du Temple eschatologique (Ez 40–48; Qumran, spéc. les nombreux fragments sur la «nouvelle Jérusalem»), ou encore celui de la destinée finale des justes et des méchants (1 Hénoch), balancent entre réalité terrestre et réalité céleste, entre l'établissement d'un Royaume sur la terre ou dans le ciel (Isaïe et Qumran). Selon la meilleure vraisemblance, cette oscillation reflète une diversité d'opinions, mais aussi la

---

1. Parmi les aperçus les plus récents, voir J.J. COLLINS *et al.* (eds.), *Mysteries and Revelations: Apocalyptic Studies since the Uppsala Colloquium*, Sheffield, JSOT Press, 1991; F.J. MURPHY, *Apocalypses and Apocalypticism: The State of the Question*, in *CR:BS* 2 (1994) 147-179; R. PENNA (éd.), *Apocalittica e origini cristiane*, in *Ricerche Storico-Bibliche* 7/2 (1995) 5-18; D.S. RUSSELL, *Prophecy and Apocalyptic dream: Protest and Promise*, Peabody, Hendricksen, 1994; P. SACCHI, *L'apocalittica giudaica e la sua storia*, Brescia, Paideia, 1990, spéc. pp. 323-361; R.E. STURM, *Defining the Word «Apocalyptic»: A Problem in Biblical Criticism*, in M. L. SOARDS (ed.), *Apocalyptic and the New Testament*. FS J.L. Martyn, Sheffield, JSOT Press, 1989, pp. 17-48.

gestation graduelle d'une pensée qui se précise au fil du temps. L'histoire du thème du Fils de l'homme est significative à cet égard.

2. La littérature apocalyptique se distingue ensuite par la modalité de
la communication entre Dieu et l'homme: Dieu communique avec l'être
humain par *révélation*. Il ouvre le ciel, se manifeste à un personnage
important du passé (Abraham, les douze Patriarches, Hénoch, Moïse,
Esdras; voir aussi la rédaction finale de Ez 1) et il lui révèle ses projets,
depuis la fondation du monde jusqu'à la fin des temps.

3. Le troisième élément qui caractérise l'apocalyptique est son *imaginaire*, lui-même lié à un *style littéraire* particulier. Elle utilise un réper-
toire exubérant de figures et de couleurs par lesquelles elle révèle – d'une
manière encore voilée – le sens progressif de l'histoire, jusqu'à la pleine
manifestation du plan de Dieu (*'ēṣāh*; μυστῆριον) caché jusqu'alors.

Ces éléments sont rassemblés dans plusieurs livres écrits au cours des
derniers siècles avant notre ère et aux deux premiers siècles de notre ère.
Il faut ajouter que le mot «apocalyptique» ne désigne pas seulement un
ensemble littéraire, mais aussi un système de pensée caractéristique
d'une époque (*Zeitgeist*). À partir du VIᵉ siècle av. J.-C., l'attente d'un
profond renouvellement national et institutionnel marquait le peuple juif.
Cette espérance a inspiré les sages de l'école deutéronomiste, avec leur
vision cyclique de l'histoire, ainsi que les cercles sacerdotaux, avec leur
perspective d'une restauration totale et radicale. Elle a inspiré tout autant
le deutéronomisme de type prophétique et le prophétisme eschatologique, mais aussi certains cercles sapientiaux, qui ont développé des spéculations sur la Sagesse, médiatrice entre Dieu, d'une part, et la création
et l'histoire, de l'autre.

Ces considérations préliminaires vont à présent nous permettre de préciser la nature apocalyptique de l'eschatologie du livre de la Sagesse et
le stade d'évolution auquel elle est arrivée[2].

I. L'ESCHATOLOGIE DU LIVRE DE LA SAGESSE

Sg 1–6

La thématique eschatologique du livre est développée d'une façon
particulière dans les six premiers chapitres[3], qui forment la première sec-

---

2. Cette thématique n'est pas entièrement neuve. Voir déjà M. CONTI, *Sapienza*,
Roma, Edizioni Paoline, 1981, p. 16; J. FICHTNER, *Die Stellung der Sapientia Salomonis
in der Literatur und Geistesgeschichte ihrer Zeit*, in ZNW 36 (1937) pp. 113-132; P. GRE-
LOT, *L'eschatologie de la Sagesse et les apocalypses juives*, in À *la rencontre de Dieu.
Mémorial A. Gelin*, Le Puy, Mappus, 1961, pp. 165-178.

3. M. CONTI, *Sapienza*, pp. 51-108; M. GILBERT, art. *Sagesse de Salomon*, in DBS,

tion de l'ouvrage. Sa délimitation fait l'objet d'un large consensus. Elle est déterminée par la discussion serrée de l'auteur sur le thème du destin final des justes et des impies, dans l'au-delà. La structure de la section se présente ainsi:

- 1,1-12.13-16: introduction; les derniers versets forment une transition vers l'argument suivant.
- Chap. 2: discours des impies, qui nient l'existence d'un au-delà de la mort (vv. 1-9) et persécutent le juste (vv. 10-20); jugement du discours des impies (vv. 21-24).
- Chap. 3–4: suite de diptyques qui opposent le juste et l'impie.
- Chap. 5: la confrontation finale des justes et des impies, récompense pour les uns et condamnation pour les autres.
- 6,1-21: texte en inclusion avec Sg 1, où l'auteur exhorte pour la deuxième fois ceux qui gouvernent la terre (6,1, cf. 1,1) à tenir en grande estime la Sagesse. Il prépare ainsi le thème de la deuxième section (6,22–8,21; chap. 9).

L'allure eschatologique du texte ressort clairement de sa structure concentrique, telle que le P. Gilbert[4] l'a proposée:

A *Exhortation*:
  - Dieu se révèle, la Sagesse se cache; rechercher– enquête judiciaire
B *Projet des impies*:
  - introduction: création, immortalité, jugement de l'auteur
  - discours: – sens de la vie, mode de vie
             – attaque contre le juste
  - conclusion: jugement de l'auteur, création incorruptibilité
C *Dyptiques*:
  mort des justes – impies
  vertueux sans enfants – enfants d'adultères (bis)
  mort prématurée du juste – impies
B' *Bilan des impies*:
  - introduction: juste – impies
  - discours: – triomphe du juste
             – mode de vie, sens de la vie

t. XI, Paris, 1991, col. 65-69.94; C. LARCHER, *Études sur le livre de la Sagesse* (EB), Paris, Gabalda, 1969, pp. 301-327; ID., *Le livre de la Sagesse ou la Sagesse de Salomon* (EB), t. I, Paris, Gabalda, 1983, p. 163. Larcher, qui limite la première partie du livre aux chap. 1–5, écrit: «Dans cette section qui prolonge différents thèmes eschatologiques de l'Ancien Testament dans un contexte apocalyptique et les transpose sur un plan transcendant, la condition humaine est éclairée par la révélation des secrets desseins de Dieu»; cf. R.J. MILLER, *Immortality and Religious Identity in Wisdom 2–5*, in E.A. CASTELLI et H. TAUSSIG (eds.), *Reimagining Christians Origins*. FS B.L. Mack, Valley Forge, PA, Trinity, 1996, pp. 199-213; A. SCHMITT, *Zur dramatischen Form von Weisheit 1,1–6,21*, in *BZ* n.s. 37 (1993) pp. 236-258; W. WERNER, *«Denn Gerechtigkeit ist unsterblich».* *Schöpfung, Tod und Unvergänglichkeit nach Weish 1,11-15 und 2,21-24*, in G. HENTSCHEL et E. ZENGER (eds.), *Lehrerin der Gerechtigkeit. Studien zum Buch der Weisheit*, Leipzig, Benno, 1991, pp. 26-61.
    4. M. GILBERT, art. *Sagesse* (n. 3), col. 70.

> – conclusion:
>> impies – justes
>> Dieu et le combat cosmique final
> A' *Exhortation*:
>> – enquête judiciaire
>> – la Sagesse se révèle: la rechercher; incorruptibilité

Sg 6,22–9,18

À première vue, cette section n'a aucune portée eschatologique directe. Des indices intéressants en ce sens peuvent cependant être relevés, dès les premières lignes du texte.

Le sujet anonyme de l'introduction (6,22-25) – est-ce déjà Salomon, qui parle certainement à partir de 7,1? – énonce son programme en des termes significatifs. Il veut dire la nature et l'origine de la Sagesse (τί δέ ἐστιν σοφία καὶ πῶς ἐγένετο, v. 22a), et «lever le secret», c'est-à-dire révéler ses μυστήρια (v. 22b). Ces mystères sont en relation avec le projet que Dieu mène depuis le début de la création et jusqu'à l'époque actuelle. Ils concernent aussi la nature et l'origine de la Sagesse elle-même, qui impliquent – le découvrirons – sa transcendance, sa préexistence et sa visée eschatologique.

Après cette introduction, Salomon traite son sujet en sept points. Encore une fois, pour M. Gilbert[5], ceux-ci sont disposés d'une manière concentrique:

A	7,1-6	l'origine de Salomon est semblable à celle de tous les hommes
B	7,7-12	il a prié pour obtenir la Sagesse
C	7,13-22a	la communication d'un savoir de Dieu à Salomon
D	7,22b–8,1	éloge de la Sagesse
C'	8,2-9	Salomon veut épouser la Sagesse
B'	8,10-16	conséquences de cette union
A'	8,17-21	Salomon se décide à prier pour la Sagesse

Le chap. 9, enfin, contient la grande prière de Salomon: tout ce qui précède prépare, semble-t-il, cette prière royale. Salomon prie le Dieu des pères et lui demande la Sagesse avec laquelle il a agi dans la création (vv. 1-3) et dans l'histoire (vv. 8-9). Ce texte annonce déjà la thématique de la troisième section. Quoi qu'il en soit, ce qui importe pour nous dans cette deuxième section, c'est est la présentation de la Sagesse comme une personne qui habite avec Dieu dans le ciel (cf. 9,4: δός μοι τὴν τῶν σῶν θρόνων πάρεδρον σοφίαν) et qui, en même temps, peut habiter sur la terre. C'est cette médiation entre le ciel et la terre, entre Dieu et

---

5. M. GILBERT, art. *Sagesse* (n. 3), col. 69-70.

l'homme, qui permet de regarder au-delà de la situation présente, et donc d'envisager les *eschata,* la destinée ultime de toute chose.

Sg 10 et 11–19

À notre avis, et bien que cette proposition ne fasse pas l'unanimité, Sg 10 fait partie de la troisième section. On peut considérer ce chapitre, soit comme une introduction à ce qui suit, soit comme le début du développement historique des chap. 11–19[6].

Le chap. 10 propose un résumé historique à la manière de Si 44–49 et de 1 M 2,49-60. Il montre la Sagesse[7] à l'œuvre dans l'histoire, et plus précisément depuis l'époque des Patriarches (vv. 1-14) jusqu'à l'Exode et son acteur principal, Moïse (vv. 15-21). Le même événement de l'Exode est ensuite développé aux chap. 11–19. Certes, le chap. 10 raconte l'action de la Sagesse, alors que les chapitres suivants mettent Dieu en scène. Il faut cependant considérer la troisième section du livre comme unifiée par la thématique de l'action de Dieu en faveur de son peuple, qu'il œuvre directement ou par la médiation de sa Sagesse. Les analogies avec Si 44–49 et de 1 M 2,49-60, relevées ci-dessus, témoignent en faveur de cette compréhension du texte. Le panorama historique est, par ailleurs, une forme littéraire répandue dans la littérature apocryphe ou extra-biblique contemporaine de la Sagesse de Salomon (Jubilés, Testament des Douze Patriarches, etc.), comme on le verra plus loin.

Le long développement des chap. 11–19 est considéré par nombre d'auteurs comme un *midrash,* c'est-à-dire un commentaire édifiant de l'Exode. Il n'est pas la simple répétition du récit: on y reconnaîtra plutôt une réflexion théologique sur la manière dont Dieu traite les justes (les Hébreux) et les impies (les Égyptiens)[8]. Cela correspond au sujet de la première section: la destinée des uns et des autres. Certes, le récit de l'Exode propose un regard sur le passé, et donc sur une réalité inscrite dans l'espace et le temps. Cependant tant la structure du récit de la Sagesse (une série de sept ou de cinq diptyques)[9] que la symbolique employée – l'eau et le feu (16,15-29), les ténèbres et la lumière (chap. 17),

---

6. H. ENGEL, «*Was Weisheit ist und wie sie entstand, will ich verkünden*». *Weish 7,22–8,1 innerhalb des* ἐγκώμιον τῆς σοφίας *(6,22–11,1) als Stärkung der Plausibilität des Judentums angesichts hellenistischer Philosophie und Religiosität,* in G. HENTSCHEL, *Lehrerin,* pp. 67-102; E. HAAG, *"Die Weisheit ist nur eine und vermag doch alles". Weisheit und Heilsgeschichte nach Weish 11–12, ibid.,* pp. 103-155; C. LARCHER, *Le livre de la Sagesse,* t. I (n. 3), pp. 120-123.

7. Remarquons la répétition du pronom αὕτη aux vv. 1.5.6.10.13.15.

8. Cf. 10,20: «Aussi les *justes* dépouillèrent-ils les *impies*», ainsi que 16,16-17.

9. M. GILBERT, art. *Sagesse* (n. 3), col. 72-73; C. LARCHER, *Le livre de la Sagesse,* t. I (n. 3), p. 121.

la Parole toute-puissante de Dieu (ὁ παντοδύναμος σου λόγος, 18,14, évoquant 9,4) qui descend du trône céleste – impliquent une connotation métahistorique. Le traitement différencié des justes et des impies de l'Exode devient ainsi l'archétype du sort final des uns et des autres, comme l'a dit la première section du livre[10].

II. Le caractère apocalyptique de l'eschatologie du livre de la Sagesse

Ce qui précède nous permet à présent d'affirmer la dimension apocalyptique du livre de la Sagesse, de montrer comment elle contribue à l'unité foncière de l'ouvrage, et enfin d'établir de quel stade historique et conceptuel l'imaginaire apocalyptique de celui-ci témoigne.

Rappelons, tout d'abord, que l'apocalyptique, entendue comme *Zeitgeist*[11] qui s'exprime dans des écrits, résulte de l'interaction de trois composantes de la culture et de la littérature juives[12]: le sens de l'histoire, lié à une conception cyclique du temps (écrits Dtr et P), le prophétisme, qui annonce le Jugement d'Israël et de toutes les nations, et enfin la sagesse. Cette dernière met l'histoire et le prophétisme en relation avec la connaissance. Plus précisément, elle envisage, avec les deux autres composantes, une connaissance quasi ésotérique du dessein secret de Dieu, qui doit se réaliser dans l'histoire, avec le concours de la création entière. Il s'agit donc de connaître l'«âme» de l'histoire, des mystères naturels de la création et de mystères surnaturels que Dieu révèle à son élu ou à ses élus.

Précisément, la première section du livre de la Sagesse (1,1–6,21) révèle la destinée effective des hommes, tant celle des justes que celle des impies. Quant au sens ultime de la vie et au scandale de l'injustice qui semble frapper tant d'hommes, cette révélation dépasse l'amer et mélancolique constat de Qohélet: «Je regarde encore toute l'oppression qui se fait sous le soleil: voici les pleurs des victimes, et elles n'ont pas de consolateur… Alors, je félicite les morts qui sont déjà morts plutôt que les vivants qui sont encore vivants» (Qo 4,1-2). De même, elle va au-delà de la réponse de foi de Job, qui déclarait: «Je ne te connaissais que par ouï-dire, mais maintenant mes yeux t'ont vu» (Jb 42,5).

---

10. Cf. 16,13: «Oui, c'est toi qui commandes à la vie et à la mort, qui fais descendre aux portes de l'Hadès et en fais remonter». Voir P. Beauchamp, *Sagesse de Salomon: de l'argumentation médicale à la résurrection*, in J. Trublet (éd.), *La Sagesse biblique*, Paris, Cerf, 1995, pp. 175-186.

11. Cf. J. Fichtner, *Die Stellung* (n. 2).

12. Cf. H. Engel, *«Was Weisheit ist»* (n. 6), p. 85; M. Nobile, *Introduzione all'Antico Testamento. Introduzione alla letteratura veterotestamentaria*, Bologna, Edizioni Dehoniane, 1995, pp. 123-124.

Dès les premières phrases du livre, la Sagesse interpelle les puissants de la terre, à la manière des grands prophètes israélites. Elle les invite à aimer la Justice: non seulement quelques décisions de justice dans la vie ordinaire, mais la Justice tout court, qui est l'égale de la Sagesse (1,1.4), don de Dieu qui se révèle (1,2). Cette Justice identifiée à la Sagesse est révélation divine, et c'est à sa lumière qu'il est possible de connaître le sort des justes et les impies, par-delà les apparences.

Une telle idée appartient en propre à l'apocalyptique. Comme plusieurs auteurs l'ont observé, elle imprègne des textes comme le premier livre d'Hénoch, et en particulier le «Livre des Paraboles» (1 Hén 37–71)[13]. Les trois «paraboles» de l'ouvrage ont en commun l'annonce du Jugement divin. La première annonce l'événement; la deuxième envisage le sort des pécheurs; quant à la troisième, elle parle de béatitude promise aux élus. L'importance de cette œuvre ne peut être minimisée. Ni son insertion postérieure dans le cycle d'Hénoch, ni la figure du «fils d'homme» (1 Hén 46; 48) ne prouvent que ce texte est d'origine chrétienne[14]. Comme l'ont montré P. Sacchi, S. Chialà et d'autres, le Livre des Paraboles est une œuvre juive, probablement essénienne, composée à la fin du Ier siècle avant J.-C. ou dans les premières années du siècle suivant. L'écrit est donc à peu près contemporain du livre de la Sagesse. Il n'est pas étonnant que la communauté chrétienne ait pu le remanier ensuite: les motifs qui y sont développés appartiennent à l'imaginaire religieux de tout le judaïsme, auquel le mouvement chrétien se rattache. En tout cas, le Livre des Paraboles garde son caractère juif. Ce n'est pas par hasard que Sg 4,10-14 le cite en évoquant la figure du patriarche Hénoch: «Il a su plaire à Dieu, qui l'a aimé, et, comme il vivait parmi des pécheurs, il a été emporté. Il a été enlevé, de peur que la malice n'altérât son intelligence ou que la perfidie n'égarât son âme; car la fascination du mal obscurcit le bien et le tourbillon de la convoitise gâte une âme ingénue. Devenu parfait en peu de temps, il a fourni une longue carrière. Son âme était agréable au Seigneur, aussi l'a-t-il retirée en hâte d'un milieu dépravé».

La deuxième section du livre de la Sagesse (6,22–9,18) présente, elle aussi, un grand intérêt dans le cadre de notre recherche.

---

13. Pour cette relation et pour celles qui suivront avec d'autres livres apocryphes et qumraniens, cf. LARCHER, *Études* (n. 3), pp. 103-132; cf. aussi S. CHIALÀ, *Libro delle Parabole di Enoc*, Brescia, Paideia, 1997.

14. Comme l'affirme J.T. MILIK, *The Books of Enoch. Aramaic Fragments of Qumran Cave 4*, Oxford 1976; pour toutes ces questions, voir S. CHIALÀ, *Libro delle Parabole* (n. 13), pp. 22-82, avec sa bibliographie récente, ainsi que P. SACCHI, *Introduzione del curatore [à Hénoch éthiopien]*, in P. SACCHI (ed.), *Apocrifi dell'Antico Testamento*, Milano, Tea, 1990, pp. 42-44.

La figure de Salomon, dont le rôle est central dans cette section, fait le lien entre la première et la troisième parties du livre. Il est roi, à l'égal des interlocuteurs auxquels l'auteur s'était adressé dans la première section (6,1-11, qui fait inclusion avec 1,1-5), mais il est un roi déjà reconnu comme juste et sage. Bien mieux, c'est «le roi» par excellence, l'archétype de ceux dont parle 6,9-21: «C'est donc à vous, souverains, que je m'adresse, pour vous apprendre la sagesse et vous empêcher de tomber; car ceux qui gardent saintement les choses saintes seront reconnus saints, et ceux qui s'en laissent instruire y trouveront leur défense. Ainsi, désirez-les, mes paroles; aspirez après elles: elles vous instruiront».

La royauté de Salomon ne peut se réduire à l'ordre politique: elle s'exerce avant tout sur le plan moral. Salomon est le roi par excellence, parce qu'il appartient au groupe des justes, auxquels la Sagesse annonce: «Ils recevront de la main du Seigneur la couronne royale de la gloire et le diadème de beauté» (τὸ βασίλειον τῆς εὐπρεπείας καὶ τὸ διάδημα τοῦ κάλλους ἐκ χειρὸς κυρίου, 5,16).

Le caractère central du personnage de Salomon est lié à la dimension proprement apocalyptique du livre. Salomon a l'autorité[15] des grands héros du passé comme Hénoch, les douze Patriarches, Moïse et Daniel. En d'autres termes, il est un élu de Dieu, qui lui révèle sa Sagesse, avec ce qu'elle comporte: le plan caché de Dieu depuis la création du monde et son déroulement dans l'histoire. Tout cela s'inscrit dans la ligne de Pr 8 et Si 24, qui font parler la Sagesse personnifiée[16]; en ce qui concerne la révélation que Dieu octroie à quelques personnages célèbres du passé, voir encore le premier livre d'Hénoch, mais aussi le Testament des Douze Patriarches, les Jubilés, l'Assomption de Moïse, l'Apocalypse de Baruch et 4 Esdras. Le caractère grec de la Sagesse dont parle Salomon (7,22–8,1) ne contredit pas la présence d'un imaginaire juif, à la fois dans la structure et dans le vocabulaire de l'ouvrage. Celui-ci s'inscrit dans le contexte de l'hellénisme, qui mélange d'une manière extraordinaire la culture grecque et les cultures sémitiques.

De toute manière, Salomon s'exprime à la première personne, à la manière des grands personnages de la littérature apocalyptique (Daniel, Hénoch, Esdras, Baruch, etc.). Par la grâce de Dieu et la médiation de sa

---

15. D. DIMANT, *Pseudonymity in the Wisdom of Solomon*, in N. FERNÁNDEZ MARCOS (ed.), *La Septuaginta en la investigación contemporánea* (V Congreso de la IOCS), Madrid, 1985, pp. 243-255.

16. C. LARCHER, *Études* (n. 3), pp. 329-349.398-414, et aussi J.M. HADLEY, *Wisdom and the Goddess*, in J. DAY et al. (eds.), *Wisdom in Ancient Israel*, Cambridge, Cambridge University Press, 1995, pp. 234-243 (réponse critique à l'hypothèse de la déesse préexilique proposée par B. LANG, *Wisdom and the Book of Proverbs: An Israelite Goddess Redefined*, New York, 1986).

Sagesse, il dispose d'une connaissance portant sur toutes les réalités possibles, qu'elles soient naturelles ou surnaturelles, cachées ou manifestes, scientifiques ou morales:

> Que Dieu m'accorde d'en parler à son gré et d'émettre des pensées dignes de ses dons, puisqu'il est lui-même le guide de la Sagesse et qu'il dirige les sages; nous sommes en effet dans sa main, nous et nos discours, et toute notre intelligence et toute notre habileté. C'est lui qui m'a donné la science vraie de ce qui est (αὐτὸς γάρ μοι ἔδωκεν τῶν ὄντων γνῶσιν ἀψευδῆ), qui m'a fait connaître la structure du monde et les propriétés des éléments... Tout ce qui est caché, tout ce qui se voit, je l'ai appris, car c'est l'Ouvrier de toutes choses qui m'a instruit, la Sagesse (ὅσα τέ ἐστιν κρυπτὰ καὶ ἐμφανῆ ἔγνων ἡ γὰρ πάντων τεχνῖτις ἐδίδαξέν με σοφία) (7,15-21).

On considère souvent que la troisième section du livre (chap. 10–19) s'ouvre après la prière du roi Salomon (chap. 9), et nous avons marqué plus haut notre accord avec cette proposition. Il convient à présent d'éclairer cette articulation du texte.

Le long discours de la troisième section est-il prononcé par l'auteur du livre, comme on le pense généralement?[17]. Nous ne le croyons pas. 10,1 marque le début d'une nouvelle section, qui a pour objet l'action de la Sagesse (chap. 10) et de Dieu (chap. 11–19) dans l'histoire d'Israël. L'auteur y exprime-t-il sa réflexion personnelle? Il nous semble plutôt que 10–19 forme la suite cohérente du discours de Salomon sur la Sagesse. Dans la seconde partie du livre, le roi sage a décrit la Sagesse en elle-même; à présent, dans la troisième partie, il dit son action comme Esprit (cf. 9,17) ou puissance divine dans l'histoire, d'Adam à Moïse et à l'Exode. Le texte donne un indice simple et surprenant en faveur de cette lecture: le locuteur des chap. 10–19 continue à s'adresser à Dieu à la seconde personne (11,4.8.10.20-22.23, etc.), comme la prière du chap. 9[18].

En d'autres termes, l'auteur qui développe le discours des chap. 10–19 est aussi celui du livre dans son ensemble, mais il a revêtu le personnage fictif de Salomon[19], dépositaire d'une révélation sur l'«âme» de l'histoire sainte, grâce à la Sagesse donnée par Dieu (9,17; cf. Si 24).

La réécriture de récits bibliques antérieurs est un genre littéraire bien attesté à l'époque du livre de la Sagesse. Les Jubilés (écrit à composante apocalyptique datant de la fin du IIe siècle av. J.-C.), reprennent le livre de la Genèse, dont le contenu est raconté à Moïse par un ange. Le Testa-

---

17. Par exemple M. CONTI, *Sapienza*, p. 135; M. GILBERT, art. *Sagesse* (n. 3), col. 73; C. LARCHER, *Le livre de la Sagesse*, t. III (EB, n.s. 5), Paris, Gabalda, 1985, p. 651.

18. LARCHER lui-même l'a relevé, parlant de la troisième section comme du cadre d'une grande prière d'action de grâce: *Le livre de la Sagesse*, t. III (n. 17), p. 651, sans toutefois y voir la continuation de la prière de Salomon.

19. Voir la n. 14.

ment des Douze Patriarches (œuvre composite, rédigée du IIe siècle avant J.-C. au début de l'ère chrétienne), rapporte le testament que chacun des douze fils de Jacob a laissé à ses descendants. Le *Liber Antiquitatum Biblicarum* du Pseudo-Philon (œuvre juive écrite au tournant de l'ère chrétienne), raconte l'histoire biblique, d'Adam à David. L'Écriture elle-même utilise le même procédé de réécriture des récits antérieurs, comme l'attestent Si 44–49, 1 M 2,51-64 et, d'une certaine manière Tb 14,4-7; dans le Nouveau Testament, on peut mentionner He 11, où l'auteur présente à des chrétiens hésitants les grands croyants de l'histoire du salut.

Chacun de ces textes présente des caractéristiques apocalyptiques, ou tout au moins l'esprit parénétique qui marque le prophétisme de cette époque, entendu comme un charisme donné par Dieu aux personnages bibliques et aux textes qui en parlent (cf. Si 44–49). C'est l'esprit de prophétie qui, à travers des personnages célèbres et souvent fictifs, révèle le passé pour éclairer le présent et l'avenir immédiat[20]. Telle est, précisément, la mentalité apocalyptique.

Ce qui précède nous permet d'affirmer que le livre de la Sagesse de Salomon est une œuvre sapientielle apocalyptique[21], ou même apocalyptique tout court. L'ouvrage, qui peut être daté du tournant de l'ère chrétienne environ, permet d'entrevoir le stade auquel les spéculations juives de cette époque, nourries de culture grecque, avaient porté les traditions historiques, prophétiques et sapientielles de la Bible. Il s'y exprime un ensemble complexe de représentations et de procédés littéraires que, par commodité, nous pouvons rassembler sous la dénomination d'«apocalyptique».

Ce que nous retirons de cette vision des choses, c'est l'unité d'horizons ou d'arrière-plans culturels et religieux du judaïsme et du christianisme naissant[22].

Pontificium Athenaeum Antonianum   Marco NOBILE
Via Merulana, 124
I-00185 Roma

20. Le Xe Congrès des biblistes véterotestamentaires italiens s'est tenu à Rocca di Papa (Rome), du 8 au 10 septembre 1997, sur le thème de l'esprit de prophétie et la manière dont il était compris dans le judaïsme de la fin de l'ère ancienne. Cet esprit, qui donnait leur autorité à ce qui deviendra les livres canoniques, affectait tant l'imaginaire apocalyptique que le caractère sapientiel des ces œuvres (voir Daniel). Les actes du Congrès paraîtront en 1999 dans la revue *Ricerche Storico-Bibliche* (Edizioni Dehoniane, Bologna).

21. M. CONTI, *Sapienza* (n. 2), p. 16, mais aussi C. LARCHER, *Le livre de la Sagesse*, t. III (n. 17), p. 651.

22. P. DUMOULIN, *Le livre de la Sagesse à la charnière des deux Testaments: l'actualité du «midrash» de Sg 11–19*, in *Rivista Teologica di Lugano* 1 (1996) 227-255.

LA RÉFLEXION SUR LE SENS DE LA VIE EN SG 1–6
UNE RÉPONSE AUX QUESTIONS DE JOB ET DE QOHÉLET

Le thème de la vie dans le livre de la Sagesse a déjà été abordé plus d'une fois, en lien avec la question de la mort et du destin de l'être humain après celle-ci[1]. À ce sujet, l'influence des philosophies grecque et juive a été souvent soulignée, alors que la relation avec les livres de Job et de Qohélet n'a pas retenu d'attention particulière[2]. Depuis longtemps, les exégètes remarquent des affinités de vocabulaire entre les livres de la Sagesse et de Qohélet, mais ils les tiennent pour mineures par rapport à d'autres parallèles bibliques ou profanes, jugés plus pertinents[3]. Dans cet article, nous reprendrons l'examen de ce dossier, afin de vérifier si le livre de la Sagesse ne répond pas aux questions de Job et de Qohélet.

Au seuil de l'enquête, il convient de délimiter les sections qui développent le thème de la vie et sa philosophie. Les six premiers chapitres de l'ouvrage, on le sait, développent d'une manière particulière la réflexion sur le sens de la vie: celle-ci figure avant tout dans les discours des impies, qui tiennent une place importante dans cette première partie du livre; ce sont d'ailleurs ces textes qui contiennent la plupart des références à Job et à Qohélet.

I. DÉLIMITATION DES PÉRICOPES

Pour de nombreux auteurs, la structure de Sg 1–6 est concentrique[4]. On observe en particulier un parallélisme entre les chap. 2 et 5, qui traitent plus proprement de la question du sens de la vie. Nous faisons nôtre

---

1. Cf. A SISTI, *Vita e morte nel libro della Sapienza*, in *BibOr* 25 (1983) 49-61; G. SCARPAT, *La morte seconda e la duplice morte*, in *Paideia* 42 (1987) 55-62; M. KOLARCIK, *The Ambiguity of Death in the Book of Wisdom 1–6. A Study of Literary Structure and Interpretation*, Roma, Pontificio Istituto Biblico, 1991.
2. À l'exception de P. W. SKEHAN, *Studies in Israelite Poetry and Wisdom*, Washington, The Catholic Biblical Association of America, 1971, pp. 191-236.
3. Cf. C. LARCHER, *Études sur le livre de la Sagesse* (EB), Paris, Gabalda, 1969.
4. Plusieurs schémas sont proposés. On comparera: M. GILBERT, art. *Sagesse de Salomon (ou le Livre de la Sagesse)*, in *DBS*, t. XI, Paris, Letouzey et Ané, 1986, col. 58-114, spéc. col. 65-71: A (1,1-12); B (1,13–2,24); C (3,1–4,20); B' (5,1-23); A' (6,1-21); KOLARCIK, *The Ambiguity of Death* (n. 1), p. 62: A (1,1-15); B (1,16–2,24); C (3,1–4,20); B' (5,1-23); A' (6,1-21); A. SCHMITT, *Zur dramatischen Form von Weisheit 1,1–6,21*, in *BZ* N.F. 37 (1993) 236-258, spéc. pp. 236-237: A (1,1-15); B (1,16–2,24); C (3,1–4,19); B' (4,20–5,23); A' (6,1-21).

le schéma proposé par V. Kolarcik, qui résume par un schéma les résultats d'études antérieures:

a	2,1b-5	5,9-13	a'
b	2,6-11	5,6-8	b'
c	2,12-20	5,4-5	c'

Dans la structure concentrique de Sg 1–6, les discours des impies jouent un rôle de premier plan. Les affirmations sur la fugacité de la vie reviennent surtout en 2,1b-5 et 5,9-13:

2,5   σκιᾶς γὰρ πάροδος ὁ καιρὸς ἡμῶν
5,9   παρῆλθεν ἐκεῖνα πάντα ὡς σκιὰ

En 2,6-11 et 5,6-8, les impies exposent leur projet de vie:

2,7   οἴνου πολυτελοῦς καὶ μύρων πλησθῶμεν
5,7   ἀνομίας ἐνεπλήσθημεν τρίβοις καὶ ἀπωλείας

En 2,12-20 et 5,4-5, l'auteur développe l'opposition entre les impies et le juste, opposition qui aboutit à la gloire des justes:

2,16b μακαρίζει ἔσχατα δικαίων καὶ ἀλαζονεύεται πατέρα θεόν
5,5   πῶς κατελογίσθη ἐν υἱοῖς θεοῦ καὶ ἐν ἁγίοις ὁ κλῆρος αὐτοῦ
      ἐστιν;

De plus, ὁ βίος αὐτοῦ (2,15a) est parallèle à τὸν βίον αὐτοῦ (5,4c). Un parallélisme structurel relie les chap. 2 et 5[5], qui ils doivent donc être examinés en même temps.

Le centre littéraire des six chapitres se confond avec l'unité C (3,1–4,20), qui n'a pas de parallèle. En éclairant le destin final des justes et des impies, ces deux chapitres bouleversent les valeurs traditionnelles et montrent le sens authentique de la vie.

C'est la structure de Sg 1–6 qui attire notre attention sur les chap. 2 à 5; cependant le contexte littéraire et philosophique a aussi son importance pour comprendre comment les principes de la vie sont différents pour le juste et pour l'impie.

II. LE PROJET DE DIEU (1,13-14; 2,23-24)

Les textes du livre de la Sagesse opposent sans cesse le projet de Dieu et les projets des impies. Le dessein de Dieu sur la Création et sur l'être

5. F. PERRENCHIO, *Struttura e analisi letteraria di Sapienza 1,1-15*, in *Salesianum* 37 (1975) 289-335, spéc. pp. 299-300; ID., *Struttura e analisi letteraria di Sapienza 1,16–2,24 e 5,1-23*, in *Salesianum* 43 (1981) 3-43, spéc. pp. 33-37; SCHMITT, *Weisheit 1,1–6,21* (n. 4), p. 252.

humain est ordonné à la vie (1,13-14) et à l'incorruptibilité (2,23-24); les impies, en revanche, sont attirés vers la mort, et même leur existence vouée au plaisir n'est qu'un paradoxe. L'antithèse entre le projet de Dieu et ceux des impies caractérise le contexte théologique du discours sur le sens de la vie.

La philosophie de la vie exprimée dans le livre de la Sagesse se fonde sur les thèmes conjoints de la Création et de la seigneurie de Dieu sur le cosmos (1,13-14). Aucun homme ne doit chercher la mort et la ruine par sa mauvaise conduite (1,12), car Dieu n'a pas fait la mort (1,13a). M. Gilbert a souligné que, dans ce passage, «l'auteur paraphrase négativement le mot de synthèse qui commence et achève le récit de Gen 1: "Dieu a fait le ciel et la terre"»[6]. L'idée centrale du texte, c'est que la mort n'appartient pas au projet originel de Dieu. Sg 1,13b insiste sur ce point, lorsqu'il dit que Dieu ne se réjouit pas de la ruine des vivants. Cette conviction est exprimée à nouveau en 6,18-19 par le mot ἀφθαρσία, c'est-à-dire l'incorruptibilité, qui offre à l'être humain une vie éternelle heureuse. À la fin de la première partie du livre, c'est la Sagesse elle-même qui assure l'immortalité (6,17-20). Le thème est encore repris en 11,24–12,1, où l'auteur reconduit tout à l'amour de Dieu. C'est dans l'amour qu'il faut chercher la source de la Création pour la vie[7]: Dieu aime ses créatures parce que son Esprit incorruptible est présent en tout être vivant. C'est dans ce contexte théologique qu'il faut situer la réflexion sur le sens de la vie, approfondie d'une façon particulière en Sg 2,1-5 et 5,9-13.

III. Les projets des impies

En Sg 1,16, la particule adversative δέ exprime l'antithèse opposant le projet de Dieu et ceux des impies, qui n'acceptent pas les principes théologiques traditionnels et opposent leur conception nihiliste à la doctrine de la Création pour la vie.

Brièveté et tristesse de la vie (2,1-5; 5,9-13)

Lorsqu'ils présentent la vie humaine comme brève et triste, les impies expriment une idée souvent développée dans les cultures hellénistique et latine. Sur ce point, les exégètes font le plus souvent référence à Sénè-

---

6. M. Gilbert, *La relecture de Gn 1–3 dans le livre de la Sagesse*, in L. Derousseaux (éd.), *La Création dans l'Orient Ancien* (LD, 127), Paris, Cerf, 1987, p. 324.

7. *Ibid.*, pp. 332-336.

que, *De brevitatae vitae*, et ils soulignent volontiers l'importance de
cette question dans les controverses de la littérature païenne[8]. En revanche, l'affirmation de la brièveté de la vie a peu de parallèles dans l'Ancien Testament[9], sinon dans la littérature sapientiale. Outre des parallèles
mineurs (Qo 2,3.22-23; 6,12), deux textes surtout entrent ici en ligne de
compte: Jb 10,20 et 14,1-2, auxquels on peut encore ajouter Ps 39,5-7.
Dans le premier de ces passages (Jb 10,20), Job adresse à Dieu des questions relatives à la vie considérée dans son déroulement, de la naissance
à la mort:

18	*Oh! Pourquoi m'as-tu fait sortir du sein?*
	J'aurais péri alors: nul œil ne m'aurait vu,
19	*je serais comme n'ayant pas été,*
	du ventre on m'aurait porté à la tombe.
20	*Et ils durent si peu, les jours de mon existence!*
	Place-toi loin de moi, pour me permettre un peu de joie,
21	*avant que je m'en aille sans retour*
	dans la région des ténèbres et de l'ombre épaisse,
22	*où règnent l'obscurité et le désordre,*
	où la clarté même ressemble à la nuit sombre.

(Jb 10,18-22)

Job pose ces questions dans le contexte d'une perception négative de
Dieu, qu'il décrit comme un être mystérieux et hostile (vv. 13-17).

Dans le deuxième passage (Jb 14,1-2), le thème de la fugacité de la
vie s'exprime à nouveau par l'idée de brièveté, puis à l'aide d'une image
végétale: la fleur qui naît et se flétrit aussitôt. L'affirmation initiale des
impies quant à la brièveté de la vie peut être la traduction de Jb 14,1
TM: אָדָם יְלוּד אִשָּׁה קְצַר יָמִים וּשְׂבַע־רֹגֶז. Le v. 2b ajoute à cette métaphore
celle de l'ombre qui fuit. Ailleurs, le livre de Job exprime encore la vanité de la vie par le thème de l'inquiétude permanente de l'homme.

Un autre texte apparenté à Sg 2,1-5 appartient au Psautier: le Ps 39,5-
7, méditation métaphysique et morale sur l'être humain et le sens de sa
vie[10]. Le pessimisme du psalmiste rejoint la protestation de Job, lorsqu'il
dénonce la réussite scandaleuse de l'impie, alors que lui-même périt: le
succès de l'impie infirme tragiquement la doctrine de la rétribution. Notons que le Ps 39 et le livre de Job présentent aussi des affinités sur le
plan littéraire: le verbe rare בלג est attesté à la fois en Jb 10,20-21 et Ps
39,14, avec la même portée: «pousser un soupir de soulagement»[11].

---

8. G. SCARPAT, *Libro della Sapienza*, Brescia, Paideia, 1989, pp. 136-137.
9. KOLARCIK, *The Ambiguity of Death* (n. 1), pp. 114-119.
10. Voir à ce sujet G. RAVASI, *Il libro dei Salmi*, Bologna, Edizioni Dehoniane, t. I,
1985, p. 707.
11. Voir aussi Ps 102,12; 109,23; 144,4.

Pour exprimer la fugacité de la vie humaine, le psalmiste utilise aux vv. 6.7.12 le mot הֶבֶל, ce qui le rapproche aussi de Qohélet.

Ces textes qui illustrent la fugacité de la vie humaine par la métaphore de l'ombre présentent une constante: ils s'intéressent tous à la question de la rétribution et dénoncent comme injuste la prospérité insolente du pécheur. Les impies de Sg 2,1 parlent, eux aussi, de la fugacité de la vie. Cependant leur réflexion va dans un autre sens, car elle les conduit au nihilisme. Ils fondent leur opinion sur la négation de l'au-delà: personne ne peut délivrer l'être humain du pouvoir de l'Hadès, si bien que, face à la mort, il n'a aucun espoir de salut. Le mot ἴασις (v. 1b) rappelle l'image de Dieu qui guérit le juste de la maladie et le sauve de la mort[12]. En employant la négation οὐκ ἔστιν, les impies polémiquent contre les textes bibliques qui proclament la foi en Dieu comme sauveur et libérateur[13]. À ce propos, G. Scarpat cite le Ps 29,3-4 LXX (κύριε ὁ θεός μου, ἐκέκραξα πρὸς σέ, καὶ ἰάσω με· κύριε, ἀνήγαγες ἐξ ᾅδου τὴν ψυχήν μου)[14]. Nous faisons nôtre cette interprétation de Sg 2,1b comme proclamation d'athéisme qui débouche sur une anthropologie nihiliste (vv. 2-5).

Le hasard (2,2a)

Les impies nient la seigneurie divine sur l'existence humaine à l'aide de l'adverbe αὐτοσχεδίως, qui exprime une conception mécaniciste de la vie. Ce terme est synonyme de αὐτομάτως[15]. Sa dérivation de l'épicurisme est affirmée par tous les auteurs. On peut aussi relever l'absence de parallèle dans l'Ancien Testament: ce mot n'apparaît pas dans la LXX. L'idée de «hasard» est cependant exprimée par Qohélet (פֶּגַע, 9,11), au sens d'un événement qui tombe tout à coup sur l'homme[16]. On peut expliquer l'adverbe αὐτοσχεδίως par l'expression ἐκ τοῦ παρατυχόντος[17], proche par le sens de פֶּגַע, (כִּי־עֵת וָפֶגַע יִקְרֶה אֶת־כֻּלָּם Qo 9,11)[18]. Certes, lorsqu'il parle du hasard, Qohélet le fait à propos de la

---

12. Cf. SCARPAT, *Libro della Sapienza* (n. 8), pp. 138.172-172.

13. Cf. SKEHAN, *Studies in Israelite Poetry* (n. 2), p. 221. L'auteur fait référence à d'autres textes: Jr 14,19; 30,13; Na 3,19; Pr 6,15; 29,1; Si 3,28; 2 Ch 21,18 LXX; Jg 5,12 LXX; Si 21,3 LXX; Jr 31(48),2 LXX; Ps 37(38),4.8 LXX.

14. SCARPAT, *Libro della Sapienza* (n. 8), p. 172.

15. Cf. C.L.W. GRIMM, *Commentar über das Buch der Weisheit*, Leipzig, Hochhausen und Fournes, 1837, pp. 41-42.

16. Sur ce thème, voir V. D'ALARIO, *Liberté de Dieu ou destin? Un autre dilemme dans l'interprétation du Qohélet*, in A. SCHOORS (ed.), *Qohelet in the Context of Wisdom* (BETL, 136), Leuven, University Press-Peeters, 1998, pp. 457-463.

17. GRIMM, *Das Buch der Weisheit* (n. 15), p. 42.

18. P. MAIBERBER, art. פֶּגַע, in *TWAT*, t. VI, Stuttgart, 1989, col. 501-508, spéc. col. 506.

mort, alors que les impies du livre de la Sagesse le font au sujet de la naissance. Les deux textes se rejoignent cependant, car ils évoquent l'un et l'autre un événement du cycle de la vie humaine qui survient sans le concours de la volonté humaine. Voilà pourquoi Sg 2,2 utilise le verbe γίγνομαι[19], qui dit l'irruption de l'homme dans ce monde. Le hasard – qui échappe même à la volonté des dieux, selon la pensée grecque – détermine l'origine de la vie.

L'imaginaire de l'inconsistance (2,2b-3; 5,9b-11)

Après la mort, qui conclut le cycle de son existence, l'être humain ne laisse aucune trace de sa présence (ἐσόμεθα ὡς οὐχ ὑπάρξαντες, Sg 2,2b). On peut rapprocher cette expression de Jb 10,19a TM: לֹא־הָיִיתִי אֶהְיֶה. Les exégètes mentionnent d'autres passages proches de Sg 2,2b: Si 44,9c; Is 41,11-12 LXX. Ce n'est pourtant qu'en Jb 10,18-22 qu'on retrouve dans une combinaison si singulière les idées de Sg 2,1-2 sur la fugacité de la vie. Le texte de Jb 10,18-22 montre, en effet, plusieurs points communs avec Sg 2,1-5: la brièveté de l'existence humaine, l'inéluctabilité de la mort sans retour, et enfin la métaphore de l'ombre. L'idée de la fugacité de l'existence humaine est reprise en Sg 5,9-13a[20], à l'aide de cinq métaphores: l'ombre, la nouvelle, le navire, l'oiseau et la flèche. Ces images évoquent le caractère éphémère que les impies attribuent à l'existence de tous les hommes. Les métaphores du navire et de l'oiseau reviennent aussi en Jb 9,26 LXX (ἦ καὶ ἔστιν ναυσὶν ἴχνος ὁδοῦ ἢ ἀετοῦ πετομένου ζητοῦντος βοράν). Tous les auteurs considèrent que les comparaisons de Sg 5,9b-11 prennent appui sur Jb 9,25-26. Mais que vaut ce rapprochement? En Jb 9,25, l'image du messager rapide évoque le caractère fugitif et éphémère de la vie, et cette considération est renforcée par les comparaisons du navire et de l'aigle. Il faut cependant observer que Jb 9 ne parle pas de la vie humaine en général, mais des jours du juste souffrant. Le discours des chap. 9 et 10 a pour objet la justice de Dieu, que Job conteste: les actions divines lui paraissent arbitraires, car elles se fondent sur la force plus que sur le droit. Job met en cause le principe de rétribution: Dieu fait périr l'innocent comme le coupable (9,22) et livre la terre au pouvoir de l'impie (v. 24). Ce constat plonge l'homme souffrant dans un profond découragement (v. 21). Le discours du juste du livre de la Sagesse se trouve aux antipodes des propos de Job! Il n'est donc pas étonnant que les idées exposées par Job et par Qohélet soient placées en Sg 2,1-20 sur les lèvres de l'impie.

---

19. SCARPAT, *Libro della Sapienza* (n. 8), p. 174.
20. SKEHAN, *Studies in Israelite Poetry* (n. 2), p. 197.

L'idée de l'inconsistance de l'esprit humain apparaît plusieurs fois, en effet, dans ces deux livres. M. Gilbert a observé que l'expression ἐν ῥισὶν ἡμῶν (Sg 2,2c), «dans nos narines», peut faire référence à Gn 2,7, où le narrateur affirme que Dieu «insuffla dans les narines de l'homme une haleine de vie»[21]. La même phrase peut aussi être rapprochée de Jb 27,3[22], où Job reconnaît que le souffle vient de Dieu. Par cette affirmation, l'homme souffrant conteste la justice de Dieu, qui l'a privé de ses droits (vv. 1-2); ici comme dans l'ensemble des discours de Job, le motif de la fragilité humaine recèle une pointe polémique, car il entre dans le cadre d'un conflit avec Dieu, dont la toute-puissance écrase l'homme.

Dans le livre de Qohélet, le souffle vital, présenté comme fumée, a le même sens que chez Job. En effet, le sens primitif du mot הֶבֶל évoque le brouillard, la brume ou la vapeur[23], et le thème de la vanité de toute chose est relié à celui de la toute-puissance de Dieu.

Toujours en Sg 2,2cd, le mot πνοή est associé au λόγος, lui aussi éphémère. La même liaison apparaît en Qo 1,2-11, texte qui met en lumière la vanité du cosmos et de l'existence humaine, tout soulignant la fragilité du דָּבָר. Au v. 8, centre de la péricope, ce mot דָּבָר signifie probablement la «parole», comme le confirme la traduction de la LXX (λόγος)[24]. Qo 1,8b souligne la fragilité du דָּבָר de l'homme, cette parole qui fatigue, car elle ne peut jamais comprendre toute la réalité.

Dans le livre de Qohélet, le texte le plus important sur la vanité de l'esprit humain se trouve au chap. 3. Les vv. 19-21 placent l'homme et la bête sur pied d'égalité, car la רוּחַ de l'homme est du même ordre que celle de l'animal: tous ont le même sort, le même souffle, le même lieu[25]. La question rhétorique du v. 21 peut être comprise en rapport avec la question de la destinée ultime de l'être humain. Tant le stoïcisme que l'apocalyptique juive sont sensibles à la perspective d'une survie de l'homme après la mort. Qohélet, en revanche, ne voit pas la supériorité de l'humain sur la bête; il veut s'en tenir aux données de l'expérience et partage ainsi avec les sceptiques le refus d'une vision métaphysique de

---

21. GILBERT, *La relecture de Gen 1–3* (n. 6), p. 325.

22. Cf. C. LARCHER, *Le Livre de la Sagesse ou la Sagesse de Salomon* (EB, n.s. 1), t. I, Paris, Gabalda, 1983, p. 97; SCARPAT, *Libro della Sapienza* (n. 8), p. 175.

23. J.-J. LAVOIE, *La pensée du Qohélet. Étude exégétique et intertextuelle* (Héritage et Projet, 49), Québec, Fides, 1992, p. 212.

24. Reconnaissons cependant que le même mot דָּבָר peut aussi se traduire ici par «réalité»; cf. L. SCHWIENHORST-SCHÖNBERGER, *Nicht im Menschen gründet das Glück (Koh 2,24). Kohelet im Spannungsfeld jüdischer Weisheit und hellenistischer Philosophie*, Freiburg i.Br., Herder, 1994, pp. 35-36.

25. LAVOIE, *La pensée du Qohélet* (n. 23), pp. 87-88.

la réalité[26]. En Qo 3,20 comme en Sg 2,3, la poussière de la terre révèle la vérité finale de l'homme. Les deux textes font référence à Gn 3,19 LXX (ἕως τοῦ ἀποστρέψαι σε εἰς τὴν γῆν, ἐξ ἧς ἐλήμφθης· ὅτι γῆ εἶ καὶ εἰς γῆν ἀπελεύσῃ). L'image de la cendre (τέφρα, *hapax* dans le livre de la Sagesse) interprète par le langage de la poésie et de la philosophie grecque un thème biblique qui se rencontre aussi en Gn 18,27 et Si 17,32[27]: l'homme et la terre. Pour les commentateurs, la dispersion du souffle (πνοή, 2,2c; πνεῦμα, 2,3b) «comme l'air inconsistant» (ὡς χαῦνος ἀήρ, 2,3b), serait, en revanche, sans équivalent dans l'Ancien Testament; par conséquent, ils ne remarquent pas que la terminologie et l'imaginaire de la vanité sont très proches de Qohélet.

L'oubli (2,4; 5,5)

Un autre thème familier à Qohélet apparaît en Sg 2,4: la critique d'une certaine conception de la mémoire et, en particulier, de la Tradition. Alors que le souvenir du passé permet au juif de fonder son espérance, Qohélet lui oppose le primat du quotidien. Sa perception du temps est focalisée sur le présent: l'avenir est un mystère dont la connaissance appartient à Dieu seul, et le passé lui-même échappe à l'être humain, qui perd assez vite le souvenir des événements. Les impies de Sg 2,4 reprennent le même argument pour justifier une conception hédoniste de la vie. Le motif de l'oubli (καὶ οὐθεὶς μνημονεύσει τῶν ἔργων ἡμῶν, v. 4b) rejoint plusieurs passages de Qohélet (1,11; 2,16; 8,10; 9,5.14-15)[28]. L'image du nuage (v. 4c) fait allusion à Jb 7,9 (ὥσπερ νέφος ἀποκαθαρθὲν ἀπ' οὐρανοῦ), ou, comme le pense Larcher[29], à la fois à Jb 7,9 et Jb 9,26.

Pour exprimer la fugacité de la vie humaine, les impies emploient au v. 5 l'image de l'ombre, attestée, elle aussi, dans les livres de Job et de Qohélet. Outre Jb 14,2b, texte déjà mentionné plus haut, cette métaphore apparaît en Jb 8,9 LXX (σκιὰ γάρ ἐστιν ἡμῶν ἐπὶ τῆς γῆς ὁ βίος), mais aussi et surtout dans le livre de Qohélet, où le motif est récurrent (2,17.23; 3,19-21; 4,3-4; 6,12; 7,15; 9,9; 11,10). Relevons en particulier Qo 6,12a (יְמֵי־חַיֵּי הֶבְלוֹ וְיַעֲשֵׂם כַּצֵּל), où l'on retrouve comme en Jb 14,2 la comparaison de l'homme avec l'ombre. Pour Podechard[30], le mot

26. Sur l'épistémologie de Qohélet, voir M. V. Fox, *Qohelet and His Contradictions* (Bible and Literature Series, 18; JSOTSS, 71), Sheffield, Almond, 1989, pp. 79-120.

27. SCARPAT, *Libro della Sapienza* (n. 8), p. 175.

28. G. BOCCACCINI, *Il tema della memoria nell'ebraismo e nel giudaismo antico*, in *Henoch* 7 (1985) 165-192, spéc. pp. 187-189.

29. LARCHER, *Le livre de la Sagesse* (n. 22), p. 224.

30. E. PODECHARD, *L'Ecclésiaste* (EB), Paris, Gabalda, 1912, p. 362.

כַּצֵּל se réfère au sujet («l'homme»), et non au complément («les jours»). Il peut donc traduire: «Car qui sait ce qui est bon pour l'homme dans la vie, durant les jours de sa vie que, pareil à l'ombre, il passe?» Cette comparaison renforce l'idée de vanité, que Qohélet énonce au v. 11a à propos des paroles humaines: celles-ci ne font qu'accroître la vanité. Au v. 11b, Qohélet formule la question qui forme la conclusion de la première partie du livre (1,3–6,9): «Quel profit pour l'homme?» Les questions du v. 12, en revanche, introduisent à la deuxième partie de l'ouvrage (7,1–11,6), qui a pour thème la raison humaine et sa capacité de comprendre à la fois ce qui est bon dans la vie immédiate et ce qui arrivera ensuite «sous le soleil». Dans ce verset, אַחֲרָיו pourrait faire référence à l'avenir historique, alors qu'en 3,22 le même mot se rapporte sûrement au sort de l'être humain après la mort. Sans doute Qohélet connaît-il les perspectives développées à ce sujet dans l'apocalyptique; il préfère cependant en appeler à l'expérience, en relevant que, face à la mort, il n'y a aucune différence, ni entre l'homme et la bête (3,16-22), ni entre les justes et les impies (9,2). C'est l'absence de toute rétribution, aussi bien dans le temps de la vie qu'après la mort, qui lui permet d'affirmer la vanité de toute chose. Pour Qohélet, la question de l'avenir ne concerne pas la possibilité d'une vie après la mort, mais plutôt «la possibilité de vivre pleinement avant la mort»[31].

Toujours à propos de Sg 2,5, le concept de καιρός peut avoir été emprunté à la pensée de Qohélet, où le mot עֵת est utilisé dans le cadre d'une vision déterministe du temps (voir Qo 3,1)[32], également perceptible dans ce verset. Les commentateurs préfèrent en général citer Si 17,2[33], qui exprime en toute clarté la fixation divine du temps. Avant le Siracide, cependant, déjà Job et Qohélet ont souligné que la mort est irrévocable. Sg 2,5 trouve ainsi un parallèle en Jb 7,9b-10 LXX: ἐὰν γὰρ ἄνθρωπος καταβῇ εἰς ᾅδην, οὐκέτι μὴ ἀναβῇ οὐδ'οὐ μὴ ἐπιστρέψῃ ἔτι εἰς τὸν ἴδιον οἶκον. Ce texte rapproche l'idée selon laquelle personne ne peut revenir en arrière et la métaphore du nuage, qui revient en Sg 2,4c. Jb 10,21 relie en outre l'idée de l'irréversibilité à la métaphore de l'ombre. Sg 2,5a peut leur avoir emprunté cette même idée[34]. De plus, si l'expression σκιᾶς γὰρ πάροδος prend ici le sens de «trajet, parcours, circuit»[35], elle renvoie à une vision circulaire du temps, caracté-

---

31. LAVOIE, *La pensée du Qohélet* (n. 23), p. 69, n. 29.
32. J. BLENKINSOPP, *Ecclesiastes 3,1-15: Another Interpretation*, in *JSOT* 66 (1995) 55-64, spéc. pp. 58-59.
33. Ainsi, SCARPAT, *Libro della Sapienza* (n. 8), p. 177.
34. Cf. LARCHER, *Le Livre de la Sagesse* (n. 22), p. 227.
35. Telle est la proposition de LARCHER, *Le Livre de la Sagesse* (n. 22), pp. 225-226.

ristique de Qohélet (cf. 1,4-11)[36]. Par le mot σκιᾶ, l'auteur du livre de la
Sagesse «évoque l'idée d'une vie inconsistante et fragile, s'évanouissant
sans laisser de traces, mais il incline cette idée dans un sens particulier:
le temps de l'homme est non seulement court (cf. 1c), mais déterminé
d'avance d'une façon rigide: on peut le comparer au trajet de l'ombre du
jour; la mort survient au terme fixé, celui-ci ne peut être retardé et il est
immuable pour tous»[37]. Qohélet expose la même conception de la vie et
de la mort (3,1-15; 9,11-12); il établit, en effet, une relation serrée entre
la mort, le destin et le temps, ce qui rejoint certains courants – stoïciens,
en particulier – de la philosophie grecque[38].
Le déterminisme de la pensée des impies s'exprime enfin par la métaphore du sceau (Sg 2,5c). Ici, l'auteur fait probablement allusion à Jb
14,5 TM (וְלֹא יַעֲבוֹר). La même métaphore revient encore en Jb 9,7, pour
dire l'action de Dieu, qui marque les étoiles de son sceau.

IV. LES PLAISIRS DE LA VIE

L'exhortation de Sg 2,6 à jouir des biens de l'existence est un *topos*
de la littérature pessimiste, qui relève de la réflexion sur la vanité de la
vie; les rapprochements avec la littérature profane sont nombreux. En ce
qui concerne l'Ancien Testament, les parallèles les plus directs se trouvent en Is 22,13 et Qo 9,7[39]. Ainsi que Larcher le fait remarquer, ces
deux textes véhiculent des différents messages. Celui d'Isaïe, qui voit
l'appel à la joie comme une expression d'impiété, est très proche de notre passage. Qo 9,7, en revanche, a une portée positive[40], puisque la joie
de vivre est un don offert par Dieu à l'homme, qui réalise ainsi sa vocation existentielle. Une lecture attentive montre pourtant que Qo 9,7-9
forme le véritable parallèle de Sg 2,6-9. Plusieurs éléments sont communs aux deux textes, en effet: l'impératif δεῦτε οὖν (Sg 2,6), qui peut
correspondre à δεῦρο φάγε (Qo 9,7 LXX); l'appel à la joie (εὐφρο-
σύνη), qui se rapporte aux considérations sur la fugacité de la vie; les

---

36. Cf. Vittoria D'ALARIO, *Il libro del Qohelet. Struttura letteraria e retorica*
(RivBibS, 27), Bologna, Edizioni Dehoniane, 1993, pp. 69-80.
37. LARCHER, *Le Livre de la Sagesse* (n. 22), p. 227.
38. Cf. P. MACHINIST, *Fate, miqreh, and Reason: Some Reflections on Qohelet and
Biblical Thought*, in Ziony ZEVIT et al. (eds.), *Solving Riddles and Untying Knots:
Biblical, Epigraphic and Semitic Studies in Honor of Jonas C. Greenfield*, Winona Lake,
IN, Eisenbrauns, 1995, pp. 159-175; BLENKINSOPP, *Ecclesiastes 3,1-15* (n. 32), pp. 58-59.
39. Qo 11,7-10 doit être considéré comme un parallèle indirect.
40. Cf. J. Y. S. PAHK, *Il canto della gioia in Dio. L'itinerario sapienziale espresso
dall'unità letteraria in Qohelet 8,16–9,10 e il parallelo di Gilgameš, Me. III*, Napoli,
Istituto Universitario Orientale, 1996, pp. 197-272; V. D'ALARIO, *Dall'uomo a Dio.
L'itinerario della sapienza nella ricerca di Qohelet*, in *PSV* 35 (1997) 39-50.

symboles du vin et du parfum comme expressions de la joie de vivre; la motivation finale (ὅτι αὕτη ἡ μερὶς ἡμῶν καὶ ὁ κλῆρος οὗτος, Sg 2,9c; ὅτι αὐτὸ μερίς σου ἐν τῇ ζωῇ σου, Qo 9,9d LXX). Le mot μερίς traduit sans doute l'hébreu חֵלֶק, que Qohélet utilise bien souvent (2,10; 2,21; 3,22; 5,17.18; 9,6.9; 11,2), et en particulier dans le contexte de l'appel à la joie de vivre (3,22; 5,17; 9,9); l'auteur désigne par ce terme le rôle que Dieu assigne à l'homme dans la vie[41]. Sg 2,9c adjoint à μερὶς ἡμῶν un parallèle: ὁ κλῆρος οὗτος, «cet héritage»; il évoque ainsi Is 57,6 LXX (ἐκείνη σου ἡ μερίς, οὗτός σου ὁ κλῆρος). En Sg 3,14d et 5,5 également, le mot κλῆρος exprime non seulement le «sort» ou le «lot» que les justes ont reçu en partage, mais aussi la disposition gracieuse de Dieu. L'association des mots μερίς et κλῆρος est encore attestée en Is 57,6; Jr 13,25; Dt 10,9; 18,1. Larcher commente: «Pour cette raison surtout, les impies semblent bien parodier des formules bibliques rappelant l'appartenance spéciale des Israélites à Dieu. Ils renieraient donc maintenant les privilèges de l'élection et de l'Alliance, avec les obligations qui en découlent; les juifs n'apparaissent en aucune façon comme la "part" privilégiée du Seigneur, et c'est également une illusion que de choisir celui-ci comme son "lot" ou d'attendre de lui un "sort" favorable ici-bas ou dans l'au-delà»[42]. Les parallèles entre Sg 2,9b et les textes de Qohélet seraient donc secondaires et indirects. On fera cependant remarquer que, seul, le livre de Qohélet associe le thème de la vanité de la vie au motif de la «part», en faisant référence aux joies de l'existence. À notre avis, le livre de la Sagesse associe intentionnellement les allusions à Qohélet et à Isaïe pour présenter le message de Qohélet sous un jour défavorable; le vocabulaire qu'il utilise se révèle très proche, en effet, des paroles que l'Ancien Testament prête volontiers aux impies.

V. L'OPPRESSION DU JUSTE

Pour le livre de la Sagesse, l'hédonisme des impies aboutit à la violence envers le juste appauvri, la veuve et le vieillard (2,10). Le choix de ces catégories traditionnelles révèle combien les impies s'opposent au projet de Dieu, orienté vers la défense des plus pauvres. La force prime le droit: telle est la règle des impies (2,11). Sur ce point, le parallèle avec Jb 12,6 a bien souvent attiré l'attention des exégètes; dans ce texte, Dieu est placé sous le pouvoir des impies, qui le réduisent à l'impuissance.

41. D. MICHEL, *Untersuchungen zur Eigenart des Buches Qohelet* (BZAW, 183), Berlin-New York, de Gruyter, 1989, pp. 118-125.
42. LARCHER, *Le livre de la Sagesse* (n. 22), pp. 235-236.

Un autre parallèle se trouve en Jb 12,16a, où l'homme souffrant dit le pouvoir exercé par Dieu (παρ' αὐτῷ κράτος καὶ ἰσχύς): de toute sa puissance, il opprime de la même manière le juste et les impies et se révèle ainsi comme le véritable ennemi du juste.

Qo 4,1-3 offre un troisième parallèle à Sg 2,11, négligé par les critiques. Dans ce texte, l'auteur souligne l'absence d'un גֹאֵל qui soulage la douleur des opprimés[43]: les oppresseurs détiennent la force, et leurs victimes n'ont pas de consolateur. Notons que la LXX traduit כֹּח par ἰσχύς, terme également utilisé en Sg 2,11.

Le motif de la force comme norme de la justice divine se retrouve encore en Sg 12,16a (ἡ γὰρ ἰσχύς σου δικαιοσύνης ἀρχή)[44]. Ce texte veut-il répondre à la question de Job, qui nie la justice de Dieu?

VI. LA CONNAISSANCE DE DIEU

Le verbe ἐνεδρεύειν (Sg 2,12) signifie «traquer, dresser une embûche». On le retrouve en Ps 9,30 LXX et Jb 24,11 LXX, deux textes qui abordent un problème de théodicée: pourquoi Dieu n'intervient-il pas pour défendre les opprimés? Job déplore que Dieu n'exerce pas sa justice sur la terre. Soulignant l'inégalité sociale, il oppose deux groupes: les oppresseurs, qui disposent de la force et de la richesse, et leurs victimes. Jb 24 s'ouvre par une question sur la connaissance des temps divins: «Pourquoi Shaddaï n'a-t-il pas des temps en réserve, et ses fidèles ne voient-ils pas ses jours?» (v. 1). C'est précisément la prétention d'une telle connaissance de Dieu que les impies reprochent au juste, en Sg 2,13. Mais de quoi parlent-ils? D'après le contexte immédiat (vv. 12-16a) leur reproche pourrait viser la connaissance pratique de Dieu par la fidélité à la Torah?; le v. 16b, cependant, évoque le sort final des justes, et le v. 22 suppose que le juste connaisse les mystères de Dieu, c'est-à-dire le plan divin avec, surtout, le destin des justes, et pas seulement la pratique de la Loi[45]. Cette problématique est développée dans Qohélet, qui se demande plusieurs fois s'il est possible de connaître l'œuvre de Dieu, et donc l'avenir: «Je vois qu'il n'y a rien de mieux pour l'homme que de jouir de ses œuvres, car telle est sa part; qui, en effet, lui donnera de découvrir ce qui arrivera par la suite?» (3,22; voir aussi 6,12; 7,14;

---

43. Cf. F. BIANCHI, *Essi non hanno chi li consoli (Qo 4,1)*, in *RivBib* 40 (1992) 299-307.

44. Cf. J. VÍLCHEZ LINDEZ, *Sapienza*, Roma, Borla, 1990, p. 181, qui renvoie à 12,16a.

45. Voir à ce sujet M. GILBERT, *La connaissance de Dieu selon le livre de la Sagesse*, in J. COPPENS (ed.), *La notion biblique de Dieu. Le Dieu de la Bible et le Dieu des philosophes* (BETL, 41), Gembloux, Duculot, 1976, pp. 191-210.

8,7; 10,14). Sa réponse à cette question est négative: l'être humain ne peut connaître le dessein de Dieu; il ne peut prédire l'avenir et, sur ce point, le juste et l'impie partagent la même incapacité. Qohélet fait ici montre d'un scepticisme destructeur des valeurs traditionnelles de la sagesse biblique, et son radicalisme risque de déboucher sur un pur nihilisme. Le livre de la Sagesse, en revanche, s'attache à défendre la Tradition: ce sont les impies qui, dans leur aveuglement, méconnaissent les mystères de Dieu, alors que le juste, dépositaire de la Sagesse donnée par Dieu, comprend qu'il existe une rétribution dans l'au-delà.

VII. L'ÉPREUVE

Une autre allusion au livre de Job se rencontre en Sg 2,20b, où les impies se proposent de montrer au juste que sa foi n'est pas fondée sur les faits. Le juste en appelle à une ἐπισκοπή de Dieu, qui le sauvera; ce terme traduit l'hébreu פְּקֻדָּה, «inspection, visite, intervention favorable ou punitive» (Jb 10,12)[46], mais il peut aussi signifier «enquête, examen» (Jb 31,14). Les impies parlent avec ironie de cette intervention de Dieu, qui ne se produira jamais. Ils veulent démontrer que les événements suivent un cours fatal et que la mort, inexorable, est définitive. Ils nient jusqu'au bout l'existence d'une Providence et la rétribution dans l'au-delà: la mort du juste doit donc montrer d'une manière irréfutable la validité de leur théorie nihiliste.

Le démenti des faits: tel est l'argument principal de Job (cf. 21,29-30) et de Qohélet, qui fondent sur l'expérience leur critique de la doctrine de la rétribution. Pour le livre de la Sagesse, cependant, cette expérience n'est qu'illusion: ἔδοξαν ἐν ὀφθαλμοῖς ἀφρόνων τεθνάναι (3,2)[47]. La foi a le primat sur l'expérience sensible, qui n'est pas l'expérience ultime; en effet, la mort n'est que le passage à une existence meilleure.

VIII. LA RÉPONSE DE LA SAGESSE

Les chap. 3 et 4, qui forment le centre littéraire de la première partie du livre de la Sagesse, répondent aux affirmations des impies en opposant à leur nihilisme une conception positive de la vie humaine.

---

46. Ici, le mot פְּקֻדָּה revêt un sens positif de «protection»; cf. SCARPAT, *Libro della Sapienza* (n. 8), p. 195.

47. Cf. KOLARCIK, *The Ambiguity of Death* (n. 1), pp. 82-84.

Les justes dans la main de Dieu (3,1)

Sg 3,1 propose une réflexion sur le sort des âmes des justes (δικαίων δὲ ψυχαί), en réponse à la vision nihiliste développée par les impies au chap. 2. Les impies ont affirmé que nous sommes nés par pur hasard et qu'il n'existe aucune Providence. La Sagesse répond que le juste est dans la main de Dieu. Déjà Qo 9,1a avait exprimé cette idée (בְּיַד הָאֱלֹהִים אֲשֶׁר הַצַּדִּיקִים וְהַחֲכָמִים וַעֲבָדֵיהֶם), mais il avait aussitôt ajouté que l'être humain ne sait ni l'amour ni la haine, et que tout devant lui est vanité (v. 1b). La locution בְּיַד הָאֱלֹהִים peut revêtir différents sens, en Qohélet comme dans l'Ancien Testament en général: «être sous le pouvoir de Dieu», qui a créé toute chose (Is 66,2; Jb 12,9; Sg 11,17), «être sous la protection de Dieu», en cette vie (Dt 33,3; Is 50,2; Ps 31,6; 89,22), «être sous la protection de Dieu», après la mort (cf. Sg 3,1). À ce propos, D. Michel a observé une relation entre Qo 9,1.4.5.6 et Sg 3,1.4.9.14, où l'on retrouve les mêmes motifs: «être dans la main de Dieu», «espoir», «amour», «connaissance» et «part»[48]. Il est difficile d'établir si Qo 9,1 parle de la vie terrestre de l'homme ou de sa vie après la mort; dans les deux cas, cependant, il nie que l'être humain puisse connaître les intentions de Dieu à son égard: son Jugement est insaisissable. Sg 3,1 répond au scepticisme de Qohélet en affirmant que les âmes des justes sont dans la main de Dieu.

Le sort des justes et celui des impies (3,2-9)

Pour Qo 9,2-3, le juste et l'impie sont livrés au même destin: il n'existe pas de rétribution équitable pour la conduite humaine sur cette terre, et la mort – anéantissement sans retour – frappe tous les hommes d'une manière identique. Le livre de la Sagesse veut réfuter cette thèse. La mort est passage à une vie meilleure (3,1-3), qui comble l'espérance des justes (v. 4). Ces derniers seront dans la gloire de Dieu et auront ainsi leur récompense (vv. 5-9). Les impies, en revanche, subiront une peine conforme à leur mauvais agir (vv. 10-12). L'espérance des justes est comblée (v. 4b), car leur vie trouve son sens dans la tension vers les biens de l'au-delà; l'espérance des impies, en revanche, est vaine et illusoire. Tout ce passage rappelle à la fois le langage et la problématique de Job et de Qohélet sur le thème du bonheur[49]. Le mot ἐλπίς (Sg 3,11) est

48. MICHEL, *Untersuchungen zur Eigenart* (n. 42), p. 180: «Inhaltlich läßt sich der zitierte und gebrüfte Satz "Die Gerechten und die Weisen und ihre Werke sind in der Hand Gottes" vorzüglich mit der von um dargelegten Auslegung von 9,2-10 vereinen, wenn er den Sinn haben kann: "Die Gerechten und Weisen und ihre Werke sind *auch nach dem Tode* in der Hand Gottes".

49. Cf. A. MATTIOLI, *Felicità e virtù. La dottrina della Sapienza nel brano macarico*

sans doute une réminiscence de Job 7,6 LXX (ὁ δὲ βίος μου...
ἀπόλωλεν ἐν κενῇ ἐλπίδι, cf. 14,7; 17,15); Job appliquera plus loin ce
déni de l'espérance à l'être humain en général: c'est en vain qu'il pour-
suit le bonheur jusqu'à la mort[50], qui est définitive (17,10-16). Les trois
amis de l'homme souffrant affirme, au contraire, la ruine de l'espoir du
méchant (8,13; 11,20). Le livre de la Sagesse s'accorde avec leur thèse,
mais sa perspective est plus large, car elle s'ouvre sur la rétribution de
l'au-delà. Il répond ainsi aux affirmations de Job lui-même et de
Qohélet, qui déploraient l'absence d'une juste rétribution accordée aux
justes et aux impies.

Le scandale de la prospérité des impies (3,10-12; 4,3-6)

Sg 3,11b, qui dit la vanité de la vie des impies, rappelle le langage de
Qohélet: leurs efforts sont vains et leurs œuvres inutiles. L'auteur reprend le vocabulaire de Qohélet au sujet de la vanité des entreprises humaines, mais il l'applique exclusivement au sort des impies.

Le livre de la Sagesse aborde ensuite (v. 12) le thème de la prospérité
des méchants, qui faisait scandale aux yeux de Job. Pour montrer l'absence de toute rétribution équitable, Job mettait en lumière le bonheur
tranquille des impies et de leur famille (21,11). Ici, tout au contraire, les
femmes des impies sont folles et leurs enfants sont pervers: pour eux, la
procréation n'est pas bénédiction, mais malédiction. Cela explique que
la stérilité soit dite «heureuse», lorsqu'elle va de pair avec la vertu
(vv. 13-15).

Dans la ligne de ce qui précède, les vv. 16-19 répondent à une autre
question de théodicée: la durée de la vie des enfants d'impies. L'auteur
envisage deux possibilités, introduites respectivement par ἐὰν τε γὰρ et
ἐὰν τε. C'est la première hypothèse qui attire notre attention: les descendants des méchants ont une longue vie, ce qui rejoint les discours de
Job (Jb 21,7-24). L'homme souffrant demandait: «(Voit-on) le vent le
chasser comme une paille, un tourbillon l'emporter comme la bale?»
(v. 18). Sg 5,14a répond: «Oui, l'espoir de l'impie est comme la bale
emportée par le vent». Ce texte fait lui-même allusion à Is 29,5 LXX[51];
encore une fois, l'image de fugacité et d'inconsistance est appliquée aux
seuls impies et rappelle le langage théophanique (cf. Is 29,6).

---

per le sterili e gli eunuchi (Sap 3,13–4,6), in V. REALI et al. (eds.), *Gesù apostolo e
sommo sacerdote. Studi biblici in onore di T. Ballarini*, Casale Monferrato, Marietti,
1984, pp. 23-49.
     50. J. LÉVÊQUE, *Job et son Dieu. Essai d'exégèse et de théologie biblique* (EB), Paris,
Gabalda, 1970, t. I, p. 297.
     51. LARCHER, *Le Livre de la Sagesse* (n. 22), p. 378; voir aussi Ps 1,4; 34,5.

L'hypothèse de la longue vie des impies est également envisagée en Qo 8,12a, en lien avec le thème de la rétribution. Qohélet en vient à constater: «il y a des justes qui sont traités selon la conduite des méchants et des méchants qui sont traités selon la conduite des justes» (v. 14). Le livre de la Sagesse répond au scandale dénoncé par Qohélet en dépassant le schéma théologique de la rétribution temporelle.

L'immortalité dans le souvenir (4,1.19)

Sg 4,1 oppose à la nombreuse progéniture des impies une fécondité plus précieuse, celle qui est assurée au juste par la vertu. Dans ce contexte, le thème du souvenir est interprété d'une façon originale, car il est gage d'immortalité, bien plus qu'une postérité innombrable. Le livre de la Sagesse répond ainsi à la question posée par Qohélet, sans pour autant recourir à la solution traditionnelle. La fécondité charnelle dont parlait Job est dépréciée, tandis qu'une autre fécondité est exaltée par sa relation à la vertu. Le motif du souvenir doit être compris dans un sens large: il ne vise pas seulement de la mémoire des hommes, mais embrasse aussi celle de Dieu. Au souvenir éternel du juste (4,1), le v. 19 oppose celui des impies, qui périt faute d'avoir cultivé la moindre valeur durable. C'est la réplique à 2,4a: l'oubli dans la mémoire des hommes est le châtiment assigné par Dieu aux méchants. Remarquons en outre que 4,19 fait inclusion avec le v. 1b par la reprise du mot μνήμη. Par ce procédé, le thème de l'oubli est enrichi d'une signification plus large, car il concerne désormais la mémoire de Dieu, qui n'enregistre pas les noms des impies. Leur existence ne se prolongera pas dans le bonheur de l'au-delà, et leur sort final sera la ruine totale (5,21-23).

CONCLUSION

Lorsque Sg 1–6 déploie sa réflexion sur le sens de la vie humaine, il répond consciemment aux questions posées par Job et par Qohélet au sujet de la rétribution. Cette conclusion peut s'appuyer sur la qualité des allusions, qui sont systématiques et ne s'expliquent pas par la simple reprise du thème commun de la fugacité de la vie. En effet, la plupart des références à Job (voir en particulier Jb 9,25-26; 10,18-22; 14,1-2; 24,11) et à Qohélet (surtout Qo 8,10; 9,5.14-15) sont liées des questions de théodicée. Le livre de la Sagesse lit les critiques de la justice de Dieu exprimées par Job et par Qohélet comme autant d'expressions d'impiété: ce sont les méchants qui refusent l'idée d'une seigneurie de Dieu sur la vie individuelle et sur l'histoire. D'autre part, l'auteur adopte la distinction traditionnelle entre les justes et les impies. En conséquence, il applique le motif de la fugacité de la vie aux méchants, et non à tous les hommes. Le souvenir, qui ne s'attache pas aux impies, assure la survie des justes; sa mise en valeur permet de répondre aux critiques de Job et de Qohélet. À l'expérience commune, qui ne voit pas le juste rétribué pour ses œuvres, le livre de la Sagesse oppose sa foi dans l'intervention ultime de Dieu, qui donnera au juste une vie heureuse après la mort.

Il nous semble donc que la relation du livre de la Sagesse avec ceux de Job et de Qohélet ne doit pas être sous-estimée: elle permet d'éclairer sa pensée relative à la rétribution et de la distinguer plus nettement d'autres courants de la littérature sapientiale.

Via Epomeo, 257   Vittoria D'ALARIO
I-80126 Napoli

FROM *ΔΙΚΑΙΟΣΥΝΗ* TO *ΑΘΑΝΑΣΙΑ*
(WIS 1,1.15)

SOME INTRODUCTORY ASPECTS

Before we begin to analyze our subject it is important to bear in mind some general issues.

1. Fidelity to the biblical tradition, openness to the Hellenistic culture.

In spite of a sophisticated vocabulary, in spite of a rhetoric feature in the exposition of the subject, the author appears to be a Jew faithful to the biblical tradition. On the other hand, and despite the biblical humus of the exposition, with constant references to the Scripture[1], and in spite of some cryptic cultural antagonism, the author appears to be someone who is open to the cultural values of his environment[2].

This aspect is important when studing the relationship between δικαιοσύνη and ἀθανασία. For the author of Wisdom the history of Israel provides a paradigmatic example of the experience of righteous individuals or a righteous people, though it is only an illustration of the working of the universe. The primary distinction is not between Israel and the gentiles, but rather between the righteous (δίκαιοι) and the impious (ἀσεβείς). While Israel is presented as the paradigm of the righteous, it is not necessarily an exclusive model[3].

---

1. But it is also a strange thing that one of the distinctive features of Wisdom is its unwillingness to name any of the characters in its story. Even the biblical heroes in 10,1-21 remain anonymous, although identifiable from Scripture, and at no point does the author identify himself, or «God's children» as Jewish. It is possible to interpret this phenomenon as a deliberate abstention from ethnic labels in the interest of a universal typology of «the just» and «the unjust».

2. In this sense it is unexpected that *Wisdom* can be used as an example of that literature which has cultural antagonism as its dominant and determinative characteristic. As J.M.G. BARCLAY claims, *Jews in the Mediterranean Diaspora. From Alexander to Trajan (323 BCE-117 CE),* Edinburg, 1996, p. 184: «The predominant theme in the *Wisdom of Solomon* is in fact the social conflict and cultural antagonism between Jews and non-Jews». Authors like C. LARCHER, *Études sur le Livre de la Sagesse,* Paris, 1969; J.M. REESE, *Hellenistic Influence on the Book of Wisdom and its Consequences,* Rome, 1970 and others have shown that the author of *Wisdom* in his theological concepts, especially in his anthropology and belief in immortality was clearly influenced by Hellenistic philosophy and culture as well as in his vocabulary and writing style. The author of *Wisdom* was convinced that the old could be expressed in a new form, and that the new form would be more readily accepted by his more intellectually demanding contemporaries.

3. Cf. J.J. COLLINS, *Between Athens and Jerusalem: Jewish Identity in the Hellenistic Diaspora,* New York, 1986, esp. pp. 183-186.

2. Importance of the concept of life

The Jewish Diaspora to which the Book of Wisdom was addressed needed to reacquire hope in the future, trust in the living and vivifying God. It is Κύριος, only Him who gives life. This hope comes to its climatic expression in the following text:

> But the righteous live forever;
> their reward is in the Lord,
> and the most High has them in his care (5,15).

In a more or less explicit and direct way life is a basic theme of the theology, anthropology and eschatology of Wisdom as it appears in its discussion of God as Creator[4] and Saviour[5]. Moreover, there is a great deal of emphasis in this work on God's universal providence and mercy. The repeated stress on God's care for his whole creation (1,13-14; 6,7; 9,1-3; etc.) is expressed in this address to God:

> For you are merciful to all
> because you are all-powerful,
> and you overlook the sins of humanity,
> to lead them to repentance.
> You love everything in existence,
> and you loathe nothing of what you have made...
> You spare everything because they are yours,
> O Lord, lover of life;
> For your immortal spirit is in all things (11,23-12,1).

Within his wisdom conception of cosmos and history our author describes different ways of obtaining means to reach life: the σοφία[6], the

---

4. Cf. for example, 1,13-14: «For God did not make death (... θάνατον οὐκ ἐποίησεν) ... he created all things that they might endure (... ἔκτισεν γὰρ εἰς τὸ εἶναι τὰ πάντα)». God creates man to share his life according to the positive teaching of 2,23: «Because God created man for immortality (ἀφθαρσία), and made him an image of his own proper being» (εἰκόνα τῆς ἰδίας ἀϊδιότητος ἐποίησεν αὐτόν).

5. The righteous man considers himself God's son (2,18); God protects the righteous by visiting him (2,20). God is portrayed as God of the fathers and Lord of mercy (9,1: Κύριος τοῦ ἐλέους). God spares all because «they are yours» (ὅτι σά ἐστιν), o Sovereign Lord, lover of living beings (φιλόψυχε) (11,26). The author of Wisdom uses the bipolar expression «life-death» to synthetize all that is said in pericope 16,5-15 about the merciful divine power of a God who is the saviour of all (16,7: πάντων σωτῆρ): «For you have the power of life and death» (16,13a: Σύ γὰρ ζωῆς καὶ θανάτου ἐξουσίαν ἔχεις).

6. Pericope 6,1-21, an exhortation to seek σοφία, which brings immortality and sovereignty, is open to an eschatological perspective in the last two verses: «Thus the desire for wisdom leads to the kingdom (ἐπιθυμία ἄρα σοφίας ἀνάγει ἐπὶ βασιλείαν)... Honour wisdom so that you may reign forever» (τιμήσατε σοφίαν ἵνα εἰς τὸν αἰῶνα βασιλεύσητε).

λόγος[7], the πνεῦμα[8]; etc. But for the author of Wisdom the main path to life is through δικαιοσύνη: to love justice means to love God, to share his ἀθανασία.

Δικαιοσύνη is a central theme of the whole work, though it is only discussed explicitly in the first section (1,1-6,21)[9]. Nevertheless, the author gives a dramatic character to death in its plural ambiguity as a pedagogical procedure that is in line with the wisdom tradition (physical

---

7. God by his λόγος created everything: ὁ ποιήσας τὰ πάντα ἐν λόγῳ σου (9,1). By his λόγος God stops the ἀσεβείς to save the δίκαιοι (12,9). The Egyptians are slain by locusts and flies, but Israel survives a serpent attack through the bronze serpent, symbol of salvation (16,5-14). The author additionally comments on the fact: «For it was neither herb nor emollient that cured them, but your word (ὁ σός λόγος), o Lord, that heals all» (16,12). And inspired by *Dt*-LXX 8,3 (though Wisdom in this case uses ῥῆμα and not λόγος) says that the sons loved by the Lord are preserved by his word (16,26); etc.

8. The use of πνεῦμα by our author is relatively frequent: twenty times according to the register of E. HATCH – H.A. REDPATH, *A Concordance to the Septuagint and the Other Greek Versions of the Old Testament (Including the Apocryphal Books)*, t. II, Graz, [3]1975. I have not been able to look up in T. MURAOKA, *A Hebrew/Aramaic Index to the Septuagint: Keyed to the Hatch and Redpath Concordance*, Grand Rapids, 1998. On the contrary, Proverbs uses πνεῦμα only once, *Sirach* eight times. It is the spirit that brings man up (1,5); it is a φιλάνθρωπον πνεῦμα who acts as σοφία (1,6). The spirit fills the world and holds all things together (1,7). The gift of the spirit goes together with that of wisdom (7,7). Πνεῦμα also acts as the creating and saving power of history (11,20). The spirit is the vivifying presence of God in everything (12,1); etc. So the spirit in *Wisdom* is a presence of life: τὸ γὰρ ἄφθαρτον σου πνεῦμα ἐστιν ἐν πᾶσιν (12,1).

9. It is obvious that the organization of Wisdom according to perceived themes is not sufficient for uncovering the theological importance of its specific terms and ideas. An analysis of the literary structure clarifies the limitations of the larger units, and brings about a greater focus on the relationships between the smaller units as well as providing solid and fertile ground on which to appreciate the author's poetic sensitivity. Cf. J.M. REESE, *Plan and Structure in the Book of Wisdom*, in *CBQ* 27 (1965) 391-399, where he speaks about «material arranged in a concentric manner», especially with regard to the cc. 1–6. Reese was the first to recognize the author's skillful use of the rhetorical device of *inclusio* in order to mark off many sections of his work, and his attempt to structure the book on that basis. A recent detailed analysis of *Wisdom's* structure is provided by M. GILBERT, *Sagesse de Salomon (ou Libre de la Sagesse)*, in *DBS*, t. XI, Paris, 1991, col. 58-120. The article is divided into seven parts (I: *Le texte;* II: *La structure littéraire;* III: *Le genere littéraire;* IV: *L'unité du livre;* V: *La datation;* VI: *Tradition biblique et culture hellénistique;* VII: *Lecture théologique du livre)*. The largest category is devoted to the study of the literary structure of *Wisdom* (13 columns). Gilbert questions the unity of 1,1-15 because of his observation of the ties between 1,13-15 and 2,23-24 (see col. 66). For a subtle study of the literary structure of Wisdom 1–6 see that of M. KOLARCIK, *The Ambiguty of Death in the Book of Wisdom 1–6: A Study of Literary Structure and Interpretation*, Rome, 1991. According to Kolarcik, a careful reading of Wis 1,1–6,21 reveals the author's sustained employment of the metaphorical image of a trial scene. In contrast to the allowing panegyric of wisdom that beckons the reader in the second and central part of the book, the introductory six chapters employ the negative image of judgment and death in an attempt to deflect him from a cynical outlook bred by utter despair and which leads to the adoption of a strategy of exploitation and oppression of one's fellows.

death, eschatological death, individual death, collective death[10], intellectual death[11] etc.). The description of the causes which provoke death (the sin, which provokes the eschatological death, death as the natural end of man, death as the consequence of the primeval fall; etc.) also has in a dramatic tone. The presence of the devil as an agent of death is absolutely secondary[12]. As it will be seen, the death referred to in Wis 1,13 and 2,24, is not a physical but rather a spiritual or «ultimate» death. Through the mouthpiece of Solomon, the author presents mortality as a human condition which does not provoke despair but rather provides an opening for wisdom and intimacy with God[13].

For didactic incisiveness the author of Wisdom emphasises the importance of death. Death, in its different aspects, is seen as a breaking, an aggression, a perversion, a punishment, etc. And it is precisely this spectacular character that at a given moment could induce one to believe that the main theme of Wisdom is death. Although death is an important matter of the work, it is not the most important one. In fact it derives from the main subject, live[14], which serves as the nucleus around which the three parts of the Wisdom of Solomon are organised[15].

10. The whole chapter 16, for instance, could be considered a typification of collective death: 1-4 describes the hungering of the Egyptians as a result of the hideousness of the creatures sent to plague them, whereas Israel, after only briefly suffering desire, came to enjoy the exotic delicacy of quail food; in 16,5-14, the Egyptians are slain by locusts and flies, but Israel survives a serpent attack through the bronze serpent, symbol of salvation; in the last antithesis, 15-29, the Egyptians are plagued by thunderstorms, while Israel is fed by a rain of manna. There follow other antitheses between the Egyptians and the Israelites (17,1–18,25; 19,1-9).

11. The inability to know and to recognize the God's existence (τὸν ὄντα, the Existent One) from visible goods (13,1) could be considered an intellectual death. Those who worship nature are chided for not searching beyond visible reality, for the beauty and dynamic character only imply supreme Author.

12. Death attributed to the devil's envy (2,24) constitues only a mythical-ornamental reference to Gen 3, without any importance neither for the literary structure nor for the general teaching of the work. The devil (mentioned only in 2,24) does not play any determinative role in the teaching of *Wisdom,* on the contrary it is rather a hinderance. Nevertheless the mention of the devil likely reflects a concern that God not appear directly responsible for the existence of evil. Cf. F. RAURELL, *Angelologia i demonologia en Is-LXX,* in *RevCatTeol* 2 (1977) 1-30.

13. Only in the third part of *Wisdom* (11-19), in the interpretation of the exodus, with digressions on false worship, does the author treat the physical death of Israel's enemies explicitly as punishment. Thus, on the surface level of the text, the author does not draw clear, unequivocal distinctions between the different notions of death, a lack of precision partly accounted for by the literary form of the book, which unfolds the argument dramatically rather than through straightforward philosophical exposition.

14. The author of *Wisdom* employs twenty-eight terms ca. to describe the world of the death; on the contrary he makes use of nine words to describe life. For example: ἀθανασία, αἰών, βίος, ζῆν, σώζειν, ἀφθαρσία, βασιλεύειν, etc. Even in two key terms such as ἀθανασία and ἀφθαρσία the statement of life is based on a negative: not-death, not-corruption.

15. The ambiguity of death has been the subject of the very useful study of Wisdom

3. Importance of the concept of justice

Although our analysis is limited to the first part of Wisdom (1,1-6,21), our textual sample provides sufficient evidence to demonstrate that the author is intent on the matter of the different behaviour of the δίκαιοι and of the ἀσεβείς with regard to the God's δικαιοσύνη. Consequently the author wants to provide an answer to the problem of life and death which concerns both, righteous and impious. Both of the groups are confronted with God's δικαιοσύνη, a key term of Wisdom's structure and thought[16]. If the members of these two groups are qualified

1–6 by M. KOLARCIK, *The Ambiguity of Death in the Book of Wisdom* (n. 9). Says Kolarcik: «The author sustains an operative function of death's ambiguity throughout the argumentation. The ambiguity of death stems from two different perspectives regarding the understanding of mortality. This first level of ambiguity constitutes a phenomenological source, for the reality of physical death is open to diverse interpretations and attitudes. It solicits a response on the part of each individual. A second level of ambiguity arises from the author's own employment of the terms for death with different connotations, namely that of mortality, physical death as punishment and ultimate death. There are two responses that the ambiguity of death evokes in the unfolding of the author's argumentation. The natural fear of physical death is transferred in the course of the argument to a fear of ultimate death. This ultimate death is the real negative motive the author presents for mobilising the reader's attention to love justice and to seek God. Secondly the metaphor of the real scene explains the author's pedagogical reason for sustaining a surface ambiguity of death. The surface ambiguity within the sustained image of a trial challenges the reader to look behind the appearances of physical death. The exhortation is constructed with the metaphor of a trial scene in order to lead the reader into a critical examination of the negative force that hinders loving justice and seeking God –a fear and rejection of mortality that leads to ultimate death, the privation of divine life» (p. 186). Nevertheless we could speak correlatively of the ambiguity in the concept of life: physical life, «ultimate» life, moral life, intellectual life, individual life, collective life, etc. Moreover, while divine causality on life is almost total, on the contrary divine causality on death is more limited. In this sense there is certain asimetry.

16. Wisdom uses eleven times the term δικαιοσύνη: 1,1.15; 2,11; 5,6.18; 8,7.7; 9,3; 12,16; 14,7; 15,3. We may interpret this number as being relatively high, at least in comparison with Job (nine times), Sirach (five times), Ecclesiastes (only once). The author also attaches a specific weight to the term δίκαιος (27 times): 2,10.12.16.18; 3,1.10; 4,7.16; 5,1.15; 10,4.5.6.10.13.20; 11,14; 12,9.15.19; 14,30; 16,17.23; 18,7.20; 19,16.17. The word ἄδικος appears 10 times: 1,8; 3,19; 4,16; 10,3; 12,12.23; 14,30.31; 16,19.24. We find also ἀδικία (twice): 1,5; 11,15, and once ἀδικεῖν. The adverb δικαίως appears three times: 9,12; 12,15, 19,13. Δικαστής is used twice: 6,1; 9,7. The verb δικάζειν arises once (B): 2,9. These are the different morphological forms of the root δικα- recorded by E. HATCH – H. REDPATH, *A Concordance to the Septuagint*, t. I (n. 8). The use of the root δικα- in Wisdom is significant for its number as well as for the variety of forms employed. A very exciting topic, though not always convincing is that proposed by D. SEELEY, *Narrative, the Righteous Man and the Philosopher. An Analysis of the Story of Δίκαιος in Wisdom 1–5*, in *JSP* 7 (1990) 55-78. According to Seeley, the story of δίκαιος in Wis 1–5 shows a combination of Jewish and Hellenistic motifs that causes both traditions to be read in a new light. Seeley describes four examples of such combinations. The first concerns the reason death entered human existence. Here the combination is not smooth since Wis 1,16 blames idolatry, and 2,1-5 philosophical error. More congruent are the Jewish and Hellenistic backgrounds to Wisdom's description of the wicked hedonists. Similarly, the fate of the righteous finds an echo in the sad fate of

as δίκαιοι and ἄδικοι (very often ἀσεβείς) it is due to the type of relationship that they have with δικαιοσύνη. Nevertheless, the author of
Wisdom does not express the weight of the contrast between the two
groups as much with the antithetic binomial δίκαιοι-ἄδικοι as with the
binomial δίκαιοι-ἀσεβείς[17]. Through the antithesis δίκαιος-ἀσεβής
the total behaviour of man is described: the totality of human actions
which are in accordance with/or against the will of God, often described
as δικαιοσύνη. The triumph of the δίκαιοι over the ἀσεβείς is described by the author as the triumph of God's δικαιοσύνη over death,
chiefly in 1,1-6,21 and in 11,2-19,22. Obviously, in the second part of
the book (6,22-11,1: the nature and power of wisdom and Solomon's
quest for it), the contrast between δίκαιοι-ἀσεβείς is practically absent.

I. THE LOVE OF THE ΔΙΑΚΑΙΟΣΥΝΗ: 1,1a

The role of «inclusio» played by the term δικαιοσύνη in 1,1a and
1,15 helps to better grasp the place and significance, given by the author
to the δικαιοσύνη as ἀθάνατος in section 1,1-15. The force of its contents and the poetic richness with which the subject is handled can be
appreciated in the literary structure:

the pious philosopher and the violent end of the prophets. Both traditions also describe
how God tests those who are close to him (Wis 3,6) and how the righteous will be exalted
after death (Wis 4,16-5,5).

17. In Wisdom is used the term ἄδικος ten times (1,8; 3,19; 4,16; 12,12.23;
14,30.31; 16,19.24); but only six times ἄδικος establishes some direct contrast with
δίκαιος. On the contrary, ἀσεβής represents the deepest and strongest contrast with
δίκαιος. In fact, in Wisdom the ἀσεβής is that person who acts with the absolute contempt of the God's will understood as δικαιοσύνη. Moreover the ἄδικος despises the
δίκαιος, the person open to the God's δικαιοσύνη. Among the fourteen times in which
Wisdom uses ἀσεβής (1,9.16; 3,10; 4,3.16; 5,14; 10,6.20; 11,9; 12,9; 14,16; 16,16.18;
19,1) only once (14,16) does it not refer to a wicked person, but rather to a bad custom. In
all of these instances the author does not qualify ἀσεβής because his ideas or his attitude
but because his behaviour which offends both the Lord's δικαιοσύνη and δίκαιος. It
may seem strange however Wisdom never uses ἀσεβής which, at least theoretically,
seems to have been more useful to express the antithesis «pious-impious», εὐσεβής-
ἀσεβής. The term was probably not strong enough to express the correct behaviour before God and His will. The Vulgate always translates ἀσεβής as *impius* and δίκαιος as
iustus except in 12,18, where *verus* is read probably due to a christianizing reading attentive to Mt 27,43: «Confidit in Deo, liberet nunc, si vult eum; dixit enim; quia filius Dei
sum». The text of *Wis* 2,18 is read as follows by the Vulgate: «Si enim *verus* filius Dei
est suscipiet illum et liberabit eum de manu contrariorum». *Mt* 27,43 must also be explained by the reading of *Ps* 21,9. On the contrary, the term ἄδικος is translated by the
Vulgate as *iniustus*, when reference is made to an individual, however as *iniquus* when
refering to a group or to the actions (*Biblia Sacra iuxta Vulgatam Versionem*, ed. B.
Fischer–H.F.D. Sparks–W. Thiele, recensuit R. Weber, t. II, Stuttgart ³1983).

Introduction (1,1a): ἀγαπήσατε δικαιοσύνην
Inclusio (1,15): δικαιοσύνη γὰρ ἀθάνατος ἐστιν

Even the fact that verse 15 is «monostico» (only one line) stresses the central place of δικαιοσύνη within the unity 1,1-15 as an introduction of the first part of Wis 1,1-6,21. The formal circularity points out the closing of the pericope 1,1-6,21 started with the exhortation: ἀγαπήσατε δικαιοσύνην, which finds a logical conclusion in the final substantive sentence: δικαιοσύνη γὰρ ἀθάνατός ἐστιν[18].

In the three imperatives of 1,1 (ἀγαπήσατε, φρονήσατε, ζητήσατε) there is the same grammatical complement of action: Κύριος. In 1,1a Κύριος is present implicitly: «Love justice» (of the Lord). The omission of Κύριος gives strength and doctrinal cohesion to the verse and illuminates the importance of δικαιοσύνη. In 1b the name Κύριος is explicit: «Be mindful of the Lord (Κυρίου) in goodness». Here the term Κύριος serves as a bridge between 1a and 1c; it makes it possible for the implicit to become explicit and for the explicit pronominal (αὐτός) of 1c to become an implicit one in symmetry with 1a. But in the three «stichi» Κύριος is the object of the three imperatives. All this helps to see that in v. 1a is dealt with the δικαιοσύνη τοῦ Κυρίου.

The imperative is repeated three times[19], with three verbs which describe the total dynamic trend of man towards God. This form allows us to perceive the urgency and importance of the central theme of the work, from the very beginning (of the story) although δικαιοσύνη that sometimes could erroneously seem that is in a second place in comparison with σοφία. But in fact, σοφία in this concrete background means

18. The first six chapters of Wisdom are organised according to an intentional concentric structure of large unities, subiunities, repetitive and antithetic images. In regard to our subject, as it has already been said before, the following structure seems convincing:

    A [1,1-15] – A' [6,1-21]
    B [1,16-2,24] – B' [5,1-23]

The «inclusio» of δικαιοσύνη within unity 1,1-15 is contested, as we have already seen by M. GILBERT, *Sagesse de Salomon* (n. 9): «Sg 1,1-12 forme une unité, mais 1,12 ouvre sur 1,13-15, qui offre plusiers liens avec 2,23-24 et un seul avec 1,1. Autrement dit, Sg 1,13-15 est-il une conclusion de 1,1-15, parallèle à la conclusion de la pèricope suivante ou constitue-t-il l'introduction de la péricope suivante?» (col. 66). The answer to the Gilbert's question has been already given with what has been said before. Moreover the delimitation of unity 1,1-15 must not been understood with rigidity. The ties between 1,1 and 1,15 do not exclude some references between 1,13-15 and 2,23-24. However it is necessary to recognize the «monostica» nature of 1,15, which helps to uncover the importance of δικαιοσύνη. The emphasis comes from the formal circularity that closes pericope 1,1-15.

19. This imperative is not in present, but in aorist, and in all cases it does not weaken the idea that the action has to continue. Moreover the imperative acts as an intensitive in the exhortation.

man's condition and attitude before the divine δικαιοσύνη[20]. Thus σοφία at times appears as the way to reach δικαιοσύνη.

The verb ἀγαπᾶν thus opens the Book of Wisdom, is the first term which gives it a special dynamism, a dynamism which gets stronger due to imperative mood: ἀγαπήσατε. This initial dynamism pervades the entire book[21], and is especially noteworthy us the first part (1,1-6,21), which ends in 6,21 with the exhortation ἀγαπήσατε σοφίαν, recalling 1,1a: ἀγαπήσατε δικαιοσύνην. While in 1,1a the subjects are οἱ κρινόντες τὴν γῆν, in 6,21 they are οἱ τύραννοι λαῶν. This kind of «inclusio» with regard to 1,1a has been held by the Vulgate: «Diligite sapientiam» (6,21; in 1,1a: «Diligite iustitiam»). In 1,1a the subjects are «qui iudicatis terram», in 6,21: «reges populi».

The following two imperatives of 1,1 (1,1b and 1,1c) further explain how δικαιοσύνη must be loved. In 1b the author expounds how a first disposition to love the Lord's δικαιοσύνη is to think of the Lord with benevolent goodness: φρονήσατε περὶ τοῦ κυρίου ἐν ἀγαθότητι. The verb ἀφρονέω defines and describes the will to consider all things and events under criterions of benevolence because they involve the cosmos and history which belong to the Lord[22].

20. Cf. 7,28: «For God loves (ἀγαπᾷ) nothing so much as the man who lives (συνοικοῦντα) with wisdom». In 7,27 we read that the σοφία renders the holy souls friends of God and prophets. The basis is God's ἀγάπη which makes man righteous and friend of God, and so like the prophets, provides witness of God's ἀγάπη. According to 1,6 σοφία which helps man to live in communion with δικαιοσύνη, is a φιλάνθρωπον πνεῦμα. There is a sort of mutual immanence through the σοφία. The author of Wisdom chose the σοφία figure as the mediator of his own message to his contemporaries. As has already been noted, σοφία was the perfect bridge between the exclusive nationalistic tradition of Israel and the universalist philosophical tradition which appealed so strongly to the Jewish youth of Roman Alexandria. Cf. G. HENTSCHEL – E. ZENGER (ed.), Lehrerin der Gerechtigkeit, Leipzig, 1991, especially pp. 134-151.

21. This dynamism is perceptible in the reading of the nine times in which the author uses ἀγαπᾶν: 1,1a; 4,10; 6,12; 7,10.28; 8,3,7; 11,24; 16,26. In 4,10, for instance, δίκαιος is loved by God, who makes him share his life. In 8,7 the author speaks of the love of righteousness (εἰ δικαιοσύνη ἀγαπᾷ τις). In both the use of ἀγαπᾶν and the two times in which ἀγάπη is used (3,9, 6,18) the prevalent concept is that of faithfulness to love. Such is the meaning of 3,9: «Those who trust in him will understand truth (συνήσουσιν ἀλήθειαν) and the faithful will abide him with love» (ἐν ἀγάπη προσμενοῦσιν αὐτῷ). In 6,18 the relationship between the ἀγάπη and the keeping of laws is explicitly established, which means to reach ἀφθαρσία by God (6,19).

22. All true φρονέω come from God: 6,15; 8,6.21. In 8,8-21 φρόνησις is the necessary condition to achieve the acknowledgment of σοφία and of ἀθανασία (8,17-18). In this sense the φρονεῖν περὶ τοῦ κυρίου ἐν ἀγαθότητι is the first condition to ἀγαπᾶν δικαιοσύνην. In 1QS 1,5 «make the fidelity, the righteousness and the right» are described as members of the community those who: לשות אמת וצדקה ומשפט בארץ (Die Texte aus Qumran, Hebräissh und Deutsch, herausg. von E. Lohse, München, 1964). Regarding ἀγαθότης, it is a term only used in Wisdom (1,1; 7,26; 12,22) and in Sirach (45,23). In Wis 7,26 σοφία is described as an image of the goodness» of God (εἰκὼν τῆς

The third imperative in 1,1c completes the idea of a total and exclusive orientation towards the Lord: «seek him with sincerity of heart» (ἐν ἁπλότητι καρδίας ζητήσατε αὐτόν). The three imperatives reciprocally explain themselves because the object of the action is the same: Κύριος. The sentence ζητήσατε αὐτόν has the same wealth of expression as that of the verb ζητεῖν in the other texts of Wisdom where this verb is used[23]. Since the imperatives of 1,1b (φρονήσατε) and of 1,1c (ζητήσατε), which explain the first imperative of 1,1a (ἀγαπήσατε) by magnifying it are juxtaposed with two modal expressions ἐν ἀγαθότητι (1,1b) and ἐν ἁπλότητι (1c) they reveal the author's interest to expound the meaning of ἀγαπᾶν δικαιοσύνην[24]. The two imperatives of 1,1b

ἀγαθότητος αὐτοῦ). It will be by means of this σοφία that the righteous will uncover the δικαιοσύνη as σωτηρία. In the article ἀγαθός (ἀγαθοεργέω, ἀγαθαποιέω, ἀγαθοσύνη, φιλάγαθος, ἀφιλάγαθος) by W. GRUNDMANN in *TWNT*, t. I, 10-18 the term ἀγαθότητος is not recorded, possibly because is either not used in the NT or because Wisdom and Sirach do not belong to the protestant canon. Philo considers the goodness and sovereignty the highest divine attributes: ἔλεγ μοι κατὰ τὸν ἕνα ὄντως ὄντα θεόυ δύο τὰς ἀνωτάτω εἶναι καὶ πρώτας δυνάμεις ἀγαθότητα καὶ ἐξουσίαν (PHILO, *De Cherubim* 27, F. H. Colson ed., t. II, Cambridge, MS, 1979).

23. Except once (19,17), the seven times in which ζητεῖν is employed in Wisdom (1,1; 6,12.16; 8,2.18; 13,6; 19,17) it always has a religious meaning: to seek God or his σοφία. In each of these texts ζητεῖν describes the aspiration and trend of the man's will towards that which carries him to discover God's will and to syntonize with him. Furthermore it is by means of σοφία that the δίκαιος illuminates and so is able to reach the δικαιοσύνη τοῦ κυρίου and enjoy its soteriological benefits. The strong tie between ζητεῖν and σοφία is explained by P. BEAUCHAMP, *Épouser la Sagesse – ou n'épouser qu'elle? Une énigme du Livre de la Sagesse*, in M. GILBERT (ed.), *La Sagesse de l'Ancien Testament*, Leuven, ²1990, 347-369. Beauchamp writes on p. 349: «La deuxième partie du Livre de la Sagesse présente une autre face du problème. La sagesse y est recherchée comme épouse, et nulle autre épouse n'y est recherchée». According to Philo ζητεῖν includes an intellectual research and the heart's movement to God: οἱ γὰρ ζητοῦντες καὶ ἐπποθεοῦντες θεὸν (PHILO, *De Abrahmo* 87, F.H. Colson ed., t. VI, Cambridge, MA, 1966).

24. These two imperatives, soul of the chiasmic nature of the two sentences, form a graphic parallelism with the sentence of 1,1a about the love for righteousness. Probably the addressee of the Book of Wisdom were witnesses and also moving spirits of the growing use of *shema*, the morning and evening recitation of Deut 6,4-9: «And you shall love the Lord your God with all your heart, and with all your soul and with all your might» (v. 5) (καὶ ἀγαπήσεις κύριον τὸν θεὸν σοῦ ἐξ ὅλης τῆς καρδίας σοῦ καὶ ἐξ ὅλης τῆς ψυχῆς σοῦ καὶ ἐξ ὅλης τῆς δυνάμεως σοῦ). In both Wisdom and Deuteronomy the «philosophic reason» to love God is the same as the reason to love the δικαιοσύνη, the σοφία and the ἀλήθεια. For the Jewish readers of *Wisdom*, though they were in a Hellenistic milieu it should be surprising that to translate the Hebrew terms of the root אהב the LXX used ἔρως and ἐράσθαι verbs frequently employed in the classic and Hellenistic Greek only seven times. Usually LXX use ἀγαπᾶν, ἀγάπη ἀγάπησις, ἀγαπητός, on the contrary they seldom read as φιλία and φιλεῖν. Where Philo would say ἐρᾶν τὴν σοφίαν (PHILO, *Quis rerum divinarum heres sit* 14, F.H. Colson ed., t. V, Cambridge, MS, 1978), *Wisdom* speaks about ἀγαπᾶν τὴν σοφίαν. While in classic and Hellenic Greek the terms of the root ἀγαπᾶν signify a love of acceptance and respect, in the LXX they often take on a new meaning. Cf. T. SÖDING, *Das Wortfeld der Liebe im paganen*

and 1,1c, with the two aforementioned modal expressions, seem to echo the deuteronomic teaching of the tendency towards God in a total and absolute way. The reading of texts such as Deut 4,29 would be illustrative: «But from there you will seek the Lord, your God (καὶ ζητήσετε ἐκεῖ κύριον τὸν θεόν ὑμῶν), and you will find him, if you search after him with all your heart and with all your soul». Moreover the author seems to have a vision like that of the prophets according to whom «to search for the Lord» is the same as «to search for justice». Therefore in Zeph 2,3: «Seek the Lord, all you humble of the land (ζητήσετε τὸν κύριον πάντες ταπεινοὶ γῆς)...» is to seek righteousness (ζητήσετε δικαιοσύνην)[25].

Thus from the very beginning from the first verse of the first chapter, the Wisdom's author presents the grounds for the division of the mankind in which God is operating: that of the men (δίκαιοι) who love the δικαιοσύνη, and that of the men (ἀσεβεῖς) who move away from the δικαιοσύνη.

II. THE ΔΙΚΑΙΟΣΥΝΗ IS IMMORTAL (1,15)

We have already spoken of the character of «inclusio» of Wis 1,15 in relation to Wis 1,1a because the presence of δικαιοσύνη. However between 1,1a and 1,15 there is no textual element which does not concern the two literary extremes of this first structural subunity of the first part of the work (1,1–6,21). On the contrary, the vv. 2-14 are intended to explain the solemn imperative of the beginning (ἀγαπήσατε δικαιοσύ-νην) and to define the simple but effective sentence of the conclusion-«inclusio» of the v. 15: δικαιοσύνη γὰρ ἀθάνατος ἐστιν.

V. 2 establishes a thematic-explanatory connexion with v. 1 and with vv. 3-15. After having strongly exhorted the addressees to love justice, the author feels the necessity to give some theological grounds solely to psychologically move his readers. The Lord's behaviour is described in positive terms[26].

und biblischen Griechisch: Philologische Beobachtungen an der Wurzel «agap-», in *ETL* 68 (1992) 284-330, chiefly on pp. 299-317; S. G. POST, *A Theory of Agape; on the Meaning of Christian Love*, Oxford, 1990, especially 12-23.

25. The coincidence between seeking the righteousness and seeking the Lord also exist in other texts such as Isa 51,1: Ἀκούσατε μου, οἱ διώκοντες τὸ δίκαιον καὶ ζητοῦντες τὸν κύριον. The MT also uses two different verbs: רדף and בקש to express the seeking of justice (צדק) and the seeking of the Lord (יהוה) respectively.

26. Examples of such a tone can be seen in 11,24 and 12,19 where we are told that the God's mercy is a model-lesson for Israel, teaching them that the righteous man must be humane. God loves all that exists, loathing what he has created (11,24), and as the lover

V. 2a: «For he lets to be found...»[27] (ὅτι εὑρίσκεται). The reader still feels the presence of the correlative verb in the v. 1c: ζητήσετε. We have here the teaching of reciprocity, implying both divine initiative and the active responsibility of man, a teaching well developed by LXX Proverbs, which seems to be known by Wisdom's author[28].

V. 2b: «manifests himself...» (ἐμφανίζεται). As in the precedent «stico» God's initiative is also stated here. It will be further explained in detail in 6,13: «She (σοφία) hastens to make herself known to those who desire her»[29]. The verb ἐμφανίζειν of 1,2b emphasizes the idea of illumination which is often present within the world of the divine δικαιοσύνη, perceived by man by means of σοφία, described as φῶς[30].

On the contrary, the ἀσεβείς notice in 5,6 that the light of righteousness (τὸ τῆς δικαιοσύνης φῶς) did not shine on them; the impious speak of the same righteousness that the author invites them to love her from the very beginning of the work: φρονήσατε δικαιοσύνην (1,1a)[31].

of all that lives, he spares all. We have here a faint intimation of the Middle Stoic doctrine of φιλανθρωπία, which is fully elaborated in the writings of Philo. His norms and values are the common coinage of Hellenism: an admirable παιδεία, a life of piety and the pursuit of virtue in accordance with nature. But for Philo nowhere are such norms attained or such values cherished as among the Jews, where they are to be found embedded in their sacred texts and practiced in their ancestral customs. Whatever his reclusive tendencies, and however risky his allegorical method, Philo is remembered as a philosopher of and for the Jewish community.

27. It seems more appropriate to translate εὑρίσκεται as «For he *lets* to be found...» because so is held by the Lord's initiative. Many english versions read: «For he is found by those...» The Vg translates: «Quoniam invenitur ab his...»

28. Cf. for instance, Prov 8,17: «I love those who love me, and those who seek me find me» (ἐγὼ τοὺς ἐμὲ φιλοῦντας ἀγαπῶ, οἱ δὲ ἐμὲ ζητοῦντες εὑρήσουσιν) Gets also illustrative 16,8: «Who seeks the Lord will find knowledge with justice» (ὁ ζητῶν τὸν κύριον εὑρήσει γνῶσιν μετὰ δικαιοσύνης). The term γνῶσις as in the biblical patterns expresses more than a simple noetic knowledge: it is something tied to the experience of the soteriological presence of God. For Wisdom's author knowledge is dynamic acceptance, insuring in action; it is appetitive as well as perceptive. In the Book of Wisdom it is usually implied that one cannot know unless one has a desire of the object known. The members of the community of Qumran boast about being called those who «know» the will of God as קרצ, as תורה, as דה (1QH 9,9; 11,14, 14,15, etc.).

29. In this knowledge as interior illumination light comes from σοφία. In 6,12 the author says something like that written in 1,2: «Wisdom is radiant and unfaiding and she is easily discerned by those who love her (τῶν ἀγαπάντων αὐτὴν) and she lets to be found by those who desire her» (καὶ εὑρίσκεται ὑπὸ τῶν ζητούντων αὐτὴν). This text of 6,12 has many similarities to that of 1,1-2: the verbs ἀγαπᾶν, εὑρίσκειν and ζητεῖν present in both texts, and the common idea of the divine initiative. However in 6,12 the place of Κύριος and of δικαιοσύνη becomes σοφία.

30. The author of Wisdom has appropriated the verb ἐμφανίζειν. In fact, of the eleven times is used by the Greek Bible, four belong to Wisdom (1,2; 16,21; 17,14; 18,18); and of the seven times that the Greek text uses ἐμφανής, three belong to Wisdom (6,22; 7,21; 17,14).

31. In Wis 6,17-20 the author goes round the same idea: the love for δικαιοσύνη, for the observance of the laws as expression of the God's will. Therefore ἀγάπη τήρησις

After clearly presenting the Lord's disposal to be found and to manifest himself in 1,2a and 1,2b, the author asserts that God must neither be tempted nor must men distrust him (1,2b). In fact, man tempts God when he has no confidence in him, or in his soteriological power. The author takes interest in the verb πειράζειν, which he uses 7 times (1,2; 2,17.24; 3,5; 11,9; 12,26; 19,5)[32]. No other book of the wisdom literature uses the verb πειράζειν as frequently as does the Wisdom of Solomon: Proverbs only once, Ecclesiastes twice, Sirach 6 times. In almost all of these texts prevails the idea that when God delivers the righteous in temptation it is for pedagogical reasons: temptation reveals a man's true disposition and will toward God, and thus it is a discovery. On the contrary, when man tempts God it is because he does not recognise his power, because he does not take his saving will seriously, as it is said in 1,2a. The second negative behaviour must be avoided so that the Lord can be *found*, and he *reveals* himself is not to be lacking confidence in God (1,2b). With the use of the verb ἀπιστεῖν the author presents the theological basis of the general organising confrontation and contraposition in Wisdom between the δίκαιοι and the ἀσεβεῖς, with their respective conceptions of God, of man, of life, of death, etc[33]. Thus not to *distrust* God is in this case the same as to love righteousness (δικαιοσύνη), and so man becomes open to that power which God makes feel as σωτηρία, implying ἀφθαρσία and ἀθανασία.

After having explained in 1,1-2 what it means to love δικαιοσύνη now in 1,3-12 the author describes by contrast what it means not to love her. In 1,1-2 it is implicitly understood that the lovers of the

νόμων (6,18a) and brings with incorruptibility, ἀφθαρσία (6,18b), which brings God nearer: ἐγγύς εἶναι ποιεῖ θεοῦ (6,19).

32. The verbs πειράζειν and πειρᾶν sometimes lend each other part of their respective morphological form and they can also change over semantically. For this reason in some dictionaries such as E. HATCH – H. REDPATH, *A Concordance to the Septuagint*, t. II, 1115 the two forms are presented as identical. In Wis 2,17 the ἀσεβεῖς tempt God by testing the righteous; they want to see if God will help him. They tempt God by exhibiting disbelief as the Israelites did in the episode of the scouts (Nm 14,22) and as appears in its classic form in the story of Massah (Ex 17,1-7, alluded to in Pss 78,17f; 95,8f; Deut 6,16). Cf. S. LYONNET, *Le sens de πειράζειν en Sap 2,24 et la doctrine du péché originel*, in *Bib* 39 (1958) 27-36.

33. Wisdom uses the verb ἀπιστεῖν with the meaning of «to be unbelieving», «to distrust» four times (1,2; 10,7; 12,17; 18,13). The author uses this verb to negatively illustrate the behaviour of the impious (ἀσεβής), in contrast to the δίκαιος. The use of this verb is very much like that of Isa 7,9: «If you do not believe you will not resist» (ἐὰν μὴ πιστεύσητε οὐδὲ συνῆτε). The idea is more strongly expressed in the MT where the same root אמן is used, and so the same sound establishes the connection between believing and resisting (to subsist): תאמינו לא תאמנו אם לא. Furthermore this root, אמן semantically implies the concept of strengthening, or the idea of getting strong resting on God who is Strength.

δικαιοσύνη are the δίκαιοι. The author does not say it explicitly because of the literary demands to call the pagan rulers to love and pursue justice, while admonishing those whose deviant behaviour will inevitably result in their destruction (1,1-15). On the contrary, in 1,3-12 those who do not love the δικαιοσύνη are called ἀφρόνες, βλασφήμοι, ἀσεβεῖς. They refuse righteousness by sins of perverse *thoughts* (vv. 3-5: devious thoughts cut men off from God), by the sins of the *word* (vv. 6-11: the ἀσεβεῖς utter unrighteous things, ἄδικα) and by the sins of *work* (v. 12: they bring on destruction by the works of their hands). The author manifests clearly that not to love justice brings on destruction and death, which are understood as the definitive separation from God.

These messages are confirmed in the solemn statement of 1,13-14, which in conjunct with the interpretative resonances of Gen 1–3 compose the important and definitive affirmation of 1,15 on immortality. Verse 13, with an emphatically negative assertion introduces the strong and definitive statement of verse 14:

> 1,13a: «Because God did not make death» (ὅτι ὁ θεός θάνατον οὐκ ἐποίησεν)[34].

The author deals with the full concept of death in connection with what has been said in 1,12. In fact, man is naturally mortal, as the author reveals in 7,1a («I too, indeed, am mortal like all men»); 9,14a; 15,17. On the contrary, in 1,12 man is urged not to seek death through his behaviour; although he cannot avoid it[35].

---

34. In Wis 1,13a the verb ποιεῖν «almost» is synonymous with τίκτειν of 1,14a. We have chosen «almost» as the definition because it seems that the author reserves the verb τίκτειν to describe with conviction what God made in the beginning, a work which nobody other than God could have accomplished. Thus, though the influence of the Septuagintic vocabulary, which uses τίκτειν or ποιεῖν without distinction to translate ברא in Gen 1 (ποιεῖν appears in Gen 1,1, 1,21; 1,27 as version of ברא), the author writes τίκτειν in 1,14a to emphasise the positive action of God. Wisdom knows that ברא is used in the OT only with the deity as the subject, hence indicating a work which is distinctively divine. In Gen 1 ברא is also used for the creation of animals (1,21) and of man. Since each of these works, the production of animal life and of human life, is a new stage the word is aptly used. The author of Wisdom knows all these semantic nuances, despite his dependence on the Septuagint.

35. It seems to me that to back up the theory that 1,13a also discusses physical death because this text like 2,24 interpret the accounts of creation and of the fall as are told in Gen 1–3, is an interpretation that reads too much into the text. This kind of argumentation assumes, but does not explain it, that the author of Wisdom literally interprets the mentioned texts of *Genesis*. In this sense the position of P. GRELOT is not convincing, *L'eschatologie de la Sagesse et les apocalysses juives,* in À *la rencontre de Dieu, Mémorial A. Gelin,* Paris, 1961. Nor is the thesis of M. GILBERT, *La relecture de Gn 1–3 dans le livre de la Sagesse,* in L. DEROUSSEAUX (ed.), *La création dans l'Orient ancien* (LD, 127), Paris, 1987, pp. 323-344, convincing, although it is better formulated. On the contrary the point of view that of J. Vílchez expressed not only in his recent commentary:

1,13b: «and he does not take delight in the destruction of the living» (οὐδὲ τέρπεται ἐπ᾽ ἀπωλείᾳ ζώντων).

With a highly psychologically plastic anthropomorphism the author goes on in his reflection: God is God of life. However to be able to include with great incisiveness the two correlative extremes «life-death», he employs with a negation, as in 1,13a. Thus the God of these verses recalls the «transcendent» God of the Priestly tradition (Gen 1) and his closeness, anthropomorphically expressed by the Jahwist and Elohist tradition (Gen 2–3). In this sense it is possible to speak of a «humane» message of Wisdom[36].

Sabiduría, Estella, 1990, pp. 145-149, but also in a much older: *Sabiduría* La Sagrada Escritura. Antiguo Testamento t. IV: *Los Salmos y los Libros Salmónicos,* Madrid, 1967, seems to be much more valid: «La muerte, en su sentido pleno, trascendental, como se entiende en v. 12, no proviene de Dios, sino que es consecuencia de los pecados del hombre (cf. 2,23s)» (p. 638).

36. It seems that sometimes our author wants to inculcate his readers with the necessity to discover and to witness God's «humanity». Twice wisdom is described as φιλάνθρωπος, humane or benevolent (1,6; 7,23), and in 12,19 we are told that God's mercy is a model-lesson for Israel, teaching them that the righteous man must be humane. God knows mans' limitations, as well as his freedom as it appears in Wis 11,23-12,2. Bonaventure accurately interprets the meaning of this message in his *Commentarius in librum Sapientiae,* Opera omnia, t. VI, Quaracchi, 1893, pp. 139-171: Sap 11,23-25

«(Vers. 23…) *El misereris omnium* etc. Hic ponitur probatio divinae misericordiae; et primo probat eam per effectum *dissimulationis;* secundo, per effectum *dilectionis; Diligis enim;* tertio, per effectum *conservationis: Quomodo autem posset* etc.; quarto, per effectum *remissionis: Parcis autem.*

(Vers. 24.). *El misereris omnium,* id est, in omnibus exerces misericordiae effectum, secundum illud Psalmi: «Miserationes eius super omnia opera eius»; item: «Universae viae Domini misericordia et veritas»; item: «Misericordia Domini plena est terra». *Quoniam omnia potes;* unde omnia sunt facturae tuae et opera tua, secundum illud Psalmi: «Qui fecit caelum et terram, mare et omnia, quae in eis sunt». *Et dissimulas,* ad tempus scilicet non puniendo, peccata hominum; non dicit *angelorum,* quia peccatum angelorum statim fuit punitum; unde Isaiae decimo quarto: «Quomodo cecidisti, lucifer, de caelo, qui mane oriebaris»? *Propter poenitentiam;* unde ad Romanos secundo: «Ignoras, quia benignitas Dei ad poenitentiam te adducit»? Ezechielis decimo octavo: «Si egerit impius poenitentiam ab omnibus peccatis suis etc.; vita vivet et non morietur».

(Vers. 25.). *Diligis enim omnia, quae sunt,* scilicet bona eorum approbando et concervando; unde Genesis primo: «Vidit Deus cuncta, quae fecerat, et erant valde bona»; Glossa: «Bonus opifex opus suum diligit»; Deus autem peccatum non fecit; unde Ioannis primo: «Sine ipso factum est nihil», id est «peccatum», secundum Augustinum. Et ideo peccatum non diligit, sed odit, secundum illud Psalmi: «Dilexisti iustitiam et odisti iniquitatem». *Et nihil odisti eorum quae fecisti,* nullum scilicet reprobando.

CONTRA quod dicitur in Psalmo: «Iniquos odio habui»; item: «Odisti omnes, qui operantur iniquitatem»; item Ecclesiastici duodecimo: «Altissimus odio habet peccatores».

Sed dicendum, quod non odit facturam suam, sed facturae vitium, sicut artifex statuam, quam fecit, diligit, et tamen aliquem nodum ex parte materiae in ea existentem odit. …» (p. 183)

Cf. also G. PICO DELLA MIRANDOLA, *De hominis dignitate Heptaplus,* E. Garin ed., Firenze, 1942, p. 106: «O summam dei patris liberalitatem, summam et admirandam hominis felicitatem». He speaks about God's liberality and man's responsibility.

The negative formulation of 1,13b to emphasise God's engagement with all living beings is like that of Wis 11,24b: «And you loathe nothing which you have created»[37].

1,14a: «For he created all things that they might endure».

The tight connection of this part of the verse 14 with the verse 13 is manifested by means of the use of the consecutive-explanatory conjunctive γάρ. By saying: ἔκτισεν γὰρ εἰς τὸ εἶναι τὰ πάντα confirms what is said in v. 13a: ὅτι ὁ θεός θάνατον οὐκ ἐποίησεν. The sentence τὰ πάντα is like the complement of the intention and action of God-creator expressed with the verb τίκτω; εἰς τὸ εἶναι means the permanence in being of everything created by God[38].

1,14b: «And the creatures of the world are wholesome».

Indeed the effect of the creating action of God is that created things are wholesome: σωτήριοι αἱ γενέσεις τοῦ κόσμου. The reader may discover or perceive this half-verse as a paraphrase of Gen 1,10.12. 18.21.25.31: καὶ εἶδεν ὁ θεὸς ὅτι καλόν. In Gen 1,31 the topic for a paraphrase is still more attractive: «And God saw everything that he had made, and behold, it was very good (καὶ ἰδοὺ καλὰ λίαν)[39].

37. A formulation probably known by the author of Wisdom is that of Ezek 18,23.32: «Have I any pleasure in the death of the wicked, says the Lord God, and not rather that he should turn from his way and live? ... For I have no pleasure in the death of any one, says the Lord God; so turn and live». On Wis 11,24 see the study of G. DE CARLO, *Ami, infatti, gli esistenti tutti*. *Studio di Sap 11,24*, in *Laurentianum* 36 (1995) 416; «L'odio di Dio, che alle volte trova il suo risvolto nel castigo, non è mai rivolto contro l'uomo in quanto tale, ma contro il suo agire malvagio, Anche allora esso assume, tuttavia, un valore positivo: esprime la non connivenza di Dio con il male e la volontà di ripristinarne le relazioni giuste in seno alla comunità del popolo eletto. Sap 11,24, che considera l'atteggiamento fondamentale di Dio verso le realtà create e non in rapporto ad una categoria particolare di persone o di azioni, non ammette in alcun modo in lui la disposizione di odio».

38. All eleven times in which the expression τὰ πάντα is used in Wisdom the references concern the totality of all things created by God; the same meaning can be expressed with the term πάντα without an article. The simultaneous presence of τίκτω and πάντα seems to manifest the wish of paraphrasing the Hebrew Gen 1,1. השמים ואת הארץ את אלהים ברא. Indeed «heavens and earth» in the Semitic culture expresses the idea of totality, an idea that the author of «Wisdom expresses by means of τὰ πάντα or simply παντα, translation of כל or of הכל (cf. Eccles 3,1). The author does not use κόσμος because it is too generic. Instead he prefers τὰ πάντα as a resonance of οὐρανός καὶ γῆ (Gen 1,1).

39. Just as in classic Greek, in Hellenism as well as in great number of languages «beautiful» and «good» in the Septuagint are often found together, constituting one thing: καλός καγαθός. The LXX usually prefer to translate טוב with καλός in an ontico-aesthetic sense rather than in a ethic one. For instance, in Gen 1,31 καλός implies an ontico-aesthetic judgment: the successful work of the creation in which God enjoyed himself. Cf. F. RAURELL, *Lineamenti di antropologia biblica*, Casale Monferrato, 1986, p. 206.

The author considers the things created by God as «salvation carriers», wholesome. It seems that the term σωτήριοι has an active meaning, a kind of *nomen agentis* like σωτήρ[40]. By means of the word σωτήριοι the author presents the creatures as provided with an active energy of permanence given by the power of God Creator.

Moreover, with regard to the sentence αἱ γενέσεις τοῦ κόσμου, it can be added that by the use of σωτήριοι[41] the author seems to understand the world (κόσμος) as a platform of the relationship between man and God. It has been asserted in 1,6.7: «For wisdom is a benevolent spirit» (φιλάνθρωπον πνεῦμα). For the spirit of the Lord fills the world (τὴν οἰκουμένην). Thus, the κόσμος is seen within the soteriological sphere[42].

It is possible that the γενέσεις τοῦ κόσμου manifests a veiled allusion to the Genesis beginning as is read by Codex Alexandrinus (A): γένεσις κόσμου[43]. The point that *Wis* 1,14b uses the plural γενέσεις can reflect the Hebrew תולדות of Gen 2,4a («These are the *generations* of the heavens and the earth when they were created»), that the LXX translate and interpret in a different way[44]. Probably the author of Wisdoms knows this background, which can help to better understand the teaching of the κόσμος. Though indirectly, here the concept of blessing (ברכה-εὐλογία) so characteristic of the Jewish vision of man and the world plays an important role. The σωτήριοι γενέσεις τοῦ κόσμου and the תולדות are connected with them through the implicit concept of blessing, as source of life and of σωτηρία. The σωτήριοι γενέσεις τοῦ κόσμου are the reality and the witness of a world that thanks to them not only is living but also is the object of the divine σωτηρία, which preserves it[45].

---

40. The translation and interpretation given by M. GILBERT takes this perspective, *Il cosmo secondo il libro della Sapienza,* in G. DE GENNARO (ed.), *Il cosmo nella Bibbia,* Napoli, 1982, p. 190.

41. Both terms, thus, are tied with σώζω. Cf. W. FOERSTER – G. FOHRER, art. σώζω, in *TWNT,* t. VIII, col. 1022-1024, where it is possible to verify the scale of different meanings: to save, to preserve, to defend, etc.

42. Wis 5,14-23 apocalyptically describes God's fighting in favour of the δίκαιοι. Yet God does not fight alone: at his side are *creation* (κτίσις: «The Lord will arm the *creation* to control the enemies», v. 17) and the *world* (κόσμος: «and the *world* will join him to fight against the madmen», v. 20). Both, κόσμος and κτίσις are in the same soteriological perceptive as the σωτήριοι γενέσεις of 1,14b.

43. (A 121). Cf. J. W. WEVERS, *Genesis.* Septuaginta Vetus Testamentum Graecum, t. I, Göttingen, 1974, p. 75. The thing could surprise because the late date of the Codex Alexandrinus (s. V A.C.).

44. Indeed we find in the MT: אלה תולדות השמים והארץ, while the LXX reads: αὕτη ἡ βίβλος γενέσεως οὐρανοῦ καὶ γῆς.

45. This idea is present in the analysis of C. LARCHER, *Le livre de la Sagesse ou la sagesse de Salomon,* t. I, Paris, 1983, pp. 203-204, as can be seen in the following transla-

Thus 1,14b describes the soteriological value of the creatures in accordance with an unitarian vision of God as Creator and Saviour. The σωτήριοι γενέσεις are the pillars of the life, they assure its permanence[46]. These primary γενέσεις continue communicating life to a κόσμος which is nature and history.

> 1,14cd: «And there is no deadly poison in them and death's rulership is not on earth».

In this double negative formulation there is a rhetoric antithesis to reaffirm what has been affirmed in 1,14ab on the positivity of the creation: the creative action of God brings to existence the being, life and the goodness of all creatures. The destructive poison is not in the things but rather in the will and actions of men: «Do not court death through a deviant way of life nor bring on destruction by the works of your hands» (Wis 1,12). By the assertion of 1,14d («Death's rulership is not on earth») the author proclaims with clarity that man is responsible for his own eschatological destiny.

In 1,14c it is clearly denied that «in them» (ἐν αὐταῖς), i.e., in the γενέσεις τοῦ κόσμου exists a «deadly poison» (φάρμακον ὀλέθρου). Thus it is denied that there is an absolute «contra-sovereignty», a βασίλειον on the earth which comes from death. Indeed, death is only present when man invites it, when man brings on destruction by the works of his hands.

> 1,15: «For righteousness is immortal» (δικαιοσύνη γὰρ ἀθάνατος ἐστιν).

The inclusive character of this verse regarding to 1,1a because the term δικαιοσύνη, gets stronger with the consecutive-explanatory parti-

---

tion: «Et elles sont conservatrices les générations dans le monde», although at first sight does not seem to catch the idea of σωτήριοι (p. 195).

46. In the Book of Wisdom the doctrine of creation is not different from what we find in wisdom literature in general: wisdom literature presents a theology of its own kind. Seems unacceptable Reventlow's point of wiew, according to which the integration of wisdom into Old Testament Theology is an unsolved task that remains for the future (H. G. REVENTLOW, *Hauptprobleme der alttestamentlichen Theologie im 20. Jahrhundert*, Darmstad, 1982, p. 201). A literary analysis of texts dealing with creation supposedly shows that it is not central to Israelite faith. This doctrine is absent from most of the prophets. There are many powerful passages concerning the Lord's victory over chaos in Deutero-Isaiah (for instance, 44,24-28), but here creation is clearly subordinate to the redemption which the prophet is proclaiming to the exiles: «Your husband is your Creator... your Redeemer is the Holy One of Israel» (Isa 54,5). The God of immediate experience, i.e., wisdom experience is the Creator, who is also גֹּאֵל. Barth's formulation is curious: «Creation is the external motive of the Covenant (Gen 1), the Covenant is the internal motive of Creation» (K. BARTH, *Kirchliche Dogmatik*, t. III: *Die Lehre von der Schöpfung*, Zurich ³1950, p. 1). Cf. the interesting study of R.E. MURPHY, *Wisdom and Creation*, in *JBL* 104 (1985) 3-11.

cle γὰρ. If we connect both sentences, that of 1,15 and that of 1,1a we find a grammatically well constructed sentence:

«Love righteousness, you rulers of the earth, for righteousness is immortal».

The particle γὰρ justifies the exhortation of 1,1a and also justifies the explanation given by 1,1bc-14 of the δικαιοσύνη, of its fruits, of what separates men from God, of this God who did not make death but who created all things so that they might exist, of the wholesome character of the creatures. As it has already been pointed out the shortness of v. 1,15, «mostick» and with the substantive verb εἶναι, make it clear that the centre of the reflection is δικαιοσύνη.

In both verses (1,1a and 1,15) it is dealt with the δικαιοσύνη of God: in 1,1a we have the imperative to love righteousness, in 1,15 we are told that to love righteousness means to love the Lord. In 1,2-14 it is explained what means to place oneself correctly or uncorrectly before the δικαιοσύνη, i.e., before Κύριος: to place oneself before life or death, to choose between life and death. In the long reflection of 1,1-15 two subjective agents of history emerge: God and man. The latter one can be the δίκαιος or the ἀσεβής, according to their behaviour with regard to the δικαιοσύνη[47].

---

47. The text of 1,15 is the object of permanent discussions due to the excessive importance placed on the Vetus Latina's addition of half verse to 1,15. After *iustitia enim est immortalis,* indeed, it adds: *iniustitia autem est mortis acquisitio* (wrongly written *iustitia* by G. SCARPAT, *Libro della Sapienza,* t. I, Brescia, 1989, p. 404). Certainly it is not easy to know whether this addition is a product of the Vetus Latina itself or whether the addition was found in the Greek *Vorlage.* In any case this addition and others which are in the Vetus Latina are important for the history of the text. (There are other additions in the Vetus Latina but they seem to be secondary. So 6,1: «Melior est sapientia quam vires et vir prudens magis quam fortis»; 6,23: «Diligite lumen sapientiae omnes qui praeestis populis»; 9,19b: «Quicumque placuerunt tibi, Domine, a principio»; 11,5bc: «a defectione populi sui cum abundarent filii Israel laetati sunt»). The variant-addition of the *Vetus Latina* has no support in the MSS known today, as it appears in the critical edition by J. ZIEGLER, *Sapientia Salomonis.* Septuaginta. (Vetus Testamentum Graecum, t. XII), Göttingen ²1980, p. 97. The translators of the Veteres Latinae probably wanted «to improve» the text. The Vetus Latina's addition has been supported by C.L.W. GRIMM, *Das Buch der Weisheit,* Leipzig, 1860, who presents the following retroversion: ἀδικία δὲ θανάτου περιποίησις ἐστιν. P. HEINISCH holds the same position without asserting any argument, *Das Buch der Weisheit,* Münster, 1912. However his many efforts to support the addition do not convince the study of D. DE BRUYNE, *Étude sur le texte latin de la Sagesse,* in *Revue Bénédictine* 41 (1929) 101-133. The observation of N. Fernández Marcos in his translation *Sabiduría,* in *Sagrada Biblia.* Versión crítica sobre los textos hebreo, arameo y griego, dirigida por F. Cantera – M. Iglesias, Madrid, 1975, p. 918, nota: «El verso no tiene conexión con lo que precede y sigue: o introducimos la variante de la Vetus Latina o hemos de admitir una laguna en el texto». Neither one thing nor the other. It is sufficient to look at the literary structure of this subunity (1,1-15) and to see the inclusive character of 1,15 with regard to 1,1a.

The inclusive character with which 1,1a and 1,15 are tied through the δικαιοσύνη, all that is said in 1,bc, the exhortations of 1,12 not to court death, the statements about God who created life and who did not make death of 1,13, etc. make it clear that both verses (1,1a and 1,15) speak about the divine δικαιοσύνη which enable to benefit from the σωτηρία and to enjoy the eschatological ἀθανασία in communion with God. Therefore the invitation to love righteousness is the invitation to open oneself totally to the divine soteriological action[48].

In section 1,1-15 there is an idea which pervades all verses: the way to reach ἀθανασία is to love δικαιοσύνη. This idea is developed in 15,3: «For to know you is perfect righteousness and to recognise your power is the root of immortality».

The δικαιοσύνη is complete (ὁλόκληρος), hence bringing ἀθανασία to full communion with God as it is said in 15,2: σοί ἐσμεν.

Cardenal Vives i Tutó, 16
E-08034 Barcelona

Frederic RAURELL

---

48. Of course it is not always easy to determine when δικαιοσύνη is God's righteousness and when it is man's righteousness. It seems that the author of Wisdom likes to maintain some degree of ambiguity. Such can be seen, for instance, with 8,7: «And if any one loves righteousness, her (of σοφία) labours are virtues». In 8,7a «the loved righteousness» (εἰ δικαιοσύνην ἀγαπᾷ τις) seems to be different from the righteousness from 8,7d. In the first case is divine δικαιοσύνη, the latter belongs to the group of the moral virtues of man. We find the traditional platonic division of the four cardinal virtues in 8,7bcd (cf. PLATO, *Republica* 4,427, ed. G. Reale, t. II, Milano, 1991). But the author of Wis 8,7 follows his own division when he speaks of the ἀρηταί.

«ET COMME LE SACRIFICE DE L'HOLOCAUSTE IL LES AGRÉA»
(SG 3,6)
LES PREMIÈRES COMPARAISONS DU MARTYRE AVEC UN SACRIFICE DANS L'ANCIEN TESTAMENT

1. LA QUESTION

Avant de souffrir le martyre, Polycarpe de Smyrne compare celui-ci dans sa dernière prière à un «holocauste (ὁλοκαύτωμα) qui sera accepté par Dieu» et il supplie que sa personne mise à mort comme martyr soit acceptée (προσδεχθείην) dans la présence du Seigneur «comme un sacrifice gras et agréable» (ἐν θυσίᾳ πίονι καὶ προσδεκτῇ)[1]. Est-ce que cette comparaison du martyre avec un holocauste et une immolation liturgique a un fondement scripturaire? Le but de cette étude en honneur de Maurice Gilbert est de montrer que cette comparaison apparaît avec netteté en Sg 3,6 et et également en Dn 3,38-40 LXX et Théodotion.

Car Sg 3,6 compare le martyre avec l'oblation d'un holocauste (ὁλοκάρπωμα θυσίας), et les martyrs eux-mêmes seront agréés par Dieu comme un sacrifice (προσεδέξατο αὐτούς). En effet, Sg 3,1-6 présente le martyre des justes[2]. Le contexte est explicite: le v. 1 se place après la mise à mort des justes qui échappent désormais à la portée des tortionnaires, tandis que les v. 2-4 se situent dans la perspective des insensés au moment où ceux-ci assistaient à la mort des justes qu'ils pensaient frappés d'anéantissement et subissant un châtiment cruel. En réalité, ce fut une entrée dans la paix (v. 3b), et celle-ci confirmera que les justes avaient espéré avec raison, à l'heure de leur mort, en l'immortalité qui leur serait réservée (v. 4b). Les vv. 1-4 regardent donc le même événement, l'exécution des justes, dans deux perspectives opposées, dans celle des insensés (nous dirions: des incroyants) et dans celle des justes, condamnés à mort et entrés désormais dans l'immortalité. Les vv. 5-6 introduisent une troisième perspective, celle de Dieu[3]. Vu à partir de Dieu, en effet, il s'agissait d'une épreuve qu'il leur imposait, mais d'une

---

1. Martyrium Polycarpi, XIV, 1-2, ed. F.X. FUNK, *Patres Apostolici*, t. I Tübingen, Laupp, 1901.

2. Il est vrai que C. LARCHER, *Le livre de la Sagesse ou la sagesse de Salomon*, t. I (EB), Paris, Gabalda, 1983, p. 283 pense que «l'idée d'offrande renvoie plutôt à la vie entière des justes, offerte sans cesse à Dieu et se consumant progressivement pour lui».

3. J. VÍLCHEZ LÍNDEZ, *Sabiduría* (Nueva Bíblia Española, t. V), Estella, Editorial Verbo Divino, 1990, pp. 178-181.

petite épreuve en comparaison avec la grandeur de la récompense qu'il leur destinera en contrepartie (v. 5). L'épreuve est comparée, selon une image traditionnelle, à la purification de l'or au creuset[4]. Cette comparaison classique du métal précieux purifié par le feu au v. 6a est accompagnée d'une ligne parallèle qui ne semble pas avoir de modèle ailleurs dans la Bible[5]: «et comme le sacrifice d'un holocauste Il les agréa» (v. 6b)[6].

Deux questions se posent ici: quelle est la raison pour comparer le martyre à l'acte liturgique du sacrifice d'un holocauste?[7] En effet, dans la réalité, le martyre n'est pas une célébration liturgique, mais une mise

4. On trouve des parallèles bibliques, qumraniens et de l'antiquité gréco-latine dans D. WINSTON, *The Wisdom of Solomon* (AB, 43), Garden City, NY, Doubleday, 1979, p. 128, et dans beaucoup d'autres commentaires.

5. P. ex. WINSTON, *Wisdom* (n. 4), prolixe pour le v. 6a (12 lignes de parallèles), est laconique pour le v. 6b (une demi ligne pour commenter «il les a agréés»: un renvoi à Am 5,22 LXX). Le même silence règne ailleurs, excepté en G. SCARPAT, *Libro della Sapienza (Biblica. Testi e studi,* 1), Brescia, Paideia, 1989, p. 234.

6. D. JACOBI, *Weisheit Salomos* (JSHRZ, 3,1), Gütersloh, Mohn, 1980, p. 410, voit en Sg 3,1-6 une série de paroles de consolation conclues par une promesse prophétique de salut aux vv. 7-9. C'est ne pas voir la composition et l'unité de pensée qui marque la section des vv. 1-6, avec les trois regards sur le même événement du martyre: le regard des martyrs (l'espérance), celui des insensés (l'absurdité et la cruauté de cette mort), celui de Dieu (l'épreuve et la récompense débordante accordée). SCARPAT, *Sapienza* (n. 5), p. 234, corrige légèrement le texte en accusatif: θυσίαν, sans appui dans les manuscrits grecs: J. ZIEGLER, *Sapientia Salomonis* (Septuaginta, vol. XII,1), Göttingen, Vandenhoeck & Ruprecht, 1962, p. 102, mais en recourant à la Vetus Latina. Celle-ci est complexe et n'atteste pas de façon claire l'accusatif *hostiam*: W. THIELE, *Sapientia Salomonis* (Vetus Latina, XI/1), Freiburg i.Br., Herder, 1977, pp. 291-293; pour Augustin, cf. A.M. LA BONNARDIÈRE, *Biblia Augustiniana, A.T.:* Le livre de la Sagesse, Paris, Études augustiniennes, 1970, p. 271. La Vulgate, qui représente ici la Vetus Latina, présente elle aussi un témoignage divisé: *Biblia Sacra iuxta Latinam vulgatam versionem, Sapientia Salomonis. Liber Hiesu filii Sirach,* Romae, Typis Polyglottis Vaticanis, 1963, p. 31. En faveur du texte grec, on notera qu'en Lv 1,9.13.17 l'holocauste (κάρπωμα) est identifié au «mets consumé» (אשה, θυσία). On peut donc interpréter cet holocauste de Lv 1 comme une catégorie spéciale de l'holocauste, celui qui est en même temps un mets consumé. ὁλοκάρπωμα θυσίας signifie ainsi peut-être l'«holocauste par excellence», puisqu'à la fois holocauste et mets consumé. L'expression reste certes difficile, si bien que les deux accusatifs proposés par Scarpat d'après certains témoins de la Vetus Latina (et de la Vulgate) semblent être facilitants. Il faut noter également que le livre de la Sagesse utilise volontiers des *génitifs d'identité,* par exemple en 1,10 θροῦς γογγυσμῶν (les murmures qui sont un bruit, i.e. bruyants), 1,12 πλάνη ζωῆς (une vie qui est un égarement), 2,12 ἁμαρτήματα παιδείας ἡμῶν (notre formation qui est une suite de péchés), etc. On pourrait d'ailleurs essayer d'interpréter θυσίας en accusatif pluriel, car LXX emploie ce mot parfois au pluriel. Mais le singulier «holocauste» suivi sans conjonction du pluriel «sacrifices» serait si difficile qu'il faut écarter cet essai de solution.

7. Le P. Maurice GILBERT a publié une bibliographie monumentale sur le livre de la Sagesse, recensant également les monographies sur les passages individuels de ce livre, en C. LARCHER, *Le livre de la Sagesse ou la sagesse de Salomon* (EB), Paris, Gabalda, 1983, p. 11-48; cette bibliographie va jusqu'en 1982. Sur Sg 3,6, aucune étude monographique n'est signalée. Si j'ai bien regardé les sources bibliographiques, il n'en existe pas non plus depuis cette date jusqu'à présent (1998).

à mort injuste, un acte de violence arbitraire puisqu'il est l'assassinat d'une personne innocente. Et deuxièmement, est-ce que la Sagesse de Salomon est le témoin le plus ancien de la comparaison entre le martyre et l'holocauste?[8]

2. LE MARTYRE COMME HOLOCAUSTE

Le deuxième Livre des Maccabées (2 M 6–7) ne compare pas le martyre d'Éléazar ni celui des sept frères et de leur mère à un sacrifice. En revanche, Is 53:10 avait comparé le don de la vie que le Serviteur de YHWH a fait avec le sacrifice *'āshām:* Ce sacrifice est destiné en premier lieu au pardon de la profanation de ce qui est sacré (*ma'al*). La LXX transforme ce passage en introduisant une autre catégorie sacrificielle: le sacrifice pour le péché (περὶ ἁμαρτίας) qui est destiné principalement au pardon des transgressions[9]. En outre, dans la LXX, ce n'est pas le Serviteur de YHWH qui offre une oblation pour le péché, mais les «vous», qui sont peut-être ceux-là mêmes qui avaient pris la parole en «nous» en Is 53,1-6. L'oblation de ce «sacrifice pour le péché» (s'il s'agit bien de lui) n'est donc pas offerte par le «martyr». De toute façon, Sag 3,6 se distingue d'Is 53 par la comparaison avec un *holocauste.*

On cite volontiers Ps 50,18-19 (TM 51,18-19) comme une source possible d'inspiration pour la comparaison de Sg 3,6 du martyre avec un holocauste[10]. Mais dans ce Psaume il ne s'agit pas de martyre et les termes ne sont pas identiques. θυσία, il est vrai, est employé de part et d'autre; en revanche, l'expression ὁλοκάρπωμα θυσίας ne se trouve qu'en Sg 3,6, pour tout l'A.T. et le N.T., alors que ὁλοκάρπωμα est assez rare dans l'A.T. grec, où il correspond à *'ôlâ*. De plus, les sacrifices de Ps 51:18-19 sont offerts pour le pardon ce qui n'est pas le cas en Sg 3,6 où le contexte ne suggère pas l'expiation, mais l'hommage offert au Seigneur par l'holocauste.

Il existe cependant un passage vétérotestamentaire suggérant une comparaison entre le martyre et l'ensemble des offrandes cultuelles.

---

8. Cette deuxième question implique le problème de la datation. LARCHER, *Livre de la Sagesse* (n. 2), p. 141-161 date la Sagesse de Salomon après l'année 30 av. J.-C. SCARPAT, *Sapienza* (n. 5), p. 24, et WINSTON, *Wisdom* (n. 4), p. 23, pensent au règne de Caligula (37-41 après J.-C.), VÍLCHEZ LÍNDEZ, *Sabiduría* (n. 3), p. 63, à l'époque d'Auguste (30 avant J.-C. – 14 après).

9. *'āshām* est normalement rendu par πλημμέλεια en LXX: C. KIRCHER, *Concordantiae Veteris Testamenti Graecae, Ebraeis vocibus respondentes*, Francofurti, apud Cl. Marnium…, 1607, pp. 577-579.

10. LARCHER, *Livre de la Sagesse* (n. 2), 283; déjà C.L.W. GRIMM, *Das Buch der Weisheit* (KeH zu den Apokryphen des A.T.), Leipzig, Hirzel, 1860, p. 88.

C'est la prière d'Azarias en Dn 3,26-45 LXX et Théodotion, dans les vv. 38-40. Le v. 38 constate la disparition du culte: il n'y a plus d'holocauste (ὁλοκαύτωσις) ni de sacrifice (θυσία) ni d'offrande (προσφορά) ni d'encens ni de lieu pour présenter les prémices (καρπῶσαι) et trouver le pardon. LXX et Théodotion sont identiques en ce qui concerne les termes signifiant ces différentes oblations. Au v. 39, Azarias et ses compagnons poursuivent leur supplication en demandant d'*être agréés eux-mêmes* par Dieu (προσδέχεσθαι) avec une âme humiliée et un esprit contrit, comme ils seraient agréés s'ils apportaient des holocaustes de béliers et de taureaux et des dizaines de milliers d'agneaux gras. Ce verset correspond au Ps 50,19 (TM 51,19) qui lui aussi remplace provisoirement (cf. vv. 20-21) les sacrifices supprimés, par l'âme humiliée et le cœur contrit. Enfin, le v. 40 conclut: «Qu'ainsi se fasse *notre sacrifice (θυσία) aujourd'hui* devant toi… car il n'y a pas de honte pour ceux qui mettent leur confiance en toi». Ici, l'offrande n'est pas l'âme humiliée et l'esprit contrit, mais la personne elle-même et la foi en Dieu des trois martyrs.

La prière d'Azarias, qui se trouve dans la fournaise avec Ananias et Misaël, ne peut viser, dans la narration où elle est encastrée, que le martyre des trois jeunes gens quand ceux-ci disent (LXX) (ou quand Azarias dit pour eux, selon Théodotion) «que se fasse ainsi *notre sacrifice* aujourd'hui devant toi!» Puisque leur prière vient de constater que le culte a totalement cessé (v. 38), les martyrs désignent leur «âme humiliée et leur esprit contrit» (v. 39), mais aussi leur foi (v. 40) et donc surtout leur martyre, qui est le don de leur vie pour la foi, comme «notre *sacrifice* d'aujourd'hui», puisque ce sont cette âme humiliée, cet esprit contrit et cette foi qui les ont conduits dans la fournaise. Car ils n'ont pas voulu se sauver eux-mêmes au prix du reniement de Dieu. Dans la situation racontée, le martyre prend la place des oblations du culte supprimé[11]. Celui-ci avait exprimé la confession de Dieu. À présent, dans son absence, c'est précisément le martyre qui l'exprime.

3. La date de la prière d'Azarias

Il semble raisonnable d'assigner cette prière à l'époque de la persécution d'Antiochus IV comme le livre de Daniel lui-même. Car elle s'explique le mieux sur le fond de l'expérience effective de la profanation du temple, de la suppression du culte et du martyre des fidèles[12].

---

11. Telle est aussi l'interprétation de M. HENGEL, *The Atonement. The Origins of the Doctrine in the New Testament*, London, SCM, 1981, p. 61.

12. LXX et Théodotion sont identiques au v. 40 cité en traduction. O. PLÖGER,

4. Conclusion

1. Trois passages bibliques comparent explicitement le martyre aux sacrifices et offrandes de la liturgie célébrée à Jérusalem: Is 53,10, la prière d'Azarias et Sg 3,6. Is 53 suggère le martyre du Serviteur de YHWH plutôt qu'il ne l'exprime, et le sacrifice est offert pour le péché de la désécration de ce qui est saint. Il est expiatoire. Quant à la prière d'Azarias dans sa place narrative, elle voit le martyre prendre le relais du culte supprimé et interdit. Le culte était en effet confession de Dieu; célébrer la liturgie signifiait vénérer le Seigneur, l'adorer, lui rendre hommage. Or, c'est précisément la signification profonde du martyre! Dès lors il est légitime de comparer les offrandes de la liturgie apportées en hommage au Seigneur, au martyre, adhésion de foi à Dieu en temps de persécution, dans l'absence de la liturgie. Pour sa part, Sg 3,6 compare le martyre à l'offrande de l'holocauste parce que les deux sont agréés par le Seigneur[13], et puisque les deux expriment le même besoin d'honorer Dieu par les dons les plus grands. On ne peut affirmer une dépendance *littéraire* de Sg 3,6 par rapport à Is 53,10 et Dn 3,38-40. Les différences terminologiques et contextuels entre ces passages sont notables. Mais sur la base de ces textes on peut affirmer une théologie du martyre qui s'affirme, après un texte précurseur (Is 53), vers la fin du 2e et au Ier s. av. J.-C. Elle reconnaît au martyre une valeur égale au culte fondé par Dieu lui-même, capable de le remplacer si la persécution en empêche la célébration. Pour le développement de cette théologie, les Psaumes (40,7-8; 51,18-19) ont sans doute joué un rôle important quoiqu'en eux le martyre ne soit pas envisagé.

Du côté de la prière d'Azarias, le martyre d'un petit nombre obtient le pardon pour tout le peuple comme en 2 M 7,37-38[14]; du côté de la Sagesse, le martyre n'est pas envisagé sous cet angle, mais comme un don tellement grand qu'il se substitue à la liturgie du sacrifice fondée par Dieu. (Il n'est pas impossible d'ailleurs que pour Sg 3,6 aussi, le martyre ait une force de pardon puisque selon Lv 1,4 l'holocauste pardonne les péchés. Mais cette dimension serait tout au plus implicite.)

Zusätze zu Daniel (JSHRZ 1,1), Gütersloh, Mohn, 1973, pp. 65-70, ne propose aucune indication chronologique pour cette prière. Il suit en cela les *Introductions à l'Ancien Testament* qui renoncent à la datation de la prière d'Azarias qui est considérée comme addition au texte de Daniel.

13. «Agréer» (προσδέχεσθαι) signifie l'accueil des sacrifices en Os 8,13; Am 5,22; Mi 6,7; Ml 1,10.13; 2 M 1,26 etc.

14. En 2 M 7,37-38 le martyre est lié à l'intercession. Il donne à celle-ci une efficacité et un prix particuliers si bien qu'on peut dire que les martyrs-intercesseurs sauvent le peuple. Cf. pour ce passage J.M. van Henten, *Das jüdische Selbstverständnis in den ältesten Martyrien*, in Id. (ed.), *Die Entstehung der jüdischen Martyrologie* (Studia Post-Biblica, 38), Leiden, Brill, 1989, pp. 127-161, surtout pp. 135,142.

Ces quelques réflexions sur le martyre dans le dernier livre sapiential sont offertes en hommage au Père Maurice Gilbert qui a su rendre accessibles les trésors de la sagesse, souvent bien enfouies dans une pensée et une langue devenues hermétiques pour le monde contemporain.

Institut Biblique   Adrian SCHENKER O.P.
Miséricorde
CH-1700 Fribourg

LA SAPIENZA, PRESENTE ACCANTO A DIO E ALL'UOMO
SAP 9,9B.10C E LA FIGURA DI ISIDE

1. IL LIBRO DELLA SAPIENZA ED I MISTERI ISIACI

Il capitolo 9 costituisce, già a livello di struttura letteraria, il cuore del libro della Sapienza; alla preghiera di Salomone M. Gilbert ha riservato una grande attenzione[1]. Diversi autori ne hanno studiato anche il sottofondo greco; tra questi, però, pochi hanno approfondito il rapporto esistente tra la preghiera di Sap 9 ed i culti misterici, in particolare quelli di Iside[2]. In ogni caso, i risultati sinora raggiunti, soprattutto nell'accurato lavoro di Kloppenborg, sono stati di grande interesse: la figura della sapienza, così come ci è presentata nei capitoli 7–10 del libro della Sapienza, sarebbe stata riletta dal nostro autore attraverso categorie isiache e riproposta in questa nuova veste ai Giudei alessandrini, destinatari del libro. A motivo di questa 're-mitologizzazione' della sapienza d'Israele fatta in categorie isiache, tale sapienza viene rivitalizzata e diventa di nuovo seducente per i Giudei dell'epoca.

---

1. Cf. i due studi più importanti al riguardo: M. GILBERT, *La structure de la prière de Salomon (Sg 9)*, in *Bib* 51 (1970) 301-331; *Volonté de Dieu et don de la Sagesse (Sg 9,17s)*, in *NRT* 93 (1971) 145-166; ai lavori di Gilbert possiamo aggiungere contributi più recenti nei commentari di C. LARCHER, *Le livre de la Sagesse ou la Sagesse de Salomon*, t. II, Paris, 1984; J. VÍLCHEZ LÍNDEZ, *Sabiduría*, Estella, Navarra, 1989; G. SCARPAT, *Il libro della Sapienza*, t. II, Brescia, 1995. Per quanto riguarda la struttura letteraria si veda P. BIZZETI, *Il libro della Sapienza. Struttura e genere letterario*, Brescia, 1984, 72-74, che conferma sostanzialmente le posizioni di Gilbert.

2. Per quanto riguarda il sottofondo ellenistico di Sap 9 è da rilevare la recente e accurata analisi di G. SCARPAT, *Il libro della Sapienza* (n. 1). Per i rapporti tra Sap 9 e la figura di Iside, cf. il lavoro pionieristico di J.M. REESE, *Hellenistic Influence on the Book of Wisdom and its Consequences* (AnBib, 41), Roma, 1970, spec. pp. 36-50, e, soprattutto, i due ottimi studi di B.L. MACK, *Logos und Sophia*, Göttingen, 1973, 62-95, e di J.S. KLOPPENBORG, *Isis and Sophia in the Book of Wisdom*, in *HThR* 75 (1982) 57-84, che ha criticato il metodo seguito da Reese. Dei rapporti del libro della Sapienza con i misteri isiaci si è occupato recentemente anche H. ENGEL, in relazione però a Sap 7–8: *Was Weisheit ist und wie sie entstand, will ich verkünden. Weish 7,22–8,1 innerhalb des ἐγκώμιον τῆς σοφίας (6,22–11,1) als Stärkung der Plausibilität des Judentums angesichts hellenistischer Philosophie und Religiosität;* in G. HENTSCHEL – E. ZENGER (eds.), *Lehrerin der Gerechtigkeit. Studien zum Buch der Weisheit*, Leipzig, 1991, pp. 67-91. Più in dettaglio, cf. P. DUMOULIN, *Entre la Manne et l'Eucharistie. Étude de Sg 16,15–17,1* (AnBib, 132), Roma 1994, pp. 136-142, e L. MAZZINGHI, *Notte di paura e di luce. Esegesi di Sap 17,1–18,4* (AnBib, 134), Roma 1995; cf. ancora L. MAZZINGHI, *La barca della Provvidenza: Sap 14,1-10 e la figura di Iside*, in *Vivens Homo* 8/1 (1997) 61-90.

In questo studio, prendendo in esame una breve sezione della preghiera di Salomone (Sap 9,9-10) e, al suo interno, il tema della presenza della sapienza accanto al Signore e accanto a Salomone (9,9b.10c), ci fermeremo appunto a studiare la possibilità di una relazione tra questi testi e la figura di Iside.

2. SAP 9,9B E 10C NEL CONTESTO DELLA PREGHIERA DI SALOMONE

Gli studi di M. Gilbert hanno dimostrato come i vss 9-11 facciano parte della strofa centrale del cap. 9 (Sap 9,7-12) e siano ordinati secondo una precisa struttura concentrica. In tal modo viene posta in risalto la relazione tra il vs 9 da un lato e il vs 10c-11 dall'altro, rilevando così la centralità di 9,10ab. Dalle osservazioni di Gilbert ricaviamo come tre elementi, in particolare, siano messi in stretta relazione tra loro:

9,9a εἰδυῖα   11a οἶδεν
9,9b παροῦσα   10c συμπαροῦσα
9,9c ἐπισταμένη τί ἀρεστόν   10d γνῷ τί εὐάρεστον.
Un certo parallelismo è infine visibile tra ἐποίεις (9b) e ταῖς πράξεσίν μου (11b).

Emergono così tre temi strettamente collegati tra loro: la sapienza, che conosce i progetti[3] di Dio e comprende 'tutto'; la sapienza, presente accanto a Dio e agli uomini; la sapienza, infine, che conosce la volontà di Dio e diviene così guida e protezione per l'uomo (cf. vs 11cd). Il tema della presenza della sapienza è dunque centrale in entrambi gli sviluppi, il vs 9 e i vss 10b-11. Analizziamo adesso, più in dettaglio, le due espressioni che ci interessano:

9b καὶ παροῦσα, ὅτε ἐποίεις τὸν κόσμον.
10c ἵνα συμπαροῦσά μοι κοπιάσῃ.

Il senso dei due stichi è di per sé chiaro: la sapienza «era presente quando tu creavi il mondo»[4] (9b) ed è ugualmente accanto a Salomone per 'faticare' con lui: «perché sia presente presso di me nella mia

---

3. Con G. SCARPAT (*Il libro della Sapienza* [n.1], p. 228) intendiamo τὰ ἔργα come i «disegni», il «piano economico» di Dio. La sapienza è così fonte di rivelazione, «force morale, mais aussi lumière pour éclairer l'intelligence de l'homme» (M. GILBERT, *Volonté de Dieu* [cf. n. 1], p. 164).

4. Il termine κόσμος è molto usato nel libro della Sapienza (19 volte), ora nel senso di 'mondo' (Sap 2,24; 7,6; 14,14), ora nel senso di 'umanità' (Sap 6,24; 10,1; 14,6); nel nostro testo κόσμος ha probabilmente entrambe le sfumature; Sap 9,1 si riferisce all'intera creazione, ma il contesto della seconda strofa (Sap 9,7-12) punta verso l'umanità in particolare. Cf. G. SCARPAT, *Il libro della Sapienza*, t. I, Brescia 1989, 344s e II (n. 1), pp. 228s.

fatica» (10c)[5]. Oggetto di discussione[6] è soltanto il senso preciso di παροῦσα in 9b: Gilbert pensa a una presenza attiva della sapienza nella creazione (soprattutto a motivo del parallelismo con il vs 10 sopra ricordato). Larcher, pur non negando un ruolo attivo della sapienza nella creazione del mondo, preferisce intepretare πάρειμι nel suo senso normale di 'essere presente' (così come nelle altre ricorrenze del verbo nel libro della Sapienza: Sap 4,2; 11,11; 14,17; 19,14). Osserva Scarpat che un'indicazione sul senso della attività o passività della sapienza ci può venire soltanto da una considerazione globale del ruolo della sapienza nell'intero libro. Secondo lo stesso autore non è possibile pensare a un ruolo attivo della sapienza nella creazione del mondo, ma soltanto a una sua presenza accanto a Dio creatore; a questo riguardo Scarpat nega che in Sap 7,21 ed 8,6 l'appellativo di τεχνῖτις riferito alla sapienza vada interpretato nella linea di una sapienza creatrice. L'analisi delle fonti che sottostanno al testo che stiamo esaminando potrà fornirci ulteriori indicazioni.

3. Sap 9,9b e 9,10c e il testo di Pr 8,27.30

Uno dei testi biblici che sta alla base dell'intero capitolo 9 del libro della Sapienza è senz'altro quello di Pr 8, e, in particolare, Pr 8,22-31 (LXX)[7]. Per quanto riguarda in particolare Sap 9,9b, il termine παροῦσα sembra suggerito da Pr 8,30 (LXX: ἤμην παρ'αὐτῷ), mentre in 9,10c συμπαροῦσα proviene senz'altro da Pr 8,27 (LXX: συμπαρήμην αὐτῷ); il verbo συμπάρειμι, infatti, appare nella Settanta, al di fuori di questi due testi, soltanto in Tb 12,12AB, ma in un differente contesto. La dipendenza di παροῦσα da Pr 8,30LXX dà al verbo il senso di 'essere presente per aiutare' (cf. il latino adesse). Occorre però osservare come il nostro autore utilizzi due espressioni che nel libro dei Proverbi sono entrambe riferite al rapporto della sapienza con Dio collegandole invece l'una (παροῦσα) al rapporto della sapienza con il Signore, l'altra (συμπαροῦσα), alla relazione che essa ha con Salomone. Nell'opinione

---

5. L'idea principale dello stico è data proprio dal participio συμπαροῦσα; un'ottima traduzione è quella fornitaci dalla versione latina: *ut mecum sit et mecum laboret*; cf. G. Scarpat, *Il libro della Sapienza* (n. 1), p. 265.

6. M. Gilbert, *La structure de la prière* (n. 1), passim; C. Larcher, *Études sur le livre de la Sagesse* (EB), Paris, 1969, pp. 388-398; G. Scarpat, *Il libro della Sapienza* (n. 1), pp. 60ss; 228; 255.

7. Cf., a questo riguardo, P.W. Skehan, *The literary relationship of the book of Wisdom to earlier Wisdom writings*, in *Studies in Israelite Poetry and Wisdom* (CBQ MS, 1), Washington, 1971, spec. pp. 174s. Per il sottofondo biblico di Sap 9 si vedano i testi citati nella n. 1.

di Scarpat, il nostro Saggio eviterebbe di riferire συμπαροῦσα alla relazione Dio-sapienza per non dover considerare poi la sapienza come collaboratrice di Dio, strumento attivo della sua creazione[8]; essa è dunque presente accanto a Dio, ma, al contrario di quanto avviene nel testo di Pr, non avrebbe un ruolo attivo nella creazione.

Vi è tuttavia un'altra differenza importante tra il testo della Settanta di Pr 8,27.30 e il modo con cui il nostro autore lo utilizza. Nella Settanta di Pr 8,22-31 appare evidente come il traduttore cerchi di sottolineare, rispetto al TM, una maggiore passività della sapienza; la scelta di συμπαρήμην αὐτῷ (il pronome è assente dal TM) è fatta proprio per subordinare la sapienza a Dio[9]. In questo modo il traduttore greco non voleva correre il pericolo che si potesse vedere nella sapienza una figura divina, magari una Ma'at ebraica o forse addirittura la stessa Iside[10]. Ora nel libro della Sapienza sono assenti preoccupazioni di questo tipo. L'elogio della sapienza (Sap 7–8) ne ha infatti riformulato la figura in categorie filosofiche greche, soprattutto stoiche e, come si è detto, ha presentato una immagine della sapienza riletta proprio alla luce della figura di Iside, senza che il nostro autore senta il bisogno di giustificarsi per questo. La scelta di συμπάρειμι in Sap 9,10c non va perciò vista come un tentativo di attenuare il ruolo attivo della sapienza riferendo il verbo soltanto alla sua presenza accanto all'uomo. E' proprio infatti la presenza della sapienza, attiva accanto a Dio, che la porta ad essere attiva anche accanto all'uomo[11]; penso che il nostro autore vada perciò oltre il tema di Pr 8,22-31, rileggendolo con l'intenzione di sottolineare un ruolo più attivo della sapienza nei confronti della creazione.

---

8. Cf. G. SCARPAT, *Il libro della Sapienza*, t. II, (n. 1) p. 263. V. anche la discussione nel paragrafo precedente.

9. Ciò accade in tutta la sezione della Settanta di Pr 8,22-31; il traduttore riferisce a Dio espressioni che nel TM sono invece in relazione con la sapienza (cf. 8,23.31), oppure aggiunge il nome 'Signore', come all'inizio del vs 26, per evitare ogni possibile fraintendimento. Cf. J. COOK, *The Septuagint of Proverbs. Jewish and/or Hellenistic Proverbs? Concerning the Hellenistic Colouring of LXX Proverbs*, Leiden – New York – Köln, 1997, pp. 227s. Secondo Cook il traduttore greco dei Proverbi è «a conservative, Jewish-schooled scribe, who was anti non-Jewish, especially Hellenistic, interpretations of the creation» (p. 246). C'è chi sostiene che già nel TM di Pr 8,22-31 la sapienza avrebbe comunque un ruolo per lo più passivo: v. O. KEEL, *Die Weisheit spielt vor Gott. Eine ikonographischer Beitrag zur Deutung des meshaḥāqät in Sprüche 8,30f.*, Freiburg– Göttingen, 1974.

10. Cf. M.V. FOX, *World Order and Ma'at: a Crooked Parallel*, in *JANES* 23 (1995) 37-48: «Lady Wisdom may well be an Isis-displacement. Proverbs 8 would be appropriating formulas from Isis-speeches in order to offer a better, and deliberately distinct, substitute» (p. 47).

11. Si osservi l'uso molto ardito del verbo κοπιάω; la sapienza divina è 'collabora-trice' che si affatica per assistere l'uomo nelle sue attività e divenire così la sua guida interiore.

4. IL POSSIBILE SFONDO GRECO DELLA 'PRESENZA' DELLA SAPIENZA

Nel riprendere Pr 8,30LXX (ἤμην παρ'αὐτῷ), utilizzando il verbo πάρειμι, assente dal testo di Pr, il nostro autore introduce un vocabolo che nell'uso greco ha ben presto acquistato una evidente sfumatura religiosa[12]: sin dal linguaggio omerico, infatti, il verbo serve a descrivere la presenza degli dèi; in particolare πάρειμι indica la presenza di un dio alle cerimonie sacre fatte in suo onore. L'uso del termine παρουσία in relazione alla divinità è fin troppo noto perché ci si debba soffermare[13]. Quanto al significato, il verbo πάρειμι prende spesso la sfumatura di 'essere presente per aiutare'. Questo doppio significato, 'essere presente' e 'assistere' è proprio anche dell'altro verbo utilizzato dal nostro autore (συμπάρειμι), che di per sé non ricorre in ambito religioso[14]. Nell'ambito del giudaismo di lingua greca fa tuttavia eccezione l'opera di Giuseppe Flavio che utilizza diverse volte συμπάρειμι in relazione alla presenza e all'aiuto di Dio (τοῦ θεοῦ συμπαρόντος, Ant. 2,268; cf. Bell. V,380; Ant. 1,260; 2,340; 3,316; 10,239).

12. Caratteristica che percorre l'intero libro della Sapienza è la volontà di rileggere i testi biblici alla luce del mutato contesto culturale; ciò fa parte dello stile *midrashico* che il libro adotta, specie nella sua terza parte; sull'argomento gli studi non mancano: ricordo soltanto l'ottimo e aggiornato *status quaestionis* proposto da J. VILCHEZ LÍNDEZ, *Sabiduría* (n. 1), 27-51; recentemente sono apparsi due lavori che si occupano del carattere *midrashico* di Sap: S. CHEON, *The Exodus Story in the Wisdom of Solomon. A Study in Biblical Interpretation* (JSPS, 23), Sheffield, 1997; Cheon parla di 'rewritten Bible'; P. ENNS, *Ancient Exegesis of the Departure from Egypt in Wis 10:15-21 and 19,1-9* (HSM, 57), Harvard, 1997 affronta il modo con cui Sap rilegge i testi biblici; entrambi i lavori hanno però la tendenza a sottovalutare il contesto ellenistico del libro; cfr ancora L.L. GRABBE, *Wisdom of Solomon*, Sheffield, 1997, 39-47.
13. Cf., per numerosi esempi, CH. SPICQ, *Notes de lexicograpie néotestamentaire* (OBO, 22/2), Göttingen, 1978, 673-675; A. OEPKE, art. παρουσία, πάρειμι, in *ThW* t. V, col. 856-869; v. anche i molti esempi riportati da L. ROBERT, *Hellenica*, t. XIII, Paris, 1965, pp. 129-130, e ancora, in relazione alla παρουσία degli dèi, P.L. SCHOONHEIM, *Een semasiologisch onderzoek van parousia*, Aalten, 1953, pp. 112-116. Di passaggio notiamo come in Platone appaia l'espressione σοφίας παρούσης; in *Euth.* 280b Socrate e Clinia discutono sul valore della sapienza, riconosciuta come colei che garantisce il successo, il raggiungimento dello scopo (εὐτυχία); quando uno possiede la saggezza, non ha più bisogno di aggiungervi il successo (σοφίας παρούσης, ᾧ ἂν παρῇ, μηδὲν προσδεῖσθαι εὐτυχίας).
14. Cf., come esempio più tardo, Luciano, *Deorum Iudicium = Deorum Dialogi*, XX,15: Afrodite, parlando di stessa, afferma καὶ αὐτὴ δὲ συμπαροῦσα, «io stessa sarò presente»; ma anche in questo caso non sembra che si tratti di uno specifico uso religioso. Nei papiri il verbo è piuttosto comune, per lo più con il significato di 'essere presente'; cf. U. WILCKEN, *Urkunden der Ptolemäerzeit*, t. I-II (Leipzig–Berlin 1927), *index verborum*; F. PREISIGKE – F. BIBABEL – E. KIESSLING (eds.), *Sammelbuch griechischen Urkunden aus Aegypten* (= SB), Strassburg–Berlin–Wiesbaden, 1913, t. III, 6280,4; t. V, 7669,37; t. VI, 9216,8 etc.; cf. *Lettera di Aristea* 178; *Pseudo Focilide* 134.

L'uso di συμπάρειμι, dunque, non punta di per sé a un preciso sottofondo greco, diversamente da πάρειμι; né lo fa l'uso di κοπιάω, che nei testi greci è piuttosto raro, mentre è frequente nella Settanta. C'è però da chiedersi se il tema della presenza della sapienza accanto a Dio e, allo stesso tempo, accanto agli uomini come collaboratrice nella loro fatica, non possa trovare qualche ulteriore chiarificazione alla luce del contesto culturale e religioso alessandrino, in particolare proprio in relazione alla figura di Iside.

5. ISIDE, DEA PRESENTE E SOCCORRITRICE

Una delle caratteristiche che più contraddistinguono Iside, soprattutto l'Iside ellenizzata, è il suo essere dea salvatrice, benevola, soccorritrice, la cui presenza è apportatrice per l'uomo di grandi benefici. L'esame della figura di Iside non si rivela, a prima vista, una pista troppo feconda di prospettive per il nostro lavoro: i passi in cui la presenza benevola della dea è descritta proprio attraverso l'uso del verbo πάρειμι, infatti, non sono molti, e in nessun caso la dea appare in connessione con il verbo συμπάρειμι[15]. L'esame dei testi ci permetterà tuttavia di allargare l'analisi dall'enumerazione di semplici paralleli verbali al confronto di temi e motivi più precisi.

Prendiamo soprattutto in considerazione i quattro inni isiaci di Medinet-Mâdi, noti come le areatologie di Isidoro, databili poco prima dell'80 a.C[16].; si tratta infatti di testi che, per epoca e collocazione culturale geografica, è possibile porre a confronto con il libro della Sapienza. Leggiamo al termine del primo inno (I,32-34):

> ὅσσοι δ'ἐμ μοίραις θανάτου συνέχονται ἐν εἰρκτῇ,
> καὶ ὅσοι ἀγρυπνίαις μεγάλαις ὀχλοῦντ᾽ ὀδυνηραῖς,
> καὶ οἱ ἐν ἀλλοτρίῃ χώρῃ πλανοώμενοι ἄνδρες,
> καὶ ὅσοι ἐμ πελάγει μεγάλῳ χειμῶνι πλέουσι
> ἀνδρῶν ὀλλυμένων νηῶν κατὰ ἀγνυμενάων
> σώζονθ᾽οὗτοι ἅπαντες, ἐπευξάμενοί σε παρεῖναι.

> *«Quanti son prigionieri d'un fato ch'a morte conduce,*
> *quanti son tormentati da veglie lunghe e penose,*

---

15. Cf. L. VIDMAN, *Sylloge Inscriptionum religionis Isiacae et Sarapiacae*, Berlin 1969 (SIRIS); G. RONCHI, *Lexicon theonymon rerumque sacrarum et divinarum ad Aegyptum pertinentium quae in papyris, ostracis, titulis graecis latinisque in Aegypto repertis laudantur*, t. I-V, Milano, 1974; L. BRICAULT, *Myryonimi. Les épiclèses grecques et latines d'Isis, de Serapis et d'Anubis*, Stuttgart–Leipzig, 1996.

16. Cf. V.F. VANDERLIP, *The Four Greek Hymns of Isidorus and the Cult of Isis*, Toronto, 1972. Per ulteriori osservazioni sugli Inni di Isidoro in rapporto a Sap cf. L. MAZZINGHI, *Notte di paura e di luce* (n. 2), p. 188 e n. 83.

tutti gli uomini erranti per terra straniera ed ostile,
quanti d'inverno s'inoltran nel pelago immenso
quando essi sono distrutti, le navi lor spezzate,
tutti costoro si salvan pregandoti d'esser presente».

In questo testo il verbo παρεῖναι ha chiaramente il senso di 'essere presente per aiutare' e il contesto chiarisce bene di quale aiuto la presenza della dea è portatrice. Le situazioni dalle quali Iside salva l'uomo sono topiche per i culti isiaci: destino, morte, malattia, viaggi per terra e per mare; tutte si ritrovano nel nostro libro della Sapienza in relazione con le opere della sapienza:

– Iside salva l'uomo dalle catene del fato, cui essa è superiore[17]; per questo motivo Iside concede all'uomo la salvezza dalle malattie e dalla morte[18]. Allo stesso modo, la sapienza d'Israele salva i prigionieri (Sap 10,13-15) e libera l'uomo dalla morte (cf. tutto il capitolo 10, e, in particolare, per l'uso del verbo σῴζω, Sap 9,18 e 10,4); gli empi, invece, privi della sapienza, sono rinchiusi in un carcere (εἰρκτή) di tenebre e prigionieri di un destino ineluttabile (Sap 17,16-17)[19].

– Il tema di Iside guida dell'uomo nel suo errare (il verbo πλανάω è peraltro caratteristico del linguaggio misterico[20]) è anch'esso frequente nelle presentazioni di Iside. Lo stesso ruolo di guida (ὁδηγός, ὁδηγέω, cf. la litania isiaca di Ossirinco = *P.Oxy.* 1380,122-123) è attribuito alla sapienza proprio in Sap 9,11; cfr 10,10; 10,17 e ancora Sap 14,5 e 18,3.

– La salvezza dei marinai dal mare in tempesta è un'altra caratteristica privilegiata di Iside, dea del mare e patrona dei naviganti, soprattutto nella sua rappresentazione alessandrina[21].

La presenza della dea, richiesta da Isidoro nella preghiera (l.34) è dunque presenza portatrice di salvezza. Questo è esattamente il ruolo

---

17. Una delle più frequenti rappresentazioni isiache è proprio quella di Ἶσις Τύχη; cf. ad esempio *Inni di Isidoro*, II,1; *Aretalogia di Kymé* (= IG 12 Suppl. 5; Berlin, 1939) l. 55; Apuleio, *Met.* XI,12; il concetto è tipicamente egiziano: v. J. BERGMAN, «*I Overcome Fate, Fate Harkens to me*», in E. RINGGREN (ed.), *Fatalistic Beliefs in Religion, Folklore and Literature*, Stockholm, 1967, pp. 38-41.

18. Su Iside salvatrice cf. F. DUNAND, *Le culte d'Isis dans le Bassin Oriental de la Méditerranée*, t. III (EPR, 26/3), Leiden 1973, pp. 256-261; M. MALAISE, *Les conditions des pénétration et de diffusion des cultes égyptiens en Italie* (EPR, 22), Leiden 1972, 184-187 ed anche C.J. BLEEKER, *Isis as a Saviour-Goddess*, in *The Saviour God.* FS. O. James, Manchester, 1963, pp. 1-16

19. Per quest'ultimo testo cf. L. MAZZINGHI, *Notte di paura e di luce* (n. 2), pp. 188s; per il tema della sapienza salvatrice a confronto con la figura di Iside v. J.S. KLOPPENBORG, *Isis and Sophia* (n. 2), pp. 67-73.

20. Cf. Platone, *Fedro* 248AB; Plutarco, *De Anima* frg. 178 (= Stobeo 4.52,49).

21. Rimando ancora al mio già ricordato lavoro *La barca della Provvidenza* (n. 2).

della sapienza nel nostro libro (v. in particolare Sap 9,18 e Sap 10), ruolo che non ha paralleli nei testi biblici precedenti, mentre ne ha, e in abbondanza, nei testi isiaci.

Nel secondo inno di Isidoro troviamo un nuovo testo che descrive la presenza della dea, ancora attraverso l'uso di πάρειμι (II,5-8):

Ὅσσοι σοὶ εὔχονται ἐπ᾽ἐμπορίην τε παρεῖναι,
πλουτοῦσ᾽εὐσεβεές εἰς τὸν ἄπαντα χρόνον·
καὶ ὅσοι ἐν νούσοις θανατώδεσι μοίρῃ ἔχονται,
σοὶ εὐξάμενοι ταχέως (σ)ῆς ζωῆς ἔτυχον.

«Quanti ti pregan presente nel loro mercato,
ricchi divengon piamente pel tempo avvenire:
quanti in mortali malanni s'appressano al fato,
te pregando tua vita veloci ottennero in sorte».

In questo caso, la presenza benevola di Iside, nuovamente invocata nella preghiera, garantisce la ricchezza (ll. 5-6) e la salvezza dalle malattie (ll. 7-8). Il tema della ricchezza caratterizza anche la presentazione della sapienza all'interno del nostro libro, sulla scia già di Pr 8; ma il vocabolario usato dal nostro autore richiama da vicino le aretalogie di Isidoro: cf. *Isidoro* III,3-6 e Sap 8,18 (ἀγαθῶν-ἀγάθη, πλοῦτος, τέρψις); v. anche Sap 7,11. Il tema della guarigione dalle malattie (legato, nel testo di Isidoro, al tema già visto della vittoria sul fato) non appare in connessione con la sapienza, all'interno di Sap 7-10; è tuttavia caratteristico di Sap 16,5-14, ove certamente si può scorgere una punta polemica contro il tema degli dèi guaritori, tra i quali la stessa Iside[22].

Una terza ricorrenza del verbo πάρειμι è nel terzo inno di Isidoro (III,26-28) all'interno di un diverso contesto, relativo all'azione di giustizia di Iside, che veglia sul mondo intero e giudica gli uomini:

κόσμον ἅπαν διάγουσα, κατοπτεύουσα ἅπαντα
ἔργ᾽ἀνδρῶν ἀσεβῶν τε καὶ εὐσεβέων καθορῶσα,
εἰ δὲ καὶ ὧδε πάρει, ἰδίαν ἀρετὴν ἐφορῶσα...

«Tu che il mondo dirigi, sull'universo vegliando,
opere d'uomini empi e di pii parimenti scorgendo,
se anche qui sei presente, d'ognun la virtù sua vedendo...».

I versi 29-31 dell'inno sottolineano come tale 'presenza' della dea sia legata alla celebrazione delle sue festività. I versi 26-27 sopra citati, tuttavia, legano la presenza della dea al suo ruolo cosmico[23] e alla sua

---

22. H. MANESCHG, *Die Erzählung von der ehernen Schlange (Num 21,4-9) in der Auslegung der frühen jüdischen Literatur. Eine traditionsgeschichtliche Studie*, Frankfurt–Bern, 1981, pp. 182-187.

23. Sul ruolo cosmico di Iside cf. J.S. KLOPPENBORG (n. 2), p. 69 e n. 48 e le sue osservazioni in relazione ai possibili rapporti con il libro della Sapienza.

giustizia. Anche in questo caso ritroviamo corrispondenze tematiche con il libro della Sapienza: la sapienza percorre l'intero universo (cf. Sap 8,1) e concede a Salomone la capacità di governare con giustizia (Sap 9,3.12). Il legame tra Iside e giustizia è del resto frequente nelle aretalogie[24]. Tale connessione ritorna, ancora in relazione al verbo πάρειμι, nel testo della aretalogia isiaca di Maronea: πείθομαι δὲ πάντως παρέσεσθαι (l. 10); ma nell'aretalogia di Maronea, come negli inni di Isidoro, la presenza benevola della dea si estende ben al di là della garanzia della giustizia, abbracciando temi già visti a proposito degli inni di Isidoro[25].

Alcuni testi del libro XI delle *Metamorfosi* di Apuleio confermano l'importanza del tema della presenza benevola della dea: «En adsum tuis commota, Luci, precibus (...). Adsum tuos miserata casus, adsum favens et propitia (...) iam tibi providentia mea inlucescit dies salutaris» (XI,5-6); Iside è *praesentissimum numen* (XI,12)[26]. In questi testi emerge il forte afflato religioso e il profondo rapporto personale che lega il devoto di Iside con la sua dea[27]; tale è anche il tono che anima la preghiera di Sap 9, che, almeno da un punto di vista formale, non differisce molto dalle preghiere in uso nel mondo greco[28].

6. SAPIENZA E ISIDE: TRA CONFRONTO E DIALOGO

Dobbiamo pensare perciò di trovarci davanti a una presentazione della sapienza fatta apertamente in categorie isiache? E in questo caso, per

---

24. Cf. *Aretalogia di Maronea* ll. 24-26.38; *Kymé* 16.28; v. Y. GRANDJEAN, *Une nouvelle arétalogie d'Isis à Maronée* (EPR 49), Leiden, 1975, pp. 79ss. Secondo G. SCARPAT (*Il libro della Sapienza* [n. 1], pp. 217-219) in Sap 9,4 vi è già una polemica con la figura di Δίκη πάρεδρος di Zeus.

25. Cf. Y. GRANDJEAN, *Une nouvelle arétalogie* (n. 22), pp. 34ss.

26. Cf. anche Serapide, *praesentissimus Deus magnus*, SIRIS 361,4; t. III sec. d.C.

27. Sulla pietà del devoto di Iside e la sincerità delle aretalogie cf. Y. GRANDJEAN (n. 22), pp. 104ss; M. MALAISE, *La pieté personnelle dans la religion isiaque*, in H. LIMET – J. RIES (eds.), *L'expérience de la prière dans les grandes religions. Actes du colloque de Louvain-la-Neuve, et Liège (22-23 novembre 1978)*, Louvain-la-Neuve 1980, spec. p. 99, e, dello stesso autore, *L'expression du sacré dans les cultes isiaques*, in J. RIES (ed.), *L'expression du sacré dans les grandes religions*, t. III, Louvain-La-Neuve, 1986, spec. pp. 49s. Su questo argomento, l'atmosfera mistica dei culti isiaci in relazione alla preghiera del saggio nel libro della Sapienza, si veda lo stimolante articolo di D. WINSTON, *The Sage as Mystic in the Wisdom of Solomon*, in J.G. GAMMIE – L.G. PERDUE (ed.), in *The Sage in Israel and the Ancient Near East*, Winona Lake, IN, 1990, 383-397.

28. Cf. al riguardo G. SCARPAT, *Il libro della Sapienza* (n. 2), pp. 207-213. Anche nelle preghiere dei maghi dell'Egitto ellenizzato la struttura formale della preghiera non è diversa: cf. F. GRAF, *Prayer in Magic and Religious Ritual*, in C.A. FARAONE – D. OBBINK (eds.), *Magica Hiera. Ancient Greek Magic and Religion*, New York-Oxford, 1981, 188-213.

quale motivo? L'evidenza dei testi che abbiamo esaminato non consente una tanto rapida conclusione: la sapienza richiesta a Dio nella preghiera di Sap 9 e definita presente con Lui e con l'uomo ha soltanto alcuni tratti in comune con Iside, mentre affonda le sue radici più profonde nella tradizione d'Israele. Molte delle caratteristiche più tipiche dell'Iside ellenizzata, infatti, non si ritrovano affatto nell'immagine della sapienza descrittaci in Sap 7–10 e, soprattutto, in Sap 9: si pensi alle raffigurazioni di Isis-Thermoutis, dea della fertilità spesso identificata con Demetra, Iside che allatta Arpocrate, Iside dolente ed altri attributi isiaci caratteristici come il modo di vestire, il sistro, la cista, la corona…; nessuno di questi elementi trova corrispondenze nella sapienza di Sap 7-10. Inoltre, cosa più importante, in Sap 9, la sapienza è oggetto della preghiera del saggio, non tanto il soggetto cui egli si rivolge; la preghiera è diretta soltanto a Dio e la sapienza è un suo dono (Sap 8,21)[29].

La preghiera di Salomone ha inoltre un'altra caratteristica che ne fa un testo singolare e, comunque, profondamente israelita: Sap 9 apre l'intera 'anamnesi innica' di Sap 11–19 e introduce la riflessione sulla storia di Israele; questa prospettiva storica è il tratto più tipico del nostro autore[30]. Il rapporto tra Salomone e la sapienza rinvia pertanto al rapporto tra l'uomo e quel Signore che nella storia del suo popolo si è fatto conoscere (cf. Sap 19,22).

Una valutazione dei risultati raggiunti deve tener conto anche di queste divergenze: nel descrivere la presenza della sapienza accanto a Dio e all'uomo, il nostro autore si serve prima di tutto di testi biblici precedenti (Pr 8,22-31 in primo luogo) e non intende staccarsi dalla tradizione di Israele; eppure il linguaggio e la scelta dei temi proposti possono essere meglio compresi alla luce del sottofondo greco del testo e, in particolare, alla luce della figura di Iside. In tal modo possiamo parlare di *rilettura e attualizzazione* (potremmo utilizzare a questo punto l'aggettivo 'midrashico') di temi biblici in chiave isiaca. Uno degli scopi è certamente polemico e apologetico: il libro della Sapienza intende rafforzare i Giudei di Alessandria contro la tentazione di seguire una delle figure più seducenti che essi avevano di fronte: Iside. In questo,

---

29. In 9,9a la sapienza 'conosce' le 'opere', cioè il piano salvifico di Dio, essendo presente accanto a lui (cf. εἰδυῖα, vs 9a; ἐπισταμένη, vs 9c); in testi più tardi la sapienza verrà posta in relazione con Iside: Plutarco, cercando l'etimologia greca di Iside, ne mette in rapporto il nome con il verbo οἶδα; cf. *De Iside et Osiride* 361EF: μᾶλλον αὐτῇ τὸ εἰδέναι καὶ τὴν ἐπιστήμην προσηκούσαν. V.J. Gwin Griffiths, *Plutarch's de Iside et Osiride*, Cambridge, 1970, pp. 257s. Cf. anche Elio Aristide, *Orat*. XLV,20.

30. Cf. M. Gilbert, *La prière des sages d'Israël*, in *L'experience de la prière* (n. 25), pp. 227-243; v. anche *L'adresse à Dieu dans l'anamnèse hymnique de l'exode (Sg 10-19)*, in V. Collado – E. Zurro (eds.), *El misterio de la Palabra. Homenaje al prof. L. Alonso Schökel*, Valencia – Madrid, 1983, pp. 207-225.

l'aggancio di Sap 9 con il tema della creazione e con quello della storia d'Israele è espressione di una precisa presa di posizione e di una grande chiarezza sulla propria identità all'interno di un contesto culturale ostile[31]. Resta il fatto che la ripresa di temi isiaci avviene con tutta naturalezza, né l'autore mostra di avere problemi nel proporre linguaggio, immagini e motivi che i suoi destinatari potevano correre il rischio di travisare. La sapienza non è certamente Iside, eppure anche il Giudeo, che da Iside poteva essere sedotto, può ritrovare nella sapienza ben più di ciò che Iside gli prometteva. Allo stesso tempo, il nostro autore getta un ponte tra la sua comunità e una cultura che poteva sembrare troppo lontana, e ciò senza mai rinunziare alla sua fede. Almeno in questo è possibile continuare ad utilizzare, per il libro della Sapienza, il concetto di 'inculturazione'[32].

Facoltà Teologica dell'Italia Centrale   Luca MAZZINGHI
Via Cosimo il Vecchio 26
I–50139 Firenze

31. Recentemente J.M.G. BARCLAY ha parlato del libro della Sapienza come esempio di 'cultural antagonism' di fronte al mondo ellenistico; la cultura ellenistica del nostro autore «is enlisted in the service of a vigourous defence of Jewish particularity» (*Jews in the Mediterranean Diaspora. From Alexander to Trajan [323 B.C.E. – 117 C.E.]*, Glasgow, 1996, pp. 180-191; spec. p. 191) Ma Barclay non tiene conto, tra l'altro, del fatto che il 'nemico' della terza parte del libro non è tanto il mondo greco quanto piuttosto, quello egiziano.

32. Cf. M. GILBERT, *Le livre de la Sagesse et l'inculturation*, in AA.VV., *L'inculturation et la sagesse des nations*, Roma, 1984, pp. 1-11.

WISDOM AS WOMAN
WISDOM AND MAN, WISDOM AND GOD

It is my pleasure and honor to offer this contribution to Professor Maurice Gilbert, a man who dedicated his life to illustrating Lady Wisdom in the various stages of the Old Testament.

A passage from the latest OT wisdom book is addressed first, then relevant passages from older Biblical wisdom books. The main issue investigated is the phraseology used to describe Wisdom in her relationship to woman, to man and finally to God.

1. Wis 10,1-2

[1a] αὕτη πρωτόπλαστον πατέρα κόσμου μόνον κτισθέντα διεφύλαξεν

[1b] καὶ ἐξείλατο αὐτὸν ἐκ παραπτώματος ἰδίου

[2] ἔδωκέν τε αὐτῷ ἰσχὺν κρατῆσαι ἁπάντων

[1a] It was she that protected the first-formed father of the world, when he was created alone,

[1b] and delivered him from his transgression,

[2] and also gave him strength to rule all things[1].

Because of its position in the first place of the sentence, the pronoun αὕτη is highlighted[2]; the sentence itself is marked and is therefore translated with a cleft sentence in English ("It was she that...")[3]. The absence of the article in πρωτόπλαστον πατέρα may be due to the fact that it is a "nomen regens" (a semitism)[4]. The participle κτισθέντα is

1. The Revised Standard Version (RSV) is used, with modifications when needed.

2. From the grammatical point of view, Wis 10,1 ff. come as an exposition of the previous two verses: "Who has learned your counsel, unless you have given wisdom and sent your holy Spirit from on high? And thus the paths of those on earth were set right, and men were taught what pleases you, and were saved by wisdom" (9,17-18). These verses stand out against their context in that they are in the aorist while the preceding verses are in the present or future tenses. Compare e.g. 9,11. On structure and genre of Wis 10, consult P. BIZZETI, *Il Libro della Sapienza. Struttura e genere letterario* (RivBibS, 11), Brescia, Paideia, 1984, pp. 75-76. 172-173.

3. See my paper, *Marked Syntactical Structures in Biblical Greek in Comparison with Biblical Hebrew*, in SBFLA 43 (1993) 9-69, esp. §6.1.

4. In other similar cases, the article is either missing or present. It is missing in 10,3 (ἄδικος) and in 10,6.10.13 (δίκαιον) while it is present in 10,4.5 (τὸν δίκαιον). However, its absence is striking with reference to the "first-formed father of the world". Adam's title "first-born of the world" is also present in Jewish writings; consult L.

circumstantial to the following main verb while μόνον is an adjective with predicative function and therefore both are without article.

The verb διαφυλάσσω is said of God in the LXX, translating the Hebrew שׁמר (Gen 28,15.20; Deut 7,12; Josh 24,17; Ps 40/41,3; 90/91,11) or נצר (Deut 32,10). It is said of wisdom in Prov 2,8 (שׁמר) and again in Wis 10,12. Coupled with ἐξαιρέω, it is only found here[5]. God protects humanity either directly or through his angels as in Ps 90/91,11 (applied to Jesus in Luke 4,10).

The terms πρωτόπλαστον[6] and μόνον κτισθέντα do not indicate the same thing but the second adds the idea that the protection happened when "the first-formed father of the world" was "created alone". There is much discussion concerning the exact meaning of the latter adjective. I would note, first, that the name Adam is not mentioned (as are not the names of the Biblical figures alluded to in the following verses). Second, the "transgression" is said to be "his", not of the woman as is the case e.g. in Sir 25,24. Third, Gen 1,27 is within the horizon of the passage: "So God created man in his own image: in the image of God he created *him*; male and female he created *them*"[7]. Here – one of the most remarkable verses of the Hebrew Bible – God's image is said to be represented in the unity as well as in the sex distinction of the human being[8]. Thus,

GINZBERG, *The Legends of the Jews*, t. I-VII, Philadelphia, The Jewish Publication Society of America, 1954-1967, t. I, p. 332, and t. V, p. 253, n. 89, where the relevant texts are quoted.

5. Simple φυλάσσω coupled with ἐξαιρέω is found in Ps 139/140,5 and (with a different meaning) in Ezek 33,5.

6. Full illustration of the term πρωτόπλαστος – also present in Wis 7,1, missing in the LXX – is found in C. LARCHER, *Le livre de la Sagesse ou la Sagesse de Salomon* (EB, n.s. 3), t. 2, Paris, Gabalda,1984, p. 444, and G. SCARPAT, *Libro della Sapienza*, t. II, Brescia, Paideia, 1996, pp. 277-279.

7. The conception of Adam created androgynous is derived from Gen 1,27; see GINZBERG, *The Legends of the Jews* (n. 4), t. V, 88-89. On the androgynous Creator of the world and the *Urmensch* in gnosticism and Old-Egyptian mythology, consult J. ZANDEE, *Der androgyne Gott in Ägypten. Ein Erscheinungsbild des Weltschöpfers*, in M. GÖRG (ed.), *Religion im Erbe Ägyptens. Beiträge zur spätantiken Religionsgeschichte zu Ehren von Alexander Böhlig* (ÄAT, 14), Wiesbaden, Harrassowitz, 1988, pp. 240-278. Also see G. QUISPEL, *Anthropos and Sophia, ibidem*, pp. 168-185.

8. In the second story of creation this is indicated by the fact that the same name, in the masculine and in the feminine, is given to the man and to the woman: אִשׁ - אִשָּׁה (Gen 2,23). Before the sin, the name Adam is not significant, although the man is called in this way. It becomes significant after the sin, when for the second time a name is given to the woman. Here, the name Adam is connected to death ("till you return to the ground - הָאֲדָמָה, for out of it you were taken", 3,19) while the woman is given a name connected to life ("The man called his wife's name *Eve*, because she was the mother of all *living*", 3,20, with a word play on חַוָּה - חַי). This fact may help to better evaluate woman's subordination to man in the Genesis account; see on this J. GALAMBUSH, *'Adām from 'ădāmâ, 'iššâ from 'iš. Derivation and Subordination in Genesis 2.4b–3.24*, in M.P. GRAHAM – W.P. BROWN – J.K. KUAN (eds.), *History and Interpretation. Essays in Honour of John H.*

what is intended in Wis 10,1 is most likely the human being as man/woman – the first couple. This "first-formed father/mother of the world" is protected by wisdom from the very beginning of his/her existence.

In which sense, then, is the first human being "alone"[9]? Not in the sense of being without a partner, as in Gen 2,18: "Then the Lord God said, 'It is not good that the man should be alone [לְבַדּוֹ – μόνον]; I will make him a helper fit for him' ", but rather in the sense of being in need of help from God, as in Esther 4,17[l].17[t]: "And she prayed to the Lord God of Israel, and said: «Lord, you alone [μόνος] are our King; help me, who am alone [τῇ μόνῃ] [...] But save us by your hand, and help me, who am alone [τῇ μόνῃ] and have no helper but you, o Lord»".

This sense accords with the common Biblical idea that individuals as well as Israel need God's assistance. It also accords with the Jewish belief that Adam and Eve in Eden were protected by guardian angels and that the sin happened in their absence[10]. In Wis 10,1a, it is personified Wisdom who plays the role of the guardian angels[11]; in other words, she is the mediator of God's assistance to the first couple. If so, speculations about Adam's – similar to God's – "uniqueness" may be somehow overstated[12].

The other statement in Wis 10,1b that Wisdom "delivered him from his transgression" telescopes the subsequent story of the first couple. The deliverance may have been seen in the fact that Adam and Eve did

---

Hayes (JSOTSS, 173), Sheffield, Sheffield Academic Press, 1993, pp. 33-46. Besides, the balance between the sexes is somehow redressed by love; compare Gen 3,16 with Cant 7,10.

9. For the various interpretations see e.g. C.L.W. GRIMM, *Das Buch Weisheit* (Kett), Leipzig, Hirzel, 1860, pp. 191-192, and LARCHER, *Sagesse* (n. 6), t. II, pp. 609-612.

10. See Greek Apocalypse of Ezra 2,10-17 (J.H. CHARLESWORTH [ed.], *The Old Testament Pseudepigrapha*, t. I: *Apocalyptic Literature and Testaments*, London, Darton, Longman & Todd, 1983, p. 572); Apocalypse of Sedrach 8,1 (*ibidem*, p. 611); Life of Adam and Eve [*Vita*] 33, and [*Apocalypse*] 7,2-3 (J.H. CHARLESWORTH [ed.], *The Old Testament Pseudepigrapha*, t. II: *Expansions of the "Old Testament" and Legends, Wisdom and Philosophical Literature, Prayers, Psalms, and Odes, Fragments of the Lost Judeo-Hellenistic Works*, London, Darton, Longman & Todd, 1985, pp. 272-273).

11. On the presentation of Wisdom with angelomorphic traits in Wis 10, see C.A. GIESCHEN, *Angelomorphic Christology. Antecedents and Early Evidence* (Arbeiten zur Geschichte des antiken Judentums und des Urchristentums, 42), Leiden – Boston – Köln, Brill, 1998, pp. 98-103.

12. Among others, see P. BEAUCHAMP, *Épouser la Sagesse – ou n'épouser qu'elle? Une énigme du Livre de la Sagesse*, in M. GILBERT (ed.), *La Sagesse de l'Ancien Testament* (BETL, 51), Leuven, Leuven University Press – Peeters, ²1990, pp. 347-369. Also consult SCARPAT, *Libro della Sapienza* (n. 6), pp. 278-279; and A. COUTO, *A sabedoria na história de Adam (Sb 10,1-2)*, in *Didaskalia* 25 (1995) 169-187. Couto also thinks that the reality of Adam's sin is played down in the passage while God's mercy through Wisdom is emphasized.

not die "in the day" they ate of the tree of knowledge (Gen 2,17)[13]. The salvation of the first man is a special theme of Jewish and early Christian literature and theology[14].

Wisdom also "gave him strength to rule all things" (10,2)[15]. The same terminology is used in Esther 4,17[b] with reference to God: "O Lord, Lord, King who rules over all things (πάντων κρατῶν)". In Prov 8,16, personified Wisdom declares: "By me princes become great, and nobles govern the earth (κρατοῦσι γῆς)"[16]. Further, according to Wis 3,8 the righteous "will govern nations (κρατήσουσιν λαῶν)", and in 6,2 the rulers are addressed as "you that rule over multitudes (οἱ κρατοῦντες πλήθους)". This idea derives, of course, from the book of Genesis (1,26-28; 2,19-20; 9,1-2), where however a different terminology is employed in the LXX[17]. Other important parallel texts are Sir 17,3-4:

13. However, the intended meaning of the passage may be different. See my discussion of Gen 2,17 in *Analysis of Biblical Narrative*, in R.D. BERGEN (ed.), *Biblical Hebrew and Discourse Linguistics*, Dallas, TX, Summer Institute of Linguistics, 1994, pp. 175-198, esp. p. 196, n. 11.

14. See Life of Adam and Eve [*Vita*] 1-11, and [*Apocalypse*] 28-29 (CHARLESWORTH [ed.], *OT Pseudepigrapha* [n. 10], Vol. 2, pp. 258-262). Christian texts are quoted in W.J. DEANE, *ΣΟΦΙΑ ΣΑΛΩΜΩΝ. The Book of Wisdom, The Greek Text, the Latin Vulgate and the Authorised English Version*, Oxford, Clarendon, 1881, p. 163. Also see J. VILCHEZ LINDEZ, *Sapienciales, V: Sabiduria* (Nueva Biblia Española), Estella (Navarra), Editorial Verbo Divino, 1990, p. 300, n. 14. Add a Christian interpolation in the Testament of the Twelve Patriarchs, Simeon 6,6 (CHARLESWORTH [ed.], *OT Pseudepigrapha* [n. 10], t. I, p. 787). J.R. LEVISON, *Portraits of Adam in Early Judaism: From Sirach to 2 Baruch* (JSPS, 1), Sheffield, Sheffield Academic Press, 1988, pp. 57-61, rightly rejects a "Philonian" interpretation of Adam as both earthly and heavenly (A. Dupont-Sommer) as well as a proto-gnostic interpretation of Adam saved through a heavenly ascent (E. Peterson; E. Brandenburger; D. Georgi). However, his own interpretation of Wis 10,1b, i.e. "that Adam was 'saved' from his own transgression in the sense that he was 'preserved' from sinning by means of Wisdom" (p. 60), is not only unnecessary but also contradicts Jewish as well as Christian tradition. A similar interpretation had been rejected already by GRIMM, *Weisheit* (n. 9), pp. 192-193.

15. As rightly observed by A. SISTI, *Il Libro della Sapienza. Introduzione – Versione – Commento*, Assisi, Edizioni Porziuncola, 1992, pp. 270-271, Wis's peculiar way of telescoping the Genesis story explains the fact that the power of ruling everything accorded to humanity is mentioned after the sin, instead of before as in Gen 1,26.28.

16. MT: "By me rulers rule, and all righteous judges are noble". However, the text is normally translated according to the LXX.

17. It is instructive to follow the development of thought in Gen 1,26-28. God decides to create humanity in his own image and likeness "in order that they have dominion" (וְיִרְדּוּ – καὶ ἀρχέτωσαν) over fish, birds, cattle, all the earth and every being creeping upon it (v. 26). The actual creation is then related and it is explained that God's image consists in the distinction of the sexes (v. 27). Finally God blesses the couple saying: "Be fruitful and multiply, and fill the earth and subdue it; and have dominion (וּרְדוּ – καὶ ἄρχετε)" over fish, birds and every being creeping upon the earth (v. 28). In the second creation story (2,19-20), human sovereignty over the creatures – beasts and birds – is signified by Adam's giving them appropriate names: "God [...] brought them to the man to

According to them[18] (God) endowed them [i.e. men] with strength (ἰσχύν, cf. Wis 10,2!), and according to his image he made them. He placed the fear of them (τὸν φόβον αὐτοῦ)[19] in all living beings, and granted them dominion over beasts and birds.

and especially Wis 9,2-3:

(O God who) by your wisdom have formed man, that he may have dominion over (ἵνα δεσπόζῃ) the creatures you have made, and rule (καὶ διέπῃ) the world in holiness and righteousness, and govern in uprightness of soul [...][20].

The main features of Wisdom's care of the first couple in Wis 10,1-2 are directly attributed to God in the following excerpt from 2th-3th cent. prayers regarded as Christian adaptation of a Jewish original:

see what he would name each one of them, because in whatever way the man, who is a living being, would name it, this is its name" (2,19; see my *Analysis of Biblical Narrative* [n. 13], p. 186-187). Despite the LXX and prevalent modern interpretation, in the second creation story Adam alone is said a "living being" (נֶפֶשׁ חַיָּה, cf. 2,7), differently from the first creation story, where also the animals are designated in this way (e.g. Gen 1,20.21.24). After the flood, the original benediction is repeated to Noah and his sons: "Be fruitful and multiply, and fill the earth" (9,1). Man's dominion is not mentioned; instead, "The fear of you and the dread of you (וּמוֹרַאֲכֶם וְחִתְּכֶם - ὁ τρόμος ὑμῶν καὶ ὁ φόβος) shall be upon" beasts, birds and every being creeping upon the earth; "into your hand they are delivered" (9,2).

18. Though widespread, the reading καθ' ἑαυτόν is a textual correction; cf. P.W. SKEHAN – A.A. DI LELLA, *The Wisdom of Ben Sira* (AB, 39), New York, Doubleday, 1987, pp. 281-282.

19. Despite the singular (αὐτοῦ), the pronoun refers to the men. In fact, Ben Sira shifts from singular in 17,1 (ἄνθρωπον - αὐτόν) to plural in 17,2-3 (αὐτοῖς – αὐτούς), and again to singular in 17,4. Instead, "the fear of him (φόβον αὐτοῦ)" refers to God in 17,8 and is connected with praising him and proclaiming his great works (17,9-10). However, most MSS have the reading τὸν ὀφθαλμὸν αὐτοῦ "his eye" instead of τὸν φόβον αὐτοῦ: "He looks with favor on their hearts" (SKEHAN – DI LELLA, *Ben Sira* [n. 18], p. 279).

20. Note how human dominion over creation is interpreted in this magnificent text. As M. GILBERT wrote, "Ce texte reprend et développe l'intention première de Dieu sur l'homme selon Gn 1,26.28; mais Sg 9,2-3 ne reprend aucun des termes de Gn 1 qui utilise deux autres verbes; par contre Sg 9 prend deux verbes qui en Sg 12,15-16 serviront à décrire le mode de gouvernement divin du monde. D'autre part, les précisions 'en sainteté et justice' et 'avec droiture d'âme' paraphrasent ce que 1 R 3,6; 9,4 disait du gouvernement de David: ce dernier devient le type parfait de l'homme": *La relecture de Gn 1–3 dans le Livre de la Sagesse*, in L. DEROUSSEAUX (ed.), *La création dans l'Orient ancien. Congrès de l'ACFEB, Lille (1985)* (LD, 127), Paris, Cerf, 1987, pp. 323-344, esp. 329-330. This may help contemporary sensibility to correctly understand and appreciate the Biblical view on the relationship between humanity and the world as well as among human beings in terms of order and "submission". See my paper *Sfondo sapienziale dell'etica dei codici domestici neotestamentari*, in L. PADOVESE (ed.), *Atti del Simposio di Tarso su S. Paolo Apostolo* (Turchia: la Chiesa e la sua storia, 7), Roma, Istituto Francescano di Spiritualità – Pontificio Ateneo Antoniano, 1994, pp. 45-72.

> O Almighty God [...] who gave an implanted and written law to him [i.e. man], so that he might live lawfully as a rational being, and when he had sinned, gave him your goodness as a pledge to lead him to repentance [...][21].

> And indeed, you have given to him an implanted law to do, so that from himself, and by himself, he might have the seeds of divine knowledge. [...] But, having cared nothing for the commandment [...] you indeed rightly thrust him out from paradise. Yet in goodness, you did not overlook him who was perishing forever, for he was your work of art. But, having subjected to him the creation, You have given him, through sweat and hard labors, to provide by himself the nourishment for his own family [...][22].

Interestingly enough, in Wis 10,1-2 as well as in the rest of the book the woman is not mentioned as the wife of the sage nor are marriage and children. Only with reference to the ungodly we find a mention of wives and children (3,12.16; 4,6). However, it is difficult to prove that marriage is outside the horizon of the text since nothing is explicitly said against it or in favor of choosing personified Wisdom as the spouse of the sage with the exclusion of the woman[23]. Besides, if "the first-formed father of the world" is to be interpreted inclusively for both Adam and Eve, it seems difficult to deny that marriage is a self-evident assumption in the text as the normal way of living. For some reason, however, only the role of wisdom is elaborated.

How are we then to understand the relationship between wisdom (personified or not) and the woman? It is the aim of the present study to look at the Biblical Hebrew tradition of the wisdom books for the sake of comparison.

---

21. Apostolic Constitutions 8.9.8 (CHARLESWORTH [ed.], *OT Pseudepigrapha* [n. 10], t. II, 689).

22. Apostolic Constitutions 8.12.18-20 (CHARLESWORTH [ed.], *OT Pseudepigrapha* [n. 10], t. II, 692).

23. Having noted that in Wis 6–9 personified Wisdom is regarded as spouse, and that no other spouse is looked for, BEAUCHAMP, *Épouser la Sagesse* (n. 12), goes on to investigate the absence of the theme of fertility in Wis 6–9 also on the basis of Greek and Jewish-Hellenistic writings. He rightly observes that Wis stands out for this absence, especially if one takes into account the fact that the OT sapiential tradition strictly relates wisdom and family. Significantly, for Beauchamp, Wis was composed in a Jewish-Hellenistic environment, where one finds a clear trend toward celibacy. According to him, the third section of Wis (from chap. 10 on) conveys an eschatological vision, which seems to recommend the exclusive choice of personified Wisdom. Although the last point may be debated (see below), Beauchamp's learned and careful research is very helpful.

2. OLDER WISDOM TEXTS

Let us compare the following texts[24]:

Prov 4,7

[a]   רֵאשִׁית חָכְמָה קְנֵה חָכְמָה

[b]   וּבְכָל־קִנְיָנְךָ קְנֵה בִינָה

Sir 36,29/24

[a]   קנה אשה ראשית קנין

[b]   עזר ומבצר ועמוד משען

Prov 8,22

[a]   יְהוָה קָנָנִי רֵאשִׁית דַּרְכּוֹ

[b]   קֶדֶם מִפְעָלָיו מֵאָז

From the grammatical point of view line a of the three texts shows some similarities. In all the three cases we find, first, a voice of verb קנה; second, an object, i.e. חָכְמָה "wisdom" in Prov 4,7 and 8,22, and אשה "a woman" in Sir 36,29/24; third, an extra element consisting of רֵאשִׁית "beginning" plus another substantive. In Prov 4,7 the third element precedes the verb and the object while both in Sir 36,29/24 and Prov 8,22 it follows them. The function of the third element is disputed.

Aside from a few scholars who would analyze רֵאשִׁית חָכְמָה as a non-verbal sentence[25], this phrase is normally taken as the subject, e.g. "The beginning of wisdom is this: Get wisdom" (RSV); "The beginning of wisdom is – acquire wisdom" (JPS)[26]. Others prefer to just juxtapose the phrase to the following one: "Der Weisheit Anfang: Erwirb Weisheit"[27]. However, a different analysis is possible: רֵאשִׁית חָכְמָה is the predicative complement of the object חָכְמָה[28]. I translate:

24. What follows is already present in a seminal way in my *La casa della sapienza. Voci e volti della sapienza biblica* (Narrare la Bibbia, 2), Cinisello Balsamo (Milano), San Paolo, 1994, pp. 48-52.

25. E.g. H. Ringgren: "Wisdom is the noblest thing", and W. McKane: "Wisdom comes first", both rightly criticized by R.N. WHYBRAY, *Proverbs* (NCBC), Grand Rapids, Eerdmans, 1994, p. 77. Thus already F. HITZIG, *Die Sprüche Salomos,* Zürich, Orell – Füssli & Co., 1858: "Das Höchste ist Weisheit".

26. JPS, i.e. Tanakh: Jewish Publication Society.

27. O. PLÖGER, *Sprüche Salomos (Proverbia)* (BKAT, 17), Neukirchen-Vluyn, Neukirchener Verlag, 1984.

28. Called "predicative accusative" in H.W. SMYTH, *Greek Grammar*, ed. G.M. MESSING, Cambridge, MA, Harvard University Press, 1920, §§1613-1618.

Prov 4,7[29]

[a]   *As the beginning of wisdom*, buy wisdom,
[b]   and with all your possessions, buy intelligence.

Thus the grammatical structure of the two lines is as follows: predicative complement (a) + verb (b) + object (c) // complement (a') + verb (b) + object (c')[30].

The same construction with רֵאשִׁית as *nomen regens* functioning as predicative complement of the object is also found in Num 15,20, and probably in Lev 23,10 and 1Sam 15,21[31].

This analysis is even clearer in the text of Ben Sira[32]:

Sir 36,29/24

[a]   Buy a woman *as the beginning of (your) possession*[33],
[b]   a helper and a fortress, and a pillar of support[34].

---

29. The LXX does not have this verse and many critical scholars believe that it is a later gloss (see below). The text of all the other ancient Greek translators is as follows: ἀρχὴ σοφίας κτῆσαι σοφίαν, καὶ ἐν πάσῃ κτήσει σου κτῆσαι σύνεσιν; cf. F. FIELD, *Origenis Hexaplorum quae supersunt...*, t. II, reprint Hildesheim, Olms, 1964 (original, Oxford, 1875), p. 317.

30. W.A. VAN DER WEIDEN, *Le Livre des Proverbes. Notes philologiques* (BiOr, 23), Rome, Biblical Institute Press, 1970, pp. 44-45, takes the preposition in line b as *beth comparativum* in parallelism to line a, which he interprets as juxtaposed. He translates: "L'essence de la sagesse est: acquiers la Sagesse (comme épouse), Plus important que tout ce que tu possèdes est: acquiers l'Intelligence (comme épouse)". Thus, however, one misses the point of the verse (see below).

31. For Lev 23,10 compare LXX (καὶ οἴσετε δράγμα ἀπαρχὴν τοῦ θερισμοῦ ὑμῶν πρὸς τὸν ἱερέα) and Vulgata ("feretis manipulos spicarum primitias messis vestrae ad sacerdotem"); contrast RSV ("you shall bring the sheaf of the first fruits of your harvest to the priest") and JPS ("you shall bring the first sheaf *of* your harvest to the priest"). In 1Sam 15,21, רֵאשִׁית הַחֵרֶם can be taken as predicative complement ("the people took from the spoil some sheep and oxen *as* the best of the things devoted to destruction, to sacrifice to the Lord") or as apposition ("the people took of the spoil, sheep and oxen, the best of the things devoted to destruction, to sacrifice to the Lord", RSV).

32. See P. C. BEENTJES, *The Book of Ben Sira in Hebrew. A Text Edition of All Extant Hebrew Manuscripts and a Synopsis of All the Parallel Hebrew Ben Sira Texts* (SVT, 68), Leiden – New York – Köln, Brill, 1997, pp. 63 (Ms. B). 152 (Synopsis). In the margin: קינה (probably for קונה, participle; see Greek) for קנה, and עיר מבצר for עזר ומבצר. The Greek has: κτώμενος γυναῖκα ἐνάρχεται κτήσεως, βοηθὸν κατ' αὐτὸν καὶ στῦλον ἀναπαύσεως; Vulgata: "qui possidet mulierem inchoat possessionem, adiutorium contra illum est et columna ut requies". However, the reading קנה as imperative is supported by the parallel Prov 4,7, as already noted by R. SMEND, *Die Weisheit des Jesus Sirach*, Berlin, Reimer, 1906, p. 325, and by N. PETERS, *Das Buch Jesus Sirach oder Ecclesiasticus* (Exegetisches Handbuch zum Alten Testament, 25), Münster i.W., Aschendorff, 1913, p. 299.

33. Compare Sir 51,21: בעבור כן קניתיה קנין טוב "therefore I bought her [i.e. Wisdom] *as* a good possession", whereas the Greek does not translate the pronominal suffix and makes קנין טוב the direct object: διὰ τοῦτο ἐκτησάμην ἀγαθὸν κτῆμα.

34. In SKEHAN – DI LELLA, *Ben Sira* (n. 18), one finds a rather free rendering of Sir 36,29: "A wife is her husband's richest treasure, a help like himself, a staunch support", and the following commentary: "The Heb[rew] phrase *rēšît qinyān*, "richest treasure,"

Does this analysis also apply to Prov 8,22? The reply is yes, although there are scholars who take רֵאשִׁית as adverbial ("at the beginning")[35]. A special problem of this verse is the meaning of verb קָנָה. For the moment, I shall translate it as in the two parallel texts:

Prov 8,22

[a]   The Lord bought me *as the beginning of his way*,
[b]   ahead of his acts, of old[36].

Prov 4,7 is frequently considered both corrupt and a late insertion[37]. Actually, the text is repetitious – or rather rhetorical – but can be read as it is. Just as v. 5a is expanded in v. 7[38], so is v. 6 in v. 8. In other words, the text progresses alternately (a – b // a' – b') as is not infrequently the case in Biblical literature.

Prov 4,5-8

[a]   Buy wisdom, buy intelligence,
      do not forget, and do not turn away from the words of my mouth.
[b]   Do not forsake her, that she may keep you;
      love her, that she may guard you.
[a'] As the beginning of wisdom, buy wisdom,
      and with all your possessions, buy intelligence.
[b'] Prize her highly, that she may exalt you;
      she will honor you if you embrace her.

Despite the claim that Prov 4,7 "involves an intolerable tautology" (Toy), the point of this verse is that the first step toward "finding wisdom" is to "buy it" at the cost of all one's possessions; in other words, as a prerequisite one has to be convinced that wisdom is more precious

---

clearly derives from the middle words of Prov 8:22a: *yhwh qānānî rē'šît darkô*; note that the verb *qānānî* has the same consonants as *qinyān* [...]. Thus, by describing the wife as man's *rēšît qinyān*, Ben Sira distinctly implies that she is to be compared to Lady Wisdom, 'the firstborn of [Yahweh's] ways,' in the majestic poem of Prov 8:22-36 – a comparison that is high praise indeed" (p. 431). This commentary points to the right connection.

35. See exposition and criticism in F. DELITZSCH, *Das salomonische Spruchbuch* (Biblischer Commentar über die poetischen Bücher des Alten Testaments, Dritter Band), Leipzig, Dörffling und Franke, 1873, pp. 141-142. Here St. Jerome's reading is mentioned: *Adonai canani bresith dercho*.

36. Compare the Vulgata: "Dominus possedit me initium viarum suarum antequam quicquam faceret a principio", and contrast the LXX (which simplifies as well as complicates line b): κύριος ἔκτισέν με ἀρχὴν ὁδῶν αὐτοῦ εἰς ἔργα αὐτοῦ "the Lord created me as the beginning of his ways toward his works". For ἔκτισεν cf. Sir 1,9; 24,9.

37. See C.H. TOY, *A Critical and Exegetical Commentary on the Book of Proverbs* (ICC), Edinburgh, Clark, 1899, p. 88.

38. V. 5b parallels the last line of v. 4. Therefore, it is wise to try to understand the text as it is instead of (or, at least, before) simply re-arranging it according to the LXX or to modern taste. Contrast BHK, BHS and RSV: "do not forget, and do not turn away from the words of my mouth. Get wisdom; get insight".

than anything else (cf. 16,16) and consequently it is worthwhile to invest everything to get it. The fool may have the necessary price to buy wisdom but he will never buy it because he has no "heart", i.e. understanding (17,16). The one who has "a sensible heart" will buy wisdom (18,15)[39].

What can we learn from the similarity in the grammatical construction of the three passages? Comparing Prov 4,7 and Sir 36,29/24 we get the following matches: "buy wisdom // buy a woman"; "as the beginning of wisdom // as the beginning of (your) possession". Apparently there is a close relationship between wisdom and woman in that both are involved in a vital process for men: buying a woman leads to possession and buying wisdom leads to wisdom itself. But there is also a progress between the two because all one's possessions must be invested to buy wisdom. In other words, buying a wife is a prerequisite to buying wisdom, and the latter is, in its turn, the beginning of wisdom itself.

The parallelism between the process that leads to wisdom with that that leads to possession suggests the importance of the latter. The term קִנְיָן indicates something different from the riches that do not profit in the day of wrath (11,4; cf. 11,28). Its conveys positive connotations. It indicates what one gets through hard labor and expenses (see Gen 31,18; 34,23; 36,6). Man's קִנְיָן means the same as "his house" (Ps 105,21). God himself has his own קִנְיָן, which are "his works" of creation (Ps 104,24). Related to this, we understand that the verb קנה "to buy" is a cipher for getting something through personal effort and possessing it by rights.

A further text, Prov 24,27, can be usefully brought to bear on what we are saying: "Establish your work (מְלַאכְתֶּךָ) outside, prepare it for you in the field; afterwards you shall build your house". This text spells a further prerequisite – even preceding that of buying a wife –, which is preparing one's work in the field, apparently also a means to establish one's קִנְיָן[40]. Thus, a man "builds his own house" and acquires an honorable place in society. He also avoids the situation poignantly described in Sir 36,30/25: "Where there is no fence, the vineyard will be consumed; and where there is no wife, a man is a vagabond and a wanderer" (like Cain; see Gen 4,12.14)[41].

39. For 23,23, a close parallel to 4,7, and other related texts, I would refer to my paper, *Proverbi 23,12-25*, in *SBFLA* 47 (1997) 33-56, esp. § 3.4.

40. According to WHYBRAY, *Proverbs* (n. 25), p. 353, "This section [i.e. 24,23-34] is more miscellaneous than the preceding one". The first step toward a correct interpretation is to identify its logic of composition, which is alternate, not straightforward (as observed above for 4,5-8). Its keywords are as follows: (a) judgment (vv. 23-26), (b) field (v. 27), (a') witness (in judgment) (vv. 28-29), (b') field (vv. 30-34).

41. The Greek is slightly different: "Where there is no fence, the property will be plundered (διαρπαγήσεται κτῆμα); and where there is no wife, a man will sigh while wandering about (στενάξει πλανώμενος)".

The fear of the Lord is another – complementary, not alternative – "beginning of wisdom / knowledge" (Prov 1,7; Sir 1,14), in the sense that "the fear of God leads to wisdom. It enables a man to acquire wisdom; it trains him for wisdom"[42]. The fear of the Lord is different from terror. It is awareness of God and of his transcendent majesty and power. It is a religious attitude towards the divine. Various passages provide a series of definitions of the fear of the Lord and enumerate its advantages (Prov 2,5; 8,3; 9,10; 14,27; 15,33; 18,27; 19,23; 22,4; Job 28,28; Sir 1,11 ff., etc.). But also the fear of the Lord has something that comes "before" it: humility (Prov 15,33; 18,12; 22,4).

At this point, we can outline the whole process that leads to wisdom. On the one side, one establishes one's possession consisting of a field and a wife, and one invests all possession in order to buy wisdom; on the other side, humility leads to fear of the Lord, and fear of the Lord leads to wisdom. Lastly, "finding wisdom" designates the final stage of the process. Let us compare two relevant texts:

Prov 8,35

[a]   כִּי מֹצְאִי מָצָא חַיִּים

[b]   וַיָּפֶק רָצוֹן מֵיהוָה

[a]   For those who find me [i.e. Lady Wisdom] have found life

[b]   and (each one) has obtained favor from the Lord[43].

Prov 3,13

[a]   אַשְׁרֵי אָדָם מָצָא חָכְמָה

[b]   וְאָדָם יָפִיק תְּבוּנָה

[a]   Happy is the man who has found wisdom,

[b]   and the man who will obtain understanding.

with the following ones:

Prov 18,22

[a]   מָצָא אִשָּׁה מָצָא טוֹב

[b]   וַיָּפֶק רָצוֹן מֵיהוָה

[a]   He who has found a wife has found a good thing,

[b]   and has obtained favor from the Lord.

Prov 31,10

[a]   אֵשֶׁת־חַיִל מִי יִמְצָא

[b]   וְרָחֹק מִפְּנִינִים מִכְרָהּ

[a]   A good wife who will find?

[b]   For far beyond the jewels is her price.

42. G. von RAD, *Wisdom in Israel*, London, SCM, 1972, p. 66.
43. This is an attempt to make sense of the consonantal text. I read line a in the plural:

Again, the similarity of the terminology used for wisdom and for the woman is striking.

Taken at face value, Prov 8,22 applies to God the language employed for humans. In fact, it is difficult to interpret the verb קנה here differently from the parallel texts[44]. Does this mean that God is also subjected to the process that leads to finding wisdom? In order to answer this question we have to look at the context.

Prov 8,23-25

[23]   מֵעוֹלָם נִסַּכְתִּי
        מֵרֹאשׁ מִקַּדְמֵי־אָרֶץ
[24]   בְּאֵין־תְּהֹמוֹת חוֹלָלְתִּי
        בְּאֵין מַעְיָנוֹת נִכְבַּדֵּי־מָיִם
[25]   בְּטֶרֶם הָרִים הָטְבָּעוּ
        לִפְנֵי גְבָעוֹת חוֹלָלְתִּי

[23]   From eternity I was woven,
        from the first, from the beginning of the earth.
[24]   When there were no depths I was given birth,
        when there were no springs abounding with water.
[25]   Before the mountains had been established,
        ahead of the hills, I was given birth.

Here we find two verbs designating human generation: סכך / נסך "to weave (nerves and bones)" and חיל "to give birth"[45]. The answer to the question raised above can be found in the very fact of coupling a verb of acquisition (קנה) with these verbs of generation[46]. This means, on the one side, that God acquired Wisdom by personal effort and, on the other

מֹצְאַי מֹצְאֵי, "my finders are the finders of". The verb in the singular in line b may refer to each one of the category indicated in line a. This phenomenon is not unusual despite the remark of DELITZSCH, *Spruchbuch* [n. 35], p. 150. See e.g. my analysis of Gen 2,19 above (n. 17).

44. Aquila, Symmachus, and Theodotion: ἐκτήσατό με; Vulgata: "Dominus possedit me".

45. See the fine analysis of M. GILBERT, *Le discours de la Sagesse en Proverbes, 8*, in ID. (ed.), *La Sagesse* (n. 12), pp. 202-218. 414-415, esp. 209-211. The whole discussion is summarized more recently by G. BAUMANN, *Die Weisheitsgestalt im Proverbien 1–9. Traditionsgeschichtliche und theologische Studien* (FAT, 16), Tübingen, Mohr (Siebeck), 1996, pp. 116-122. For the 4 cases of verb *ḥyl* used anthropomorphically for God's creative power (Prov 8,24.25; Ps 90,2; Isa 45,11; Deut 32,18), consult J.A. FOSTER, *The Motherhood of God. The Use of ḥyl as God-Language in the Hebrew Scriptures*, in L.M. HOPFE (ed.), *Uncovering Ancient Stones. Essays in Memory of H. Neil Richardson*, Winona Lake, IN, Eisenbrauns, 1994, pp. 93-102.

46. In Ps 139,13, this coupling also occurs for humans: כִּי־אַתָּה קָנִיתָ כִלְיֹתָי תְּסֻכֵּנִי בְּבֶטֶן אִמִּי "For you have bought / possessed my inward parts, you have woven me together in my mother's womb".

side, that he himself is the originator of Wisdom. In other words, Wisdom did not pre-exist God's generation, as the use of a verb of acquisition might lead to conclude[47]. Thus, God is presented as the model for men while remaining God.

Prov 8,22 tells then that God "bought / acquired / possessed" Wisdom "as the beginning of his way". The term דֶּרֶךְ here means "activity"[48]; it is not different from קִנְיָן "possession" (Ps 104,24) and from מְלָאכָה "occupation" (Gen 2,2.3). The three designate the work of creation – God's "career", as it were.

The fact that before creating God acquired and generated Wisdom means that he carefully prepared himself for the work; he made a detailed plan of what he was going to create[49]. In the language of Job 28,27, God

רָאָהּ וַיְסַפְּרָהּ

הֱכִינָהּ וְגַם־חֲקָרָהּ

saw it [i.e. Wisdom] and expounded it;
he established it and searched it out.

(LXX: εἶδεν αὐτὴν καὶ ἐξηγήσατο αὐτήν, ἑτοιμάσας ἐξιχνίασεν).

This is echoed by Sir 1,9:

κύριος αὐτὸς ἔκτισεν αὐτὴν
καὶ εἶδεν καὶ ἐξηρίθμησεν αὐτὴν
καὶ ἐξέχεεν αὐτὴν ἐπὶ πάντα τὰ ἔργα αὐτοῦ

The Lord himself created her;
he saw her and apportioned her,
he poured her out upon all his works.

This "pouring" means creating everything in accordance with wisdom; thus, every creature contains something of God's wisdom. The task of humankind is to get this wisdom, and ultimately to come to know God through his creatures[50]. This happens through personal experience –

47. An echo of the Christological controversies based on this verse is found in older commentaries such as DELITZSCH, *Spruchbuch* (n. 35), pp. 141-143; and A. ROHLING, *Das salomonische Spruchbuch*, Mainz, Kirchheim, 1879, pp. 98-101.

48. Behemoth is called רֵאשִׁית דַּרְכֵי־אֵל "the first of the ways of God" (Job 40,19; LXX: ἀρχὴ πλάσματος κυρίου "the beginning of the Lord's formation").

49. This sketchy interpretation of Biblical wisdom is based on von RAD, *Wisdom in Israel* (n. 42), esp. Chap. IX entitled "The Self-Revelation of Creation", which constitutes the peak of the book. Also see my essays *Giobbe 28*, in *SBFLA* 31 (1981) 29-58, pp. 47-53; *La teologia sapienziale nel quadro dell'Antico Testamento. A proposito di alcuni studi recenti*, in *SBFLA* 34 (1984) 7-24; and *La casa della Sapienza* (n. 24), pp. 137-176.

50. Even for Qoheleth, God's work of creation is the occupation assigned to the "sons of men" (1,13), with all the hardship and joy it entails. See my reading of the book in *La casa della Sapienza* (n. 24), pp. 85-106.

through "eating" them in the language of Gen 3. The wisdom acquired is nothing else but God's wisdom. Even what humanity acquires against the will of the Creator *is* wisdom (Gen 3,22!) but brings death, not life; wisdom only brings life when it is acquired according to the will of the Creator and in obedience to him – i.e. in the "fear of the Lord".

The theme of God's relationship to Wisdom as a model for men comes up with a different language in the Solomon's prayer in Wis. In two successive waves, the prayer deals with three main points: (a) Wisdom with God, (b) request of the same Wisdom by the supplicant, and (c) Wisdom with man (actually the king). Note the similarity between a – a', on the one side, and c – c', on the other.

Wis 9,1-12[51]

[a]   O God of my fathers and Lord of mercy, who have made all things by your word,
       and by your wisdom have formed man, to have dominion over the creatures you have made,
       and rule the world in holiness and righteousness, and govern in uprightness of soul,

[b]   give me the wisdom that sits by you on your thrones, and do not reject me from among your servants.

[c]   For I am your slave and the son of your maidservant, a man who is weak and short-lived, with little understanding of judgment and laws; for even if one is perfect among the sons of men,
       yet without your wisdom he will be regarded as nothing.
       You have chosen me to be king of your people and to be judge over your sons and daughters.
       You have given command to build a temple on your holy mountain, and an altar in the city of your habitation, a copy of the holy tent which you have prepared from the beginning.

[a']   With you is wisdom, who knows your works and was present when you made the world,
       and who understands what is pleasing in your sight and what is right according to yourcommandments.

[b']   Release her from the holy heavens, and from the throne of your glory send her,
       that she may be with me and toil, and that I may learn what is pleasing to you.

[c']   For she knows and understands all things, and she will guide me wisely in my actions
       and guard me with her glory.
       Then my works will be acceptable, and I shall judge your people justly,
       and shall be worthy of the throne of my father. [...]

51. The dependence of 1Clem 61,2 on this passage has been pointed out by SCARPAT, *Sapienza* (n. 6), t. II, pp. 214-215.

The desire of Wisdom because of her intimacy with God is previously expressed in Wis in spousal terms. The supplicant has decided "to take to live with him" the Wisdom who "lives with" God[52]:

Wis 8,2-4.9

[2]   I loved her and sought her from my youth, and I desired to take her for my bride (νύμφην ἀγαγέσθαι), and I became enamored (ἐρασ-τής) of her beauty.

[3]   She glorifies her noble birth by living with (συμβίωσιν) God, and the Lord of all loved (ἠγάπησεν) her.

[4]   For she is an initiate (μύστις) in the knowledge of God, and a guide (αἱρετίς)[53] in his works. [...]

[9]   Therefore I determined to take her to live with (ἀγαγέσθαι πρὸς συμβίωσιν) me, knowing that she would give me good counsel and encouragement in cares and grief.

This is a peculiar way of interpreting the old conception that Wisdom "was beside" God (וָאֶהְיֶה אֶצְלוֹ), and "was all delights" (וָאֶהְיֶה שַׁעֲשֻׁעִים) with him during the creation, and after the creation her "delights are with the sons of men" (וּשַׁעֲשֻׁעַי אֶת־בְּנֵי אָדָם) (Prov 8,30-31)[54].

3. THEOLOGICAL HORIZON

With reference to the question raised at the end of §1, one can affirm, first, that the older wisdom books exhibit a remarkable similarity between wisdom and the woman. Second, God's relationship to pre-existent, personified Wisdom is described in human terms – he acquired and generated Wisdom; thus God is presented as the heavenly model of the sage. Third, because of the similarity just mentioned, man's search for a woman is the first step toward his search for God's wisdom.

---

52. The term συμβίωσις indicates ultimate intimacy, especially marriage, as it is clear from the equivalence of "taking as bride" (νύμφην ἀγαγέσθαι, 8,2) to "taking to live with" (ἀγαγέσθαι πρὸς συμβίωσιν, 8,9). Consult J. REIDER, *The Book of Wisdom* (Jewish Apocryphal Literature), New York, Harper & Brothers, 1957, p. 119; LARCHER, *Sagesse* (n. 6), t. II, p. 522; SCARPAT, *Sapienza* (n. 6), t. II, pp. 187-188.

53. The *hapaxlegomenon* αἱρετίς qualifies Wisdom as "guiding, advising" as illustrated by SCARPAT, *Sapienza* (n. 6), t. II, pp. 139-142. However, Wisdom's guidance is likely to concern God, not humanity, as the context shows; thus, also LARCHER, *Sagesse* (n. 6), t. II, p. 524. Wisdom can be said "a guide in all his [i.e. God's] works" because she is the plan according to which God created the universe (see §3 below).

54. As pointed out by GILBERT, *Le discours de la Sagesse* (n. 45), p. 215, the key words of Prov 8,22-31 are יהוה (God) at the beginning, אֲנִי (Wisdom) in the middle (v. 27), and בְּנֵי אָדָם (humanity) at the end.

The profound homogeneity of the woman with wisdom[55] is capable of inspiring seemingly antithetical choices: either choosing the woman of one's life without excluding the acquisition of wisdom, indeed, as the first step to it; or choosing wisdom as one's only spouse in fuller imitation of God in celibacy.

This theological horizon of the old wisdom tradition seems to be behind Wis 10,1-2. The fact that only wisdom, not the woman, is mentioned in this passage and in the book in general need not to mean a break with the wisdom tradition[56]. It may better be seen as a clearer perception that both possibilities are open. In other words, while Proverbs and Ben Sira seem not to envisage any possibility for man other than marriage as an orderly life-style that can lead to acquiring wisdom, the Book of Wisdom hints at the alternative possibility of choosing wisdom as the only spouse of the sage[57]. Despite the differences of language, the attitude is in both cases inclusive rather than exclusive.

The homogeneity of the woman with wisdom is based on the unity of wisdom itself. I mean that according to Biblical thought only one wisdom exists, and this is the wisdom of God. What is present in the creatures and what man is invited to get is God's wisdom and nothing else. Among other things, this means that the conception held by many interpreters that Biblical wisdom developed from profane to religious is a modern understanding that contradicts the OT wisdom texts, none excluded.

To the unity of Wisdom there corresponds the unity of Love as divine force of life present in creation[58]. The love that moves the two youngsters and all the creatures in the Song of Songs is none other than the all-powerful God's love:

55. We do not forget, of course, that the woman (better said, "the foreign woman", i.e. the prostitute, who because of her behavior is "foreign" to the orderly society of Israel) is also the antagonist of Lady Wisdom – Lady Folly (e.g. Prov 2,16; 5,3; 7,5).

56. This point is investigated in BEAUCHAMP, *Épouser la Sagesse* (n. 12), pp. 349 ff. I would say that the Jewish-Hellenistic trend toward celibacy may have raised the awareness of this life-style in the author of Wis.

57. A good number of similarities have been identified by various scholars between Wisdom-Sophia and Isis in Wis, sometimes even to the point of obscuring, if not ignoring, the older Biblical tradition. For a summary and balanced discussion on the subject one can refer to J.S. KLOPPENBORG, *Isis and Sophia in the Book of Wisdom*, in *HThR* 75 (1982) 57-84. Kloppenborg illustrates Wis's "reshaping of the representation of Sophia by the use of constellations of Isis-mythologoumena" (p. 79). He sees the main reason for Wis's retelling of the Jewish *Heilsgeschichte* as follows: "it helped revitalize Jewish tradition so that it could continue to provide religious identity and structure to a people under attack. But it also laid the basis for communication with the dominant group [i.e. the Greek citizens], to whose privileges and position Alexandrian Jews aspired" (p. 84).

58. I would refer to my essays, *Cantico dei Cantici e canti d'amore egiziani*, in *SBFLA* 41 (1991) 61-85, and *La casa della Sapienza* (n. 24), pp. 107-136.

Cant 8,6-7

[6]   Love is strong as death,
        jealousy is tough as the grave.
        Its flashes are flashes of fire,
        flashes of God.
[7]   Abysmal waters cannot quench love,
        neither can floods wipe it out.

The similarity of Wisdom with Love is suggested by the following expression, where the preciosity of Love is exalted above everything exactly as is the preciosity of Wisdom in, e.g., Prov 3,14-15 and Job 28,15-
19:

Cant 8,7

        If a man gave all the wealth of his house for love,
        he would be utterly scorned.

As a consequence, both the literal and the allegorical interpretation of
the Song of Songs is legitimate. The first should not offend anybody nor
the second should appear foreign to a critical mind because both are
based on God's – not humans' – Love.

Studium Biblicum Franciscanum   Alviero NICCACCI, O.F.M.
POB 19424-91193
Jerusalem

KURIOS, LE NOM INCOMMUNICABLE (SG 14,21)

Comment le judaïsme alexandrin désigne-t-il et invoque-t-il le Dieu unique? Telle est la question à l'origine de cette enquête, ici limitée au livre de la Sagesse[1]. Concrètement quel est le nom incommunicable, τὸ ἀκοινώνητον ὄνομα évoqué en Sg 14,21?

Dans le registre étendu des noms et qualificatifs divins, l'auteur de la Sagesse privilégie à l'évidence θεός (37 fois pour désigner le Dieu unique), mais κύριος est régulièrement employé (23 fois). On notera que ὕψιστος ne vient que deux fois, en parallèle avec κύριος dans les deux cas (5,15[16]; 6,3[4]). Le titre παντοκράτωρ vient une seule fois, en parallèle avec θεός (7,25)[2]. Le titre δεσπότης vient sous la forme ὁ πάντων δεσπότης en 6,7[8] et en 8,3, en 13,3 et 9 (τούτων ὁ δεσπότης, τὸν τούτων δεσπότην), et en 11,26 au vocatif. Il est relayé par le verbe δεσπόζω (9,2; 12,16 et 18).

Les titres exceptionnels, tels que γενεσιάρχης (13,3) ou γενεσιουργός (13,5), et d'autres peuvent être laissés de côté dans la présente étude, mais il faut mentionner le ὁ ὤν, sous la forme τὸν ὄντα (13,1), car il rappelle non seulement le buisson ardent (Ex 3,14 LXX), mais aussi une invocation à Dieu attestée chez le traducteur grec de Jérémie (Jr 1,6; 4,10; 14,13 et 39[32],17)[3].

Parmi les dénominations absentes, je retiens ἰσχυρός, ἱκανός[4], κύριος τῶν δυνάμεων, σαβαωθ, αδωναι. Ce sont des traductions litté-

---

1. Nous suivons l'édition de J. ZIEGLER, *Sapientia Salomonis* (Septuaginta. Vetus Testamentum Graecum, 12/1), Göttingen, 1962, ²1980, en particulier pour la numérotation des versets (qui peut différer de la concordance de Hatch & Redpath). Nous considérons aussi l'apparat critique.

2. Sur παντοκράτωρ, voir C. DOGNIEZ, *Le Dieu des armées dans le Dodekapropheton: quelques remarques sur une initiative de traduction*, dans B.A. TAYLOR (ed.), *IX Congress of the International Organization for the Septuagint and Cognate Studies, Cambridge, 1995*, Atlanta, GA, 1997, pp. 21-36.

3. Dans son édition manuelle de Jérémie, A. Rahlfs a généralise ⁎Ω d'après 4,10. J. Ziegler a raison de garder ὁ ὤν là où les manuscrits le justifient et de l'étendre à 4,10; voir E. TOV, *The Septuagint Translation of Jeremiah and Baruch. A Discussion of an Early Revision of the LXX of Jeremiah 29-52 and Baruch 1:1–3:8* (HSM, 8), Missoula, MT, 1976, p. 24.

4. Ἱκανός rend *Shadday* selon une étymologie artificielle dans des traductions tendant vers le littéralisme; voir F. ZORELL, *Der Gottesname «Shaddai» in den alten Übersetzungen*, dans *Bib* 8 (1927), 215-219; G. BERTRAM, *IKANOS in den griechischen Übersetzungen des Alten Testaments als Wiedergabe von* schaddaj, dans *ZAW* 70 (1958), 20-31. Le traducteur de Job rend Shadday par παντοκράτωρ. – Sur les noms divins, voir P.-M. BOGAERT, art. *Septante*, dans *DBS*, t. XII, fasc. 68, 1993, c. 536-692; spéc. 661-664.

rales, des hébraïsmes, que l'auteur de la Sagesse ne recherchait pas. Il faudra revenir sur αδωναι.

Reste le tétragramme, le nom propre du Dieu d'Israël, YHWH. La Bible grecque l'a rendu habituellement par κύριος, avec ou sans l'article. Toutefois les découvertes de copies juives du Pentateuque grec en Égypte et à Qumrân attestent une situation complexe qui, sous réserve de confirmations ou de compléments ultérieurs, se présente de la façon suivante:

1. La transcription du tétragramme par ιαω est très ancienne dans la Bible grecque; elle est peut-être originale[5].

2. Des manuscrits de la Bible grecque, attestant par ailleurs un texte déjà légèrement révisé sur l'hébreu, transcrivent aussi le tétragramme en hébreu carré après que le copiste grec a laissé la place libre.

3. Des manuscrits de la Bible grecque, dont le texte a été l'objet d'une révision plus drastique sur l'hébreu devenant standard, transcrivent le tétragramme en paléo-hébreu, selon une mode archaïsante attestée par ailleurs[6].

4. Plus couramment les manuscrits de la Bible grecque utilisent κύριος pour rendre le tétragramme, et il y a de sérieux indices pour affirmer que, dans le judaïsme alexandrin, assez vite sinon dès l'origine, κύριος fut la façon commune de prononcer le tétragramme, son q^eré, de même que Adonay est le q^eré perpétuel du k^etîb YHWH[7]. Rien n'empêche que κύριος ait été une ou la façon ancienne de prononcer le tétragramme dans le judaïsme alexandrin.

5. Les manuscrits chrétiens, aussi haut que l'on puisse remonter, abrègent κύριος en KC[8].

6. Αδωναι se rencontre dans la Bible grecque, mais vraisemblablement du fait de révisions ultérieures. On le trouve dans Ézéchiel fréquemment, mais pas dans les meilleurs témoins (B et 967); dans Jg 13,8 et 16,28, mais seulement dans B qui, pour ce livre, représente une révision[9].

---

5. D.E. AUNE, art. *Iao*, dans *Reallexikon für Antike und Christentum*, t. XVII, Lief. 129, 1994, cc. 1-12; P.W. SKEHAN, *The Divine Name at Qumran, in the Masada Scroll, and in the Septuagint*, dans *Bulletin of the International Organization for Septuagint and Cognate Studies*, 13 (1980), 14-44, spéc. 28-31.

6. P.W. SKEHAN, *The Divine Name* (n.5), pp. 31-32 (hébreu carré), 32-34 (paléo-hébreu).

7. P.-M. BOGAERT, art. *Septante* (n.4), col. 661-662 (bibliographie); sur Ézéchiel, voir J. LUST, אדני יהוה *in Ezekiel and its Counterpart in the Old Greek*, dans *ETL* 72 (1996) 138-145.

8. P.-M. BOGAERT, art. *Septante* (n. 4), cc. 588-589 (bibliographie).

9. Sur B dans les Juges, voir le *status quaestionis* dans P.-M. BOGAERT, art. *Septante* (n. 4), col. 588-589.

L'examen des apparats critiques ferait vraisemblablement apparaître d'autres exemples[10].

Après avoir fait ainsi l'inventaire des noms divins disponibles, il faut revenir au livre de la Sagesse.

I. LES EMPLOIS DE θεός, NOM «COMMUNICABLE»

Dans la Sagesse, les emplois de θεός se répartissent en deux grandes catégories. Le mot peut s'appliquer aux idoles. Au pluriel, c'est évident (12,24.27; 13,2.3.10). Au singulier, le contexte décide: en 14,8.15. 20(var.); 15,8.16, il s'agit des idoles. Rien de surprenant, puisque ces passages se rencontrent dans les chap. 13–15, critique appuyée de l'idolâtrie, et à la fin du chap. 12 qui prépare cet ensemble structuré et qui, en critiquant le culte des animaux, prépare le châtiment corrélatif qui suivra, par delà les chap. 13–15, au chap. 16. Nous retrouvons ici une section de la Sagesse jadis commentée magistralement par Maurice Gilbert[11].

Mais θεός désigne aussi le vrai Dieu dans de de nombreux autres passages.

Ce peut être dans le voisinage d'emplois où θεός désigne les idoles: 12,7.13.26.27; 13,1.6; 14,9.11.30; 15,1.19. La proximité n'est pas accidentelle; elle est même recherchée en 12,27 (οὓς ἐδόκουν θεούς ... θεὸν ἐπέγνωσαν ἀληθῆ) et en 14,8.9 (τὸ δὲ φθαρτὸν θεὸς ὠνομάσθη ... μισητὰ θεῷ).

On le trouve aussi en divers autres lieux, en parallélisme avec κύριος (2,13; 3,14[var.]; 8,21; 9,1.13), ou seul (1,3.6.13; 2,16.18.22.23; 3,1.5. 4,1; 5,5; 6,4[5].22[var.]; 7,15.25 [en parallèle avec παντοκράτωρ] 26.27.28; 8,3.4[proche de δεσπότης].21; 10,10; 18,13).

Θεός est utilisé au vocatif en 9,1 (θεέ parallèle à κύριε) et en apposition à un vocatif en 15,1[12].

Plus fréquent que κύριος, θεός fonctionne donc assez sensiblement comme lui. Dès l'ouverture, les deux mots sont employés comme syno-

---

10. Ainsi en Jdt 16,13 (minuscules grecs 58 et 583; nombreux témoins de l'ancienne version latine).

11. M. GILBERT, *La critique des dieux dans le Livre de la Sagesse (Sg 13–15)* (AnBib, 53), Rome, 1973; ID., art. *Sagesse de Salomon*, dans *DBS*, t. XI, fasc. 60, 1986, cc. 58-119.

12. Sur le vocatif de θεός, voir H. THACKERAY, *A Grammar of the Old Testament in Greek*, Cambridge, 1909, p. 145; R. HELBING, *Grammatik der Septuaginta. Laut- und Wortlehre*, Göttingen, 1907, p. 34; pour le Nouveau Testament, F. BLASS – A. DEBRUNNER – F. REHKOPF, *Grammatik des neutestamentlichen Griechisch*, Göttingen, [16]1984, §§ 44,2 et 147,5.

nymes, même si le premier intervient en positif (1,1), le second en négatif (1,3). Seul θεός toutefois est appliqué aux faux dieux. En ce sens,
θεός n'est pas incommunicable.

II. LES EMPLOIS DE κύριος

À la différence de θεός, κύριος désigne toujours le Dieu d'Israël.
Quelques observations stylistiques facilitent le classement. Sur les 22
(ou 23) emplois, le vocatif est employé 6 (ou 7) fois, le génitif
«adnominal» 6 fois, le nominatif 2 (ou 3) fois.

Alors que le vocatif de θεός n'est employé qu'une fois (9,1; cf. 15,1),
le vocatif de κύριος vient 6 ou 7 fois à partir de 9,1 (9,1; 10,20; 12,2;
16,12.26; 19,22; et 11,13[14 var.]).

L'emploi du génitif adnominal est toujours sans article: πνεῦμα
κυρίου (1,7), παῖδα κυρίου (2,13), ναῷ κυρίου (3,14), ὁδὸν κυρίου
(5,7), χειρὸς κυρίου (5,16[17]), θεράποντος κυρίου (Moïse, 10,16).

Hors le vocatif et le génitif adnominal, l'article est normal, surtout au
nominatif. On a περὶ τοῦ κυρίου (1,1; voir 3,14), ὁ κύριος (4,17.18;
9,13; 1,13[var.]), τῷ κυρίῳ (8,21), mais πρός κύριον (1,9), ἐν κυρίῳ
(5,15[16]), παρὰ κυρίου (6,3)[13].

L'importance de ce titre apparaîtra à l'examen de 9,1 et de 10,20,
mais elle se manifeste déjà de deux façons, positive et négative:

1. Le premier et le dernier distique de la Sagesse emploient la dénomination κύριος (1,1 et 19,22).

2. La polémique contre les idoles utilise seulement θεός, et dans ses
deux applications. Autrement dit, κύριος est absent des chap. 13 à 15.

Ces deux observations font entrevoir le caractère incommunicable du
nom κύριος. Ne serait-il pas le Nom?

III. LE NOM INCOMMUNICABLE

Les chapitres 13 à 15

En proposant la structure des chapitres 13 à 15, Maurice Gilbert a mis
en évidence la place centrale de 14,21c, τὸ ἀκοινώνητον ὄνομα λίθοις
καὶ ξύλοις περιέθεσαν. Dans cette structure, l'invocation des idoles et

---

13. Sur l'emploi de l'article, voir surtout A. DEBRUNNER, *Zur Übersetzungstechnik der
Septuaginta. Der Gebrauch des Artikels bei* κύριος, dans *Vom Alten Testament. Karl
Marti zum siebzigsten Geburtstage* (BZAW, 41), Giessen, 1925, pp. 69-78.

donc leur nom ont une place significative. Il n'est pas nécessaire de reprendre ici le tableau. Essayons de dire l'essentiel[14].

En 13,1-9 (les philosophes) et en 15,14-19 (les Égyptiens), il n'est pas question d'appellation. L'erreur condamnée est de considérer (13,2-3; 15,5) les éléments, les idoles ou les animaux comme des dieux. En revanche, dans la section centrale (13,10-15,13), l'accusation formulée d'emblée en introduction est que les idolâtres ont appelé dieux (ἐκάλεσαν θεούς, 13,10) des œuvres de mains d'hommes. Plus loin l'accusation est reprise: «le corruptible a été nommé dieu» (14,8). L'emploi du singulier, θεός, et du verbe propre, ὀνομάζω, précise et renforce le grief. On le retrouve en 14,15: «il a honoré, ἐτίμησεν, (un mort) comme un dieu». Le développement décisif sur l'origine des idoles, qui commence en 14,15, s'achève sur l'accusation solennelle: «ils ont conféré le Nom incommunicable, τὸ ἀκοινώνητον ὄνομα, à des pierres et à des (morceaux de) bois» (14,21). Inversement les idoles ne devraient être nommées d'aucune façon; elles sont «anonymes» (ἀνωνύμων εἰδώλων, 14,27).

Si la traduction de ἀκοινώνητον ne pose pas de difficulté, celle de ἀνώνυμος qualifiant les idoles en 14,27 doit être justifiée. L'adjectif peut signifier, d'après Liddell and Scott[15]: «sans nom», «sans nom d'auteur», «innommable», «qu'il est interdit de nommer», «difficile à nommer», «sans renom». La plupart des commentateurs marquent une hésitation[16]. Je trancherais en faveur de «qu'il est interdit de nommer», sans écarter les connotations péjoratives de «innommable» et de «sans renom». La vieille version latine, devenue Vulgate, a traduit: *infandorum... idolorum*[17]. Habituellement les idoles ont un nom, et leur nom est un élément essentiel de leur culte. L'évocation du nom a des propriétés magiques et constitue ipso facto une participation au culte. Refuser le culte, c'est donc aussi refuser de prononcer le nom de l'idole. Même si l'auteur de la Sagesse ne rentre pas dans cette perspective païenne, il ne peut l'ignorer. Pour lui, l'idole n'a pas de nom, car elle n'a pas d'existence. Elle ne peut être invoquée par un nom, puisqu'elle est inanimée (14,29).

14. M. GILBERT, *La critique des dieux* (n. 11), pp. 131, 136-137, 253-254, 257, et les dépliants hors-texte.
15. Voir aussi le récent supplément: P.G.W. GLARE et A.A. THOMPSON, *Greek-English Lexicon. Revised Supplement*, Oxford, 1996, p. 38.
16. M. GILBERT, *La critique des dieux* (n. 11), pp. 134-135 et 170; C. LARCHER, *Le livre de la Sagesse ou la Sagesse de Salomon*, t. III (EB), Paris, 1985, p. 838.
17. *Sapientia Salomonis*, ed. W. THIELE (Vetus Latina, 11/1), Freiburg i. Br., 1977-1985, p. 509.

Relativement au nom, le raisonnement est donc le suivant. Pour soutenir l'accusation portée – nommer dieu ce qui est corruptible –, l'auteur apporte deux raisons: 1. les idoles ne peuvent avoir de nom ni être invoquées par un nom; 2. le Nom est incommunicable.

Faut-il déduire des chap. 13–15 et de ce raisonnement que θεός est le Nom incommunicable? Il y a deux objections. La première est que θεός n'est en aucune manière un nom propre; la seconde tient à la première, mais est plus pertinente encore: θεός désigne aussi bien les idoles que le Dieu d'Israël; c'est un nom éminemment communicable. Pour avancer, il faut considérer 9,1 et 10,20.

Dieu des pères et Seigneur de miséricorde (9,1)

La grande prière du chap. 9 s'ouvre sur une invocation solennelle[18]: θεὲ πατέρων καὶ κύριε τοῦ ἐλέους. Cette formule demande un commentaire.

1. Le vocatif de κύριος est fréquent dans la Sagesse à partir de 9,1 précisément. En revanche, le vocatif de θεός est rare (9,1; cf. 15,1). Depuis le chap. 9 et surtout à partir du chap. 11, le Seigneur est le destinataire du discours, et c'est lui qui est désigné par la 2ᵉ personne du singulier.

2. L'expression «Dieu des pères» est traditionnelle et fréquente. On ne trouve jamais, sauf erreur, «Seigneur des pères». L'expression occupe diverses fonctions dans la phrase. Ici, en tête de la récapitulation de l'histoire des patriarches (10,1-14), elle est en situation.

3. L'expression κύριε τοῦ ἐλέους – tel est le texte communément imprimé[19] – est unique dans la Bible grecque, et je ne l'ai pas trouvée ailleurs[20]. Il faut noter que les meilleurs manuscrits lisent κύριε τοῦ ἐλέου(ς) σου, «Seigneur de *ta* miséricorde»[21]. La traduction habituelle est «Seigneur de miséricorde» où le génitif est qualitatif et qu'il faut comprendre «Seigneur miséricordieux». Une tournure comparable se lit en Si 44,27(45,1) ἄνδρα ἐλέους (sans correspondant exact dans l'hébreu conservé) à propos de Moïse. Si le σου est original, il faut comprendre «maître de ta miséricorde», «qui fais miséricordre quand tu le veux». Mais on peut tenir que le σου s'est ajouté en raison d'une hésita-

18. M. GILBERT, *La structure de la prière de Salomon (Sg 9)*, dans *Bib* 51 (1970) 301-331.

19. Ainsi dans l'édition manuelle de A. Rahlfs et dans l'édition critique de J. Ziegler. Je n'ai pas poussé plus loin la recherche.

20. Je n'ai rien trouvé de semblable ni dans le Nouveau Testament (sinon pour l'idée) ni dans la littérature intertestamentaire grecque et latine.

21. Σου est omis par les manuscrits lucianiques (*L*) et par C.

tion sur la déclinaison (2ᵉ ou 3ᵉ) de ἔλεος (génitif avec ou sans ς)[22]. La référence à 1 R 3,6 (2 Ch 1,8) où Salomon rappelle la grande miséricorde de Dieu à l'égard de David, source de la prière de Sg 9, explique suffisamment la mention de l'ἔλεος dans le second titre divin.

La titulature solennelle en tête de la prière emploie donc au vocatif les deux noms, Dieu et Seigneur, les plus fréquents. Elle manifeste aussi une sorte d'équivalence entre eux, ce que des parallélismes antérieurs (surtout 2,13) et postérieurs (9,13) signalent discrètement. Pour notre propos, cela ne suffit pas à départager les deux désignations dans leur prétention à être le Nom, d'autant qu'elles apparaissent sous une forme complexe: «Dieu des pères et Seigneur de (ta) miséricorde».

Et ils ont chanté, Seigneur, ton saint Nom (10,20)

Ainsi que l'a observé Maurice Gilbert, 10,20 ouvre une grande inclusion qui s'achève en 19,9, les deux versets (10,20 et 19,9) se caractérisant par l'emploi de αἰνέω (seuls exemples dans la Sagesse) et de κύριε[23]. Plusieurs détails invitent à reconnaître en 10,20 le rappel du Cantique de Moïse (Ex 15)[24]. Ce cantique emploie θεός et κύριος, mais surtout il a la formule κύριος ὄνομα αὐτῷ (Ex 15,3)[25]. Dès lors, en Sg 10,20, le Nom saint dans la phrase καὶ ὕμνησαν, κύριε, τὸ ὄνομα τὸ ἅγιόν σου s'entend soit de κύριος, soit du tétragramme lui-même (dans l'hébreu de Ex 15,3), soit encore de sa prononciation Adonay.

Retour à 14,21

Comment décider entre κύριος, le tétragramme et Adonay? On se rappellera que, en 14,21, les idolâtres sont accusés d'appliquer le Nom à leurs dieux. S'il est vrai que αδωναι et le tétragramme (sous diverses formes ιαω, ιαυε, etc.) se retrouvent dans des grimoires magiques et des textes gnostiques (au sens le plus large)[26], ces noms propres n'y sont pas, à proprement parler, attribués à d'autres dieux. En revanche, tout le monde s'accorde pour reconnaître que κύριος est un titre largement utilisé pour désigner des divinités importantes et des princes divinisés[27].

---

22. H. THACKERAY, *A Grammar* (n. 12), p. 158 et n. 4.
23. M. GILBERT, art. *Sagesse de Salomon* (n. 11), col. 72.
24. Tous les commentaires l'observent.
25. La formule se retrouve surtout chez Isaïe, Jérémie et Amos, mais le contexte est différent.
26. D.E. AUNE, art. *Iao* (n. 5), col. 6-8 (attestations diverses pour Iao et Adonay).
27. Pour faire bref, je renvoie à W. F[AUTH], art. *Kyrios*, dans *Der Kleine Pauly. Lexikon der Antike*, t. III, Stuttgart, 1969, cc. 413-417 (la bibliographie rappelle L. Cerfaux).

Kyrios a donc la particularité d'être simultanément un *titre* des dieux païens et le *Nom* propre du Dieu des juifs. Le risque était donc constant que le Nom incommunicable soit profané.

CONCLUSIONS

1. C'est bien κύριος, prononciation du tétrgramme, qui est pour l'auteur de la Sagesse le Nom incommunicable. La question de la «communicabilité» et de la profanation se pose parce que κύριος est en même temps un titre attribué par les païens à leurs dieux et à leurs princes et le Nom propre de YHWH, le *q^eré* perpétuel du tétragramme.

2. Si cette conclusion vaut pour la Sagesse, elle vaut aussi pour le milieu juif alexandrin de son auteur et de ses premiers destinataires au début de notre ère (date et milieu acceptés communément aujourd'hui). Le judaïsme utilisait déjà alors κύριος en lieu et place du tétragramme. Cela a été montré pour Philon d'Alexandrie, contemporain probable de l'auteur de la Sagesse[28].

3. En conséquence, il ne faudrait pas trop vite croire, sur la foi des rares témoins grecs bibliques trouvés en Égypte et à Qumrân qui emploient ιαω ou le tétragramme hébreu, que l'usage de κύριος pour le tétragramme dans les manuscrits bibliques grecs est d'introduction chrétienne. Il est infiniment plus probable que les chrétiens ont privilégié un des anciens usages juifs[29].

Louvain-la-Neuve, Maredsous   Pierre-Maurice BOGAERT

---

28. N.A. DAHL et A.F. SEGAL, *Philo and the Rabbis on the Names of God*, dans *JSJ* 9 (1978) 1-28; A. PIETERSMA, *Kyrios or Tetragram: A Renewed Quest for the Original LXX*, dans A. PIETERSMA and Cl. COX (eds.), *De Septuaginta*. Studies in Honour of J.W. Wevers, Toronto, 1984, pp. 85-101; spéc. 92-93.

29. Ainsi déjà R. HANHART, dans *Orientalische Literaturzeitung* 73, 1978, c. 42. – Seule l'abréviation K̄C̄ (et des autres *nomina sacra*) est presque certainement d'origine chrétienne.

BEN SIRA – QOHELET – QUMRAN

WOMEN AS SNARES
A METAPHOR OF WARNING IN QOH 7,26 AND SIR 9,3

Qohelet and Ben Sira seem to have educated the (young) people in
search or in need of instruction (cf. Qoh 12,9; Sir 51,23). Among the
many themes they treat of, there is a reference to women described as
snares, because of which the authors have been thought misogynists by
some scholars[1]. These texts read respectively:

> And I find *woman* more bitter than Death,
> she is a *snare*,
> her heart is a net, and her arms are chains (Qoh 7,26: *NJB*).
>
> Do not go near a loose *woman*,
> or you will fall into her *snares* (Sir 9,3: *NRSV*).

Every literary phrase, be it complete or not, has a meaning in itself,
but the meaning intended by the author could be something other than
that of the literary phrase itself, for he can use such a phrase in order to
illustrate or deepen his own perspectives. This is all the more true, if any
author uses a metaphor in a certain context[2]. It is important, in this regard, to define the function of the metaphor. The purpose of this paper is
to deal with the literary role of the expression "women as snares" in our
texts and to search for the sages' real meaning.

QOH 7,26

Expressing his personal *findings*, structured in a triple assertion[3],
Qohelet seems, in 7,26[4], to reflect, to say the least, his personal negative

1. H. MCKEATING, *Jesus ben Sira's Attitude to Women*, in *ExpT* 85 (1973-74) 85-87,
is of the opinion that Ben Sira, one of the wisdom writers "who always make the assumption: the woman is the seducer" (p. 86), is a misogynist. On the contrary, M. Gilbert concludes in his article which appeared in 1976: "À la lumière de tous ces textes, il semble
difficile de parler encore d'un Ben Sira misogyne": *Ben Sira et la femme*, in *RTL* 7
(1976). 441. For an understanding of Qohelet as misogynous or anti-feminist, cf. F.
DELITZSCH, *The Book of Ecclesiastes, Commentary on the Old Testament in Ten Volumes,*
vol. VI, Edinburgh, Eerdmans, 1877, reprinted 1984, pp. 332-334; J.A. SOGGIN, *Introduzione all'Antico Testamento* (BCR, 14), Brescia, Paideia, ⁴1987, p. 487.
2. Cf. C.V. CAMP, *Woman Wisdom as Root Metaphor: A Theological Consideration*, in
K.G. HOGLUND et al. (eds.), *The Listening Heart. Essays in Wisdom and the Psalms in Honor
of Roland E. Murphy, O. Carm* (JSOTSS, 58), Sheffield, JSOT Press, 1987, pp. 48-49.
3. At XLVI° *Colloquium Biblicum Lovaniense* in 1997, we took an opportunity to
present the structure and significance of Qoh 7,23–8,1a. We will take here some of the
main arguments discussed there.
4. The reference to woman as a snare in 7,26 stands in a literary unit 7,23–8,1a, where

views in regard to women[5], which views might have been shared by other men in the society of that day.

v. 26   And I understand that more bitter than death is the woman,
           if she is a snare, her heart a net, her hands bonds.
           He who pleases God escapes her, but the sinner is captured by her.

v. 27-28   See, I have found – says Qohelet, adding one thing to another to
           find out a conclusion – that "my soul has sought continuously,
           but I have not found out: "One man among a thousand I found,
           but a woman among all these I have not found".

v. 29   See, this alone I found that God made human beings straightfor-
           ward, but they pursued many questionable things[6].

The text does not say, in concrete, anything about whether or not Qohelet has met during his life any man ensnared by a woman, resulting in his death[7]. Qohelet's own experiment only attests that he knew a woman could act as a snare[8]. This is in accordance with the traditional wisdom, according to which a woman, or, better, an evil woman (Prov 6,24) could be a "deep pit"[9]. If such a woman demonstrates the quality expressed in 7,26bβc ("she is a snare, her heart a net, her hands bonds"), then she would surely be a definite danger to man: she would be more bitter than death! In wisdom literature the wickedness of certain women (cf. Sir 25,19) is said to be able to reduce a man even to death or lead him down to Sheol[10]. The wise Qohelet (12,9) understands such a situation. This means that the description of woman as a snare in Qohelet may represent the possible reality of certain women leading

Qohelet begins to introduce his own past intellectual experiment accompanied by wisdom and ends with rhetorical questions: "Who is so wise?", "Who knows the meaning of the [above mentioned] matter?" (8,1a). These rhetorical questions are linked closely to the first chapter of the Book and to 8,16ff. In effect, Qohelet affirmed that his quest for wisdom ended in failure (cf. 1,13-17). Because he has never pretended to know everything, he confesses that "the crooked cannot be made straight" (1,15; cf. 7,13). And later, Qohelet underscores again that no sage is able to comprehend all that happens under the sun (cf. 8,16–9,10).

5. Cf. H.P. MÜLLER, *Neige der althebräischen »Weisheit«. Zum Denken Qohäläts*, in *ZAW* 90 (1978) 252; M.V. FOX, *Qohelet and His Contradictions* (Bible and Literature Series, 18), Sheffield, JSOT Press, 1989, p. 243.

6. On חשבנות 'questionable things', see C.F. WHITLEY, *Koheleth – His Language and Thought* (BZAW, 148), Berlin-New York, de Gruyter, 1979, p. 70.

7. The particle אשר is to be parsed as a conditional nuance (cf. Lev 4,22; Deut 11,27). The conditional clause envisages a circumstance in which an evil woman could create a more-bitter-situation than death; this understanding of the text does not permit us to see whether or not Qohelet has personally met any person ensnared by a woman, nor to regard the author as a misogynist.

8. The Hebrew word חטא does not have a moral significance in this context. Cf. R.E. MURPHY, *Ecclesiastes* (WBC, 23a), Dallas, Word Books, 1992, p. 76.

9. Cf. Prov 22,14; 23,27; cf. 18,7. See further Ps 9,16; Isa 24,18.

10. Cf. Prov 5,1-5.20-23; A. MEINHOLD, *Die Sprüche. Teil 1: Sprüche Kapitel 1–15* (ZBK AT, 16.1), Zürich, Theologischer Verlag, 1991, pp. 102.106.

men to death. But it is not necessarily the author's own view of women[11].

One might question: Who then will be ensnared by such a woman? Qohelet gives the answer to this problem: "the sinner is captured by her" (v. 26d; cf. 2,26). In other words, one who does not follow the way of wisdom, but pursues the way of folly will be her victim[12]. The author does not seem, however, to have any intention to underscore such a characteristic of women. In effect, Qohelet never gives any definition of the moral quality of woman as such, apart from the assertion that all humans, represented by "the just and the wise", are full of wickedness (רע) in their lifetime and all destined to death (9,1-3). Qohelet only knows the very fact that he has not yet found out the truthfulness of the saying of v. 28b. Qohelet's wisdom did not suffice to apprehend the traditional sayings despite his scientific method: "My soul has sought continuously, but I have not found out". He never agrees with the saying which affirms the inferiority of woman to man (cf. the rhetorical questions in 8,1a).

In reality, the assertion of v. 26d not only represents Qohelet's own comment to v. 26a-c which can be a quotation[13], but also serves significantly in choosing the right way on the part of his male students who seek the love of a woman (cf. 9,9). Qohelet's recommendation to his male students to live all their fleeting days in the company of their own wives (cf. Prov 5,18b-19), suggests that the author does not have any misogynous perspective about women in general[14]. His recommendation is in accordance with the Old Testament appreciation of the benefits a good wife brings: "He who finds a wife finds a good thing"[15]. The author accepts also the conventional wisdom, which gives importance to the partnership in life: "Two are better than one, because they have a good reward for their toil. Again, if two lie together, they keep warm; but how can one keep warm alone?" (Qoh 4,9.11).

---

11. Qohelet puts together here his own opinion and that of others; cf. D. MICHEL, *Qohelet* (EdF, 258), Darmstadt, Wissenschaftliche Buchgesellschaft, 1988, p. 153.

12. For an understanding of "woman" in Qoh 7,26 as Lady-Widsom, cf. Th. KRÜGER, *«Frau Weisheit» in Koh 7,26?*, in *Bib* 73 (1992), p. 402. But see further O. LORETZ, *"Frau" und griechisch-jüdische Philosophie im Buch Qohelet (Qoh 7,23-8,1 und 9,6-10)*, in *UF* 23 (1991) 261-262.

13. V. 26a-c can be an old *topos* celebrated in the wisdom literature; cf. Prov 7,27; 5,4 with 9,13. R.E. MURPHY, *Ecclesiastes* (n. 8), p. 76, refers to Prov 2,16-19; 5,1-4; 7,22-23; 9,13-18. Cf. J. VÍLCHEZ LÍNDEZ, *Eclesiastes o Qohelet*, Estella (Navarra), Verbo Divino, 1994, p. 326.

14. Cf. J.Y.S. PAHK, *Il canto della gioia in Dio. L'itinerario sapienziale espresso dall'unità letteraria in Qohelet 8,16-9,1- e il parallelo di Gilgameš Me. iii* (SMDSA, 52), Napoli, Istituto Universitario Orientale, 1996, pp. 250-258; H.F. RICHTER, *Kohelets Urteil über die Frauen. Zu Koh 7,26.28 und 9,9 in ihrem Kontext*, in *ZAW* 108 (1996) 591-593.

15. Cf. Prov 18,22; cf. Sir 26,1-18; 36,22-25.

The teachings of Qohelet are not to demonstrate whether a woman might be dangerous to man or not. Rather, the author studies the traditional wisdom (cf. Qoh 12,9-10) regarding women and sees – objectively – in v. 26abα a possible danger which they might be to his students. Therefore, the reader is challenged to see the tragedy which a woman may cause and to remain as one "who is pleasing to God" (v. 26). The real intention of the author appears to consist in encouraging the students to remain "good" (טוב) before God; that is to act in the right way in saving themselves from a wicked woman. If this is the case, then the usage of the metaphor "snares" serves to warn the readers to avoid the situation where a woman acts as a snare. Consequently, Qohelet uses the expression "woman as snare" not in its usual metaphorical meaning but rather as a warning to his students to avoid such a woman and so to remain "good".

SIR 9,3

In the midst of a group of distichs that offer various counsels concerning conduct with women[16], Ben Sira recognizes, in 9,3, a situation similar to Qoh 7,26, which could occur between his readers and women. Ben Sira is in line with the wisdom tradition which is attentive to the compromising complications that can arise from relations with women[17]. Ben Sira warns not to go near a strange woman, adding a motive clause:

> Do not go near[18] a strange woman,
> lest you fall into[19] her snares[20] (Sir 9,3).

16. Ben Sira writes about woman as mother, widow, wife, daughter, adulteress, or prostitute; see the arguments advanced by W.C. TRENCHARD, *Ben Sira's View of Women. A Literary Analysis* (Brown Judaic Studies, 38), Chico, CA, Scholars Press, 1982. Instead, Qohelet does not make any specific distinction in this regard.

17. A. MINISSALE, *Siracide (Ecclesiastico)* (Nuovissima Versione della Bibbia dai testi originali, 23), Roma, Edizioni paoline, 1980, pp. 69-70.

18. According to MS A אל קרב. Greek text has μὴ ὑπάντα, which reads the verb קרה ("to meet"). Cf. R. SMEND, *Die Weisheit des Jesus Sirach*, Berlin, Reimer, 1906, p. 82.

19. In Greek ἐμπίπτω (נפל in Hebrew) is used in the metaphoric sense in the Bible; cf. N. CALDUCH-BENAGES, *En el crisol de la prueba, Estudio exegético de Sir 2,1-18* (Asociación Bíblica Española, 32), Estella (Navarra), Editorial Verbo Divino, 1997, pp. 238-239. See Sir 25,13, where Ben Sira asserts that "a sinner's lot may fall upon her". The verb used in this motive clause is a typical term which describes the man-woman relationship.

20. The term מצודה, from the root צוד ("to hunt"), denotes, in the primary sense, a hunting net, a snare to catch animals. From this ordinary sense, there derives a metaphoric sense, applied to a woman, who, with her seductive power, can catch a man, resulting in his being put in a dangerous situation, even in danger of death. See Prov 6,25 (תצור) where this kind of metaphor is used. Cf. P.W. SKEHAN, *Tower of Death or Deadly Snare?*, in *CBQ* 16 (1954) 154; *TWAT*, t. IV, p. 1083.

The counsel of Ben Sira centers thus on the אשה זרה (strange woman[21]) who appears as a married woman (v. 19) behaving like a prostitute (v. 10)[22] and so manifesting the same features as the woman mentioned several times in Proverbs[23]. The idea of going near a strange woman "conveys the notion of a person's rendezvousing with the woman in question for the purpose of sexual activity"[24]. It is attested in the Old Testament that the Hebrew verb קרב[25] has the meaning "to come close (for sexual intercourse)". In addition, the explicit reference to the prostitute in v. 6 makes it very probable that it conveys the scene of a person submitting to the seductiveness of a prostitute by engaging in sexual intercourse with her.

The characteristics of such a woman are clearly defined by the immediate context: she could be a "snare". The author shares the traditional Israelite wisdom about an adulterous woman. The counsel of the Book of Proverbs is typical:

But in the end she is bitter as wormwood,
    sharp as a two-edged sword.
Her feet go down to death;
    her steps follow the path to Shĕ'ōl (Prov 5,4-5: *NRSV*).

Right away he follows her,
    and goes like an ox to the slaughter,
or bounds like a stag toward the trap
    until an arrow pierces its entrails.
He is like a bird rushing into a snare,
    not knowing that it will cost him his life (Prov 7,22-23: *NRSV*).

The author of these passages of Proverbs gives the impression that men should be extremely cautious when associating with women, for certain women can demonstrate the qualities of "bitter as wormwood",

---

21. A. BRENNER, *Some Observations on the Figurations of Woman in Wisdom Literature*, in H.A. MCKAY – D.J.A. CLINES (ed.), *Of Prophets' Visions and the Wisdom of Sages. Essays in Honour of R. Norman Whybray on his Seventieth Birthday* (JSOTSS, 162), Sheffield, JSOT Press, 1993, p. 193, n. 4, is reluctant to clarify the hebrew term זרה, preferring it thus untranslated. Cf. J. COOK, אשׁה זרה (*Proverbs 1–9 Septuagint): A Metaphor for Foreign Wisdom?*, in *ZAW* 106 (1994) 458-476.

22. Cf. Prov 7,10-27; W.C. TRENCHARD, *Ben Sira's View* (n. 16), p. 119. It is difficult to determine the juridico-social condition of the strange woman. It is a subject much discussed among the scholars. See V. D'ALARIO, *Le donne nei libri sapienziali*, in *Libri sapienziali e altri scritti* (Logos. Corso di studi biblici, 4), Torino, 1997, p. 415, with bibliographical notes.

23. Prov 2,16; 5,3.20; 7,5; 22,14; 23,27; P.W. SKEHAN – A.A. DI LELLA, *The Wisdom of Ben Sira* (AB, 39), New York, Doubleday, 1987, p. 218.

24. W.C. TRENCHARD, *Ben Sira's View* (n. 16), p. 119.

25. Cf. Gen 20,4; Lev 18,6.19; Deut 22,14; Isa 8,3; Ezek 18,6; P.W. SKEHAN – A.A. DI LELLA, *The Wisdom* (n. 23), p. 218.

"sharp as a two-edged sword", whose "feet go down to death", whose "steps follow the path to Sheol" (cf. Prov 5,10f; 6,26.32-35). He who follows such a woman or "goes near the door of her house" (Prov 5,8) is "like a bird rushing into a snare" (Prov 7,23). The consequences of such behavior are so grave that it cannot be regarded as trivial or casual. The young man invited to eat the victim will himself become the victim[26].

For Ben Sira, a man captured by such a (wicked) woman risks his own life, as is the case with birds caught in snares. The concern of the author seems to be meeting a strange woman with the intention of having sexual relations. In case the reader goes near (for intercourse) and meets (as if by chance)[27] a strange woman, he will inevitably fall into her snares[28].

This idea of falling into the snares of women is further illustrated in the next verse, where Ben Sira warns the reader not to consort with a prostitute female musician (cf. Sir 9,4-5; Isa 23,15-16), since she may capture him by her tricks: "Do not dally with a singing girl, or you will be caught by her tricks" (9,4).

Now, in Sir 9,3, the text itself does not refer directly to the result of this "being fallen into her snares", i.e. a sexual encounter with a strange woman. One might think of the loss of inheritance (cf. Sir 9,6). But if one considers the similar situation of Prov 7,10-27, a prostitute is expected to lead a man into a snare, depriving him of his life.

Ben Sira does not say anything about how and who can avoid such a 'strange woman'. But it is significant that the author of the long recension in the Greek version (26,19-27) contrasts the pious wife with the godless one[29]. That this latter represents a "prostitute" (γυνὴ μισθία: lit. a payed woman) is made clear in 26,22, where she is placed

---

26. Cf. L. ALONSO SCHÖKEL – J. VÍLCHEZ LÍNDEZ, *I Proverbi*, Roma, Borla, 1988, pp. 266-267.

27. For this nuance of the verb קרב and קרה, see P.W. SKEHAN – A.A. DI LELLA, *The Wisdom* (n. 23), pp. 21.218.

28. As regards the negative aspects of women, references are made in such passages like these: 25,13.16.18.19.20.23.25; 26,6.7.8. Among these verses, Ben Sira mentions the evil/wickedness of woman in relation to (1) his personal thought (25,16); (2) her husband (25,19). The term "evil/wicked woman" is not mentioned by itself, except in relation to the persons around her.

29. M. GILBERT, *Ben Sira* (n. 1), pp. 436-437, asserts that the author of this verse is offering advice against intermarriage, putting in question the religious quality of wife. For the understanding of intermarriage prohibitin in Graeco-Roman Palestine, see L.J. ARCHER, *Her Price is beyond Rubies. The Jewish Woman in Graeco-Roman Palestine* (JSOTSS, 60), Sheffield, JSOT Press, 1990, pp. 127-129, who is of the opinion that "intermarriage in the fifth century was condemned not only for 'religious' reasons but also because of the resultant 'racial' impurity": p. 128. Gilbert observes further that Ben Sira "ne parle jamais de la qualité de croyante de l'épouse" (p. 442).

in opposition to a "married woman": "a pious wife is given to the man *who fears the Lord*" (εὐσεβὴς δὲ δίδοται τῷ φοβουμένῳ τὸν κύριον[30]: 26,23b). The author of these verses is offering advice to "fear the Lord" to those who want to get a pious wife or those who do not want to be given to a wicked woman. According to the context, it seems likely that the emphasis here is chiefly on the proper way for the young men to live; they should remain faithful in God!

Returning to our texts, Ben Sira speaks about women to his male audience[31], but even though he speaks of women, "he views them primarily in relationship to men"[32]. This being so, it seems inevitable to think that Ben Sira adopts such a topos as "snares" in relation to women for the obvious purpose of reinforcing the traditional counsels that young men should not become involved with strange women. This means that the description of "snares" in Sir 9,3 only serves to warn the readers against any dangerous contact with strange women.

As Gilbert notes, conjugal harmony is approved not only by Ben Sira, but also by God and by human beings in general[33]. Lest a youngster wish to end like "an old fool who commits adultery" (25,2) and whose lifestyle Ben Sira hates, he has to prepare himself by becoming a person who has the fear of the Lord (25,6).

Different from the Greek text of Ben Sira cited above, Qohelet does not link the "fear of the Lord" directly with his consideration of women. But as already noted above, he is explicit in pointing out that he who can avoid her is the "one who pleases (טוב) God", but he who is taken by her is the "sinner" (7,26d). One might ask, however, if there could be a connection between the "fear of the Lord" and "good before God"? We observe first of all the connection between "fear of the Lord" and the substantive רצון ("favor", "pleasure") in Sir 2,16a[34]: "Those who fear the Lord seek to please him". On the other hand, the wisdom tradition suggests that "the good (טוב) obtain favor from the Lord" (Prov 2,12a).

---

30. The Greek of Ben Sira is taken from J. Ziegler's critical edition, *Sapientia Iesu Filii Sirach* (Septuaginta, XII,2), Göttingen, Vandenhoeck & Ruprecht, ²1980.

31. It has been observed that the perspective regarding women expressed in this text is male-centered, as is the case with Qohelet. Cf. A. BRENNER, *Some Observations* (n. 21), pp. 192-208; N. LOHFINK, *Kohelet* (NEchtB), Würzburg, Echter Verlag, ³1986, p. 58 (= *Qohelet*, Brescia, Morcelliana, 1997, p. 103).

32. Cf. R. SMEND, *Die Weisheit* (n. 18), p. XXII; A. MINISSALE, *Siracide* (n. 17), p. 23; A.A. DI LELLA, *Women in the Wisdom of Ben Sira and the Book of Judith: A Study in Contrasts and Reversals*, in J.A. EMERTON (ed.), *Congress Volume. Paris 1992* (SVT, 61), Leiden-New York-Köln, Brill, 1995, pp. 39-40; *ABD*, vol. 6, p. 944.

33. Cf. M. GILBERT, *Ben Sira* (n. 1), p. 433.

34. For a recent detailed study of Sir 2,16, cf. N. CALDUCH-BENAGES, *En el crisol de la prueba* (n. 19), pp. 212-218.

If this is the case, the Greek text of Sir 26,23b: "a pious wife is given to the man who fears the Lord" has the meaning of "a pious wife is given to the good". We may then paraphrase Qoh 7,26d: One who pleases and fears God escapes her, but the sinner is taken by her".

CONCLUSION

Both Qohelet and Ben Sira are aware of the wickedness of certain women (cf. Sir 25,19) as well as the positive aspect of life with a wife. They understand that one who belongs to the group of sinners will fall into the snares of a wicked woman. While Qohelet urges his readers to be "good" before God so as to escape from a woman who is a snare, Ben Sira advises his readers never to go near a strange woman, lest they be caught in her fatal snare. The authors' purpose in using the metaphor of "women as snares" taken from tradition, seems to be to instruct their male students on the proper way to live. The description of women as snares in both authors, seems to have the common and, at the same time, primary purpose of underscoring an ethical attitude before God on the part of the readers.

The Catholic University of Korea   Johan Yeong Sik PAHK
Song Sim Campus
43-1 Yokkok 2-dong, Wonmigu,
Puchon City, Kyonggido 420-743
South Korea

DER WEISE UND DAS VOLK
IN KOH 12,9 UND SIR 37,23

Für die Deutung der ersten Hälfte des Epilogs des Koheletbuches (Koh 12,9-11) ist es entscheidend, ob Kohelet hier (vielleicht gegen damalige Bestreitungen) unter die חכמים eingeordnet oder ob er ihnen zwar zugeordnet, aber dann doch als einer, dem noch weitere Qualitäten zukamen, auch wieder von ihnen abgehoben werden soll[1]. Ein wichtiges Element für die Entscheidung dieser Frage ist die Aussage in 12,9b:

עוד למד דעת את־העם

Was tat Kohelet, wenn er »das Volk Wissen lehrte«? Dazu: War das, was er tat, etwas, was alle taten, die man mit dem Wort חכם kennzeichnen konnte? »Lehrten« damals die חכמים das »Volk« Wissen? Oder tat Kohelet etwas, was die anderen חכמים nicht taten?

Daß wir in den Büchern des hebräischen Kanons keine Aussage finden, die mit dem lexematischen Material von Koh 12,9b den חכמים eine Lehrertätigkeit oder gar breite Volksbelehrung zuschriebe, läßt sich durch Konkordanzuntersuchung leicht feststellen. Durch eine solche Untersuchung glaube ich darüber hinaus an anderer Stelle nachweisen zu können, daß hier auf Formulierungen für eine Institution der Torabelehrung durch umherziehende Beamte und Priester in den Städten des persisch-hellenistischen Juda zurückgegriffen wird. Das war nötig, um das für Jerusalem und Judaia neue Phänomen einer *Wanderphilosophentätigkeit* überhaupt benennen zu können[2]. Das heißt, in Koh 12,9 würde – sogar mit gewissen Formulierungsproblemen – von einer Qualität Kohelets gesprochen, die *nicht* jedem חכם zukam.

Nun gibt es einen Text bei Ben Sira, der den beschriebenen Befund wieder in Frage zu stellen scheint. Ihm möchte ich mich in dieser Festschrift zu Ehren des großen Sirachspezialisten Maurice Gilbert näher zuwenden.

---

1. Vgl. N. LOHFINK, *Zu einigen Satzeröffnungen im Epilog des Koheletbuches*, in A. A. DIESEL u. a. (Hg.), *»Jedes Ding hat seine Zeit...« Studien zur israelitischen und altorientalischen Weisheit, Diethelm Michel zum 65. Geburtstag* (BZAW, 241), Berlin, de Gruyter, 1996, pp. 131-147.

2. Die entscheidende Belegstelle ist 2 Chr 17,9, doch muß man als Hintergrund den gesamten Sprachgebrauch untersuchen. Bei der genannten Studie handelt es sich um eine Untersuchung des ganzen Koheletepilogs, an der ich noch arbeite. Für einen Zusammenhang von Koh 12,9 und 2 Chr 17,7-9 vgl. J.L. CRENSHAW, *Urgent Advice and Probing Questions. Collected Writings on Old Testament Wisdom,* Macon, Georgia, Mercer, 1995, pp. 248f.

Wenn ich recht sehe, hat erstmalig Kurt Galling für die Deutung von Koh 12,9b auf Sir 37,23 aufmerksam gemacht[3]. Seitdem fehlt der Hinweis in den Kommentaren selten[4]. Er bleibt zwar stets kurz, beeinflußt aber meist die Deutung. Diese Parallele, so wird offenbar unterstellt, könne zeigen, daß man von einem guten חכם Belehrung des Volkes erwartet habe. Hans Wilhelm Hertzberg hat mit dieser Stelle ausdrücklich gegen Gordis argumentiert, wobei er allerdings übersieht, daß Gordis nicht mit einer volksbildnerischen Lehrtätigkeit Kohelets, sondern nur mit Volksbeeinflussung durch sein Schrifttum rechnet[5].

Wer Sir 37,23 für die Deutung von Koh 12,9 heranzieht, müßte zunächst wohl darauf hinweisen, daß er sich auf einen Text beruft, der nach vorherrschender Auffassung *jünger ist als Kohelet* (und wohl auch sein erster Epilog — bei der zweiten Hälfte des Epilogs sieht die Lage vielleicht anders aus). Bei Ben Sira sind Weisheit und Tora schon in einem ganz anderen Ausmaß als in den Weisheitsschriften der hebräischen Bibel einander genähert. Das Buch selbst ist ein Zeugnis für die Verschmelzung auch bei der gesellschaftlichen Weitergabe dieser Größen. Es gab also genau in dem Bereich, um den es geht, innerhalb weniger Generationen, ja vielleicht Jahrzehnte, Verschiebungen und Änderungen. Natürlich kann eine fast sprichwörtlich klingende Aussage bei Ben Sira durchaus einen schon lange vorhandenen Zustand benennen. Aber wenn man sich für Verhältnisse zur Zeit Kohelets auf das beruft, was der spätere Ben Sira voraussetzt, müßte man angesichts der Gesamtlage Gründe nennen. Eine solche Begründung hat keiner der Autoren, die Sir 37,23 zur Deutung von Koh 12,9 heranziehen, auch nur angedeutet.

Auch wäre festzuhalten, daß der Betrieb einer eigenen Schule durch Ben Sira — was man, obwohl der Fall nicht völlig klar ist, aus dem בית מדרש von Sir 51,23 erschließen kann — noch nicht das darstellt, was unter »Belehrung des Volkes« zu verstehen wäre.

Sodann wäre es sicher gut, den *Text* genauer zu inspizieren, auch in seinem *Kontext*. Sir 37,23 ist uns hebräisch erhalten, und zwar in zwei Geniza-Exemplaren, in einem der beiden allerdings erst am Rande hin-

---

3. K. GALLING, *Prediger Salomo,* in M. HALLER und K. GALLING, *Die Fünf Megilloth* (HAT, 1,18), Tübingen, Mohr, 1940, p. 89.

4. Vgl. W. Zimmerli in H. RINGGREN und W. ZIMMERLI, *Sprüche / Prediger* (ATD, 16,1), Göttingen, Vandenhoeck, ³1980, p. 244; H.W. HERTZBERG, in Ders. und H. BARDTKE, *Der Prediger / Das Buch Esther* (KAT, 17,4-5), Gütersloh, Mohn, 1963, p. 218; A. LAUHA, *Kohelet* (BKAT, 19), Neukirchen-Vluyn, Neukirchener Verlag, 1978, p. 218; R.N. WHYBRAY, *Ecclesiastes* (NCBC), Grand Rapids, Eerdmans, und London, Marshall, Morgan & Scott, 1989, p. 170.

5. HERTZBERG, p. 218: »Wir wissen, daß gerade das Lehren die eigentliche Beschäftigung eines חכם war; daher heißt es Sir 37,23 ויש חכם לעמו נחכם פרי דעתו נאמן, eine Stelle, die der erwähnten Meinung von Gordis widerspricht.«

zugefügt. Erhalten ist er in D, und am Rande hinzugefügt ist er in B. Da es sich in 37,22-24.26[6] deutlich um eine durchkonstruierte Spruchkomposition handelt, ist es am besten, diese vier Verse zunächst einmal als eine Einheit ins Auge zu fassen (37,22 und 24 finden sich außer in B und D auch in Manuskript C, 37,26 nur in C und D)[7]:

פרי דעתו על גויתו:	22 יֵשׁ חכם לנפשׁו יחרם
פרי דעתו בגויתם:[8]	23 ויֵשׁ חכם לעמו יחכם
ויאשׁרהו כל רואיהו:	24 חכם לנפשׁו ישׂבע תענוג
ושׁמו עומד בחיי עולם:	26 חכם עם ינחל כבוד

22 Es gibt den Weisen, der *für sich selbst* weise ist:
   die Frucht seines Wissens zeigt sich an *seinem* Leib.
23 Es gibt den Weisen, der *für sein Volk* weise ist:
   die Frucht seines Wissens zeigt sich an *ihrem* Leib.
24 Der Weise *für sich* sättigt sich an Glück,
   und selig preisen ihn alle, die ihn sehen.
26 Der Weise *fürs Volk* gewinnt ein Erbteil von Ehre,
   und sein Name hält sich ins ewige Leben.

Dieses strenge Spruchgefüge wird nun – in einzelnen Zeugen an wechselnder Stelle (nach 37,23 oder nach 37,24) – in der hebräischen und griechischen, nicht jedoch in der syrischen Texttradition durch den kommentierenden Seitengedanken des Verses 37,25 unterbrochen:

וחיי ישׁרון[9] ימי אין מספר:	25 חיי אנושׁ ימים מספר

25 Das Leben des (einzelnen) Menschen: zählbare Tage,
   doch das Leben von Jeschurun: unzählbare Tage.

Diese wohl *sehr frühe Erweiterung* führt nicht nur die Zeit- und Ewigkeitsdimension ein, die dann im abschließenden Spruch 37,26 entscheidend ist, sondern gibt zugleich eine klare Deutung dessen, was in 37,23 und 26 mit עמו und עם gemeint sein soll: *Jeschurun/Israel*. Ohne diese Klarstellung könnte man das עמו von 37,23 im Kontext durchaus

6. Ich halte mich an die Smend-Ziegler-Zählung für die Septuaginta.
7. Da ich historisch frage, diskutiere ich den hebräischen Text. Für die hier verfolgten Fragen sind die dortigen Varianten in 37,24 und 25 unwichtig, und ich begründe meine Entscheidung nicht näher.
8. Diese hebräisch doppelt bezeugte Lesung wird meist zugunsten einer vom Griechischen her konstruierten Konjektur נאמן aufgegeben. Sie sei eine sekundäre Angleichung an das Ende des vorangehenden Verses. Doch allein die gewundene Argumentation von Di Lella legt es schon nah, bei בגויתם zu bleiben. Vgl. P. W. SKEHAN und A.A. DI LELLA, *The Wisdom of Ben Sira* (AB, 39), New York, Doubleday, 1987, p. 435. Dem übersetzenden Enkel war die Passage zu eintönig, und er hat im ganzen ein wenig frei übersetzt. Das wird alles sein.
9. So D. Dagegen liest B עם ישׂראל. Textkritisch hat D die ungewöhnlichere Lesart, während B den Bezug zur textlichen Umgebung noch deutlicher herausstellt. Doch der Sache nach ist dieser auch bei der vorzuziehenden Lesart von D voll da.

auch als »seine Verwandtschaft, seine Familie« übersetzen, auch wenn die umfassendere Bedeutung »Volk« natürlich nie ausschließbar ist. Vermutlich ist dies einer der Gründe, weshalb der Spruch in das so strenge Gefüge eingeschoben wurde.

Da das sehr früh geschah, spiegelt sich vielleicht eine Hinwendung der traditionellen Weisheit auf die Größe Israel, die in den wenigen Jahrzehnten zwischen Großvater und Enkel vor sich ging. Das würde in die Periode passen, denn es sind die Jahre des Makkabäeraufstandes. Doch ist natürlich auch nicht ausgeschlossen, daß schon der Großvater eine eigene ältere Spruchkomposition bei der Herstellung seines Buches kommentierend stärker auf Israel bezogen hätte[10]. Auf jeden Fall zeigt diese Erweiterung des Textes, daß die *Referenz* von עמו und עם ursprünglich nicht ganz eindeutig war. Das schafft nach der Zeitfrage eine zweite Unsicherheit, will man Sir 37,23 zur Erklärung von Koh 12,9 heranziehen.

Doch noch wichtiger ist die Feststellung, daß die ganze Spruchkomposition samt Erweiterung *nirgends vom Weisen als Lehrer* spricht. Es geht in viel allgemeinerer Form stets darum, wem ein חכם seine Bildung und sein Wissen zugutekommen läßt. Dann werden sofort die Effekte ins Auge gefaßt: Wohlergehen des Leibes, Bewunderung, Ehre, weiterlebender guter Name. *Wie* der חכם sein Wissen Frucht bringen läßt, wird nicht näher reflektiert. Es wird nicht gesagt, er tue das als Lehrer. Um Erklärungskraft für Koh 12,9 zu gewinnen, läge aber alles daran, daß auf die Weitergabe des Wissens durch Lehrtätigkeit hingewiesen würde, mindestens bei den Sprüchen, die von einem »חכם für sein Volk« handeln. So kann man aus Sir 37,22-26 nichts für Koh 12,9 folgern.

Daß – wenn überhaupt an bestimmte Weisen, das Wissen Frucht bringen zu lassen, gedacht wird – eher anderes im Blick ist, zeigt der *umfassendere Kontext*. Sir 37,1-6 handeln von der *Freundschaft*. Genauer: Sie fragen nach dem guten Freund[11]. Von da aus wird als nächstes Thema das des guten *Ratgebers* assoziiert[12]. Es wird in 37,7-15 abgehandelt.

---

10. Dann müßte es aber schon aus der Hand von Ben Sira verschiedene Fassungen gegeben haben, oder die syrische Übersetzung hätte den Vers gestrichen.

11. Zu Sir 37,1-6 vgl. G. SAUER, *Freundschaft nach Ben Sira 37,1-6*, in F.V. REITERER (Hg.), *Freundschaft bei Ben Sira. Beiträge des Symposiums zu Ben Sira Salzburg 1995* (BZAW, 244), Berlin, de Gruyter, 1996, pp. 123-131. Zu allen Texten über die Freundschaft vgl. O. KAISER, *Was ein Freund nicht tun darf. Eine Auslegung von Sir 27,16-21*, ebd., pp. 107-122.

12. Zu »Rat« bei Ben Sira vgl. F.V. REITERER, *Gelungene Freundschaft als tragende Säule einer Gesellschaft. Exegetische Untersuchung von Sir 25,1-11*, in REITERER, *Freundschaft*, pp. 133-169, spez. p. 158f.

Am Ende steht, daß man vor allem dem eigenen Gewissen trauen und auf Gott vertrauen soll. Der zwischenmenschliche Rat kommt also ziemlich schlecht weg, und passend schließt sich in 37,16-18 eine Übergangspassage über die Bedeutung und Gefährlichkeit der *menschlichen Zunge* an. Offenbar ist das Thema des Ratgebers noch nicht abgeschlossen. So beginnt nun eine Phänomenologie der verschiedenen Typen jenes Menschen, der in der damaligen Gesellschaft als der *gegebene Berater* gilt, nämlich des חכם. Sie erstreckt sich von 37,19 bis 37,26, hat also unseren Text 37,22-26 als zweite Hälfte. Vorher wird ein anderer typologischer Gegensatz beim Phänomen חכם behandelt: Weise, die andere gut beraten, sich selbst aber nicht beraten können, stehen in polarer Opposition zu Weisen, deren guter Rat nicht angenommen wird. Dem folgt, zunächst chiastisch eingeführt, unser Text: Weise für sich selbst und Weise für ihr Volk. Zusammen: Es geht hier offenbar um den *Rat* des חכם. Von Lehre und Belehrung ist keine Rede. Erst recht nicht von breiter Volkserziehung[13].

Der ganze Zusammenhang geht von privaten persönlichen Beziehungen aus. Nur am Ende, gerade in unserem Text, weitet sich der Blick aufs Volk. Der Rat des חכם, so sehr er zunächst ins Private gehört, kann also durchaus eine breite Öffentlichkeit erreichen.

Aus anderen Stellen des Buches wird noch stärker deutlich, wie das geschieht. Der Ort des Rates des חכם ist die Versammlung der Gemeinde. Denn die Weisheit

öffnet ihm inmitten der Versammlung (בתוך קהל) den Mund (Sir 15,5).

Vom Gegentyp des חכם, den Arbeitern, heißt es:

Zum Rat des Volkes werden sie nicht hinzugezogen,
sie ragen nicht hervor in der Versammlung.
Auf dem Stuhl des Richters sitzen sie nicht,
Gesetz und Recht durchschauen sie nicht.
Sie können auch die Lehren der Weisheit nicht entfalten,
noch findet man sie unter den Vorstehern (Sir 38,32d.33)[14].

All diese negativen Aussagen sind vom positiven Bild des חכם aus entworfen. Sie zeigen deutlich den Ort, wo dieser zum Nutzen des gan-

---

13. J. MARBÖCK, *Weisheit im Wandel. Untersuchungen zur Weisheitstheologie bei Ben Sira* (BBB, 37), Bonn, Hanstein, 1971, p. 126, findet zu 37,19-26 nur die sehr vage Aussage von den »Weisen« als »Menschen, die auf irgendeine Weise auf andere Einfluß ausüben wollen.« Im anschließenden Abschnitt über Weisheit und »Unterweisung« erwähnt er Sir 37 nicht – sicher zu Recht.

14. Bei der Vorlagenrekonstruktion des hebräisch nicht erhaltenen Textes folge ich SKEHAN – DI LELLA, p. 448.

zen Volkes in die Öffentlichkeit hineinwirkt[15]. Der Gedanke, daß der חכם die Aufgabe hätte, die Arbeiter durch Mitteilung seiner eigenen דעת gewissermaßen in sein eigenes Bild hineinzuverwandeln, ist auch hier nicht vorhanden. Im Zusammenhang wird geradezu betont, wie wichtig auch die Arbeiter mit ihren spezifischen Leistungen für das Gemeinwesen sind. Es wird aber herausgestellt, daß sich das Leben des חכם und das Leben des Handarbeiters nicht vereinbaren lassen.

Das ist dann doch wohl eine etwas andere Sicht als die von Koh 12,9. Dort geht es zweifellos nicht um beratende Tätigkeit, selbst nicht um solche in großer Versammlung und zu Nutzen des ganzen Volkes. Sondern es ist echte Belehrung gemeint – wie immer sie im einzelnen dann zu denken ist. Für so etwas als typische Tätigkeit des חכם zur Zeit Kohelets ist aber – gegen die Meinung vieler jüngerer Koheletkommentare – Sir 37,23 keineswegs ein brauchbarer Beleg, so schön und tief der Text in sich selbst ist.

Offenbacher Landstraße 224   Norbert LOHFINK S.J.
D-60599 Frankfurt am Main

---

15. Diese Darstellung erscheint J. G. GAMMIE als so signifikant, daß er vor allem von ihr aus Schlußfolgerungen für den »Beruf« von Ben Sira wagt. Er hält ihn für einen »lay jurist and scribe«. Vgl. ders., *The Sage in Sirach,* in Ders. und L. G. PERDUE (Hg.), *The Sage in Israel and the Ancient Near East,* Winona Lake, Eisenbrauns, 1990, pp. 355-372, spez. pp. 364-368.

LE LIVRE DE BEN SIRA
ET LES MANUSCRITS DE LA MER MORTE

Dans un remarquable *status quaestionis* récent sur le Siracide, M. Gilbert écrivait: «Une étude d'ensemble sur les rapprochements entre Ben Sira et Qumrân fait encore défaut. Sur le rôle des Qumrâniens dans l'élaboration d'Hb II, thèse prônée par C. Kearns…, manque également une étude systématique»[1]. Ces quelques pages n'ont certainement pas la prétention de combler ce vide. Mais dans un volume d'hommage au Professeur M. Gilbert, qui nous a si bien introduit dans l'approche de ce livre, nous osons esquisser quelques éléments de réponse à ce souhait, ou du moins y apporter quelques précisions en attendant la publication officielle de tous les manuscrits du Désert de Juda, qui seule permettra une recherche plus complète et nuancée. Mais dans un premier temps, il importe avant tout de faire le point des acquis commencé par M. Gilbert[2]. Pour ce faire, nous passerons en revue les manuscrits retrouvés, les citations et points communs qui supposent une dépendance des seconds par rapport à Ben Sira.

I. LES MANUSCRITS HÉBREUX DU LIVRE DE JÉSUS BEN SIRA

Jusqu'à la fin du siècle dernier, le livre du Siracide n'était connu que par des versions, principalement grecques, latines et syriaques. Mais on savait qu'il avait existé un texte hébreu, comme le rapportent le premier traducteur grec, son petit-fils, dans le *Prologue* (v. 22) et Jérôme dans sa préface aux livres salomoniens (*Patrologia Latina* XXIX pp. 427s); dans le manuscrit aux mains de Jérôme le livre précédait l'Ecclésiaste et le Cantique[3]. En témoignent aussi des citations de l'ouvrage dans la lit-

---

1. M. GILBERT, Art. *Siracide*, in *DBS*, t. XII, Paris, Letouzey et Ané, 1996, 1389-1437, col. 1415.
2. Voir encore M. GILBERT, *The Book of Ben Sira: Implications for Jewish and Christian Traditions*, in Sh. TALMON (ed.), *Jewish Civilization in the Hellenistic Roman Period*, Philadelphia, Trinity Press International, 1991, pp. 81-91.
3. Voir GILBERT, *The Book of Ben Sira* (n. 2), pp. 85-87. Si le livre portait bien comme titre *mšlym*, n'aurait-il pas pu alors être confondu avec celui des Proverbes qui précède le Cantique et Qohelet ? Quoi qu'il en soit, il est probable que ce Sira en hébreu provienne des découvertes faites dans la région de Qumrân sous Caracalla (211-217), dont Origène avait eu connaissance, voir R. DE VAUX, *Postscriptum, La cachette des manuscrits hébreux*, in *RB* 56 (1949), 234-37 pp. 236s, du même, *Les grottes des manuscrits hébreux*, in *RB* 56 (1949) 586-609, p. 592, J.T. MILIK, *Ten Years of Discovery in the Wilderness of Judaea* (Studies in Biblical Theology, 26), London, SCM, 1959, p. 19 n. 2.

térature rabbinique et dans le *sefer ha-galûy* de Saadiyah Gaon au Xe siècle[4].

Les manuscrits du Caire

De 1896 à 1982 furent découverts parmi les manuscrits de la *genizah* de la synagogue qaraïte du Vieux Caire des fragments du livre hébreu de Ben Sira qu'on pense, à juste titre, être des copies des Xe-XI/XIIe siècles de manuscrits retirés peu avant 800 d'une grotte (de Qumrân) près de Jéricho[5]. Ces copies sont de trois sortes:

- Les manuscrits B, E et F portent un texte en stichométrie: un stique par ligne avec séparation des deux hémistiches par une césure.
- Les manuscrits A et D présentent un texte en écriture continue.
- Le manuscrit C qui est aussi en écriture continue, pourrait être un florilège et ne pas remonter à un original «qumranien».

La graphie en continu ou en stichométrie est déjà celle du scriptorium qumranien pour ce genre littéraire. On comparera par exemple le manuscrit le plus récent des Proverbes, 4QProverbes[a] (4Q102) en stichométrie, et 4QProverbes[b] (4Q103) le manuscrit le plus ancien – du milieu du II[e] siècle av. J.-C. – en écriture continue, sans qu'il soit nécessaire de faire appel aux manuscrits de Ben Sira de Qumrân et de Masada du Ier s. av. J.-C. (voir *infra*). Les manuscrits B et E confirment l'ordre des chapitres connus du syriaque et du latin.

---

4. Voir S. SCHECHTER, *The Quotations from Ecclesiasticus in Rabbinic Literature*, in *JQR* 3 (1891), pp. 682-706: 24 citations, A.E. COWLEY – A. NEUBAUER, *The Original Hebrew of a Portion of Ecclesiasticus (XXXIX.15 to XLIX.11) Together with Early Versions and an English Translation, Followed by the Quotations from Ben Sira in Rabbinical Literature*, Oxford, Clarendon, 1897, pp. XIX-XXX: 79 citations. Mais seuls 19 hémistiches sur 106 correspondent à la terminologie des manuscrits hébreux du Caire, les 87 autres sont des paraphrases plus ou moins libres sans grande correspondance de vocabulaire, sans doute parce que les auteurs, ne disposant pas du livre, dépendent d'une tradition orale ou de traductions. En revanche, Saadiyah Gaon cite 26 hémistiches pratiquement dans la forme du Ms A du Caire et un autre plutôt *ad sensum*, voir A. DI LELLA, *The Hebrew Text of Sirach. A Text-Critical and Historical Study* (Studies in Classical Literature, 1), London-The Hague-Paris, Mouton and Co, 1966, pp. 95s.
5. Sur cette découverte, voir la lettre du Patriarche Timothée Ier à Serge, Métropolite d'Elam, in O. BRAUN, *Ein Brief des Katholikos Timotheos I über biblische Studien des 9 Jahrhunderts*, in *Oriens Christianus* 1 (1901) 299-313, et R. DUVAL, *Une découverte de livres hébreux à Jéricho*, in *Revue sémitique d'épigraphie et d'histoire ancienne* 10 (1902) 174-179. Cette identification à une grotte de Qumrân explique aussi la présence de deux copies du Document de Damas et du Testament de Lévi en araméen parmi ces manuscrits et l'existence d'un texte hébreu de Ben Sira du temps de Saadiyah Gaon au Xe s., alors que ce livre qui n'est pas régulièrement transmis par les rabbanites, n'est guère connu d'eux que par des paraphrases.

Les manuscrits de Qumrân

a. 2Q18

En 1952, la grotte 2 de Qumrân a fourni les premiers fragments hébreux du livre, renforçant l'hypothèse de l'origine des copies qaraïtes. Le manuscrit 2Q18, daté de la seconde moitié (troisième quart) du Ier s. av. J.-C[6]., porte un texte en disposition prosodique d'identification certaine grâce au manuscrit A de la *genizah* du Caire: fragment 2 = Si 6,20-31. Le fragment appartenant à la partie gauche d'une feuille (couture) porte des points d'encre pour les réglures assurant des traces de 14 lignes[7]. Malgré les maigres finales des seules lignes 9-10 et 13, la nature du texte préservé assure l'ordre des versets retenu par le grec contre le manuscrit A du Caire qui intercale les deux stiques de 27,5-6 en lieu et place de 6,23-25. Même sans restes écrits préservés, les trois lignes du fragment 2,4-6 devaient contenir les trois versets 6,23-25[8]. Mais, comparé au Ms A, ce fragment porte une variante (?) non relevée en lisant *n]kḥ* qui est plus qu'une graphie défective, mais encore un masculin. Aussi, au lieu de restaurer *hy' n]kḥ* (Baillet)[9] avec le Ms A *hy' nkwḥh*, devrait-on lire *hw' n]kḥ*, reprenant le substantif masculin de 22a: *ky hmwsr kšmh kn hw'*. Le grec a lu σοφία, substantif féminin[10].

Le fragment 1 est difficilement localisable, étant donné l'état fragmentaire du texte hébreu de Ben Sira. L'éditeur hésite entre deux possibilités: en 6,14-15, ou 1,19-20. En faveur de 6,14-15 qui a sa préférence, il invoque l'indice matériel du fragment et en faveur de 1,19-20, un long intervalle à première vue difficile en 15a. Les auteurs donnent leur préférence à 1,19-20[11], qui est loin de s'imposer. Matériellement, une lec-

---

6. Voir M. BAILLET, *Planches*, in M. BAILLET, J.T. MILIK et R. DE VAUX, *Les 'Petites Grottes' de Qumrân, Texte* (DJDJ, 3), Oxford, Clarendon, 1962, pp. 75-77.

7. On n'a pas affaire nécessairement au coin inférieur gauche, malgré BAILLET, *Les 'Petites Grottes'* (n. 6), p. 75, puisque nulle trace de marge inférieure n'est préservée, contrairement au fragment 1.

8. Avec M. BAILLET. La transcription de P.C. BEENTJES, *The Book of Ben Sira in Hebrew. A Text Edition of All Extant Hebrew Manuscripts and a Synopsis of All Parallel Hebrew Ben Sira Texts*, (SVT, 68), Leiden, Brill, 1997, pp. 123 et 133-34, ne donne pas une idée exacte de la disposition du texte de 2Q18, frg. 2, en plus d'une faute de transcription en 6,22: *]kh* pour *]kḥ*.

9. BAILLET, *Les 'Petites Grottes'* (n. 6), suivant le Ms A du Caire. De même P.W. SKEHAN, *The Acrostic Poem in Sirach 51:13-30*, in *HTR* 64 (1971) 387-400, p. 400, lit deux fois *kn hy'* et *hy' n]kḥ*.

10. Comme la confusion des *waw/yod* est plus que difficile dans un manuscrit du Moyen Âge alors qu'elle est très fréquente dans une copie du Ier siècle av. J.-C., il est probable que la faute du manuscrit A vient d'une lecture fautive de l'original (*hw'* > *hy'*) entraînant ensuite la correction du masculin en féminin *nk(w)ḥh*. Pour d'autres erreurs de ce genre, voir DI LELLA, *The Hebrew Text* (n. 4), pp. 97-101.

11. Par exemple M.H. SEGAL, *Ben Sira in Qumran*, in *Tarbiz* 33 (1963-1964) 243-

ture '*yn* est préférable à '*rk,* si on note la cassure et la distension du cuir portant la hampe de lettre et si on relève l'épaisseur du trait de la tête de la lettre à gauche de la haste en bordure de la cassure. *Yod* est bien préférable à *reš*: comparé à 2,10, la haste est à peine plus longue, mais dans cette écriture les modules des lettres sont variables, et le ductus doit l'emporter pour un déchiffrement correct. De plus, pour *twmkyh,* on aurait dû avoir des traces de *waw* alors que la microfiche semble laisser entrevoir des éléments de la tête de *qof.* Aussi, sans être certain et à défaut de mieux, le placement en 6,14-15 paraît bien préférable. La disposition assez lâche du début du v. 15 peut tenir au module plus grand des lettres et à l'écart variable entre les mots ou à un défaut de la surface, à une rature… Quoi qu'il en soit du fragment 1, le fragment 2 suffit à assurer l'identification du manuscrit.

b. 11QPs[a] XXI 11 – XXII 1 = Si 51,13-30

En 1956, on découvrit parmi les rouleaux assez bien conservés de la grotte 11 un recueil liturgique daté de la première moitié du Ier s. de notre ère[12], contenant outre des psaumes bibliques et des compositions apocryphes, le poème alphabétique en écriture continue de Si 51,13-19[…]30. Ce passage est compris entre le Ps 138,18 et un hymne acrostiche à Sion. En plus de la ligne 18 de la col. XXI, manquent 6 autres lignes qui devaient contenir les autres stiques alphabétiques. Quoi qu'il en soit, avec les deux mots manquant du stique *kaf* et les deux derniers mots en XXII 1, la moitié du poème est au moins conservée, si ce n'est encore des indications pour le stique acrostiche *lamed.* Même une fois reconnue la supériorité du grec sur la transmission corrompue de l'hébreu du Ms B pour ce passage[13], la restauration de ce dernier d'après le grec à l'ordre partiellement remanié ne va pas sans difficulté. La proposition de Skehan, qui ne tient pas compte du *lamed* préservé sous le *nun* de '*tbwnn,* est bien trop longue[14]. Seraient matériellement possibles l.

246, p. 243, la *Traduction Œcuménique de la Bible,* Paris, Le Cerf, Paris, [3]1989, p. 2141, GILBERT, *Siracide* (n. 1), col. 1394, C. MARTONE, *Ben Sira Manuscripts from Qumrân and Masada,* in P.C. BEENTJES (ed.), *The Book of Ben Sira in Modern Research. Proceedings of the First International Ben Sira Conference 28-31 July 1996, Soesterberg. Netherlands,* (BZAW, 255), Berlin/New York, de Gruyter, 1997, pp. 81-93, (p. 82). Cet auteur laisse entendre par «in both manuscripts» (p. 83) que le Ms A du Caire est copié en stichométrie, ce qui n'est pas le cas.

12. GILBERT, *Siracide* (n. 1), col. 1324, écrit par erreur «entre 100 et 50 av. J.-C.».

13. Bien des auteurs s'accordent à en faire une pure rétroversion du texte syriaque.

14. SKEHAN, *The Acrostic Poem* (n. 9), p. 388, propose *b'bwr kn l' ʾzbh*; il en est de même de *lb qnyty mtḥlh b'bwr kn lw' ʾgzbnh* de J. A SANDERS, *The Sirach 51 Acrostic,* in A. CAQUOT – M. PHILONENKO (ed.), *Hommages à André Dupont-Sommer,* Paris, Maisonneuve, 1971, pp. 429-438, (p. 432). La trace du *lamed* appartient à peu près sûrement au deuxième hémistiche, non au premier comme le reconstruit T. MURAOKA, *Sir. 51,13-30:*

18: [*wbnqywn mṣ'tyh lb qnyty 'mh mr'š]l[kn l]'[*"zbh ou w]l[' ']'[zbh*.
La ligne 17 a donné lieu à diverses lectures, à commencer par l'édition:
prš[et *pth[ty*[15], mais la lecture *pth[* est certaine; il faut sans doute comprendre *ydy pth[h]š'rh* (comparer Ms B *š'ryh*) *wm'rmyh...*, préférable à
ydy pth[ty m]rwm wbm'rmyh (avec le grec). On aurait un autre indice
appuyant la lecture du syriaque en accord avec le Ms B contre le grec
pour πρὸς ὕψος *-(l)mrwm* (voir l. 16). Mais le texte hébreu de 11QPs[a],
qui représente une forme assez proche de l'original, n'appuie pas spécialement le caractère sexuel des images que nombre d'auteurs ont cru y
trouver[16]. En ce sens, mais il fallait s'y attendre, cet acrostiche pré-
qumranien n'a rien à voir avec la sublimation du célibat des membres de
la Communauté.

Le manuscrit de Masada (Mas1[h])

Le 8 avril 1964, l'expédition dirigée par Y. Yadin découvrit dans les
ruines de Masada des fragments d'un rouleau de Ben Sira[17], qui cou-
vrent les chapitres 39,27 à 44,17 mais sans restes de 39,33 à 40,7[18], 40,9-
10, 22-25 et 43,26-28 et 30-33[19]. Le manuscrit daté du début du Ier siècle

An Erotic Hymn To Wisdom ?, in *JSJ* 10 (1979) 166-178, (p. 176), suivi par Martone, *The Ben Sira* (n. 11), p. 84.

15. J.A SANDERS, *The Psalms Scroll of Qumrân Cave 11 (11QPs*[a]*)* (DJDJ, 4), Oxford, Clarendon, 1965, p. 42: *prš[ ]m'rmyh* et *'l.?*, et p. 80: *pth[ty... w]m'rmyh* et *'l....* . Ces lec-tures ont laissé des traces ensuite. I. RABINOWITZ, *The Qumran Hebrew Original of Ben Sira's Concluding Acrostic on Wisdom*, in *HUCA* 42 (1971) 173-184, (p. 175): *prš[ty.... wb]m'rmyh 'tbwnn kpy hzkwty qbl[tyh??*, mais *hbrwty 'l[* de Sanders est certain, MARTONE, *The Ben Sira* (n. 11), p. 84: *prš [...] m'rmyh*, SKEHAN, *The Acrostic Poem* (n. 9), p. 388: *pthh š'rh wbm'rwmyh* (sic) et *'lyh*. M. DELCOR, *Le texte hébreu du Cantique de Siracide LI,13 et ss. et les anciennes versions*, in *Textus* 6 (1968) 27-47, pp. 31 et 36: *pth[ty... w]m'rmyh*, Muraoka, *Sir. 51,13-30* (n. 14), p. 176: *pth .... m'rmyh* et *l...*. On ne comprend pas la lecture de BEENTJES, *The Book of Ben Sira* (n. 8), pp. 125 et 178: *pt[ ]'rmyh*, ni la coupure de 51,20 qui ne tient plus compte des acrostiches avec *yod* et *kaf*.

16. SANDERS, *The Psalms Scroll* (n. 15), pp. 83-85, *The Sirach 51* (n. 14), pp. 433s, DELCOR, *Le texte hébreu* (n. 15), pp. 36s, MURAOKA, *Sir. 51,13-30* (n. 14), MARTONE, *Ben Sira Manuscripts* (n. 11), pp. 86s. Ainsi, dans ce stique, le grec n'a pas eu à éviter les termes trop explicites en ce sens, puisque l'hébreu ne les portaient pas! Par ailleurs, Martone, (pp. 87s) reprend sans nouveaux arguments la conclusion de Sanders sur l'inauthenticité de ce Psaume en Ben Sira, mais voir GILBERT, *The Book of Ben Sira* (n. 2), p. 83, qui estime que cet acrostiche peut servir de conclusion au livre tout aussi bien que la composition alphabétique de Pr 31,10-31 en Proverbes. Cela est fort vraisemblable.

17. Y. YADIN, *The Ben Sira Scroll from Masada*, Jerusalem, Israel Exploration So-ciety, 1965 (reprinted from *Eretz-Israel* 8 [1965] 1-45).

18. L'édition de Yadin contient un certain nombre d'erreurs de lecture, et la ligne I 23 correctement déchiffrée appartient à 40,8, non à 40,10, voir la recension de P. SKEHAN, in *JBL* 85 (1966) 260.

19. Voir J.T. MILIK, *Un fragment mal placé dans l'édition du Siracide de Masada*, in *Bib* 47 (1966) 425-426, voir encore J.M. BAUMGARTEN, *Some Notes on the Ben Sira Scroll from Masada*, in *JQR* 58 (1968) 323-327, J. STRUGNELL, *Notes and Queries on 'the*

av. J.-C[20]., est disposé en stichométrie, comme le manuscrit, d'un genre comparable 4QProverbes[a] du Ier siècle av. J.-C[21]., et est quelque peu antérieur à la copie du même type de 2Q18. Comme Ben Sira n'a pas été retenu dans le canon rabbanite au IIe siècle après J.-C., il est très probable que ce rouleau trouvé à Masada provienne de Qumrân, tout comme le rouleau des *Širôt ʿolat haššabbat*, emportés dans ce nid de résistance par les derniers rescapés des réfugiés du désert de Juda[22]. On en voudrait comme indice le remplacement à une époque ancienne du tétragramme encore utilisé dans l'original par *ʾdny* (en écriture défective) en 42,15 et 17c (Ms B *ʾlhym*), 42,16 et 43,5 (Ms B *yyy* et *ʾlywn* dans la glose marginale en 43,5), 43,10 (Ms B *ʾl*, grec ἁγίου) ou par un suffixe *npl'wtyw* en 42,17b et déjà dans la *Vorlage* du grec (Ms B *yyy*, glose marginale suffixe d'un prédicat supplémentaire). Les scribes qumraniens utilisent ces mêmes procédés de substitutions dans leurs propres compositions (comparer 4Q521), etc. La copie de Masada suppose donc déjà une certaine révision, ne serait-ce qu'à ce niveau, mais apparemment non encore intervenue dans la copie contemporaine traduite par le petit-fils[23].

Ben Sira Scroll from Masada', in *Eretz-Israel* 9 (1969) 109-119, même si toutes les remarques ne sont pas à retenir, beaucoup sont recevables, P. SKEHAN, *Sirach 40,11-17*, in *CBQ* 30 (1968) 570-572, du même, *Sirach 30,12 and Related Texts*, in *CBQ* 36 (1974) 535-542, (pp. 541 s.). Mais le fragment isolé en VI 25 ne semble pas appartenir à 43,30.

20. Voir YADIN, *The Ben Sira Scroll* (n. 17), p. 4 et n. 11, citant les opinions de F. M. Cross et N. Avigad. On ne comprend pas la proposition de MARTONE, *Ben Sira Manuscripts* (n. 11), p. 88: «écriture hérodienne entre 40 av. et 20 A.D.»! Cette écriture est tout à fait comparable à celle de 4Q521, voir É. PUECH, *Qumrân Grotte 4 XVIII*, (DJD, 25), Oxford, Clarendon, 1998.

21. Voir P. SKEHAN, *Qumrân. IV Littérature de Qumrân – A. Textes bibliques*, in *DBS*, t. IX, Paris, Letouzey et Ané, 1978, col. 818.

22. GILBERT, *The Book of Ben Sira* (n. 2), p. 84, écarte cette hypothèse, estimant que cette découverte prouverait que Ben Sira était lu aussi par d'autres juifs. Et cela expliquerait les citations dans les anciens écrits rabbanites. Mais ces citations peuvent fort bien provenir d'autres copies comme celle qui a servi à la traduction grecque à la fin du IIe siècle av. J.-C. Aussi, le lien du rouleau de Masada avec Qumrân nous paraît bien plus probable, les derniers résistants non esséniens auraient-ils pensé emporter dans cette cachette des rouleaux qu'ils estimaient non normatifs ou si peu représentatifs? Le milieu rabbanite a ensuite tenu ce livre pour autorisé, *Babli, Baba Qamma* 92, *Sanhédrin* 100b (rabbi Yoseph), ou plus souvent prohibé, *Yerushalmi, Sanhédrin* X 1 (rabbi Aqiba). Quoique peu connu, Ben Sira est parfois cité par les rabbins, voir M. R. LEHMANN, *11QPs[a] and Ben Sira*, in *RQ* 11 (1982-1984) 239-251, (pp. 243-245).

23. Ces indications montreraient que les copies des Mss B et A du Caire ont été faites sur un manuscrit antérieur au milieu du IIe siècle av. J.-C. et partiellement corrigé d'après une autre copie d'un peu postérieure mais encore de graphie défective (par ex. *ʾdny*), voir BAILLET, *Les 'Petites Grottes'* (n. 6), p. 75. En effet, dans nombre de cas, le tétragramme n'a pas été corrigé, voir 10,22; 40,26 et 51,1 dans l'expression bien connue *yr't yhwh*, excepté en 40,27 et en Ms A 9,16; 10,12 (*yr't 'lhym*), de même en *lpny 'lhym* (14,16, Ms A) ou encore Ms B en 45,2 *'lhym* mais *yyy* en marge, etc. En 51,15, Ms B porte *ʾdny* qu'on ne retrouve pas en 11QPs[a] XXI 13 dans une autre phraséologie (voir le grec). On aurait un témoignage du début du processus en cours. Pour les cas de tétragramme retenus

Quoi qu'il en soit, l'importance de ces fragments vient d'abord de leur ancienneté. Ils sont les plus anciens retrouvés, datant d'à peine un siècle après l'original, soit une génération après la traduction du petit-fils de Ben Sira. Étant donné les passages substantiels préservés qui, de plus, recoupent de larges portions du Ms B, il est enfin possible d'apprécier la valeur des manuscrits médiévaux, d'une part, et des différentes traductions: grec I et II, syriaque et latin, d'autre part. Comme il a déjà été noté à plusieurs reprises, ce manuscrit confirme dans l'ensemble le texte hébreu du Ms B et spécialement la valeur des gloses marginales, bien qu'on doive juger cas par cas[24]. Et dans un grand nombre de cas, parfois impossibles à évaluer étant donné la difficulté de retrouver le mot original parmi les synonymes possibles, il s'accorde avec le grec. Cet accord se retrouve dans les cas où manquent des versets dans le Ms B: 40,12; 41,22; 42,5,18c-d,22; 44,12 ou avec le Ms B contre le grec en 42,11e, mais le grec et Ms B s'accordent contre le manuscrit de Masada en 44,16 à propos d'Hénoch[25]. En revanche, dans nombre de cas, MasSira s'accorde avec le Ms B contre le grec dans la séquence des versets, ou d'autres fois avec le syriaque contre le grec, prouvant ainsi que le syriaque ne dépend pas du grec mais d'un manuscrit hébreu lui-même assez révisé.

Suite à ces remarques, MasSira et indirectement les manuscrits de la *geniza* peuvent donc revendiquer une origine qumranienne qui, avec 2Q18, sont alors les seuls restes du texte hébreu de Sira mais transmis par les Esséniens, et désormais ne font plus exception que les rares citations plus ou moins *verbatim* des rabbanites qui n'ont pas retenu ce livre dans leur liste officielle. Toutefois, ces différentes copies d'origine qumra-nienne (qui explique la disposition stichométrique ancienne), n'en font pas un livre essénien. Le témoignage de ces anciens manuscrits hébreux du Siracide prouve qu'avec les manuscrits du Caire, on a affaire à des co-pies du texte original, certes parfois révisé, mais pas à une retraduction du grec. Enfin, ce texte proche de celui traduit par le petit-fils accrédite le texte grec court ou grec I avant les diverses révisions[26] du livre.

---

en hébreu, voir Z. BEN ḤAYYIM (ed.), *The Book of Ben Sira. Text, Concordance and an Analysis of the Vocabulary*, Jerusalem, Academy of the Hebrew Language – Shrine of the Book, 1973, pp. 157s. La disposition stichométrique renforcerait cette remarque.

24. Voir à ce sujet les listes relevées par l'éditeur, YADIN, *The Ben Sira Scroll* (n. 17). Le tableau 1 (pp. 7-8 de l'hébreu) rassemble les 51 cas (41,12 excepté) où le manuscrit recoupe les gloses marginales contre le Ms B, le tableau 2 (p. 9) les 37 cas (42,14 et 22 exceptés) où le manuscrit reprend le texte du Ms B contre les gloses marginales, et le ta-bleau 3 (pp. 11-13) les 88 cas (43,23 et 25 exceptés) où le manuscrit diverge du texte du Ms B et des gloses.

25. Sur ce sujet, voir YADIN, *The Ben Sira Scroll* (n. 17), p. 38.

26. Pour le point sur la complexité de la transmission et des révisions du texte de Ben

II. Citations

Les manuscrits hébreux découverts au cours du dernier siècle prouvent déjà, nous l'avons souligné, que le texte hébreu du Siracide composé entre 195 et 175 av. J.-C. était connu des Esséno-qumraniens, très probablement même avant que le livre passe à la communauté juive d'Égypte (Alexandrie?) par la traduction grecque du petit-fils de Sira, peu après 132 av. J.-C.

L'identification d'un stique du Siracide dans le manuscrit sapientiel hébreu 4Q525 (*Béatitudes*) au style et au contenu par ailleurs si proches, en est une confirmation supplémentaire. Dans le fragment très mal conservé de 4Q525 25,4, nous avons lu et restauré avec certitude[27]:

אל תהי זולל וסו]בא ומא]ומה אין בכיס

«Ne sois ni glouton ni iv]rogne alors qu'il n'y a [rien dans la bourse!»

Cette maxime nous paraît provenir de Si 18,33, plutôt qu'être un proverbe isolé appartenant au fond commun de la littérature de sagesse. En effet, il y a trop de points de contacts entre 4Q525 – pourtant bien mal conservé – et Ben Sira pour que l'auteur qumranien[28] n'ait pas cité son prédécesseur, de la génération de son père. 4Q525 2 ii 2 insiste sur la recherche de la sagesse tout comme Si 14,20 ss. Dans les deux compositions, la sagesse s'identifie à la Loi, Si 24,22 ss et 4Q525 2 ii 4. En outre, le syntagme *twrt 'lywn* se retrouve en 4Q525 2 ii 4 et Si 41,4,8; 42,2 et 49,4 (en hébreu), voir encore νόμος ὑψίστου en 9,15; 19,17; 23,23; (24,23); 38,34; 44,20; ajouter 11QPsᵃ XVIII 14 (= Psaume syriaque II) et *Testament des Douze Patriarches, Lévi* 13,1 mais nulle part ailleurs dans la Bible[29] (Sagesse = Loi est une innovation de Ben Sira).

Sira, voir GILBERT, *Siracide* (n. 1), col. 1407-1412. Les gloses marginales en persan du Ms B ne prouvent rien quant à l'origine du manuscrit à la base de la copie. La présence de qaraïtes en Palestine et en Babylonie est bien connue, voir DI LELLA, *The Hebrew Text* (n. 4), pp. 96-97.

27. PUECH, *Qumrân Grotte 4* (n. 20), pp. 164-165.

28. Dans l'édition de 4Q525, *Qumrân Grotte 4* (n. 20), pp. 117-119, nous avons donné les arguments en faveur d'une composition essénienne de ce texte de sagesse, soulignant en particulier l'usage exclusif de *'l* et *'lwhym*, voir ci-dessus les remarques à propos du tétragramme dans le Ms B et les gloses marginales et MasSira. Mais il y a bien d'autres approches de la sagesse qui recoupent les points de vue qumranien connus par ailleurs. Le manuscrit semble être le produit de la première génération esséno-qumranienne, peut-être du Maître instruisant ses disciples, tel un maître de sagesse.

29. *Contra* J.C.R. DE ROO, *Is 4Q525 a Qumran Sectarian Document?*, in S.E. PORTER and A. EVANS (eds), *The Scrolls and the Scriptures. Qumran Fifty Years After* (JSPS, 26), Sheffield, Academic Press, 1997, pp. 338-367 (pp. 340 et 345). Le lecteur doit savoir que cet auteur donne la numérotation des fragments et des lignes d'après une édition pirate, fautive et incomplète, qui n'est pas la numérotation de l'édition officielle.

III. ALLUSIONS ET CONTACTS

Outre cette caractéristique, plusieurs autres rapprochements ou points de contacts ont déjà été soulignés[30], mais ils relèvent plutôt de citations communes à divers livres bibliques que d'emprunts directs au Siracide. Toutefois, l'influence du Siracide sur la littérature qumranienne est réelle. On peut encore signaler la sentence de Si 11,8 en 4Q525 14 ii 22-24 et 1QS VI 10-11 sur l'écoute avant de répondre, de Si 22,27 et 28,18 en 4Q525 14 ii 26-28 sur les dangers de la langue, de Si 12,6 en 1QS VIII 6-7, CD VII 9/ XIX 6 et 1QM XI 13s sur la rétribution à rendre aux impies que Dieu hait (voir 1QS I 4,10,...), de Si 21,20 en 1QS VII 14 sur le rire bruyant du sot, de Si 49,16 en 1QS IV 23a, CD III 20, 1QH IV 27 (= XVII 15) sur la gloire d'Adam en tant que créé par Dieu lui-même, ou encore de Si 11,14 (33,12,14s) en 1QS III 15s sur Dieu principe de tout, bien et mal, vie et mort. L'on sait combien le dualisme va être un point développé dans le milieu essénien[31]. Mais en Ben Sira, le bien et le mal ne dépendent pas encore de forces maléfiques.

Ces rapprochements de vocabulaire et les affinités de pensée indiscutables soulignent tout au moins une proximité dans l'espace et le temps, soit en gros le judaïsme palestinien de IIe siècle av. J.-C., et très probablement une influence du *Siracide*, de préférence à une simple tradition

---

30. Voir J. CARMIGNAC, *Les rapports entre l'Ecclésiastique et Qumrân*, in *RQ* 3 (1961-1962), 209-218. À ce propos, GILBERT, *Siracide* (n. 1), col. 1414, écrit: «Ben Sira faisait partie, selon Carmignac, de la littérature proprement Qumranienne». Cela est inexact, puisque Carmignac résume ainsi sa pensée (p. 218): «Cela (les différences) empêche au moins d'affirmer de façon définitive que l'*Ecclésiastique* fasse partie de la littérature proprement qumranienne», et en n. 29: «le dernier chapitre... si indépendant du reste de l'ouvrage... offre tant de rapprochements avec les textes de Qumrân que l'on pourrait plus facilement envisager qu'il ait bel et bien été composé à Qumrân», et enfin «Si les recherches ultérieures confirmaient que l'*Ecclésiastique* n'a pas été composé au sein de la communauté de Qumrân,...». Les rapprochements à des degrés divers ne soulignent que la proximité des deux milieux.

31. M.E. LEHMANN, *Ben Sira and the Qumran Literature*, in *RQ* 3 (1961-1962) 103-116, pp. 109-110, a relevé une liste de mots ou expressions idiomatiques caractéristiques du langage de Ben Sira et de Qumrân: *sgr* (au *nif'al*), *'bny ḥpṣ, šbyb, šw'h wmšw'h, dltym wbryḥ, pt' pt'm*, rares et dispersés dans l'un ou l'autre livre biblique, et surtout *kwr npwḥ, mwṭ* (au *hitpa'el*), *yšyš – zqn, šb'tym, yhm lbb, rz, gwr, šḥt, mqwh, ṣrr ḥyym, m's, hgh, m'md* et *mmšlt, qṣ, mw'd* en relation avec *tqwph*. Voir aussi S. IWRY, *A New Designation for the Luminaries in Ben Sira and in the Manual of Discipline (1QS)*, in *BASOR* 200 (1970) 41-47, *gdyl* en 1QS X 4 et Si 43,5 (Ms B, *gdwl* MasSi), D.J. HARRINGTON, *Wisdom at Qumran*, in E. ULRICH and J. VANDERKAM (eds), *The Community of the Renewed Covenant. The Notre Dame Symposium on the Dead Sea Scrolls*, Notre Dame, IN, University of Notre Dame Press, 1993, pp. 137-152, pp. 146 ss; N. CALDUCH-BENAGES, *Trial Motif in the Book of Ben Sira with Special Reference to Sir. 2,1-6*, in *The Book of Ben Sira in Modern Research* (n. 11), pp. 135-151 (p. 140): l'image du creuset – *mṣrp* pour la purification en Ben Sira et à Qumrân, etc.

orale, sur les écrits qumraniens[32], influence qu'on peut affiner encore à l'aide de quelques exemples plus précis.

Hymne

Même si des formules liturgiques assez fixes ont dû exister très tôt, il est assez remarquable de noter les formulations parallèles entre les débuts d'Hymnes d'action de grâces de Si 51,1-2 et de 1QH XI 20 s (= III 19 s)[33].

1QH XI 20-21	Si 51,1-2
20 אודכה אדוני	1 אודך אלהי אבי ...
כי פדיתה נפשי	כי פדית ממות נפשי
משחת	2 חשכת בשרי משחת
ומשאול אבדון 21 העליתי	ומיד שאול הצלת נפשי

Si l'attribution de cet hymne qumranien au Maître de Justice ne semble pas exclue[34], un demi-siècle environ le séparerait de Si 51. La dépendance de la phraséologie ne surprend alors aucunement.

Béatitudes

En préparant la publication de 4Q525, il est apparu clairement que le fragment 2 ii portait la fin d'un passage centré sur un thème particulier: des béatitudes ou macarismes. La colonne ii 1-6a ne compte plus que des restes de 5 béatitudes dont 4 de type court et une de type long[35]. Une étude de la composition, des style et genre littéraire a montré que ce manuscrit portait en fait un paragraphe composé de 8 béatitudes de type court groupées en deux strophes de 4 et une neuvième de type long égale à une strophe de 4. Ce paragraphe est suivi d'un développement intro-

---

32. Une influence de la littérature qumranienne sur Ben Sira est chronologiquement hors de question. Bien que la date de sa composition soit débattue, il est peu probable que le corpus sapientiel de Qumrân (1Q26, 4Q415, 416, 417, 418, 423) soit dans ce cas. Son origine essénienne est aussi discutée et elle pourrait se situer entre Ben Sira et le début de l'essénisme à cause d'une forte perspective dualiste et eschatologique, voir D.H. HARRINGTON, *Two Early Jewish Approaches to Wisdom: Sirach and Qumran Sapiential Work A*, in *JSP* 16 (1997) 25-38.

33. Voir aussi LEHMANN, *Ben Sira* (n. 31), p. 107. Nous citons les Hymnes de la grotte 1 d'après la nouvelle organisation du rouleau, voir É. PUECH, *La croyance des Esséniens en la vie future: immortalité, résurrection, vie éternelle? Histoire d'une croyance dans le Judaïsme ancien*, 2 t. (EB, n.s. 21-22), Paris, Gabalda, 1993, pp. 335-419.

34. Voir PUECH, *La croyance* (n. 33), p. 366.

35. É. PUECH, *4Q525 et les péricopes des béatitudes en Ben Sira et Matthieu*, in *RB* 98 (1991) 80-106, et du même, *Qumrân Grotte 4* (n. 20). Mais il est faux de dire que «ll. 3b-7 constituent une seule béatitude» (DE ROO, *Is 4Q525* [n. 29], p. 358) puisqu'après un *vacat*, commence en 6b-10 un développement portant sur l'ensemble du passage.

duit par *ky* (ll. 6b-10). Un tel groupement de macarismes a un parallèle plus tardif en Mt 5,3-12 mais aussi un antécédent en Si 14,20-27 (+ 15,1 ss: *ky*...). Les autres macarismes de Ben Sira sont de facture habituelle: 26,1; 31(34),15 (LXX); 48,11 (LXX); 50,28; 25,(7b),9 (LXX), mais 34(31),8 comprend un hémistiche positif suivi d'un négatif et 25,8 et 28,19 (LXX) un hémistiche positif suivi de 3 hémistiches négatifs comme en 4Q185 1-2 ii 13-14. 4Q525 2 ii 1-6a connaît ce genre de structure: les macarismes courts sont composés d'un hémistiche positif suivi d'un hémistiche négatif, alors que le macarisme long comprend, après un hémistiche introductif positif, 4 hémistiches positifs suivis de 4 négatifs. En 4Q525 2 ii chaque strophe compte 31 mots[36] dont 15 dans les hémistiches positifs et 16 dans les négatifs.

Une telle structure aussi bien ciselée, assurément reprise dans la présentation grecque de Mt 5, n'est pas due au hasard. L'auteur semble l'avoir trouvée pour la première fois en Si 14,20-27 qu'on peut maintenant étudier avec quelque précision en hébreu même grâce au Ms A du Caire. La transmission a peu altéré sa forme originelle, les corruptions principales sont au v. 21b: *wbtbwntyh* métathèse pour *wbntybtyh* (avec le syriaque et Pr 3,17), au v. 22a: *lṣ't* infinitif, corruption probable pour le participe *wyṣ'* [37] et v. 22b: addition de *kl* (absent du grec, latin et syriaque). Le passage comprend 8 stiques positifs introduits par un seul *'šry*, groupés en deux strophes de 4 stiques ou 23 mots par strophe, elles-mêmes composées de deux sous-strophes aux structures parallèles, comme nous l'avons montré ailleurs. Aussi, étant donné la forte influence de Ben Sira que l'on retrouve dans bien d'autres compositions qumraniennes et le groupement unique de 8 béatitudes du même type, une influence directe de Ben Sira sur la structure et le contenu sapientiel du passage est là encore hautement probable.

L'alliance sacerdotale et l'alliance davidique

Le livre de Ben Sira finit par l'eulogie de la gloire de Dieu dans le monde, Si 42,15-43,33, et dans l'histoire, Si 44–49. Dans l'éloge des an-

---

36. Ce même chiffre de 31 mots se retrouve dans une strophe de macarismes du rouleau des Hymnes 1QH[a], voir PUECH, *4Q525 et les péricopes* (n. 35), p. 90, ou É. PUECH, *The Collection of Beatitudes in Hebrew and in Greek (4Q525 1-4 and Mt 5,3-12)*, in F. MANNS and E. ALLIATA (eds), *Early Christianity in Context. Monuments and Documents*, (Collectio Maior 38), Jerusalem, Franciscan Printing Press, 1993, pp. 353-368, (pp. 357 et 361).

37. Voir PUECH, *4Q525 et les péricopes* (n. 35), p. 92: addition du *waw*/ *yod* au-dessus de la ligne donnant l'aspect d'un *lamed* mais *wyṣ'* est nécessaire pour lier les deux sous-strophes, et ensuite correction de la finale de l'infinitif, voir *supra* la correction au féminin en 6,22 (Ms A).

cêtres, l'ordre chronologique habituellement respecté de Hénoch à Néhémie, Si 44,16 à 49,13, revient sur Hénoch, Joseph, Sem, Seth et Adam
en 44,14-16 comme une inclusion de cette vaste fresque, pour finir avec
le grand prêtre Simon, fils d'Onias, son contemporain, Si 50,1ss. Toutefois, dans ce tableau se trouve une anomalie, la chronologie est quelque
peu bouleversée en 45,23-26: passant du prêtre Aaron à Pinhas, à David
et de nouveau à Pinhas pour retrouver ensuite l'ordre historique avec
Josué en 46,1. Mais cet anachronisme est certainement intentionnel,
cherchant à rattacher à l'alliance sacerdotale (*bryt šlwm*) avec Aaron-
Pinhas et leurs descendants celle avec David (*bryt 'm dwd*) et ses fils par
succession directe[38], alors que ces notions sont précisées mais séparé-
ment et à leur place attendue en 45,7 (*ḥq 'wlm*) pour Aaron et en 47,11
(*qrnw, ḥq mmlkt*) pour David. Plusieurs passages bibliques ont déjà rapproché explicitement l'alliance de la royauté et l'alliance du sacerdoce:
Jr 33,17-22 et Za 6,9-14; 4, comparer aussi 1 Ch 17,14 et 2 S 7,16, 1 Ch
29,22 et 1 R 1,39 où la pérennité des deux alliances ou institutions est
assurée dans l'avenir. Cette présentation prépare le messianisme
bicéphale de *Jubilés* 31 et des textes qumraniens par la suite[39].

Si Ben Sira (grec) n'explicite guère ses idées messianiques (voir cependant Si 36,1-17), en revanche, le Psaume hébreu inséré après 51,12
en témoigne[40], vv. 12h-j:

> h Louez celui qui rebâtit sa ville et son sanctuaire, car éternel est son amour,
> i Louez celui qui fait pousser une corne à la maison de David, car...,
> j Louez celui qui a choisi les fils de Sadoq comme prêtre(s), car...

Même si le Psaume n'est pas de Ben Sira, comme il semble[41], il s'in-
sère logiquement dans la suite du passage, Si 45,25. Comme il apparaît
dans l'éloge d'Aaron, de Pinhas et de Simon, Ben Sira tient le sacerdoce
en très haute estime et, sans laisser de côté cependant l'alliance avec

---

38. L'hémistiche 45,26c en hébreu est corrompu mais il n'est pas trop difficile d'y
reconnaître l'original qui est à la base de la phraséologie du grec: *nḥlt hmlk lbnw lbdw*
devenu *nḥlt 'š lpny kbwdw* (préférable à *bkwrw*) = κληρονομία βασιλέως υἱοῦ ἐξ υἱοῦ
μονοῦ. De même v. 24b où le grec porte ἁγίων καὶ λαοῦ αὐτοῦ, mais (*w*)*'mw* qui pourrait aussi bien se comprendre «avec lui» que «son peuple».

39. Pour un état de la question, voir É. PUECH, *Messianisme, eschatologie et résurrection dans les manuscrits de la mer Morte*, in *RQ* 18 (1997) 255-298, pp. 265-86, mais
nous n'avons pas insisté sur ces passages de Ben Sira comme précurseurs.

40. L'authenticité de ce psaume modelé sur le Ps 136 a été mise en question, car ce
dernier n'est connu que de l'hébreu seul (Ms B).

41. Voir DI LELLA, *The Hebrew Text of Sira* (n. 4), pp. 101-105, J. TRINQUET, *Les
liens 'sadocites' de l'écrit de Damas, des manuscrits de la mer Morte et de l'Ecclésiastique*, in *VT* 1 (1951) 287-292, p. 290: «Authentique ou inauthentique, ce psaume par sa
présence dans les fragments hébreux de l'Ecclésiastique paraît indiquer qu'au moins
ceux-ci furent entre les mains des 'fils de Sadoq'.» Cela n'exige pas une composition
antérieure à 171/170 av. J.-C. (meurtre d'Onias III), mais tout aussi bien du milieu du siècle ou peu après, voir note suivante.

David et sa descendance, le sacerdoce sadocite en particulier, puisqu'on lit en 50,24 (hébreu):

«Que sa miséricorde demeure fidèlement avec Simon et maintienne pour lui l'alliance de Pinhas qui ne sera rompue ni pour lui ni pour sa descendance comme les jours des cieux»[42].

Ce Psaume a une coloration directement messianique alors que les autres passages de Ben Sira en restent aux deux alliances. Mais en sont-ils si éloignés? L'accent mis sur le sacerdoce en fait l'élément dominant comme c'était le cas du vivant de l'auteur, sans oublier l'alliance royale[43]. N'y avait-il pas là une pierre d'attente de premier ordre pour la réception de ce livre dans le milieu essénien qui, après la perte du sacerdoce sadocide et l'opposition anti-hasmonéenne, ne pouvait qu'espérer l'avènement de deux messies?

Élie

La communauté essénienne attendait de fait la venue de deux messies, le messie d'Aaron qui avait la préséance et le messie d'Israël, que devait accompagner le prophète (1QS IX 10-11)[44]. Des textes qumraniens, 4Q521 2 iii en particulier, en renvoyant à Ml 3,23-24, font explicitement référence au Nouvel Élie. Mais la figure d'Élie *redivivus*, le prophète eschatologique, n'est pas absente de Ben Sira 48,11 (grec et hébreu), dans la forme la plus ancienne, avant les additions de Grec II, à lire certainement[45]:

42. Ce passage est-il rédigé du vivant de Simon (au passé cependant en 50,1-5) ou de ses descendants (Onias III?) ou de son fils, Simon III qui exercera le grand sacerdoce de 159 à 152 et qui est très probablement à identifier au Maître de Justice, voir É. PUECH, *Le grand prêtre Simon (III), fils d'Onias (III), le Maître de Justice?*, in B. KOLLMANN, W. REINBOLD, A. STEUDEL (eds.), *Antikes Judentum und frühes Christentum*. FS H. Stegemann (BZNW, 97), Berlin, de Gruyter, 1999, pp. 137-138, On comprendrait que ce passage n'ayant plus de raison d'être après l'expulsion des sadocides ait été changé par le traducteur grec.
43. J. PRIEST, *Ben Sira 45,25 in the Light of the Qumran Literature*, in *RQ* 5 (1964-1966) 111-118, p. 118: Ben Sira n'est ni un qumranien ni un proto-qumranien, mais un prédécesseur dont le milieu des Ḥasidim a servi d'intermédiaire. Le rappel des deux alliances préparait certainement la voie au messianisme des générations postérieures, aussi la réponse par la négative comme le propose A. CAQUOT, *Ben Sira et le messianisme*, in *Semitica* 16 (1966) 43-68, paraît trop tranchée.
44. Voir PUECH, *Messianisme, eschatologie* (n. 39), pp. 282-286.
45. Comme nous l'avons montré ailleurs, E. PUECH, *Ben Sira 48:11 et la résurrection*, in H.W. ATTRIDGE, J.J. COLLINS, T.H. TOBIN (eds), *Of Scribes and Scrolls. Studies on the Hebrew Bible, Intertestamental Judaism, and Christian Origins presented to John Strugnell in the occasion of his sixtieth birthday*, (College Theology Society Resources in Religion, 5), Lanham – New York – London, 1990, pp. 81-90, et PUECH, *La croyance*, I (n. 33), pp. 74-76. On ne comprend pas la lecture de BEENTJES, *The Book of Ben Sira* (n. 8), p. 86, qui ne reflète pas l'état du manuscrit, *ttn* est certain.

כ[י] תתן חז[י]ם [וי]חיה: אשר ראך ומת

«Heureux qui te verra avant de mourir, car tu rendras la vie [et] il revivra.»

Comme cette lecture rend compte de tous les états successifs du texte en grec, syriaque et latin, elle doit être originelle, et elle se coule parfaitement dans un stique régulier.

Après avoir fait l'éloge du prophète historique qui arracha même un homme à la mort et au Shéol (48,5), vient la mention de la figure du prophète eschatologique qui, ayant été enlevé au ciel, doit revenir avant le jour du Jugement apaiser la colère divine, exhorter à la conversion et rétablir les tribus d'Israël (48,9-10). Le passage affirme que ceux qui seront témoins du retour d'Élie et viendront à mourir après avoir reçu la prédication du prophète, ressusciteront pour les récompenses au jour du Jugement et de la restauration. Ces conceptions sont corroborées par le passage sur Élisée ensuite, 48,13 (hébreu).

Ainsi, dans l'éloge des pères où s'exprime davantage sa sensibilité personnelle que dans les maximes de sagesse, Ben Sira rappelle la pérennité des deux alliances sacerdotale et royale et la préparation du Jour de Yahvé par la venue du prophète comme un cheminement vers le messianisme bicéphale et la croyance à la résurrection des justes qui seront reprises par les Esséniens et les Pharisiens[46].

Additions d'origine essénienne?

Livre lu et recopié à Qumrân comme le prouvent les différentes découvertes de manuscrits en hébreu, 2Q18, MasSi et les copies de la *geniza* du Caire, il ne serait pas surprenant que çà et là des additions aient pu être insérées. S'il n'est pas le lieu d'étudier l'ensemble des additions au texte du Siracide, on doit au moins relever les remarques déjà faites à ce propos. Certains ont tenu les additions du Grec pour une recension pharisienne[47], d'autres les rapportent à l'école d'Aristobule[48]. Mais il a été proposé que l'addition des deux stiques de 16,15-16, connus des manuscrits en minuscule grecs 248 et 106, de la

---

46. Ces conceptions ne sont pas spécialement aux antipodes des doctrines pharisiennes en matière d'eschatologie et de messianisme, comme le laisse entendre GILBERT, *Siracide* (n. 1), col. 1415. Mais elles préparent les développements dans le milieu pharisien, qui ne viendra que plus tard.

47. Voir J.H.A. HART, *Ecclesiasticus: the Greek Text of Codex 248, edited with a textual commentary and prolegomena*, Cambridge, University Press, 1909, pp. 272-320.

48. A. SCHLATTER, *Das neu gefundene hebräische Stück des Sirach. Der Glossar des grieschischen Sirach und seine Stellung in der Geschichte der Jüdischen Theologie* (BFCT, 1,5-6), Gütersloh, 1897, et G.L. PRATO, *La lumière interprète de la Sagesse dans la tradition textuelle de Ben Sira*, in M. GILBERT (éd.), *La Sagesse de l'Ancien Testament* (BETL 51), Leuven, University Press – Peeters, 1990, 317-346, pp. 341ss.

Peshitta et du Ms A du Caire mais absents du latin, proviennent du milieu essénien[49].

> [15] Dieu a endurci le cœur de Pharaon pour qu'il ne le reconnût pas
> afin de faire connaître ses œuvres sous le ciel.
> [16] À toute la création (G)/ ses créatures (S-H), sa pitié se manifeste,
> il a partagé sa lumière et les/ses (G/S-H) ténèbres entre les fils d'Adam/
> les hommes.

Comme illustration de 16,14b: «Il arrivera à chacun selon ses
œuvres», l'addition cite l'exemple de Pharaon qui ne connut pas Dieu
dont les œuvres sont manifestes (Ex 5,2; 7,3), transformant la proposition relative en finale (G et S, Ms A imprécis): «pour qu'il ne le recon-
naisse pas». Si le v. 16,15 prolonge la partie historique démonstrative de
16,6-11b, le v. 16,16 reprend l'idée de rétribution de 16,11c-14: à misé-
ricorde-pardon et colère-correction correspondent lumière et ténèbres.
L'endurcissement du cœur de Pharaon introduit une partition de type
déterministe (un copiste – Ms A a changé ḥškw en šbḥw), comparable à
l'enseignement de l'*Instruction sur les deux esprits* en 1QS III 13-IV
26: «Il (Dieu) a créé l'homme pour la domination du monde et il lui a
attribué deux esprits grâce auxquels il doit se conduire jusqu'au moment
de sa visite. Ce sont les esprits de vérité et de perversité. Grâce à la
source de lumière (il existe) des générations fidèles mais à cause de la
fontaine de ténèbres des générations perverses» (III 17-19), et «et il les
a répartis aux fils d'homme pour la connaissance du bien et du mal, ainsi
Dieu fait tomber les sorts pour chaque vivant selon son esprit au moment
de la rétribution» (IV 26). L'addition de Si 16,16 s'inscrit pleinement
dans cette ligne de pensée.

De la même veine sont les antithèses qui prolongent 11,14 «bien et
mal, vie et mort, pauvreté et richesse viennent de Yahvé» dans l'addition 11,15-16[50]:

> (Ms A) [15] Sagesse, science et intelligence de la parole viennent de Yhwh,
> péché (corruption pour amour) et chemin de droiture viennent de Yhwh.
> (G,Syh,L) Sagesse, science et connaissance de la loi viennent de Yhwh,
> amour et voies des bonnes œuvres viennent d'auprès de lui.
> [16] Sottise (Ms A)/ erreur et ténèbres sont créées pour les pécheurs,
> ceux qui se complaisent dans le mal vieillissent dans le mal.

Ces développements dualistes présents à la fois dans le Ms A du Caire
et dans les additions des versions ne peuvent guère provenir que du milieu essénien qui tenait ce livre en grande estime.

---

49. M. PHILONENKO, *Sur une proposition essénisante dans le Siracide (16,15-16)*, in
Orientalia Suecana 33-35 (1984-1986) 317-321.
50. Voir PRATO, *La lumière interprète* (n. 48), pp. 353s.

Parmi les manuscrits de la mer Morte, il faut certainement distinguer les compositions esséniennes des livres qui ont une origine autre et qui sont sans doute plus anciens. Le livre de Jésus Ben Sira dont plusieurs copies en hébreu d'origine qumranienne plus ou moins directe ont été retrouvées, appartient à ce dernier groupe, mais il a fait une forte impression sur les Qumraniens et laissé des empreintes dans leurs propres compositions bien au-delà des écrits de sagesse proprement dits. Copié et recopié, des révisions devenaient inévitables dans le milieu essénien et plus tard dans les versions des communautés chrétiennes qui reçurent ce livre sans difficulté. Mais une étude exhaustive des additions doit encore être menée pour déterminer leur origne propre et leur transmission.

École Biblique et Archéologique Française   Émile PUECH
POB 19053   CNRS – CRFJ
Jérusalem

INDEXES

ABBREVIATIONS

ÄAT	Ägypten und Altes Testament
AB	Anchor Bible
ABD	*Anchor Bible Dictonary*
AnBib	Analecta Biblica
ANET	Ancient Near Eastern Texts Related to the Old Testament
ANRW	W. Haase – H. Temporini (eds.), *Aufstieg und Niedergang der Römischen Welt*
AOAT	Alter Orient und Altes Testament
ATANT	Abhandlungen zur Theologie des Alten und Neuen Testaments
ATD	Die Alte Testament Deutsch
ATSAT	Arbeiten zu Text und Sprache im Alten Testament
BAR	*Biblical Archaeology Review*
BASOR	*Bulletin of the American Schools of Oriental Research*
BBB	Bonner Biblische Beiträge
BBST	Z. Ben-Hayyim (ed.), *The Book of Ben Sira. Text, Concordance and an Analysis of the Vocabulary*, Jerusalem, 1973
BCR	Biblioteca de Cultura Religiosa
BDB	F. Brown – S.R. Driver – C.A. Briggs, *A Hebrew and English Lexicon of the Old Testament*
BET	Beiträge zur biblischen Exegese und Theologie
BETL	Bibliotheca Ephemeridum Theologicarum Lovaniensium
BEvT	Beiträge zur Evangelischen Theologie
BFCT	Beiträge zur Förderung christlicher Theologie
BHK	*Biblia Hebraica* (ed. R. Kittel)
BHS	*Biblia Hebraica Stuttgartensia* (eds. K. Elliger – W. Rudolph)
Bib	*Biblica*
BiblTheolBull	*Biblical Theology Bulletin*
BibOr	*Bibbia e Oriente*
BiOr	*Bibliotheca Orientalis*
BJ	*La Bible de Jérusalem*
BJRL	*Bulletin of the John Rylands Library*
BK(AT)	Biblischer Kommentar
BN	*Biblische Notizen*
BVC	*Bible et Vie Chrétienne*
BZ	*Biblische Zeitschrift*
BZAW	Beihefte zur Zeitschrift für die Alttestamentliche Wissenschaft
BZNW	Beihefte zur Zeitschrift für die Neutestamentliche Wissenschaft
CahÉv	Cahiers Évangile
CBC	Cambridge Biblical Commentary
CBQ	*Catholic Biblical Quarterly*
CBQMS	Catholic Biblical Quarterly, Monographs Series

CR:BS	*Current Research: Biblical Studies*
CRB	Cahiers de la Revue Biblique
CRINT	Compendia Rerum Iudaicarum ad Novum Testamentum
CuBíbl	*Cultura Bíblica*

DB	*Dictionnaire de la Bible*
DBAT	*Dielheimer Blätter zum Alten Testament*
DBS	*Supplément au Dictionnaire de la Bible*
DCH	D.J.A. CLINES (ed.), *The Dictionary of Classical Hebrew*, Sheffield, 1993ss
DDD	K. VAN DER TOORN – B. BECKING – P. VAN DER HORST, *Dictionary of Deities and Demons in the Bible*, Leiden, 1990
diss.	Dissertation
DJDJ	Discoveries in the Judaean Desert of Jordan

EB	Echter Bibel
EB	Études Bibliques
EdF	Erträge der Forschung
EeT	*Église et Théologie*
EHAT	Exegetisches Handbuch zum Alten Testament
EKK	Evangelisch-katholischer Kommentar zum Neuen Testament
EPR	Études préliminaires aux Religions Orientales dans l'Empire Romain
EstBíbl	*Estudios Bíblicos*
ETL	*Ephemerides Theologicae Lovanienses*
ExpT	*The Expository Times*

FAT	Forschungen zum Alten Testament
FRLANT	Forschungen zur Religion und Literatur des Alten und Neuen Testament
FS	Festschrift
FzB	Forschungen zur Bibel

HAL	L. KOEHLER – W. BAUMGARTNER (neu bearbeitet von W. BAUMGARTNER *et al.*), *Hebräisches und Aramäisches Lexicon zum Alten Testament*, Leiden, 1967-1990
HALE	*The Hebrew and Aramaic Lexicon of the Old Testament. The new Koehler-Baumgartner in English*, t. I, Leiden, 1994
HAR	*Hebrew Annual Review*
HAT	Handbuch zum Alten Testament
HBS	Herders Biblische Studien
HSAT	H. HERKENNE – F. FELDMANN (eds.), *Die Heilige Schrift des Alten Testaments*
HSM	Harvard Semitic Monographs
HThS	Harvard Theological Studies
HTR	*Harvard Theological Review*
HUCA	*Hebrew Union College Annual*

ICC	International Critical Commentary

IEJ	*Israel Exploration Journal*
IG	Inscriptiones Graecae
JAAR	*Journal of the American Academy of Religion*
JANES	*Journal of the Ancient Near Eastern Society, Colombia University*
JBL	*Journal of Biblical Literature*
JEA	*Journal of Egyptian Archaeology*
JNES	*Journal of Near Eastern Studies*
JNSL	*Journal of Northwest Semitic Languages*
JQR	*Jewish Quarterly Review*
JSHRZ	Jüdische Schriften aus hellenistisch-römischer Zeit
JSJ	*Journal of the Study of Judaism in the Persian, Hellenistic and Roman Period*
JSOT	*Journal for the Study of the Old Testament*
JSOTSS	Journal for the Study of the Old Testament, Supplement Series
JSP	*Journal for the Study of the Pseudepigraphs*
JSPS	Journal for the Study of the Pseudepigraps, Supplements
JTS	*The Journal of Theological Studies*
KAT	Kommentar zum Alten Testament
KeH	Kurzgefaßtes exegetisches Handbuch
KEK	Kritisch-exegetischer Kommentar über das Neue Testament
KK	Kurzgefaßter Kommentar zu den Heiligen Schriften
LAPO	Littératures Anciennes du Proche-Orient
LD	Lectio Divina
NAB	*New American Bible*
NCBC	The New Century Bible Commentary
NEchtB	Neue Echter Bibel
NRSV	*The New Revised Standard Version*
NRT	*Nouvelle Revue Théologique*
NT	*Novum Testamentum*
NTS	*New Testament Studies*
OTA	Old Testament Abstracts
OTL	Old Testament Library
OTS	Oudtestamentische Studien
PBSB	Petite Bibliothèque des Sciences Bibliques
PIB	Pontificio Istituto Biblico
PRSt	*Perspectives in Religious Studies*
PSV	*Parola Spirito e Vita*
QD	Quaestiones Disputatae
RAC	Reallexikon für Antike und Christentum
RB	*Revue Biblique*

REJ	*Revue des Études Juives*
RevCatTeol	*Revista Catalana de Theologia*
RHPR	*Revue d'Histoire et de Philosophie Religieuses*
RivBib	*Rivista Biblica*
RivBibS	Supplementi alla Rivista Biblica
RQ	*Revue de Qumrân*
RSR	*Recherches de Science Religieuse*
RTL	*Revue Théologique de Louvain*
SBFAnalecta	Studium Biblicum Franciscanum Analecta
SBFLA	Studium Biblicum Franciscanum Liber Annuus
SBLDS	Society of Biblical Literature Dissertation Series
SBLSCS	Society of Biblical Literature Septuagint and Cognate Studies
SBLSP	Society of Biblical Literature Seminar Papers
ScotJT	*Scottish Journal of Theology*
SDC	Scripture Discussion Commentary
SJOT	*Scandinavian Journal of the Old Testament*
SKG.G	Schriften der Königsberger Gelehrten Gesellschaft. Geisteswissenschaftliche Klasse
SMDSA	Series Minor. Dipartimento di Studi Asiatici
STDJ	Studies in the Texts of the Desert of Judah
SVT	Supplements to Vetus Testamentum
TDOT	*Theological Dictionary of the Old Testament*
ThD	*Theology Digest*
ThW	→ TW
ThZ	*Theologische Zeitschrift*
TOB	*Traduction œcuménique de la Bible*
TP	*Theologie und Philosophie*
TUAT	Texte aus der Umwelt des Alten Testament
TWAT	*Theologisches Wörterbuch zum Alten Testament*
TWNT	*Theologisches Wörterbuch zum Neuen Testament*
UF	Ugarit-Forschungen
VD	*Verbum Domini*
VT	*Vetus Testamentum*
WBC	Word Biblical Commentary
WUNT	Wissenschaftliche Untersuchungen zum Neuen Testament
ZA	*Zeitschrift für Assyriologie*
ZAH	*Zeitschrift für Althebraistik*
ZAW	*Zeitschrift für die Alttestamentliche Wissenschaft*
ZBK	Zürcher Biblische Kommentar
ZNW	*Zeitschrift für die Neutestamentliche Wissenschaft*
ZTK	*Zeitschrift für Theologie und Kirche*

INDEX OF AUTHORS

INDEX OF BIBLICAL REFERENCES

30,14	38	33,15	135 136	35,19	172 173 174
30,16	38	33,16–39,11	65		175 175 176
30,17	38	33,16-18	65 66 67 169		177
30,21	42	33,19	67 84 171	35,20-24	173
30,23	42	33,20-32	85	35,20-21	174
30,25-27	70	33,20-24	84	35,20	177
30,25-26	67	33,20	76 79 84 85	35,22	175
30,27	67		86 88	35,23-24	175
30,28-32	84	33,25-32	85	35,23	170 173
30,28	76 79 84	33,25	85	35,24	173
30,33-40	85	33,26	85	36	59 219
30,39	76	33,28	85	36,1-22	172
30,40	4	33,30	85	36,1-17	66 67
31(34),2	79	33,31	79 85	36,1	226
31(34),5	81	33,33	171	36,8	122
31(34),9-13	84	34(31),1	168	36,10	92 122 123
31(34),10	67 220	34(31),8	421	36,11	122
31(34),11	80	34(31),12-13	67	36,12	222
31(34),12	59	34(31),13	92 107 123	36,13-14	219
31(34),15	79 421	34(31),16	102	36,13	92 122 123
31(34),18	79	34(31),18–35(32),10	171	36,15	92 123
31(34),21	11 12 13	34(31),21-35	227	36,16-22	99
31(34),22	67 171	34(31),27	92 122 124	36,16	67 70
31(34),31	79	34(31),26	171	36,17	222
32,1-4	104	35,1-20	59	36,18-19	219
32,1-2	105	35,1-2	104	36,20	99 100
32,1	93 104	35,1	59 93	36,22-25	399
32,2	93 104	35,2	59 93	36,27-29	49
32,3	73 93 104	35,3	59	36,29	375 376 378
	105	35,4	59 93	37,1-6	81 408
32,4	93 104 105	35,5	171	37,1	59 69
32,6	93	35,6	172	37,2	79
32,7	93	35,11	173	37,3	67 69 79 92
32,8	17 19 20 80	35,12-24	169		122 123
32,11	8 10	35,12-23	173	37,6	80
32,14–33,18	135	35,12-13	177	37,7-15	408
32,15	166	35,12	173 175 177	37,16-18	409
32,16–33,2	163	35,13-15	172	37,18	107 134
32,17-18	166	35,13-14	173	37,19–26	409
32,17	9	35,13	92 122 123	37,22-26	408 409
32,18	48	35,14	175	37,22-24	407
33(30),16-19	64	35,15-18	170	37,22	407
33(36),1-13	99	35,15	173 175	37,23	405 406 407
33(36),1	92	35,16	172 178		408 410
33(36),8-9	227	35,17-18	173 178	37,24	407
33,2	165	35,17	172 177	37,25	407
33,5	167	35,18-19	177	37,26	407
33,12	419	35,18	175	38,1-15	228
33,14	135 419	35,19-20	174	38,1-7	228

44–49	33 34 56 216	45,6-26	86 216 226	46,13	92 123 183
	218 267 307	45,6-25	218		188
	312 421	45,6-22	86 187 216	46,14	122
44,1–49,13	232		221	46,15	183 187
44,1–45,28	184	45,6-14	87	46,18	4 231
44,1–45,26	224	45,6-7	216	46,20	183 188
44,1-15	185	45,6	76 86 87 88	47,1-11	225 228
44,1-7	185		187 188	47,1	183 189
44,1	65 66 67	45,7-13	216	47,4	220
44,2	92 121 122	45,7	220 422	47,7	231
	220	45,8	220	47,8-10	228
44,3-6	185	45,9	222	47,8	92 122 123
44,3	188	45,11	222	47,9-10	189
44,4	187	45,12	225 227	47,11	122 422
44,6-22	190	45,13-17	217	47,12-22	143
44,7	185 220	45,15-22	87	47,13	190 219 228
44,8-9	141	45,15	24 87 186	47,16	228
44,8	185 186		187 221 223	47,20	187
44,9	185 186		225	47,21	205
44,10-15	185	45,16	17 19 20 21	47,22	188
44,10	186		223	47,23-25	187
44,12	186 416	45,17	187	47,24	205
44,13	186	45,20-22	217	48,1	17 183 188
44,14-16	422	45,23-26	212 422	48,5	423
44,14	186	45,23-25	87 217 221	48,8	183 188
44,15	186	45,23	92 187 188	48,9-10	423
44,16–49,13	422		226 338	48,10	183 190
44,16–45,25	184	45,24-25	187 225	48,11	66 67 104
44,16-23a	186	45,24	186 187 217		421 423
44,16	56 416		225 226 422	48,13	92 122 123
44,17–45,25	184	45,25-26	138		183 423
44,17	186 187	45,25	186 188 217	48,15-16	187
44,18	186 222		222 422	48,16	188
44,20-21	186	45,26–50,24	184	48,17	196 213 219
44,20	57 186 416	45,26	217 422	48,22–49,10	182 183
44,21	87 186	46,1–49,10	183 184 187	48,22	187
44,22	186		188	49,1-13	184
44,23-26	190	46,1-12	184	49,1	17 21 22 24
44,23	186	46,1	92 122 123		25 228
44,23c-45,5	187		188 422	49,2	228
44,24-25	186	46,3	122	49,3	187
44,27(45,1)	392	46,5	10 11 13	49,4	187 188 189
45	171 224	46,6	122 173		416
45,1-5	87 186	46,7	187	49,5	213
45,1	188 223	46,9	187	49,6	190
45,2	416	46,10	188	49,7	4 92 122 123
45,3	187	46,11	187 188		188
45,4	57	46,13–49,10	184	49,9	188 190
45,5	187	46,13-14	188	49,10	183 184 188

SUBJECT INDEX

BIBLIOTHECA EPHEMERIDUM THEOLOGICARUM LOVANIENSIUM

* = Out of print

*1. *Miscellanea dogmatica in honorem Eximii Domini J. Bittremieux*, 1947.
*2-3. *Miscellanea moralia in honorem Eximii Domini A. Janssen*, 1948.
*4. G. PHILIPS, *La grâce des justes de l'Ancien Testament*, 1948.
*5. G. PHILIPS, *De ratione instituendi tractatum de gratia nostrae sanctificationis*, 1953.
6-7. *Recueil Lucien Cerfaux. Études d'exégèse et d'histoire religieuse*, 1954. 504 et 577 p. FB 1000 par tome. Cf. *infra*, n°s 18 et 71 (t. III).
8. G. THILS, *Histoire doctrinale du mouvement œcuménique*, 1955. Nouvelle édition, 1963. 338 p. FB 135.
*9. *Études sur l'Immaculée Conception*, 1955.
*10. J.A. O'DONOHOE, *Tridentine Seminary Legislation*, 1957.
*11. G. THILS, *Orientations de la théologie*, 1958.
*12-13. J. COPPENS, A. DESCAMPS, É. MASSAUX (ed.), *Sacra Pagina. Miscellanea Biblica Congressus Internationalis Catholici de Re Biblica*, 1959.
*14. *Adrien VI, le premier Pape de la contre-réforme*, 1959.
*15. F. CLAEYS BOUUAERT, *Les déclarations et serments imposés par la loi civile aux membres du clergé belge sous le Directoire (1795-1801)*, 1960.
*16. G. THILS, *La «Théologie œcuménique». Notion-Formes-Démarches*, 1960.
17. G. THILS, *Primauté pontificale et prérogatives épiscopales. «Potestas ordinaria» au Concile du Vatican*, 1961. 103 p. FB 50.
*18. *Recueil Lucien Cerfaux*, t. III, 1962. Cf. *infra*, n° 71.
*19. *Foi et réflexion philosophique. Mélanges F. Grégoire*, 1961.
*20. *Mélanges G. Ryckmans*, 1963.
21. G. THILS, *L'infaillibilité du peuple chrétien «in credendo»*, 1963. 67 p. FB 50.
*22. J. FÉRIN & L. JANSSENS, *Progestogènes et morale conjugale*, 1963.
*23. *Collectanea Moralia in honorem Eximii Domini A. Janssen*, 1964.
24. H. CAZELLES (ed.), *De Mari à Qumrân. L'Ancien Testament. Son milieu. Ses écrits. Ses relectures juives* (Hommage J. Coppens, I), 1969. 158*-370 p. FB 900.
*25. I. DE LA POTTERIE (ed.), *De Jésus aux évangiles. Tradition et rédaction dans les évangiles synoptiques* (Hommage J. Coppens, II), 1967.
26. G. THILS & R.E. BROWN (ed.), *Exégèse et théologie* (Hommage J. Coppens, III), 1968. 328 p. FB 700.
27. J. COPPENS (ed.), *Ecclesia a Spiritu sancto edocta. Hommage à Mgr G. Philips*, 1970. 640 p. FB 1000.
28. J. COPPENS (ed.), *Sacerdoce et célibat. Études historiques et théologiques*, 1971. 740 p. FB 700.

29. M. DIDIER (ed.), *L'évangile selon Matthieu. Rédaction et théologie*, 1972. 432 p. FB 1000.
*30. J. KEMPENEERS, *Le Cardinal van Roey en son temps*, 1971.

SERIES II

31. F. NEIRYNCK, *Duality in Mark. Contributions to the Study of the Markan Redaction*, 1972. Revised edition with Supplementary Notes, 1988. 252 p. FB 1200.
32. F. NEIRYNCK (ed.), *L'évangile de Luc. Problèmes littéraires et théologiques*, 1973. *L'évangile de Luc – The Gospel of Luke*. Revised and enlarged edition, 1989. X-590 p. FB 2200.
33. C. BREKELMANS (ed.), *Questions disputées d'Ancien Testament. Méthode et théologie*, 1974. *Continuing Questions in Old Testament Method and Theology*. Revised and enlarged edition by M. VERVENNE, 1989. 245 p. FB 1200.
34. M. SABBE (ed.), *L'évangile selon Marc. Tradition et rédaction*, 1974. Nouvelle édition augmentée, 1988. 601 p. FB 2400.
35. B. WILLAERT (ed.), *Philosophie de la religion – Godsdienstfilosofie. Miscellanea Albert Dondeyne*, 1974. Nouvelle édition, 1987. 458 p. FB 1600.
36. G. PHILIPS, *L'union personnelle avec le Dieu vivant. Essai sur l'origine et le sens de la grâce créée*, 1974. Édition révisée, 1989. 299 p. FB 1000.
37. F. NEIRYNCK, in collaboration with T. HANSEN and F. VAN SEGBROECK, *The Minor Agreements of Matthew and Luke against Mark with a Cumulative List*, 1974. 330 p. FB 900.
38. J. COPPENS, *Le messianisme et sa relève prophétique. Les anticipations vétérotestamentaires. Leur accomplissement en Jésus*, 1974. Édition révisée, 1989. XIII-265 p. FB 1000.
39. D. SENIOR, *The Passion Narrative according to Matthew. A Redactional Study*, 1975. New impression, 1982. 440 p. FB 1000.
40. J. DUPONT (ed.), *Jésus aux origines de la christologie*, 1975. Nouvelle édition augmentée, 1989. 458 p. FB 1500.
41. J. COPPENS (ed.), *La notion biblique de Dieu*, 1976. Réimpression, 1985. 519 p. FB 1600.
42. J. LINDEMANS & H. DEMEESTER (ed.), *Liber Amicorum Monseigneur W. Onclin*, 1976. XXII-396 p. FB 1000.
43. R.E. HOECKMAN (ed.), *Pluralisme et œcuménisme en recherches théologiques. Mélanges offerts au R.P. Dockx, O.P.*, 1976. 316 p. FB 1000.
44. M. DE JONGE (ed.), *L'évangile de Jean. Sources, rédaction, théologie*, 1977. Réimpression, 1987. 416 p. FB 1500.
45. E.J.M. VAN EIJL (ed.), *Facultas S. Theologiae Lovaniensis 1432-1797. Bijdragen tot haar geschiedenis. Contributions to its History. Contributions à son histoire*, 1977. 570 p. FB 1700.
46. M. DELCOR (ed.), *Qumrân. Sa piété, sa théologie et son milieu*, 1978. 432 p. FB 1700.
47. M. CAUDRON (ed.), *Faith and Society. Foi et société. Geloof en maatschappij. Acta Congressus Internationalis Theologici Lovaniensis 1976*, 1978. 304 p. FB 1150.

48. J. KREMER (ed.), *Les Actes des Apôtres. Traditions, rédaction, théologie,* 1979. 590 p. FB 1700.

49. F. NEIRYNCK, avec la collaboration de J. DELOBEL, T. SNOY, G. VAN BELLE, F. VAN SEGBROECK, *Jean et les Synoptiques. Examen critique de l'exégèse de M.-É. Boismard,* 1979. XII-428 p. FB 1000.

50. J. COPPENS, *La relève apocalyptique du messianisme royal. I. La royauté – Le règne – Le royaume de Dieu. Cadre de la relève apocalyptique,* 1979. 325 p. FB 1000.

51. M. GILBERT (ed.), *La Sagesse de l'Ancien Testament,* 1979. Nouvelle édition mise à jour, 1990. 455 p. FB 1500.

52. B. DEHANDSCHUTTER, *Martyrium Polycarpi. Een literair-kritische studie,* 1979. 296 p. FB 1000.

53. J. LAMBRECHT (ed.), *L'Apocalypse johannique et l'Apocalyptique dans le Nouveau Testament,* 1980. 458 p. FB 1400.

54. P.-M. BOGAERT (ed.), *Le livre de Jérémie. Le prophète et son milieu. Les oracles et leur transmission,* 1981. *Nouvelle édition mise à jour,* 1997. 448 p. FB 1800.

55. J. COPPENS, *La relève apocalyptique du messianisme royal. III. Le Fils de l'homme néotestamentaire.* Édition posthume par F. NEIRYNCK, 1981. XIV-192 p. FB 800.

56. J. VAN BAVEL & M. SCHRAMA (ed.), *Jansénius et le Jansénisme dans les Pays-Bas. Mélanges Lucien Ceyssens,* 1982. 247 p. FB 1000.

57. J.H. WALGRAVE, *Selected Writings – Thematische geschriften. Thomas Aquinas, J.H. Newman, Theologia Fundamentalis.* Edited by G. DE SCHRIJVER & J.J. KELLY, 1982. XLIII-425 p. FB 1000.

58. F. NEIRYNCK & F. VAN SEGBROECK, avec la collaboration de E. MANNING, *Ephemerides Theologicae Lovanienses 1924-1981. Tables générales. (Bibliotheca Ephemeridum Theologicarum Lovaniensium 1947-1981),* 1982. 400 p. FB 1600.

59. J. DELOBEL (ed.), *Logia. Les paroles de Jésus – The Sayings of Jesus. Mémorial Joseph Coppens,* 1982. 647 p. FB 2000.

60. F. NEIRYNCK, *Evangelica. Gospel Studies – Études d'évangile. Collected Essays.* Edited by F. VAN SEGBROECK, 1982. XIX-1036 p. FB 2000.

61. J. COPPENS, *La relève apocalyptique du messianisme royal. II. Le Fils d'homme vétéro- et intertestamentaire.* Édition posthume par J. LUST, 1983. XVII-272 p. FB 1000.

62. J.J. KELLY, *Baron Friedrich von Hügel's Philosophy of Religion,* 1983. 232 p. FB 1500.

63. G. DE SCHRIJVER, *Le merveilleux accord de l'homme et de Dieu. Étude de l'analogie de l'être chez Hans Urs von Balthasar,* 1983. 344 p. FB 1500.

64. J. GROOTAERS & J.A. SELLING, *The 1980 Synod of Bishops: «On the Role of the Family». An Exposition of the Event and an Analysis of its Texts.* Preface by Prof. emeritus L. JANSSENS, 1983. 375 p. FB 1500.

65. F. NEIRYNCK & F. VAN SEGBROECK, *New Testament Vocabulary. A Companion Volume to the Concordance,* 1984. XVI-494 p. FB 2000.

66. R.F. COLLINS, *Studies on the First Letter to the Thessalonians,* 1984. XI-415 p. FB 1500.

67. A. PLUMMER, *Conversations with Dr. Döllinger 1870-1890.* Edited with Introduction and Notes by R. BOUDENS, with the collaboration of L. KENIS, 1985. LIV-360 p. FB 1800.

68. N. LOHFINK (ed.), *Das Deuteronomium. Entstehung, Gestalt und Botschaft / Deuteronomy: Origin, Form and Message*, 1985. XI-382 p. FB 2000.

69. P.F. FRANSEN, *Hermeneutics of the Councils and Other Studies.* Collected by H.E. MERTENS & F. DE GRAEVE, 1985. 543 p. FB 1800.

70. J. DUPONT, *Études sur les Évangiles synoptiques.* Présentées par F. NEIRYNCK, 1985. 2 tomes, XXI-IX-1210 p. FB 2800.

71. *Recueil Lucien Cerfaux*, t. III, 1962. Nouvelle édition revue et complétée, 1985. LXXX-458 p. FB 1600.

72. J. GROOTAERS, *Primauté et collégialité. Le dossier de Gérard Philips sur la Nota Explicativa Praevia (Lumen gentium, Chap. III).* Présenté avec introduction historique, annotations et annexes. Préface de G. THILS, 1986. 222 p. FB 1000.

73. A. VANHOYE (ed.), *L'apôtre Paul. Personnalité, style et conception du ministère,* 1986. XIII-470 p. FB 2600.

74. J. LUST (ed.), *Ezekiel and His Book. Textual and Literary Criticism and their Interrelation,* 1986. X-387 p. FB 2700.

75. É. MASSAUX, *Influence de l'Évangile de saint Matthieu sur la littérature chrétienne avant saint Irénée.* Réimpression anastatique présentée par F. NEIRYNCK. *Supplément: Bibliographie 1950-1985,* par B. DEHANDSCHUTTER, 1986. XXVII-850 p. FB 2500.

76. L. CEYSSENS & J.A.G. TANS, *Autour de l'Unigenitus. Recherches sur la genèse de la Constitution,* 1987. XXVI-845 p. FB 2500.

77. A. DESCAMPS, *Jésus et l'Église. Études d'exégèse et de théologie.* Préface de Mgr A. HOUSSIAU, 1987. XLV-641 p. FB 2500.

78. J. DUPLACY, *Études de critique textuelle du Nouveau Testament.* Présentées par J. DELOBEL, 1987. XXVII-431 p. FB 1800.

79. E.J.M. VAN EIJL (ed.), *L'image de C. Jansénius jusqu'à la fin du XVIIIe siècle,* 1987. 258 p. FB 1250.

80. E. BRITO, *La Création selon Schelling. Universum,* 1987. XXXV-646 p. FB 2980.

81. J. VERMEYLEN (ed.), *The Book of Isaiah – Le livre d'Isaïe. Les oracles et leurs relectures. Unité et complexité de l'ouvrage,* 1989. X-472 p. FB 2700.

82. G. VAN BELLE, *Johannine Bibliography 1966-1985. A Cumulative Bibliography on the Fourth Gospel,* 1988. XVII-563 p. FB 2700.

83. J.A. SELLING (ed.), *Personalist Morals. Essays in Honor of Professor Louis Janssens,* 1988. VIII-344 p. FB 1200.

84. M.-É. BOISMARD, *Moïse ou Jésus. Essai de christologie johannique,* 1988. XVI-241 p. FB 1000.

84ᴬ. M.-É. BOISMARD, *Moses or Jesus: An Essay in Johannine Christology.* Translated by B.T. VIVIANO, 1993, XVI-144 p. FB 1000.

85. J.A. DICK, *The Malines Conversations Revisited,* 1989. 278 p. FB 1500.

86. J.-M. SEVRIN (ed.), *The New Testament in Early Christianity – La réception des écrits néotestamentaires dans le christianisme primitif,* 1989. XVI-406 p. FB 2500.

87. R.F. COLLINS (ed.), *The Thessalonian Correspondence,* 1990. XV-546 p. FB 3000.

88. F. VAN SEGBROECK, *The Gospel of Luke. A Cumulative Bibliography 1973-1988,* 1989. 241 p. FB 1200.

89. G. THILS, *Primauté et infaillibilité du Pontife Romain à Vatican I et autres études d'ecclésiologie*, 1989. XI-422 p. FB 1850.
90. A. VERGOTE, *Explorations de l'espace théologique. Études de théologie et de philosophie de la religion*, 1990. XVI-709 p. FB 2000.
91. J.C. DE MOOR, *The Rise of Yahwism: The Roots of Israelite Monotheism*, 1990. *Revised and Enlarged Edition*, 1997. XV-445 p. FB 1400.
92. B. BRUNING, M. LAMBERIGTS & J. VAN HOUTEM (eds.), *Collectanea Augustiniana. Mélanges T.J. van Bavel*, 1990. 2 tomes, XXXVIII-VIII-1074 p. FB 3000.
93. A. DE HALLEUX, *Patrologie et œcuménisme. Recueil d'études*, 1990. XVI-887 p. FB 3000.
94. C. BREKELMANS & J. LUST (eds.), *Pentateuchal and Deuteronomistic Studies: Papers Read at the XIIIth IOSOT Congress Leuven 1989*, 1990. 307 p. FB 1500.
95. D.L. DUNGAN (ed.), *The Interrelations of the Gospels. A Symposium Led by M.-É. Boismard – W.R. Farmer – F. Neirynck, Jerusalem 1984*, 1990. XXXI-672 p. FB 3000.
96. G.D. KILPATRICK, *The Principles and Practice of New Testament Textual Criticism. Collected Essays*. Edited by J.K. ELLIOTT, 1990. XXXVIII-489 p. FB 3000.
97. G. ALBERIGO (ed.), *Christian Unity. The Council of Ferrara-Florence: 1438/39 – 1989*, 1991. X-681 p. FB 3000.
98. M. SABBE, *Studia Neotestamentica. Collected Essays*, 1991. XVI-573 p. FB 2000.
99. F. NEIRYNCK, *Evangelica II: 1982-1991. Collected Essays*. Edited by F. VAN SEGBROECK, 1991. XIX-874 p. FB 2800.
100. F. VAN SEGBROECK, C.M. TUCKETT, G. VAN BELLE & J. VERHEYDEN (eds.), *The Four Gospels 1992. Festschrift Frans Neirynck*, 1992. 3 volumes, XVII-X-X-2668 p. FB 5000.

SERIES III

101. A. DENAUX (ed.), *John and the Synoptics*, 1992. XXII-696 p. FB 3000.
102. F. NEIRYNCK, J. VERHEYDEN, F. VAN SEGBROECK, G. VAN OYEN & R. CORSTJENS, *The Gospel of Mark. A Cumulative Bibliography: 1950-1990*, 1992. XII-717 p. FB 2700.
103. M. SIMON, *Un catéchisme universel pour l'Église catholique. Du Concile de Trente à nos jours*, 1992. XIV-461 p. FB 2200.
104. L. CEYSSENS, *Le sort de la bulle Unigenitus. Recueil d'études offert à Lucien Ceyssens à l'occasion de son 90ᵉ anniversaire*. Présenté par M. LAMBERIGTS, 1992. XXVI-641 p. FB 2000.
105. R.J. DALY (ed.), *Origeniana Quinta. Papers of the 5th International Origen Congress, Boston College, 14-18 August 1989*, 1992. XVII-635 p. FB 2700.
106. A.S. VAN DER WOUDE (ed.), *The Book of Daniel in the Light of New Findings*, 1993. XVIII-574 p. FB 3000.
107. J. FAMERÉE, *L'ecclésiologie d'Yves Congar avant Vatican II: Histoire et Église. Analyse et reprise critique*, 1992. 497 p. FB 2600.

108. C. BEGG, *Josephus' Account of the Early Divided Monarchy (AJ 8, 212-420). Rewriting the Bible*, 1993. IX-377 p. FB 2400.

109. J. BULCKENS & H. LOMBAERTS (eds.), *L'enseignement de la religion catholique à l'école secondaire. Enjeux pour la nouvelle Europe*, 1993. XII-264 p. FB 1250.

110. C. FOCANT (ed.), *The Synoptic Gospels. Source Criticism and the New Literary Criticism*, 1993. XXXIX-670 p. FB 3000.

111. M. LAMBERIGTS (ed.), avec la collaboration de L. KENIS, *L'augustinisme à l'ancienne Faculté de théologie de Louvain*, 1994. VII-455 p. FB 2400.

112. R. BIERINGER & J. LAMBRECHT, *Studies on 2 Corinthians*, 1994. XX-632 p. FB 3000.

113. E. BRITO, *La pneumatologie de Schleiermacher*, 1994. XII-649 p. FB 3000.

114. W.A.M. BEUKEN (ed.), *The Book of Job*, 1994. X-462 p. FB 2400.

115. J. LAMBRECHT, *Pauline Studies: Collected Essays*, 1994. XIV-465 p. FB 2500.

116. G. VAN BELLE, *The Signs Source in the Fourth Gospel: Historical Survey and Critical Evaluation of the Semeia Hypothesis*, 1994. XIV-503 p. FB 2500.

117. M. LAMBERIGTS & P. VAN DEUN (eds.), *Martyrium in Multidisciplinary Perspective. Memorial L. Reekmans*, 1995. X-435 p. FB 3000.

118. G. DORIVAL & A. LE BOULLUEC (eds.), *Origeniana Sexta. Origène et la Bible/Origen and the Bible. Actes du Colloquium Origenianum Sextum, Chantilly, 30 août – 3 septembre 1993*, 1995. XII-865 p. FB 3900.

119. É. GAZIAUX, *Morale de la foi et morale autonome. Confrontation entre P. Delhaye et J. Fuchs*, 1995. XXII-545 p. FB 2700.

120. T.A. SALZMAN, *Deontology and Teleology: An Investigation of the Normative Debate in Roman Catholic Moral Theology*, 1995. XVII-555 p. FB 2700.

121. G.R. EVANS & M. GOURGUES (eds.), *Communion et Réunion. Mélanges Jean-Marie Roger Tillard*, 1995. XI-431 p. FB 2400.

122. H.T. FLEDDERMANN, *Mark and Q: A Study of the Overlap Texts*. With an *Assessment* by F. NEIRYNCK, 1995. XI-307 p. FB 1800.

123. R. BOUDENS, *Two Cardinals: John Henry Newman, Désiré-Joseph Mercier*. Edited by L. GEVERS with the collaboration of B. DOYLE, 1995. 362 p. FB 1800.

124. A. THOMASSET, *Paul Ricœur. Une poétique de la morale. Aux fondements d'une éthique herméneutique et narrative dans une perspective chrétienne*, 1996. XVI-706 p. FB 3000.

125. R. BIERINGER (ed.), *The Corinthian Correspondence*, 1996. XXVII-793 p. FB 2400.

126. M. VERVENNE (ed.), *Studies in the Book of Exodus: Redaction – Reception – Interpretation*, 1996. XI-660 p. FB 2400.

127. A. VANNESTE, *Nature et grâce dans la théologie occidentale. Dialogue avec H. de Lubac*, 1996. 312 p. FB 1800.

128. A. CURTIS & T. RÖMER (eds.), *The Book of Jeremiah and its Reception – Le livre de Jérémie et sa réception*, 1997. 332 p. FB 2400.

129. E. LANNE, *Tradition et Communion des Églises. Recueil d'études*, 1997. XXV-703 p. FB 3000.

130. A. DENAUX & J.A. DICK (eds.), *From Malines to ARCIC. The Malines Conversations Commemorated*, 1997. IX-317 p. FB 1800.
131. C.M. TUCKETT (ed.), *The Scriptures in the Gospels*, 1997. XXIV-721 p. FB 2400.
132. J. VAN RUITEN & M. VERVENNE (eds.), *Studies in the Book of Isaiah. Festschrift Willem A.M. Beuken*, 1997. XX-540 p. FB 3000.
133. M. VERVENNE & J. LUST (eds.), *Deuteronomy and Deuteronomic Literature. Festschrift C.H.W. Brekelmans*, 1997. XI-637 p. FB 3000.
134. G. VAN BELLE (ed.), *Index Generalis ETL/BETL 1981-1997*, forthcoming.
135. G. DE SCHRIJVER, *Liberation Theologies on Shifting Grounds. A Clash of Socio-Economic and Cultural Paradigms*, 1998. XI-453 p. FB 2100.
136. A. SCHOORS (ed.), *Qohelet in the Context of Wisdom*, 1998. XI-528 p. FB 2400.
137. W.A. BIENERT & U. KÜHNEWEG (eds.), *Origeniana Septima. Origenes in den Auseinandersetzungen des 4. Jahrhunderts,* 1999. XXV-848 p. FB 3800.
138. É. GAZIAUX, *L'autonomie en morale: au croisement de la philosophie et de la théologie*, 1998. XVI-739 p. FB 3000.
139. J. GROOTAERS, *Actes et acteurs à Vatican II*, 1998. XXIV-602 p. FB 3000.
140. F. NEIRYNCK, J. VERHEYDEN & R. CORSTJENS, *The Gospel of Matthew and the Sayings Source Q: A Cumulative Bibliography 1950-1995*, 1998. 2 vols., VII-1000-420* p. FB 3800.
141. E. BRITO, *Heidegger et l'hymne du sacré*, 1999. XVI-787 p. FB 3600.
142. J. VERHEYDEN (ed.), *The Unity of Luke-Acts*, 1999. XXV-828 p. FB 2400.
143. N. CALDUCH-BENAGES & J. VERMEYLEN (eds.), *Treasures of Wisdom. Studies in Ben Sira and the Book of Wisdom. Festschrift M. Gilbert*, 1999. XXVII-463 p. FB 3000.
144. J.-M. AUWERS & A. WÉNIN (eds.), *Lectures et relectures de la Bible. Festschrift P.-M. Bogaert*, 1999. XLII-482 p. FB 3000.
145. C. BEGG, *Josephus' Story of the Later Monarchy (AJ 9,1–10,185)*, 1999. forthcoming.
146. J.M. ASGEIRSSON, K. DE TROYER & M.W. MEYER (eds.), *From Quest to Q. Festschrift James M. Robinson*, 1999. FB 2400.

PRINTED ON PERMANENT PAPER • IMPRIME SUR PAPIER PERMANENT • GEDRUKT OP DUURZAAM PAPIER - ISO 9706

ORIENTALISTE, KLEIN DALENSTRAAT 42, B-3020 HERENT